3-24 8l

Culture in Context

Culture in Context

Selected writings of Weston La Barre

Duke University Press   Durham, N.C.   1980

To the willfully blind who remain my friends

Contents

Introduction

1. Clinic and Field

The kind of anthropologist one becomes depends greatly, beyond motivation and need, on his view of the nature of his data. There is long and basic disagreement among anthropologists as to whether their discipline is potentially a science or, more properly and essentially, one of the humanities— whether human data are quantifiable and able to yield durable "hard" scientific generalization, or whether by their nature these data are overly malleable to the motivations of the researcher, set in his own ethnographic time and psychological life-space.

Among methods anthropology might borrow from other sciences, the *experimental method* would seem to be wholly repugnant, out of a decent humanistic concern for the data, other human beings. Besides, since the experimenter is himself a human being and motivated to find his own psychic homeostasis, the "controlled experiment" tends to control out of his data his own anxieties and prevents the very edifications an unmanipulated naturalism might give him. A further difficulty with the experimental method, and I think an insurmountable one, is that anthropologists enculturated to one culture could hardly frame objective and culture-free hypotheses concerning another culture or cultures.

Consider the sociologist. At one time, notably at the early University of Chicago, sociologists were actually field workers, entranced and open-ended observers of subcultures in their own society, and they produced such fine naturalistic studies as *Gold Coast and Slum, The Saleslady, The Jack-Roller*[1] and others, which the anthropologist can still admire. The tradition is not yet extinct (in a sense, in the phenomenological approach of Goffman, Luckman, and others), and yet most contemporary sociologists would prefer to think of themselves more prestigefully as quantifying scientists, with "testable" hypotheses. Now, any such hypothesis derives from common sense, a basic "insight" (unwitting awareness of his own culture). That is, one wants a *plausible* hypothesis that, it is to be hoped, will find verification. But to be plausible the hypothesis must derive from that covert consensus, unexamined contemporary local ethnography. Lest the sociologist be detected in obviousness, the hypothesis is muffled in an arcane and fatuous pomposity of vocabulary, and any obviousness of his conclusions merely testifies to the soundness of the method. Thereupon the sociologist sets out to "collect his data"—commonly a noun entity to be measured against a predicated adjectival quality— to be calibrated against the opinions of his selected "subjects." Next he brings heaps of protocols, puts them on punch-cards, and lays them at the feet of the

Originally published in George S. Spindler (ed.), *The Making of Psychological Anthropology* (Berkeley: University of California Press, 1978), pp. 258–99. Reprinted by permission.

Truth Machine untouched by human mind. Finally he pushes the button, and Science emerges. The more elaborated the programming "model" (his equations), the more "sophisticated" his results. But he does not seem to realize that his results have already been programmed by a far more sophisticated (or sophistic) computer, his mind—the unexamined, motivated, enculturated, time-serving human mind.

If the sociologist is lucky, his results will indicate an overlap of two intersecting circles—never concentric, unless he has produced an authentic tautology, though the more tautological the more impressive—the common area of which can be expressed statistically (if the circles are not even tangent he has flubbed it). That is, his new scholasticism has discovered and measured a semantic overlap, a pooled consensus of the connotations and denotations of a noun and an adjective in selected tribesmen's minds. It is an obscure recognition of this circularity and ethnocentricity in what the sociologist has been doing, chasing his tail in his own back yard, that is at the heart of the anthropologist's characteristic and chronic vexation with the sociologist. The man and his machine have labored mightily and brought forth: contemporary folklore. He has not only discovered, but what is more *proven*, a fragment of ethnography much more expeditiously produced by simple old Chicagoan ethnography. He has discovered the obvious, however pretentiously, to which all can agree. Can the sociologist ever be even the folklorist of his own society, unless he discovers and acknowledges that this is what he is really doing? The anthropologist can congratulate himself that at least he has flung a much wider net upon the human than has the sociologist. But ignoring for the moment the enormous cross-cultural differences in doing even this, is it possible that the anthropologist can ever do more than simple ethnographic description?

In a spirit of fun, but also with a modicum of ironic seriousness, I wrote an account of Professor Widjojo,[2] a fictive native ethnographer visiting the "Usans" (pronounced either "Us-ans" or "U.S.A.-ans" as one chooses, since no phonemic table was provided by Widjojo), who attended an occidental *futbol* game and systematically misinterpreted all he saw in terms of what he thought were Usan categories. The battle over the sacred pigskin produced fallen warriors, but these were miraculously resurrected (evidently in accordance with Christian myths) under the aegis of an Alma Mater and her animal totem, the animal mascot of the men's society, aided by the magical chants of the moiety-communicants. The totem was not, however, of an exogamous group, for careful diachronic kinship studies showed that communicants as often married within as outside of the totemic Alma Mater moieties, etc., etc. The *koktel parti* after the ceremony was even more grotesquely misunderstood, though, in all fairness, by that time as a participant observer Professor Widjojo may have become tiddly.

The spectacle of the sociologist should chasten the anthropologist. Is he, too, imprisoned in the nature of the cultural situation when he attempts to play the scientist? Is he, too, not to be trusted to frame objective scientific hypotheses, even after the most earnest and compendious bird watching? Early anthropology is replete with examples in which, having an ax to grind, the anthropologist sets up a hypothesis, subtly or flagrantly ethnocentric, and then sets out on a world tour for confirmation. Sir James George Frazer, no field-worker to be sure, is usually cited as a notorious example of this tendency since he assumes, *a priori* and unexamined, a "psychological unity of man-kind" which is precisely what should be established first, empirically and in-ductively, before using an Australian myth, say, to explain folklore in the Old Testament,[3] as though it had any ethnographic relevance whatever.

This "daisy-picking" method tears the datum brutally from its tribal con-text, and (without our espousing Malinowski's antihistorical and antiareal tunnel-vision that would treat each single culture as explainable sufficiently and only in terms of itself) surely we have learned from functionalism the critical significance of *context*. Indeed, surprisingly, Frazer sometimes succeeds in illuminating an apocopated or overly terse Old Testament myth, such as "The Origin of Death," when citing a nearby African Semitism, relevant pre-cisely because it is related in ethnographic space and historic time. Otherwise, depending as it does on unproven psychological unity—which Malinowski's insistence on the *sui generis* nature of each tribe does much to destroy—Fra-zerian comparativism is quite useless as distribution studies. My point is not a now uselessly didactic beating of a dead horse, but a necessary polemic one. For Freudian psychology, which I employ, also depends on unities—but here rooted in demonstrably pan-human biology, a psychology founded presum-ably overmuch in biology, for which Freud has been so roundly criticized. As for Malinowski's "synchronic" shibboleth, often the meaning of a dysfunc-tional element is to be found in the history of a culture. The understanding of a society's culture depends as much on ethnographic history as does the Freudian understanding of personality through individual history. Lack of method is no excuse to erect Trobriand lack of literacy into a rigidly antihistorical principle. Indeed, in a similarly "historyless" hemisphere, Sapir[4] brilliantly summarized many sound and useful techniques for discovering *Time Perspective in Abo-riginal American Culture*.

It is usually assumed that Frazerism is defunct. But what are we to think of the implied unity-of-mankind psychologism of the French Jungian who, after a few weeks of rapid travel through Bororo country, sits in Paris and spins out volume after volume of myths from his own mind? And what are we to think of Chomskian universalism, even when at last jounced from its Indo-European back yard into Finnish and Samoan studies? All languages, we are told, show a mystic sameness—which shows that Chomsky as little understands the unique quiddities of languages as Lévi-Strauss does those of cultures, for neither lan-guage nor culture is quasi-neurological. But when Chomskians are pressed to elucidate this mystical sameness, it turns out that all languages have sound, sense, and structure—which means that language is by definition oral (and not, as has been wickedly suggested, modulated flatus, which is within the realm of biological possibility though not of the tautological definition of language) and has a finite number of discriminable gamuts of sound or phonemes, varied as these are, instead of white noise; that sense is necessary for any communication, and that is what communication is, transduction of meaning; and that, finally, languages are structured, alarmingly incommensurate as these structures are. If the generalized Chomskian "similarities" are not these tautological banalities, we get at best such universals as something functionally resembling pronouns—as if man were a social primate, though divided up into discrete metazoan bodies, and some men talk to and about others! What hath God wrought? The human mind grinds everywhere with the same cogs!

As to other scientists whose methods the anthropologist is invited to emulate, consider the experimental psychologist. But when Wundt went into his laboratory to contrive the "controlled experiment" did not his hypotheses subtly control out of the data everything anxiety-laden that would teach the psychologist anything properly *psychological* about *people?* Instead of the bread of psychological understanding of human beings, we get from them the stone of a disguised neuroanatomy and neurophysiology of birds and animals, with human analogies at best on this crude biological level of perception, sensation, and learning. But rats and pigeons lack infantile dependency of any significant amount, they lack the nuclear family, the incest taboo, symbolism, language, and culture—in fact all the species-specific traits that make human beings human. Or when social psychologists actually do use people in their "experiments," say, in measuring attitudes through (culture-bound, deductive) questionnaires, are these "attitudes" true statistical comparables, and are they not still buzzing with unexamined quiddities and semantic incommensurabilities? Questionnaires are no more than Gallup polls that pool and mask the many remaining dynamically significant differences in individuals, and are at best unwitting ethnography—or psychiatry. For example, some die-hard opinions about Mr. Nixon seem to reveal only irrational oedipal dispositions toward authority figures or the degree of personal psychopathy of the pollee.

Only the clinical psychologist, far less prestigefully "scientific" than the experimental psychologist, continues to observe the unmutilated naturalistic phenomenon, the individual person with his idiosyncrasies, and allows him through a structurally *meaningless* Rorschach card to speak projectively of himself and his own meanings, or through the diagnostically useful MMPI to display a sizeable number of the varying psychiatric components of his unique personality configuration, in similarly open-ended fashion. Experimental psychologists, one observes, are self-recruited from among individuals who have appreciable psychological problems that evidently motivate them to psychological research. Honest compulsives, they obscurely suspect the truth is not in them, so they armor themselves more and more with protective method. However, since self-therapy is largely impossible, academic psychology becomes a kind of institutionalized compulsion neurosis: a new method-obsessed scholasticism that to obtain the reliable has given up the threateningly significant. (Of course a different character diagnosis can similarly be given for most anthropologists.) For good reasons clinically blind, the experimentalist can be elaborately scornful of the naturalistic "hunch artist" clinician who states precisely the psychological dynamics that arouse the experimentalist's anxieties, which his "method" successfully avoided.

Here one is reminded of the scorn often meted out to the clinically oriented culture and personality anthropologist, whose statements about group-ethos are said to mask constantly remaining differences among finer categories of individuals; indeed, Sapir himself, the founder of culture and personality studies, noted that as we refine these social categories more and more, the closer we get to the psychological individual. Oddly enough, anthropologists are happily content to make large *ethnographic* generalizations about generic group behavior, but are curiously alarmed at *psychological* statements about generic ethos. However, "culture" and "personality" are both abstractions, on different levels,[5] *from the same data*, reverberant inter-individually influenced behavior in a social animal. Culture is the abstraction of the regularities of behavior among members of a group—resulting from the influence of individuals upon individuals.[6] Personality is an abstraction of the regularities of behavior in an individual—resulting from the influence of individuals upon an individual. Those who denigrate culture as an abstraction should remember that Society and Structure are equally abstractions from the same socially reverberant behaviors of the same animal. It is simply a matter of the abstraction one feels comfortable with and allows no invidious name-calling with respect to "abstraction."

Because of the semitautologous relationship of culture and personality, society and structure, it early occurred to me that a concept of the "social cynosure" would be dynamically more significant than the "modal personality" and similar concepts. The cynosure is not the modal person, not the "successful" or otherwise desirable to become, not even the most to be emulated person in the society, but simply the one who receives the most massive and continuous *attention* in any society. Cynosures in American, Chinese, central Australian, British, Indonesian, Japanese, African, Aztec, Indian, German, American Indian, French, classic Greek, Balinese, and Northwest Coast cultures were examined, with indications of how the study of these cynosures afforded insights into the dynamics and structure of their respective societies. Contemporary feminists might relish my sympathy with women in our society as clotheshorses, male consumer-appanages, and mere sex objects in male games of invidious prestige, in this my first paper written at Duke University, with notes hastily sketched on the back of an envelope from the Dean, when I was suddenly asked to address one of Gillin's anthropology classes as part of the slave-market scrutiny of a potential new academic property. But I also brought into evidence both businessmen and consumers as unwitting victims of our system. Although the article has been anthologized and also published in French, the concept of cynosure has been used, to my knowledge, only by Warren Morrill in Bucknell. The concept had not been a mere renaming of the familiar concept of ethos, and both the English and French versions appeared in obscure publications.[7]

The glory of anthropology is its comparative perspective. Perhaps one could take the position that the "experiments" in being human have already been made for us in the naturalistic ethnographic world, and with more extravagant differences than any culture-bound experimenter could imagine. Onerous as cultural difference is intellectually, the historically looming disappearance of ethnographic difference is in a sense frightening. Cultural imperialism in a world village may produce the monolithic which still remains, in fact, merely a culture—which is the reason why any utopian who becomes omnipotent had better be one hundred percent omniscient and omnibenevolent as well! For only the spectacle of cultural difference has enabled us to discover the fact of culture itself.

We have ventured to dissect the sociologist and the psychologist. What are the anthropologist's motivations and behaviors, beyond the obvious wish to escape his own stultifying and punitive culture, in the discontent with his own civilization? Edmonson[8] has shrewdly observed that "in its nativistic aspect anthropology is nascent internationalism." If so, is the anthropologist actually bent on the destruction of his data? Anthropology is basically a reaction to the intellectual crisis posed by the Renaissance, the massive encounter—first the classic past, and later world horizons opened by trade—with the fact of other cultures, alarmingly varied in space and time, and consequent attempts to attain some nomothetic rock of ages amidst the sea of idiographic relativism. Like every other voyager, the anthropologist passes between Scylla and Charybdis, between the rock of dogma and the whirlpool of mysticism in Joyce's metaphor, the institutionalized and the subjective "truth" respectively. The metaphor is even more painful than it first appears: the monster consumes whatever human passes by, the whirlpool engulfs it. The relativist flounders, but every would-be nomothete distorts and transforms. In a sense, consumed by dogma, the anthropologist *becomes* the man-eating monster on the rock and turns ethnography into its own substance, which surely constitutes no scientific superiority over swirling in a sea of relativism.

Perhaps the only intellectual escape is honestly to recognize the predicament: the nomothetic aspect of any culture as a postulational system is a psychic defense mechanism—which is why we detest this defeatist insight. But cultural truth is no more apodictic than a Riemannian, Bolyaian, Lobachevskian or Euclidean Fifth Postulate—including the private culture of the anthropologist and his need for intellectual homeostasis. He is inescapably a symbol-manipulator. "Man depends on symbols because he cannot endure a threat to his powers of comprehension."[9]

Anthropologizing thus resembles the behavior of participants in a crisis cult, the intellectual crisis inherited from the Renaissance. A fifty-year perspective on the history of anthropology shows it to be, ironically, quite like the history of any other science. Kuhn[10] has shown us that science "progresses" not in a steady, cumulative, linear fashion but by a series of disjunctive leaps, when, after a crisis of reigning "normal" science, men suddenly begin to look at the world with new hypothetic myths. In our urge to be scientific we should not ignore the predicament of the other sciences! Nor are we entitled to be epistemologically condescending to Tillich[11] when, after a masterly and courageous survey of existentialism, he obdurately leaps to the postulate of a "God beyond God." Human wishing is only more nakedly exposed in religion than in science, the defense against nescience.

However repugnant to our intellectual pretenses, the dour recognition that anthropologizing is crisis behavior, as in any other science, is intended with deadly seriousness. Consider only how, phenomenologically, we *behave*. The last fifty years of anthropology is not so much an unbroken cumulative endeavor as it is disconcertingly like a straggling parade of charismatic characters and their entourage. When viewed in context, the statement of each messianic *guru* makes each anthropology into a species of autobiography, or lyric poetry. The personal motive is even embarrassingly exposed, as in eminent anthropologists anyone could name. And from Malinowski to Lévi-Strauss there is an unmistakable aura of the messianic, certainly in the reflex behavior of journeyman communicants who during a period of "normal" science dutifully repeat and prove the master's dicta. This is not meant as contumely. It is only that the more eminent the leader, the more his clientele expose the fact in their behavior, and both Malinowski and Lévi-Strauss were in their day inarguably very eminent anthropologists.

Consider the case of Malinowski. Staunch Boasians like Lowie[12] responded to the meteoric rise of Malinowski with a truly vituperative tone, all the more remarkable in this ordinarily judicial-minded, good gray historian of ethnological theory. Malinowski makes "apocalyptic utterances" in "messianic mood," his "favorite pastimes" consisting in "battering down wide open doors . . . or petulantly deriding work that does not attract him." Malinowski "thumbs his nose at technology, flouts distribution studies, sneers at recognition of the past"—and all his acolytes piously respond. Disdaining any larger human context, areal or distributional, that might help make sense of his chosen people, Malinowski "treats each culture as a closed system except insofar as its elements correspond to vital biological urges." For Malinowski, however, unlike Durkheim, this windowless-monad society was not the unit, and "Malinowski came to regard the family as the fundamental unit in all human society." But Malinowski never attempted an adequate human biology beyond this vague postulate. As to any psychoanalytic ground for this postulate (another anathema to Lowie), although Lowie mistakenly thought Malinowski a representative of this school, Malinowski was quite inadequately informed in this area and plainly anti-psychoanalytic, which makes it grossly unfair to use Malinowski as a whipping-boy for it.[13]

Like Radcliffe-Brown, Malinowski "avowed a disdain, largely but by no means uniformly indulged in practice, for history"—and acolytes learn to chant the cant word "diachronic" pejoratively. For a presumably biology- and psychology-based theorist, Malinowski also curiously disdained the individual, though Radcliffe-Brown, remarkably considering his derivation from Durkheim, later included the individual as a legitimate object of anthropological inquiry. Like Radcliffe-Brown, Malinowski considered that any particular culture "is normally a systematic or integrated unit in which every element has a distinct function"—ignoring the fact that many elements are plainly dysfunctional, or even functionally irrelevant as inherited from past culture-history. Worse yet in the view of contemporary anthropologists, like the notorious Bastian, Malinowski would apply anthropology to colonial government. For Lowie, when "functionalism is reduced to what it is—a worthy program for ascertaining what intracultural bonds may exist," Malinowski remains "an ethnographic provincial" with an "adolescent eagerness to shock the ethnological bourgeois."

Thus from an eminent contemporary of Malinowski. Regard, again, his fate at the hands of his students. Considering that, for whatever reasons, their distinguished mentor had fallen into neglect, a group of Malinowski's students[14] joined in writing an intended rehabilitation of his reputation. But each specialist, in turn, concluded that Malinowski did not really understand kinship, or handled economics inadequately, or linguistics or whatever, though all could at last enthusiastically agree that, after all, as even Lowie conceded, Malinowski was a superb field worker. But then even this laudatory consensus evaporated on the lamentable publication, posthumously in 1967, of *A Diary in the Strict Sense of the Term*[15] in which it transpired that Malinowski really "hated his niggers" and preferred to cling to companionship with European colonials, to waste his time reading cheap romantic novels, or to suffer Portnoy's complaint. It looks very much as though, diachronically, Malinowski had become the Scyllan monster.

The extremeness of the range between messiah and monster may lead one to wonder whether it pays to become an eminent anthropologist, even if one could. Better to remain the hierodule of the reigning cognitive king! Stay "normal" scientist and be counted "sound"! The unreasonable and unrealistic range of attitudes toward another prominent colleague, Margaret Mead, is another case in point. The phenomenon is also current in the career of Lévi-Strauss, who, although incompletely translated at this writing, by some younger American anthropologists has already been solemnly pronounced "dead." In none of the social sciences, I suggest, is there such a swift passage between hyperdulia and contumely as in anthropology. Field work at the next yearly convention of the American Anthropological Association should confirm or disconfirm this hypothesis.

If eminence is a function of other anthropologists' opinions, then this should be a proper arena of inquiry. Perhaps anthropologists could learn some anthropology through scrutiny of themselves. This is a growing concern, most ably exemplified in Devereux's sophisticated study of countertransference to one's data,[16] but also evidenced in recent writings of other sensitive anthropologists.[17] Is it that, by definition self-alienated from his own culture, the maverick anthropologist has a consequently inordinate thirst for conformity to the current culture of fellow-anthropologists?[18] There is certainly a marked professional camaraderie among these social exiles. But such an explanation for a perhaps peculiarly American need to belong does not accord with the savage one-upmanship hierarchy of British social anthropologists, who in their fun and games often appear more tiresomely eager to advance the anthropologist than anthropology as a discipline. Or is this latter merely a matter of the notorious rudeness in British establishment circles, employed to keep others in their proper place? Or is it a question of the paucity of Oxbridge university jobs? Again, why is it that the French can tolerate only one ranking official intellectual at a time, now Sartre, now Lévi-Strauss? But prestigeful academic jobs are not plentiful in classical studies either, and I seem to discern far more decorous an urbanity and even polemic grace among Hellenists, who appear resigned to being ethnologists who are merely humanists. Or do all anthropologists suffer a fanatically religious *odium theologicum* because anthropologizing is everywhere truly crisis cult behavior, still attempting to surmount the Renaissance trauma? Laymen constantly and eagerly interrogate us for the truth, and in the public eye it all makes anthropology seem an excitingly fast-moving game, and the anthropologist a waggish fellow. Certain it is that anthropology obeys Kuhn's rules, often with unseemly alacrity.

Thus far, this phenomenological ethnology of ethnologists would appear only to expose motives. But every scientist has motives, and we do not darkly question physicists and chemists about theirs. The reason is that these scientists are not people studying people, and it remains true that the motives of "social scientists" should always be carefully scrutinized, lest they discover only what they *need to*, autobiographically. By analogy, but far more exquisitively, the psychiatrist must know himself, through a rigorous and often painful didactic analysis, *for he will not be able to see in his patients what he cannot afford to see in terms of his own defenses.* He must constantly ask, "What am I doing in saying this or asking that?"—that is, he must carefully watch his own countertransference to the patient. ("Am I seeking power over my patient? Am I showing what I know, indulging in one-upmanship? Am I being impermissively aggressive, in terms of my own needs and not my patient's? Why am I vexed with him at this moment? What anxieties does he arouse in me, and why? Am I projecting my own meaning, or patiently seeking his? And however firmly clear I finally am about the pattern, have we shared enough examples of it from his behavior now for the patient to be able to see his patterns despite his defenses? Can the patient bear the insight at his present anxiety level, or should we wait?"—etc., etc.) As a psychiatrically oriented anthropologist, I find the imperative of self-awareness inexorably imposed also on all anthropologists.

What are the alternative *methods* anthropologists use, and hence what are the subtypes of anthropologists? Largely, I think, the difference between the anthropological scientist (nomothete) and the anthropological humanist (idiographic naturalist) ultimately resolves into whether he chooses to use numbers or words as his model. What are the differences between numbers and words?

In the hands of physical scientists, number can undeniably accomplish spectacular results. In 1950, H. C. Urey examined a Jurassic belemnite roughly 150 million years old. From the isotopes of oxygen present, and their amounts, he was able to show that the animal was hatched in the spring, lived almost four years, and died in the spring; and that, during its lifetime, the temperature of the water in which it lived ranged from 68 to 70 degrees Fahrenheit in summer, and from 59 to 64 degrees in the winter. What an elegant scientific demonstration this is! How devoutly we would wish to be able to do this in the social sciences!

Now, the reason Dr. Urey was able to sustain these astonishing insights with confidence was that the *last significant difference* between the comparables consists in the differences between the isotopes of oxygen. Having no other differences, the isotopes were then fit to be counted and compared: number itself is only one step further denuded of all qualities. Knowing the biochemistry of organisms, Urey could make these statements because an atom of isotope X of oxygen is observed *always* to behave exactly like another atom of this isotope under the same circumstances of temperature. Indeed, the laws of chemistry are based on quite daring extrapolations: all isotope X atoms of an element behave exactly alike whenever they occur in time. So too in physics: if we observe anything with respect to magnetism-gravity in our portion of the universe, and are sure we are dealing with comparables, in this case energy-mass, then we can extrapolate the same principles to the farthest galactic system.

The elegance and precision of the physical sciences has led to quite premature attempts to take over the statistical methods of the physical sciences into the social sciences—premature largely because we sorcerer's apprentices have nowhere in our analyses reached anything like the *last significant difference* among "comparables" in the human data we observe. This statement is not to be taken as an indiscriminate attack on the use of quantitative techniques as such, but only to maintain a proper respect for them. All we insist upon (and numerologists think they have) are authentic comparables. It also helps to know qualitatively what we are measuring. The famous example from physical anthropology is Dixon's measurement and correlation of three indices of the head and nose, surely an "objective" and exact enough procedure. Thereupon Dixon[19] found "Melanesians" among the Pueblo Indians and "Australoids" in South America. What a superb method to trace racial, and hence cultural diffusions! The quietus on this scholasticism was rendered by Boas,[20] in his study of the children of immigrants in New York: children of dolichocephalic Italians became successively more brachycephalic the younger they were in the

family, whereas children of brachycephalic Ashkenazim Jews became successively more dolichocephalic. And now long shelves of patient craniometric
studies became waste paper for they had been measuring what was not genetically there. (Had they had illegitimate racist motives that anthropological reality failed to sustain?) One German scientist perfected over two hundred such
indices! If only he had had the computer then, we would doubtlessly have had
the triumph of computeroscopy for all time.

Social scientists often believe they are dealing with admissable comparables
in their data because they have *defined* them as such. But there's the rub: words
have now entered the picture. I firmly believe that, just as one is seemingly
born a Platonist or an Aristotelian, a Parmenidean or a Heraclitean,[21] so apparently one is born a quantifier or a qualifier, possibly even through comparative
brain-hemisphere dominance. Quantifiers say qualifiers do not understand
numbers. But qualifiers say that quantifiers do not understand words *or* numbers. In any case, numbers-minded and word-minded persons do differ widely
in their judgment of what constitutes authentic comparables in the social sciences. Numbers, say the rigorously verbal-minded, can be manipulated only if
the comparables are denuded *in nature* of every other single quality but one
and have qualitatively reached the level of "last significant difference." Words
cannot be made to jump through numerical hoops. They unfortunately cannot
be made comparables "by definition" because words are slippery in their Protean connotations and denotations, and a Procrustean lopping off of heads
and feet does a certain damage to the human data.

Eagerly quantitative individuals shirk all the remaining *and perhaps functionally significant* differences in their still-global data in order to reach their
putatively number-stark "comparables"—but qualifiers believe they have thus
mutilated and impoverished their data. The problem is peculiarly insuperable
with respect to ethnological data: perhaps one must be born into a culture in
order to handle its categories with any astuteness connotatively and denota-
tively. Besides, emic *pattern* and *context* are what we should really attend to
(data orientation), not fragmental etic numerical manipulation (method orientation). But may we not legitimately compare apples with oranges if we have
rigorously *defined* both as "fruits" and not "vegetables"?

No, says the verbally minded person, acutely sensitive to the semantic arbitrariness and cultural subjectivity of such labels in any verbally defined category. Any etic mode is one possible butchering of the world, admits the emic-
conscious person, and perhaps the Boston mode is as good as the differing
butchering method of Omaha meat packers when it comes to the eating, depending only on one's preferences for cuts of meat. But any etic mode is ethnographically *irrelevant* when it ignores native context and pattern in the
living culture. And it mixes up the desired scientific truth with the observed
ethnographic fact. Further, can we be sure that we are correct in categorizing
something as economic when it is more importantly religious in native eyes?
Again, is not every etic enterprise an attempt (wished) to translate (transmog-

rify) sometimes irrational(?)—(!)—human behavior into what is cognitively comfortable (rational) to the researcher (the old Renaissance trauma again)? For all our yearning loyalty to science, is not social science always subtly ethnocentric? Given our motives, cognitive homeostasis, is it really possible to be scientific about ourselves and others? Perhaps it is. But it means becoming clinical, and perhaps only humanist in the process.

Now, by no means are all nomothetic endeavors necessarily quantifying, any more than the designation "empirical" belongs exclusively to the quantifiers, as many of them seem easily to assume. There are many nonquantifying ways of being empirical. Consider the superb work of nonquantifying psychological experimentalists such as McClean on functional brain areas, or the productive naturalism of Dement on REM states. The clinical is a case in point. Ordinarily we would readily agree, a valid generalization necessitates $N + 1$ instances for it to be minimally established—and yet Freud's case of "Little Hans" did not really need Ferenczi's case of "Little Arpad" to prove what can easily stand on its own as a complex and self-consistent organic whole. To my mind, also, the Indo-Europeanist Bender sufficiently established that "-ock" is an archaic dualizing suffix in the single word "buttock" and does not really need the reduplicated pluralizing of "ballocks" to prove it, for this repluralizing merely confirms again that the suffix is archaic and now nonfunctional. Similarly, Malinowski's contrast of lagoon versus deep-sea fishing in the Trobriands alone is sufficient to establish a useful heuristic principle, widely applicable to secular versus magico-religious behaviors elsewhere. It is not really necessary to make an exhaustive statistical study of all inhabited Pacific atolls in order to use this insight, though it might be good for a grant.

There is also something to be said for expertise, and for being massively "soaked in the data." Many good ethnographers can confidently reply to the query, "How would the Bobobobo you studied react in this situation?" even though they might need to correct some implicit and irrelevant assumption of the questioner. Shall long experience count for nothing in making sound judgments? The "intuition"—nothing mystical but literally "imbedded learning"— of medical diagnosticians is sometimes of so high an order that the doctor can merely walk through his waiting room and know with assurance that "this is a gall-bladder case." His well-programmed mind has worked almost instantaneously to sort into a meaningful whole a complex of observations that he might even have difficulty in verbally articulating bit by bit without long explanation.

I once witnessed a brilliant Rorschacher, on the basis of a scant handful of responses, state flatly, "This man has a tumor in his right frontal lobe"—and upon operation a right-frontal tumor was found and removed. The procedure seems almost magical to those ignorant of Rorschach technique. But it produced verifiable results. The Rorschacher may later, somewhat painfully, point out consistent "organic signs" in the protocol—and did you notice the lack of speech slurring there would have been if it were on the left?—etc., etc. The

Rorschach test may sometimes seem to be only window-dressing for sheer clinical insight. But the Rorschacher meanwhile is surely demonstrating the ability to operate with "large W's" that is a sign of intelligence itself. Some individuals have this reticulated mode of clinical insight. Many linear thinkers do not. Nor may they have the experience and the open Gestalt preparedness to see the data that are waiting there.

Counting does have its uses in the social sciences. But in anthropology cultures are molar complexes, with reticulated meanings—that informants can tell us about best. Numbers here can only operate with etically fragmented shards assembled from maimed wholes. The less trivial and the more complex the data, the less legitimately available is the quantitative method. Besides, relevant quantifying can only operate on the basis of prior insight. Statistical voyagers from atoll to atoll would be mere camp followers of a masterly Malinowskian insight. The cultural statistician, curiously, cares little for insights into functioning wholes but seems principally enamored of his method. "Have method, will travel"—and from guru to guru as these kaleidoscopically change. "Empirical sociology" is already a mere branch of statistics, which is the main subject. However, we repeat, social science statistics are often useful in proving what we already know. Or think we know.

It may be impossible to show the numbers-minded why their manipulations are so unsatisfactory in the social sciences. Their statistical operations may be mathematically impeccable, the equations marvelously "sophisticated" (read, complex), but they have missed the boat. I have in mind here Whiting's[22] elegant Rube Goldberg contraption for explaining circumcision—in such rainy *kwashiorkor*-afflicted regions as, say, the *locus classicus* deserts of the pastoral-Semitic Near East, with polygyny thrown in free. In my view, the Semites have already explained the real motive for circumcision in their abundant documents, though it depends on only a single constantly reiterated and deeply imbricated symbol, the immortal snake.[23] If etically defined research later discovers that the wives of circumcised men have a lower incidence of cervical cancer, that is very interesting, and a triumph of etic science for us. But it is not the late-Old Stone Age motive for circumcision.

What is wrong with the quantifier is not only his locus of meaning but also his unexamined semantic predicament. Who cares about seventy percent truths anyway? This simply means that the numerical baskets are thirty percent full of irrelevant noncomparables. Some qualitatively undiscerned cobblestones have somehow gotten in with the apples and the oranges. The supposed entities turn out to have been only slippery words after all. They have evidently been dealing with something else, perhaps only round things. In the early days of anthropology, assuming that a field worker is manufactured through mere attendance at classes, Boas used to ask a single question of students returning from the field: "Did you find your Indians?" The question to be asked of the quantifying social scientist is, "Have you found your entities?" Are verbally defined data enough? Are words entities?

By no means. Let us push words to their limits. Take the quantifiably test-able question, "How many seats are chairs?" Quantifiers too easily believe that *definition* safely confines discrete numberlike entities that can then be manipu-lated numerically. But how do words behave semantically? Is a "seat" a chair, bench, bar stool, or something in a car, ski lift, train or plane? Is it an elective office in the legislature, a country place, a capital? Is a seat the rear of one's pants, or a privilege one buys at a ball game or concert for various prices depending on its location, has free on the floor in front of the TV, struggles to keep on a horse or tractor, but (depending on sexist training) should not keep when a lady is present? For that matter, is a "chair" a kind of formal public leadership, usually exercised standing up—no, it is a "bench" on the judiciary, *other* people stand up and the process begins when the man sits down, or when several judges sit, not on one bench but in separate swivel chairs—or is the chair what a judge gives murderers to their dismay, or a university professor-ship one avidly seeks and exercises mostly standing up, leaning on a podium or sitting affably on the corner of a table? As for "table," that favorite object of philosophers, well, that is a protean word we should probably table here.

In vain the quantifier insists, "This is ridiculous; we all know what I mean!" But do we? As very speakers of the same complexly connotative and denotative language, we amiably consent, perhaps unwittingly, that a seat is a chair is a bench is a table, and much else besides. At best, quantifying here is merely the impressive manipulation of already covertly accepted comparables, a *fait ac-compli*, so why bother?—but here we are back again at the sociologists' over-lapping circles. Consequently, for me, the main interest in a quantifying article lies in the proposition the author intends to prove. And of course he will, since negative results do not display his astuteness in framing hypotheses, and scho-lastic exercises in not-even-tangent circles are unpublishable. Meanwhile the only plausible "models" rest on prior consensus, which is unexamined ethnog-raphy.

For this, and other reasons, "problem-oriented" field work, even when un-quantified, is so often dubious, especially if the results are "positive." How do we know which island to select for such research? Are Arapesh and Mundugu-mor and Tchambuli all waiting there on one island to illustrate one's problem? Or would our crudely statistical probability sense feel more comfortable if Redd adventitiously found Tribe A in Ulan Bator, White found Tribe B in Kuala Lumpur, and Blu Tribe C in Uttar Pradesh—and no one was even look-ing for them? How did one fieldworker, setting up a theoretical paradigm while in New Guinea, presciently know the missing link would be found in Bali? Mead has borne much of the onus for her presumably psychoanalytic field work—but how accurately and justly, since much of it has been devoted to systematically "disproving" Freud's chief propositions: that passage from childhood to adulthood is for Oedipal reasons inevitably marked by the tur-moil of adolescence, that psychic ontogenesis universally follows biological paradigms, and that masculinity and femininity are psychologically shaped by the vicissitudes of the kind of body one has?

Authentic field work, I submit, is far more open-ended, discursive, and multi-dimensional. In not going to the field armed with prefigured questionnaires (which find only what they are shaped to find), culture-bound hypotheses (one is motivated to verify), models (based on what verbal analogies), and problems (whose?), anthropological field work is more like the naturalism of the clinical method. Beyond the hypothesis that human beings can communicate about themselves if only one listens and watches, how much does one really know beforehand when he goes to a new tribe, beyond a vague perception of his own somehow universal humanity? But from this he must constantly delete his own cultural presuppositions, as the clinician must constantly subtract his personal countertransference distortions. The associations are the patient's, the meanings the informant's. Learning a culture is much like learning an unknown language, with all kinds of unguessed symbols, structures, semantics. We guess that the language communicates. But we have to learn it.

Field work on cultural wholes is much like a double-acrostic puzzle—and if anthropology is so much like a game, ignoring for the moment why we play it, what are the rules of the game we are playing? In a double-acrostic puzzle we are given a number of blanks, prefigured by the culture so to speak, the meanings of which we laboriously piece together with what we find out from our informants. Their meanings and their contexts make up the answers. In a double-acrostic puzzle, each fragmentary meaning is part of a larger consistent whole: each word that satisfies the meaning occupies an exact number of spaces, and the puzzle maker, the society studied, directs us to place each meaningless phoneme into a statement; each letter-space is keyed to a larger pattern of meaning. Each definition-word is rigorously governed by the sense of the final statement and, as so often in field work, it may be that one is not sure of the right meaning until very late in the game. But as meaning gradually begins to emerge, one can read back and forth from diagram to definition, as well as the other way. Further, in a classic double-acrostic, the initial acronyms of the definitions, read vertically, give the name of an author and his book title. All these consistencies control the final solution; in anthropology, whatever consistencies are involved in biology, economics, religion, and a kinship system—all the functional relationships that knit a culture into a consistent whole—control and criticize the answer.

Now, the person who is busy with double-acrostic ethnographizing is scarcely concerned with scrutinizing his single steps (any more than the diagnostician is), or in making explicit why he assumes what he does. He easily discards a minor false inference, for he has no large ego-involvement in a fragmentary part-hypothesis. He knows, for example, that in an English sentence -- --- is likely to be o-f t-h-e, but he could be mistaken. It could be "to, at, by, on, in, if, as, or" etc., plus "the"—or it could be something else again. He can only establish this by minute and implicit computer-fast *ad hoc* hypotheses (constantly checking with his informant), and then testing back and forth constantly for consistency, meaning, and relevance. The inferences that crowd upon him are so low-level as hardly to deserve the name of hypotheses!

Part of his sense of procedure is contributed to by his awareness of the characteristic way single letters combine in the language (English words do not end in q, nor begin with ng). Let us say it is his morphophonemic sense, here close to a "clinical sense" (the clinician does not expect manic warmth in a schizophrenic, an hysteric denies the obvious and a compulsive is only pretending to seek it, a paranoiac does not load himself with depressive guilt, etc.). Perhaps the double-acrostic puzzle solver is indeed a "hunch artist"—but is not the physical scientist allowed even more grandiose hypotheses? He is not so much interested in procedures in his own mind as in relevance in his subject's. He knows that false solutions will be thrown out by their internal inconsistency with the whole (no one can "fake" a Rorschach). Thus, if the t-h-e he inferred turns out to be a-r-e, he has to erase part of it and try again. It is the multidimensional controlling consistencies that force a meaningful answer upon him. It is not irresponsible hunch artistry because the rules of the game (his clinical "methodology") will trip up all false hasty inferences. The pattern that emerges may still have minute errors left, but the chance of two completed solutions to a double-acrostic being both correct is astronomically remote. The clinician and the Rorschacher, the ethnographer and the analyst are all alike here: they soak themselves in the unreconstructed data, in naturalism as uncontaminated by the examiner as is humanly possible, in minute synthetic working on the richly reticulated qualitative details of holistic pictures. As hungry as the next man for nomothetic heurisms, I trust them all only with a benevolent skepticism and feel my feet more on the ground with sustaining idiographic detail. My model is Antaeus, not Pythagoras.

When a Definition is guessed, pencil it in the spaces given. Then write in the letters again in the puzzle Diagram, distributed as directed (A94, A12, A57, A81). In "O" for example, the word for "law-seeker" might be "plaintiff" since the number of letters fits—but it must obey other consistencies. For, when completed, the Diagram will read across horizontally (1, 2, 3, 4, etc.) as a complete sentence quotation from a book; further, the first letters of the Definitions (A, B, C, D, etc.) read vertically will give both the author and the title of the book from which the quotation is taken (there is no other "vertical" rationale, as in a crossword puzzle, but because of complex internal consistencies one *knows* he has the right answer and does not need to wait until next week's filled-in Diagram). One may make low-level hypothecations back and forth between Diagram and Definitions: for example, M74 and G75 in the Diagram/G might be "of"—or "it" or "is" or "he"—but it must fit the Definitions. So, too, E71, O72, Q73 might be "who"—or "for" or "she" or "the" or "but"—but always depending on fit both with the sentence-meaning and the Definitions. Correct meanings will be constantly rewarded with new

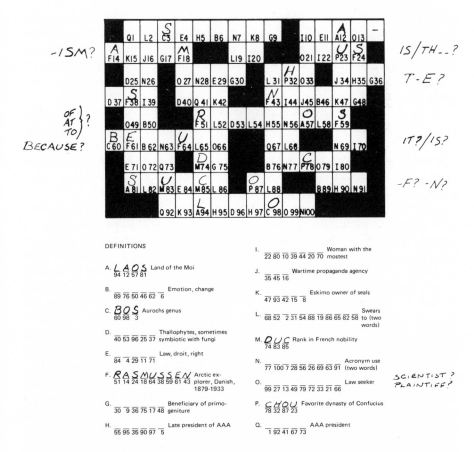

-ISM?

OF
AT }?
TO
BECAUSE?

IS/TH--?

T-E?

IT?/IS?

-F? -N?

DEFINITIONS

I. _ _ _ _ _ _ _ Woman with the
   22 80 10 39 44 20 70 mostest

A. L A O S Land of the Moi
   94 12 57 81

J. _ _ _ Wartime propaganda agency
   35 45 16

B. _ _ _ _ _ _ Emotion, change
   89 76 50 46 62 6

K. _ _ _ _ _ _ Eskimo owner of seals
   47 93 42 15 8

C. B O S Aurochs genus
   60 98 3

L. _ _ _ _ _ _ _ _ _ _ Swears
   68 52 2 31 54 88 19 86 65 82 58 to (two
                                   words)

D. _ _ _ _ _ Thallophytes, sometimes
   40 53 96 25 37 symbiotic with fungi

M. D U C Rank in French nobility
   74 83 85

E. _ _ _ _ _ Law, droit, right
   84 4 29 11 71

N. _ _ _ _ _ _ _ _ Acronym use
   77 100 7 28 56 26 69 63 91 (two words)

F. R A S M U S S E N Arctic ex-
   51 14 24 18 64 38 59 61 43 plorer, Danish,
                              1879-1933

O. _ _ _ _ _ _ _ _ _ Law seeker
   99 27 13 49 79 72 33 21 66

G. _ _ _ _ _ _ _ Beneficiary of primo-
   30 9 36 75 17 48 geniture

P. C H O U Favorite dynasty of Confucius
   78 32 87 23

H. _ _ _ _ _ _ _ Late president of AAA
   55 95 35 90 97 5

Q. _ _ _ _ _ AAA president
    1 92 41 67 73

SCIENTIST?
PLAINTIFF?

insights, as in field work, until, gradually, an irrefutable meaning will emerge, for any incorrect inference will be brought up short by inconsistency with the multiple logic of the method.

The reader, having inevitably put together the opinions evidenced in this paper, should now have some idea of where I stand as an anthropologist: not a scientist if, as usually in the social sciences, "scientist" means only the quantifier, for these quantifiers seem to me monumentally naive semantically and quite hopeless in understanding what numbers are and can be made to do. Not an experimentalist, since social science hypotheses tend so painfully to display autobiographical origins and motivations, and are, I think, inescapably ethnocentric. Instead, the anthropological holism I seek requires biology, primatology, human biology, folklore, anatomy, archaeology, linguistics, clinical psychology, *belles lettres*, history, psychiatry, art, and any other discipline that promises perspective on our complex human data; one is not impressed by what any of the "social sciences" have given us to date, and I think I know why they have not. For me, the books of Job and Genesis, *Moby Dick* and

Ulysses, the Parthenon and Senlis, Mozart and Bloch are all equally texts in anthropology, and I would as soon learn about the human from *Lophophora williamsii* as from a schizophrenic girl or a half-mad Siberian shaman. If anthropological holism means *Nil humanum alienum a me puto*, I would aspire to be called a humanist, if one ever knew enough about the human animal to deserve the appellation.

By training primarily an Americanist taught by Sapir, Spier, Wissler, Murdock, and Osgood, I have also benefited from the cultural anthropology of the Indonesianist Kennedy, the Africanist Herzog, and the Polynesian Te Rangi Hiroa (Sir Peter Buck), but could never get enough of Asia, though I lived for some years in China, India and Ceylon, and have visited Japan, Taiwan, Hong Kong (all three twice), Thailand, Singapore, and central Malaysia. An insatiable traveler, I have lived and traveled for six months in Bolivia, Chile, British Guiana, Peru, and Brazil, as well as visiting the Caribbean four times in Cuba, Puerto Rico, Bermuda (twice, for a total of two months), and have traveled across Africa twice, from the Gold Coast to Khartoum and from Cairo to Casablanca. I know most of the large cities and many of the college towns of the United States from many speaking tours and scientific congresses, as well as Canada (including Nova Scotia) and twice Mexico. Whatever linguistics I know came from Sapir and Bender, a Princeton professor who wrote all the etymologies of the second unabridged Webster, and the Anglo-Saxonist Elsasser, as well as the language teachers of the five languages I can speak adequately. Bender thought I should be a linguist when he sent me to Sapir, but at Yale slightly older graduate students already there were Voegelin, Whorf, Swadesh, Newman, Haas, and others, and after the culture shock of a course in Navaho with Sapir, I never aspired to compete with these formidable older colleagues in linguistics, though I remained an avid Indoeuropeanist as far as my abilities permitted and have lived and traveled over the years in twenty-five countries of Europe. My favorite tribes are the classic Greeks and the Jews, partly for technical reasons but also because they are my intellectual ancestors.

But the major influence on my anthropological thinking has been analytic psychiatry. Sapir considered that no one was prepared for certain kinds of field work, such as religion and culture-and-personality studies, unless he knew analysis thoroughly. Hence it was the fashion in the thirties at Yale to undergo a didactic analysis, and reading the classic works of Abraham, Jones, and Ferenczi was taken seriously. A post-doctoral fellowship year as research intern at the Menninger Clinic confirmed this interest, and I later had two more analyses, including a violently negative transference to a celebrated New York analyst, from whom I finally learned only decades afterward on my own. My third therapist made me his colleague in teaching at the Medical School of the University of North Carolina at Chapel Hill, and my wife and I have long been colleagues in psychiatry there and at Duke University and have published together.[24] Trained as a parachuter for the Office of Naval Intelligence, I was kidnapped from duty with them in Calcutta, Kunming, and Chungking by the

Office of Strategic Services, successively in the China-Burma-India unit in Delhi and the South East Asia Command in Kandy where I spent a much-remembered seven months (every anthropologist has a Goona-Goona land, and mine was Ceylon), and ended up attached to the Staffs of the Commander Destroyers Atlantic Fleet in Casco Bay and the Commander-in-Chief Atlantic Fleet in Bermuda; no warrior, I hasten to add, even parachuting was for me primarily a profoundly psychological experience, and my jobs were invariably in intelligence. I have taught anthropology at Rutgers, in summer sessions at Washington Square College, Wisconsin, Northwestern, Minnesota, North Carolina (also for some years in the UNC Medical School), and am now the James B. Duke Professor of Anthropology at Duke University. I have been a Sterling Fellow of Yale and a Guggenheim Fellow (also fellow of the Santa Fe Laboratory of Anthropology, American Museum of Natural History and Yale Institute of Human Relations, SSRC, Viking Fund, and twice NSF), and the initial recipient of the Róheim Award. As editor-in-chief of the *Landmarks in Anthropology* series, I have edited some 129 books in approximately 178 volumes. One of the professional honors I count highest has been my being invited some twenty times as consultant in the three-day semiannual conferences of the Group for the Advancement of Psychiatry, founded by William Menninger after the war, working with the Committee on Adolescence with whom I have also published.[25] In consequence of being an anthropologist with psychiatric training, I am pleased to be called on for such rewarding chores as speaker on a panel with Robert Stoller and the Johnson-Masters team at the American College of Psychiatrists in New Orleans, with Linus Pauling and Stanley Szurek on the President's Panel of the American Orthopsychiatric Association in San Francisco, and more recently as incumbent of the Simmel-Fenichel Lectures in Los Angeles. In descent, I am of so-called Old American pre-Revolutionary stock, including the Quaker divine John Woolman and Pennsylvania Dutch grantees of William Penn in Lancaster County. But the bar sinister in my French patronymic family was burned at the stake in 1766 at the age of eighteen in Abbeville, from which strain I may have inherited a certain maverick streak; his grandfather was Governor of New France just after Frontenac and lost a disastrous war with the Iroquois, which swung this powerful tribe to the side of the infant American colonies. Perhaps like him I am a spectacularly poor administrator, and (as was darkly alleged of my spiritual father, Edward Sapir) much prefer to "waste my time on students"—being delighted to help choose as departmental chairman a lady who promptly became president-elect of the American Anthropological Association. I like to think these mongrel origins make a case for "hybrid vigor," improved again in three stunning children by my marriage to a descendant of Danish sod house pioneers in frontier Minnesota, herself then the editor of a professional journal in New York and lately a winner of the Isabel Carter Award. *Haec sunt mea gaudia*, to which must be added extreme good fortune in my friends.

The *apologia pro opera sua* can best be done by simply exposing the methods used. *Native American Beers*,[26] my first professional article, was a distribution study, made from leftover data on psychotropic substances zealously compiled in one of twenty-two appendices to my doctoral dissertation; my thesis advisor, Leslie Spier, suggested I publish it in the *American Anthropologist* (he edited it at that time). This earliest effort achieved the distinction of a brief news article in *The New York Times*, affording the kind of feedback and appreciation so encouraging to a young writer. Although the article, like the dissertation itself, was thoroughly an example of then "normal" science, in my more innerdirected later efforts I have come to value the famous but little regarded words of Henry David Thoreau: "Why should we be in such desperate haste to succeed, and in such desperate enterprises? If a man does not keep pace with his companions, perhaps it is because he hears a different drummer. Let him step to the music which he hears, however measured or far away."

The Peyote Cult[27] was modeled after Spier's admirable study of the Sun Dance, though the study of peyotism afforded abundant oral history, collected by myself and generous colleagues, with no need to rely on statistical study of trait-distributions as Spier had. The publication of this dissertation by five publishers in over a dozen imprints and new editions, and three languages, though gratifying, is the result merely of a later unanticipated interest of the counterculture in its subject matter, for the book has no merit of innovation in method and is largely a meticulously compiled ethnography only. In this connection it is amusing that, when setting up a new tribal peyote cult, Indians have repeatedly consulted the rather jejune descriptive core of the monograph for details, with the result that scarcely any culture change in ritual has occurred in the past fifty years. This is further discomfiting, since one hardly expected to be the prophet in a religion of the book—for what if the young graduate student had made some error, thus to mislead later generations! Fortunately the conjectural elements, notably those on the Red Bean Cult, have been amply supported by archaeologists from Campbell and Troike to Adovasio and Fry.[28] In some cases, fieldworkers on specific tribes have tended to push back the date of acquisition to earlier cult-bringers; but peyotism has often been introduced several times into a tribe, and such field work is a useful refinement of my own. I have myself had second thoughts on the provenience of peyotism and wish we had more information from the little-known tribes of Texas and northeastern Mexico for another look at the matter. Spier was rigidly antipsychological and allowed no such material in the published version, edited while I was in South America, though some surreptitious psychological glints did get by in a few footnotes. And I learned, as does every graduate student, that no one should count himself a free agent intellectually in his doctoral dissertation. Indeed, both Róheim[29] and Hultkrantz[30] criticized the book—and quite rightly—for its dearth of individual psychological materials, though in the end I can scarcely be justly accused of being antipsychological. For myself, I prefer to the original text the again mounting appendices to the book, for these five- and ten-year supplements allow more perspective and reassessment.

Once interested, perhaps one is always interested in a subject, and out of this grew the concept of a New World "narcotic complex" (I would now prefer the term "psychotropic" as being more accurate),[31] and an ethnological understanding of the Old World/New World problem of botanical statistics on psychotropic plants; when a botanist noted the New World natives knew some eighty psychotropic plants, whereas the Old knew only a half-dozen, though the Old World was longer inhabited by men, had a larger land area, and certainly as varied plants and climates as the New, I suggested that perhaps the reason was that, ethnographically, American Indians in their concepts of "medicine power" were in a sense culturally programmed to discover psychotropic plant sources of such power.[32] Another study gives a larger perspective on American psychotropics.[33] It is a matter of some pride that on my second field trip, his first, I took along a Harvard undergraduate named Richard Evans Schultes, who after more than a dozen years of field work in Amazonia has become the ranking authority[34] on the ethnobotany of New World psychotropic plants, as I may be of the ethnology.

My first properly psychological, indeed psychiatric, paper was *The Psychopathology of Drinking Songs*,[35] a rather light-hearted scrutiny of limericks collected at Princeton beer parties and at Mory's at Yale, showing the content of the "normal unconscious" when the superego is liquidated in alcohol. It seemed that limerick singers were preoccupied with, of all things, Oedipal revolt, lampooning of authority figures, youthful atheism, male and female sexuality (including perversions and fixations), auto-erotism, anality, coitus and its variants, and (often unintended) pregnancy and other anxieties. The study was first presented as a paper at an evening meeting of the senior staff at the Menninger Clinic, none of whom appeared startled at its disclosures, though it achieved attention in an article with the clever title "Beneath Genteel Externals" in a weekly news magazine.

Some Observations on Character Structure in the Orient: I. The Japanese[36] was a psychoanalytically oriented culture and personality study, based on War Relocation Authority internees at Topaz, Utah, and on wartime interrogation of Japanese prisoners in the Red Fort at Old Delhi during the war. Anthropologists and sociologists, plainly upset by its analytic clinical approach, have long found it a convenient target as a presumably "early impressionist" culture and personality study, without any method beyond hunch-ethnography. It was not. Roiled by the method, critics quite failed to discern the method. The method was deductive. Observing that the Japanese encountered were markedly compulsive, I carefully listed all the traits which clinical work indicates are characteristic of the compulsive personality, together with the life history vicissitudes that ontogenetically and regularly produce the compulsive. Thereupon, voluminous ethnographic data were cited in order to ascertain whether there was a deductive matching between the clinical and the ethnographic. There was. QED, I thought. But I did not know then the degree of anxiety and danger aroused in people by a method that unpleasantly informs them of what they do not want to know about themselves. However, a baker's dozen of later studies of the Japanese ethos, using the Rorschach and other more acceptable methods, have uniformly demonstrated the the the Japanese are, surprisingly, compulsive. Since that time, of course, there are many younger[37] psychological anthropologists quite adequately qualified to use analytic theory; and Margaret Mead,[38] at the outset of her masterly summary of the work of a large psychological congress at Houston in 1968, stated that in four decades of culture and personality studies the basic stratum of theory has been the psychoanalytic. Twenty years was a long time to wait.

Curiously, a second and longer such study, on the Chinese, much more discursively ethnographic despite its implicitly analytic method, aroused no such indignation and it has been placidly anthologized and excerpted ever since. The experience taught me that method is what alerts colleagues, not the subject matter delineated: the method is the message. But it takes stamina for the young anthropologist to stand in a rain of contemporary disfavor. *The Aymara of the Lake Titicaca Plateau, Bolivia*[39] would be, if nothing else, a thoroughly standard ethnography. The fate of this monograph is curious. John Gillin, a superbly qualified reviewer, was assigned the book. But shortly afterward he was to undergo a potentially grave major operation, and my reaction to my old friend and admired predecessor at Duke University was, "John, please don't bother about it now!" Gillin sturdily survived the operation for some decades, and the book was never reassigned from so obviously appropriate a reviewer. Although it was a Memoir of the American Anthropological Association, the monograph was never reviewed and is almost entirely unknown. To me this was a minor and perhaps undeserved professional disaster, since long argument with the Memoir editor, John Alden Mason, had finally succeeded in including a long section on the uncustomary subject of "Native Knowledge, or Folk Sciences." These included ethnometeorology, ethnohistory (read, folk history), ethnobotany, ethnoanatomy and ethnophysiology, ethnoanthropology, ethnopsychology, ethnoethnology, and ethnogeography. Since the Aymara are specialists in it, ethnomedicine required additional, separate treatment and further articles, while the data on ethnobotany were so voluminous as to require a separate monograph, published in my favorite Italian city, Firenze. As a result, I have long privately thought that "the new ethnography" was not so new after all, being already present in this monograph of 1948, indeed in still earlier articles of 1942 and 1947.[40]

Publication of my Aymara field work has taught me, if nothing else has, the sometimes wide discrepancies between one's own and others' judgments of his work. As a last scraping of the bottom of the barrel, there were left some field notes on the potato taxonomy of the Aymara which, not valuing them much, I published in an obscure and now extinct journal.[41] But the fantastically omnivorous Lévi-Strauss found it! It is the only work of mine he has ever cited (though I did send him *The Human Animal* in thanks for his serving as my NSF sponsor in Paris), but I nevertheless remain puzzled to find it in the canon of the younger social anthropologists. The Aymara have an interesting binomial system of plant nomenclature, but I had never *done anything* in writing this article, I had only carefully reported voluminous categories of the Aymara, and to them belonged any credit! Perhaps sheer information is still the more to be valued than the fanciest "method" in ethnography, of which this paper had quite none at all. Consequently, any kudos with respect to the Aymara field work has come from a simple reportorial minor article, not from innovations in an unknown book.

Other Aymara work concerned their ethos.[42] I found them "truculent, hostile, silent, and unsmiling in all their dealings with whites." Now, field work in the barren and cold windswept Titicaca plateau, as in many other places, is admittedly not pleasant physically. After several experiences of attempted kindness met with treachery, I began to blame myself and to be concerned with "countertransference." What, possibly, was I myself contributing to this untoward judgment? I had always liked the straightforward temperament of the Plains Indians among whom I had worked on two earlier field trips. Postfield library work, however, quickly revealed that earlier students had expressed still harsher judgments. A Frenchman found them "cruel, awkward, and repulsively ugly" (Grandidier, in 1861); a Scot, "silent, and uncommunicative, intensely suspicious and distrustful' and filled with "deep-rooted and inveterate hatred" (Forbes, 1870); an American, "more sullen, and more cruel" than the Quechua, and "a people notoriously morose, jealous, and vindictive" (Squier, 1877); and another Frenchman, "hard, vindictive, bellicose, rebellious, egotistical, cruel, and jealous . . . lacking in will, except the will to hate" (Walle, 1914). Indeed, shortly before my stay, another American had considered them "the most difficult of all Andean peoples to cultivate . . . disagreeable . . . dishonest and generally unreliable. . . . Here is a rare opportunity for the ethnologist who is looking for a tough job" (Hewlett, 1938). Better to have gone to Wetar in Indonesia, as I had at first planned, until it was learned that Du Bois was going to Alor! One writer even invoked for the Aymara a degenerative "racial or ethnic disease" (Adams, 1915). Indeed, the Aymara themselves had a word, *qaiya*, for their sullen melancholy. I returned several times to the problem, to measure these multi-national "subjective" assessments of ethos against "projective" data in the form of the Aymaras' own folktales. A 100 percent sample of tales, collected earlier for linguistic studies, was examined and finally a psychological-historical explanation was offered for the findings: "If the Aymara, as evidenced in their folk tales (and indeed throughout the rest of their culture), are apprehensive, crafty, suspicious, violent, treacherous, and hostile, one important reason for this may be that such a character structure is an understandable response to their having lived for perhaps as long as a millenium under rigidly hierarchic and absolutist economic, military, and religious controls"—successively of the ancient Colla empire (when chiefs were carried in litters), the conquering Inca, the Conquistadores, the colonial Spanish, and the postcolonial Bolivians. Curiously, in the last two decades, younger Aymarists (Heath, Plummer, Carter, Cole, Hickman) have taxed me with giving a wholly inaccurate picture of the Aymara, whom they found friendly, cheerful, and cooperative during the post-Revolution field work of these students. Moreover, the new fieldworkers are mutually consistent in the matter. Was a whole generation of earlier workers mistaken, despite the range of time and variety of nationalities represented? Perhaps this only demonstrates that ethos, a learned complex, is not necessarily stable diachronically and that nongenetic ethos can be as changeable as culture. The ethnographic "experiment" here prepared for us by history, I would observe, has given results not inconsistent with the findings of clinical psychologists when describing the contrastive effects on children's groups of authoritarian versus permissive treatment by adults. Historically, the Bolivian peasant rebellion seems in fact to have been one of the few authentic revolutions in Latin America, with real changes between the thirties and the sixties in basic politico-economic structure beyond the usual mere circulation in personnel. If this is true, the answer may remain culture-historical: with drastic change in social conditions, the Aymara ethos has apparently veered 180 degrees. Since the new Aymarists are manifestly competent and mutually consistent, any humanist will be thoroughly gratified with their findings.

The Human Animal[43] was a first venture into anthropological holism, into what I did not then but might now call the "ethology of culture." The experience of all my major book manuscripts, save for The Aymara, has uniformly been rejection by a dozen publishers each. The first version, of article length, was rejected by Benedict, as advisory editor of Psychiatry, for being "too Spencerian." However, like most students of the Boasian tradition, I had been restive with ethnography as mere piles of ethnographic information, and was in search of some unifying principle. Could this not be done by putting together physical anthropology, ethnology, and linguistics, and trying to make sense of the whole? But my generation of graduate students had been rigorously drilled to accept that biology (race) and culture have two entirely distinct modes of filiation, biological and sociological, and never the twain could meet. Perhaps, also, an honorable field-oriented anthropology had totally failed to sustain racist superstitions. Nevertheless, could not an adequately species-specific human biology encompass all these aspects of man? This biology I found in analytic psychology—which was doubly to damn it. Melville and Frances Herskovits, citing their own successful encounter with the formidable Boas over Africanisms in the Americas, encouraged my heresy, without necessarily agreeing with it. One celebrated physical anthropologist jeered at this heretical holism and strongly urged rejection by the ultimate publisher. But a stubborn editor, since established as one of the foremost publishers of anthropological materials in the United States, Alexander Morin, with whom it is only fair to say I rewrote the book, persisted. A comforting irony is that several physical anthropologists, including my irate reader, have since compiled symposia on man's biological adaptations to culture and the species-specific grounds in human biology for culture-bearing. Of later physical anthropologists, Frederick Hulse, James Spuhler, and Alice Brues have most elegantly handled these ideas. As Heller[44] has noted, the history of an idea is to begin as heresy, and to end as a commonplace banality. But again the irony of the Japanese study: the conclusions were readily adopted, but the method of reaching them contemned.

They Shall Take Up Serpents: Psychology of the Southern Snake-Handling Cult[45] was forced on me as ethnography lying virtually at my front door, since an interstate conference of snake-handling churches was held in 1948 in Durham, North Carolina. My relationship with the organizer of the conference, the snake-handling minister "Beauregard Barefoot," was long and clinically edifying, though I ended up with a certain humanistic sympathy for him and his poor-white clientele, and the snake-handling cult itself was reassurance to me that anthropologists would not necessarily be technologically unemployed with the final acculturation of the last "untouched" tribe in highland New Guinea or central Amazonia. The method of the book was quite simple and clear from its divisions: first, the ethnography and history of the cult movement, then its Old World origins and symbolisms in the Old Testament, and finally the autobiography of the snake-handling preacher, which was of necessity treated as a clinical document. The study furthered my understanding of the relationship between personality and culture, and the data dynamically illustrated Freud's observation that hysteria and psychopathy are two sides of the same coin, for the acting-out leader and his repressed clientele were symbiotically made for each other. Cultist snake-handling has largely died out, as I predicted, in the urbanizing and industrializing Piedmont, but a number of workers are studying the continued persistence of snake-handling in Appalachia, among whom I consider the present authority on the snake-handling cult to be Steven Kane, now a graduate student at Princeton.

Another interest has been kinesics and nonverbal communication. *The Cultural Basis of Emotions and Gestures*[46] has been considerably anthologized, but I now regard *Paralinguistics, Kinesics and Cultural Anthropology*[47] and *Ethology and Ethnology*[48] as more developed studies. An international conference at Royaumont on dreams—and especially association there with the psychologist William Dement and the Hellenist E. R. Dodds—further stimulated my interest in the relationship of REM state dreams to the charisma and visionary innovations of the culture-hero founders of crisis cults.[49] As a prolific reviewer, I consider the book review an art form, demanding much of the discipline of a short story or *haiku*. Of mine, the favorite half-dozen that best succeed in saying what I wanted to, may be still worth reading.[50]

The culmination of a holistic interest in human biology and culture is my major work, *The Ghost Dance: The Origins of Religion*.[51] It is a complex book, with several main themes. Anthropologists have long puzzled over the definitions, taxonomy, and institutionalization of magic and religion, but it seems to me that the difference lies not so much in differing real objectivities in the outside world as in their being basically different subjective ways of apperceiving the unknown. That unknown is here less outside than inside man. Since religion appears to be inclusively and exclusively human, its roots must lie in human biology, and these sources can be studied ontogenetically through dynamic psychiatry, as well as "phylogenetically" though archaeology, explicit history, comparative ethnography, and species-specific human biology. Further, no earlier anthropologist had ever concerned himself with the question *why magic and religion have such emotional plausibility*, since both are so often in manifest conflict with explicit rational experience. These origins lie emotionally in the ontogenetic development of each individual personality, and as universally as the developmental stages in neotenous *Home sapiens*. Indeed, the universally present *types* of magic, I believe, must ultimately rest on the universal human experiences of learning to walk and to talk. To walk is to learn an impressive new voluntary control of one's body and much of the material environment, a potency that includes "alloplastic" evolution as a peculiarly human evolution culturally. But, regressively in crises of ego-technique controls, this valid and experienced control of one's organism is illegitimately extrapolated if it is supposed that control of part of an enemy's substance, his exuviae, means affecting his now-discrete organism. Exuvial or contagious magic thus misconstrues the nature of organism. Similarly, to talk is to discover the almost magical power of symbols in adapting to and even managing other human beings. But this valid and experienced power does not operate, as homeopathic magic assumes, through mere verbal means, on the puppet that merely *symbolizes* the enemy, for this is falsely to extrapolate the nature of symbols. Thus, exuvial magic misapprehends the nature of organic things, effigy magic the nature of symbols. Again, since in sober fact all our information about the "supernatural" comes exclusively from charismatic personalities, our relation to which can be examined psychiatrically, why not then examine cultural crisis situations, in which dependency on personal authority is substituted for our experience of reality. Since the *de facto* source is always clear, why not give up *de jure* wranglings over *truth* arrived at by unexaminable "supernatural" means, and instead study naturalistically these charismatic utterances as clinical and ethnographic *fact*, together with a study of these vatic culture heroes and the socio-cultural conditions under which they operate. An earnest cultivation of the scientist's careful discrimination between what is inside (hypothesis) versus what is outside (phenomena) could only end in perceiving that the secular is adaptive to "outside" but the sacred only to "inside" realities. The contrast of sacred and secular, religious and rational, is further the contrast of two experienced epistemological modes, REM state and waking state.

This rigorously secular approach to religion implies ultimately a benevolently skeptical attitude even toward culture itself, and as such is perhaps shocking. A medical student taking a reading course with me in psychoanalytic psychiatry, after he had read *The Ghost Dance* remarked amazedly, "Sir, you would say *anything* if you thought it was true!" When I survey the customary reaction to my often ungenteel and group-unchastened statements, perhaps his amazement is justified with respect to religion, the understanding of which has been traditionally so hampered by our emotional vested interests, and hence by the privileged position we give religion as presumably unexaminable subjective human experience. But the subjective *is* examinable clinically. The procedure is likely to infuriate all true believers, and many other people besides, but I had long since decided in lone battle that I knew what I knew about secular psychiatry. The locus of the "*super*natural" world is the "*sub*conscious" mind, as projected in the crisis-cult revelation-vision of the leader while in a dissociated state; but REM dreams and all other dissociated states are equally open to secular scrutiny.[52] The Ghost Dance is one type of the seemingly endless and ubiquitous crisis cults in societies suffering cultural trauma (the discovery of the fallible defensive nature and limitations of one's own culture). But the social context of these traumata also can be examined, both historically and ethnographically as well. With insights derived from psychiatrically sophisticated human biology into the nature and purpose of culture, and the abundant comparative ethnography of crisis cults in their social context, insights gained into culture heroes and their charisma can then be applied to our own Graeco-Hebraic tradition. Charisma, which seems to be a "supernatural" *rightness* streaming from the charismatic individual, is merely the emotional welcomeness of his message, *déjà vu* in the prepotent unconscious wishes of each communicant. A somewhat startling discovery on examination of occidental culture-history was that Platonism and the whole Great Tradition in Western philosophy and religion can be traced and unmistakably demonstrated continuously clear back to Old Stone Age origins. In another book I intend to pursue study of this tenacious *continuity* of culture, in the context of an amazingly widespread superstition about ourselves, before embarking on the third work of a proposed trilogy, begun by *The Human Animal* and continued in *The Ghost Dance*, to be titled *The Singing Head*.

Reference Notes

1. H. W. Zorbaugh, *Gold Coast and Slum* (Chicago: University of Chicago Press, 1929); Frances R. Donovan, *The Saleslady* (Chicago: University of Chicago Press, 1929); and Clifford R. Shaw, *The Jack-Roller* (Chicago: University of Chicago Press, 1930).
2. "Professor Widjojo Goes to the Koktel Parti," *New York Times Magazine*, 9 December 1956, 17ff.; republished, "Totemistic Celebrations," *The College Years*, ed. A. C. Spectorsky (New York: Hawthorne Books, 1958), pp. 396–98; R. W. Hoffmann and R. Plutchik, eds., *Controversy* (New York: G. P. Putnam's Sons, 1959), pp. 129–32; "The Koktel Parti," *Background and Foreground*, ed. Lester Markel (Great Neck, N.Y.: Channel Press, 1960), pp. 256–61; "Professor Widjojo's Field Trip to the Us-ans," *Duke Alumni Register* 50 (January 1954), 4–7.
3. Sir James G. Frazer, *Folklore in the Old Testament* (London: Macmillan, 1919), 3 vols.
4. E. Sapir, *Time Perspective in Aboriginal American Culture, A Study in Method* (Ottawa: Canada Department of Mines, Geological Survey Memoir 90 [#13 Anthropological Series], 1916); reprinted, New York: Johnson Reprint Corp., 1968.

5. M. E. Spiro, "Culture and Personality, The Natural History of a False Dichotomy," *Psychiatry* 14 (1951), 19–46.

6. W. La Barre, *The Ghost Dance: Origins of Religion* (New York: Doubleday, 1970; London: Allen & Unwin, 1972); revised paperback edition (New York: Delta Books, 1972), pp. 46–48.

7. W. La Barre, "Social Cynosure and Social Structure," *Journal of Personality* 14 (1946), 169–83; reprinted in *Personal Character and Cultural Milieu*, ed. D. G. Haring (Syracuse: Syracuse University Press, 1956), pp. 535–45, now chap. 8, this volume; "Cynsures (points de mire) et structures sociales," *Revue de Psychologie des Peuples* 8 (1953) 362–77; Warren Morrill, "Social Cynosure and Cultural Adaptation," *Anthropology Tomorrow* 6 (April 1960), 8–12.

8. M. S. Edmonson, "Nativism, Syncretism and Anthropological Science," *Nativism and Syncretism* (New Orleans: Middle American Research Institute, Tulane University, Publication 19, 1960, 183–203), pp. 186–88.

9. Barbara G. Myerhoff, *Peyote Hunt: The Sacred Journey of the Huichol Indians* (Ithaca: Cornell University Press, 1974), p. 230.

10. T. S. Kuhn, *The Structure of Scientific Revolutions* (Chicago: University of Chicago Press, Phoenix Books, 1962).

11. Paul Tillich, *The Courage To Be* (New Haven: Yale University Press, 1952).

12. Robert H. Lowie, *The History of Ethnological Theory* (New York: Farrar & Rinehart, 1937), pp. 230–42.

13. Lowie cited in W. La Barre, "The Influence of Freud on Anthropology," *American Imago* 15 (1958), 281, 292–94. See also S. Axelrod, review of Hendrick, *American Anthropologist* 61 (1959), 548–49; and a letter of R. Benedict to M. Mead, *An Anthropologist at Work* (Boston: Houghton Mifflin, 1959), p. 305.

14. R. W. Firth, ed., *Man and Culture: An Evaluation of the Work of Bronislaw Malinowski* (London: Routledge & Kegan Paul; New York: Humanities Press, 1957). Ronald Cohen (review of M. Gluckman, *American Anthropologist* 67 [1965], 954) wonders "why a man who in the passage of time had been so wrong on so many counts, had during his lifetime been hailed as such an all-encompassing leader not only of his discipline, but of western intellectual life as a whole."

15. B. Malinowski, *A Diary in the Strict Sense of the Term* (New York: Harcourt Brace and World, 1967).

16. G. Devereux, *From Anxiety to Method in the Behavioral Sciences*, with a preface by W. La Barre (The Hague: Mouton, 1967), *Angst und Methode in den Verhaltenswissenschaften*, W. La Barre (München: Hanser Verlag, 1973).

17. R. M. Wintrob, "An Inward Focus: A Consideration of Psychological Stress in Field Work," *Stress and Response in Field Work*, ed. F. Henry and S. Saberwal (New York: Holt, Rinehart & Winston, 1969), pp. 63–76; A. N. J. den Hollander, "Social Description: The Problems of Reliability and Validity," *Anthropologists in the Field,* ed. D. G. Jongmans and P. C. W. Gutkind (Assen: Van Gorcum, 1967; New York: Humanities Press, 1970); Eleanor Bowen (Laura Bohannan), *Return to Laughter* (New York: Harper & Sons, 1954); Fred Gearing, *Face of the Fox* (Chicago: Aldine Press, 1970); Kenneth Read, *High Valley* (New York: Scribners, 1965); G. W. Berreman, *Behind Many Masks* (Ithaca: Society for Applied Anthropology Monographs, 4, 1962); Hortense Powdermaker, *Stranger and Friend* (New York: Norton, 1966); W. La Barre, *The Ghost Dance*, pp. 52–53; Barbara Gallatin Anderson, "Adaptive Aspects of Culture Shock," *Abstracts*, 67th Annual Meeting of the American Anthropological Association, 1968, p. 4; G. D. Spindler, ed., *Being an Anthropologist: Field Work in Eleven Cultures* (New York: Holt, Rinehart & Winston, 1970); M. Freilich, ed., *Marginal Natives: Anthropologists at Work* (New York: Harper and Row, 1970).

18. La Barre, *Ghost Dance*, pp. 4, 52–53, 289–90.

19. R. B. Dixon, *The Racial History of Man* (New York: Scribners, 1923).

20. F. Boas, "Changes in Bodily Form of Descendants of Immigrants," *Race, Language and Culture* (New York: Macmillan, 1940), pp. 60–75.

21. La Barre, *Ghost Dance*, pp. 507–8, fn. 23.

22. J. W. M. Whiting, "Effects of Climate on Certain Cultural Practices," *Explorations in Cultural Anthropology: Essays in Honor of George Peter Murdock*, ed. W. Goodenough (New York: McGraw-Hill, 1964), pp. 511–44.

23. W. La Barre, *They Shall Take Up Serpents: Psychology of the Southern Snake-Handling Cult* (Minneapolis: University of Minnesota Press, 1962; New York: Schocken Books, 1969), pp.

78–84, 107. See also, W. La Barre, "The Snake-Handling Cult of the American Southeast," Goodenough, *Explorations*, pp. 309–33, reprinted in *Bobbs-Merrill Reprint Series in Anthropology*, 1971.

24. Maurine and Weston La Barre, "The Worm in the Honeysuckle; A Case Study of a Child's Hysterical Blindness," *Social Casework* 47 (July 1965), 399–413, reprinted as chap. 11, this volume; "The Triple Crisis: Adolescence, Early Marriage, and Parenthood," *The Double Jeopardy, The Triple Crisis* (New York: National Council on Illegitimacy, 1969).

25. *Normal Adolescence: Its Dynamics and Impact* (New York: Scribners, 1948, GAP Report No. 68); *Come Costrire l'Adolescente Normale: La curiosità l'esigenza di libertà la maturazione sessuale* (Milano: Ferro Edizione, 1969); *Ungdommen og Samfunnet, En bok om vanlig ungdom for foreldre, oppdragene, ungdomsledere og de unge selv* (Oslo: H. Aschenhoug & Co., 1969); *Dinamica da Adolescencia, Aspetos biologicos, culturais e psicologicos* Sao Paolo: Editora Culturix, 1970). Other articles on childhood and adolescence: W. La Barre, "Toward World Citizenship," *Survey Graphic* 85 (March 1949), 153–56, 187–89, reprinted as a training document (Washington: State Department Foreign Service Institute, 1949); "Child Care and World Peace," *The Child* 13 (1949), 156–57, also reprinted as an FSI training document; "Wanted: A Pattern for Modern Man" (New York: National Committee for Mental Health pamphlets, 1949), reprinted in *Child-Family Digest* 1 no. 3 (August 1949), 17–31, and in *Sociology: A Book of Readings*, ed. S. Koenig, R. D. Hopper, and F. Gross (New York: Prentice-Hall, 1953); "The Age Period of Cultural Fixation," *Mental Hygiene* 33 (1949), 209–21; "The Family, Its Functions and Future," *Child-Family Digest* 2 (June 1950), 3–16; "The Family: Fundamentals versus Filigree," *Child-Family Digest* 5 (July 1951), 3–13; "Family and Symbol," *Psychoanalysis and Culture: Essays in Honor of Geza Roheim*, ed. G. W. Wilbur and W. Muensterberger (New York: International Universities Press, 1951), pp. 156–67; "Appraising Today's Pressures on Family Living," *Journal of Social Casework* 32 (1951), 51–57; "Self Respect and Mental Maturity," *Child-Family Digest* 13 (September 1955), 3–16, reprinted in Michigan Society for Mental Health *Mental Health Bulletin* 12 no. 2 (1955), 1–6; "The Social Worker in Cultural Change," *Social Welfare Forum*, 1957, pp. 179–93; "The Social Cell," *Saturday Review* 38 no. 17 (23 April 1955), 17, reprinted *Child-Family Digest* 12 (June 1955), 74–76; "The Patient and His Families," *Casework Papers* (New York: National Conference on Social Welfare, Family Service Association of America, 1958), pp. 61–71, reprinted, *Child-Family Digest* 18 (January-February 1959), 9–18, also reprinted as chap. 10, this volume; "Adolescence: Lesson in History," *Child Study* 36 (1959), 10–15; "How Adolescent Are Parents?" *National Parent-Teacher, The PTA Magazine* 54 (December 1959), 4–6; "Relations Between Parents and Children," *Understanding Family Dynamics* (Pittsburgh: Family Living Institute, 1960), reprinted *Child-Family Digest* 19 (July-August 1960), 15–16, and "Les relations entre les parents et les enfants," *Medicine et Hygiene* (Geneva, Switzerland), 20 no. 559 (30 July 1962), 604–6; "The Well-Disciplined Parent," *Christian Home*, 20 no. 2 (February 1961), 12–14, reprinted in *Adult Teacher* 14 no. 5 (May 1961), 4–6; "The Trouble with Young People Nowadays is . . .," *Carnegie Review* 10 (January 1967), 3–12; "Adolescence, the Crucible of Change," *Social Casework* 50 (January 1969), 22–26; "Authority, Culture Change and the Courts," *Loyola Law Review* 18 no. 3 (1971–1972), 481–92, reprinted as chapter 9, this volume.

26. W. La Barre, "Native American Beers," *American Anthropologist* 40 (1938) 224–34; "Aboriginal Americans Liked Their Liquor," *New York Times*, 6 March 1938.

27. W. La Barre, *The Peyote Cult* (New Haven: Yale University Publications in Anthropology, 19, 1938); reprinted (Hamden, Conn.; Shoe String Press, 1959, 1964, 1968, 1970, 1975; New York: Schocken Books, 1969, 1970, 1975). For defenses of peyotists see Franz Boas, A. L. Kroeber, A. Hrdlicka, J. P. Harrington, M. R. Harrington, W. La Barre, V. Petrullo, R. E. Schultes, Elna Smith, and Chief Lookout, "Statement against the Chavez Senate Bill 1349," *Congressional Record*, 8 February 1937; and W. La Barre, D. P. McAllester, J. S. Slotkin, O. C. Stewart, and S. Tax, "Statement on Peyote," *Science* 114 no. 2970 (30 March 1951), 582–83. For reviews see W. La Barre of J. S. Slotkin, *The Peyote Religion*, in *American Anthropologist* 59 (1957), 350–60; of D. F. Aberle and O. C. Stewart, Navaho and Ute Peyotism, *American Anthropologist* 60 (1958), 171; of C. B. Dustin, "Peyotism and New Mexico," *Western Folklore* 21 (1962) 211; and the film review of Peter Furst, "To Find Our Life: The Peyote Hunt of the Huichols of Mexico," *American Anthropologist* 72 (1970), 1201.

28. W. La Barre, "Mescalism and Peyotism," *American Anthropologist* 59 (1957) 708–11; T. N. Campbell, "Origin of the Mescal Bean Cult," *American Anthropologist* 60 (1958), 156–60;

R. C. Troike, "The Origin of Plains Mescalism," *American Anthropologist* 64 (1962), 946–63; J. M. Adovasio and G. F. Fry, "Prehistoric Psychotropic Drug Use in Northeastern Mexico and Trans-Pecos Texas," Paper, *Seventy-First Annual Meeting, American Anthropological Association*, Toronto, 1972, mimeographed.

29. G. Róheim, Review, *Psychoanalytic Quarterly* 8 (1939) 248–49.

30. Ake Hultkrantz, in "Twenty Years of Peyote Studies," *Current Anthropology* 1 (1960), 45–60, p. 57.

31. W. La Barre, "The Narcotic Complex of the New World," *Diogenes* 48 (1964), 125–28, reprinted in *Bobbs-Merrill Reprint Series in the Social Sciences*, 1969 and 1971; "Le complexe narcotique de L'Amerique autochtone," *Diogène* 48 (1964) 120–34; "El complejo narcótico de la América Autóctona," *Diógenes* 48 (1964) 102–12. The term "psychotropic" is suggested in *Twenty Years*, p. 54 (p. 204, in 1964 and later editions of *The Peyote Cult*). See also Carol C. Barber, "Peyote and the Definition of Narcotic," *American Anthropologist* 61 (1959), 641–46.

32. W. La Barre, "Old and New World Narcotics: A Statistical Question and an Ethnological Reply," *Economic Botany* 24 no. 1 (1970), 73–80.

33. W. La Barre, "Hallucinogens and the Shamanic Origins of Religion," in *Flesh of the Gods: The Ritual Use of Hallucinogens*, ed. P. T. Furst (New York: Praeger, 1972), pp. 261–78; "Anthropological Perspectives on Hallucination and Hallucinogens," *Hallucinations: Behavior, Experience, Theory*, ed. R. K. Siegel and L. J. West (New York: John Wiley and Sons, 1975), pp. 9–52.

34. Richard Evans Schultes and Albert Hofmann, *The Botany and Chemistry of Hallucinogens* (Springfield, Illinois: Charles C Thomas, 1973).

35. W. La Barre, "The Psychopathology of Drinking Songs," *Psychiatry* 2 (1939) 203–12; "Beneath Genteel Externals," *Time*, 10 July 1939. In "the largest collection of limericks ever published," G. Legman (*The Limerick, 1700 Examples, with Notes, Variants, and Index*, Paris: Hautes Etudes, 1953) incorporated my long manuscript collection, but gave credit for those in the *Psychiatry* article. Other psychiatric articles: W. La Barre, "Primitive Psychotherapy in Native American Cultures: Peyotism and Confession," *Journal of Abnormal and Social Psychology* 24 (1947), 294–309, reprinted in *Bobbs-Merrill Reprints in the Social Sciences*, 1965; "The Apperception of Attitudes," *American Imago* 6 (1949), 3–43; "Obscenity: An Anthropological Appraisal," *Law and Contemporary Problems* 20 (1955), 533–43, reprinted as chap. 13, this volume; "Psychoanalysis in Anthropology," *Science and Psychoanalysis*, ed. J. J. Masserman (New York: Grune & Stratton, 1961), vol. 4, pp. 10–20; "Transference Cures in Religious Cults and Social Groups," *Journal of Psychoanalysis in Groups* 1 (1962), 66–76; "Confession as Cathartic Therapy in American Indian Tribes," *Magic, Faith, and Healing*, ed. Ari Kiev (New York: Free Press, 1964), pp. 36–49; "Geza Roheim," *Psychoanalytic Pioneers*, ed. F. Alexander, S. Eisenstein, and Martin Grotjahn (New York: Basic Books, 1966), pp. 272–81; "Clinical Approach to Culture," *Contemporary Psychology* 11 (1966), 397–98; "Personality from a Psychoanalytic Viewpoint," in *The Study of Personality, An Inter-Disciplinary Approach*, ed. E. Norbeck, D. Price-Williams, and W. M. McCord (New York: Holt, Rinehart and Winston, 1968), pp. 65–87, reprinted as chap. 5, this volume; "Anthropological Perspectives on Sexuality," *Sexuality: A Search for Perspective*, ed. D. L. Grummon and A. M. Barclay (New York: Van Nostrand, Reinhold Co., 1971), pp. 38–53, reprinted as chap. 6, this volume; "Culture and Personality: An Overview," *Psychotherapy and Social Science Review* 5 no. 11 (1971), 17–19.

36. W. La Barre, "Some Observations on Character Structure in the Orient: I. The Japanese," *Psychiatry* 8 (1945), 319–42, reprinted in *Japanese Character and Culture*, ed. B. S. Silberman (Tucson: University of Arizona Press, 1962), pp. 325–59; "Some Observations on Character Structure in the Orient: II. The Chinese," *Psychiatry* 9 (1946), 215–37 and 375–95; a portion of this has been reprinted as "Chinese Food and Drink," *Alcohol Intoxication: Social Attitudes and Controls*, ed. R. G. McCarthy (New Haven: Yale University Center of Alcohol Studies, 1954). A third in the series, on India, lies on my five-foot shelf of unpublished manuscripts.

37. "The Influence of Freud on Anthropology," *American Imago* 15 (1958), also chap. 7, this volume, was intended to continue the survey by Clyde Kluckhohn, "The Influence of Psychiatry on Anthropology in America during the Past One Hundred Years," in *One Hundred Years of American Psychiatry*, ed. J. K. Hall, G. Zilboorg, and H. A. Bunker (New York: Columbia University Press, for the American Psychiatric Association, 1944). The survey should be continued from 1958 to the present by some qualified young anthropologist.

38. M. Mead, "Problems and Progress in the Study of Personality," in Norbeck, Price-Williams, and McCord, eds., *The Study of Personality*, 373.

39. W. La Barre, *The Aymara Indians of the Lake Titicaca Plateau, Bolivia* (Menasha, Wisconsin: Memoirs of the American Anthropological Association, 68, 1948). "The Uru of the Rio Desaguadero," *American Anthropologist* 43 (1941), 493–522, and "The Uru-Chipaya," *Handbook of South American Indians*, ed. J. H. Steward (Washington: Bureau of American Ethnology, Bulletin 143), II, 575–83, 1946—were also products of this field trip.

40. W. La Barre, "Aymara Biologicals and Other Medicines," *Journal of American Folklore* 64 no. 252 (1951), 171–78; *Materia Medica of the Aymara, Lake Titicaca Plateau, Bolivia* (Firenze: Istituto Botanico dell'Università, 1960, *Webbia* 15 no. 1 [1959], 47–94). But my interest lay still earlier in "Folk Medicine and Folk Sciences," *Journal of American Folklore* 55 no. 218 (1942), 197–203, and "Kiowa Folk Sciences," *Journal of American Folklore* 60 (1947), 105–14.

41. W. La Barre, "Potato Taxonomy among the Aymara Indians of Bolivia," *Acta Americana* 5 (1947), 83–103.

42. *Aymara Indians*, pp. 39–40; "Aymara Folktales," *International Journal of American Linguistics* 16 (1950), 40–45; "Aymara Folklore and Folk Temperament," *Journal of the Folklore Institute* 2 (1965), 25–30; "The Aymara: History and Worldview," *Journal of American Folklore* 79 no. 311 (1966), 130–44, and in *The Anthropologist Looks at Myth*, ed. John Greenway (Austin: University of Texas Press, 1966), pp. 130–44. See also John F. Plummer, "Another Look at Aymara Personality," *Behavior Science Notes* 1 no. 2 (1960), 55–78.

43. W. La Barre, *The Human Animal* (Chicago: University of Chicago Press, 1954; Phoenix Books, 8th impression, 1968); *L'Animal humain* (Paris: Payot, 1956); an Italian edition is in press (Milano: Bompiani, 1975). Portions of the English edition have been reprinted as: "Strange Patterns of Marriage," *Science Digest* 36 no. 5 (November 1954), 23–26; "Universal Biological Features in the Family," *Marriage and Family in the Modern World*, ed. Ruth S. Cavan (New York: Crowell, 1960), pp. 16–19; "People Are Different," *Midway* 7 (1961), 62–83; "Human Abilities," *Perspectives on the Social Order*, ed. H. L. Ross (New York: McGraw-Hill, 1963), pp. 48–51; "Superstition and the Soul," *Prose as Experience*, ed. T. C. Altschuler, M. M. McDonough, and A. J. Roth (Boston: Houghton-Mifflin, 1965), pp. 180–92; "The Human Animal in Biological Perspective," *Culture Shock*, ed. P. K. Bock (New York: Knopf, 1970), pp. 5–15. Further articles developed from viewpoints in *The Human Animal*: "The Biosocial Unity of the Family," *Exploring the Base for Family Therapy*, ed. N. W. Ackerman, F. L. Beatman, and S. L. Sherman (New York: Family Service Association of America, 1961), pp. 5–13; "Introduction to the Science of Man," *Anthropology Today* (Del Mar: CRM Books, 1971), pp. 5–21; "The Development of Mind in Man in Primitive Cultures and Society," *Brain and Intelligence: The Ecology of Child Development*, ed. F. Richardson (Hyattsville, Md.: National Educational Press, 1973), pp. 21–38.

44. Erich Heller, *The Disinherited Mind* (Baltimore: Penguin Books, 1961), p. 232.

45. See reference note 23; also W. La Barre, "Snake-Handling: The Present and Recent Past," *Readings in Anthropology: The Evolution of Human Adaptations*, ed. P. J. and G. H. Pelto, and J. J. Poggie, Jr. (New York: Macmillan, 1976), pp. 373–78.

46. W. La Barre, "The Cultural Basis of Emotions and Gestures," *Journal of Personality* 16 (1947), 49–68; reprinted in *Selected Readings in Social Psychology*, ed. S. H. Britt (New York: Rinehart, 1949), pp. 49–56; *Personal Character and Social Milieu*, ed. D. G. Harding (Syracuse: Syracuse University Press, 1949: 489–506; 1956: 547–63); *Bobbs-Merrill Reprint Series in the Social Sciences*, 157, 1961); *Modern Sociology: An Introduction to the Study of Human Interaction*, ed. A. W. and H. P. Gouldner, J. R. Gusfield, and K. Archibald (New York: Harcourt, Brace and World, 1964), pp. 26–32; *Workbook in Group Dynamics*, ed. Jeanne Noble (New York: New York University Bookstore, 1968), pp. 49–68; *Interpersonal Dynamics, Essays and Readings in Human Interaction*, ed. W. G. Bennis, E. H. Schein, F. I. Steele, and D. E. Berlin (Homewood, Illinois: Dorsey Press, 1968), pp. 197–205; *Selected Readings*, ed. Phillip L. Stern (New York: Associated Educational Services Corp., 1969); *Make Men of Them*, ed. Charles G. Hughes (Chicago: Rand McNally, 1972), pp. 94–104; *Communicating Interpersonally: A Reader*, ed. R. W. Pace, B. E. Peterson, and T. R. Radcliffe (Columbus, Ohio: Charles E. Merrill Publishing Co., 1973); *Man and Culture*, ed. James M. Henlin (Boston: Holbrook Press, 1974); *The Social Aspects of the Body*, ed. T. Polhemus (New York: Random House, 1974); D. P. Gilfillan, *Nonverbal Behavior* (Evanston, Illinois: Northwestern University, 1974); *Anthropological Aspects of Movement*, ed. Martha Davis (New York: Arno

Press, 1975); and "Die kulturelle Grundlage von Emotionen und Gesten," *Kulturanthropologie*, ed. W. E. Muhlmann and Ernst W. Muller (Köln-Marienburg: Kiepenheuer & Witsch, 1966), pp. 264–81.

47. W. La Barre, "Paralinguistics, Kinesics, and Cultural Anthropology," *Approaches to Semiotics*, ed. T. A. Sebeok, A. S. Hayes, and M. C. Bateson (The Hague: Mouton, 1964), pp. 191–220, reprinted as chap. 16 this volume; *The Human Dialogue, Perspectives on Communication*, ed. F. W. Matson and Ashley Montagu (New York: Free Press, 1967), pp. 456–90; *Intercultural Communication: A Reader*, ed. L. A. Samovar and R. E. Porter (Belmont, California: Wadsworth Publishing Co., 1972), pp. 172–80; and "Paralinguistica e Cinesica e Antropologia culturale," *Parlinguistica e Cinesica*, ed. T. A. Sebeok, A. S. Hayes, and M. C. Bateson (Milano: Bompiani, 1970), pp. 279–321.

48. W. La Barre, "Ethology and Ethnology," *Semiotica* 6 (1972), 83–96. Related publications: "Comments on the Human Revolution," *Current Anthropology* 5 (1964), 147–50, reprinted in *Bobbs-Merrill Reprints in the Social Sciences*, 1965; "Some Comments Concerning Hockett's and Ascher's Contribution on the Human Revolution," *Current Anthropology* 7 (1966), 201–3; "Comments on Proxemics," *Current Anthropology* 9 (1968), 101–2, reprinted in *Culture: Man's Adaptive Dimension*, ed. Ashley Montagu (New York: Oxford University Press, 1968), pp. 50–55.

49. W. La Barre, "El sueño, el carismo y el héroe cultural," *Los Suenos y las Sociedades humanas*, ed. L. Echávarri (Buenos Aires: Editorial Sudamericana, 1964), pp. 453–61; "The Dream, Charisma, and the Culture Hero," *The Dream and Human Societies*, ed. G. E. von Grunebaum and Roger Caillois (Berkeley: University of California Press, 1966), pp. 229–35; *Le Rêve et les Sociétés humains*, ed. R. Caillois et G. E. von Grunebaum (Paris: Gallimard, 1967), pp. 205–21.

50. W. La Barre, reviews of D. G. Mandelbaum (ed.), "Selected Writings of Edward Sapir," *Survey Graphic* 86 no. 263 (May 1950); Rattray Taylor, "Sex in History," *Book Find News*, November 1955; Charles Winick, "Dictionary of Anthropology," *Southern Folklore Quarterly* 21 (1957), 322–23; Ashley Montagu (ed.), "Man and Aggression," *American Anthropologist* 71 (1969), 912–15; R. L. Birdwhistell, "Kinesics and Context: Essays on Body Motion Communication," *American Journal of Sociology* 77 (1972), 999–1000; E. F. Torrey, "The Mind Game: Witchdoctors and Psychiatrists," *Social Casework* 55 (1974), 57–58; W. McKee Evans, "To Die Game: The Story of the Lowry Band, Indian Guerrillas of the Reconstruction," *American Anthropologist* 76 (1974), 409–10; and Rene Girard, "Violence and the Sacred," *Journal of Psychological Anthropology* 1 no. 4 (Fall 1978), 517–20.

51. *The Ghost Dance* (see reference note 6); W. La Barre, "Materials for a History of Studies of Crisis Cults," *Current Anthropology* 12 (1971), 3–44. See also "Les mouvements réligieux nés de l'acculturation en Amérique du Nord," Histoire des Religions, tome 2, *Encyclopédie de la Pléiade* (Paris: Gallimard, 1969) 29:1–40.

52. W. La Barre, "Anthropological Perspectives on Hallucination and Hallucinogens," in R. K. Siegel and L. J. West (eds.) *Hallucinations*.

I. Psychotropics

2. Anthropological Perspectives on Hallucination, Hallucinogens, and the Shamanic Origins of Religion

Because of great cultural variety in concepts and social contexts regarding certain mental states which, moreover, are easily confused with one another, it is important to delimit the phenomena we seek to discuss. The etymology of terms, we shall presently see, is already an exercise in cross-cultural ideology.

"Illusion" is a false mental appearance made by some actual external cause acting on the senses but capable of conceptual correction. Thus, mistaking a tree in the dark for a man is an illusion, of which the subject may be disabused by various forms of reality testing; emphasis is on the ready correctability of an illusion. "Delusion" is a fixed false concept occasioned by external stimuli; but these stimuli are so consistently misconstrued that delusion remains largely insusceptible to correction. Thus, a strongly held belief that one's food is "poisoned," based on some imagined taste or appearance, is a delusion. Both illusion and delusion are based on the Latin *ludere*, "to play." "Illusion" implies the innocent subjective misinterpretation of a fact and exists only as a noun. But "to delude," as a transitive verb, means sometimes intentionally to befool the mind or judgment, to make sport of, beguile, or mislead. "Delusion" easily suggests a demonological view of causality, as of some ill-intentioned external *anima* or spirit actively deceiving the subject—a view rejected by modern psychology which sees the subject "projecting" demons as a way of disclaiming psychic responsibility for his own thought productions. In this sense one is always self-deluded. Illusion and delusion vary along a scale of increasing psy-

My half century of professional interest in the relation of hallucinogens to visionary religions was adventitiously overtaken, in the 1950s, by a youthful generation's interest in secular hedonic drug use. The present rewritten essay draws upon many of my earlier studies and (with the essays on cannabis and soma following) represents my most compendious summary and perspective on the ethnography of psychotropic drugs.

This chapter is a condensation of "The Narcotic Complex of the New World," *Diogenes* 48 (1964), 125–38, reprinted by permission; "The Dream, Charisma, and the Culture Hero," in G. E. von Grunebaum and R. Caillois (eds.), *The Dream and Human Culture* (Berkeley: University of California Press, 1966), pp. 229–35, reprinted by permission; "Old and New World Narcotics: A Statistical Question and an Ethnological Reply," *Economic Botany* 24 (1970), 73–80, reprinted by permission; "Hallucinogens and the Shamanic Origins of Religion," in Peter T. Furst (ed.), *Flesh of the Gods: The Ritual Use of Hallucinogens* (New York: Praeger, 1972), pp. 261–78, reprinted by permission; and "Anthropological Perspectives on Hallucination and Hallucinogens," in R. K. Siegel and L. J. West (eds.), *Hallucinations: Behavior, Experience and Theory* (New York: John Wiley & Sons, 1975), pp. 9–52, copyright © 1975 John Wiley & Sons, reprinted by permission of the editors and John Wiley & sons.

chological intensity, subjective needfulness, and relative incorrectability. These features are dynamically important, both psychiatrically and cross-culturally.

"Hallucination" derives from the Latin deponent or half-passive verb *alucinari*, "to wander in mind"—again dependent on archaic animistic notions to which modern psychology does not subscribe. In careful present-day usage, hallucination indicates a false appearance, in sensory form, hence seemingly external, but occasioned by an internal condition of the mind, the central suggestion of the term being its subjectivity and groundlessness. Hallucinations can occur in any sensory modality, whether visual, auditory, olfactory, gustatory, tactile, or kinesthetic, and they may sometimes be synesthetic—that is, input in one sensory modality is perceived in terms of another, as when a peyotist hears the sun come up with a roar, or when ritual drumming lifts the hearer up into the air. Since all men are accustomed to believe their senses, it is the *sensory* form of its presentation that gives hallucination its psychic conviction.

Two other terms must be examined before we travel cross-culturally: possession and trance. "Possession" implies the now wholly inadmissable demonological notion that the body in such a state is possessed or held by an invading alien spirit. The seeming externality of the force derives from the fact that it is ego-alien; that is, it comes from "primary process" mentation, erupting from its usual locus, the unconscious mind, into the conscious ego. "Trance" derives from Latin *transitus*, "a passage," in turn from *transire*, "to pass over," namely to go into another psychic state, to swoon half-dead, to undergo rapture (being taken away) or ecstasy (the soul's standing outside the body). This word also is entangled with false animistic notions now discarded, but in medicine "trance" is still used to designate a cataleptic or hypnotic state of partial consciousness or high suggestibility.

These etymologies already descry comparative ethnography along a time line within a Western tradition. Consequently, many who use these terms uncritically do so because they are victims of archaic categories of thought. It would therefore seem scholastic confusion further to divide "possession" into supposed subtypes, as some students have done, when we no longer espouse the ideology of possession itself. The ancient notion of a trance as a state in which an ec-static or body-separable soul (brainless mind or organismless life) wanders in space and time has long since been banished from psychology; all the supposed attributes of the soul can be better explained in terms of the sciences.[1] The superstition obtains credence nevertheless from the hallucination in certain drug-states that the subject stands off and views his own body from outside (kinesthetic-proprioceptive delusion); from the ecstatic shaman's "journey" into distant places; from the dream, in which the psyche seems to travel in far places and past times—and, indeed, even from reverie or memory. In each case, other persons can testify that the "absent-minded" subject's body remained in the same place throughout. The cut-off from local and current sensory-input, characteristic of the REM-state dream, is also contributory to the belief; and again in each case the "altered state of consciousness" is falsely equated with the veritability of ordinary waking consciousness.

Similarly, with such ethnographic complexes as shamanism, ancient and near-universal in the world, we should note that the only valid subdivisions of shaman (black and white, bird and reindeer) are those provided by natives themselves. To label shamans genuine or false is to foment bogus problems, since we do not accede to shamanistic suppositions themselves. For us properly to perceive diverse ethnographic phenomena all the way from Haitian *vodun* to the Amerindian vision quest requires conceptual clarity and awareness of our own cognitive maps. It is better to use our own experimentally derived terms to maintain self-critical control of theory and implication.

A few other terms that disclose ethnography may be examined. "Revelation" refers to a supposed human contact with a "supernatural" world, whether this contact be through trance, vision, possession, or whatever. In this sense of course all religions are "revealed," and all our alleged information about the supernatural is only the statements made about this realm by self-designated authorities: shamans and visionaries, prophets and priests, and other "seers." A "vision" is a seen hallucination, and since sight is the predominant sense in primates, both dreams and hallucinations are ordinarily visual. "Prophecy" is to "speak forth" with the voice of the god or spirit, whose "medium" or mere *porteparole* the inspired ("breathed-into") enthusiast ("god-inside-belabored") may temporarily be. "Divination" makes statements of supposed fact in past, present, or future time through the aid of spirit-helpers. "Prognostication" is spirit-given "foreknowledge" of events or alleged precognition. "Clairvoyance" is to "see clearly" beyond the range in space and time of the workaday mind and eye. All these alleged phenomena can be subsumed under subsequent scientific descriptions and, accepted as fantasies, can serve psychiatric understanding.

It is evident that any sound cross-cultural understanding has awaited the discernment of an authentic and verifiably cross-cultural phenomenon. This necessary psychological tool is offered by new understanding of the dream. The dream is not only a pan-human psychic state;[2] it occurs in all the warm-blooded mammals and birds so far investigated. We are far from a complete knowledge of the physiological and psychological functions of the dream. Nonetheless, present understanding of the dream profoundly illuminates a whole universe of human beliefs and social institutions; such understanding embraces both the revolutionary psychiatric insights of Freud and the new experimental psychology of REM states.[3]

As a first rough approximation, the human mind can be said to exist in two relatively distinct and different states of being: wakefulness and sleep. The major difference between them is that the waking mind ordinarily has full access to sensory input, hence is adaptively environment oriented. It is highly significant that in experienced "sensory deprivation,"[4] as in a subject suspended in a tank of body-warm water as isolated and shielded from all sensory stimuli as possible, thus deprived of customary complex information from the outside world, the wakeful mind promptly begins to project its own contents onto the blank screen of consciousness. In a word, the individual hallucinates.

In ordinary sleep, the mind is by some neural process normally cut off from sensory input. Mental activity continues in ordinary sleep, with a momentum still fairly realistic and matter of fact, although thoughts are somewhat apocopated and fragmentary. But in the REM state of "paradoxical sleep" there erupts an extraordinary discontinuity with the waking state and even with ordinary sleep. Objectively, and visibly to the observer, the sleeper displays a curious "rapid eye movement" (hence the acronym REM), a restless skittering of the eyeballs behind closed lids—as if, psychologically, a "seer" were seeing without sight. Subjectively, the sleeper "dreams," as can easily be ascertained by waking him during the REM state. By EEG measurements and other psychophysical signs the brain is oddly and unexpectedly more furiously active in the REM state than it ever is when the subject is awake.

Paradoxical sleep is paradoxical indeed. In the REM state the mind seems to "be in business for itself"—and the outside real world takes the hindmost. Aristotle long ago observed that dreams lack the element of critical judgment (to epikrīnon).[5] Deprived of edifying restraint and editing by environing reality, in this state too, as in sensory deprivation, the central nervous system hallucinates. REM sleep is a "spree of the id"—a freewheeling of the central nervous system in a kind of "primary process thinking" otherwise most visible in dereistic schizophrenic fantasy. Indeed, Kant suggested that "the lunatic is a wakeful dreamer," and Schopenhauer that "a dream is a short-lasting psychosis, and a psychosis is a long-lasting dream."[6]

Subjects who are REM deprived over protracted periods (by being awakened each time the eyes or EEGs indicate dreaming) appear to build up a REM need proportionate to the amount of deprivation, a need which they indulge by prolonged dreaming at the next opportunity for sleep. It is as though waking thought produced some serotonin-like toxin or metabolic product that only REM activity could neutralize. In fact, the cerebrospinal fluid of a REM-deprived cat, when injected into another cat, produces abnormally high REM activity in the second animal. Ethanol tends to repress REM dreaming, thus giving rise to the provocative suggestion that delirium tremens in chronic alcoholics is an explosive return to hallucination out of deferred REM need. Given at bedtime, d-amphetamine sulfate considerably reduces the amount of REM activity during sleep. Can the paranoid hallucinations of chronic "speed freaks" be owing to a similarly frustrated REM need? By contrast, LSD seems to exert a specifically stimulating effect on the REM mechanism.[7]

All these differential psycho-pharmacological facts should be carefully attended to for their possible bearing on varied ethnographic behaviors. Mescaline and psilocybin both induce wakefulness but seem to produce either a simulacrum of REM or a hallucinatory REM substitute, because their use may be followed ultimately by a deep, dreamless sleep. The fomenting of REM or

REM-like activity may account in part for the subjectively "therapeutic" effects of the use of these drugs, much as in intentionally induced "sleep therapy" in psychiatry. The residual gentle happiness that may last for weeks after psilocybin is clearly such a psychological phenomenon, since it persists long after any possible pharmacological effect or immediate euphoric action on the pleasure center of the brain. And some hallucinogens appear to release deep, affectively toned memories, but these provide for a more leisurely contemplation of "inner space" than haphazard or unremembered dreams afford, since under mescaline and psilocybin the subject is conscious, and since the effect that follows is the same as that which normally comes after refreshingly well-dreamt sleep. Of course the same release of "primary process" material that cannot be handled may cause severe upset or even psychosis of varying length in other individuals, or even in the same individual at other times (hence the "bad trip"). In this context, the experimentally little-known *Amanita* intoxication appears first to produce a two-hour "sleep"—during which, however, the subject is conscious of every sensory occurrence; afterward he "awakens" to hallucinate actively for eight to ten hours.

Psilocybin, peyote, and perhaps other hallucinogens produce a curious double consciousness such that without diminishing the convincingness of an open-eyed visual hallucination, "another part of the mind" can be firmly aware that "I am hallucinating." The suggestion is that these drugs may differentially affect sensory and cognitive brain regions or brain functions. In some subjects, visual hallucinations promptly and regularly recur some 20 to 30 minutes after ingestion of psilocybin, with auditory hallucinations being at their peak some two to four hours later, whereas tactile, kinesthetic, olfactory or gustatory hallucinations occur only sporadically and in no discernible time sequence. Some subjects hallucinate realistic though distorted persons, objects, or scenery; others see only complex geometric patterns and forms. Still others report that they "never" have visual hallucinations under psilocybin, except for the "ec-static" seeing of their own bodies as if from outside.

Some hallucinogens produce specific response to sound, as to shamanic drumming and singing, which may have ethnographic relevance. Some, as noted later, evoke peculiarly red or yellow or "painted" hallucinations; other macropsia, and still others micropsia, which may affect the shaping of myths about giants or "little folk." Bufotenin (5-OH-dimethyltryptamine), a hallucinogen present in toadskins as well as in the Amazonian-Antillean narcotic snuff (*Anadenanthera peregrina*) and in some higher plants and animals, seems specifically to promote a feeling of flying through the air—a factor to be taken into account in reports of shamanistic "journeys" among paleo-Siberians, and in witches' flights in late medieval Europe. Any similar cross-cultural psychophysical constants in the hallucinatory process (as opposed to symbolic content) will increase our confidence in inferences based on such psychic uniformitarianism.

Hallucinogens evidently produce pharmacodynamic variants of the normally occurring dream state. Several other phenomena give dimension to our understanding of REM states. Some individuals are afflicted with the curious ailment of narcolepsy, once thought to be mere overpowering attacks of daytime sleep but now regarded as persistent occurrences of specifically REM states; significantly, the eyeballs skitter in narcolepsy too. Again, experimenters have taped subjects' eyelids open and have demonstrated that REM dreaming can occur with the eyes wide open. The dreamer gives the uncanny impression of being wide awake, although judging from the EEGs he is undoubtedly asleep. Open-eyed "sleep-walking" is probably akin. Normal reverie (literally "dreaming") or ruminative woolgathering sometimes partakes of this catatonic-schizophrenic quality of wideawake daydreaming. Clinical experience shows that a catatonic may be hallucinating at the very moment he is talking with another person. Again, a late-night reader may suddenly become aware that what he is reading is outrageously inapposite to what went before and indeed preposterous in itself. He finds that his eyes are closed: he has been dreaming.

Experiments in sensory deprivation demonstrate how very greatly waking sanity depends on constant wavelets of sensory experience lapping on the shore of consciousness, so to speak, defining the body image and conscious ego. Even the absence of one sensory modality, such as hearing, may induce pathology. A further instance is that of the deaf person; deprived of the chief means of social intercourse, language, the person who cannot hear commonly has mildly paranoid delusions. Again, a guilt-laden and self-preoccupied college student walking across the campus may have delusions of reference when other students, too far away for him to hear their speech, suddenly laugh. Projective phenomena, both in deaf man and student, are dynamically akin to the paranoiac's hallucination of hearing accusatory voices. The same phenomenon is evidently the case in primitives' hallucinations.

So important is language for social communication that occasionally clinics receive acute cases of psychotic "culture shock." A soldier has brought home an alien wife, perhaps to a small and isolated town where she has no culturally similar others, and after perhaps a very short time the alien wife has a psychotic episode, usually with depression and hallucinatory experiences of a mild to severe paranoid-persecutory nature. Cases of culture-shock suicide have even occurred in privileged diplomatic circles where no literal social deprivation exists. And self-perceptively honest anthropologists know the depressive-paranoid stage that comes early in isolated fieldwork and is another form of culture shock: much of the self is socially mirrored and must be continuously reaffirmed.[8]

Even the most hardened sociopath can become "stir crazy"—often from the social and indeed massive sensory deprivation in prolonged solitary confinement,[9] sometimes in pitch dark; habits of compensatory hallucination may continue long after this cruel but not unusual punishment has ceased. A lonely child, deprived even of a dog, may invent a truly hallucinatory "imaginary companion."[10] A sufficiently normal Admiral Byrd in the South Pole hut described in *Alone*, and other individuals isolated from other people for long periods, especially in featureless landscapes, have had hallucinatory experiences of this nature. A famous case is that of Captain Joshua Slocum. This hardy man sailed around the world alone at the turn of the century, and once in a North Atlantic gale hallucinated a bearded man taking the wheel as Slocum himself was forced below by sickness. At first Slocum thought the intruder was a pirate, but he later told Slocum he was the pilot of Columbus's *Pinta* and would return whenever needed. Despite the vividness and obviously reassuring function of the experience, the tough-minded captain knew it was an hallucination. An "imaginary presence" also haunted Sir Ernest Shackleton and his companions in the Antarctic. Stypulkowski, a Russian confined in Lubyanka Prison, experienced such hallucinations, as did Christiana Ritter during her long winter isolation, and Jan Baalsrud, a wounded Norwegian resistance fighter, who spent 27 days before rescue alone on a mountain plateau.[11]

These well-attested hallucinatory experiences of psychiatrically normal men and women may be invoked for an understanding of similar phenomena among preliterate peoples. For example, prominent in both Americas and indeed also among many paleo-Siberian tribes is the ancient supernatural "vision quest."[12] Usually about the time of puberty, with whatever accompanying anxiety or stress, the individual goes alone to some remote place where he fasts and struggles to stay awake, typically for four days and four nights. During this time he may receive an hallucinatory "vision" that gives him great medicine-power, embodied in his medicine bundle, collected on the same vigil. So important is this vision that it may give direction, normal or pathological, for the rest of his life.[13] The shamanic vision quest is so ubiquitous and ancient in Eurasia and the Americas that it is evidently of at least Mesolithic cultural horizons. It is suggested here that the intentionally sought supernatural vision is either a sensory-deprivation hallucination in a lonely place or a literal REM dream fomented by ritual sleeplessness.

Hallucination would appear to be implicated in such "ethnic psychoses" as *kayakangst*, *windigo*, and "Arctic hysteria." Kayakangst[14] comes to the hunter out alone in his kayak on the featureless sea; there is a trancelike lowering of the consciousness from a kind of hypnotic fixing (of foveal vision?), along with curious kinesthetic shifts of body image and body ego. This disoriented and disorganizing experience can be deeply frightening, and panic ensues, together with acute phobic and conversion-hysteric symptoms. Kayakangst may be related to the "windigo psychosis"[15] that seizes lonely hunters in winter among high-latitude Algonquian Indians in the northern United States and Canada. Windigo is culturally stylized, for the hunter is believed to be possessed by the spirit of a cannibal giant whose bones are made of ice, and when the windigo-possessed hunter returns without game he attempts to bite chunks out of the flesh of his campmates. One thinks here of the initiate's possession by the Cannibal Spirit in the main winter dance of the Kwakiutl: the ritually psychotic initiate must be lured back from the woods with corpse flesh, to be tamed into Cannibal Society membership.[16] One wonders what tragic horrors of Hyperborean forced cannibalism may lie behind these violent ritual exorcisms.

In Tungusic "olonism" in Siberia, the brooding adolescent also runs off into the woods and becomes entangled in a bush or tree, whence he must be brought back and exorcised of his demonic spirit-hallucinations (and here again one thinks of Odin, bound on his shamanic initiate's ordeal tree). The pattern is so widespread as to argue immense, I think Stone Age, antiquity. In Tibeten *chöd*[17] the candidate for shamanic vision goes into a wild and lonely spot, preferably to a place where violent death has occurred; and in Malayan *mejapi*[18] (literally "to hide oneself"), flight into a lonely spot in the forest is also the pattern.

The motif of loneliness and social, sometimes also sensory, deprivation seems to be constant in these ethnographic behaviors. Many Arab folktales tell of encounters with evil *jinn* in the featureless desert; and Jacob, when alone, seems to have wrestled with one of these Semitic demons and to have extorted procreative power at the ford of the Jabbok river. His experience seems to be similar to the phenomenon described by Hippocrates[19] of a man, traveling in a wild and lonely place, who was seized by terror on seeing an apparition—for is not "panic" the possession by Pan, the god of lonely places? In all these events, hallucination appears to be interpreted as spirit encounters. But a demon is psychologically as real as the phobic projection to the outside of one's own psychic processes, experienced now as hallucination.

A near-universal explanation of disease is that it is possession by an evil spirit, perhaps sent by an enemy or god (Kali, Apollo). An example might be taken from the Devil Dance of the Sinhalese. Here the shaman takes the appropriate one of a set of 19 masks—say, the black mask with lolling tongue, bulging eyes, and fearsome fangs at the corner of the mouth, representing the cholera spirit—and frightens the disease spirit from its victim by a dramatic, knee-spread shamanic dance. The Navaho night chanter uses a ground painting of sand into which to cast the disease spirit, and afterward the painting is destroyed. Aymara Indians project disease spirits into objects they leave at a path crossing, there to be caught and carried out of the vicinity by the next passerby.[20] Jesus used magic verbal formulas to cast evil spirits out of a possessed man into the Gadarene swine. Self-referent, narcissistic man believes that everything in nature, even disease, is caused by the omnipotent acts of manlike entities. Spirits and demons are hallucinated everywhere to account for all happenings in nature, but demons and spirits are manlike because they are made of men's own psychic stuff. In fact, a surprisingly good case could be made that much of culture is hallucination: the concerted "seeing" of mind-tailored clothes on the naked emperor, nature.

Repeated fieldwork on many continents produces the conviction that all the defense mechanisms described by Freud occur universally among all men as psychic processes, quite apart from wide differences in symbolic content and cultural context. By far the most common defense of all seems to be simple denial, the shutting-off of manifest unwelcome facts, perhaps because that is what all men habitually do in dreams and visions, as well as in the dereistic crisis-cult religions based on such revelations. Self-aware or psychiatrically sophisticated anthropologists may come to conclude that the simpler peoples, or for that matter most simple people everywhere, are chronic hysterics. That is, projective denial of unwelcome fact or hallucination of wish are conspicuous and common in the species.

The intense suggestibility of a subject under hypnosis is well known. The subject will act out all manner of absurd suggestions made by the hypnotist, yet later retain no memory of his acts. Or, at a covert cue from the hypnotist, the subject who has just come out of a hypnotic trance will perform some act quite compulsively and have no idea why he is "compelled" to do it. The persistent naïveté of the hysteric personality is quite astonishing. Indeed, Freud gained his first major insights in the famous case of Dora,[21] who naively laid out her transparent psychodynamics with no immediate insight into them whatever. Although hypnosis was used (and still is in fieldwork),[22] Freud later abandoned it as a therapeutic technique because it involved neither the conscious ego of the patient nor democratically shared understanding. But many a facile montebank, lacking Freud's integrity, still obtains symptomatic cure without insight or personality change, through his thus cheaply omniscient and easily omnipotent suggestion to hysteric patients. Easy insight and simple suggestion are the stock in trade of primitive witch doctors and other tribal therapists.[23] Similarly, any psychotropic effect on the patient by his medicines can be rationalized as proof of his power.

Both phobic and conversion hysterics use the defense of projection. The phobic hysteric projects some unwanted evil aspect of the psyche into an as-if-outside person or spirit—a true "dissociation" of psychic components normally integrated in the healthy personality. Similarly, the conversion hysteric projects and transforms psychic anxiety into as-if-physical pain, thenceforth showing *la belle indifference* of the conversion hysteric to psychic pain. The Greeks divined the symbolic erotization of organs through displacement, by theorizing a wandering womb (*hysteron*) reappearing now here, now there, as a cause of symptoms in conversion hysteria. The primitive medicine man meets the dissimulation of hysterics by shamanic histrionics: he obliges fantasy by sucking out some foreign body, a stick or stone or feather that had been "causing" the sickness (to psychiatrists, the symbolic nature of the "foreign body" is plain, both in hysteria and in paranoia). But the earnest general practitioner, who can honestly find no physical evidence of illness, in exasperation finally pronounces the pain as "here, there, everywhere, but mostly in the neck." And since truly psychic pain has been banished from the hysteric's consciousness and transformed into pseudo-physical pain, the *belle indifference* leaves the concrete-minded doctor unconvinced of any pain as she gives, with evident gratification, the endless long organ-recital of her illnesses, any handful of which, if real, would long since have left her a corpse. (How difficult it is to see that mental illness is mental!) But here the surgeon is often psychiatrically as naive as the witch doctor, seduced into involvement with the patient's system: rejected in her self-diagnosis, the hysteric then shops around from surgeon to surgeon to remove each successively erotized naughty organ in turn. The conversion hysteric denies and projects (somatizes) anxiety: she *hallucinates* pain. In fact, after literal hysterectomy, with no more sinful body parts that can be spared to punish or extirpate, the hysteric commonly becomes psychotic, since all the surgery has not removed the psychic cause, and her psychic defense-by-conversion fails.

The gambit of hallucination in hysteroids is clear. The phobic hysteric can remain deliciously, moreover morally, preoccupied with the fictitious man under the bed she wishes were really in it, yet she can be innocently unaware of her denial, dissociation, and projection. She fears her own disclaimed inner wish as though it were outside; she excretes the unbearable noxiousness from her conscious psyche by dissociation and projective denial. Similarly, conversion allows one to hallucinate the "attack" of illness as though the organ inside were wicked, not the guilty wish. Surely devils and demons everywhere, inside or out, are projective hallucinations![a]

Habitual hysteroid denial and projection sometimes result in the dramatic "multiple personality."[b] In this dissociative state, two or more distinct, indeed contrastive, personalities seem alternately to "take possession" of the conscious mind. The availability of this phenomenon for demonological interpretation is manifest. But from a psychiatric point of view it is, rather, just another instance of the dissociative states to which the hysteroid is susceptible (for multiple personality is a hysteroid, not schizoid phenomenon). Psychodynamically, we would suggest, "possession" is not so much invasion by an alien psyche as it is the overwhelming of conscious ego function by ego-alien primary process mentation, a sort of stylized REM-hallucinosis or auto-suggestion to which poorly integrated hysterics are prone in the service of unconscious wish. Consequently, most primitive and most simple-minded people appear hysteroid to more integrated, sophisticated minds.

a. And, just as surely, the hysteric will call the analyst unwelcomely describing her behavior to her, "a dirty old man"—quite as the psychopath will claim that "Freud says we should get rid of all repression so we can do anything we want guilt-free," and the paranoiac will decide that the therapist is part of the great plot against him. Primitive therapy, commonly, is thus only symptomatic cure, rarely enough abreaction, and almost never true cure of psychodynamics through insight, since the medicine man joins in with his patient's system and cossets it. And since his system is his defense, the religionist (and indeed any right-thinking man in any society) is impervious to any analysis of his cult-behavior (and culture at large is, in part, defense mechanism too).

b. Lay notions of psychiatric syndromes are often grotesque. Of a piece with the superstition that "hysteria" is a kind of screeching mania, instantly cured by a slap on the face ("Thanks, I needed that"), is the cliché that the schizophrenic has a "split personality." On the contrary, schizoids are notably in close contact with "primary process" id material; hysteroids just as notably are not. Moreover, consciousness of conflict is no evidence of "split personality" but is a hallmark of normality.

Anthropologists have long noted that most societies divide their culture into the "holy" and the "profane," either conceptually, or in their behavior, or both. The profane or secular is the realm of mundane workaday technology, of ego control, of relatively low emotional charge, and of constantly evolving adaptation to the environment. The secular world is one that we can all see and point to and talk about. In material culture, this secular world is not merely intersubjective but even intertribal, with the consequence that any material-culture adaptation of one society is potentially borrowable by the whole human species and with relative ease, whereas societies battle to the death over differences in sacred culture. Since secular culture is clearly implicated in the differential survival of competing societies, it would appear that this material kind of secular adaptation to the environment accumulates and evolves like any other animal adaptation. Material culture is rarely lost but is built upon and refined. Sacred culture, however, is in fact constantly changing, despite fervent faith in its perdurability.

By contrast with secular adaptation to the environment, the sacred is a realm of adaptation to inner anxieties, of high emotional potential, of positions the more heatedly defended the less defensible they are by common sense. Some of these inner anxieties, for example those concerning death, doubtless exist in all human beings; hence, faith in an animistic, separable, and indestructable soul is a well-nigh pan-human phenomenon. But some inner anxieties are created by variable and changing elements and socialization pressures in cultures themselves, or by idiosyncratic vicissitudes in individual enculturation. Thus, whereas secular material culture is highly communicable and diffusable, sacred culture is often ineffable, inexpressible, and uncommunicable, whether inter-tribally, tribally, or personally; hence, sacred culture does not manifest cumulative evolution for the species ecologically, but only adaptation to changing cultural pressures and psychological differences.

The secular world is that of the *ob-ject*—literally, the thing that is "thrown across" the path of our animal wish. The sacred world is that of the *sub-ject*,— that is, the experience that is "thrown under" us, the ground of our conscious being, the basis of our apperception, our culture-specific humanity, and each learned personality. The secular world is perforce convincing, if only because the ob-ject very commonly frustrates raw animal wish. Hence, we must adapt to it if we would stay in business as an animal. But the subjective world is convincing too: we *trust* subjective personality because every last shred of it is based either on inherited animal adaptations or on individual life-experience of the world. One's personality has been, all of it, honestly, if sometimes painfully, learned. Freud made a dichotomy between the Pleasure Principle of subjective feeling and gratification (early mediated by the nurturant mother, and nonincestually returned to in the wife), as opposed to the Reality Principle of sternly obdurate objects (of which the first paradigm is the father, frustrator like the real world, and surrogate of society in the growth of conscience or dominating superego).

The secular world of objects presents itself to our senses persistently, unasked for and obdurately, while we are awake. By contrast, we are closer to the subjective world of the self when we are divested of sensory input from the outside. That is to say, the subjective self emerges most purely in states of sensory deprivation, when the blank screen of consciousness has projected upon it only the individual hallucinatory subjective self, without sensory correction or editing, without reality testing or any such objective "noise." This hallucinatory projection, we have seen, can be demonstrated in sensory-deprivation experiments, with the subject suspended in a warm, soundless, sightless tank like a synthetic womb. The same hallucinatory projection comes to us spontaneously at night in dreams, in the REM state of sleep, when the mind is cut off from the sensory body-ego and is furiously "in business for itself" cognitively. Experientally, therefore, both the sacred and the secular world are as real to us as are sensory experience and dreaming, and as sleeping and waking.

Nevertheless, our sacred and secular worlds are quite commonly in conflict, just as wish and perception often are. It is the twin experiences of waking and dreaming that first made man an epistemologist. What can a man believe? This is his dilemma. An organism that gave up all subjective insistence on its essential organic homeostasis would soon cease to be an organism: it would be uncontained dead matter, undisturbed by life or consciousness. On the other hand, no open system like an organism can maintain its improbable existence unless it adapts to and constantly borrows its energies from the outside, and at least temporarily monitors its adaptation to the environment. In complex organisms like ourselves, perhaps sleeping and waking are themselves ultimately responses to the ecological fact of night and day, catabolism and anabolism, for all warm-blooded species are alternately wide awake and sleeping, and all have discernible REM states and are thus able to dream. It may even be that the possibility of sleep is the enabling factor behind complex waking life itself. Further, dreaming may be the ultimate source of innovative culture, so conspicuous in the species, and like art or play occasionally provides patterns of behavior "preadaptive" to some new aspect of the Unknown. Culture is the human speciation, for all that it may be as random and blind as the mutation of genes.

Among human institutions, science is closest to a pure type of conscious animal adaptation. Science is the cognitive state of mind we strive most strenuously to base on our secular experience of objects and to divest of the subjective and the wished-for. Science is the state in which we try most objectively to communicate about the nature of what we sense and see. But in order to see and to communicate, scientists must have both hypotheses and symbolic languages—both of these being subjective human artifacts—so that it is quite unclear to what degree science is cumulative adaptive knowledge, like viable genes and snowballing material culture, or merely a succession of disjunctive cognitive maps, no more real than the group dreams we call languages or cultures. Certainly scientific thinking does change through time;[24] hence, we must ruefully suspect that it too may never have salt safely on the tail of that volant cosmic bird Truth, contaminated as science must always be by group-hypotheses and culturally given symbol-systems.

Among human institutions, in turn, religions of the supernatural perhaps represent the purest form of subjective social wish, for in the supernatural we deny the natural world, and in religion we willingly ignore the mundane in our yearning for the idea(l). A religion is a kind of group dream, the subjective poetry in which, supporting one another's faith or need to believe, we strive desperately to believe. That a large component of every religion is *willful belief* is shown in the fact that adherents to such crisis cults as the nineteenth-century Ghost Dance religion of the Plains Indians or the twentieth-century Cargo Cult of Melanesia[25] coerce men to believe in what "common sense" already knows to be untrue: what never does and never will come to pass. Crisis cults, like group schizophrenias, are constantly dereistic and, for all their emotional seductiveness, ultimately nonadaptive. The Xosa Millennium, for example, has never arrived in South Africa, in spite of the unilateral bargain with fate by men who dutifully destroyed all their crops and killed all their animals to make the millennium arrive and the hated white man depart. As to the personal wish for immortality, many still await the return of the man who died but did not die, the man who really was God, and a god who was himself sacrificed to Himself for others' sins toward himself/Himself—all of which propositions would seem to contain a sufficient modicum of the inconsistent and the improbable. Plainly, religion is a way men have of bearing one another's emotional burdens and of trying to cope with their unresolved and perhaps unresolvable fears in an inhuman and absurd universe—that is, an environment not pre-edited in the individual's special interest, as was the womb-Eden and the tendentiously protective family of the human child, neither of which states of grace can we really unlearn.

Sacred knowledge is commonly traceable, even by natives themselves, to an origin in revelation given to the ancestors or to some similarly charismatic individual, such as a shaman, visionary prophet, or other culture hero believed to have been in communication with an unseen, "supernatural" world. In actual fact, all men live alternately in two psychological states of being, that of waking life and that of the REM-hallucination or dream. The realms of sacred and secular are at least as "real" as man's two psychic worlds. If the secular tends to maintain sensory-enforced loyalty to the Reality Principle, the sacred insistently strives to maintain a warmly nurturant attitude toward subjective and arbitrary organic need, thus primarily indulging the Pleasure Principle. For most men, the dream is the only escape from their often unwilling imprisonment in obdurate waking space and time, and in their bondage to the senses. If one world seems to be remolded nearer to the heart's desire, it is no wonder that we balk at attributing reality only to the vexatious waking world. All men dream. It is not a matter for invidious contumely, but simple recognition of the way things are. Dream-knowledge of this "inner space" prepares men for belief in the sacred and the supernatural. Revelatory dreams are close to myth, which is the dream-thinking of a society, much as the dream is the mythology of the individual. Dreams and myths are thus similar, if only because much of mythology originates in the dreams of individuals. Australian Bushmen themselves equate dream-time with the eternal myth-time that is mysteriously brought back in ritual: "alchuringa-time" is as timeless as the unconscious mind, quite as half-forgotten childhood is the eternal private myth-time still at work beneath the conscious mind of the adult.

It is the delectability of dream-wish that lends it credibility. But only a lowered critical threshold gives dreams their more intense "deeper reality." Dreaming is as inescapable and inevitable as the fact that one brings his whole learned self to acts of friendship and love. The schizoid seer doubtless knows his id-self far better than do we normals. But what good is it to gain one's own soul in eternal dream, yet lose the whole waking world? We need not be reactively antirational just because rational critique often demonstrates that men are sometimes disenchantingly nonrational. Let no one denigrate the dream. But let everyone be epistemologically tidy about the location of these various realities: the *super*natural is wholly housed in the *sub*conscious.

The *mysterium tremendum et fascinosum* in religion is therefore human, not divine, love known in childhood though it be, and fear. Every religion is the dramatization on a cosmic scale of the fears, loves, and longings the child felt in his experience of his parents in the nuclear family, that pan-human phenomenon. And every religion, in the last analysis, is the beliefs and behaviors of identifiable men. Hence every sacred cult can be studied in secular terms— group-cults, by anthropology and sociology; the visionary originator or communicant, by psychology and psychiatry. Throughout history, extravagant attention has been paid to the nature of the gods, whose nature it is to be quite inaccessible to examination insofar as their origins lie in the unconscious. The locus of the "supernatural" is consistently misidentified. The result of this preoccupation with the "gods" is that there is very little consensus concerning the sacred, insofar as cultural and individual experience are variable. At the same time, we have paid relatively little attention to the impresarios of gods, the prophets and shamans, who in fact are available for scrutiny.

Indeed, each contemporary crisis cult shows a new "origin" of religion in a living visionary's revelation. All our "knowledge" of the supernatural derives *de facto* from the statements made by these visionaries (i.e. shamans, for the priests merely administrate the ecclesia established upon shamanistic revelation). Thus, in this secular world, we need only examine the peculiar vatic personality of the visionary as it is manifested in an "altered state of consciousness" in order to understand religion psychologically; and we have only to scrutinize the function of this personality in groups in order to understand religion anthropologically. The "information" purveyed by the vatic shaman concerning the "supernatural" is really only information about himself, misconstrued as divine revelation. Since, in his trance state, the alleged Cosmic Unknown remains totally and studiously unknown to his sleeping senses; the real Unknown, unknown to himself, is the unconscious self of the visionary. Like the paranoid schizophrenic, the vatic personality pretends to be talking about the grandiose outside world, but he is really talking grandiosely in symbolic ways only about his narcissistic self and his inner world. The mystic pretends to discard his sensory self in order to meld with the cosmic Self; but in discarding his senses he abjures his only connection with the cosmos and narcissistically re-encounters only himself. The realities he expounds are inside him, not outside in the world. He reveals only inner space, not outer space, in his revelation. But neither he nor his communicants can afford this discernment, since such an insight would destroy the defensive function his "revelation" performs for all concerned.

The REM dream of the shaman is therefore a fragment of his autobiography; a cult is the Rorschach protocol of the society. Any meaning is a function of the seer, not of the meaningless (since unknown) Unknown. Thus, the diffusion of a cult is in all ways precisely like the diffusion of a culture, from individual to individuals; and if we understood the function of cults, we would probably understand the function of cultures. Every established *ecclesia* of the majority began in a minority crisis cult of one, in real historic, not supernatural time; and his cult spread and diffused historically, sometimes until it became the Established Religion, whose priests (as opposed to visionary shamans) are merely the nonecstatic journeymen officiants of routinized established cults. Since every religion in historic fact began in one man's "revelation," the crisis cult is *characteristically* dereistic, autistic, and dreamlike precisely *because* it had its origin in the dream, trance, "spirit" possession, epileptic "seizure," REM sleep, sensory deprivation, or other visionary state of the shaman-originator. All religions are necessarily "revealed" in this sense, inasmuch as they are certainly not revealed consensually in secular experience.

But we need still to explain psychologically the diffusion of the dereistic in social terms. A private neurosis or psychosis is the pathological operation of the defense mechanisms of a confused and troubled individual under stress. A religion is in origin the defense mechanism of a society in confused and crisis-torn times. In states of crisis-cult helplessness, the prophet provides the omniscience, the shaman the omnipotence, that the people need. "God" is often clinically paranoiac because the shaman's "supernatural helper" is the projection of the shaman himself. The personality of Yahweh, so to speak, exactly fits the irascible personality of the sheikh-shaman Moses: the voices of Yahweh and Moses are indistinguishable. Of course, shamans do not always have an easy time of it. If the dereistic dreamer arouses too much anxiety, people call him crazy, just as people must put themselves at a psychological distance from the frightening and uncanny schizophrenic. But if the dreamer largely allays anxiety in the society, then he is the shaman-savior, a culture hero. Thus it is that outsiders to the society cannot tell the difference between a psychotic and a vatic personality. Only the society itself can discriminate between its psychotics and its shaman-saviors, not realizing that both may be the same.

Hence other allegedly supernatural elements in religion can be seen in completely naturalistic terms. "Charisma," that supernatural animal magnetism that seems to stream compellingly from the sacred vatic personage or religious innovator, is really a quite secular circumstance psychologically. The compelling force comes not from the great man as he voices new supernatural Truth: he speaks only to the powerful anticommonsensical fantasy already present in the unconscious wish of each communicant: commonly, Let Time's Arrow Reverse Its Flight, or Let Onerous Actuality Be Undone. The voice of the vatic has an "uncanny" consistency with each one's private wish; his phatic message is psychic actuality already, in a sense *déjà vu* to his communicants. They are now overwhelmed by the supernatural authority of the wished-for. The charismatic leader is the liberator who unlocks hidden wish; hence some psychopathic leaders can release psychopathic behavior in mobs that is usually repressed in the individuals composing the mob. When individuals emotionally abdicate the ego functions of reality testing in favor of wishful belief, they sometimes also abandon the superego repressions in their behavior. The leader of the mob and the mob itself mutually sanction each one's mob behavior.

The psychological voltage of the leader's charisma is the exact measure of his emotional appeal. Any uninvolved bystander, either one alien to the tribe or a tribesman with his own reality testing intact, can clearly perceive the dubious reality-status of the group dream, whether new or old. But he may express insight only at his peril. With often incredibly savage and nobly justified wrath, True Believers turn and rend the skeptic for his sin of unbelief. Fanatic faith obscurely realizes that it is mistaken in its fantasies, for denied common sense tells it so. But just as the psychoanalyst who exposes the defense mechanisms of his neurotic patient must expect an annihilating blast of anger in return, so also the unwary freethinker who naively offers reality testing to the cult mob (when this is the last thing it wants) must expect his own human sacrifice in order to verify their Truth.

True Believers are authoritarian personalities because they are infantile dependents on the divine authority of the shaman, not mature assessors of their own judgments. Fundamentalists abjectly depend on past tribal culture, not on their own contemporary common sense: every Fundamentalism is an intellectual lobotomy. "God" is only the infantile shaman's-eye view of a father he has not grown emotionally into, a child's psychic recreation of his Creator. The "omnipotence" of the paranoid shaman, possessing or being possessed by the father-power, serves a similar function for the True Believer. The unreal omnipotence of the shaman is the reciprocal of the unreal helplessness of the cultist; the omnipotence of charismatics only feeds on the supposed impotence of men.

We are so accustomed to belief in gods (or at least in our own True God) that we forget Durkheim's insight: supernatural projections can derive only from the secular historic reality-states of societies. Anthropologically speaking, the post-Alexandrian High God as "Emperor of the Universe" could not possibly be present in the Paleolithic cave of Trois Frères because these ancient Magdalenian hunters had never known the secular political structures first created in the Alexandrian world: a supernatural "King of kings" must await the political creation of kingship. The so-called High God that some scholars of the Viennese *Kulturkreislehrschule* thought to find in the Old Stone Age cave is merely a projection backward in time of their own Catholic theology, with the added gain of a reassuring *semper et ubique* as though ethnology confirmed theology.

In such ethnographic situations, one authentic Stone Age painting serves us better than even the contemporary theological truth of the matter. The "Dancing Sorcerer" of Trois Frères (and the many similar masked figures in other Stone Age caves) is simply the animal-masked dancing shaman of prehistoric hunting peoples. Any subsequent "Master of Animals" supernaturalized to his model is exactly the sacred projection we would expect, given the secular anxieties, ecological relevancies, and social organization of small bands of ancient hunters. The Dancing Sorcerer himself is only a man dressed up in animal skins, shamanizing in the hunter's small world. He is the group shield from anxiety. He simply pretends (but with no necessary intent to deceive) to be able to do what they need to believe he can do: he has the power to dance success that the hunter cannot always achieve in the uncertain hunt, and he controls the fertility of the animals hunted so that they will always be abundant.[c] He simply "controls" what people cannot. Nothing more. He is not the High God, Creator of the Cosmos, because the concept of cosmos did not exist until later Greek times. Besides, the shamanistic world-view takes the world for granted; the shaman merely manages the changing aleatory elements in it, the life and death of men and animals, the weather, and the like.

The Dancing Shaman is at most a shamanic trickster-transformer; the cave artist at Lascaux perceives an unevenness in the rock wall, and on this he paints the animal into existence deep in the womb of the earth. He literally

c. Since human lives seem to continue indefinitely as long as man can feed on the lives of animals (hence Paleolithic cave art is mainly concerned with the fertility-replacement and the availability of the animals hunted), perhaps the naively wished-for reincarnation or re-embodiment of the life of animals actually preceded the notion of human immortality. Our earliest clear notion of the latter is in the shamanist Orphic religion, probably of central European inspiration among Paleolithic-Neolithic peoples, revived in the Dionysian and Eleusinian Mysteries. The Dionysian eating of the cult animal would be the rite of hunters in the communal or sacrificial feast that makes hunters of one flesh (though Dionysus was later syncretized with a wine-god that gives all men ecstasy). The Eleusinian Mysteries are clearly agricultural, and recently R. Gordon Wasson (*The Road to Eleusis*, with Albert Hofmann and Carl A. P. Ruck, New York: Harcourt Brace Jovanovich, 1978) has suggested that another psychotropic drug than wine was used in the latter Mysteries, but here through grain-smut LSD in the sacramental wafers. Christianity, in the wafer and the wine, continues the symbolism of both Mysteries, all concerned with human immortality. In any case, European prehistorians argue convincingly for the immensely greater antiquity of the "animal bone cult" or hunters' ritual at the site of the kill, designed to bring back the animal incarnate; certainly the bone-cult is intercontinental in spread.

only creates what he "conceives"—out of a half-reality he has perceived. His wish apperceives and magically transforms into reality the animals needed by his group. The Dancing Sorcerer is only the artist-creator, like the mythological trickster-transformer of the California Indians. He is like the Oceanic *tu-hunga*, the shaman-craftsman who sings his canoe into existence from a tree and builds a new structure into the structure of the world with the aid of his creative magic formulas. Even the Indic great god Shiva merely dances the world into shape with his transformer's magic (and one component of this syncretized god is Pasupati, master of animals). Classic "great religion" deities still bear many marks of their shamanic origins also. Manlike Zeus, for example, the majestic Cloud Compeller and cosmic rain god of classic Athens, was once only a man, a shaman who could make rain with the help of his spirit familiar, the Eagle, the great Thunderbird so ancient that he is found intercontinentally in the northern hemisphere on Mesolithic horizons.

That this picture of the ancient shamanic hunters' religion is not a projective fantasy of our own is indicated in the fact that the religion of all hunting peoples known in early modern times has remained this same simple shamanism, consistent with both the hunters' world-horizons and his life-anxieties. Eliade[26] has massively demonstrated that shamanism is still found among the ethnographically conservative peoples of Oceania and on all continents except Africa, he thinks; but Nadel[27] has found true possession shamanism in Africa as well. In Africa, indeed, ancient weather shamans have grown into the rain kings of the Sudan and into divine kings like the Pharaohs in Egypt; and in South America and elsewhere in the New World, man-god shamans still grandiosely control the cosmic weather. In the Paleolithic Ur-culture that Kluckhohn[28] discerned in the whole world, it is quite plain that there were shamans before there were gods. For gods are only charismatic power-wielding shamans, hypostatized after death and grown in stature with the increased world horizons.

Greek Zeus the fire-juggler still has the many Ovidian animal metamorphoses of the ancient shamanic fertility demon. His brother Poseidon, Owner of the Sea Animals, still carries the antique trident of the old Eurasiatic shaman, still found in the eighteenth century among various Paleo-Siberian tribes. The Greek nature gods are manlike for the simple reason that they were once men, mere human shamans. And, like other shamans, Greek gods still had their old animal familiars, Zeus the eagle, Apollo the wolf, Athena the owl and serpent, Artemis the stag and bear, Hermes the snake, Proteus the seal, and so forth. In Greece, dead shamans who still controlled aspects of nature became the Immortals who do the same; but in India, the Indo-European cognates of these shamans stayed human or, more exactly, the old Brahmanic shaman-bards persisted as human man-gods or living deities, and indeed the whole thrust of Indic religion is for the self to merge into the Self and man to become god.

The control of fertility by the Paleolithic Master of Animals lingers on in the attributes of Zeus, a god of many dalliances with all manner of animals, goddesses, and humans. Zeus had the multiple-glans oak as his tree; and Apollo was lord of fertility (like Krishna) among his kine. In old Judaic tradition, Abraham's wife Sarah was given fertility late in old age by a mysterious manlike daemon-visitor; and we have seen how, at Jabbok, Jacob wrested from his angel-adversary the gift of countless progeny for Israel. This old Semitic place-deity of the deep Jabbok gorge as "husband of the land" is not unlike the artist-inseminator of the earth-womb in European caves, or the Greek fertility daemon, the snake found so abundantly in pre-Olympian religion by Jane Ellen Harrison.[29]

In the Pentateuch, Moses and Aaron were still represented as snake-shamans at the court of the Pharaonic rain king, in shamanistic rivalry with his magicians. Moses turned his shaman's staff into a snake and back again, he afflicted Egypt with pestilence and other magic plagues, he parted the Red Sea with his shaman's staff, he set up in the desert a brazen Nehushtam or serpent image of his Familiar, he struck water with his rod from a rock in the wilderness, he held up his rod in long battle to gain victory—all like the magic shaman he was, or perhaps compound of several traditional shamans, since one Moses served the volcano-spirit adopted from the Kenites. Judaism, in fact, is ultimately the revelation of the shamanic Moses, and the composite Mosaic snake-bull-volcano god grew into the Most High, as Israel grew into a united kingdom under the Saul-David-Solomon line—but not without the aid of the shaman Samuel and a local Canaanite shamaness, "a woman who hath a familiar spirit" and "saw gods ascending out of the earth" (I Samuel 28:7, 13), the Witch of Endor. The growth of Yahweh into Jehovah was all in good Durkheimian fashion, with the magnitude of projected gods exactly commensurate in scale with each new contemporary political structure. The Hellenized Paul, in turn, transformed Jesus the Charismed into the Universal God, through Paul's epileptic vision on the road to Damascus.

Whether myth begets ritual or ritual begets myth in the social diffusion of the seer's vision is a question that will doubtless be argued indefinitely by anthropologists. The descriptive fact remains that, psychologically, *the wide-awake acting out of the myth in ritual adds a kind of veridity to it*, accompanied as it is by kinesthetic body-image conviction (in dancing and other ceremonial acts), often enriched by waking sensory input: visual (witnessing of the drama), auditory (music and the intoning of sacerdotal formulas), olfactory (incense), and even gustatory (ritual imbibement). Ritual is a technique groups have of magically pretending what is not true (though the social consequences may be real enough): that at christening a soul is saved from eternal hell-fire by a few apotropaic drops of tap water; at baptism human sin is undone and washed away by more massive ablution; at communion eating the god's flesh and drinking his blood (magically transubstantiated of course from ordinary foodstuffs) negates metazoan death entirely; at a puberty ritual there emerges an adult man or woman (proven of course by autonomous endocrine events the rite "causes"); blood-brother rituals make blood kin of men who are not; at marriage two persons are spiritually united forever (with no needful subsequent working at it); a sheepskin in an archaic tongue and long banal speeches creates a learned person, and so on. Individuals evidently participate in rituals with varying degrees of critical loss of ego function, depending in part perhaps on whether one is the *pièce de résistance* in the ritual or merely a jaded onlooker. And yet the whole intent and function of ritual appears to be coercive group wish to hallucinate reality.

Indignant objection to these statements about ritual—calling cynical what is merely cool case-hardened objectivity—only demonstrates that there are varying degrees of conviction in the efficacy of acting out various magic wishes, which is the only point we wish to make here. Likewise, calling an officiant shaman or pseudo-shaman is a statement only of relative belief within the observer, not a discrimination of objective difference in psychic function for the ritual participants. No man can criticize, since he cannot experience, another's hallucination. What ritual *does* for the participants is the critical psychological issue.

Dark night, with a flickering fire, is the best time for ritual. The long ecstatic drumming and singing of the Siberian shaman, his uncanny replication of the bird calls of his attendant spirits, ventriloquism of voice against the reverberant cone of the skin tent, [d] magic shaking of the tent itself, loss of sleep, shamanic calls and antiphonal response by participants—all these induce an empathic half-hypnosis of the whole group. It has been suggested[30] that music itself began in the singing of shamans, who wanted a special language other than speech with which to address the supernaturals. Music is almost the *sine qua non* of ritual: rhythm, song, and other contrived appeals to the senses seduce belief. Since humanly configurated sound is customarily in the form of semantic speech, music is the perfect Rorschach stimulus for pseudo-communication of meaning in reverie: we hallucinate to music meanings that are evoked only in the private mind. Pronounced rhythm in song and dance, especially in crowd situations, may constitute "sensory overload," and hence induce an altered state of consciousness.[e] In ritual, compulsive act "confirms"

d. The most compelling shamanistic performance known to this writer is the chanting of Tantric rituals by Tibetan abbots, recorded in 1968 by Huston Smith of the Massachusetts Institute of Technology. The style of singing is said to be possible only to lamas of the Gyume and Gyáto monasteries of Lhasa. The singing, to invoke fearsome cosmic demons, is in incredibly virtuoso male coloratura, with melisma on the single syllable Om, in prodigiously *basso profundo sostenuto* two octaves below middle C and lower—against which *organon* the soloist cantillates or "double sings," evidently by opening and closing resonance chambers in the skull, producing timbre change in high-frequency harmonics of remarkable amplitude simultaneously with the deep canto firmo bass tones. Such part-singing by a single voice is multi-dimensional "monotone" indeed, illustrating with so much in a single note the *multum in parvo* doctrine of Tantric Buddhism. The experience is so unbelievable to one conversant with the physics of sound as to seem hallucinatory.

e. A. Neher, "A physiological explanation of unusual behavior in ceremonies involving drums," *Human Biology* 34 [1962], 151–60) has argued that primitive drumming (and other rhythmic sensory stimuli synergistic with physiological rhythms) induces trance; see also R. J. Strobos,

obsessive belief. That belief is the wished-for, and that others join in mutual support of belief together make ritual a hypnotic-hallucinatory social substitute for reality.

It is now evident that the earlier designation of REM and waking states as only contingently polar and contrastive states of mind was a necessary caution. Hypnosis, hysteria, and hallucination in dream, vision, delusion, and trance show manifestly infinite gradations in "altered states of consciousness" with respect to their relative proportions of dereistic REM versus sense-nourished contact with reality. It is often difficult to assess accurately the relative proportion of these factors in exotic ritual and ritual curing, since our own cognitive maps, reality testing, and level of ego-functioning all intervene to distort judgment. But since our minds operate variously between the poles of deep dreaming and wakened consciousness, we may safely suspect that so also do the minds of our ethnographic subjects.

This raises the problem of cross-cultural criteria of normality. The ease with which individuals designated as abnormal in our society may function in other societies is well known to anthropologists. In India, for example, the mildly to severely schizoid individual is preadapted, so to speak, to a *saddhu*'s role as holy ascetic, whereas in extroverted Western societies schizoid trends are highly visible socially. Yet among us, hypomania and even markedly sociopathic behaviors either pass unnoticed or are highly esteemed in business and political circles, much as obsessive traits are admired in academe. Again, in classic China, normal occidental male aggressiveness is obtrusively painful, upsetting, and contemned.

As Ruth Benedict has noted in her celebrated essay on *Anthropology and the Abnormal*, homosexuality in our society exposes the individual to conflicts we tend to identify with neurotic disposition,

> . . . but these consequences are obviously local and cultural. Homosexuals in many societies are not incompetent, but they may be such if the culture asks adjustment of them that would strain any man's vitality. Wherever homosexuality has been given an honorable place in any society, those to whom it is congenial have filled adequately the honorable roles society assigns to them.[31]

Benedict cites the classic Greeks, among whom homosexuality was presented "as one of the major means to the good life," as "the most convincing statement of such a reading of homosexuality." In the same vein but somewhat differently in cultural context, transvestism in Indian *berdaches* of both Americas was regarded as evidence of marked supernatural status.[32]

"Acousticomotor Seizures," *Electroencephalography and Clinical Neurophysiology* 14 (1962), 129–31. But Steven Kane ("Ritual Possession in a Southern Appalachian Religious Sect," *Journal of American Folklore*, 87 no. 346 [1974], 293–302) considers trance in the snakehandling religion a complexly over-determined phenomenon, not adequately explained by this *simpliste* and reductionist physiological view.

Cultural relativity of judgment extends to other psychic states. For example, epilepsy is a fear-shadowed and undesireable state in modern industrial societies. Yet in the classical world and in the ancient orient it was a blessed sign of visitation by a god. In many Moslem societies an epileptic habitus is necessary to authenticate the holy man—so much so that the ambitious aspirant must be able to produce at least the protective coloration of epilepsy if he is not so gifted naturally. It is the *dissimulation* of such states that leads outsiders to judge fraudulence in some shamans, which is no proof that the dissociative state itself is not the authentic *fons et origo* of the institution. Meanwhile, conviction among the shaman's clientèle is the functionally significant matter. The Shasta Indian shamaness is chosen by her constitutional liability to trance states. Cataleptic skill is essential to Siberian shamans, and in Zulu candidates a stylized neurosis is needed. Benedict notes that a "culture may value and make socially available even highly unstable human types [which] force upon us the fact that normality is culturally defined . . . [and] every culture besides its abnormals of conflict has presumably its abnormals of extreme fulfillment of the cultural type."[33]

In the all-important function of intermediary with the sacred supernatural world in any society, a developed tendency to hallucination in vision or trance is indispensable. In a convincing study of shamanism by the Korean psychiatrist Kwang-iel Kim, the author claims that despite modernization and acculturation to Confucianism, Buddhism, and Christianity in turn, in Korea the archaic "shamanistic passion remains without any change among the masses." An estimated 100,000 shamans in South Korea alone means one shaman for every 314 persons. The priestly shaman is hereditary, but the "charismatic shaman" must suffer *sin-byung* ("disease of god") or possession by an ancestral spirit, which Dr. Kim regards psychiatrically as a "depersonalization syndrome." This depersonalization resolves "incestuous fantasy with symbolic marriage to ancestral gods whose image is parental . . . compensating their inferiority feeling with elevation of their status from the humble to the higher" one of spouse-hood with the god. Psychiatric significance is also evident in the twenty-four-hour curing ritual *goot*, with shamanistic dancing, trance, and oracular pronouncements by the god. "Catharsis, abreaction, suggestion and hypnotism, as well as transference to [the] shaman are the main mechanisms of [the] shaman's psychotherapeutic approach . . . other essences [of which] are the trance state of participants during group dancing," adding group-psychotherapy to the shaman's empathized compassion. Dr. Kim interestingly considers that "the vicious cycle of projection" in the shamanic worldview reinforces a paranoid tendency already present in the *ethos* of the people; moreover "the weakening of the ego function by dependency on suggestion by the shaman prevents any gaining of insight"—thus indicating the close fit of the institution with Korean culture and personality. Anthropologists, Kim notes, tend to emphasize "the positive function of shamanism as a culturally integrated system," but as a psychiatrist he deplores the enhancement of "a paranoid cultural system."[34]

Cross-cultural studies of dissociative states are not new. In a half-century-old classic on *Possession, Demoniacal and Other among Primitive Races, in Antiquity, the Middle Ages, and Modern Times*, T. K. Oesterreich is at pains to argue "the constant nature of possession throughout the ages."[35] In his "somnambulistic form," normal individuality is replaced by another, but with no memory in the subject; in his "lucid form" the subject does not lose consciousness. The two forms are evidently only degrees of dissociation. Oesterreich also discusses the relation of possession and obsession (in European psychiatry the latter rubric includes compulsive acts as well), and "voluntary and involuntary possession amongst primitive peoples, so-called shamanism." Although differing degrees of conscious ego participation are alluded to, the only cross-cultural constant would be REM-like hallucination of possession demons, no doubt of phobic- or conversion-hysteric or paranoid nature.

Bourguinon has edited an anthology[36] concerning the relation of social change to religious beliefs and institutions in which altered states of consciousness are exploited. She uses two systems of classification: (1) that of Roland Fischer who examines states of consciousness varying on a continuum with respect to degree of central nervous system arousal (thus a neurophysiological model); and (2) that of Arnold Ludwig,[37] who presents a classification based on modes of inducing modification in CNS activity (thus a psychobiological model).

> In spite of the great variety of states included in this classification, Ludwig finds that they share a series of 10 general characteristics: alterations in thinking, disturbed time sense, loss of control, change in emotional expression, change in body image, perceptual distortion, change in meaning or significance (that is, the attributing of heightened significance to subjective experiences, ideas, or perceptions in this state), sense of the ineffable, feelings of rejuvenation, and hypersuggestibility.[38]

Bourguignon classifies altered states of consciousness culturally into two categories, which she calls "possession trance" (belief in spirit invasion) tending toward public and ritual manifestation, and "trance" (typically hallucinatory, with visions) which may be private. Both, she maintains, involve learning to greater or lesser but always significant degrees; and, statistically, each type is associated with different degrees of complexity in society, as well as clustering in ethnographic regions, thus suggesting both historical diffusion and ecological factors.

In a comprehensive ethnographic, human-biological, psychiatric holistic approach, I have noted that all religions begin in the hallucinatory revelation of an individual, accounted "charismatic" to the degree that his message coincides with the unconscious wishes of his clientele, and that every established religion began as a "crisis cult" when contemporary secular culture failed to provide resolution of overwhelming anxieties. Crisis cults derived from massive acculturation have arisen in great numbers in the postcolonial world. But more fundamentally, I believe, the propensity to magic cults and religions derives from the psychobiological neoteny of the human animal, since each individual has passed through a magical (patterned on talking and walking) and a religious (nuclear-familial) stage of ego-differentiation to which, under stress, he may regress. World-view is thus a function of ego-differentiation and consequent psychosexual maturation.[39] Similarly, cultural institutions roughly manifest *degrees of hallucinosis* in their epistemological grounds.

Since compendious volumes have been written on hallucinatory trance and possession states—notably by Oesterreich, Prince, and Bourguignon—we attempt here only a representative sampling of the comparative ethnography of dissociated states, in roughly areal sequence, to indicate their range and scope. By the fifth edition of his *Lehrbuch* in 1896, Emil Kraepelin,[40] the great taxonomist of modern psychiatry, had already included an appendix on such anomalous ethnic syndromes as "Arctic hysteria," amok, and latah, and in 1925 Freud[41] published "A Neurosis of Demoniacal Possession in the Seventeenth Century," thus giving rise to what might be termed "comparative psychiatry," subsequently developed by the culture-and-personality school of anthropology stemming from the work of Edward Sapir.[42] An influential report by F. E. Williams on the New Guinea "Vailala Madness" (which included hysteroid hallucination) and another by James Mooney on the Ghost Dance (which began in shamanic visions) drew attention to the frequent origin of cults in individual trance experiences. A considerable anthropological interest in crisis cults ensued. I have provided an extensive bibliography.[43]

Raymond Prince discussed possession cults in relation to "social cybernetics"; Bourguignon, the world distribution and patterns of possession and trance states; Davidson, the psychiatric significance of trance cults; the Mischels, psychological aspects of spirit possession; Akstein, kinetic trances and therapeutic ritual dancing; Lee, the complex sociology of Bushman trance performances; and Harper, spirit possession and social structure.[44]

Regionally in the Americas, we have the ethnopsychiatry of hallucinations among Chicano populations by Schepers, and by Henney on the Shakers of St. Vincent, whose cult hallucinations, most interestingly, are induced by ritual sensory deprivation. One of many such acculturational rites with possession and glossolalia, the Apostolics of Yucatan, has been studied by Goodman. The snake-handling cult of the southeastern United States, has been monographed together with individual case histories by La Barre and by Kane; these manifest not only hysteroid trance and glossolalia but also fire-handling, which Kane has discussed also psychophysiologically. For the Caribbean, *vodūn* trance in Haiti has been much studied by a number of scholars and is perhaps best understood as quasi-therapeutic acting out by low-status persons under the guise of possession by cult spirits, some having discernible African origins. Similar cults include *Umbanda* and others in Brazil.[45]

For Africa, Greenbaum has given a descriptive analysis of possession trance, with valuable ethnographic references in 14 Negro tribes, also analyzing their social correlates. Bourguignon has summarized divination, trance, and spirit-possession in sub-Saharan Africa; Collomb et al. have discussed the socio-therapeutic aspects of the *n'doep* initiation into the possession society of the Wolof and Lebou of Senegal; Gerlach related possession hysteria among the Digo of Kenya to the changing roles of men and women in a new market-economy; and Giet et al. studied spirit possession and faith healing among the Ghion of Ethiopia. The sociopsychological implications of spirit possession among the Sidamo of southwest Ethiopia were investigated by John and Irene Hamer; and Gussler reported on social change, ecology, and spirit possession among the South African Nguni. Lee notes the relevance of Zulu concepts of psychogenic disorder; Lombard treats possession cults in Black Africa, especially among the Hausa; Sangree relates spirit possession to marriage stability in Irigwe; and Wintrob relates sexual guilt to culturally sanctioned delusions in West Africa and discusses psychosis in association with possession by genii in Liberia. Since the foregoing is only a sampling of the rich materials available from Africa, it is useful to have Zaretsky's bibliography on spirit possession and mediumship in Africa.[46]

In northern India spirit possession is in the cultural context of illness, according to the Freeds. Obeyesekere sees possession in Ceylon as the cultural idiom of mental illness. The same appears true of the whole Indic area, in which ritual exorcism of demons is the traditional cure. In Bali, trance dancing is a highly stylized drama in which, suddenly grasping his snaky *kris* dagger, the dancer attempts to assault the masked witch Rangda—but, gorgonized by a gesture from her, he falls senseless, and the kindly bumbling male figure Barong aids the trance-stricken dancer to a slow recovery. Scholars regard Balinese trance-dancing as an abreaction of violent rage against the teasing and rejecting mother of the knee-child at the birth of a younger sibling.[47]

In Oceania, hallucination as an experience of the supernatural is the idiom of cultural cognition among Filipino peasants, according to Jocano. Leonard notes transformations of the traditional spirit mediums in Palau under cultural change. Langness sees possession in the New Guinea highlands as an ethnic psychosis; Salisbury, however, regards it somewhat differently among the Siane of New Guinea. The psychiatry of highland New Guinea is in any case a complex matter.[f] The mysteriously localized endemic *kuru* is now firmly estab-

---

f. The rhizome of *Kaempferia galanga* is used in New Guinea as the hallucinogen *maraba*; and the Papuans use the leaves and bark of *Galbulimima belgraveana* (sometimes mixed with *Homalomena ereriba* leaves as *agara*), which intoxicates with spectacular visions and later dreamlike somnolence; it contains several isoquinoline alkaloids (W. A. Emboden, *Narcotic Plants*, [New York: Macmillan, 1972], pp. 25–26). The "mushroom madness" of some highland groups has been thought by several authorities to come from the eating of *nonda*, various hallucinogenic *Boletus* species of mushrooms (R. Heim and R. G. Wasson, "La folie des Kuma," *Cahiers du Pacifique*, 6 [1964], 3–27; *idem*, "The 'mushroom madness' of the Kuma" [Harvard], *Botanical Museum Leaflets*, 21 no. 1 [1965], 1–36; M. Reay, "Mushroom madness in the New Guinea Highlands," *Oceania*, 31 [1960], 135–39; *idem*, "'Mushrooms and collective hysteria," *Australian Territories*, 5 [1965], 18–21; Emboden, *Narcotic Plants*, pp. 25–26).

lished by the Gajdusek group as a slow-acting virus disease of the central nervous system, spread by endocannibalism of insufficiently cooked human brains. "Wild man" behavior, on the other hand, appears to be an institutionalized means of violent abreaction of culturally imposed tensions, according to Newman.[48]

Sufficient data have now been presented to indicate that various native cults and religions are closely and often associated with trance, possession, visions, sensory deprivation, REM states, hallucinations, and other such "altered states of consciousness," and that, moreover, such states occur everywhere in the world, among all races, and in context with quite varied cultural dispensations. These dissociated conditions of the human mind are, like dreaming, undoubtedly pandemic in the species. Now, very possibly, the vast majority of "supernatural" experiences can be traced to such endogenous or autonomous psychological states. Nevertheless, there is one very powerful impetus to hallucination—one, indeed, found in the whole shamanic visionary complex that can be traced back to a Paleolithic Ur-religion—that has yet remained unmentioned in this discussion: the proven ability of psychotropic drugs to produce convincing hallucinatory experiences. That is, some individuals, "spiritually" quite ungifted in spontaneous visionary skill, are nevertheless capable of authentic hallucinations, given pharmacodynamic help. We believe, with some other anthropologists, that the use of potent botanical hallucinogens has been a real and important vehicle of shamanistic ecstasy, not only in modern ethnographic time but also in prehistoric antiquity. In demonstration of this, we will make first a rapid survey of relevant Old World psychotropic drugs and then proceed to the convincing evidence in the archaic New World, in its special context with shamanic religion.

There appears to be no human society so simple in material culture as to lack some sort of mood-altering drug as an escape from the workaday world. Even the primitive Australians used *pituri* (*Duboisea hopwoodii*) as a narcotic; in larger amounts, they put the same drug into waterholes to stupefy emus, permitting hunters to run them down and club them for food. And the Bantu hallucinogen *iboga* (*Iboga tabernenthes*) of West African cults in the Gabun and Congo appears to have been borrowed from more primitive Pygmy hunters.[49] The *kanna* (*Mesembranthemum* spp.) euphoriant and hallucinogen of South Africa was chewed, and later smoked, by the Hottentot. Botswana Bushmen use *kwashi* bulbs (*Pancratium trianthum*) as an hallucinogen. There is even a narcotic bamboo grub in Amazonia, to match the hallucinogenic "dream fish" (*Kyphosus fuseus*) caught off Norfolk Island by native Melanesians.[50]

Many stimulants have long been in customary secular use in the Old World as well as in the New. *Coffea arabica* (Abyssinian coffee), *Camelia sinensis* (Himalayan tea), *Cola acuminata* (African cola nut), *Paullinia yoco* and *P. cupana* (Orinocan and Amazonian *pasta guarana*), *Ilex guayusa* (used by Indians of the eastern slope of the Ecuadorean Andes), *Ilex paraguayensis* (Paraguayan *maté*), and *Theobroma cacao* (Mayan cocoa or "food of the gods") all contain caffeine or caffeine-like alkaloids, but all are ignored here as being neither hallucinogens nor in ritual religious use—though perhaps, as is possible, their onetime employment in a prehistoric sacred context has since been overshadowed by common secular use. This caution is necessary, for although the narcotic and mild hallucinogen *kava* (*Piper methysticum*) was used aboriginally only in a secular social-status ritual in Polynesia, it has recently been reported by a student of mine, Robert Gregory, in use in a cultural revitalization movement in Tannu, New Hebrides (Melanesia). Betel (*Areca catechu*) is widely used in the Indic cultural sphere, both mainland and insular, but for secular enjoyment only. Two nutmegs (*Myristica fragrans, M. malabarica*) from the seed, and mace from the aril of the same plants, are violently hallucinogenic in sufficient quantities and have been used in the Indic medicine *made shaunda* since Auyrvedic times; otherwise, these have served as condiments only since Arabs introduced them to the West in the early centuries of Christianity, and they have never with certainty been used as a ritual hallucinogen, doubtless because of their toxicity.[51]

Christian Europe has been traditionally hostile to the consumption of hallucinogens. A possible reason is the survival of the practice of using a number of the most powerful ones—for example, belladonna (*Atropa belladonna*), mandrake (*Mandragora officinarum*), and henbane (*Hyoscyamus niger*)—from pagan times on into European witchcraft. Belladonna has been used as a potent poison since early classical times. Renaissance ladies are said to have used it to produce enlargement of the pupils, which men found attractive (since such enlargement occurs naturally in either sex when sexually attracted), hence belladonna ("beautiful lady") is indirectly an aphrodisiac, provoking un-Christian lust. Mandrake, despite its toxicity, was a panacea in medieval folk medicine, being used as a sedative and hypnotic agent in treating nervous disorders and acute pain. A magic plant in folklore, Greek and Hebraic alike, mandragora was surrounded with many legends and greatly feared. The forked root was named *Alraune, Erdmännchen*, and *Erdweibchen* from the fancied resemblance of the "Hexenkraut" to the human figure, and it was used as an amulet and in all kinds of profane medieval European magic. An animal was employed to drag out the dangerous root, yet even so the man-plant's screams at deracination would drive a person mad. Mandragora was used as an analgesic in surgery, but it had also a wide reputation as an aphrodisiac, as does the similarly shaped ginseng (*Panax Schinseng*) in the Sinitic cultural realm. Belladonna, mandrake, and henbane were all reputedly used in witches' brews,[52] and were therefore connected with the Evil One. All contain hyoscyamine, a powerful hallucinogen, which gives the peculiar sensation of flying through the air, as on a witch's broom, or on a shamanic journey, among other effects. The use of toads in witches' brews is interesting, since, as we noted earlier, the skin of some toads contains bufotenin, a hydroxy-tryptamine that is highly hallucinogenic. The virtually panic fear of "toadstools" by some Europeans may also derive from reaction to pagan times, for the use of hallucinogenic

Amanita mushrooms even antedated (and culturally influenced) the Greek and other Indo-European gods originating in northern Eurasia, *Amanita* being thought to have been born of divine thunderbolts.[53]

But the European fear of psychotropics, and even of new foods such as potatoes, sometimes passed all reason. King James I of England was as much exercised over tobacco as he was over witchcraft: tracts of his time allege that smokers' brains, after their early death, would be found to be blackened with soot. Again, early in the present century, children were forcefully adjured not to eat even a single berry of the much-cultivated vine called "love apple," for it would surely kill them, probably within the hour, since it was botanically related to "the deadly nightshade." Children nevertheless persisted in eating the fruit, and no child ever died of eating love apples, for, bred to larger and tastier varieties, tomatoes are even a better source of Vitamin C than the ritual orange juice, being both cheaper and more stable to oxidation and cooking. Meanwhile, after an interim of worldwide approbation and even praise of tobacco (by now thoroughly entrenched in the economic and political establishment), medical scientists have come to agree with King James, though with better evidence, on the dangers of smoking.

Again—to the credit of European morality—municipal councils and national governments were deluged with petitions against the opening of the new coffeehouses or cafés in seventeenth-century Europe. Savants averred that coffee was a strong poison and that on Judgment Day all coffee drinkers would arise from their graves "as black as coffee grounds." But King Gustavus Adolphus of Sweden took twin brothers, both murderers, and condemned them to death, the one by drinking "fatal" doses of coffee, the other of tea, and appointed a medical commission to watch and report on their condition. The brother criminals both developed palpitations from the enormous doses given them, but both outlived their doctors, until the tea drinker died—at the age of 83. Voltaire, a passionate coffee drinker himself, remarked that "coffee is a deadly poison, but it acts slowly" which he proved by dying at the age of 84. The consumption of coffee has since spread insidiously over half the world, although the downfall of civilization is no longer blamed exclusively on its use.

Coffee is otherwise edifying to the anthropologist, accustomed as he is to detached awareness of cultural contexts. Originally, the sugar-containing coffeeberry of Christian Abyssinia had been fermented into an alcoholic drink, of a sort that later Moslem religion fanatically prohibited. But religious prohibition never stopped the coffeeberry. By dry roasting, Moslems converted some of its substances into a complex of chemical stimulants that are even now not exhaustively known to science; and in this new form, sometimes with added sugar, coffee drinking spread over the Arabic world (coffee, sugar, and alcohol are in origin all Arabic words), and with Christian contact in the late medieval crusades, into Europe. Here, as we have seen, coffee became so widely established, even among otherwise respectable folk, that they ignore the psychotropic properties of the drug (a related *Rubiacea* of the tropical rain forest of

Puerto Rico is even hallucinogenic), and most hardened drinkers freely and shamelessly admit psychological dependency.

Cross-cultural paradoxes are as instructive as cross-generational ones. Despite its much-proved danger, we accept alcohol blandly, but rabidly reject marihuana for its as yet unproved dire danger, since unknown euphoriants must surely be more dangerous than known ones. By contrast, Moslems rigidly forbid the drinking of alcohol, although narcotic drugs, even dangerous ones, are acceptable to them. In fact, all the Moghul emperors of India were addicted to opium, a habit they acquired from their fellow Moslems in Persia,[54] and the use of hashish is well-established among Moslems of Africa and Asia. On this matter we are capable of a certain ethnocentric smugness and blindness. We consider the Near-Eastern custom of giving opium to children while the mother is absent from the home to be quite outrageous. However, an earlier generation in America admired the parental concern and care represented by giving paregoric in "soothing syrup" to babies, and laudanum to teethers— yet both substances are opium derivatives, such as were used by degenerate literary men like De Quincey and Baudelaire.[g] And many persons are aware that a popular and now worldwide Atlanta proprietary (still called a "tonic" in New England) once contained both cocaine and cola drugs, from Andean and African natives respectively.

Again, among American Indians, hallucinogens are in the hands of the social and religious establishment, and are administered to adolescents to invoke proper awe for the sacred institutions of their adult mentors—a somewhat different context from drug use by our adolescents with contracultural intent. Yet at the end of the last century, it was the pinnacle of the establishment— ladies—who were widely the unwitting addicts of successive derivatives of opium in their elixirs.[55] The staunch pillar of the Women's Christian Temperance Union might combat female troubles with a "vegetable compound," the alcoholic content of which varied in different periods up to 19 percent—while her beleaguered husband got, at best, only 10 percent in his beer. The final irony, however, rests in today's worthy taxpayer settling down to his beer, enjoying the manly bite of the hops, while righteously railing at the bearded "pot-smoking freak" he has the misfortune to call son. But hops (*Humulus lupulus*) and marihuana (*Cannabis sativa*) are the only members of the dioecious family Cannabaceae,[56] the female of which produces the resins cannabinol and lupulin—both mild narcotics suspected of producing psychological depen-

---

g. The nineteenth-century poets, Francis Thompson and Samuel Taylor Coleridge, were also addicted to opium. The classicist F. R. Jevons (in "Was Plotinus Influenced by Opium?" *Medical History*, 9 [1965], 374–80) has shown that the neo-Platonist philosopher, on his own evidence and that of his students, was an opium addict, as were also the celebrated physicians Avicenna and Paracelsus. In distinction from these, Hugo, Gauthier, and Mallarmé were members of *Le Club des Hachichins* in Paris (Ch. R[ice], "Historical Notes on Opium," *New Remedies*, 5 [August 1876], 229–32, 6 [May 1877], 144–45, and 6 [July 1877], 194–95). The herb known to Rabelais as "pantagruelion" has been alleged to be cannabis by N. Marty-Laveaux and also by L. Faye (*Rabelais botaniste*, Angers: Cosnier et Lachèse, 1854).

dency. High moral dudgeon has here only a fragile basis: hop drinker and hippie smoker are pharmacodynamically brothers under the skin. Nor does history give time-depth precedence or prestige to hop-drinker at the expense of the pot-smoker, but rather the reverse. Indeed, the European plant hops may be only a late additive to Levantine-originated beer—the *Oxford English Dictionary* gives 1440 for its first appearance in England, and the drug was introduced to England from Flanders between 1520 and 1524—whereas hemp is certainly one of the oldest cultigens of man. Although the *smoking* of marihuana is probably post-Columbian only, the *ingesting* can be documented back to the Bronze Age and probably beyond (see the essay on *cannabis* in the present volume).

Several legendary plants of the Mycenaean Greeks have been suspected of being hallucinogens. Whatever the witch Circe gave Ulysses' men to make them hallucinate themselves as animals may remain forever unknown. Whatever Hermes gave Ulysses himself to avoid this contretemps is scarcely any better known. The fabulous black-rooted and white-flowered *moly*, sovereign herb of Homer used by the gods themselves, is really unknown, for the *moly* of Dioscorides and Theophrastus was only the innocent *Allium subhirsutum*, the wild garlic of Mediterranean peoples. *Nepenthe*, which makes men forget sorrow, is likewise obscure botanically. A plant of Egyptian origin—"In it the Greeks met Zeus face to face"—has been equated with everything from *Papaver somniferum* to Bugloss (Greek "ox-tongue"), a Boraginaceous species (by a writer in 1699)—whereas botanists have given the name *Nepenthe* to pitcher plants mostly of oriental provenience!

We can only hazard a guess at the plant of Homer's "Lotus Eaters." Their most plausible locale is in Tripoli and nearby African islands, to judge from a later people with similar name. But "lotus" can scarcely be the water lilies *Castalia caerulea* and *C. Lotus* that are often figured, for some reason, in old Egyptian temples. Still, the lotus is also prominent in Indian iconography, as a seat for Hindu deities; and the same lotus had spread early with nirvana-seeking Buddhism, via central Asia to China and Japan. The lotus of Homer (*Od.* ix, 90ff) was identified by later Greek writers with a North African shrub, the descriptions of which many modern botanists have thought to indicate the *jujube* tree (*Zizyphus Lotus* of Linnaeus). But would nonhallucinogenic *jujube* fruits be enough to keep Ulysses' men from their Penelopes in Ithaca so long after leaving Troy? The name "lotus" has been applied also to the *nelumbo* (the *Nelumbo Nelumbo* of Linnaeus), the sacred bean which, for unknown reasons tantalizing to scholars, was rigorously proscribed to followers of the nebulous half-shaman Pythagoras. Whatever they were botanically, *moly, nepenthe,* and the *lotus* are all presented in such contexts as to raise question of their being ancient but lost hallucinogens.[57]

With fair certainty none of them could have been opium, for this narcotic has been well and separately known since the earliest times. Opium (Greek *opos*, "juice" from the milky sap of the lightly cut partly ripened seed capsule) is known only from the opium poppy (*Papaver somniferum*), a flowering annual not known in the wild state, hence perhaps an ancient cultigen of *P. setigerum*, which is indigenous in the Mediterranean region. The main ingredient is morphia (from Morpheus, the Roman god of sleep), usually employed in medicine as various morphine salts, but two dozen other alkaloids have been found in opium. Mediterranean use is far older than the Odyssey episode, in which a compassionate older woman gave Telemachus opium to lessen grief at the supposed death of his father. The Ebers Papyrus (ca. 1500 B.C.) copied references to opium from a source at least a thousand years earlier; indeed, the earliest Sumerian cuneiform tablets mention its use. But opium is still older than writing.

Recently, remains of poppy capsules have been excavated in prehistoric camp sites in the Rigi Mountains of Switzerland. Other archeological finds of the seeds and capsules of *Papaver somniferum* have been most numerous in the prehistoric Lake Dwellings of Switzerland: of seventeen Neolithic finds, most were in Switzerland, but some were in southwest Germany, north Italy, and the Murcielagos Cave in Spain. The Swiss Robenhausen Neolithic contains poppy seeds, and ten other finds are from the Swiss Bronze Age. *Papaver setigerum* seeds are found in five Bandkeramic settlements (Oekoven, Aldenhoven, Lamersdorf, Garsdorf, and Langweiler) in Germany; and *P. somniferum* at Langweilen and Wickrath in Iron Age contexts, also at Fifield Brabant in southern England, and Hallstatt-period finds in Biskupin, Poland— thus indicating expansion of use into northern Europe during the Iron Age, probably from prehistoric Switzerland. Poppy seeds are rich in oil, but contain no opium; and *setigerum* seeds might have been used only in Neolithic cooking, but *P. somniferum* capsules indicate the cultigen and probable narcotic use. In any case, unambiguous evidence is found in early artifacts. Representations of the poppy capsule are archeologically ancient in religious iconography of Mycenaean and Minoan date: for example, the body of an early Greek bronze vase is shaped like a poppy capsule, and a terracotta head from Knossos bears a headdress of incised capsules.[58]

Opium was well known from classical times through the Middle Ages. Paracelsus carried opium in the pommel of his sword and named the alcoholic tincture *laudanum* ("that which is to be praised"); another physician-addict, Avicenna, died in Persia of opium poisoning in 1037. Opium was probably brought to India in the Arab invasion of the eighth century. European traders took opium to China, but for long afterward none was grown in China. The British East India Company forced poppy cultivation in China in the eighteenth century, from which eventuated the Opium Wars of 1840 and 1861. As late as 1923, two-thirds of the arable land in Yunnan Province grew opium; in the capital city Yunnanfu (Kunming), 90 percent of the men and 60 percent of the women were said to be addicts. In Shensi and Kansu provinces, opium was the principal crop that could be sold at a distance for a profit. In Red China, opium consumption has reportedly been greatly diminished, no doubt owing to savage reprisals, including decapitation; but *montagnard* tribes in Laos and Thailand were stimulated to take up poppy cultivation under the impetus of the Viet Nam war. In the nineteenth century, cultivation had returned massively to the Near East, notably Turkey, with the French Mediterranean port of Marseilles the chief center for processing into heroin (diacetyl morphia) for the world trade.

Opium and its derivatives constitute the main, and perhaps the only, indisputably addictive narcotic drugs. Yet, curiously in view of its known hallucinogenic effects, opium, so far as ethnographic knowledge goes, appears never to have been used ritually (unless pre- and protohistoric peoples are an exception). Opium appears to have been employed only medicinally as an anodyne and such, and secularly as a euphoriant—in both instances undoubtedly because opium is a true narcotic, promoting sleep, which would not lend opium to ritual use, unlike mescaline, psilocybin, and (to a degree) soma, during which intoxications the subject is awake. Thus, in the form of heroin, it constitutes the chief "hard drug" of illicit commerce, and chief target of anhedonic Christendom.[59] In this connection, an interesting but very little-known drug should be mentioned.[h] In Southeast Asia, especially in Bangkok and Singapore, *Mitragyna speciosa*, a rubiaceous (coffee family) plant is sold as *kratom* ("leaves") or *mambog* (syrupy infusion), either as an opium substitute or withdrawal agent.[60]

In vivid contrast to opium, the long-mysterious soma of the *Rig Veda* was without question the major religious hallucinogen of ancient Eurasia and one, moreover, that has exerted an incalculable influence on later religions. In their oral form, the earliest Vedic hymns date from about 1800 B.C. But once the Aryans entered India around 1500 B.C., the identity of the plant (which does not grow south of the Himalayas) was lost and never rediscovered in Hinduism, despite much discussion in the endless *Brahmanas* or priestly commentaries on the *Vedas*, and during centuries of European Sanskritic scholarship. In the *Rig Veda* only priests drank ritually prepared soma, which conferred divinity on the Brahmanic "living gods" much as in Greek legends the gods, originally shamans too, obtained immortality by imbibing odorous "ambrosia" with "nectar" (the latter probably pan–Indo-European mead, traces of which use reach even as far back as a Spanish Paleolithic rock painting).[61]

Ever since Sanskrit was discovered by eighteenth-century Europeans, soma has been the apparently insoluble riddle lying at the heart of Vedic studies. In 1968, with only the word *soma* and the *Rig Veda* hymns to proceed on (the *Brahmanas* were manifestly useless), R. Gordon Wasson solved the riddle,

---

h. The excessive difficulty of obtaining samples for pharmacodynamic assessment by local university biochemists, as a potential aid in cure of opium addiction, is an example of the narcophobic legacy, exploited politically by an earlier administration in Washington. Similarly, in 1974, only two experiments on humans with nonaddictive and nontoxic psilocybin were in progress, and these not for therapeutic ends, though psilocybin gives promise of use, adjunctive to psychotherapy, in severely obsessive-compulsive patients.

with overwhelming evidence that illuminates much of ancient Eurasiatic religion, in one of the most admirable triumphs of modern scholarship.[62] Chapter 4 reviews the evidence by which he traces soma to the *Amanita* mushroom.

If Wasson's interlocking and self-consistent evidence holds,[63] then the hallucinogenic mushroom *Amanita* was being invoked as a divine inebriant in northern Eurasia long before the Indo-Europeans left their homeland, in the Chalcolithic or early Bronze Age, to scatter from Ireland to Ceylon. It is a common fallacy of historians to suppose, just because Christianity became officially the religion of the mainline great tradition, that the suppressed Old Religion disappeared without a trace. On the contrary, throughout the Middle Ages and into contemporary England there has survived the witches' coven, an old fertility cult of women centering around an ancient horned god (now the cloven-hooved and horned Evil One), which may trace back to the Paleolithic "Cogul dance" and a tradition unbroken in France from the Paleolithic Trois Frères Dancing Sorcerer down to the Celto-Roman horned god Cernunnus, equated then with the underworld god of spirits and wealth, Pluto.[64] Similarly, apart from the classic Greek gods' imbibing of ambrosia and the Brahman priests' use of soma, there are other unmistakable traces of the survival of the *Amanita* cult of the Old Religion. St. Augustine (354–430 A.D.) still bitterly censured the heretic Manichaeans for their fungus eating, and Manichaeism was a powerful though repressed religious force, active from Spain to China, that influenced Eurasia for at least twelve centuries. Indeed, the Chinese, in a twelfth-century text, refer to Manichaeans who *eat red mushrooms*. And the indigenous Taoist religion still remembered the mysterious *ling-chih*, "mushroom of immortality," which even the great emperor Shih-huang searched for in vain.

Although nectar and ambrosia of the immortals survived in the legends of the classic Olympian sky-gods of state religion, still another tradition was strong in chthonic folk religion from eighth-century B.C. Orphism of central Europe to the Hellenistic mystery cults that shaped early Christianity. The core of the Dionysian Mysteries was eating the flesh (as a bull god) and drinking the blood (as a wine god) to obtain Orphic immortality, the same promised in the central Christian sacrament. The sacramental meal has a hoary antiquity both in Paleolithic Europe and Neolithic Asia Minor. But the present writer finds it difficult to believe that maddened Maenads were driven to wild night dancing on mountain tops and tearing a live god-animal to bits from simple eating of a cereal wafer in the Eleusinian Mysteries—unless the "bearded one" were some such ancient ritual grain as spelt (*Triticum spelta*) that was subject to a fungus infection like the LSD-producing smut *Claviceps purpurea* on rye.[65] The whole thrust of Indo-European religion, among religions at large, may well be the rather specialized goal of obtaining immortality—through eating and drinking substances, some of which are undoubtedly ancient hallucinogens. And behind all these later religious traditions, both Indic and European, looms the very old Eurasiatic soma.

At one time, alcoholic mead[i] was a sacred substance, giving immortality to Greek gods, along with soma, as "nectar and ambrosia." But in prohibiting alcoholic drinks, Hindus have now lost both. When ritually symbolized as the blood of the wine-god Dionysus, alcohol in the West was sacred well into the Hellenistic period, and so it remained in the Christian Eucharist. Otherwise, in the Mediterranean world of Europe and Africa, alcohol became secularized— indeed, in more potent form after Renaissance Italians learned to distill wines into brandies, perhaps under Arabic stimulus, and in northern Europe beers into whiskies. By contrast with both sacralizing and secularizing, in the Asiatic and African Moslem world alcohol became rigorously forbidden by religion— though cannabis was not proscribed, and the potentially hallucinatory qat (*Catha edulis*) might even be used immediately before prayer. Qat is a minor hallucinogen of East African and South Arabian habitat, brought by Yemenites to Israel. It contains three alkaloids—cathenine, cathedrine, and cathine—the last its main ingredient, the same as in *Ephedra vulgaris*, which produces euphoria, loquacity, diminished hunger and, finally, sleepiness. The aftereffects include apathy, anorexia, and depression; the side-effects, palpitation, sweating, and thirst. Occasionally qat produces psychosis, with incoherence, excitation, and schizophreniform visual and auditory hallucinations, much like amphetamine. These effects, similarly, subside a few days after stopping intake.[66]

The relation of hallucinogens to American Indian religions represents a special case in the New World. To understand the nature and scope of the problem, it is first necessary to locate the American Indian in a proper time-perspective. In this investigation, geological, archeological, genetic, botanical, linguistic, and cultural evidences must all remain consistent, and in fact all enrich our insight into the problem. The effort is worthwhile because some rather startling perspectives emerge.

The Paleo-Indian "big game hunters" were perhaps contemporary with, or somewhat later than, the mid-Paleolithic hunters in the Old World, and they

---

i. In the Germanic branch of Indo-European, the mead-words refer to the fermented drink made from honey (Early Modern English also *meath*, from Middle English *mede, methe*, from Anglo-Saxon *medu, meodu* = Old Frisian, Danish, Middle Low German *mede* = Old High German *metu, mito*, Middle High German *mete, met* = Icelandic *mjödhr* = Swedish, Danish *mjöd* = Gothic **mid-us* (not recorded except in Greek transcription as given by Priscus as the name at the Hunnish court A.D. 448 for a drink which there took the place of wine). Irish *meadh* ("mead") may have borrowed semantically from English, because the Welsh *medd* (becoming ultimately English "metheglin," from Welsh *meddyglyn* = *medd* plus *llyn* "liquor") would seem to indicate that, like the other European subfamilies, the Celtic mead-word meant only "honey." Compare Old Slavonic *medu*, honey, wine, Old Bulgarian *medú*, honey, wine; but Russian *medú*, honey, Lettish *meddus*, honey, Sanskrit *madhu*, honey, sugar. However: Lithuanian *midus*, mead, *medus*, honey; and Zend *madhu* = Persian *mai*, wine = Greek *méthu*, mead (from which ultimately "amethyst," a gem supposed to prevent drunkenness). These learned etymologies (from the *Oxford English Dictionary*, microtype edition, p. 1751, and the *Century Dictionary-Encyclopedia*, p. 3740) would seem to suggest that many Indo-Europeans preferred to take their honey as mead, by the "simply add water" technique, and waiting.

both hunted mammoths and other large game. But the 30,000 B.P. dates suggested by some students, based on charred baby mammoth bones found in California, would seem to imply a Neanderthaloid physical type with a Mousterian culture of the Lower Paleolithic. However, no trace of Neanderthal remains among American Indians, who are uniformly of modern *Homo sapiens* type, have been found. Nor are any skeletal remains of New World Neanderthals available. And of the material culture of the Big Game Hunters, archeologists are able as yet to report only Folsom, Clovis, and other spear-points, because, like their contemporary Old World hunters, the pre-bow-and-arrow Paleo-Indians hunted on foot armed only with spears, whether thrown or in hand. Conservative opinion among Americanists would therefore suggest Indian origins in at best only post-Aurignacians, early Upper Paleolithic, when the African Capsian-period bow and arrow first came via Spain into western Europe. Even so, sufficient time must be allowed for the diffusion of the bow from western Europe to eastern Asia. And evidence exists that even Mesolithic peoples were still straggling into the Americas; witness the scattered but distant occurrence of pottery in Middle and South America.[j]

Although essentially Asiatic Paleo-Siberians, the Akmak people[67] early hunted in interior Alaska and on the tundra of "Beringia" at the height of the last glaciation some 20–18,000 years ago, when so much water was tied up in glacial ice that the continents were connected by this 1,300-mile-wide dry-land

j. Agricultural Neolithics as Amerindian ancestors would be far too late, for many reasons. Most convincingly, there exist in the Old and New Worlds no plants cultivated in common, with the possible exception of two *Gossypium* species (cotton) independently cultivated; the Oceanic–New World yam is alleged on dubious and controvertible evidence. The Paleo-Siberian hunters, easily proven ancestral with plentiful evidence of all kinds, had no agriculture; like them the first Indians were hunters and gatherers only, and Indians themselves later independently invented agriculture in the Americas with quite different cultigens.

The peopling of Polynesia from America is a romantic fiction, for which the evidence is all negative: racially, Polynesians are caucasoids, with in some areas admixtures of negroids, but Amerindians are early unspecialized mongoloids (they lack, for example, the specialized later mongoloid epicanthic fold). In addition to having no common cultigens, no common linguistic stocks are traceable, as should be the case. In fact, Polynesian languages are Malayo-Polynesian (Austronesian), with insufficient dialecticization to argue any great time-depth. By contrast, despite millennia of time-depth, reconstructed proto-Athapaskan can be equated with Asiatic proto-Sinitic, and so perhaps can some other linguistic stocks be traced in both Asia and America. Besides, on the evidence of their own genealogies, Polynesians entered Oceania far too late, in half-remembered protohistoric A.D. centuries, to have had any influence on early American hunters or, for that matter, later agriculturalists. One critical fact is that Indians were not Oceanic navigators (they plied only interior waterways, and were at most only island-hoppers of the Antillean chain), but the Polynesians were spectacular navigators who populated islands from Madagascar off southeast Africa to Easter Island in the Pacific. Actually, the reverse direction, *from* Polynesia *to* America is more plausible. Given the sporadic occurrence of Oceanic traits in America (barkcloth, blowgun, and some dozens of others, all precisely traits not widely diffused in the Americas as they might be had they originated there), it would seem quite possible that Polynesians, capable of pinpointing remote Oceanic islands in their navigation, could in occasional boatloads have hit the barn-door of coastal North and South America, if thrown off course by storms. Meanwhile, if far horizons are desired, Oceanic posture-dancing looks more Indic than Indian, and the stratified Polynesian social structure is much more south Asiatic than the open system of the aboriginal Indian hunters—all of which culture traits consist better with racial, linguistic, and other evidences.

corridor and the rest of the New World was blocked to man by an all-Canadian glacier that began to gap only about 14,000 years ago. Most authorities, therefore, now date the first massive invasion of proto-Indians to the "Magdalenians" of Lake Baikal sites in Siberia, whose culture can be traced westward to the classic Magdalenians of western Eurasia; the mid-palatal ridge of Cro-Magnons and that of some American physical types would conform with this thesis.

On the basis of culture traits universal or near-universal from Alaska to Patagonia (bow, spear-thrower, dog), it is evident that the trickling southward of post-Aurignacian, bow-using, Paleo-Siberian hunters continued on into the Mesolithic (sporadic pottery), at which time, many believe, Eskimos now in both Asia and America blocked further incursions of Asiatic peoples and cultures. This picture is fully confirmed archeologically, in Asiatic-American semi-subterranean houses from Siberia to Alaska and also in the American Southwest; and linguistically (tonemic Apache-Navaho is cognate with Tibeto-Burman-Chinese tone languages of Asia); and culturally (the conical tipi-wigwam extends from western Asia across Siberia to the central Algonkians of the Great Lakes, snow vehicles are of similar type from Finland to Maine, so too the sweat-lodge even beyond these limits; and in religion (the circumboreal "bear ceremonialism," Tungusic olonism and the Asiatic-American vision-quest complex, shamanism); and folkloristically (the Eurasiatic-American lightning-eagle, the "magic flight" motif, the Orpheus legend); and even botanically[k] (the absence of aboriginally shared cultigens, and domesticates beyond the Mesolithic dog.[68]

The ethos of American Indians was and essentially remained that of hunters. Even the famed prestige-warfare of the Plains (certainly not a case of Marxian class-warfare, or struggles over means of production like the bow) may have derived from the hunting ethos. When invidious prestige could no longer be based on hunting of animals as inordinately plentiful and easily accessible as the Plains buffalo, then the more difficult and dangerous hunting of men themselves (surely not demanded by any "territorial imperative" based on competition for scarce game) preserved the old invidious prestige pattern of hunters

---

k. The botanist Oakes Ames (*Economic Annuals and Human Cultures*, Cambridge: Botanical Museum of Harvard University, 1939, p. 11) argued that the domestication and spread of corn and other old cultigens in America demanded more than the 10,000 B.P. date then allowed by anthropologists for the entry of Indians into the Americas; modern archeology would now concede that he was right. In retort courteous, a tantalizing botanical fact is offered: *the only hallucinogenic plant used in both Old and New Worlds is the narcotic mushroom*, though these are of different species, *Amanita muscaria* in Asia and *Psilocybes* (and others) in Mexico. Could there be "cultural memory" in America of the Asiatic psychotropic plant? Surely the thunderbird-eagle and thunder-engendered mushrooms as folk-beliefs in both hemispheres lend countenance to this conjecture—and what, indeed, is the tricontinental bear-ceremonialism (traceable to east-Alpine Stone-Age caves) than "cultural memory"? Further, though the time-span is less gigantic, the ethnobotanist William Merrill, puzzled that some Indians requested sweet barley-water from fur-traders in preference to firewater, was led to discover that some Plains Algonkians had remembered the maple sugar of their onetime Woodlands habitat (William Merrill, unpublished ms., about 1960).

intact—but joined, as we shall see, by other aboriginal elements in generic Indian culture like the "power" quest.

For a more basic example of the persisting hunter ethos, Indian economic and social status everywhere—even to the *potlach* giveaway feasts of the wealthy Northwest Coast fishermen, even to the economic take-and-give in Amazonia of the "great house" chief who receives game and captive women from the young hunters which he then redistributes, and even to the stored tax hoards of the royal Inca communal state given out in time of need—all were ultimately based on the invidious ability of hunters to provide shared largesse for their dependents.[1]

In this male-centered hunting society, curiously, *quite like food*, a boy's manhood itself and manly prowess in hunting and war and sexuality, all *come as gifts from the outside*, from the stronger ones—that is, as "medicine power" from the outer generalized supernatural (Siouan *wakan*, Algonkian *manitou*, Iroquoian *orenda*, e.g.) and not from any endogenous endocrine entelechy within. The young vision-seeker, abstaining from food and sleep, and sometimes undergoing other punishments, plaintively begs the supernatural to witness his powerlessness and, as a suppliant, with tears running down his face, he beseeches the Power to take pity on his weakness and to *give him* what it takes to be a man. At puberty this power was *acquired*, either struck in by lightning, or bought in another man's medicine-bundle, or imbibed by the individual, whether in the individual vision quest, the shamanic spirit-possessed ecstasy, or the invariably, therefore, *sacred* eating, drinking, snuffing, or smoking of psychotropic plants. In one northern-Algonkian tribe, medicine power may even be obtained through ritual coitus with a great warrior's wife! But in every instance, medicine power is a *commodity* to be *obtained*.

Even in the advanced hierarchic agricultural societies of the Aztec of Mexico and the Chibcha of Colombia, with the hunter's generalized supernatural-now-become-personalized gods (medicine-bundle spirits, grown in complexer socie-

---

1. From the *Philosophes*, encyclopedists, and other eighteenth-century utopians down to the early nineteenth-century Romantic movement, the image of the American Indian, with obvious polemic tendentiousness in then-contemporary Europe, has been of open-handed communalist hunters' generosity. But this ethnographic truth neglects the obverse of the coin: the inveterate and deep-rooted psychological *dependency* of the rest of the band on the great hunter—a dependency early transferred to the Indian trader as source of goods, and to California and Paraguayan missions, then in North America to the Indian agent, and now on reservations to the Indian Office bureaucracy, with land claims on guilty Americans that might seem exorbitant, considering that Americans through their labors had created the increased land values. The once-proud hunters and warriors-without-weapons are now, sadly, a rural proletariat of the psychologically (and culturally) most dependent kind. It is no accident that peyotism since 1870 (anciently a deer-hunting and first-fruits rite) diffused almost universally in the Plains and beyond, still accompanied by both a ritual meal and the traditional feast by the donor. It might even be argued that the notorious Indian vulnerability to alcohol is consistent with the inveterate vision-quest for "medicine power" *from outside*, and their deep dependence on the psychotropic experience as another such power from outside. Any attempt to "better" the plight of the Indian must take into account, beyond romanticism or guilt, the *culturally built-in* psychological dependency of the American Indian.

ties first to the tribal palladia of the Plains Sun Dance, and thence into indivi-
duated gods in an empire, as fearsome and autocratic as the ruler himself—for
example, the Aztec god of war whom the bravest war-captive impersonated
for a year before being sacrificed—these gods still needed to be fed spirit-
power like food, from human-sacrificial victims. The Aztec captured these victims for god-food in war, the Chibcha bought them in lively trade with their
neighbors. Much as Andeans brought tribute to the deified Inca, so also in
their religion the Aztec and Chibcha brought human-spirit food-power to their
gods. To obtain victims was the chief motive of Aztec warfare: "impersonated"
is perhaps misleading, because the brave captive-warrior's spirit *became* part
of the war-god who ate it. Farther north, scalping, and farther south, headhunting had the same motive, the acquisition of spirit-power from scalp or
shrunken head, whether for the individual or for the tribe. *Mos saecula, mos
religiosa*: men need "power" in all male activities, and gods need power from
spiritual food to remain gods.

Spirit-power must be hunted, quite like flesh-food. In the Huichol long hunting trip in "quest for our life," Elder Brother Deer is symbolically assimilated
directly to the psychotropic peyote plant, and the first one seen on the pilgrim-
age by the shaman is shot with bow and arrow quite as if it were a deer. And,
when shrunken into its corky cone below ground during drought, peyote is
Deer's footprints. Again, on the shamanic level, it strikes us strange that the
doctor takes the medicine rather than the patient. But the medicine man is
taking a supernatural medicine that enables him to shamanize: to prognosticate, for divination, for clairvoyance, or to diagnose the human or physical
cause of an illness. If the cause is physical, like an embedded claw or feather,
he provides physical treatment (sucks it out). If the cause is spiritual, he uses
counter-magic. When he does give medicine to patients, in a sense the shaman
is sharing his "medicine" with them, not unlike a hunter sharing his kill. Moreover, in Indian belief, the shaman-visionary has power over an illness manifestly because he had earlier recovered from the same illness himself through
his supernatural power. As a result, patients whom he has cured characteristically then join the "medicine society" of the successful shaman, in a psychic
sodality quite like Alcoholics Anonymous. A cure is an initiation into the society. For example, if the vision-gained "bear power" of the shaman cures his
illness, then the patient joins his shaman's Bear Society; the cure was a magic
ritual the patient has learned, if, like the shaman, he recovers.

For the American Indian, the presence of any psychotropic effect in a plant
is plain evidence of its containment of supernatural "medicine" or spirit-shak-
ing "power." One introjected the power exactly as he ate food. This principle
was true of even so mildly psychotropic a drug as tobacco, though some *Nicotiana* species (*N. rustica, N. bigelovii, N. attenuata, N. trigonophylla*, e.g.)
often contain far larger amounts of nicotine than the mild commercial *N. ta-
bacum*. For instance, among the Warao of Venezuela and elsewhere in South
America, the *bahanarotu* shamans used tobacco in truly hallucinogenic amounts

to travel in trance states to the *bahana*-spirit realms in the eastern cosmic vault, and to feed with smoke the *kanabo* (ancestral spirits) and the *hoarotu* (spirits of dead shamans), or to initiate new *hoarotu* into shamanhood.[69] The native American tobaccos were used wherever *Nicotiana* species, wild or cultivated, will grow—which is to say from southern Canada to northern Patagonia—in cylindrical or elbow pipes, in cigarettes or cigars, or snuffed, chewed with lime, or drunk in infusion.[70] As typical examples, Amazonian postadolescent youths dipped a spatula into a thick tobacco syrup in the men's palaver-pot and licked it off, to sanction adherence (under supernatural penalty) to conventionally "unanimous" tribal vote; and an Iroquois lucky enough to meet a "tobacco-begging spirit" in the woods, after suitable gifts of tobacco, would carve the face of the supernatural on a living basswood tree and later use the power-laden mask in long-house "False Face Society" ceremonies (masks, of course, everywhere in the world promote a sense of identification with, or possession by, gods and spirits). The plentiful evidence would suggest, in fact, that tobacco was the supernatural plant par excellence of the American Indian. Such near-universal use argues not merely great time-depth for tobacco in the Americas, but also the wide acceptability of the plant in the generic religious ideology of American shamanism.

Beyond the enormous diffusion on two continents of the use of a single psychotropic plant like tobacco is the great variety of others, often of widespread diffusion and great time-depth as well. The entire aboriginal Southeast, including the northern half of Florida, the Arawakan Great and the Cariban Lesser Antilles, used *Ilex vomitoria* (*I. cassine* and *I. yaupon*), which Indians boiled down into a heroically strong stimulant and emetic Black Drink. Virginia and Carolina tribes used it in the "huskinaw" or ritual puberty initiation of boys; and Creeks mixed tobacco with their Black Drink for purification before important councils and sacred rites like the corn harvest busk.[71] It is probable that the botanically related *Ilex paraguayensis* in South America was also aboriginally used in ritual, before becoming the common South American secular stimulant *maté*; indeed, *I. guayusa* has been found recently in a Tiahuanacoid tomb of highland Bolivia which is C_{14}-dated to the fifth century.[72]

The violently hallucinatory and toxic daturas were so widespread and so deeply entrenched in aboriginal American ritual use as to provide an exemplary overview in detail of the various ways in which psychotropics and hallucinogens in general were used in the New World. In Virginia, the "Jamestown"[m] or jimson weed was taken as "wysoccan" (probably *D. stramonium*)

---

m. The name "Jamestown" or jimson weed did not arise from the native Virginian tribal use of *wysoccan*. Rather, it comes from the behavior of British soldiers, sent to Jamestown in 1676 to put down Bacon's Rebellion, who ate young shoots of datura as a pot green and for several days became amusingly intoxicated. In 38–37 B.C., during a retreat, Antony's legion had a similar experience with a European datura (R. Beverly, *History of Virginia, by a Native Inhabitant of the Place* (2nd ed., London: B. and S. Tooke, 1722). The use of daturas since prehistoric times in the Old World is documented in R. E. Schultes and A. Hofmann, *The Botany and Chemistry of Hallucinogens* (Springfield, Ill.: Charles C Thomas, 1973), pp. 166–67.

in the puberty ordeals for boys. Confined for long periods, they were given "no other substance but the infusion or decoction of some poisonous, intoxicating roots [and] they became stark, staring mad, in which raving condition they were kept eighteen or twenty days [and were said to] unlive their former lives" and to begin manhood by losing all memory of ever having been boys.[73] Algonkian and other Eastern Woodlands tribes also may have used the thorn-apple as a hallucinogen in initiatory rites.[74]

In the Southwest, the ancient Aztec *toloache* (*D. inoxia* = *D. meteloides* of older sources, but *D. discolor* and *D. wrightii* were also valued hallucinogens) was also used by the Cocopa, Havasupai, Hopi, Navaho, Pima, Walapai, Yuma, and Zuñi of the Southwest; again, in California, by the Akwa'ala, Cahuilla, Chumash, Diegueño, Gabrieleño, Luiseño, Miwok, Mohave, Mono, Salinan, Serrano, and Yokuts. The distribution of datura use is continuous with that in northwestern Mexico among the Cora, Opata, Tepecano, and Tepehuane (the Aztec used it to stupefy sacrificial victims); and its use extends southward into Andean and Amazonian South America. Zuñi rain priests and the heads of two medicine societies "owned" and were exclusively allowed to gather *D. inoxia*; to commune with bird spirits at night, they put the powdered root into their eyes; the rain priests chewed the roots to ask ancestral spirits to intercede for rain (the greatest "aleatory anxiety" among these agricultural-isis). Besides such use as a hallucinogen, Zuñi valued *a'neglakya* as an anesthetic and analgesic for broken bones and serious wounds; medicine men also gave it to clients to discover robbers by divination. Besides employment in puberty ceremonials, the typical Californian use, tribes of the Yuman stock used datura to induce dreams for predicting the future. Yokuts usually took the seeds only once in a lifetime, but shamans had to undergo yearly intoxication to keep in practice. Navaho eat the root for divination and prophecy, but the Hopi used it in doctoring. In southern California, the Akwa'ala, Yuma, and Eastern Mono ate datura for luck in gambling; Central Miwok do not eat it but think a dream about datura brings luck in gambling. "Of the remaining tribes of the area who used it ceremonially, some features were held in common: (1) datura was not taken before puberty, (2) it was usually administered to a group, and (3) a supernatural helper, sometimes an animal, was sought."[75] In southwestern California, datura was strongly ritualized in the Chungichnich cult of the Luiseño, Diegueño, Cahuilla, and tribes of the San Joaquin basin and Sierra Nevada, in a male puberty rite that Kroeber[76] thinks overlay older nonritual use in a wider area. White Mountain Apache and Tarahumare used datura in their *tesquino* maize beer. Tepehuano used it instead of peyote; indeed, the aboriginal areas of datura and peyote use are mutually exclusive.[77] But Tepecano prayers implicate *toloache* with maize and the sun, much as in Mexican peyotism, and the Pima had a jimson weed deer hunting song, as in Huichol peyotism.[78]

In South America, the arborescent *Datura* species (*D. candida, D. sangui-*

narea of the Andean highlands of Colombia southward to Chile, and *D. suaveolens* of the warmer lowlands) are never found wild, and all are evidently ancient cultigens, given their chromosomal aberrancy and extreme variation into several hundred cultivars or "races."[79] The Chibcha, Choco, Ingano, Kamsá, Siona, and Kofan of Colombia, the Quechua of Ecuador, Peru, and Bolivia, the Mapuche-Huilliche of Chile, the Canelo, Piojo, Omagua, Jivaro, and Zoparo of eastern Ecuador—all use datura hallucinogens in daily life, the Mapuche as a correctional medicine for unruly children, the Jivaro to bring ancestral spirits to admonish recalcitrant youth in datura hallucinations. Chibchans mixed daturas (including perhaps *D. aurea*, as well as their other two) with maize chicha beer, giving it to wives and slaves of chiefs and warriors to induce stupor before burial alive with husband or master. Indians at Sogamoza, Colombia, used *D. sanguinea* in sacred rituals at the Temple of the Sun, as did Quechuans to communicate with ancestors and the spirit world, and in Matucanas (Peru) to reveal treasures in *huaca* tombs. Initial intoxication on the scopolamine and other tropane alkaloids in daturas is so violent that physical restraint is needed before users pass into hallucinatory sleep, with dreams that are interpreted by shamans in order to diagnose disease, identify thieves, and prognosticate events of tribal concern. Beyond botanical evidence, the antiquity of datura use is proven by the remains of the drug in a Tiahuanacoid period shaman's tomb in Peru.[80]

The Amerindian hallucinogen earliest known to Europeans was of course *Anadenanthera* [formerly *Piptadenia*] *peregrina*, an Antillean narcotic snuff of the Caribbean Taino, *cohoba*, used for spirit communication, and mentioned in a letter of Columbus in 1496. The main area of use, however, is that of the Orinocan *yopo* (von Humboldt's *niopo?*)[81] the indole hallucinogens of which initially cause unconsciousness; then, as the limbs and head droop, users may see the world "upside-down and men walking with their heads downwards," according to a colonial observer.[82] However, the highly narcotic *parica* snuffs are made of the blood-red sap of *Virola* species trees (Puinave *yaki* and Kuripako *yato*); these are taken by shamans for diagnosis and treatment of disease, divination, and prognostication, among the Burusana, Makuna, Kabuyari, and others of the Vaupés drainage. In the headwaters of the Orinoco and north of the Rio Negro, the Waiká groups (Kirishaná, Shirianó, Karauetari, Karimé, Parahuri, Surará, Pakidái, Yanömamö[83] and others use *Virola* snuffs they variously call *epena*, *ebene*, or *nyakwana* "in excessive—even frightening— amounts" in daily use as a hallucinogen.[84] In addition to use in snuffs by these tribes, *Virola* is recently known as an oral hallucinogen among the Bora of Peru.[85]

South American snuffs are still somewhat confused in the botanical and anthropological literature,[86] but Peruvian *vilca* and *cébil* in northern Argentina may be *A. colubrina*. *Cytisus* (*Genistus*) *canariensis*, the Old World "genistus" used as decorant-foliage by florists, is a minor hallucinogen apparently employed only by Yaqui shamans in Mexico—suggesting, as with Mazatec *Salvia divinorum* and perhaps Tepehuano *Cannabis sativa*, a continuing Indian readiness to use newly available hallucinogens. Despite its restricted area of modern use, only recently discovered, *Salvia divinorum* nevertheless may be the psychotomimetic *pipilsintzintli* of the Aztec, a mint like *Nepeta cataria*, the catnip so loved by cats.[87]

If cohoba snuff was the earliest known, the oldest presently known Indian narcotic is the newly discovered Texas buckeye *Ungnadia speciosa*, found in northeast Mexican and trans-Pecos caves in association with Folsom points and stratigraphically below abundant Red Bean (*Sophora secundiflora*) specimens in ritual context. But the buckeye is so highly toxic that later and successively less toxic hallucinogens like the Red Bean, peyote, and psilocybe mushroom in turn may have been gradually substituted in ritual use.[88] Archeologically, the buckeye is dated C_{14} to a remarkable 8500 B.C., the Red Bean to the range 8440–8120 B.C., peyote as yet only to A.D. 810–1070, but mushroom stones indicating ritual use of narcotic mushrooms in highland Guatemala conservatively to 1000 B.C. The Red Bean was used by the Tarahumare and other Mexican tribes, the Southwestern Apache, and the Texan Tonkawa in historic times, and in the Plains also by Comanche, Delaware-Caddo, Iowa, Kansa, Omaha, Pawnee, Ponca, and Wichita.[89] The Iowa had a Red Bean Dance in the spring in which initiates bought membership into a medicine society, but the Pawnee were their source for the cult; Pawnee initiates painted themselves and danced with peculiar jumping movements to the music of musical bows and gourd rattles. A large number of beans were "killed" by pounding and boiling in a pot with herbs said to make the powerful decoction milder in action; a cup or two of it stupefied and caused everything to look red.[90] Heavy taboos were laid on the red-medicine-bundle owners. Numerous similarities led La Barre to hypothecate that a "Red Bean Cult" had preceded and perhaps influenced the later peyote cult,[91] a supposition later confirmed archeologically and botanically by Campbell, Troike, Adovasio and Fry, and Schultes.[92] Peyotism, of course, is too well known to need more than mention here.[93]

Likewise the universal Andean ritual use of coca (*Erythroxylon coca*), the source of cocaine (early used in experiments by Freud), is well documented in Americanist sources.[94] The widespread Amazonian use of the "vine of the spirits," *Banisteriopsis caapi*, earlier only poorly known ethnographically, has been abundantly documented by Harner and his associates in *Hallucinogens and Shamanism*,[95] and by others.[96] Since the interested reader may now be referred to easily accessible monographs on some American hallucinogens, attention here has been focused on lesser known and newly discovered ones. For example, a mescaline-containing Peruvian cactus, "San Pedro" or *cimora* (*Trichocereus pachanoi*), is used in folk healing.[97] According to seventeenth-century Jesuit sources, the Yurimagua of Peruvian Amazonia had a potent beverage made from a "tree fungus," possibly *Psilocybe yungensis*.[98] The Guege, Acroa,

Pimenteira, and Atanayé of eastern Brazil formerly made "a miraculous drink," *ajuca* or *vinho de jurema*, from *Mimosa hostilis*, which gave "glorious visions of the spirit land," and was used especially before going to war.[99] *Brunfelsia* species were apparently used in psychotomimetic drinks by the Kachinahua of Brazilian Amazonia; but the Kofan and Jivaros of Colombia and Ecuador employed them only as additives to their basically *Banisteriopsis* "yajé" or *natemä* drink.[100] The general Amazonian custom of mixing drinks makes botanical identification of hallucinogens very difficult. The spiny shrub *latué* or *árbol de los brujos*, "witchdoctor's tree," (*Latua pubiflora*, which contains hyoscyamine and scopolamine) was used in central montane Chile to produce delirium, hallucinations, and, sometimes, permanent insanity; it is said that shamans could produce madness of any chosen duration, according to the dose.[101] Schultes discovered an anomalous monotypic genus *Methysticodendron amesianum*, known only in clones and called *culebra borrachera*, in the Sibundoy valley of Colombia, which he considered allied to the tree daturas.[102] The Kofan and Kashinahua of Amazonia use two *Psychotria* species (coffee family) which they call *nai-kawa* and *matsi-kawa*, elsewhere sometimes added to ayahuasca.[103]

Even in more easily accessible North America, there are some little-known but interesting plant "medicines." The Cree and other Canadian Indians chew flag root or sweet calomel (*Acorus calamus*) to lessen fatigue on long journeys; the plant contains aserones similar in structure to mescaline, and in larger doses produce an LSD-like experience.[104] Northwest Indians chewed *Lycopodium selago* fern for its narcotic effects, three stems intoxicating, and eight rendering a man unconscious; the Calpella considered their "sleeproot," red larkspur (*Delphinium nudicaule*), a powerful soporific.[105]

Of all regions in the world, perhaps the Nahuatl culture area of Mexico had the largest number of psychotropic plants in native use.[n] The Aztec had pre-Columbian *chocolatl* (*Theobroma cacao*, originally from Amazonia, probably via the Maya),[106] and *ololiuhqui* (the seeds of *coatlxoxouhqui*, *Rivea corymbosa*, a morning-glory containing d-lysergic acid amide or ergine): "When the priests wanted to commune with their gods and to receive a message from them, they ate [*ololiuhqui*] to induce a delirium, during which a thousand visions and satanic hallucinations appeared to them."[107] They also had *peyotl* (*Lophophora williamsii*, but the Aztec term referred also to other cacti and noncacti);[108]

---

n. But Schultes, on botanical, and La Barre, on ethnographic grounds have agreed that the Colombian area of Chibchan cultures—comprising along with the well-known Aztec and Inca, the little-known *third* of the "high cultures" in the Americas—may well rival in time the Mexican culture area (R. E. Schultes, "Mexico and Colombia: Two Major Centers of Aboriginal Use of Hallucinogens," *Journal of Psychedelic Drugs*, 9 [1977]; W. La Barre, *Journal of Psychedelic Drugs* 9 [1977], 351). And not to be forgotten as containing possible new hallucinogens is the enormous *materia medica* of the Aymara in the Incan area (W. La Barre, "Materia medica of the Aymara, Lake Titicaca Plateau, Bolivia," *Webbia* [Firenze: Instituto Botanico dell'Università], 15 no. 1 [1959], 47–94).

picietl (probably *Nicotiana rustica*);[109] *pipiltzantzantli* (the hallucinogenic mint *Salvia divinorum*);[110] *pulque*, (a beer made from the sap of mescal, *Agave amercana*);[o] *sinicuichi* (*Heimia salicifolia*, a little-known narcotic from highland Mexico, producing especially auditory hallucinations that "help to remember events that took place many years earlier . . . even prenatal events," and that give a yellow cast to everything seen);[111] *teonanácatl*, the famous "flesh of the gods," a group of *Conocybe, Panaeolus, Psilocybe*, and *Stropharia* mushroom species, some of which Wasson discovered still in use in Mazatecan shamanism;[112] *teyhuinti*, narcotic mushrooms "that cause not death, but madness that on occasion is lasting . . . with night-long visions are they sought, awesome and terrifying";[113] *tlitliltzin*, the seeds of *Ipomoea violacea*, a morning-glory yielding LSD-like alkaloids;[114] *toloatzin*, Mexican *toloache, Datura inoxia*;[115] and *yauhtli* ("Rosa maria" or marihuana)—but all these leave unidentified the colonial ethnographer Sahagun's *aquiztli, atlepatli, mixitl, quimichpatli, tenoxoxoli, tlapatal, tochtetepi*, and *tzintzintlapatl*. Nor do even these exhaust the Mexican list alone. For example, the Chontal of Oaxaca used the leaves of the sacred *thle-pelakano*, "leaf of god" (*Calea zacatechichi*) as a hallucinatory narcotic, and more undoubtedly remain to be discovered.[116]

So numerous, in fact, are Amerindian hallucinogens that in 1964 La Barre postulated a "New World narcotic complex" extending from a mid-United States latitude southward to include most of the Andean and Amazonian regions (on evidence discovered since, the area should be enlarged to include the Orinocan drainage and parts of Canada).[117] This complex is inextricably bound to Indian shamanism.[118] In 1963 and again in 1966, Schultes raised the pertinent question: since hallucinogens are found as alkaloids, glucosides, resins and essential oils in Fungi and cacti and in the seeds, leaves, barks, stems, flowers, roots, and saps of many angiosperm species distributed with botanical indiscrimination in both hemispheres, why should New World natives know many scores of psychotropic plants, whereas the Old World had scarcely half a dozen? The reason for the marked discrepancy in hemispheric narcotics is not immediately apparent; in point of fact, one might reasonably expect the re-

---

o. Indians lacked distilled alcoholic "fire water" brandies and whiskeys, but had many pre-Columbian beers and wines: mescal *Agave*-beer (Southwestern tribes of the Yuman stock, Kaibab Paiute, Apache groups' *tulapai, tulpi* = Aztec *pulque*, Huichol *nawa, tepache, toach*, Tarahumare *tshawi* = *tesvino* of northern Mexico); Southwestern, Mexican and Caribbean *pitahaya* (from fruits of the *Cereus giganteus*; cf. Papago sahuaro-cactus *huaren*, Gallibi *huicú*); Mexican *colonche* (*Opuntia tuna, O. Ficus Indica*): Yuman *pissiona* (from parched, ground grain); Southwestern and Mexican *sotol* (*Dasylirion* spp., "bear-grass"); Mexican *atolle*, Quechuan *asua*, Bolivian Chiriguano *cangui*, Caribbean Taino *chicha* (extended as a generic name by the Spanish colonials), Gran Chaco *kiwa*, all made variously from *Zea mays* or Indian corn; *algoroba* beer (*Prosopis alba, P. pallida*, and *P. juliflora* [mesquite bean]); Mayan *balché* (a bark-flavored mead; cf. Nicarao and Chirotega of Nicaragua *mazamorro*, made of honey and ground corn; Amazonian *cachiri*, Brazilian *cauim, pajuarú*, British Guianan *paiva* or *paiwari* (fermented juice of *Jatropha manihot*, Brazilian arrowroot or tapioca); Ecuadorian Jivaro *ui*, Canellos *chontaruru*, Tapajós region *taroba* (*Guilielma* chonta-palm species); South American *tusca* (from *Acacia aroma*), etc. For modes of preparation, see W. La Barre, "Native American Beers," *American Anthropologist*, 40 (1938), 224–34.

verse to be true. Certainly the Old World has a considerably larger land mass than the New, fully as varied environments, and hence the apparent possibility of a greater number and variety of plants. Further, as we can see from our dating of the incurrence of Indians into the New World, men and protomen who might have discovered the properties of plants that are psychotropic have existed for an incomparably longer period in the Old World—from the Australopithecines and *Homo habilis* onward, and indeed the trend is to push protohuman dates still further backward in time, whereas New World time-horizons are only Mesolithic or at best late Paleolithic. Thus both botanical and paleontological discoveries serve only to widen the discrepancy in Old/ New World psychotropic plants used by man.

Of the perhaps 800,000 plant species, Schultes points out that among the 200,000-500,000 angiosperms only about 3,000 are known ever to have been used directly as human food; and that of these last, only about 12-13, all of them cultigens, really stand between man and starvation. Small as this number is, the provenience of the major food plants is reasonably balanced between those of Old and New World origin—which highlights again the discrepancy in known narcotics. Psychotropics may be seen in biochemical perspective, since "we find, likewise, that the number of species providing men with narcotic agents is very small. Between four and five thousand species are now known to be alkaloidal (*apud* R. F. Raffauf), and we must realize that constituents other than alkaloids—glucosides, resins, essential oils, and others— may also be responsible for narcotic activity. Probably no more than sixty species, including Cryptogams and Phanerogams, are employed in primitive and advanced cultures for their intoxicating effects. Of these, only about twenty may be considered of major significance.[119] Only four or five narcotic cultigens are commercially important, and they are unknown in the wild state, indicating long association with man. Surely, there are no systematic ecological, floristic, histological, or chemical differences so that "natural occurrence" could explain the discrepancy.

There are several enmeshed components in an adequate cultural explanation, and perhaps no single-factor ethnologic-historical explanation is possible. The answer is complex. Indians were aboriginally hunters and gatherers in both Americas, and they largely retained the essential ethos of hunters and gatherers even in the religion of advanced local agriculturalists. It may be that plant gathering is more conducive to new plant discoveries than is the case with comfortably agricultural peoples—especially in the Old World, in which newer agriculture-based religions appear to have modified, overlayed or supplanted many of the older hunting religions, a matter perhaps again of greater time-depth in Old than in New World culture history. As hunters, Indians essentially kept the religion of hunters, that is, shamanism, with basic ideologies still discernible even among later agriculturalists. Shamanism and the vision quest may depend appreciably on hallucinogens. But the more codified and established priestly religions both need and tolerate shamanistic individualism the less. (In America, the firm resistance of Pueblo priesthoods to native alcoholic and hallucinogenic substances—moreover, abundant all around them geographically and used by neighboring Athapaskan and Yuman tribes—may be a case in point).*p* Thus, in shamanistic hunting societies that seek "power" visions, Indians are in a sense *culturally programmed* to seek and to use hallucinogens.[120] In any case, as we have seen, Indian religions are deeply disposed to value visionary and psychotropically induced "altered states of consciousness."

The importance of prior culture-areal culture should also be noted. With most of their specific tribal cultures now largely gone, Indians bearing residual traces of generic Plains-areal culture in common still regard the hallucinations produced by eating *peyotl* (an Aztec term for *Lophophora williamsii*) as visionary proof of the presence of the supernatural—even though the native trade-introduced plant grows nowhere in the area of Plains culture. In fact, a good case has been made that peyotism spread so rapidly in the Plains after 1870 because the tribes there were in a sense "preadapted" to peyotism. Ruth Shonle predicted that peyotism would spread as far as the aboriginal vision quest of the Plains; and this is precisely what subsequently happened. Interestingly, it is only the most Plains-like of the Pueblos, the Taos, to which (though with much conflict lasting over several centuries) peyotism has spread. Again, even in other Pueblos, there are strong echoes still of the shaman's ancient relationship to psychotropic plants. Among the Zuñi, for example, *a'ne-glakya* (*Datura stramonium*) is used to achieve trance states, to "listen to the voices of birds," to cure and to divine, as well as to make rain—in other words, in traditional shamanic ways. Evidently the "aleatory" anxiety of agriculturalists is the weather, not the contingencies of the hunt. But they still use datura.

An exhaustive monograph on the ethnography of Amerindian psychotropic drugs still remains to be written, and can scarcely be attempted here, in part because much continues to be learned. But Peter Furst has provided an excellent, scholarly and readable "introduction to some of the hallucinogenic drugs in their cultural and historical context"[121] in his *Hallucinogens and Culture*. The present essay has sought only to demonstrate these propositions:

1. that all the dissociative "altered states of consciousness"—hallucination, trance, possession, vision, sensory deprivation, and especially the REM-state dream—apart from their cultural contexts and symbolic content, are essentially the same psychic states found everywhere among mankind;

2. that shamanism or direct contact with the supernatural in these states (that

---

p. That prior tribal culture outweighs in importance simple ecology would seem to be indicated in the fact that in the same culture-area the Cherokee of North Carolina retain much of their rich *materia medica* of plant origin, whereas the Catawba of South Carolina are culturally impoverished in this respect (Cherokee consequently call the Catawba "ignorant," and Catawba call the Cherokee "superstitious" in the use of plant simples).

is, contact with "primary process" mentation arising from the unconscious) is the *de facto* source of all revelation, and ultimately of all religions;

3. that psychotropic drugs, far more than we have realized, are commonly adjunctive to these states; and

4. that, for a complex of reasons, although evidence is plentiful even in old Indic and European religions, the Eurasiatic-American shamanic complex shows these relationships most clearly and compendiously.

Epistemologically, the life-guiding and decision-making authority for American Indians is the individually experienced supernatural "power" in the "altered states of consciousness" in their vision quest, often to be sought through the use of actively psychotropic drugs. Their cognitive map is that of mystics, perhaps, but they were also pharmacodynamically pragmatists: some plants house spirits and psychedelic forces. By contrast with this faith in altered states of consciousness, the epistemological authority for belief among rational occidental men, ever since Heraclitus and the pre-Socratic nature philosophers, has been found in the common *koine* world of group-validated intersubjective experience, as opposed to the private world of the vision or dream. These are quite different cognitive maps. And yet we should remember that if our vested interest in rational establishment controls vision, nevertheless vision bursts the cognitive establishment, even in the history of science. The wisdom of knowing we might be wrong distinguishes the scientist from the tribalist.

So-called divine revelation from some spirit land is merely the result of tapping the id-stream of primary process thinking, and such revelation should be approached not as a cosmological but as a psychiatric phenomenon. What we seem to experience as an external "supernatural" *mysterium tremendum et fascinosum* appears to be external and objective only because it is presented in sensory-hallucinatory form, since our senses are the customary conduit of information from the outside environment. Furthermore, we see ghosts dance because of specific universal experiences occurring in the development of the human animal. That is, we bring from each individual family-nurtured past a mode of response to the supposed Stimulus, the nature of the Unknown being projected, not perceived. Technically, supernatural information is misapprehended information about the mind itself. The Mystery is in fact only our own brains, often in an altered state of consciousness: experiencing the "supernatural" is only a functionally dissociated and differentiated state of mind.

In the human sciences, those in which men study themselves, we do not yet know who we are. The motive for our researches may well determine what we find. The true believer will encounter only a *consensus gentium* for such sacred superstitions as the belief in animism, surely the most absurd and most punished error in the history of *sapiens*, the triple paradox: that all things can think, that thinking can be disembodied from any thing, and that thinking (soul, spirit) is a thing more immortal than matter—whereas actually mind is only and always a contingent and temporary function of a thing, the brain. However, the detached skeptic may find shocking though edifying new information, from an unanticipated quarter, about his own tendentious psyche and social self. Comparative ethnography can be a potent ally in helping us delimit and calibrate our own more exotic experiences—that is, if we maintain a firmly scientific, benevolent skepticism toward ethnic data (including our own), instead of indulging a voraciously gullible appetite for miracle. What we accumulate then is only soberly empirical confirmation of perhaps unwelcomely learned and limiting idiosyncrasies in the mental behavior of the species. The *Mysterium tremendum et fascinosum* of religion is really the naively unexamined human mind, which has forgotten the individual formative history of its longings. Indeed, the authoritarian personality of the fundamentalist right thinker is actually seeking, not comprehension of self and world, but group-confirmed fantasies—of revelation, charisma, god-like projected parents, and the soul—all of which are amenable to a purely secular scrutiny. We should therefore not expect other tribes, however multiplied, to provide grounds for belief or to permit us to shop around for alternative fantasies, when all they can provide are data for this skeptical scrutiny. But we are willingly seduced by wish, and in the alternate inhabiting of two psychic worlds all mankind is kin. In hallucinosis, cultural or chemical, we need postulate no fatuous "separate reality," for it is always our selfsame selves but in varying psychic states.

Reference Notes

1. W. La Barre, *The Human Animal* (Chicago: University of Chicago Press, 1954), pp. 267–302; idem, *The Ghost Dance: Origins of Religion* (rev. ed. New York: Delta Books, 1972), pp. 367–74.
2. J. S. Lincoln, *The Dream in Primitive Cultures* (Baltimore: Williams & Wilkins, 1935); W. La Barre, "The Influence of Freud on Anthropology," *American Imago* 15 (1938), 316, fn. 55, reprinted as chap. 7, this volume; D. Eggan, "The Significance of Dreams for Anthropological Research," *American Anthropologist* 51 (1949), 177–98; idem, "Dream Analysis," in B. Kaplan (ed.), *Studying Personality Cross-Culturally* (Evanston, Ill.: Row, Peterson, 1961), pp. 551–57.
3. E. Aserinsky and N. Kleitman, "Regularly Recurring Periods of Eye Mobility and Comcomitant Phenomena During Sleep," *Science* 118 (1953), 273–74; W. Dement, "Studies on the Function of Rapid Eye Movement (Paradoxical) Sleep in Human Subjects," in M. Jouvet (ed.), *Aspects anatomo-fonctionnels de la physiologie du sommeil* (Paris: Centre de la Recherche Scientifique, 1954); C. Fisher, "Dreams, Images and Perception: A Study of Unconscious-Preconscious Relationships," *Journal of the American Psychoanalytic Association* 4 (1956), 5–48; W. Dement and N. Kleitman, "Cyclic Variations in EEG During Sleep and Their Relation to Eye Movements, Bodily Motility, and Dreams," *Electroencephalography and Clinical Neurophysiology* 9 (1957), 673–90; idem, "The Relation of Eye Movements During Sleep to Dream Activity: An Objective Method for the Study of Dreaming," *Journal of Experimental Psychology* 53 (1957), 339–46; W. Dement, "The Effect of Dream Deprivation," *Science* 131 (1960), 1705–7; N. Kleitman, "The Nature of Dreaming," in G. E. W. Wolstenholm and M. O'Connor (eds.), *The Nature of Sleep* (Boston: Little, Brown, 1961),

pp. 349–63; idem, *Sleep and Wakefulness* (Chicago: University of Chicago Press, 1963); C. Fisher and W. Dement, "Studies in the Psychopathology of Sleep and Dreams," *American Journal of Psychiatry* 119 (1963), 1160–68; W. Dement and C. Fisher, "Experimental Interference with the Sleep Cycle," *Canadian Psychiatric Association Journal* 8 (1963) 400–5; W. Dement, "Dreaming: A Biologic State," *Modern Medicine*, July 5, 1965, 184–206; idem, "Recent Studies on the Biological Role of Rapid Eye Movement Sleep," *American Journal of Psychiatry* 122 (1965), 404–8; W. Dement and S. Greenberg, "Changes in Total Amount of Stage Four Sleep as a Function of Partial Sleep Deprivation," *Electroencephalography and Clinical Neurophysiology* 20 (1966), 523–26; W. Dement et al., "The Nature of the Narcoleptic Sleep Attack," *Neurology* 16 (1966), 18–33; H. P. Roffwarg et al., "Ontogenetic Development of the Human Sleep-Dream Cycle," *Science* 152 (1966), 604–19; E. L. Hartman, *The Functions of Sleep* (New Haven: Yale University Press, 1973).

4. W. H. Bexton et al., "Effects of Decreased Variation in the Sensory Environment," *Canadian Journal of Psychology* 8 (1954), 70–76; J. C. Lilly, "Illustrative Strategies for Research on Psychopathology in Mental Health," *Group for the Advancement of Psychiatry*, Symposium No. 2 (1956), 13–20; J. A. Vernon et al., "Visual Hallucinations During Perceptual Isolation," *Canadian Journal of Psychology* 12 (1958), 31–34; L. Goldberger and R. R. Holt, "Experimental Interference with Reality Contact," *Journal of Nervous and Mental Disease* 127 (1958), 99–112; D. Wexler et al., "Perceptual Isolation: A Technique for Studying Psychiatric Aspects of Stress," *AMA Archives of Neurological Psychiatry* 79 (1958), 225–33; B. D. Cohen et al., "Sensory Isolation: Hallucinogenic Effects of a Brief Exposure," *Journal of Nervous and Mental Disease* 129 (1959), 486–91; J. L. Wheaton, "Fact and Fancy in Sensory Deprivation," *Aeromedical Review* 5 (1959), np.; S. J. Freedman and M. Greenblatt, "Studies in Human Isolation," *U. S. Armed Forces Medical Journal* 11 (1960), 1330–1497; S. J. Freedman et al., "Perceptual and Cognitive Changes in Sensory Deprivation," *Journal of Nervous and Mental Disease* 132 (1961), 17–21; A. J. Silverman et al., "Psychophysiological Investigations in Sensory Deprivation," *Psychosomatic Medicine* 23 (1961), 48–60; P. Solomon, et al., *Sensory Deprivation* (Cambridge: Harvard University Press, 1961); P. Solomon and J. Mendelson, "Hallucinations in Sensory Deprivation," in J. L. West (ed.), *Hallucinations* (New York: Grune & Stratton, 1962); C. A. Brownfield, *Isolation: Clinical and Experimental Approaches* (New York: Random House, 1965); J. P. Zubek (ed.), *Sensory Deprivation: Fifteen Years of Research* (New York: Appleton-Century-Crofts, 1969).

5. La Barre, *Ghost Dance*, pp. 55–60.

6. J. Moreau de Tours, *Du hachiche et de l'alienation mentale* (Paris: Fortin, Massin, 1845); N. Rosenzweig, "Sensory Deprivation and Schizophrenia: Some Clinical and Theoretical Similarities," *American Journal of Psychiatry* 116 (1959), 326–29; M. Katan, "Dream and Psychosis: Their Relationship to the Hallucinating Processes," *International Journal of Psycho-Analysis* 41 (1960) 341–51; Kleitman, *Sleep and Wakefulness*, p. 106; La Barre, *Ghost Dance*, pp. 67–68; Fisher, in Kleitman, "Patterns of Dreaming," in T. J. Teylor (ed.), *Altered States of Awareness* (San Francisco: Freeman, 1973), p. 50.

7. Dement, in Jouvet, p. 587; R. Greenberg and C. Pearlman, *Delirium Tremens and Dream Privation* (Washington, D.C.: Association for the Psychophysiological Study of Sleep, 1964); Roffwarg, *Ontogenetic development*, p. 614.

8. La Barre, *Ghost Dance*, pp. 51–54.

9. C. Burney, *Solitary Confinement* (London: Clerke and Cockeran, 1952).

10. C. Vostrovsky, "A Study of Imaginary Companions," *Education* 15 1895), 393–98; N. A. Harvey, *Imaginary Playmates and Other Mental Phenomena* (Ypsilanti, Mich.: State Normal College, 1919); E. B. Hurlock and M. Burnstein, "The Imaginary Playmate: A Questionnaire Study," *Journal of Genetic Psychology* 41 (1932), 380–92; M. Svendsen, "Children's Imaginary Companions," *Archives of Neurology and Psychiatry* 32 (1934), 985–99.

11. J. Slocum, *Sailing Alone Around the World* (New York: Century, 1900); F. Shackleton, *South: The Story of Shackleton's Last Expedition, 1914–17* (New York: Macmillan, 1920), p. 209; R. Byrd, *Alone* (New York: Putnam, 1938); W. Gibson, *The Boat* (Boston: Houghton Mifflin, 1954); C. E. Ritter, *A Woman in the Polar Night* (New York: Dutton, 1954); H. Lindemann, *Alone at Sea* (New York: Random House, 1958), pp. 19, 128, 144, 152, 157–59, 161, 171; Solomon et al., *Sensory Deprivation*; La Barre, *Ghost Dance*, pp. 53–54.

12. Ruth Benedict, *The Concept of the Guardian Spirit in North America* (Menasha, Wisc.: American Anthropological Association, Memoir 29, 1923; idem, "The Vision in Plains Culture," *American Anthropologist* 24 (1922), 1–23.

13. W. La Barre, *The Peyote Cult* (New Haven: Yale University Publications in Anthropology, 19, 1938), pp. 95–104; idem, *Ghost Dance*, p. 140.

14. Z. Gussow, "A Preliminary Report of 'Kayakangst' Among the Eskimos of West Greenland: A Study of Sensory Deprivation," *International Journal of Social Psychology* 9 (1963), 18–26; K. I. Taylor and W. S. Laughlin, "Sub-Arctic Commitment and 'Kayak Fear,'" Paper presented at the 62nd Annual Meeting, American Anthropological Association, San Francisco, 1963.

15. V. Barnouw, "A Psychological Interpretation of a Chippewa Origin Legend," *Journal of American Folklore* 68 nos. 267–69 (1955), 73–85, 211–23, 341–55; S. Parker, "The Windigo Psychosis in the Context of Ojibwa Culture and Personality," *American Anthropologist* 62 (1960), 603–24; R. Fogelson, "Psychological Theories of Windigo 'Psychosis' and a Preliminary Model Approach," in M. E. Spiro (ed.), *Culture and Meaning in Cultural Anthropology* (New York: Free Press, 1965), pp. 74–99; J. M. Cooper, "The Cree Witiko Psychosis," in A. Dundes (ed.), *Every Man His Way* (Englewood Cliffs, N.J.: Prentice-Hall, 1968), pp. 288–92; La Barre, *Ghost Dance*, p. 66.

16. F. Boas, *The Social Organization and Secret Societies of the Kwakiutl Indians* (Washington, D.C.: Report of the U.S. National Museum for 1895, 1897, 311–738), pp. 436–62; R. Benedict, *Patterns of Culture* (Boston: Houghton-Mifflin, 1934), pp. 173–222.

17. S. M. Shirokogoroff, *Psychomental Complex of the Tungus* (London: Kegan Paul, Trench, Trübner, 1935); La Barre, *Ghost Dance*, pp. 171–75; J. Schnier, "The Tibetan Lamaist Ritual: Chöd," *International Journal of Psycho-Analysis* 38 (1957), 402–40.

18. J. Van der Kroef, "Messianic Movements in the Celebes, Sumatra, and Borneo," in S. L. Thrupp (ed.) *Millenial Dreams in Action* (The Hague: Mouton, 1962), pp. 80–121.

19. E. R. Dodds, *The Greeks and the Irrational* (Berkeley: University of California Press, 1951), p. 117.

20. W. La Barre, *The Aymara Indians of the Lake Titicaca Plateau, Bolivia* (Menasha, Wisc.: American Anthropological Association, Memoir 68, 1948), p. 221.

21. S. Freud, *Collected Papers*, 5 vols. (London: Hogarth Press, 1924–1950), III:13–146.

22. G. A. Agogino, "The Use of Hypnotism as an Ethnologic Research Technique," *Plains Anthropologist* 10 no. 27 (1965), 31–36.

23. La Barre, "Influence of Freud," fn. 95, pp. 325–26, also chap. 7, this volume; I. Galdston (ed.), *Man's Image in Medicine and Anthropology* (New York: International Universities Press, 1963); A. Kiev (ed.), *Magic, Faith, and Healing* (New York: Free Press, 1964).

24. T. S. Kuhn, *The Structure of Scientific Revolutions* (Chicago: University of Chicago Press, Phoenix Books, 1962).

25. J. Mooney, *The Ghost Dance Religion and the Sioux Outbreak of 1890* (Washington, D.C.: Bureau of American Ethnology, 14th Annual Report, part 2 [1896], 641–1136). F. E. Williams, "The Vailala Madness and the Destruction of Native Ceremonies in the Gulf Division, Port Moresby," *Territory of Papua: Anthropological Reports* no. 4, 1923; idem, "The Vailala Madness in Retrospect," in E. E. Evans-Pritchard, R. Firth, B. Malinowski, and I. Schapera (eds.), *Essays Presented to C. G. Seligman* (London: Kegan Paul, Trench, Trübner, 1934).

26. M. Eliade, *Shamanism: Archaic Techniques of Ecstasy* (New York: Pantheon Books, Bollingen Series 76, 1964); idem, "Recent Works on Shamanism: A review article," *History of Religions* 1 (1961), 153. For refutation of Eliade's exclusion of Africa, see also note 46 below.

27. S. F. Nadel, "A Study of Shamanism in the Nuba Mountains," *Journal of the Royal Anthropological Institute* 7 (1946), 25–37; La Barre, *Ghost Dance*, p. 186, fn. 4.

28. C. Kluckhohn, "Recurrent Themes in Myths and Mythmaking," in Alan Dundes (ed.), *The Study of Folklore* (Englewood Cliffs, N.J.: Prentice-Hall, 1965), pp. 158–68.

29. J. E. Harrison, *Prolegomena to the Study of Greek Religion* (Cambridge: Cambridge University Press, 2nd ed., 1908).

30. S. F. Nadel, "The Origins of Music," *Musical Quarterly* 16 (1950), 538–42; but cf. La Barre, *Ghost Dance*, p. 421.

31. R. Benedict, "Anthropology and the Abnormal," *Journal of General Psychology* 10 (1934), 64. See also G. Devereux, "Normal and Abnormal: The Key Problem of Psychiatric Anthropology," in J. B. Casagrande and T. Gladwin (eds.), *Some Uses of Anthropology: Theoretical and Applied* (Washington, D.C.: Anthropological Society of Washington, 1956), pp. 3–32.

32. La Barre, *Ghost Dance*, pp. 139–41, 156–58.

33. Benedict, *Anthropology and the Abnormal*.

34. K. Kim, "Psychoanalytic Consideration of Korean Shamanism," [Journal of the] *Korean Neuropsychiatric Association* 11 no. 2 (1972), 121–29.

35. T. K. Oesterreich, *Die Bessessenheit* (Halle: Wendt und Klauwell, 1922). Translated as *Possession, Demoniacal and Other, among Primitive Races, in Antiquity, the Middle Ages, and Modern Times* (New York: Richard R. Smith, 1930; University Books, 1966). See also I. M. Lewis, *Ecstatic Religion: An Anthropological Study of Spirit Possession and Shamanism* (Middlesex, England: Penguin Books, 1971).

36. E. Bourguignon, *Religion, Altered States of Consciousness, and Social Change* (Columbus: Ohio State University Press, 1972). See also idem, "The Self, the Behavioral Environment and the Theory of Spirit Possession," in M. E. Spiro (ed.), *Context and Meaning in Cultural Anthropology* (New York: Free Press, 1965); idem, *A Cross-Cultural Study of Dissociational States* (Columbus: Ohio State University Research Foundation, 1968); and idem, "Dreams and Altered States of Consciousness in Anthropological Research," in F. L. K. Hsu (ed.), *Psychological Anthropology* (Cambridge, Mass.: Schenkman, 1972). Cf. A. F. C. Wallace, "Mental Illness, Biology and Culture," in Hsu, *Psychological Anthropology*.

37. R. Fischer, "Prediction and Measurement of Perceptual-Behavioral Change in Drug-Induced Hallucination," in W. Kemp (ed.), *Origin and Mechanisms of Hallucinations* (New York: Plenum Press, 1970), pp. 303–32; cf. P. H. Van der Walde, "Trance States and Ego Psychology," in R. Prince (ed.), *Trance and Possession States* (Montreal: R. M. Bucke Memorial Society, 1968), pp. 57–68. A. Ludwig, "Altered States of Consciousness," in R. Prince, *Trance and Possession States*.

38. Bourguignon, *Religion*, p. 7.

39. W. La Barre, "The Dream, Charisma, and the Culture-Hero," in G. E. von Grunebaum and R. Callois (eds.), *The Dream and Human Societies* (Berkeley: University of California, 1966), pp. 229–35; idem, *Human Animal*, pp. 303–4, 357; idem, "Psychoanalysis and the Biology of Religion," *Journal of Psychological Anthropology* 1 (1958), 57–64.

40. G. Zilboorg and G. W. Henry, *A History of Medical Psychology* (New York: Norton, 1941).

41. S. Freud, "A Neurosis of Demoniacal Possession in the Seventeenth Century," *Collected Papers*, 4:436–72.

42. La Barre, "Influence of Freud," pp. 278–80, 309–11, 318–26. See also chap. 7, this volume.

43. W. La Barre, "Materials for a History of Studies of Crisis Cults," *Current Anthropology* 12 (1971), 3–44.

44. R. Prince, "Possession Cults and Social Cybernetics," in Prince, *Trance and Possession States*, pp. 157–65; E. Bourguignon, "World Distribution and Patterns of Possession States," in Prince, *Trance and Possession States*, pp. 3–34; W. D. Davidson, "Psychiatric Significance of Trance Cults," Paper presented at the 118th Annual Meeting of the American Psychiatric Association, New York, 1965 (reviewed in *Transcultural Psychiatry Research Review*, 3 [1966], 45–47); W. Mischel and F. Mischel, "Psychological Aspects of Spirit Possession," *American Anthropologist* 60 (1958), 249–60; D. Akstein, "Kinetic trances and their Application in the Treatment and Prophylaxis of Psychoneuroses and Psychosomatic Diseases," Paper presented at the Fourth World Congress of Psychiatry, Madrid, September 1966 (Reviewed in *Transcultural Psychiatry Research Review* 5 [1968], 74–75); R. B. Lee, "The Sociology of Bushman Trance Performances," Paper presented at the Second Annual Conference of the R. M. Bucke Memorial Society on Possession States in Primitive Societies, Montreal, 4–6 March 1966; E. B. Harper, "Spirit Possession and Social Structure," in B. Ratman (ed.), *Anthropology on the March* (Madras: Thompson and Co., 1962 (Reviewed in *Transcultural Psychiatry Research Review* 1 [1964], 107–8).

45. E. Schepers, "Psychiatry and Folk Evaluations of Hallucinations and Other Psychiatric Symptoms Among Chicano Populations," Paper presented at the 71st Annual Meeting of the American Anthropological Association, Toronto, 1972 (*Abstracts*, p. 105); J. H. Henney, "The Shakers of St. Vincent: A Stable Religion," in Bourguignon, *Religion*, pp. 219–63; F. D. Goodman, "Apostolics of Yucatan: A Case Study of a Religious Movement," in Bourguignon, *Religion*, pp. 178–218; W. La Barre, *They Shall Take Up Serpents: Psychology of the Southern Snake-Handling Cult* (Minneapolis: University of Minnesota Press, 1962; New York: Schocken Books, 1969); S. M. Kane, "Ritual Possession in a Southern Appalachian Religious Sect," *Journal of American Folklore* 87 no. 346 (1974), 293–302; idem, "These Signs Shall Follow Them that Believe: Toward an Understanding of Holiness Snake Handling, Fire Handling and Strychnine Drinking," Paper presented at the 75th Annual Meeting of the American Anthropological Association, Washington, D.C., 1976; G. E. Simpson, "The Acculturative

Process in Jamaican Revivalism," in A. F. C. Wallace (ed.), *Men and Cultures* (Philadelphia: University of Pennsylvania Press, 1960); A. Kiev, "Spirit Possession in Haiti," *American Journal of Psychiatry* 118 (1961), 133–38; L. Mars, "La crise de possession et la personalité humaine en Haiti," *Revue de Psychologie des Peuples* 17 (1962), 6–22; K. Ravenscroft, "Spirit Possession in Haiti: A Tentative Theoretical Analysis," Unpublished thesis, Yale University (Reviewed in *Transcultural Psychiatry Research Review* 14 [1963], 51–52); E. D. Wittkower, "Spirit Possession in Haitian Vodun Ceremonies," in ibid., 53–55; idem, *Acta Psychotherapeutica* (Basel), 12 (1964), 72–80; E. Douyou, "La crise de possession dans le vaudou Haitien," Unpublished thesis, Université de Montréal, 1965 (Reviewed in *Transcultural Psychiatry Research Review*, 2 [1965], 155–59; R. Ribeiro, "Possessão: Problema de etnopsicologia," *Boletim do Instituto Joaquin Nabuco de Pesquisas Socials* 5 (1960), 2–44; E. Pressel, "Umbanda in São Paulo: Religious Innovation in a Developing Society," in Bourguignon, *Religion*, pp. 264–318; E. Willems, "Religious Mass Movements and Social Change in Brazil," in D. B. Heath (ed.), *Contemporary Cultures and Societies of Latin America* (2nd ed., New York: Random House, 1974), pp. 452–68.

46. L. Greenbaum, "Societal Correlates of Possession Trances in Sub-Saharan Africa," in Bourguignon, *Religion*, pp. 39–57; idem, "Possession Trance in Sub-Saharan Africa: A Descriptive Analysis of Fourteen Societies," in ibid., pp. 58–87; E. Bourguignon, "Divination, transe et possession en Afrique transsaharienne," in A. Caquot and M. Leibovici (eds.), *La Divination* (Paris: Presses Universitaires de France, 1968); H. Collomb et al., "Aspects socio-thérapeutiques du 'N'doep' cérémonie d'initiation à la société des possédés chez les Lebou et les Wolof du Senegal," *Neuro-Psychiatrie* [Université de Dakar], 14–16 (reviewed in *Transcultural Psychiatry Research Review* 1 [1964] 136–37); L. P. Gerlach, "Possession Hysteria Among the Digo of Kenya," Paper presented at the 64th Annual Meeting of the American Anthropological Association, Philadelphia, 1965 (*Abstracts*, p. 23); R. Giel et al., "Faith Healing and Spirit Possession in Ghion, Ethiopia," *Transcultural Psychiatry Research Review* 5 (1968), 64–67; J. Hamer and I. Hamer, "Spirit Possession and Its Socio-Psychological Implications Among the Sidamo of Southwest Ethiopia," *Ethnology* 5 (1966), 392–408; J. Gussler, "Social Change, Ecology, and Spirit Possession Among the South African Nguni," in Bourguignon, *Religion*, pp. 88–126; S. G. Lee, "Some Zulu Concepts of Psychogenic Disorder," *Journal for Social Research* 1 (1950), 9–18; idem, "Spirit Possession Among the Zulu," in J. Beattie and J. Middleton (eds.), *African Mediumship and Society* (New York: Africana Publishing, 1970); J. Lombard, "Les cultes de possession en Afrique noir et le Bori Hausa," *Psychopathologie Africaine* 3 (1967), 419–39 (reviewed in *Transcultural Psychiatry Research Review* 6 [1969], 65–69); W. H. Sangree, "Spirit Possession and Marriage Stability in Irigwe, Nigeria," Paper presented at the 67th Annual Meeting of the American Anthropological Association, Seattle, 1968; R. M. Wintrob, "Psychosis in Association with Possession by Genii in Liberia," *Psychopathologie Africaine* 2 (1966), 249–58 (reviewed in *Transcultural Psychiatry Research Review* 5 [1968], 55–59); idem, "Sexual Guilt and Culturally Sanctioned Delusions in West Africa," Paper presented at the 123rd Annual Meeting, American Psychiatric Association, Detroit, 1967 (reviewed in *Transcultural Psychiatry Research Review* 4 [1967], 149–52); I. I. Zaretsky, *Bibliography on Spirit Possession and Spirit Mediumship* (Berkeley: University of California Department of Anthropology, mimeograph, ca. 1970).

47. S. A. Freed and R. S. Freed, "Spirit Possession as Illness in a North Indian Village,"*Ethnology* 3 (1964) 152–71; G. Obeyesekere, "The Idiom of Demonic Possession," *Social Science and Medicine* 4 (1970), 97–111; J. Belo, *Trance in Bali* (New York: Columbia University Press, 1960).

48. F. L. Jocano, "Varieties of Supernatural Experiences Among Filipino Peasants: Hallucination or Idiom of Cultural Cognition," Paper presented at the 123rd Annual Meeting, American Psychiatric Association, San Franciso, 1970 (reviewed in *Transcultural Psychiatry Research Review* 8 [1971], 43–45); A. P. Leonard, "Spirit Mediums in Palau: Transformations in a Transitional System," in Bourgignon, *Religion*, pp. 129–177; L. L. Langness, "Hysterical Psychosis in the New Guinea Highlands: A Bena Bena Example (New Guinea)," *Psychiatry* 28 (1965), 258–77; idem, "Rejoinder to R. Salisbury," *Transcultural Psychiatry Research Review* 4 (1967), 125–30; idem, "Possession and Ethnic Psychosis—A Cross-Cultural View," Paper presented at the Second International Congress of Social Psychiatry, London, 1969; "On Possession in the New Guinea Highlands," *Transcultural Psychiatry Research Review* 6 (1969), 95–100; R. Salisbury, "Possession Among the Siana (New Guinea)," in ibid. 3 (1966), 108–116; idem, "Salisbury Replies," in ibid. 4 (1967), 130–34; idem, "On Possession in the

New Guinea Highlands," ibid. 6 (1969), 100–102; D. C. Gajdusek and V. Zigas, "Kuru: Clinical, Pathological and Epidemiological Study of an Acute Progressive Disease of the Central Nervous System Among Natives of the Eastern Highlands of New Guinea," *American Journal of Medicine* 26 (1959), 442–69; P. L. Newman, "'Wild Man' Behavior in a New Guinea Highlands Community," *American Anthropologist* 66 (1964), 1–19.

49. J. W. Fernandez, "Politics and Prophecy: African Religious Movements," *Practical Anthropology* 12 (1965), 71–75; idem, "Symbolic Consensus in a Fang Religious Movement," *American Anthropologist* 67 (1965), 902–9; idem, "*Tabernanthe Iboga*: Narcotic Ecstasies and the Work of the Ancestors," in P. T. Furst, *Flesh of the Gods*, pp. 237–60; H. G. Pope, Jr., "*Tabernanthe Iboga*—An African Plant of Social Importance," *Economic Botany* 23 (1969), 174–84; Emboden, *Narcotic Plants*, pp. 28–32; R. E. Schultes and A. Hofmann,*The Botany and Chemistry of Hallucinogens* (Springfield, Ill.: Charles C Thomas, 1973), pp. 139–41.

50. Schultes and Hofmann, *Hallucinogens*, pp. 206–7; Emboden, *Narcotic Plants*, pp. 29–32, 49.

51. G. Weiss, "Hallucinogens and Narcotic-like Effects of Powdered Myristica (Nutmeg)," *Psychiatric Quarterly* 34 (1960), 346–56; A. T. Weil, "Nutmeg as a Narcotic," *Economic Botany* 19 (1965), 194–217; idem, "Nutmeg as a Psychoactive Drug," in D. Efron, B. Holmstedt, and N. S. Kline (eds.), *Ethnopharmacologic Search for Psychoactive Drugs* (Washington, D.C.: Public Health Service Publication No. 1645, 1967), pp. 204–14; A. T. West, "The Use of Nutmeg as a Psychotropic Agent," *Bulletin on Narcotics* 18 no. 4 (1966), 15–23; R. E. Schultes, "The Botanical Origins of South American Snuffs," in D. Efron et al. (eds.), *Search*, pp. 185–201, 215–29; Schultes and Hofmann, *Hallucinogens*, pp. 66–70.

52. M. J. Harner, "The Role of Hallucinogenic Plants in European Witchcraft," in M. J. Harner (ed.), *Hallucinogens and Shamanism* (New York: Oxford University Press, 1973), pp. 125–50; Schultes and Hofmann, *Hallucinogens*, pp. 161–63, 181–82, 185–87.

53. R. G. Wasson, "Lightning-Bolt and Mushrooms: An Essay in Early Cultural Exploration," in *To Honor Roman Jakobson* (The Hague: Mouton, 1956), pp. 605–12.

54. P. G. Kritikos and S. P. Papadaki, "The History of the Poppy and of Opium and Their Expansion in Antiquity in the Eastern Mediterranean Area," *Bulletin on Narcotics* 19 no. 3 (1967), 17–38, and 19 no. 4 (1967), 5–10.

55. G. Sonnedecker, "Emergence of the Concept of Opium Addiction," *Journal Mondial de Pharmacie* 3 (1962), 275–90; 4 (1963), 27–43.

56. Schultes and Hofmann, *Hallucinogens*, pp. 53–59; *Century Dictionary*, p. 2880.

57. *Century Dictionary*, pp. 3525, 3826, 3967; *Oxford English Dictionary*, pp. 1667, 1833, 1912–13; Emboden, *Narcotic Plants*, pp. 14–23; Emboden, in Furst, *Hallucinogens and Culture*, p. 219.

58. J. Renfrew, *Palaeoethnobotany: The Prehistoric Food Plants of the Near East and Europe* (New York: Columbia University Press, 1973), pp. 161–63; Emboden, *Narcotic Plants*, pp. 21–22, Figs. 1, 2.

59. Anonymous, "The Cultivation of the Opium Poppy in Turkey," *Bulletin on Narcotics* 2 no. 1 (1950), 13–25; Anon., "History of Heroin," ibid. 5 no. 2 (1953), 13–16; Ch. R[ice], "Historical Notes on Opium," *New Remedies* 5 (1876), 229–32; 6 (1877), 144–45, 194–95; I. C. Chopra and N. R. Chopra, "The Abolition of Opium Smoking in India," *Bulletin on Narcotics* 9 no. 3 (1957), 1–7; P. G. Kritikos and S. P. Papadaki, "The History of the Poppy and of Opium and Their Expansion in Antiquity in the Eastern Mediterranean Area," ibid. 19 no. 3 (1967), 17–38, 19 no. 4 (1967), 5–10.

60. Emboden, *Narcotic Plants*, pp. 13–14.

61. La Barre, *Ghost Dance*, pp. 159, 435; La Barre, in Furst, *Flesh of the Gods*, pp. 261–78. The rock painting of a Paleolithic honey-gatherer at the Cueva de la Araña, Bicorp, Valencia, in Charles Singer, E. J. Holmyard, and A. R. Hall (eds.), *A History of Technology* (New York: Oxford University Press, 5 vols., 1954–58 [with Trevor I. Williams, vols. 2–5]), I:275, Fig. 177.

62. R. G. Wasson, *Soma, Divine Mushroom of Immortality* (New York: Harcourt Brace Jovanovich, 1968); W. La Barre, review, *American Anthropologist* 72 (1970), 368–73.

63. R. G. Wasson, "The Divine Mushroom: Primitive Religion and Hallucinatory Agents," *Proceedings of the American Philosophical Society*, 102 no. 3 (1958), 221–23; idem, "The Divine Mushroom of Immortality," in Furst, *Flesh of the Gods*, pp 185–200; idem, "What Was the Soma of the Aryans?," ibid., pp. 201–13.

64. M. A. Murray, *Witch Cults in Western Europe* (London: Oxford University Press, 1921); idem, *The God of the Witches* (New York: Doubleday-Anchor, 1960); R. G. Wasson and V. P. Wasson, *Mushrooms, Russia and History* (New York: Pantheon, 1957, 2 vols.), I:117, 190–91; La Barre, *Ghost Dance*, pp. 257, 410–16; M. J. Harner "The Role of Hallucinogenic Plants in European Witchcraft," in M. J. Harner (ed.), *Hallucinogens and Shamanism* (New York: Oxford University Press, 1973), pp. 125–50.
65. La Barre, *Ghost Dance*, pp. 468, 470–71.
66. J. P. Hes, "On the Use of *Catha edulis* Among Yemenite Jews," *Journal of the Israel Medical Association* 78 no. 6 (1970), 283–84; reviewed in *Transcultural Psychiatry Research Review* 8 (1971), 62.
67. Douglas D. Anderson, "A Stone Age Campsite at the Gateway of America," *Scientific American* 218 no. 6 (1968), 24–33; J. B. Griffin, "Some Prehistoric Connections Between Siberia and America," in J. R. Caldwell (ed.), *New Roads to Yesterday: Essays in Archaeology* (New York: Basic Books, 1966), pp. 277–301, originally in *Science* 131 (1960), 801–912; G. R. Willey, "New World Prehistory," in Caldwell, *New Roads*, pp. 302–32; and idem, "New World Archeology in 1965," *Proceedings of the American Philosophical Society* 110 no. 2 (22 April 1966), 140–45.
68. La Barre, *Ghost Dance*, pp. 121–27.
69. J. Wilbert, "Tobacco and Shamanistic Ecstasy Among the Warao Indians of Venezuela," in Furst, *Flesh of the Gods*, pp. 55–83.
70. C. Wissler, *The American Indian* (2nd ed., New York: Oxford University Press, 1922), p. 25, Fig. 6; H. E. Driver, *Indians of North America* (2nd ed., Chicago: University of Chicago Press, 1970), Map. 10.
71. E. M. Hale, *Ilex cassine, the aboriginal American tea* (Washington, D.C.: Department of Agriculture, Bulletin 14, 1891); Wissler, *American Indian*, pp. 195, 239; W. La Barre, *The Peyote Cult* (Yale University Publications in Anthropology, 19, 1938), pp. 26, 39, 55, 96, 131, 133 fn. 14; J. Lawson, *History of North Carolina* (Richmond, Va.: Garrett and Massie, 1951), pp. 253–54; Driver, *Indians*, pp. 107, 115, 304, Map 14.
72. R. E. Schultes, "*Ilex guayusa* from 500 A.D. to the Present," *Ethnologiska Studier* 32 (1972), 115–38 (Göteborg: Göteborgs Etnografiska Museum).
73. W. E. Safford, *Daturas of the Old World and New: An Account of their Narcotic Properties and their Use in Oracular and Initiatory Ceremonies* (Washington, D.C.: Smithsonian Institution Annual Report for 1920, 1922, pp. 557–58.
74. Schultes and Hofmann, *Hallucinogens*, p. 167.
75. La Barre, *Peyote Cult*, p. 135.
76. A. L. Kroeber, *Anthropology* (New York: Harcourt Brace, 1923), pp. 309–11; idem, *Handbook of the Indians of California* (Washington, D.C.: Bureau of American Ethnology, Bulletin 78, 1925), pp. 462, 589, 593, 605, 614.
77. La Barre, *Peyote Cult*, pp. 136–37; Driver, *Indians*, p. 113, Maps 13 and 14.
78. P. T. Furst, "To Find Our Life: Peyote Among the Huichol Indians of Mexico," in Furst, *Flesh of the Gods*, pp. 136–84; B. G. Myerhoff, *Peyote Hunt: The Sacred Journey of the Huichol Indians* (Ithaca: Cornell University Press, 1974); M. Benzi, *Les derniers adorateurs du peyotl* (Paris: Gallimard, 1972); idem, *à la quête de la vie* (Paris: Chêne, 1977).
79. Schultes and Hofmann, *Hallucinogens*, pp. 168–79.
80. S. H. Wassén, "Ethnobotanical Follow-Up of Bolivian Tiahuanacoid Tomb Material and of Peruvian Shamanism, Psychotropic Plant Constituents, and Espingo Seeds," *Göteborgs Etnografiska Museum Årstryck, 1972, 1973, 35–52.
81. S. R. Altschul, *The Genus Anadenanthera in Amerindian Cultures* (Cambridge: Harvard Botanical Museum, 1972).
82. Schultes and Hoffman, *Hallucinogens*, pp. 84–93.
83. N. A. Chagnon, P. LeQuesne, and J. M. Cook, "Yanömamö Hallucinogens: Anthropological, Botanical and Chemifindings," *Current Anthropology* 12 (1971), 72–74; R. E. Schultes, "The Botanical Origins of South American Snuffs," in D. Efron, B. Holmstedt, and N. S. Kline (eds.) *Ethnopharmacologic Search for Psychoactive Drugs* (Washington, D.C.: Public Health Service Publication No. 1645, 1967.
84. Schultes and Hofmann, *Hallucinogens*, p. 72.
85. R. E. Schultes, "*Virola* as an Oral Hallucinogen Among the Bora of Peru," [Harvard] *Botanical Museum Leaflets*, 25 no. 9 (1977), 259–72.
86. R. E. Schultes, "A New Narcotic Genus from the Amazon Slope of the Colombian Andes,"

ibid. 17 (1955), 1–11; O. Zerries, "Medizinmannwesen und Geisterglaube der Waika-Indianer des Oberen Orinoko," *Ethnologica* 2 (1960), 485–507; S. H. Wassén, "The Use of Some Specific Kinds of South American Indian Snuff and Related Paraphernalia," *Etnologiska Studier* 28 (1965), 1–116; G. Seitz, "Epena, the Intoxicating Snuff Powder of the Waiká Indians and the Tukano Medicine Man, Agostino," in D. Efron, et al., *Search*, pp. 315–38; Wassén, "Indian Snuff," pp. 233–89; R. E. Schultes and B. Holmstedt, "The Vegetal Ingredients of the Myristicaceous Snuffs of the Southwest Amazon," *Rhodora* 70 (1968), 113–60; R. E. Schultes, "The Plant Kingdom and Hallucinogens," *Bulletin on Narcotics* 21 no. 3 (1969), 3–13; 21 no. 4 (1969), 15–27; 22 no. 1 (1970), 25–53; idem, "The New World Indians and Their Hallucinogenic Plants," *Bulletin of the Morris Arboretum* 21 (1970), 3–14; Schultes and Hofmann, *Hallucinogens*, pp. 70–83; G. T. Prance, "Notes on the Use of Plant Hallucinogens," *Economic Botany* 24 (1970), 62–68.

87. B. Jackson and A. Reed, "Catnip and the Alteration of Consciousness," *Journal of Genetic Psychology* 207 (1969), 1349–50.

88. J. M. Adovasio and G. F. Fry, "Prehistoric Psychotropic Drug Use in Northeastern Mexico and Trans-Pecos Texas," Paper presented at the 71st Annual Meeting of the American Anthropological Association, Toronto, 1972.

89. La Barre, *Peyote Cult*, pp. 105–9; Schultes and Hofmann, *Hallucinogens*, pp. 96–101.

90. A. Skinner, "Societies of the Iowa, Kansa, and Ponca Indians," *American Museum of Natural History, Anthropological Papers* 11 (1915), 679–740; idem, "Ethnology of the Iowa Indians," *Museum of the City of Milwaukee Bulletin* 5 (1926), 181–354.

91. W. La Barre, "Mescalism and Peyotism," *American Anthropologist* 59 (1957), 708–11. J. H. Howard, "The Mescal Bean Cult of the Central and Southern Plains: An Ancestor of the Peyote Cult," *American Anthropologist* 59 (1957), 75–87.

92. T. N. Campbell, "Origin of the Mescal Bean Cult," *American Anthropologist* 60 (1958), 156–60; R. C. Troike, "The Origin of Plains Mescalism," *American Anthropologist* 64 (1962), 946–63; R. E. Schultes, "An Overview of Hallucinogens in the Western Hemisphere," in Furst, *Flesh of the Gods*, pp. 31–32.

93. Ruth Shonle [Cavan], "Peyote, the Giver of Visions," *American Anthropologist* 27 (1925), 53–75; La Barre, *Peyote Cult*; J. S. Slotkin, *The Peyote Religion* (New York: Free Press, 1956; Driver, *Indians*, Map 13.

94. Wissler, *American Indian*, Fig. 6, p. 26; Anonymous, "Coca Chewing, Geography and Nutrition," *Bulletin on Narcotics* 2 no. 4 (1950), 2–13; A. A. Buck, T. T. Sasaki, J. J. Hewitt, and A. A. Macrae, "Coca Chewing and Health: An Epidemiological Study Among Residents of a Peruvian Village," *Journal of Epidemiology* 88 (1968), 159–77; F. Guerra, *The Pre-Columbian Mind: A Study into the Aberrant Nature of Sexual Drives, Drugs Affecting Behavior, and the Attitude Toward Life and Death* (London: Seminar Press, 1971).

95. M. Dobkin de Rios, *Visionary Vine: Psychedelic Healing in the Peruvian Amazon* (San Francisco: Chandler, 1972); idem, "Curing with Ayahuasca in an Urban Slum," in M. J. Harner (ed.), *Hallucinogens and Shamanism*, pp. 67–85; M. J. Harner, "The Sound of Rushing Water," in ibid., pp. 15–27; K. M. Kensinger, "*Banisteriopsis* Use Among the Peruvian Cashinahua," in ibid., pp. 9–14; C. Naranjo, "Psychological Aspects of the Yagé Experience in an Experimental Setting," in ibid., pp. 176–90; J. Siskind, "Visions and Cures Among the Sharanahua," in ibid., pp. 29–39; G. Weiss, "Shamanism and Priesthood in Light of the Campa Ayahuasca Ceremony," in ibid., pp. 40–47.

96. C. V. Morton, "Notes on Yajé, a Drug Plant of Southeastern Colombia," *Journal of the Washington Academy of Sciences* 21 (1931), 485–88; G. Reichel-Dolmatoff, "The Cultural Context of an Aboriginal Hallucinogen: *Banisteriopsis caapi*," in Furst, *Flesh of the Gods*, pp. 84–113; Schultes and Hofmann, *Hallucinogens*, pp. 114–18.

97. C. Gutiérrez-Noriega and G. C. Sanchez, "Alteraciones mentales producidas por la *Opuntia cylindrica*," *Revista de Neuropsiquiatria* [Lima] 10 (1947), 422 ff.; C. Gutiérrez-Noriega, "Area de mescalinismo en el Peru," *America Indigena* 10 (1950), 215; M. Dobkin de Rios, " *Trichocereus pachanoi*: A Mescaline Cactus Used in Folk Healing in Peru," *Economic Botany* 22 (1968), 191–94; idem, "Folk Healing with a Psychedelic Cactus in North Coastal Peru," *International Journal of Social Psychiatry* 15 (1969), 23–32; idem, "Fortune's Malice: Divination, Psychotherapy, and Folk Medicine in Peru," *Journal of American Folklore* 82 no. 324 (1969), 132–41; D. Sharon, "The San Pedro Cactus in Peruvian Folk Healing." in Furst, *Flesh of the Gods*, pp. 114–35.

98. Schultes and Hofmann, *Hallucinogens*, pp. 39, 41, 51.

99. Ibid., pp. 94–96.
100. Ibid., pp. 163–66.
101. Ibid., pp. 182–85.
102. Ibid., pp. 186–91; Schultes, *A New Narcotic Genus.*
103. Schultes and Hofmann, *Hallucinogens*, pp. 194–96.
104. Ibid., pp. 200–201.
105. A. Weiner, *Earth Medicines—Earth Foods: Plant Remedies, Drugs and Natural Foods of the North American Indians* (New York: Macmillan, 1972), pp. 101–2.
106. Emboden, *Narcotic Plants*, p. 87.
107. F. Hernandez, *Nova plantarum, animalium et mineralium Mexicanorum Historia* (Roma: B. Duersini e Z Masotti, 1651); Schultes and Hofmann, *Hallucinogens*, pp. 144–45.
108. La Barre, *Peyote Cult*, pp. 124–25.
109. Driver, *Indians*, Map 10.
110. Schultes and Hofmann, *Hallucinogens*, pp. 158–59.
111. Emboden, *Narcotic Plants*, p. 54; Schultes and Hofmann, *Hallucinogens*, pp. 135–37.
112. S. A. Borhegyi, "Miniature Mushroom Stones from Guatemala," *American Antiquity* 26 (1961), 498–504; Schultes and Hofmann, *Hallucinogens*, pp. 36–52; R. G. Wasson, "The Hallucinogenic Mushrooms of Mexico and Psilocybin: A Bibliography," [Harvard] *Botanical Museum Leaflets*, 20 (1962), 25–73.
113. Hernandez, in Schultes and Hofmann, *Hallucinogens*, p. 38.
114. Ibid., pp. 147–53.
115. Ibid., p. 168.
116. Emboden, *Narcotic Plants*, p. 65.
117. La Barre, *Ghost Dance*, pp. xiv–xv, 124–35, 154, 160, 363, 468.
118. W. La Barre, "Hallucinogens and the Shamanic Origins of Religion," in Furst, *Flesh of the Gods*, pp. 261–68; idem, *Ghost Dance*, pp. 133, 161; P. T. Furst, "Introduction," in *Flesh of the Gods*, p. viii; J. Wilbert, in ibid., p. 83.
119. Schultes, *Botanical Sources*, p. 147; idem, "Hallucinogenic Plants of the New World," *Harvard Review* 1 (1963), 18–32; idem, *Native Narcotics*; idem, "The Search for New Natural Hallucinogens," *Lloydia* 26 (1966), 295; idem, "Ein halbes Jahrhundert Ethnobotanik amerikanischer Hallucinogene," *Planta Medica* 13 (1965), 125–57; idem, "The Place of Ethnobotany in the Ethnopharmacologic Search for Psychotomimetic Drugs," in D. Efron et al., *Search*, p. 36.
120. W. La Barre, "The Narcotic Complex of the New World," *Diogenes* 48 (1964), 125–38; idem, "Le complexe narcotique de l'Amerique autochtone," *Diogène* 48 (1964) 120–34; idem, "El complejo narcótico de la America autóctona," *Diógenes* 48 (1964), 102–12; R. E. Schultes, "Native Narcotics of the New World," *The Pharmaceutical Sciences*, 3rd Lecture Series, 1960 (Pt. V, Pharmacognosy) 143.
121. P. T. Furst, *Hallucinogens and Culture* (San Francisco: Chandler and Sharp, 1976), quotation from back cover.

3. History and Ethnography of Cannabis

The hemp plant is one of the oldest cultivated fiber plants in the Old World. Appearing in various forms distributed through various cultures—*cannabis, charas, dagga, diamba, ganja, gonjo, hashish, injaga, kancha, kanebosm, kif, maconha, marihuana, mbanga, umburu, zamal*—it is also one of the most widespread psychotropic plants in historic and protohistoric use among mankind, rivaled only by tobacco.

All the Indo-European languages have dialectically equivalent terms for hemp: Anglo-Saxon *henep, hænep,* Middle English *hemp,* Danish and Middle Low German *hennep,* Icelandic *hampr,* Swedish *hampa,* German *hanf,* Polish *konop,* Bohemian *konope,* Old Bulgarian and Russian *konoplya,* Lithuanian *kanapes,* Lettish *kenepa,* Irish *canaib,* Persian *qinnab,* Greek *kannabis,* Latin *cannabis,* French *chanvre,* and Sanskrit *çana.* An earlier anthropologist, Berthold Laufer, believed that the Indo-European term for hemp was a loan word from ancient Finno-Ugrian and Turkic stocks of north central Eurasia; but "Scythian," by some etymologists (doubtless influenced by an early mention in Herodotus), has also been the proposed donor of the term to the several Indo-European languages independently. However, since the appropriate linguistic rules for sound-change appear to have been followed, the word would seem very old in Indo-European, rather than multiply borrowed. Again, if as the anthropologist Sula Benet proposes, the cannabis terms are borrowed from a Semitic language, then there is the problem of a seemingly pan–Indo-European term diffused from ancient northern Eurasia. And cannabis, of course, grows wild in north central Eurasia, whence the Indo-Europeans came. That the terms are manifest dialectic equivalents would constitute the solidest possible evidence for the antiquity of the word, since the undivided neolithic Indo-Europeans began to migrate (spreading prehistorically all the way from Ireland to Ceylon) and to break up dialectically in the early Bronze Age.[1]

Care must be taken to discriminate in sources the textile use of the plant ("canvas" for example is a term cognate with cannabis) from its use as a drug. But the drug use is also very old. As opposed to its applications as a textile, its early psychotropic use is proven by archeological finds of leaves and fruit scales in a Bronze Age urn field at Wilmersdorf in Germany, and of burnt seeds in bronze vessels at Pazaryk in the Altai region of Siberian Russia, which strontly suggest narcotic use since these parts contain the maximum cannabi-

Portions of this chapter have appeared in "Anthropological Views of Cannabis," in Gretel H. Pelto and Pertti J. Pelto (eds.), *Reviews in Anthropology* 4 (1977), 237–50, which was an essay-review of Vera Rubin (ed.), *Cannabis and Culture* (The Hague: Mouton, 1975), to which compendium I am much indebted. Reprinted by permission.

nol, whereas the textile fibers are in the larger stems and not the flower heads.[2] Thus, archeological evidence of the appropriate time period and geographical area agrees with the independent linguistic evidence for the great antiquity of cannabis in northern Eurasia. Indeed, on purely documentary evidence the Chinese have valued the hemp narcotic since the middle of the seventh millennium B.C.; and in the emperior Shen Nung's pharmacopoeia of 2737 B.C., cannabis was described as an important medicine. Assyrians burned it as an incense in the sixth century B.C. Hindu Ayurvedic medicine has used it from the ninth century A.D. onward, although hemp was known in India at least as early as the fourth century B.C. The *Avesta*, our oldest Iranian textual authority for the drug, first mentioned the intoxicating resin in 500 B.C. And in 480 B.C., Herodotus (iv: 142) referred to the use of hemp as a narcotic by the Scythians of southern Russia, who threw the seeds on heated rocks in their sweat-baths and shouted with joy on inhaling the steamy smoke.[3]

The economics and botany of cannabis, in particular its ecology and provenience, should be noted, as a necessary background for its diffusion, history, and other matters. The hemp plant is diœcious, that is, with the sexes usually in separate individuals. However, the widespread and originally Mexican term, "[planta] mari[a]-juan-a" is probably not, as once conjectured by the present writer, from the doublet of "Maria" and "Juan," a folk reflex of this botanical fact, although the attribution of separate sex to near-related plants is ethnographically common among Mexican and Plains and Southwestern Indians, whether legitimately or oftener not.[4] More plausibly, *marijuana* may derive from a Chinese word for hemp, brought by Chinese coolie laborers in western Mexico. The common Caribbean term *grifos*, I believe, comes directly from the Spanish *grifos*, "kinky" or "twisted," perhaps after the appearance of the female plant's flower heads that produce the bulk of the resinous hashish. *Grifos*, as locally pronounced, came from American Puerto Rico to New York's Harlem, there anglicized as "reefers" in the 1920s, or as "Mary Warners" from the Mexican *marijuana*. Other terms not relevant to the botany of cannabis will be discussed below, when they are of value in tracing the historical diffusion of the drug.

Botanically, Linnaeus' classification of Cannabis as a monotypical genus has been largely accepted since 1753, though in 1914 the *Century Dictionary* sagaciously lists "two known species, *C. sativa* and *C. Indica*." Cannabis taxonomy has been much debated since it is highly polytypical. Hemp is now seen, both by Russian botanists and Schultes, as comprising three species, *Cannabis sativa*, *C. indica*, and *C. ruderalis*—a view based partly on neglected evidence from Lamarck and partly on recent cytological work—although there are many further polymorphous ecotypes and differing cultivars. The ancestors of hemp, unlike those of many other cultivated plants, may still be growing wild, in this case in remote central Asia.[5]

Since prehistoric times, hemp was used for clothing in Europe, but gradually it was displaced by other very old textile fibers such as linen (*Linum usitatis-*

simus) and Near-Eastern cotton (*Gossypium herbaceum*, originally from India). The fiber of hemp is coarse and inflexible compared with these, but because of its high tensile strength it was valued and widely used in making ropes and canvas. The need for large amounts of rope to hoist and furl canvas on sailing ships greatly increased hemp cultivation during the days of exploration and trade in sailing ships. Ancient use of hemp fiber for cordage, and for the oily seeds in porridges, had been in small local cultivation. Commercial production of textile hemp has been mainly in Russia, where it was grown as early as the seventh century B.C.; in Canada since 1606, the earliest in North America being in Nova Scotia, brought by Louis Hébert, Champlain's apothecary; and in the thirteen colonies in the eighteenth century. At one time, in the early American republic, farmers were forced to grow hemp under penalty of fine; it is said that British prohibition of local growing in favor of their own trade monopoly was a major cause of the Revolution. Both England and somewhat later Spain had introduced colonial cultivation, the latter in Mexico, Peru, and Colombia though only Chile produced any commercial quantity—in order to break the Russian monopoly on hemp. With the coming of the steamship, need for rope and canvas on windjammers greatly diminished. But hemp, which readily reproduces itself as a weed and takes kindly to waste places in both temperate and hot dry climates, escaped from cultivation and now grows wild in many parts of the world, including much of the United States.

The first documented medical use of cannabis, as noted earlier, is found in a Chinese herbal text of the second century A.D., but other evidence indicates central-Asiatic shamanistic use from prehistoric times.[6] Medical and sacred use in India also predates written records (*Atharva Veda*, 1400 B.C.; compare the *Avesta*, in which hemp occupies the first place in a list of 10,000 medicinal plants of the doctor Thrita). These ancient areas of use agree well with the putative botanical origin of the plant in central Asia.

But the term *kanebosm* occurs as early as both the Aramaic and the Hebrew versions of the Old Testament, hemp being used for ropes in Solomon's temple and in priestly robes, as well as the seed-oil for anointing, and hemp was carried as merchandise in ancient Biblical caravans. Indeed, the ubiquitous Scythians were in Palestine in the seventh century B.C., where they aided the Medes and the Babylonians to defeat the Assyrians, and even threatened to invade Egypt. Cannabis was in ritual use as early as classic Assyria (*qunnabu*), and in Babylon (*kanbun* in Chaldean). The fact that use by the highly mobile Scythian groups, known as "Ashkenaz" to the Hebrews[7] in the Caucasus area intervening between Asia Minor Semites and northern Eurasiatic Indo-Europeans, suggests that Indic, European, and Semitic use might early have been nearly simultaneous. However, though important as diffusors, Scythians need not have been originators, since the scope of the problem is far wider. The great antiquity and enormous spread of cannabis—stretching from northern Europe through Siberian Asia to China, and southward to India, Asia Minor, and Southeast Asia (Thai *kancha*, Cambodian *kâncha*, Laotian *kan Xa*, and Vietnamese *ĉan ha*)[8] —lends countenance to the present writer's belief that cannabis was part of a religio-shamanic complex of at least Mesolithic age, in parallel with an equally old shamanic use of soma, the hallucinogenic mushroom (for which see the following chapter in this volume).

The use of hemp in a religious context is early enough to support this view. The Soviet archeologist S. Rudenko believes that the Bronze Age Wilmersdorf and Pazaryk finds indicate that cannabis was used ritually in funeral services similar to those of the Scythians of Herodotus 2,500 years ago. Indeed, the connection with funeral practices still remains in folk customs of eastern Europe, where a handful of seeds is thrown into a fire at hemp harvest as an offering to the dead.

> Hemp never lost its connection with the cult of the dead. Even today in Poland and Lithuania, and in former times also in Russia, on Christmas Eve when it is believed that the dead visit their families, a soup made of hemp seeds, called *semieniatka*, is served for the dead souls to savor.

Other folk customs in Europe, in Bible lands, and in Africa are also summarized by Sula Benet.[9]

Since early times, cannabis has been used in other religious cults, most notably in India but also, later, in Africa. The ancient sacred book of the Aryans, the *Atharva Veda*, called it a "liberator from sin" and "heavenly guide." The major Hindu god Shiva was notoriously fond of hemp, and the plant is still sacred in many temples, where it is grown in gardens. In India, the use of cannabis as a narcotic has been continuous since prehistoric times.[a] *Bhang* (hemp leaves) and *charas* (the resin that, under certain climatic conditions, occurs even on the leaves and stems) are mixed with tobacco and smoked in a *chilam* or funnel-shaped pipe, often jointly by a group on social occasions. *Bhang* is also drunk in variously spiced *thandai* drinks infused in water or milk, eaten in the form of small balls (often as jaggery or palm-sugar candies), and in *hari* ["god"] *gulfi*, native green ice cream. Holy men use cannabis in all three forms, after the example of Shiva, and the yearly *Shivaratri* festival in March is celebrated with the use of these in various forms by the populace. Candies called *majun* are made of cannabis with sugar and spices, sometimes with added datura or opium.[b] *Ganja*, made of the dried pistillate tops from

---

a. One is tempted to suggest that even if cannabis were indeed not as early as Mohenjodaran-Harappan India (suspiciously adjacent geographically to Mesopotamian Sumeria and/or to Scythian southwest Asia), whence the shamanic Paśupati "master of animals" prototype of pot-loving Shiva emerged, then cannabis might just as well have been brought by the first Aryan invaders, given the pan–Indo-European extent of the hemp-word. In such an event, despite the incalculably great influence of the *Rig Veda* (earliest literate recording of any Indo-European tongue), soma-ambrosia was lost to the Brahmanic man-gods, while cannabis still remained the soma of the poor.

b. S. and Ved Prakash Vatuk have reported on *chatorpan* in Uttar Pradesh, India, as a culturally conditioned form of addiction to certain sweetmeats and salty-spicy snacks, which have consequences quite like those found in alcoholism and drug addiction. "The *chatora* acquires an urge for these expensive delicacies, gradually neglects other foods and spends considerable cash on them. Eventually he resorts to sale of jewelry, land and other possessions and even illegal activities

cannabis races rich in resin, is usually smoked, such smoking being probably a post-Columbian practice from the New World. The eating of *ganja* leaves and *charas* resin, in various forms, is more prevalent among Hindus, whereas the smoking of *charas* is more usual among Moslems; but *charas* may also be eaten, sometimes mixed with opium. Besides the water and milk infusion in *thandai* drinks mentioned above, sometimes an alcoholic tincture is drunk, although pious Hindus and Moslems both abjure alcohol. And sometimes various fats, used to absorb the cannabinol but contaminated with chlorophyll, are the greenish paste base from which highly spiced honeyed sweetmeats are made; references to these are common in Persia and North Africa. The poor in India use cannabis leaves in folk medicine and as a reputed aphrodisiac.[10]

Along with many other plants, cannabis has been suggested as a candidate for the celebrated lost soma of the Rig Veda. But hemp does not fit at all the botanical descriptions of this god-making intoxicant, addressed in ecstatic apostrophes in this earliest of the Vedas, dating in oral form to 1,800 B.C. On the contrary, since the classic work of Wasson, soma has been firmly established as the hallucinogenic mushroom *Amanita muscaria*, still in shamanic use in central Siberia according to eighteenth-century and later ethnographers.[11] (See the following chapter.) Furthermore, the identity of cannabis as *bhang*, *charas*, and *ganja* has never at any time been in question, and India has clearly been the major center for diffusion of narcotic hemp-use in historic times.

Pakistani hemp use is virtually the same as the Indian. Cannabis has been used there traditionally for centuries, equally in rural and urban areas, but is now said to be confined virtually to adult males; the average age of subjects in Lahore is 44 years, with a range of 29–75, which suggests ingrained establishment acceptance. Long since acclimatized in Moslem India, the narcotic use of hemp carries no social or moral stigma, and whereas alcohol in any form became tabooed to high-caste Hindus and to Moslems in India-Pakistan, hemp (and indeed opium) never was. Any currently growing concern among the educated classes of Pakistan "is unquestionably borrowed from Western publications in the field."[12] In fact, it seems probable that Moslem Indians, after the great expansion of Islam in post-seventh-century times, were the vehicles of early diffusion westward, and not Hindu Indians, the conservative members of which do not travel overseas.

Greek knowledge of cannabis use among other peoples came from the north, not the east. Indeed, their term could have come with the first Indo-European invaders. Thebans made a drink of cannabis that was reputed to have opium-like properties. The Hellenistic physician Galen recorded general use of cakes which, if eaten to excess, were intoxicating; while the traveler Herodotus was

---

to support his habit, precipitating his own and family's economic and social decline" (See reference note 10). Folk stories and beliefs, and even Hindu fiction all testify to the reality of *chatorpan* addiction, and yet the substances involved are alleged to be only highly pleasant foods. But W. Emboden (*Narcotic Plants*, [New York: Macmillan, 1972] p. 14) reports that cannabis is made into the candy *dwamsec*, and there is reasonable question whether *chatorpan* is simply a food.

of course writing about Scythians in southern Russia. But "there is no evidence that cannabis was used by ancient Greeks for commercial, ritual, or euphoriant purposes."[13]

In thirteenth-century Asia Minor, the *hashishin*—whence our words "assassin" and "hashish"—were politico-religious murderers, given the drug by the terrorist leader al-Hasan ibn-al-Sabbah, the "Old Man of the Mountains," for assassination of Christian leaders in the Crusades. The well-known account by the Italian Renaissance traveler, Marco Polo, may have given rise to the unfair association of euphoriant hashish with violent crimes such as murder. But hashish was given in seclusion to the young commando-candidates as a foretaste of Paradise, in order to motivate them to face dangers for a holy cause. They did not necessarily face their difficult and dangerous enterprises while in intoxicated states. But, interestingly enough, in 1964 Kiluawa crisis-cultists in the Congo were accused of hashish intoxication during their terrorist attacks on whites.[14]

Syrian mystics appear early to have carried hashish into Africa, first bringing it to Egypt. But for east and south Africa, Arab traders may have brought cannabis directly from India. Du Toit "hypothesizes that cannabis and the pipes used were diffused by Arab traders during the first centuries A.D., and that once it had been introduced it spread to other parts of the continent. While other writers have suggested that cannabis use in Africa, south of the Sahara, is comparatively recent, [Du Toit's] hypothesis is bolstered by Nicolaas van der Nerwe's article on an archeological find in Ethiopia of fourteenth century pipe bowls containing cannabis residue."[15] The hypothesis of African pipe-smoking in the fourteenth century must, however, run the gauntlet of Americanist opinion that the smoking of plant narcotics would be post-Columbian, after the pattern of Amerindian tobacco smoking.

Terminologically, there are three distinct cannabis provinces: South Africa (*dagga* terms), east-central (*bangi* and variants, from "Bengal"), and West African (*diamba* and variants). Diffusion to sub-Saharan Negro Africa is clearly later than in Moslem north Africa. *Dagga* may have been brought to Khoisan-speaking South Africa only with the incursion of the protohistoric, precolonial Bantu Negroes. Nevertheless, in sub-Saharan Africa cannabis has an important role in magic and religion. West Africa, under Moslem influence, was earlier acquainted with the drug and in turn gave hemp-use to Brazil, since the word used there, *maconha*, was brought with black slaves from Angola.[16]

As in North Africa, cannabis has been used as a narcotic since the middle of the twelfth century in Egypt, in which country laws against eating hashish have been traditionally draconian. At the turn of the fourteenth century, the Sultan punished hashish-eaters by pulling out their teeth, yet a quarter of a century later public consumption was a fashionable matter and talking about it was quite uninhibited. But again in our mid-century, in Egyptian laws of 1960–66, to cultivate, possess, buy, sell, import, export, transport or offer hashish in illicit traffic in Egypt is punishable by death, or by hard labor for life and a fine of £3,000–10,000.[17]

By contrast, further west in North Africa, in Morocco, "grown in large quantities in the Rif and smoked by a fairly high proportion of native adult males, *kif* ranks, along with citrus fruit, lumber, cotton, and palmetto fiber, as one of the area's chief cash crops."[18] Although technically illegal, use of *kif* in Morocco meets much less severe legal sanctions among devout Moslems than does Quran-prohibited alcohol, the elite use of which, especially of Scotch, appears to be increasing. *Kif*-smoking in North Africa by American and other emigré litterateurs seems to have been borrowed directly from the prevalent native users. Nevertheless, whether from the same North African sources, hemp-smoking in France is surprisingly early, for the "pantagruelion" of Rabelais was very probably cannabis, thus in use much prior to nineteenth-century Parisian litterateurs.[19] This evidence appears consistent with an early North African use in Moslem countries, and only a later diffusion in sub-Saharan Black Africa.

In 1888, for example, Kalamba-Mukenge, chief of the Baluba, brought cannabis into the conquered parts of the Congo in order to unite the people in a new cult of Bena-Riamba, "Sons of Cannabis." In Ruanda, even in 1959–60, the use of hemp was confined to the men of a tiny, despised and backward group, the Twa, comprising less than 18 percent of the population.[20] But in Réunion Island in the Indian Ocean, slaves brought *zamal* from Madagascar, and immigrants to Réunion from South India used it ritually. Later, secular use by literary people for hedonistic purposes is found in Réunion, here influenced by the French writers Baudelaire and Gauthier who formed, together with Victor Hugo and others, the famous Parisian *Club des Hachichins*.[21] France, therefore, had the earliest *haut monde* use of hemp as a narcotic in western Europe. The French psychotropic use of hashish has been attributed to soldiers returning from the Napoleonic campaign of 1798 in Egypt, but good evidence exists for its introduction far earlier, by soldiers returning from the Crusades between the eleventh and thirteenth centuries. Certainly the sixteenth-century physician Rabelais was familiar with the analgesic and antibacterial qualities of cannabis, only recently rediscovered and reported in the pharmacological literature.[22]

Though long grown for its fiber in Mexico, the rediscovery of the narcotic use of hemp there, as we have seen, appears to have been stimulated by emigrant oriental laborers. In colonial America also, the general use of hemp as a narcotic seems to have been unknown. In the United States, awareness of the potential drug use of cannabis is quite certainly from outside influences, probably through intermediate sources in the Caribbean originating in imported labor from India, or if not via the Caribbean, then from direct contacts with India through trade to the international port of New Orleans. In the 1920s and early 1930s, the demimonde of jazz musicians knew "muggies," "joints," and "Mary Janes," as soon also did Bohemians and a limited few visiting college students in Greenwich Village, who came there to listen to early jazz. Transients among jazz musicians, originally from New Orleans, spread knowledge of muggies, as in New York, to other large cities such as Chicago and San Francisco along with the new proletarian music, jazz. But comparatively little public stir was created then. Only in the 1950s, with the rise of the so-called counterculture of disaffected Beatniks in San Francisco, did the use of "pot," "tea," or "grass" become widespread and widely publicized among middle-class college students. The Vietnam War spread use of the more potent hashish (as well as heroin, an opium derivative), both from nearby oriental sources (richer, for ecological reasons, in hashish gums than western sources), ultimately among all classes of the young.[23]

Rubin has noted two major historic streams of cannabis use, the ancient, peasant one exemplified by the Hindu "*ganja* complex," the other the only century-old upper- and middle-class "psychedelic" use dating back to the Club des Hachichins in Paris and diffused in the United States and Canada in the present mid-century as the "marihuana complex." While secular use for pleasure was present in both traditions of use, anciently the psychotropic religious use of cannabis was priestly and shamanic. However, it is our opinion that the elitist influence has been overemphasized, and the folk tradition too minimized. Rubin surmises that after it was "apparently introduced to the United States by Mexican laborers about the turn of the century and taken up by black stevedores and jazz musicians, a furor about marihuana use—probably tinged with racist attitudes—was raised in the wake of the moral reform movements in the 1920s."[24]

However, it is clear that East Indian and other sailors brought hemp-smoking to New Orleans, not Mexican laborers, and from the waterfront roustabouts it spread easily to black jazz musicians in the adjacent "barrel-house" red-light district, whence pot-smoking, along with jazz, spread upriver and to both coasts, as described above. The opprobrium was therefore not specifically racist, but was associated rather with the "immoral" context of jazz origins in New Orleans (the original meaning of "jazz" itself supports this interpretation). And certainly the first minor diffusion in the '20s and '30s was firmly associated with jazz musicians such as Gene Krupa, and with collegians who came to hear early jazz performances. From the first to last, diffusion was not from elitist Parisian litterateurs, but with the newly emerging folk music, itself of lower-class social origins (including, in this interpretation, other "have-nots," both drop-outs and adolescents, as underdogs to the unbudging Establishment of the time). The brouhaha and scandal came only with the later marihuana-smoking by middle- and upper-class youth, thence downward in age to high school "teeny boppers" and outward to antiestablishment youth in Europe and South America, influenced by their youthful American prototypes. Thus, the "marihuana complex" as well as the *ganja* complex" should be regarded as a folk rather than an elitist movement.

In any case, this critique of recent middle-class history of the North American use of cannabis should not obscure the other authentic folk traditions in Mexico, the Caribbean, and in South America. In Costa Rica, apparently another center, with Puerto Rico and Jamaica, for diffusion in the western hemisphere, cannabis use was early well established in lower-class use, before it spread rapidly in the 1960s through the middle and upper sectors of society, among which at least 25 percent of college students there are now marihuana users.[25] Thus, on the whole, the literacy of elitist Great Traditions sometimes obscures the power and persistence of folk traditions.

Because of the ready availability of marihuana growing wild, and many signs pointing to an increasing and perhaps ultimately uncontrollable use of the drug,[26] some thoughtful citizens, including eminent anthropologists, have suggested legalizing cannabis because of the unenforceability of any prohibition law.[27] The alarmist attitudes toward cannabis seem clearly traceable to American sources. The remote North Indian kingdom of Nepal provides exact critical evidence for this. As Fisher writes:

> Cannabis has been grown in Nepal, in both wild and cultivated varieties, for an extremely long time; but its uses, and attitudes toward them, have begun to change in recent years.
>
> Traditionally, Hindu yogis (more often than not pilgrims from India) have used cannabis as an aid to meditation, and male devotees use it as a symbol of fellowship in their frequent *bhajans*. It is also used by older people of many castes to while away the time when they are too old to work in the fields and, until recently only secretly, by younger people in search of fun.
>
> The advent of the hippie era brought increased cultivation, greatly inflated prices, and large-scale smuggling into the provinces of northern India. Over an approximately eight-year period the attitudes of young, middle-class, urban Nepalis changed to the extent that smoking *ganja* (marihuana) or *charas* (hashish) came to be regarded as a novel, acceptable, and pleasurable mark of sophistication.
>
> All dealers' licenses were revoked on July 6, 1973, and at present it is illegal to buy, sell, or cultivate (but not to use) cannabis. Three factors contributed to this government crackdown: (1) Nepalese alarm that their own youth were being corrupted by cannabis; (2) United Nations pressure to join other "respectable" nations in outlawing cannabis; and (3) U.S. pressure for narcotic control.

Earlier, in Nepal, use was so far accepted that

> Cannabis even functions as a tranquilizer for children. It is sometimes mixed with sweets and given to children to help them sleep or keep them quiet while, for example, a mother works in the fields. By giving her child a small amount of *ganja* in forms such as *agnikumar* or *jatikari*, she keeps him less active and less likely to get into trouble while she is occupied in other ways.[28]

(This use of hashish is quite paralled to the use of opiates in "soothing syrups" given to fretful or teething babies in the nineteenth and early twentieth centuries in America).

Latin American countries do not always reflect the influence of attitudes in the United States.[29] Cultivation, marketing, and consumption appear to be relatively recent innovations on the north coast of Colombia (though growth for fiber dates to colonial days). In none of these three activities are the persons involved either deviant, parasitic, or marginal elements socially. Since members of the upper class who staff the patronage government customs posts are implicated, cannabis traffic is accepted as just another contraband activity, in the comfortable Latin-American spread between official premise and actual practice, for it is technically illegal. In Colombia, neither consumption nor merchandising seems to be connected with stressful social or economic changes. Alcohol is the traditional and actual drug of choice for business negotiation, social relations, and religious celebration. But since a bottle of alcohol costs a laborer's full-day wages, "cannabis may be related to economic deprivation resulting from exploitative wage levels." However, we are told that in Brazil "certain sectors of the population tend to increase their use of marihuana or other hallucinogenic drugs when the going gets rough."[30]

The epidemiology and folk beliefs about the effects of hemp-use are varied. Judgments are likely to be influenced by the caste and class membership of both judges and judged; important also is the length of historical time during which cannabis has been used in the particular region. In India,

> although it is true that the use of hemp drugs is not looked down upon among Hindu castes, there is no evidence of physical dependence. People use these drugs sometimes as a means of recreation but usually there is no desire to continue usage nor is there any tendency to increase the dosage. Only occasions of festivity and ceremonial functions are meant for using these drugs in most cases. The number of users is negligible.[31]

In Nepal, "*Ayurvedic* practitioners believe that too much cannabis, like too much alcohol, can have deleterious effects and that overindulgence can result in madness, weight loss, and decreased semen."[32] In India, "the use of cannabis suggest[s] effects on the personality associated with prolonged use: loss of desire to work, loss of motivation, and loss of judgment and intellectual functions"[33] but in this case it is hard to say which is cause and which effect.

In Canada

> the Addiction Research Foundation of Ontario conducted a survey of 1,200 randomly selected adults (persons 18 years of age and over) in Toronto in the spring of 1971 and found that 8.4% had used cannabis at some time during the previous twelve months, and that half of these had done so seven or more times during this one year period. Of greater import—as regards future incidence of use figures—was the study's finding that the extent of cannabis use was inversely related to age: approximately 30% of the respondents between 18 and 25 years of age had used canna-

bis during the previous year, while only about 10% of those between 26 and 35 and only 1% of those 36 years of age or over had done so (Smart and Fejer, 1971).[34] While Toronto survey findings cannot be appropriately generalized to the entire country, the incidence of use in this city is likely typical of that of Canada's larger metropolitan areas and suggests a significant increase over the 3.4% "ever used" rates found by the Commission's national adult survey in 1970.

At the same time, "The Commission was unable to find any evidence that cannabis use was a significant factor in aggression, violence or nondrug crime in Canada."[35]

In the United States, the National Commission on Marihuana and Drug Abuse was established by the Congress in 1970, in somewhat polemicized and politicized circumstances. A survey subsequently showed that

of all adults, 15% reported that they had ever used marihuana, while 5% stated that they were currently using it. Among the youth (12–17 years old), 14% had ever used and 6% reported current use. Interestingly, proportions of users increased during the late adolescent years to 27% (18–25 years old). There was a steady decline in number of users with advancing age (19%, 26–35 years; 9%, 36–49 years; 6%, over 50 years).[36]

Use does not vary significantly with race; Jews and Catholics are only slightly overrepresented as compared to Protestants (perhaps because the first two are more urbanized); male users predominate over female 2 to 1 among adult users, but the sex differential is diminishing among youthful users. Users tend to be represented more frequently among clerical and professional workers in the higher socioeconomic brackets; the use of marihuana increased with the level of formal education attained; but 75 percent of the 18- to 25-year-old users were not students.

The chemistry of cannabis is still not sufficiently understood. "Relatively little is known regarding the drug effects of marihuana in man, *vis-à-vis* the different methods of preparing the plant material prior to actual use."[37] There are numerous reasons for our ignorance, beyond the effects of mode of preparation. There may be subtle as as well as frank pharmacological differences, because the quantities of active chemicals vary widely in different species and ecotypes, and because tetrahydrocannabinol is by no means established as the chief pharmacodynamic factor. For example, the whole marihuana fluid extract is approximately three times as potent as equivalent amounts of tetrahydrocannabinol. Again, the absorption of THC is three times more effective when smoked than when taken by mouth. Moreover, "Presently there is an ever-increasing body of evidence which points to the fact that there may be heretofore uncharacterized biologically active constituents present in hemp."[38] Added to these uncertainties, it is a fact that, in both the Princeton and the Toronto studies of street drugs, a high percentage of the alleged hallucinogens were tested as other than what they were sold to be, and many of these would have had highly unanticipated effects if taken. Possible teratogenic effects of cannabis, and in what amounts, are inadequately known for man. The same may be said for the lethal intravenous amount, though it has been calculated that 200 mg. of THC would be needed for a 70 kg. man.[39] Nor do we really know from sufficient sampling and controls what may be the possible effects of varying long-term usage in varying amounts and in varying methods of use.

Psychopharmacodynamically, there are ambiguities and contradictions as well. Since THC is soluble in body-fats, the effect of a given use seems cumulatively dependent upon prior use, and quite widely varying subjective reports are available as a result. In the (New York City) *Mayor's Committee on Marihuana* report in 1944 ("the LaGuardia Report") and other studies,

> the effects of cannabis cited include: anxiousness followed by euphoria, a sense of well-being, and excitement; rapidly changing emotions; heightened sensory awareness; feelings of enhanced insight; fragmented thought; impaired short term memory; altered perception of time and space; altered sense of identity; increased desire for food; restlessness and hyperactivity followed by a relaxed, slightly drowsy state and sleep.[40]

However, the reader will be well advised to note that not all these effects appear always or ever in the same or in different individuals. Furthermore, in different climatic and/or cultural areas, the physiological effects apparently vary. In Jamaica there was no evidence of any effect of smoking cannabis on the relationship between oxygen consumption and work done (i.e., metabolic function was unaltered); but, after smoking, both resting and submaximal heart rates were increased, and thus heart rates were high relative to the work load after smoking.[41] The "amotivational syndrome" reported from use in the United States does not appear to occur in Jamaica where, indeed, and apparently with success, marihuana is often smoked before addressing oneself to a difficult task. As to subjective attitudes,

> the farmers with whom we worked insist that cannabis-induced alterations in perception and action are associated with quality work. One weeds more completely and forks better, they say, after smoking cannabis. In Valley this achievement, if, indeed, it occurs with cannabis use, is achieved at the expense of time, space, and energy.[42]

One might be reduced, then, to choosing between subjective peace of mind and objective fact—in which case, marihuana-smoking is not the only institution that induces vehemently differing opinions concerning validity and efficacy as, indeed, varied stances on sacred subjects are also wont to do.

Again, ethos and temperament may require different results:

> Prior to the outbreak of middle-class drug epidemic, various European observers speculated as to cultural explanations for the choice of alcohol versus cannabis. Bouquet (1950 and 1951) and Porot (1942) both concluded that hashish was suitable for the dreamy, contemplative temperament of the Moslem, where alcohol fitted the aggressive, outward-oriented Westerner. Stringaris (1939) observed that alcohol spreads readily in

hashish cultures but not the reverse. The most complete development of this theme is provided by Carstairs (1954) in his explanation of why, in India, the aggressive, action-oriented Rajputs drank alcohol while the passive introspective Brahmins preferred *bhang*.[43]

The cultural anthropologist may quibble that the matter may not be so simple: (1) which is cause, and which effect; and (2) what might be the obvious influence of religious taboos, that of both Hindus and Moslems on alcohol use but not on cannabis, and that of puritanical Christian prohibition of drugs, but not of the older, established use of alcohol. Again,

> cannabis is usually the drug of the have-nots and alcohol the chosen drug of the establishment. It has frequently been suggested that this correlation is no accident, that in fact, there is a causal relationship involved. Two main reasons for this correlation are usually suggested: either (1) that the effect of cannabis is such that it enables the failure to retreat from the world and forget his failures; or (2) that the effect of the drug is such that it actually interferes with his motivation to succeed, or if not his motivation to succeed, his efficiency and productivity, so that in fact he doesn't get on in the rat-race. . . . Is the relationship between cannabis use and low socioeconomic status a causal one and, what is the relationship between cannabis and alcohol? Is it possible that in some situations cannabis may be a desirable alternative to alcohol?[44]

Perhaps these explanations may not be so simple either: can differential use be the *result* simply of economic status, since alcohol *costs* more than marihuana?

> Or, in the last analysis, is the difference primarily temperamental? Alcohol after all is a sedative and is needed by those who develop high anxiety levels while striving and competing, those with high levels of aggression, high belligerence. While cannabis is a complex drug, it is a stimulant and euphoriant, also something of a sedative and something of a hallucinogen. It may be that this is needed more by the less aggressive folk—those unable to communicate, tending to inaction, to dreaming, seekers after meaning.[45]

And when all this is said, what, in a democracy, should be done by legislators, judges, and policemen—commonly not all of the same socio-economic class or with the same political, economic, or social power—to say nothing of the public at large, to decide and control the wishes and propensities of others, in all conditions of life?

Two of the few objective and well-documented effects of cannabis in humans are the enlargement of scleral blood vessels and the mild decrease in intraocular pressure, for which reasons it has been suggested that marihuana might be useful in the treatment of glaucoma. But meanwhile no assured answers may be given to a number of basic questions, and the possibility remains that, medically, marihuana, in the respective amounts and manner of use, may be every bit as dangerous as tobacco.

Reference Notes

1. H. H. Bender, *The Home of the Indo-Europeans* (Princeton: Princeton University Press, 1922); P. Thieme, "The Indoeuropean Language," *Scientific American*, 199 no. 4 (October 1958), 63–74; Marija Gimbutas, "The Indo-Europeans: Archeological Problems," *American Anthropologist* 65 (1963), 815–36.
2. S. Benet, "Early Diffusion and Folk Uses of Hemp," in V. Rubin (ed.), *Cannabis and Culture* (The Hague: Mouton, 1975), pp. 30–49, p. 42; C. Stefanis, C. Ballas, and D. Madianou, "Sociocultural and Epidemiological Aspects of Hashish Use in Greece," in ibid., p. 304; Hui-Lin Li, "The Origin and Use of Cannabis in Eastern Asia: Their Linguistic-Cultural Implications," in ibid., pp. 51–62.
3. W. La Barre, *The Peyote Cult* (New York: Schocken, 1969), pp. 12–14, 21, 106, 138, 200.
4. Benet, "Hemp," p. 40; J. Fisher, "Cannabis in Nepal: An Overview," in Rubin, *Cannabis and Culture*, pp. 247–55.
5. R. E. Schultes, W. M. Klein, T. Plowman, and T. E. Lockwood, "Cannabis: An Example of Taxonomic Neglect," in Rubin, *Cannabis and Culture*, pp. 21–38; G. E. W. Wolstenholme and J. Knight (eds.), *Hashish: Its Chemistry and Pharmacology* (Boston: Little, Brown, 1965); R. E. Schultes and A. Hofmann, *The Botany and Chemistry of Hallucinogens* (Springfield, Ill.: Charles C Thomas, 1973). pp. 53–65.
6. W. A. Emboden, "Ritual Use of *Cannabis sativa* L.: A Historical-Ethnographic survey," in P.T. Furst (ed.), *Flesh of the Gods: The Ritual Use of Hallucinogens* (New York: Praeger, 1972), pp. 214–36.
7. Benet, "Hemp," pp. 39–42.
8. M. A. Martin, "Ethnobotanical Aspects of Cannabis in Southeast Asia," in Rubin, *Cannabis and Culture*, pp. 63–75.
9. Benet, "Hemp," p. 43.
10. R. J. Bouquet, "Cannabis," *Bulletin on Narcotics* 2 no. 4 (1950), 14–30 and 3 no. 1 (1951), 22–43; I. C. Chopra and N. R. Chopra, "The Use of the Cannabis Drugs in India," *Bulletin on Narcotics* 9 no. 1 (1957), 4–29; K. A. Hasan, "Social Aspects of the Use of Cannabis in India," in Rubin, *Cannabis and Culture*, pp. 235–46. Ved Prakash and Sylvia Vatuk, "Chatorpan: A Culturally Defined Form of Addiction in North India," *Transcultural Psychiatry Research Review* 4 (1967), 27–30.
11. R. G. Wasson, *Soma: Divine Mushroom of Immortality* (New York: Harcourt, Brace & World, 1968); W. La Barre, essay-review in *American Anthropologist* 72 (1970), 368–73; W. E. Emboden, *Narcotic Plants* (New York: Macmillan, 1972), p. 16.
12. M. A. Khan, A. Abbas, and K. Jensen, "Cannabis Use in Pakistan: A Pilot Study of Long-Term Effects on Social Status and Physical Health," in Rubin, *Cannabis and Culture*, pp. 345–54.
13. Stefanis et al., *Hashish Use in Greece*, p. 305.
14. Emboden, *Narcotic Plants*, p. 15; W. La Barre, *The Ghost Dance: Origins of Religion* (New York: Delta Books, 1972), pp. 308, 323.
15. Rubin, in *Cannabis and Culture*, p. 5; B. M. du Toit, "Dagga: The History and Ethnographic Setting of *Cannabis sativa* in Southern Africa," in ibid., pp. 81–116; N. J. van der Merwe, "Cannabis Smoking in 13th-14th Century Ethiopia: Chemical Evidence," in ibid., pp. 77–80.
16. R. Cordeiro de Farias, "Use of maconha (*Cannabis sativa*, L.) in Brazil," *Bulletin on Narcotics*, 7 no. 2 (1955), 5–19; A. R. de Pinho, "Social and Medical Aspects of the use of Cannabis in Brazil," in Rubin, *Cannabis and Culture*, pp. 293–302; H. W. Hutchinson, "Patterns of Marihuana Use in Brazil," in ibid., pp. 173–83.
17. A. H. Khalifa, "Traditional Patterns of Hashish Use in Egypt," in ibid., pp. 195–205. See also M. I. Soueif, "Hashish Consumption in Egypt, with Special Reference to Psychosocial Aspects," *Bulletin on Narcotics* 19 no. 2 (1967), 1–12.
18. R. Joseph, "The Economic Significance of *Cannabis sativa* in Moroccan Rif," in Rubin, *Cannabis and Culture*, pp. 185–93. See also A. Benabud, "Psycho-pathological Aspects of the Cannabis Situation in Morocco," *Bulletin on Narcotics* 9 no. 4 (1951), 1–16; P. Palgi, "The Traditional Role and Symbolism of Hashish Among Moroccan Jews in Israel and the Effect of Acculturation," in Rubin, *Cannabis and Culture*, pp. 207–16.
19. L. Faye, *Rabelais Botaniste* (Angers: Cosnier et Lachèse, 1854).
20. H. Codere, "The Social and Cultural Context of Cannabis Use in Rwanda," in Rubin, *Cannabis and Culture*, pp. 217–226; J. M. Watt, "Dagga in South Africa," *Bulletin on Narcotics*

13 no. 3 (1961), 9–14; T. Asuni, "Socio-psychiatric problems of cannabis in Nigeria," *Bulletin on Narcotics*, 16 no. 2 (1964), 17–28.

21. J. Benoist, "Rèunion: Cannabis in a Pluricultural and Polyethnic Society," in Rubin, *Cannabis and Culture*, pp. 227–34.

22. T. H. Mikuriya, "Marihuana in Medicine: Past, Present and Future," *California Medicine* 110 (January 1969), 3–40; R. Mechoulam (ed.), *Marihuana: Chemistry, Pharmacology, Metabolism and Clinical Effects* (New York: Academic Press, 1973).

23. C. Winick, "The Use of Drugs by Jazz Musicians," *Social Problems* 3 (Winter 1959–1960) 240–53; idem, "Marihuana Use by Young People," in E. Harms (ed.), *Drug Addiction in Youth* (New York: Pergamon Press, 1965), pp. 19–35; E. Marcovitz and H. J. Myers, "The Marihuana Addict in the Army," *War Psychiatry* 6 (1964), 382–91; W. H. McGlothlin and S. Cohen, "The Use of Hallucinogenic Drugs Among College Students," *American Journal of Psychiatry* 122 (1965), 572–74; J. T. Carey, "Marihuana Use Among the New Bohemians," *Journal of Psychedelic Drugs* 2 (1968), 79–92.

24. Rubin, in *Cannabis and Culture*, p. 7.

25. W. E. Carter and W. J. Coggins, "Chronic Cannabis Use in Costa Rica: A Description of Research Objectives," in ibid., pp. 389–98.

26. J. R. Gamage and E. L. Zerkin, *A Comprehensive Guide to the English Language Literature on Cannabis (Marihuana)* (Beloit, Wisc.: STASH Press, 1965); O. J. Kalant, *The Cannabis (Marihuana) Literature* (Toronto: Addiction Research Foundation Bibliographic Series No. 2, 1968).

27. N. S. Kline, "Introduction: The Psychology, Philosophy, Morality, and Legislative Control of Drug Uses," in D. Efron, B. Holmstedt, and N. S. Kline (eds.), *Ethnopharmacologic Search for Psychoactive Drugs* (Washington, D.C.: Public Health Service Publication no. 1645, 1967), pp. xvii-xix, 1–2. See also Louis Bozzetti and Jack Blaine, "Memories, Reflections and Myths: The American Marihuana Commission," in Rubin, *Cannabis and Culture*, pp. 521–29; W. H. McGlothlin, "Sociocultural Factors in Marihuana Use in the United States," in ibid., pp. 531–47; and J. Kaplan, "Intersections of Anthropology and Law in the Cannabis Area," in ibid., pp. 549–57.

28. J. Fisher, "Cannabis in Nepal: An Overview," in ibid., pp. 247, 251.

29. V. Rubin, "The 'Ganja Vision' in Jamaica," in ibid., pp. 257–66; L. Comitas, "The Social Nexus of *Ganja* in Jamaica," in ibid., pp. 119–32; J. Schaeffer, "The Significance of Marihuana in a Small Agricultural Community in Jamaica," in ibid., pp. 355–88; Carter and Coggins, "Cannabis Use."

30. W. L. Partridge, "Cannabis and Cultural Groups in a Colombian Municipio," in ibid., p. 170; Hutchinson, "Patterns," p. 181. See also B. R. Elejalda, "Marihuana and Genetic Studies in Colombia: The Problem in the City and in the Country," in ibid., pp. 327–43.

31. Hasan, "Social Aspects," p. 245.

32. Fisher, "Cannabis in Nepal," p. 251.

33. Hasan, "Social Aspects," p. 244.

34. R. G. Smart and D. Feier, "Marijuana Use Among Adults in Toronto," Unpublished ms., Toronto: Addiction Research Foundation, 1971.

35. M. Green and R. D. Miller, "Cannabis Use in Canada," in Rubin, *Cannabis and Culture*, pp. 507, 511.

36. Bozzetti and Blaine, "Memories," p. 523.

37. A. B. Segelman, R. D. Sofia, and F. H. Segelman, "*Cannabis sativa* L. (Marihuana): VI Variations in Marihuana Preparation and Usage—Chemical and Pharmacological Consequences," in ibid., p. 270.

38. Segelman et al., "Marihuana Preparation," p. 275.

39. Nahas, cited in ibid., p. 286.

40. Schaeffer, "Significance of Marihuana," p. 354.

41. Ibid., p. 381.

42. Ibid., pp. 384–85.

43. McGlothlin, "Sociocultural Factors", p. 543.

44. M. H. Beaubrun, "Cannabis or Alcohol: The Jamaican Experiment," in Rubin, *Cannabis and Culture*, p. 486.

45. Ibid., p. 493.

4. Soma: The Three-and-One-Half Millennia Mystery

Ever since the Aryans crossed the Hindu Kush into India in prehistoric times, the mystery has persisted. And ever since Sanskrit was discovered by Europeans in the eighteenth century, an apparently insoluble riddle has lain at the heart of Vedic studies: the identity of the mysterious, sacred psychotropic plant of the Brahman priests called soma.

The problem is not a minor or incidental one. The eminent French Vedist, the late Louis Renou, thought the whole of the immense *Rig Veda* is present *in nuce* in the Vedic hymns to soma. The distinguished Indo-Europeanist, Wendy Doniger O'Flaherty, states categorically that

> the Soma sacrifice was the focal point of the Vedic religion. Indeed, if one accepts the point of view that the whole of Indic mystic practice from the Upanishads through the more mechanical methods of yoga is merely an attempt to replace the vision granted by the Soma plant, then the nature of that vision—and of that plant—underlies the whole of Indian religion, and everything of a mystical nature within that religion is pertinent to the identity of the plant.

The careful scholarship of the dedicated amateur mycophile R. Gordon Wasson reads like an exciting scientific detective story. Moreover, his willingness to pursue the quest through the wide range of linguistics, archeology, folklore, philology, ethnobotany, plant ecology, human physiology, and prehistory constitutes an object lesson to all holistic professional students of man.

First of all, use of the soma plant must date at least back to the time of a common Indo-Iranian stock, since the *Avesta* refers to the cognate *haoma*. However, the plant that some students identify with *haoma* cannot be the same as soma because their *haoma* is apparently an herbaceous plant, a *haoma* substitute that completely misfits the voluminous Vedic descriptions of soma. This, of course, does not militate against the possibility, indeed the probability, that the original *haoma* plant was the same as that here identified as soma. In any case, the Vedic evidence is considerably fuller and better than the Avestan.

The earliest Vedic hymns date in their oral form from the period of about

This chapter is adapted from an article-review on R. Gordon Wasson, *Soma: Divine Mushroom of Immortality*, with a section by W. D. O'Flaherty, Ethno-mycological Studies, I (New York: Harcourt, Brace & World; The Hague: Mouton, 1968), in *American Anthropologist* 72 (1970), 368–73. Since the original work commands rare book prices, and even the commercial edition is similarly prohibitive in price to many, this résumé of the problem, the argument, and the proof is included here.

1800 B.C., so that the protohistoric horizon for soma use is probably also Indo-European. In the *Rig Veda*, only priests drank soma, and it conferred divinity on the Brahmanic "living gods." In the European tradition, the gods themselves obtained immortality through the eating of ambrosia (the curious and delicate odor of which is constantly referred to) and the drinking of *nectar* (probably mead, the cognate terms for which are pan–Indo-European). Thus, in Europe, the old weather mages, Othinn and Zeus, with their many shamanistic animal metamorphoses, developed into anthropomorphic nature gods, whereas in India the old Indo-European shaman bards remained human and became a priestly caste. The soma-haoma term, however, is Indo-Iranian only; *ambrosia* is cognate with the Indic *amrita*, indicating that a divine substance was embibed, but under different names.

If the soma-ambrosia complex is thus early Indo-European, a northern Eurasiatic provenience is suggested.[a] Here some striking philological facts emerge. Because of regular Grimm's Law-like sound shifts in Uralic languages, we can demonstrate that there was an ancient Uralic word for fly-agaric or fungus, and moreover this word was held in common with ancient Indo-European. Since the cognate Indo-European words undergo regular Grimm's Law sound changes, we can confirm the antiquity of the term but not, perhaps, the direction of the borrowing. For example, the Ugric *poŋ* is the Ostyak [*tul*]-*paŋx* ("fool's punk," with which compare Magyar "fool's mushroom," whence German "mad-mushroom") and also the Ob-Ugric *poŋx* (compare Chukchi *poŋ*); the starred form *paŋx* was proto-Uralic, which ceased to be spoken ca. 6000 B.C. But *poŋ* is also cognate with Greek *sphóngos*, *spóngé*, and the Latin *fungus*; Roman Jakobson accepts this (Holger Pedersen's) etymology for fungal words in Indo-European. If *sponge-fungus-punk* are loan words in Indo-European from the common Uralic (or vice versa), the fly-agaric *paŋx* was being invoked as a divine inebriant in northern Eurasia long before the Aryans left their ancestral home. With the antiquity of a hallucinogenic mushroom thus established, the whole complex of ecstatic shamanism in this same northern region now appears in a new light.

A related fact is the use of dried fungus as punk tinder since at least Mesolithic times, for in the Maglemosian finds at Star Carr were discovered quantities of the punk-fungus *Fomes fomentarius*. Interestingly also, in many European languages toxic mushrooms are known as "toadstools" (an associa-

a. Since the word for "wolf" and other northern animals (but not for "lion," "elephant," etc.) is original pan-Indo-European, the ancestral speakers of this linguistic stock must have come into India from the north. "Turtle" is also pan-Indo-European; but the turtle does not live north of a line through the base of the Jutland Peninsula, hence the Indo-Europeans did not originate in classic Norse lands. "Beech" is pan-Indo-European too, but the beech-tree does not grow east of a line from the Baltic to the Black Sea. Again, *laks* is pan-Indo-European for "salmon," which occurs only in the Oder and Elbe rivers of the appropriate region. Hence the early Neolithic Indo-Europeans (as established by other words) must have come originally from the Lithuania–northern Poland region before their dispersal and breakup into the Germanic, Slavic, Celtic, Italo-Greek, and other substocks.

tion possibly because toad skins contain the powerful hallucinogen *bufotenin);* and in China the fly-agaric is actually called the "toad-mushroom"! Wasson thinks that "toadstool," unspecific for toxic and other mushrooms in English, was an originally Celtic concept (crapaudin, from *crapaud* "toad," is the modern French name) for the fly-agaric in its shamanistic role, associated with great fear and awe and held under a powerful and lasting taboo. (Compare the Vogul belief that if laymen ate agaric it would kill them; and Donner says that among the Ket and Selkup only shamans and aspiring shamans could use agaric, for others would die from eating it.) St. Augustine still bitterly censured the heretic Manicheans of the Old Religion for their fungus-eating. The Chinese also refer, in a twelfth-century text, to Manicheans who *eat red mushrooms,* a telling point, as we shall see (cf. the mysterious Taoist *ling-chih,* "mushroom of immortality," which even the great emperor Shih-huang searched for in vain).

Another interesting folk complex associates the "fire" of lightning with the flint "thunderstone" and with the fire latent in both flint and fungus punk-tinder. In the very old temple of Zeus Feretrius at Rome, the cult object was a flint (*silex),* while in European folklore Paleolithic hand axes were long and widely considered to be literal "thunderbolts" from the sky. Thus, the "Funke" or residual spark struck from a flint in fire-making is identical with the fire in the lightning that produced the "thunderstone." Flint thunderstones are thus latent with the fire of Zeus for human Prometheuses to steal. The fact that lightning sometimes vitrifies silicon dioxide, far the commonest mineral on the crust of the earth and chemically identical with flint, would encourage this uranic theory, though flint is in fact geologically neptunian in origin.

Again, "toadstools" also are believed in folklore to be produced by thunder. Thus the *Funke* latent in the punk-fungus or touchwood-tinder is of the same skyey origin. In this connection, it is interesting that the Vedic fly-agaric is repeatedly called "red" and is specifically associated with Surya the Sun, with the sky-god Indra who brings rain, and with the trickster-god *Agni* (Latin *ignis,* "fire"); both toads and toadstools often appear mysteriously after rain. Punk-fungus, like flint, holds hidden fire. "Spunk" is also the essential male soul-stuff or spark of life in semen, the divine Fire or *logos* of Heraclitus from whom Plato took his doctrine of the formative Idea. (Incidentally, Marco Polo says the Mongolian Uighur tribe's Khan was born directly of punk—much as Athene sprang directly from her sire's *muellos,* the brain-marrow thought by ancients to be the source, via the spine, of animal seed.)

The Manicheans who ate mushrooms for immortality also used urine for ritual water. This practice recalls that of agaric-using Paleo-Siberian tribes who still in the last century drank the urine of the original partaker of fly-agaric in order to extend its pharmacological action—a curious behavior but one confirmed by all our best ethnographic sources on several Siberian tribes. The mysterious "Second Form" of the drink soma, then, as the urine of users, is the obvious interpretation of one puzzling Vedic verse. And, as opposed to the woolen "second filter" used to strain the mashed-up *soma* to obtain the juice, another filter is the god Indra, the first eater of soma, thence his urine as a magic drink.

In brief, implicated with a rich and complex symbolism, the use of the agaric mushroom was known to early Uralic and Indo-European peoples, under a name common to both, and eastward through various Paleo-Siberians to China. Widespread also is the connection with a sky-god, an origin of mushrooms (and thunderstones) in thunder, and fire (in flint and punk) from lightning. Far-flung as are the ethnographic evidences, their antiquity, nevertheless, suggests authentic common culture-historical origins.

On the other hand, the easy suggestion that soma was an alcoholic liquor— for soma was a plant juice of some kind that was drunk as a liquid—is quite improbable. There are many arguments against this interpretation. Soma juice was drunk immediately after ritual preparation, and there is no mention anywhere of a period of fermentation, which, if present, the ritual litigiousness of the Vedic formulae would surely have taken into account. Furthermore, a beer (starch-fermented) or wine (sugar) could be made from many substances other than one sacred plant lost after the Indo-Europeans had left their northern homeland; and it is repeatedly indicated in Vedantic texts that in India, after Aryans had left the Himalayas, the specific soma plant was no longer available. Nor is there a shred of evidence in the Vedantic Hindu tradition of the ritual use of alcohol. Quite the contrary! A *distilled* drink strong enough to induce the attested-to psychedelic effect is unlikely also, for distillation of alcohol seems to be first known in late medieval Italy, probably in Salerno about A.D. 1100. Furthermore, if *soma-ambrosia* were a mere beer or wine, why drink mead-nectar also?

Many plant sources have been suggested for soma. The leafless Sarcostemma is a favorite candidate, also *bhang* or *Cannabis indica* (philologically an Indo-European enough plant, since "hemp" and "cannabis" by Grimm's Law are cognate), Ephedra, rhubarb, etc. None of these halfhearted suggestions has carried any conviction, and all are implausible philologically, botanically, and pharmacodynamically. It is no wonder that most ranking twentieth-century scholars had come to regard the problem of soma as insoluble.

The difficulty has been partly one of method. The compendious commentaries on the *Vedas*, the priestly *Brahmanas*, written from about 800 B.C. onward, are much preoccupied with the question of *substitutes* for soma. But the substitutes used later were always known to be such. Hence, it is a mistake to suppose that the original soma was entirely similar to these *Brahmanas* substitutes or was even one of them, for all that they imitated, doubtlessly for magic reasons, one trait (such as the redness, etc.) of the original soma. It is on *Rig Veda* evidence alone that soma may be identified botanically as the ancient Aryan psychotropic plant. Another difficulty is that the abundant references to soma in the *Rig Veda* have been too easily dismissed as mere poetic metaphor, and they do seem at first blush to be inconsistent with one another. Wasson's methodological astuteness has been to use *Rig Veda* evidence alone, eschewing the tempting but wholly irrelevant prolixity of the *Brahmanas*. When taken all together and respected literally for what they say, the Vedic apostrophes to soma turn out to be quite exact and mutually consistent botanical descriptions of the mushroom *Amanita muscaria* (Fr. ex L.) Quel., the fly-agaric.

The fly-agaric first comes out from its underground mycelium looking like a little cottonwool ball. But as it expands, the enveloping white veil splits and breaks up into various patches adhering to the bright red skin underneath. Sometimes, as with rain, the patches of veil are washed off entirely to reveal a brilliant, shining red mushroom. After gathering, or when old, it loses luster and one phase is a dull tawny chestnut color. This is "the first time that a mushroom has been proposed in the Soma quest," but the evidence is overwhelming. To match each Vedic description, Wasson produces a color photograph of the mushroom in one or another of its phases—"he makes of milk his vesture-of-grand-occasion" (the early stage of milky white flocculence); "he sloughs off the asurian color that is his, he abandons his envelope" (the red pileus has split the enveloping veil in such fashion that only fragments of it remain); the vesture of *hari*, the vault of heaven clothed in storm clouds (the fiery canopy flecked with bits of the integument); Agni (fiery red, with flecks of white smoke); "the hide of bull, the dress of sheep" (the envelope in fragments adhering to the red skin); "by day the color of fire, by night silvery white" (Wasson shows two color photographs, by day and by night, of the recognizably same group of three plants—to which one might add remarks on the physiology of color vision with respect to seeing red at night); "the single eye" (the veil-free red ball-shaped state); Surya the Sun (a larger shining fiery red sphere); the tawny yellow *pávamána* (in its opened "parasol" mature golden form); "the mainstay of the sky" (a long stem supporting a white-flecked canopy); "with his thousand knobs" (a neatly polka-dotted form with studs like the cudgel of Indra); "tongue of the Way" (a long-stemmed, glans-headed specimen); and so on. Since the envelope-denuded agaric is a flaming scarlet mushroom, by ancient criteria the *Brahmanas* substitutes sought were reddish, small, leafless, and fleshy-stalked plants. But it is astonishing how exactly the *Rig Veda* has described the plant soma, when viewed as the fly-agaric. The scholarly triumph of Wasson's identification has been so decisive that the Botanical Museum of Harvard University, in May of 1969, gave a dinner at the Harvard Faculty Club, attended by distinguished botanists, Sanskritists, historians of science, and others, to celebrate the publication of this book.

But the evidence is not solely botanical. The common Uralic term for the fly-agaric is associated with its historic ethnographic use among the Ugric Ostyak and Vogul, the Uralic Samoyed, as well as the Paleo-Siberian Ket, Chukchi, Kamchadal, and Koryak—a use once also of Yukagir and Inari Lapp, with further evidence that the Finno-Ugric Hungarians and some Indo-Europeans had it too. The linguistic evidence points to a northern Eurasiatic region where

Indo-Iranian peoples could find the agaric growing and borrow its use (or the reverse) from proto-Finno-Ugric or proto-Uralic peoples—and a region likewise where Indo-Europeans could get their loan word spongos-fungus-punk from a proto-Uralic word that spread even to linguistically unrelated Pacific Siberians like the Chukchi. The philological evidence of the *Rig Veda-Brahmanas* is that in sub-Himalayan India, Brahmans could no longer find this plant of the northern homeland of the Aryans; and for all its being so highly prized, soma never lent itself to cultivation but was always found mysteriously god-engendered.

The ecological evidence is even more stunningly apposite, for it joins solidly together the mycology of both soma agaric and punk-tinder. That is, the tribes that historically, and by inference prehistorically (Indo-Aryans), used agaric all lived in the region of birch (*Betula*) species: *Amanita muscaria*, fly-agaric-soma, is a toadstool of northern birch forests; and *Fomes fomentarius*, the ancient punk-tinder of flint-using times, is the bracket fungus commonly found growing on birch trees. (One might add that, archeologically, the palynological evidence from the Maglemosian Star Carr site places it in a birch forest climatic phase, indeed some specimens at Star Carr were still attached to birch wood.) The closure of linguistic, botanical, ethnographic, and ecological evidence is exhilarating. The identification of soma with *Amanita muscaria* is definitive, and the Sanskritic puzzle of two millennia from the *Brahmanas* to this day can now be regarded as finally solved.

The evidence is perhaps wider than Wasson would venture. On excellent grounds he thinks that *teonanacatl* and agaric are thousands of years old in use, and yet he regards them each as "autonomous" in origin. But it is interesting that of the two color phases of *Amanita muscaria*, the flaming red variety, standard in Eurasia, grows in Washington, Oregon, and British Columbia as well (and also commonly in the Sierra Madre of Mexico), while the yellow variety prevails in birch forests of the rest of its range. It is true that within the Basidiomycetes, *Amanita* and the narcotic *Psilocybe, Panaeolus, Stropharia* spp. (the latter known to be in native use in Mexico, which *Amanita* is not) are quite different in appearance. And yet Mesolithic horizons are securely reached in some Paleo-Siberian and Amerindian similarities in culture—for example, the conical wigwam-tipi spreads almost continuously from the Eastern Woodlands westward to Swedish Lapland, circumboreal "bear ceremonialism" (which now appears also to be late Paleolithic in the eastern Alps), common myth motifs (e.g., the "magic flight" and Orpheus legends), the similarity of proto-Sinitic and proto-Athapaskan (and of the Eskimo and Altaic languages?), the trickster Raven in eastern Siberia and the Northwest Coast, the evident Late Stone Age time-death of the bow and arrow in the Old and New World, etc. In this context, the possibility of cultural memory or now lost legends about, or substitute stimulus-diffusion of, Siberian and American narcotic mushrooms is not wholly fantastic (n.b., the many so-called "mushroom stones" in Guatemalan archeology, which may be just that)—especially in view of fundamental similarities in shamanism and vision quest, and the fact of aboriginal use of some three dozen meridional American plant hallucinogens.

Wasson is properly conservative on other matters. Narcotic mushrooms were *not* part of the witchcraft epidemics of late medieval and Renaissance Europe. Mushrooms, for all that the "toadstool" complex seems to be of Celtic origin, were *not* implicated with the Druidic mysteries, not at least on the basis of scanty evidence now available: the Golden Bough of the sky-god's oak tree was evidently mistletoe. Mushrooms were *not* involved with the wild Viking "berserker" state (though Odman, a Swede, first proposed the idea in 1784 on the basis of his reading of Georgi and Steller, perhaps also of von Strahlenberg and Krasheninnikoff, all of whom, however, took their data from tribes in the extreme northeast of Siberia, not Scandinavia). The berserker "rage" seems rather to be related to shamanistic animal metamorphosis into the bear; besides, agaric is tranquilizing, not "berserker" in effect. And, finally, the fly-agaric mushroom is *not* implicated with the *Pilzbaum* or Romanesque "mushroom tree" or Garden of Eden scenes (e.g., the Plaincourault fresco).

In addition to the many hand-tipped color plates of *Amanita*, distribution maps, etc., the lavishness of this book permits an unprecedented and in many ways ideal boon to scholarship: at the end of the book, all the classic ethnographic sources are quoted at length in full contextual detail. The convenient availability for re-scrutiny of all this familiar ethnographic evidence only confirms the argument of the book: that the shamanistic use of the narcotic mushroom *Amanita* is of immense antiquity in northern Eurasia and elsewhere, and that the use of mushroom punk for flint-tinder is as old as the European Mesolithic. Small technicalities perhaps? But these small technicalities, soundly demonstrated, open whole new vistas into prehistory for further exploration.

The cautious scholarship and careful method of Mr. Wasson—a retired banker, formerly a partner in J. P. Morgan & Co.—may cause us to forget that as an ethnomycologist he is also an autodidact. This leads us to an interesting professional question. Mr. Wasson is fully professional in scholarly behavior, and moreover in several diverse fields. An amateur affection for data, pursued with such zeal and acumen, achieves here results really as good as the best professional work.

But there are evidently autodidacts and autodidacts. One at least, L. M. Klauber (professionally an engineer), in his magnificent two-volume monograph *Rattlesnakes*, became manifestly the world authority on his subject; Klauber, indeed, is no less than masterly in his handling of the voluminous folkloristic and complex ethnographic data on snakes. Others, like Robert Ardrey (a dramatist and freelance journalist), cut no such professional swathe on the nature of man. Professionals are quite unimpressed with the democratic vote of laymen as a criterion of "success." But professionals constitute no impenetrable Establishment. They merely respond with approval (or dismay) to the relative mastery of information and to astuteness in assessing evidence. On this score experts may even disdain professionals like Thor Heyerdahl, Desmond Morris, and J. B. Rhine.

There is also the matter of didactic preparation, autodidactic or not, for the intellectual tasks one sets himself. Benjamin Whorf, for example, was an insurance man, but he studied with the world's peer linguist, Edward Sapir, in earning his laurels as a linguist. Gordon Wasson, who later in life learned from such distinguished teachers as the mycologist Heim, the linguist Jakobson, and from Harvard's Schultes, the world's ranking authority on the ethnobotany of psychotropic plants, evidently belongs in the high company of the Klaubers and the Whorfs as a distinguished scholar in his own right. Wasson's research on soma is a thoroughly remarkable scholarly achievement, judged even by the most stringent professional standards.

This book is on all counts a magnificent one. The volume is in blue half-leather stamped in gold, and slip-covered in fine blue linen cloth. It is designed by Giovanni Mardersteig and printed in Dante type by the Stamperia Valdonega in Verona, on paper handmade by the Fratelli Magnani, with numerous color plates tipped in by hand, in an edition of 670 copies, of which 250 are available for sale in this country. This connoisseur elegance in book-making is an appropriate setting for the stature of the problem attacked and for the scholarly quality of its solution.

II. Analytic

5. Personality from a Psychoanalytic Viewpoint

It may seem strange, in a symposium on psychology, to deal specifically with the psychology of Freud, since his influence on our times is so far-reaching and so profound. In the words of the poet Auden about Freud, "If often he was wrong and at times absurd, to us he is no more a person now but a whole climate of opinion."[1] This very fact of widespread familiarity with psychoanalytic theory, often at second or third hand or even more remotely, does not guarantee, however, the accuracy of these widespread notions, for we are deeply motivated to distort some of Freud's findings. Therefore, it may be well to summarize this difficult psychology from the original sources.[2] I wish to make clear at the outset that I think Freud did make some errors—for example, in *Totem and Taboo*, in his projection of the Oedipal conflict into the purely mythological past history of mankind in his "primal horde" theory, and again in the so-called "hydraulic theory of the libido" which supposes that libidinal energy, different in amount for each individual, can be freely transferred from one organ system to another.[a] But his contribution remains the core of modern psychiatry, while parts of it are widely shared in all modern psychologies.

There are four characteristics of Freudian psychology which originally set it off from other psychologies:

(1) Psychoanalysis is the first psychology to take seriously the whole human body as a place to live in.[b] The specific experiences of this body and the vicis-

This chapter is based on a paper presented 5 November 1966 at Rice University in Houston, Texas, and was published in *The Study of Personality: An Interdisciplinary Appraisal*, ed. Edward Norbeck, Douglass Price-Williams, and W. W. McCord. Copyright © 1968 by Holt, Rinehart and Winston, Inc. Reprinted by permission of Holt, Rinehart and Winston.

a. The "primal horde" theory of the "cyclopean family" I reject on anthropological grounds: recent primatological studies have cast doubt upon it; and the animal-hunting *Australopithecines* must already have had nuclear families within the necessarily cooperating group of male hunters of large or swift game. (Weston La Barre, *The Human Animal*, Chicago: Phoenix Books [paperback], 1960, p. 346.) Kroeber, at his death the acknowledged premier anthropologist in the world, in a famous review of *Totem and Taboo* quite fairly calls it a "Just So" story, and Freud's view of totemism is universally rejected now by anthropologists as an etiological myth. Nevertheless, if we can discriminate between Freud's insight and his faulty anthropology, *Totem and Taboo* still has much to teach us. The so-called "hydraulic theory of the libido" seems to me improbable on anatomical, neurophysiological, and biological grounds alike. In this I believe I am joined by most psychologists.

b. Psychoanalysis has not statistically dismembered man into artificial and subjectively selected fragments, where critical remaining differences of the "comparables" are masked or ignored, as well as significant traits of the whole configuration lost, but has kept its eye steadily on live, whole, functioning human beings in real situations. Psychoanalysis has not retreated into a disguised

situdes of learning about it adaptively as various parts become biologically important—especially in relation to the culturally structured attitudes and requirements of a given society—profoundly shape the individual personality.[c] Personality is partly learned: its individual structure is shaped by individual experience to an amazing degree. Nevertheless, psychoanalysis is profoundly biological about basic "species-specific" givens, and sensitively oriented to the concrete social and cultural sources of learning.

(2) Psychoanalysis is the first psychology to preoccupy itself with the *purpose* (as opposed to the processes) of thinking. The pre-Freudian notion was that thinking was simply an obvious and rational way of discovering the nature of reality. Psychoanalysis has dealt a hard blow to this unexamined and comfortably confident faith, much as Copernican theory dealt a fatal blow to earth-centered astronomy, and Darwinian evolution to man-centered biology. To Freud, thinking is a far more complex matter of making peace among three competing forces. The first datum of psychology is the conscious mind. "I think, therefore, I am," said Descartes, and all of us are convinced of the reality of our own minds. But the conscious mind has been rejected by some psychologies as too "subjective" a thing to study, hence behaviorism, for one, discarded the subject matter of psychology at the very beginning. Freud called this subjective, conscious, adaptive *executive* part of the mind the "ego." But the ego, as we shall see, must serve three masters, and is not solely the obedient subject of reality alone.

First of all, there are the imperious organic demands of this kind of animal body, demands which may be deferred and disciplined but never finally frustrated if the organism is to stay healthy, alive, and reproduce itself. For example, the gratification of conscious thirst can within limits be postponed, but without water ultimately, the animal dies.[d] The sum total of these organic

---

neurophysiology that ignores "subjective" *psychological* events. And psychoanalysis has not converted itself into an overtly infrahuman animal psychology. Since rats do not have the nuclear family, incest taboos, the oedipus complex, culture, conscience, psychoses (though experimental psychologists, taking their cue from psychoanalysis, have been able experimentally to make rats and other animals neurotic), language, or articulate symbolism, it can be well argued that none of these critical human features can be encountered or discussed meaningfully in rats. Further—human defense mechanisms being what they are—the "controlled experiment" will likely control out of the experimental situation any of the dangerous and unpleasant discoveries that might edify us about humans; at best, such experiments can only "test," often in methodologically inappropriate ways, hypotheses provided by psychoanalysis, already sufficiently established clinically. Like anthropology in its nonmanipulative study of functioning groups, psychoanalysis is a naturalistic, "bird-watching" science that does not manipulate its subjects into contrived situations, but only observes. Nevertheless, purely observational studies can still be scientific: astronomy is, and without pushing one star out of orbit.

c. Since psychoanalysis is body-oriented, and since the human body is functionally a crosstural phenomenon, it is not surprising that culture-and-personality studies of group *ethos* also began within a psychoanalytic framework. The preoccupation of psychoanalysis with the purposes and symbolic content of thought further fits it, uniquely among psychologies, for the study of myth and religion. It is a pity that "social anthropology" has degenerated into a kind of "kinship algebra" obsessed with structure, since many of these human relationships might possibly have functional significance psychoanalytically.

d. Not all organic needs, of course, ever become conscious. If, for example, from hard exercise,

demands on the psyche is called the "id." When id needs are repressed, we have *neurosis* and conflicts of various kinds, with the "return of the repressed" in the form of distorted symptoms which both punish and gratify.

Secondly, the ego must adapt the organism to external reality from which the organism derives its biochemical energy, for no organism can survive unless adapted to its environment. If the ego loses its adaptive relation to reality, we have *psychosis*. And thirdly, the ego must adapt to the moral demands of a specific traditional society, not all of which demands are necessarily life enhancing or even rational. The influence of moral reality is precipitated within the mind as an arduously learned conscience or "superego." If the individual does not incorporate these moral demands emotionally and forcefully, but is only intellectually aware of his tribal customs in the way a visiting anthropologist might coldly and bloodlessly know about the customs of an alien society that do not apply to him, then we have the *psychopath*, who may be well oriented to physical reality and thoroughly indulgent of his id impulses but who is morally sick. These relations may be diagrammed simply as indicated in figure on p. 122.

The ego therefore must serve three masters at the same time: the organic id, the environmental reality, and the social superego—and the shirking of each ego task gives us, respectively, neurosis, psychosis, and psychopathy. In this view, then, the ego is not master in its own house, the mind.[e] The *purpose* of thinking is to achieve homeostasis, to preserve some kind of equilibrium or *modus vivendi* among these three kinds of demands made upon it. As everybody knows, the task is not easy or automatic.

The ego has a number of defenses which all of us use at one time or another—rationalization, denial, projection, intellectualization, and the like—but chronic overuse brings problems. Rationalization is finding good reasons for unreasonable positions we wish to hold, despite our perhaps unconsciously "knowing better," which only increases the flow of rationalizations. The extreme of this self-serving indulgence in fantasy is schizophrenia. Denial is simply "turning one's back" psychologically on unpleasant facts—a characteristic ego defense in hysteria. Projection is pretending the forbidden impulse is not

---

the CO_2 level of the blood rises, a special chemoreceptor at the entrance to the heart increases the rate of heartbeat to increase oxygen replacement in the red blood cells pumped to the lungs. There are many such automatically homeostatic "feedback" devices in the body, described in W. B. Cannon's valuable book on *The Wisdom of the Body* (New York: W. W. Norton & Company, 1932). Indeed, the forebrain may only be another such, and phylogenetically latest, homeostatic device, needed only for new or physiologically uncontrolled problems.

e. Reality figuratively says, "This is the way things are." The id says, stubbornly and obdurately and blindly, "I want." The superego says, "You should (or should not)." But only the ego says, "I shall (or shall not)." Reality and superego and id all tend to be heard as "You must" though it is only our (possibly mistaken) *view* of reality that seems to require this; the demands of conscience may sometimes be circumvented, especially if defined irrationally, but the price of conscious circumvention may be guilt or shame; and the id may be satisfied with many *alternative* sources of calories and other necessities, and not necessarily a specific food consciously desired. Only the ego is saddled with existentialist *epistemological* problems.

inside but outside one's own mind—like the hysteric old maid who looks constantly and with delicious fearfulness for the burglar under the bed she unconsciously wishes were in bed with her.

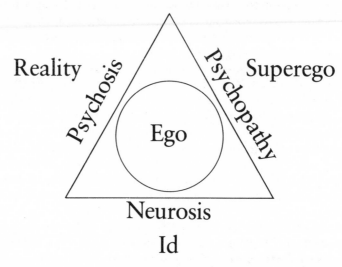

The lustful burglar has the wicked wish, not she! For, see, how busily she preoccupies herself with seeing that this wish is not accomplished? She seemingly can have her cake and eat it too: she can spend all her time in delectable fantasy, and yet not be guilty. But her symptom both punishes and gratifies. Her *phobia* is what she unconsciously desires but consciously denies and projects—and she never gets her man.*f* Fantasy is fun and not dangerous; and yet it does not really gratify in the end.

The ego has other mechanisms of defense, for example "conversion." The conversion hysteric can convert conscious psychic pain into as-if physical illness, thus achieving the characteristic "belle indifference" of the conversion hysteric, but keeping the surgeon needlessly busy cutting out one naughty organ after another. The conversion hysteric can (and often does), with smiling face and evident pleasure, give a long "organ recital" of dreadful illnesses, any one of which, if organically real, might put her at death's door, instead of allowing her to walk around and pridefully talk about it. Her "belle indifference" or surprising emotional unconcern comes from the conversion (projection) of psychic stress into a pseudo-organic illness, which *functionally*

---

f. It is a dangerous mistake to think simply that "she needs a man" because if she really did have one then she might be precipitated into psychosis—because that is what her symptom is for, to protect her from recognizing she has expanded the prohibition of an incestuously loved man (father, or sometimes brother) to include all men. The attempt by the would-be omnipotent "therapist" simply to wrest away symptoms may leave the neurotic denuded of necessary protective defenses and drive him into deeper difficulty. Well-meaning "advice" from a friend, though insightful (and especially *if* insightful), can often do great damage if this psychiatric principle is not taken into account.

substitutes for conscious anxiety. That is, the pain of operations gives punishment, but she may get sympathy too—and she has gotten rid of the symbolically wicked organ. But only symbolically. She will soon need another operation because this masochistic process has meant no dynamic cure of the *psychological* problem. Ultimately she may shop around for a surgeon (surgeons have unconscious motivations too) and have a needless hysterectomy, after which, commonly, she may have a psychotic breakdown.

Our insight into the meaning of the psychic game of the "burglar under the bed" or the hypochondria of the conversion hysteric is one reason why we get so impatient with the neurotic. We correctly perceive that the neurotic partly enjoys the symptom; hence we regard even real suffering as somehow "phony" and dismiss the neurotic as an "old crock" whose problem "exists only in the imagination." No, not in the imagination; only in the memory. Neurotics are literally sick of the past. The psychiatric problem is how to discover that past, examine and understand it. It is true the neurotic seems like the famous Hellenistic sculpture of Laocoön, in which a brawny man and his two sons struggle extravagantly with a snake, but if they would just *let go* they could probably step out of the coils and walk away. However, in this incomplete judgment we forget two facts: first, the neurotic clings to his symptoms because of what they *do for him*, protecting him from frightening insight, often plus the "secondary gain" of removing him from frightening situations and eliciting pity or indulgence—at the same time that they morally punish him with guilt and psychically needed anguish and anxiety. The patient seems to say to the analyst, "Take anything, but just let me keep my symptoms!" Secondly, because of *resistance*, the insight of an analyst or friend is by no means equivalent to insight on the part of the patient himself. The very correctness of the insight arouses his defense mechanisms. Anyone who has uselessly tried to tell a neurotic plain and obvious facts about himself knows well what "resistance" is and may agree that it takes skilled professional help to cope with it. Resistance is often extremely easy to see in other persons, and just as often impossible to see in oneself. Thus "self-analysis" is impossible beyond a very modest point, because a kind of psychic blindness arises when one gets close to really anxiety-arousing points. Similarly, resistance to "certain parts of psychoanalysis" is likely to be part-identification with the neurotic at these points because the insights apply to us too.

We have seen that in phobic hysteria there is projection of a disclaimed portion of the psyche to the outside, and in conversion hysteria projection of psychic into physical pain. Projection of erotic and aggressive impulses is also present in males, especially in paranoia. Instead of recognizing his own hostility, the paranoiac projects it into other people and then claims they are persecuting him ("persecutory mania"). Instead of recognizing his own (forbidden) unconscious wishes, he claims someone else is making "unwanted" sexual advances to him. Since the hysteric's unconscious wish is merely heterosexual, she can often get along with the relatively shallow and transparently naive defense of simple denial. But since the paranoiac's unconscious wish is homosexual, he needs the far more elaborated defenses of a completely rationalized "paranoid system" for he can afford no chink in his psychic defenses or body-image—other people would otherwise wickedly "poison" him or "stab him in the back." (Such fears are not without symbolic meaning.) Pathological jealousy means he unconsciously feels the attractiveness of another man but projects this into his own wife and falsely blames her for being attracted to him. Or, instead of recognizing his own inadequacy, he fantasies compensatory omnipotence ("megalomania"), as overprotested as he needs it to be. Or, instead of recognizing his inability to love, he believes that every woman *loves him* ("erotomania"). Likewise, paranoid suspiciousness imputes to other people one's own denied aggressive and hostile impulses, which later can be consciously felt because now "justified." The paranoiac Hitler displayed all these mechanisms in classic textbook forms.[g] (But he also had hysteric symptoms.)

The variety of defense mechanisms is almost endless. In displacement of anger toward his boss, the man bullies his wife, she nags the child, and the child kicks the cat. Intellectualization and isolation are characteristic of compulsion neuroses and obsessions, which are sometimes almost as intricate as paranoid systems, though their dynamics are otherwise somewhat different. Too tyrannical a conscience or superego may crush the ego into a *depression*, in which the ego feels weak, rejected, unlovable and unloved, helpless, and "no good." Or a rebellious ego-id team, trying to run away from an overly severe superego, can end up in the pseudo-blithesome "vacation from conscience" of frantic *mania*.

(3) The third distinguishing characteristic of psychoanalysis is that it is the first psychology to pay significant attention to the *symbolic content* of thought. The neurotic symbol is something that is not, but conveniently stands for, the upsetting reality. We can immediately see the great usefulness of the symbol, for example in dreams, where the wish may disguise itself behind the mask of the symbol, and thus achieve gratification at the same time it gets past the dream censor and hoodwinks the superego. Of course the conflict may arouse too much anxiety, and we wake up, often with the mild malaise of guilt mixed with a smug naughty sense of surreptitious gratification. Similarly in more severe conflicts, the nightmare, terror-laden, may call upon the conscious ego for help and we wake up frightened. But most of the time dreaming seems to

g. The "blood purge" of his former crony Ernst Roehm was a classic instance in Hitler of "homosexual panic" often found in seemingly meaningless murders or random paranoid massacres of many persons. The contrived "Reichstag fire" was a paranoid maneuver to project guilt and "justify" attack, as was the alleged "persecution" of Sudeten Germans, followed by the invasion of Czechoslovakia and a later mass murder of Jews that was the most psychotic enormity in all recorded history. The cult of "der schöne Adolf" in which all Nordic women were supposed to be in love with Hitler was a classic case of erotomaniacal fantasy. Hitler's sexual life can also be called in question: he was evidently a nonpracticing, unconsciously homosexual paranoid fanatic, with only a feeble or dubious heterosexuality. These and other paranoid symptoms are abundantly documented in Konrad Heiden, *Der Fuehrer* (Boston: Houghton Mifflin Company, 1944) and elsewhere.

be another homeostatic device of the mind, this one specifically to preserve sleep. Beyond dream use, massive symbol-using is one of the prime adaptive characteristics of *Homo sapiens,* and no human psychology that ignores the nature of symbolizing can hope to be a complete or even adequate psychology.

The nature of symbolizing now seems to be so widely recognized that many people indulge in amateur symbol hunting as a kind of parlor game. The dangers in this are multiple and complex. For one, there exists no absolute "universal dictionary" of previously agreed-upon dream symbols or of any other kind of symbol supposedly inherent in human minds. Hence *ad hoc* "interpretation" risks being simply wrong intellectually. It is the nature of symbol equations to be invented by man, not discovered in nature—for all that they may be unconsciously shared by people in the same society and learned like the rest of culture. Hence cross-cultural "interpretations" may simply miss the point methodologically and rise from the wrong culture base. Again, common sense can always say "Come now, X is not *really* equal to Y!"—and be right, even though we correctly perceived what the person meant it to mean unconsciously, but have now aroused someone's resistances, perhaps the subject's. Again, who is doing the symbolizing? Insofar as an unconscious meaning is not truly resident in the symbol producer's mind, we are clearly projecting a meaning of our own, the only possible source now being one's own mind. We are then not so much discovering the contents of another psyche as naively and unwittingly exhibiting one's own. Finally, *what are we doing* in this allegedly "psychoanalytic" gambit of symbol chasing: are we being voyeuristic, punitive, aggressive, seductive, hostile, oneupsman, exhibitionistic, or what? Such "wild analysis" of the amateur can be each of these unseemly activities, when lacking the constant self-scrutiny of the "countertransference" in himself as a trained analyst does it. Since the professional analyst must often spend actual weeks in discovering an unconscious meaning *through his patient's voluminous free associations* in order to be able to demonstrate it unequivocally and massively to him later, nothing is quite so painful to the sophisticate as to witness amateur symbol mongering. Besides, *motives* for doing this in the parlor are not the same as those in the doctor's office—in addition to the shameless inadequacy of the methodology. In the same manner, and for much the same reasons, nothing so much sets the professional anthropologist's teeth on edge as to hear a glib interpretation of the "symbolism" of a piece of primitive art, when the speaker knows nothing whatever about the man or the tribe that made it but is merely improvising *ad hoc* folklore; whereas the anthropologist may have spent patient months tracing *in native minds* the ramifications of a new and alien symbolic system. No one with genuine knowledge of the individual and cultural nature of symbolism would permit himself the fatuous absurdity of public amateur "interpretations." Nor, justly, is he likely to convince.

(4) A fourth characteristic of psychoanalysis involves a profound irony. We are all familiar with some of the Victorian generation's defense against Darwinian evolution. This defense is one of the shabbiest of all argumentative

dodges: it consists in an unacknowledged understanding of what a man said, with clever purpose distorting it, and then using it to demolish a straw man of one's own devising. For example, the cliché about Darwin was, "You don't think your grandfather was an ape, ha ha!, do you?" As a matter of fact, Darwin was looking for a "missing link" at each branching between man's ancestry and that of modern apes. It is a cheap triumph to demolish one's own nonsense.

But the same gambit is still commonly used against psychoanalysis. Even now, people sometimes say, "Freud thinks everything is sex, ha ha!, and you and I both know this isn't so." However, Freud long argued, and evidently without much success, that there are *other kinds of sensual pleasure* besides the sexual (genital), for example the oral pleasure of the baby's lustful suckling at his mother's breast, which we still retain in modified form in the pleasure of eating, drinking, smoking, gum chewing, talking, and the like. There is also evident pleasure in urination and defecation, but half the time we say this is not true, so Freud is wrong, and half the time we acknowledge it but call Freud a nasty man for dreaming it up.

This is what I mean by saying that we are sometimes deeply motivated defensively to distort the findings of Freud. He tells us many things we do not want to know, and against these we liberally use all the familiar defense mechanisms, including readily-joined-in ridicule insofar as we share the same aversion to self-knowledge. In this we are again like the proverbial old maid. When the analyst finally points out that she seems, on much evidence, to have real (and even legitimate) sexual wishes, she calls him a "dirty old man" (denial), probably lusting after her himself (projection)—an especially terrible matter because the analyst unconsciously represents her (forbidden) father. Similarly, the paranoid patient, or person, gets into a long "logical" argument in which he is able to rationalize everything, however preposterous. And the psychopath, in turn, falsely alleges that "Freud says you should act on all your impulses or you'll be neurotic—" this at the precise moment when the analyst is trying to point out that what the psychopath really needs is a few well-contrived inhibitions and ego-disciplined sublimations. One's peculiarly distorted view of Freud's findings may therefore be diagnostic of one's basic personality.

This brings us to the chief difficulty of Freud's psychology. Are we to suppose that people become anguishingly insane over nice, innocuous, genteel matters that we can complacently converse about in the parlor? No! People go mad over really upsetting matters like forbidden incestuous impulses, deeply unconscious homosexual wishes, murderous rage, and other such unseemly feelings. We all have forbidden wishes, it is to be hoped to a lesser degree and in more manageable forms; hence our anxieties are inevitably aroused by Freud's explanations, and hence our various defense mechanisms bristle in violently argumentative form. At this point we can only quote Shakespeare,

"Methinks the lady doth protest too much"—or in more homely fashion discern that "Where there's smoke, there's fire."

Freud first pointed out what now seems obvious to many: that there are a number of body zones besides the genital one, all capable of giving sensual pleasure, zones in fact primordially more activated and physiologically significant in time than the genital. Diffuse skin erotism is present very early, although in humans it is perhaps not so significant as it is in lower animals. There is also positive, and sometimes intense, pleasure in seeing and hearing, smelling and touching and tasting. But none of these is primary in the libidinal sense. It is because of traumatic relinquishment, painful vicissitudes in experiencing, overindulgence, or repression of these libidinal pleasures that so many people protest so fiercely their nonexistence; and because it is often so hardly won, or precarious, they protest the exclusive primacy of genital pleasure. And yet pregenital gratifications are always part of genital forepleasure (kissing, seeing, touching, and so on), such that the forepleasure is a kind of recapitulation of the libidinal history of the individual and an autobiography of the relative importance of these for the individual.

The primary libidinal zones are those of the various portal skins of the body, where pleasure is associated with successful accomplishment of an adaptive physiological duty or need. Primary in the baby suckling is the oral zone, where libidinal pleasure accompanies the satisfaction of its primary need to take in and to grow; the eye and ear are later adjuncts of "oral incorporation" as a process. Reciprocally, the normal woman obtains deep physical gratification in nursing a baby. The mutual gratification-frustration gamut of these experiences shapes the individual, quite irrationally and preverbally, as either an "oral optimist" or an "oral pessimist" in his emotional expectations of the world. Later appearing, about the time the individual begins to walk and talk and to achieve a more active body mastery, social demands invading individual body autonomy come into conflict over the anal zone; the residual emotional tone of this experience has much to do with individual awareness of self/not-self discrimination and attitudes of dominance-submission in larger social contexts later. Urethral disciplines become associated with pride, shame, and ambition. The phallic phase, about which more will be said later, is perhaps still an "imprinting" period for sexual identification and introjection of psychic maleness or femaleness; this is the time of enthusiastic discovery and valuation of one's own sex, and appropriate sex typing through emulation, learning, and identification (only when a fixated self-sex admiration becomes genitalized does it become perverse). Associated with the phallic is the oedipal phase, when the child discovers a significant figure (father) beyond the gratifying-demanding mother of the oral-anal phases; it is the emotional paradigm for all future superego relations with society; for example, individual attitudes toward religion are a revealing Rorschach of the peculiar resolution of the oedipal conflict, which underlies all rational or rationalized superstructures built intellectually upon it (war, politics, and the like). The psychological phase of genital primacy is quite the last of all. Of course none of these phases should be thought of as stations on a railway line, for they coexist and intermingle and in some form persist; but they do follow much the same sequence in most individuals.

There is a familiar phrase—"As the twig is bent, so is the tree inclined"—to which we often pay lip service, but which psychoanalysis insists on taking seriously and literally. There must be the concrete "twig," the physical body and nervous system of the baby; it is "bent" by environmental forces and grows thereafter in the distorted form; and the way the personality is "inclined" can be seen later in overt symptoms. Psychoanalysis points to specific parts of the human body significant in pleasure-rewarded learning of adaptive and necessary physiological acts; it notes characteristic features in the human environment of primary importance, the mother and father; it describes the relation of body demands (id) to the conscious mind (ego), and of the ego to society (superego) and the physical world (reality). Taking these simple postulates, psychoanalysis relentlessly pursues their corollaries, upsetting and surprising as these may be. Psychoanalysis is positivistic, empirical, phenomenological, and concrete.

Individual personality, then, according to psychoanalytic psychology, is a structure incorporating all the experiences of the ego in meeting these components of psychological reality. Each later psychological phase builds on the victories and defeats of earlier ones. Each earlier phase shapes the later, for example, oral gratification-frustration certainly influences the process of undergoing social discipline in the anal period; in turn, anal rebelliousness may carry over into and color Oedipal conflict; and the resolution of phallic-Oedipal problems deeply conditions the genital constitution of the individual.

Further, every neurosis, psychosis, and psychopathy is a major fixation at or regression to some growth stage, and represents continuing unresolved conflicts (now repressed) at one or a combination of the pregenital phases. Schizophrenia is the lack of libidinal reality of the outside world, resulting from primary frustration of oral dependency needs and the acquired fixed habit of fantasying magic-symbolic libidinal gratification instead. The schizophrenic has not been loved into, rewarded into accepting the gratifying reality and the frustrating separateness of the now present, now absent mother; he must be for himself the whole world narcissistically and libidinally. Schizophrenia is hard to cure because it represents traumata at a very archaic level of ego development, with at best only precarious development in later phases; disturbance at the pre-verbal oral object level means that in schizophrenia it is very difficult to make human contact with the therapist. Alcoholics, often literal "bottle-babies," still seek the magic ego-enhancing liquid potency, now ambiguously masculine-feminine; they commonly marry dominating women who want a phallus without a man behind it, and whom the alcoholic punishes with his provocative infantilism. Though partly an oral disturbance, alcoholism is far easier to cure than schizophrenia because there is often relatively strong growth in later phases that enables the therapist to work with and build on them.

Compulsive obsessives, fixated mainly at the anal level, are somewhat less difficult to work with than schizophrenics because of a further matured ego; but they still do much magic-symbolic thinking, have relatively feeble ego boundaries, and maintain massive resistance to the influence of another person; compulsive obsessives still struggle for complete anal-omnipotent management of the whole world as if the only reality were the body and body contents. Manic-depression is the fluctuating self-image learned from ambivalent parents in early oral-anal and other conditioning, with consequently very unstable superego-ego tonuses; depression is more susceptible to therapy than mania because of greater accessibility to outside influence, though in depression the ego is weak, whereas in mania the ego is in full flight from any constrictions. Paranoia is the (chiefly male) struggle for the father's archaic-level omnipotence and love. Hysteria (chiefly female) is oral-dependent-colored phallic conflict over possession of the father; hence the frequency of oral-pregnancy fantasies (stomach-baby) in hysteria, *anorexia nervosa* or eating disturbances, and so on—but hysteria is relatively easier to treat by therapy because of ready suggestibility and accessibility to a father authority. (Freud early used hypnosis in hysteria, but decided that only "symptomatic" or "transference" cure could result if there is no participation of the conscious ego of the patient; nevertheless, because of the relative transparency of hysteric defenses, he was able to learn much initially from hysterics). Perversions are phallic-period fixations in oral, anal, or other pregenital zone terms; they represent "genitalization" of basically oral and anal libido. And, finally, psychopathy is a superego pathology representing only part-identification and conflict with a hated (and possibly hating) father; understandably the therapist encounters built-in difficulties in working with psychopaths.

These "pure type" classic syndromes can of course also be mixed symptomatically, for there is nothing to prevent idiosyncratic mixtures of libidinal traumata in individual patients; because of this conception, analysts are less interested in pigeonholing syndromes than in understanding dynamics. By contrast with the types described above, the "genital character"—obviously another pure-type construct, since no individual has enjoyed problemless growth—can have all kinds of libidinal cakes and eat them all too. Through cumulative "amphimictic" growth in all stages he can enjoy food, drink, and people without distorting irrational components, disabling guilt, and psychic energy tied up in major unfinished battles raging in the unconscious. The mature person can enjoy lustily all body functions without antisocial hostility, be appropriately aggressive or accommodative in proper proportion and contexts, and achieve full maleness or femaleness without fear of body damage as the consequence of enjoying it. The mature person has learned to love from loving parents, whom he now sees realistically as persons and not as fearsome images in child-written dramas. Freud's definition of the mature person is one who is able to work and to love, because work we are fitted for achieves sublimation of all pregenital needs, and genital needs can be expressed directly in love.

Although following each unwelcome insight into its ultimate ramifications in many varieties of individual makes psychoanalysis both difficult intellectually and disturbing emotionally, Freud maintains that complexity is inherent in the human data and may not be oversimplified out of existence. Freud further observed that nearly all psychic events are "over-determined." That is, they have many complex and simultaneously operating causes. This complexity is demonstrated in the fact of "condensation" that may occur in a single dream symbol (another reason for not indulging in facile *ad hoc* interpretations). That is, a single symbol may quite uncannily "condense" into itself a fantastic amount of meanings when its implications are followed out in free association. The semantic complexity is an analogue of the complexity of the brain and the complexity of life experience itself.

Overdetermination and condensation mean that single-cause statements are oversimplified and probably wrong. Hence those who insist on thinking in terms of single-cause formulas have an easy straw man to set up and destroy. In each individual there is a *complex* of causes, though the component causes may differ and operate in different people in different contexts. Consequently, the findings of psychoanalysis are difficult to *generalize*, each case being in some way unique. By contrast, one atom of an isotope of oxygen may behave *identically* like another; i.e., they are in one-to-one comparability with one another and can be meaningfully discussed numerically since numbers properly can summarize and generalize only comparables. Persons who can deal only with complex data when falsely denuded to numbers will always be frustrated with the semantic irreducibility of words and meanings to numbers: the denotations and connotations are endlessly rich, like a psychiatric "complex." Psychological data are more like words than numbers. Verbal-minded people are more apt in handling psychoanalytic data, therefore, than are number-minded people. Number-minded temperaments are likely to have a vast impatience with psychoanalysis on "purely scientific" grounds. Unfortunately, the content of the Oedipus complex, for example, may be almost tiresomely similar in one patient after another, and yet each person remains unique in his complex.

Such summary formulas as the analyst is able to make about the universal human Oedipus complex—beyond its anxiety-arousing nature—must therefore lack the overwhelming convincingness of the countless corroborating details present in a single specific case. Probably no person has ever been emotionally convinced of the reality of the Oedipus complex until he has encountered it analytically in himself—though the cold intellectual fact remains that *every known human group has the nuclear-family incest-taboo.* The anthropological fact is somehow easier to accept than the psychiatric consequences of the same fact. Every human being faces the Oedipal predicament, and yet every single Oedipus complex is somehow unique. It is not that analysts are number-shy mystics but that their data do not admit of simplified reductionism. The analyst even thinks that reductionism falsifies his data, since it is the dynamic configuration that is significant. The numbering of uniquenesses ignores their significant quiddity.

If the normal reader's resistance has not yet been aroused by our rapid review of the dynamics of the various neuroses, psychoses, and psychopathies (since he shares none of these dynamics in disabling or unfaceable degree), or by our uncompromising insistence on the reality of the Oedipus complex (which is, in fact, in every human being), perhaps we can make the fact of resistance psychologically real by discussing now material certain to arouse anxiety by reason of the universality of another complex. This is an area of common experience that has been or still is acutely painful to every one of us. It is the *castration complex*, though this differs in males and females.

At some time early in life, every little boy and every little girl becomes aware of the physical differences of the other sex. For the boy this means that there are persons who do not have what he has, external genitals, a situation he can only believe results from their having lost this "normal" and taken-for-granted, indeed pleasure-giving, part of his body. The lack raises the frightening possibility that he could and might lose his too, either in punishment for guilty wishes or in punishment for forbidden pleasure. Since there are several pleasure zones in the body, castration anxiety is part of a larger "separation anxiety" from the source of gratification. At birth he suffered the "birth trauma" of losing complete gratification and protection in a physiological Eden, where every metabolic wish was continuously granted. Now he had to learn new methods of blood oxidation, heat control, nourishment and elimination (perhaps colic is so common a problem because of some difficulty in learning all at once the intricate process of digestion). As a weanling he lost the mother's breast. In toilet training he had to learn not especially welcome discipline concerning his own body contents—and now he may lose his pleasure-giving genitals also (thus castration means for the boy the specific loss of the penis, not the testes).

For the little girl, sexual difference means that she has lost what boys have, either unfairly or as a punishment. Thus she feels deprived, inferior and envious, and may even fantasy that somehow the organ will one day magically grow back. The appearance of bleeding at menstruation commonly reactivates the female castration complex at puberty, and she may feel deeply frightened at this new "proof" of her "mutilation." The uncontrollability of the flow may also reactivate cleanliness-training problems again and arouse shame. Residually, even when a grown woman she may still feel some deep fear of body damage in sexual intercourse or childbirth. (Men, too, can fear genital damage at intercourse, in the fantasy of the "vagina dentata" and the general dangerousness of woman). Because her presumed "deprivation" has always been the case, most women are able to recapture memory of earlier "penis envy," though in many women the complex becomes repressed early and comes out in various irrational symbolic demands to be treated as identical to men. "Female courage" has nothing to lose; besides, she can always exploit her advantages as a woman.

In males, however, because damage to or loss of external genitals is still a dreaded and real possibility, the male castration complex is characteristically very deeply repressed. The poignancy of male strength and courage lies in the fact that he still remains tenderly vulnerable. The castration complex in males may be further complicated by a usually still more deeply repressed envy of women and their lot, envy of their greater retention of the permitted passivity and dependence which he also enjoyed as a child but which he has had to replace with more dangerous, aggressively competitive activity; envy of the female breast, rudimentary in him, but its pleasure potential dimly discernible in analogy to penis pleasure; and even envy of the female's ability to have a baby, which both sexes early fantasy in the oral-anal terms of body experience of these other zones. The terribleness of his envy consists in its sometimes being a monstrous wish desperately defended against, to get rid of the whole problem entirely; and there are actually some few cases where men have had themselves surgically made "women."

The normal adult, however, comes to "possess" a mate. This is no idle metaphor, but a psychological reality. A man can take endless pride in what his "possession" is, a woman who has everything he lacks and cannot do—women can take mere groceries and miraculously turn them into delicious food. Remaining drab himself, he can still obtain much gratification in enhancing her femininity with clothes, furs, jewels and home, and display his successful masculine prowess at the same time. His emotionally married identification with her can even be sexual, for a loving husband commonly has great anxiety at the birth of a child (the *couvade* or "male childbirth" drama is fairly common among privitive peoples also). Consciously, he may have some guilt at what his aggressive male sexuality has "done to" her; unconsciously, his own womb-envy and castration anxiety may be aroused, even to the point of a literal new "separation anxiety" in potentially losing his pleasure-giving object at childbirth.

Conversely, a woman symbolically obtains a penis in her man. Remaining modestly feminine herself, she may still obtain great vicarious pleasure in the male aggressiveness of her man, boast of his successes, and suffer with his defeats (a woman can tenderly identify especially with defeat, for she has intimately known pain and loss in her own body). Curiously, for many normal women, having a child unconsciously symbolizes obtaining a penis; certainly in her sons she gains further foils for her vicarious enjoyment of masculinity and her fomenting of it in males she loves. Perhaps men marvel at the truly astonishing ability of feminine women to identify with loved males only because man's own conscious masculinity must deny his unconscious feminine component, so that he must loudly boast he "just cannot understand women." (But psychological fatherhood consists a great deal in learning from women.)

Sexual difference is not dangerous, after all, either to men or to women, when "possession" of a mate of the other sex represents a further amphimictic triumph. In the "genital character" that achieves a firm and unfearing self-possession of his or her sexual identity, castration anxiety is transcended. The individual loves being a man or a woman. And what is wrong with loving another different body as much as one's own? The castration complex will of course vary in individuals, depending on whether the boy has been overtly threatened with penis loss, either "playfully" in teasing or more seriously as the consequence of masturbation; whether he has been overthreatened by having a seductive hysteric mother or insecure brutal father; or whether the girl has been properly prepared for menstruation—and depending on a host of other factors, including each parent's conscious and unconscious evaluation of his own and the other sex, parental preference for another sex in the child, and so on.

The castration complex here becomes implicated again with another involving the parents, the ubiquitous Oedipus complex (often called "Electra complex" in females). The child of either sex normally has *loved oral-dependently* the mother as a source of physiological gratification. When sexuality supervenes, if a boy, the child must now give up this first love object, to retain his physical maleness in competition with the more powerful father, who properly possesses the mother as a genital but not alimentary property as the child had. To achieve psychological genitality, as described above, the boy must find substitute female objects for his love or else give up the heterosexual aim entirely and remain fixated at the same-sex-loving phallic level, as a male homosexual who stays childishly attached to mother and pretends he passively loves men orally as a pseudo-child or anally as a pseudo-woman. To become masculine like his father, the boy must give up the father's sexual love object and find another like her; he must also change his body modality of relating to females from the passive-oral to the active-genital. (Here again is manifest the fact of different zone modalities of loving, since all love is a tender concern for the source of any kind of libidinal gratification.)

The girl child, on the other hand, must change the sex of her love object from mother to father. Since she has already suffered "castration," a girl commonly has closer to consciousness her sexual fantasy about an early love of her father, a new and more powerfully protective figure for her feminine dependency, and as a male one who is able to give her a baby. But in resolving the "Electra" competition with mother—less frightening than the boy's Oedipal conflict with the father—she must next find another male than father to love. Female sexuality is consequently more complex and derived. It is also more secret and hidden, for whereas a male can never deny or be in doubt about sexual arousal, a girl may sometimes actually not know.

Boys are perhaps more fiercely embattled in growing up. They must go farther from childhood and change the most in relation to women from passive dependence to aggressive dominance; and they must constantly prove that they have made the masculine journey from child to man. But male love for women, given the fact of motherhood, is psychologically simple and transparent. The girl's coming to love men is a more intricate process and, in terms of early need gratification, more obscure than male love of women, or a female's love of her own femininity, both via mother. Why men love women is no problem: they loved their mothers. Why women love men is highly problematical. One supposition is that the girl simply transfers her childhood dependency from mother to father (Why? Because he is a stronger and more dominating protective figure of both mother and daughter, or because as a male he is more loving and indulgent of his daughter?) Another supposition is that women love men because men have what they lack, or that only a man can give them a baby. But in this, as in other explanations, psychoanalysis can perhaps properly be accused of being a male-centered psychology, for women are not just unmales but *sui generis* in their own right. Still another explanation is that the encompassing narcissistic self-love of motherhood that includes her baby also includes mothering loved men, for women physiologically have more ways of loving than men do. Perhaps men are debarred from this understanding simply because they do not have female bodies. Feminine sexuality is certainly hard to understand!

The psychological fact of experiencing different bodies, in any case, explains a number of differences in sexual temperament. Men must learn courage in order to face and to transcend castration anxiety and to achieve their masculinity and psychophysical "integrity." Nevertheless, it is the male, often the most masculine one, who is most threatened by any surgical operation or other symbolic body mutilation. In being male he is still most vulnerable. Women, already knowing pain in menstruation, defloration, and childbirth, are more stoic in facing this kind of pain—indeed, may be more accustomed to making the masochistic symbolic "bargain" with guilt in surgical operations—because pain has often been followed with pleasure and triumphs of feminine fulfilment. Thus women are sometimes polysurgical hysterics, men almost never.

Again, male masturbation is commonly more guilt laden than female masturbation, and more rigorously suppressed. The male superego is also commonly more stern and uncompromising; the female can more easily say that the rules do not apply to her because of anatomical "injustice" and therefore she has "something coming to her." Besides, males take in masculine superego demands primarily from males (chiefly father) and hence fulfill their masculinity in this process of introjection; but the process applies less to women (fathers indulge daughters more than sons, and the Electra complex and counter-complex are more direct than is Oedipal *rivalry* over the mother), and women take in part of the superego from females (that is, femininity from the mother). Male sexuality *overwhelms* obstacles, because the normal man resolves his castration complex by accepting that, once the male-imposed incest rule is respected, then active male sexuality will go unpunished by castration. The female castration complex is resolved by accepting femininity and *acquiring* a penis-bearing man. Therefore female sexuality *accepts* a gift, because the normal woman wants a baby and knows only accepting a male can give her one and thus fulfil her basic femininity. Men fear being unable to *perform* (being unable to love); women fear *being unloved* (being unlovable). Women are concrete personalities; they first love *this* man and *this* child because these symbolize narcissistic possessions or gains, although they may later generalize their love socially, but still concretely and personally. After giving up the mother—a more intense love, because once more physiological, than the girl's love for her father—men are abstractionists and generalists, and perhaps poorer monogamists than women. Men can manifest fierce respect for abstract and artificial Oedipal hierarchies such as those in the military, which women find merely ridiculous or incomprehensible and seek constantly to undermine on personal grounds. Male narcissism is derived and intensely symbolic; female narcissism is more primary and physical. Men are more commonly the symbolic creators of money, symbolic dominance-prowess, science, art, and social structures (law, the state), because only women can naively and obviously really create (grow a baby). Hence men must constantly *prove* their masculinity and fear its loss or impugning, whereas women (once having transcended the castration complex) can more passively and complacently *be* feminine. Sexual differences in social role, therefore, are not so much intellectual as motivational and emotional: individuals may differ in their position on a masculine-feminine gamut and yet still manifest definitely masculine versus feminine characteristics and trends. Besides, every individual introjects from both parents: the doctor may borrow a more-than-typical male compassion for other people from his mother while yet insisting intensely on male dominance and fatherly control of his patients; a woman can be a formidable politician while yet employing feminine wiles too.

An acknowledged and perhaps inescapable scientific difficulty with psychoanalysis is the "nonreplicability" of its data (quite apart from the uniqueness of each case). One must be present, either as analyst or analyzand, in order to *witness the data.* And, because of our normal resistances and our thinking (falsely) that we "know ourselves," it is really impossible intellectually to translate the analyst's public scientific generalizations into their full visceral-emotional reality—as when, with shock and surprise, we discover they apply to us in every inescapable detail. Both proselytizing analyzand and reluctant unanalyzed persons must admit, in all fairness, that psychological revelation and the psychiatrist's pointing out its significance both occur in a private, privileged, protected situation with no one else present; hence it is difficult to convey the transactions publicly or fully enough—again, even apart from the quite understandable defenses normal people have against insight into such fearsome and terrible things. However, for some degree of understanding, all we need do is to attend any clinical "Grand Rounds" on a psychiatric case, or listen carefully with an open mind to any psychotic in the State Hospital—in each instance deciding in safe psychological privacy whether our ability to see is not first an insight into ourselves—at least to be convinced that really desperate and dangerous matters are involved. It is in fact a demonstration of our own equilibrium and strength if we can listen without being overwhelmed by anxiety. For this reason, every psychiatrist must be carefully and exhaustively trained to know himself, since we can only afford to see clinically what we have first acknowledged in ourselves.

Psychoanalysis has several assumptions it now shares with other psychologies. First is *psychic determinism*. Everything that happens in the mind is part of a lawfully determined universe. Every psychic event has causes and effects, as inevitable as brain chemistry, no matter how multiple and obscure and complex these events are, and no matter how difficult to discover and to discern and to discuss completely. Any attempt at heated, special pleading that at least *this* event is "purely accidental" or "meaningless" points, in that very protest, the relentless finger of evidence. Consequently, full classic psychoanalysis has a very clear understanding of how and why some "neo-Freudians" like Rank and Jung and Adler have each erected their own unanalyzed portions into a system, even though they have all made contributions that can be accepted into the analytic tradition.[h]

Another discovery psychoanalysis now shares widely with other psychologies is that all that goes on in the conscious mind does not exhaust the whole activity of the mind. There is an *unconscious* part of the psychic economy that can be demonstrated in such phenomena as hypnosis, dreams, memory, multiple personality, and the like. The only uniqueness nowadays is that psychoanalysis uses the technique of "free association" in which the patient is allowed freely to fantasy and to say absolutely anything he wants to. Everyone these days knows about the many brilliant and successful *alternative* research techniques of the clinical psychologist in uncovering the same unconscious content of the mind—the Rorschach Test, the Thematic Apperception Test, and many other projective techniques. To understand these techniques is inevitably to respect them. They are justifiably regarded as powerful diagnostic tools. Therapeutically, however, old-fashioned id analysis insists that the *conscious insight of the patient* into his psychic mechanisms is necessary if the executive ego is to take charge, now with a fuller awareness and understanding of the problem.[i]

---

h. For example, Jung's early psychoanalytic understanding of schizophrenia is a magnificent and permanent contribution. By the same token, we can criticize Freud himself for being too "Jungian" in projecting the Oedipal situation once and for all back into the mythological past— whence it reaches us as a kind of Lamarckian "acquired characteristic" of the "folk unconscious!" Similar critiques can be made of Rank and Adler, and at the same time some of these apply to Freud. Any "orthodoxy" arrived at by many highly critical and keen minds lies in the unavoidable facts of human nature.

i. In the adjective "old-fashioned" I refer to classic id-analysis, which is so lengthy and expensive that, given the shortage of qualified analysts, this is nowadays best confined to research persons and those who wish to become psychiatrists. Modern "ego-analysis," though harder to conduct in the sense that it requires superlative skill of the analyst in picking out major items to deal with, often does not require "total" insight in the patient for a cure. But it is more economical

This understanding comes only from a long and patient process in which the subject brings out one example after another of a behavior which, after a while, the analyst invites the patient to compare, and then to decide for himself whether these mechanisms are really there and characteristically do operate—but only against the most intense resistance of the subject to reopening old wounds. Defense mechanisms intervene between joint sharing of these details and the belated acknowledgement of their reality. The analyst does not have to argue or indoctrinate, because the data are now open-facedly there and will certainly come up again another time. The insight of the analyst is not automatically equivalent to the patient's.

Strangely, "free association" has to be learned, the relentless intellectual and emotional honesty of saying without censorship anything that comes into the mind, however ugly, ridiculous, shameful, aggressive, obscene, or seemingly trivial. Every patient must learn this through long preliminary testing out and gradually coming to trust his psychiatrist—that absolutely anything the patient says is heard without punishment or judgment, rejection or moral indignation from the analyst. Then emerges the extraordinary phenomenon of "transference." Transference is often misunderstood to mean "falling in love" with the analyst, but this is erroneous and misses the real point of the phenomenon. What happens is that as the analyst is more and more experienced by the patient as a neutral listener who does not demand the usual adaptive and sail-trimming social protocol, gradually in more and more pure form the patient begins to treat him *as if he were* the person who was critically important to the particular problem in the past.

Examining the transference is a *research technique*, for here are laid bare the now uncensored feelings of the patient toward his parents and siblings as a child. The analyst does not fatuously think that all his patients are in love with him. On the contrary, he knows that what the patient projects onto the blank screen *has nothing to do* with the analyst's real private personality—a useful knowledge when the analyst has to absorb unjust and abusive comments as well as expressions of twisted kinds of love. In order to remain less a real person, the analyst commonly sits out of sight behind the patient lying relaxed on the couch; also, the trained analyst constantly examines his own feelings of "countertransference" for what his free-floating attention and understanding of his own unconscious can teach him about the patient—with all of which he scrupulously refrains from burdening the patient. Thus, at the patient's protestations of love, he is likely, to the surprise and edification of the patient, to point out ambivalent components of the patient's "love."

---

of time and money, though not of pain. Furthermore, much therapy is not technically "analysis" but merely "psychoanalytically oriented therapy." Indeed, many primitive techniques of curing, if dynamically sound and despite irrational native rationale, can result in cure without the conscious insight of either patient or therapist. For evidence of this, see Ari Kiev (ed.), *Magic, Faith, and Healing* (New York: The Free Press, 1964), and Marvin K. Opler (ed.), *Culture and Mental Health* (New York: The Macmillan Company, 1959).

Curious and unexpected phenomena emerge in the transference: commonly the patient treats the male analyst as if he were, say, a tenderly overprotective mother, or a female analyst as if she were a sternly authoritative father. The content of every transference statement is, in this, similar to the Rorschach Test: any "meaning" is not in the meaningless cards or the faceless nonperson of the analyst but only in the mind of the projecting subject. Again, a transference from parent to therapist may not necessarily be a loving one, since sometimes children hate their parents. A transference can be violently "negative" (hate filled) in feeling and still yield useful data, if that was the problem with the parent, though a positive transference is easier to deal with therapeutically and the patient is less likely precipitately to leave off the analysis. Meanwhile, the analyst knows that the patient's hatred does not really apply to him either, though he has painfully to teach through his neutrality that he is not in fact the hateful parent. Slowly the patient realizes that his transference statements are only his real feelings laid bare. The analyst has mirrored back the patient's own psychological visage.

It is true, of course, that transference-like phenomena do occur outside analysis, since we meet each unknown new person with our habitual feelings and experiences from the past. It is sometimes startling to realize how we unconsciously collect people to play roles in our private dramas, say, an angry, arbitrary father in a little-known but really quite benevolent and decent boss. "Falling in love at first sight" can be elicited by a single cue of similarity to the parent loved in the past (the girl has red hair like mother's) and "punch the button" for projective fantasy. But such "love" cannot, by definition, proceed from a full knowledge of the actual personality of the unknown "loved" one, and he who marries in haste can repent in leisure. "First love" is rather like a Rorschach, in which we learn mostly about ourselves, painfully, when the part-transference collapses through accumulating knowledge of the object. Authentic love can occur only in knowing both subject and object, and both accepting both mutually. Thus, to speak loosely of transference to mean affection in ordinary social situations is of course merely silly.

There is one further difficulty. Freud believed that every neurosis—and every person is technically neurotic to some degree—is a frustration of and impediment to normal growth. The neurosis is a protective scab over the crippling wound. At one time in the individual's past, the anxiety of new and then insoluble problems overwhelmed the weak but growing adaptive ego of the child. That is, he became "fixated" (massively or mildly) at that stage in his development, and still struggles now with the same buried and unresolved problem that other persons normally will have solved. Thus the "normal" person quite truly does not actively suffer from an "Oedipus complex" in the sense that it cripples him from loving other women than the mother; but he nevertheless did once face the Oedipal *predicament* which is the lot of every man. The normal man quite commonly encounters, if he is fortunate, maternal tenderness and sometimes arbitrarily loving acceptance in the woman he loves; but she is not his mother, and he is not her son. Similarly, a normal woman quite commonly encounters, if she is fortunate, paternal strength and loving protectiveness in her husband; but he is not her father, and she is not his child. It is only that mature love has its roots deep in childhood.

By contrast, the neurotic's ego is *functionally mutilated* in its ability to solve the problem, whatever it is, because the whole overwhelming conflict was finally repressed into the unconscious. And there it still boils explosively, like a soup pot with the lid tightly on, now coming out as a symptom, now as intense anxiety, and again as neurotic "acting out."*j* The whole job of therapy is to discover the old forgotten griefs and terrifying experiences and frightening impulses and woefully lost battles, then to face and understand them with the more mature resources of the now older person; first to rely on the unafraid analyst, and then to let the strengthened ego of the patient take over again the continuing task of running his own life. There is no magic in it, only intellectually honest and emotionally sincere struggle, pain, and hard work. No one can be expected to understand Freud unless he is willing and able to make, in some fashion, the perilous and frightening journey into the past. But if he can and does, he will see all these things for himself.

j. Again there is a gross misconception current about "acting out." Properly speaking, this means that the patient is not able to verbalize his problem but "acts out" his conflict in real life outside the analysis, and then tells the analyst about it later. Though not an ideal method of communication, and sometimes dangerous, acting out does provide the analyst, and the patient, with significant data which they can use by analyzing it. To use "acting out" loosely to mean merely *manifesting one's neurosis* unfortunately has become a current cliché for people who do not know what it means.

Reference Notes

1. W. H. Auden, *The Collected Poems of W. H. Auden* (New York: Random House, Inc., 1945), p. 166. This poet has a precise and sure knowledge of what Freud was about.
2. The main sources are Freud's *Interpretation of Dreams (Complete Psychological Works of Sigmund Freud*, ed. James Strachey, "Standard Edition," [London: Hogarth Press, Ltd., 1953, Vols. 4 and 5]; *Collected Papers of Sigmund Freud* [New York: Basic Books, Inc., Vol. 3, 1959]; and Avon Books; *Three Contributions to the Theory of Sex* (New York and Washington: Nervous and Mental Disease Publishing Company, 1930); also in *The Basic Writings of Sigmund Freud* (New York: Modern Library, 1938), pp. 181–549, but the Strachey translations are to be preferred, in the Basic Books paperback and *Standard Edition*); and also Freud's *The Ego and the Id* (London: Hogarth Press, Ltd., 1927), *Beyond the Pleasure Principle* (London: Hogarth Press, Ltd., 1922), *Civilization and Its Discontents* (London: Hogarth Press, Ltd., 1930)—the last three long essays also to be found in the *Standard Edition*. After Freud, the classical psychoanalytic works are *Selected Papers of Karl Abraham* (London: Hogarth Press, Ltd., 1927); Sandor Ferenczi, *Further Contributions to the Theory and Technique of Psycho-Analysis* (London: Hogarth Press, Ltd., 1926); Ernest Jones. *Essays in Applied Psycho-Analysis* (London: Hogarth Press, Ltd., 1923), and *Papers on Psycho-Analysis* (Baltimore: Williams and Wilkins Co., 1912, also Beacon [paperback]). The best introduction to Freud is

by Karin Stephen, *Psychoanalysis and Medicine, A Study of the Wish to Fall Ill* (London: Cambridge University Press, 1939); the best single-volume compendium, but for the advanced student, is Otto Fenichel, *The Psychoanalytic Theory of Neurosis* (New York: W. W. Norton & Company, 1945). A remarkable biography is by Ernest Jones, *The Life and Work of Sigmund Freud* (New York: Basic Books, Inc., 3 vols., 1953–1957; also available in paperback in abbreviated form). A magisterial understanding of Freud in his cultural context is by the distinguished Yale historian, Peter Gay, *Freud, Jews and Other Germans* (New York: Oxford University Press, 1979).

6. Anthropological Perspectives on Sexuality

Anthropology, as the comparative study of man, is a mixture of biological, historical, psychological, and social sciences. While this mixture often gives broad-scale opportunities for the interfertilization of sciences, it also forces the anthropologist to be careful about his categories and the location of his subject matter. The nature and the accurate discrimination of male/female differences within their common humanity has probably preoccupied people since the beginning of human time. We should not then be surprised if, in our complex species, the study of sexuality, like that of anthropology itself, belongs to all the above categories.

The basic biological question is, perhaps, why sexuality at all? Many single-celled species, both of plants and animals, get along without sexuality. With successful nutrition, single protozoan cells could grow larger indefinitely—except for one inexorable geometric fact. The food-obtaining and waste-excreting skin increases only as the square of the diameter of the cell, but the metabolizing volume increases as the cube, and an impasse is soon reached. However, by dividing the cell through *fission*, an economical ratio of volume to surface is restored—with the accidental advantage that two, then four, then eight . . . daughter-cells, especially if they move into different separated areas, have a better chance for survival. Reproduction through fission, however, though it brings an accidentally adaptive result from successful nutrition, has no genetic significance since all the daughter-cells are genetically identical. But if one cell lineage should happen to have a random mutation, this would still never become available to other single-cell lineages, which may meanwhile have achieved other adaptive mutations. Evolution would be stymied at its outset.

Some single-celled species, like the slipper-shaped animalcule *Paramecium*, have a halfway solution to the problem: after dividing indefinitely in a vegetative fashion, sometimes two individual *Paramecia* will moor side-by-side like a pair of rowboats and exchange nuclear genetic material, then separate, and go off again seemingly invigorated and reproducing indefinitely by fission. The system appears to have its advantages though, since one species, *Paramecium aurelia*—lest we suppose two sexes are all there can be—has eight different "sexes" and *Chlamydomonas* has ten, five "male" and five "female," all reacting with different degrees of intensity to their opposite sexes. But the only way to add the *total* advantages of two lineages is not through this halfway "en-

This chapter was originally an address given as part of a symposium for students at Ann Arbor, Michigan, on 14 January 1969, and was later published. It is from *Sexuality: A Search for Perspectives*, ed. Donald L. Grummon and Andrew M. Barclay. © 1971 by Litton Educational Publishing, Inc. Reprinted by permission of D. Van Nostrand Company.

domixis," however multiplied the sexes, but for two cells to join by *fusion* into one. Sexuality, properly speaking, begins through such fusion, and the whole vast panorama of later evolution is based upon this invention of sexuality, which alone combines adaptive heredities. Indeed, modern "eukaryotic" animal cells are based on *four* separate heredities living together in one cell—and plant cells have *five* such obligatory symbiotes! Judging from later evolution, fusion would seem to have great genetic advantages over simple fission.

Birds and animals, we observe, often have markedly contrastive male and female individuals (some Lake Titicaca fishes are sexually so dimorphous they were thought to belong to different species). These differences always have a functional significance in species-specific ecology. Take the ground-living, slow-foraging baboons of Africa and Asia. Here the larger males, who stay on the periphery of the band, have developed murderously long canine fangs to protect the whole group. Size and specialized protectiveness have come to reside in the male evidently because the occasional death of a male is less significant to the continuity of the band than that of a reproductively more precious female. Of course more males would increase the protection afforded the band, but many such large animals would bear too heavily on the food supply, which is limited because of the slow movement of the enclosed females and juveniles. The solution is given by allocating more of the nutritionally limited "biomass" of the band to a larger number of smaller females, thereby increasing reproductivity. In general then, survival of this species is facilitated by having a limited number of large protective males and a greater number of smaller reproductive females. Sexuality has adapted to ecology.

Lest it be thought that I linger too long on the protozoans, the birds, and the fishes—and will never get to the higher apes you are interested in—let me point out that these different sexual dispensations highlight our own as *only one kind* of sexuality; in short, I hope I have established beyond doubt that sexuality has always and inescapably a biological-ecological significance!

In the same African environment as baboons, and with much the same body size and foraging ecology, the anthropoid ape lineage of early man (baboons belong to a monkey lineage) adapted quite differently *by effectively changing the food-ecology*. While other primates are now know to be occasional, though largely accidental meateaters, the first "human revolution" began when the more active peripheral males temporarily separated from the band and formed active all-male groups to hunt animals for meat. The results in the adaptive evolutionary "hominization" of the species are still sexual-ecological and species-specific to a marked degree.

Anatomically, human males are generally larger, with more massive musculature and bones, and relatively fat-nude for the purpose of radiating body heat produced during the expenditure of massive amounts of energy as in hunting.[a] Longer-limbed hunting males are also adapted to a more rapid metabo-

---

a. Slow foraging primates can radiate heat slowly. Loss of primate hair in humans is a still further functional step beyond hunting males' fat-nudity. Caucasoid males are hairier than Ne-

lism physiologically, in their larger lungs and larger number of red blood cells per cubic centimeter. But shorter-legged females do not have to be adapted like wild animals to hunting, for they are technically and literally domesticates—protection from natural wild enemies, man-provided food, and selective breeding being the specific criteria for domestication—removed by the male from the wild animal state of self provision. At the same time, *group hunting*, necessary both with swift ungulates in Africa and mammoths in Europe alike, gives individual males an equity in the kill. Meat provides a higher proteid commodity for selective favoritism in sharing with females, whence the emergence of marriage regulations and kin-family. Thus, family and kin, along with the ecologically necessary social group, are everywhere the norm among human beings. With meat sharing and protection by males, human females can then specialize in prolonged maternity and child care. For group survival under primitive conditions, child bearing must have been of necessity almost continuous. The temporary mammalian teat becomes the permanent breast in the human female (the same sometimes occurs among man's other selectively bred domesticates as well). Likewise, the menstrual cycle replaces seasonal oestrus, concomitant with nonseasonal year-round breeding and sexuality-motivated family cohesion. Humans have not ditched their mammalian inheritance; they have *intensified* both sexual drive in the male and maternal care in the female. But if marriage is strongly female-motivated economically, then exclusiveness of sexual claim would appear to be male-motivated for clear biological-economic reasons, judged also from the commonness and economic base of polygyny and the comparative rarity of polyandry.

We speak of "dimorphism" of specialization in the baboon band. More properly it is "trimorphism" in the human family, biologically. The human infant, as big-brained at birth as a widened female pelvis can allow, can in turn within a family nexus *specialize in mother-nurtured infancy*. For brain growth, largely finished at birth among other primates, continues in humans for some time after birth. Even though one-seventh of the human baby's birth weight is in brain, it is still born "prematurely" (noninstinct-prepared) for a brainy learning animal, whose whole postcranial growth is largely postnatal. Moreover, brain size increases progressively as well in hominids, as we know from the fossil series, as if brains were an adaptive trait. The human family clearly makes man a new kind of animal in ecological adaptation. But dependence of infantile individuals is meanwhile a biological burden on adults, hence prolonged human infancy must have some adaptive advantage for the group. This

---

groid perhaps because they reached higher latitudes (where insulating hair would be adaptive) before the process was complete, as in Negroids remaining in the same tropical African habitat. Again, specialization in an increased darkness of skin in some Africans (from a generic primate and mammalian brown) still further facilitates diffusion of body heat, as indeed would also the marked linearity of males in some African groups. "Male bonding" and "instinctive aggression" in males from the hunting experience I consider unproven and dubious, on grounds discussed in my review of a fine Ashley Montagu-edited book, *Man and Aggression* (New York: Oxford University Press, 1968), in *American Anthropologist* 71 (1969), 912–15.

advantage, so the argument goes, is learned *culture*, which enables individuals and societies to tap the larger past experience of the whole species, as if culture and language in this big-brained social species were more adaptive than fixed instincts. It is evidently useful and necessary for adolescents as they are maturing to criticize the cultural past, for a good deal of any culture is noxious nonsense. But those who do not learn the past, in order to scrutinize and select from it in largest possible measure, would fatuously discard the essence of their humanity.

In this comprehensive biological view, then, specialized maleness and femaleness and infancy in the familial trinity are intrinsic to the species' humanity. But here, in order to pursue the same tough-minded biological argument, we must emphasize that *the ecological conditions of humanity have now changed enormously.* Quite as birth control and the control of venereal diseases have released us from taboos on sexuality necessary and useful (economically, socially, and medically) in a past situation, so also the enormous reproductive success of the family system has emancipated the female from an intenser reproductivity. The gradual emancipation of the female from the burden of reproductivity, in fact, is a biological trend visible in the whole evolution from fish to amphibians, to mammals and to primates, all from changed ecologies that procured an increasingly greater survival of their young. Indeed, human reproductivity today has become itself an ecological problem: the adaptive potential of combined family-society as an animal plan has continued this biological trend and has transformed the demographic-ecological situation from that of early human times. This in no way impugns the functional importance and the reality of these adaptations during the long hominization of man, but rather confirms them. Nor have all traces of this specialized "trimorphism" suddenly disappeared biologically from the human scene. Along with dimorphism of the sexes anatomically, careful studies have established a concomitant dimorphism psychologically.[1] It could hardly have been otherwise, and the differences cannot be suddenly wished away. It is only that the conditions of adaptation are now new, inarguably permitting the female a richer participation in the nonsexual aspects of her humanity. Sexuality thus appears to have a largely libidinal future and freedom. But Freud is still right, that "anatomy is destiny." Sexual temperament is never "purely cultural," and it is always in part inescapably biological.

Indeed, there are at least ten levels on which we can discuss human sexuality, and these can be put into three major groupings: primary, secondary, and tertiary sexuality. "Primary sexuality" means the physical-anatomical givens of sex at birth, and these are:

1. *Biological cellular sex,* that is, the XX-XY patterning of chromosomes in the individual. Recently there has been some discussion of the "supermale" type, with an anomalous XYY chromosome pattern. This condition appears with some frequency in the criminal psychopath, as though an untypical en-

dowment with Y has burdened the individual with amounts of masculine behavioral aggressivity that foredoomed him to a life of crime (but it is a simpliste view of psychopathy to regard it as simply cellular in origin).

2. *Gonadal sex*, that is whether the sex glands, ovaries or testes, produce eggs or sperm.

3. *External genital anatomy*, concerning which there is sometimes considerable ambiguity, since maleness and femaleness are based on the same embryological ground plan, and analogous genital organs are in part a matter of size, as well as of differentiated shape and function. Administration of hormones or surgery or both can correct some of these ambiguities. But often it is a matter of psychiatric and medical judgment as to what to do, depending on other factors of the individual's upbringing and personal choice. Of course, also, it is sometimes possible to change surgically the anatomically normal person of one sex into a synthetic *ersatz* specimen of the other sex, known as a "transsexual." But that is a matter of psychopathology, not of the primary sexuality being discussed here.

4. *Anatomy of the internal accessory reproductive structures.* Without sufficient study it is possible to modify external genitalia surgically, but inconsistently with the internal sexual morphology (uterus versus prostate gland, etc.).

In addition to these primary anatomical givens, there are also "secondary" sexual characteristics. These traits are those aspects of gross maleness and femaleness in texture, body proportions, and conformation, that appear most prominently at adolescence in response to increased secretion of hormones, such as wide hips versus wide shoulders, presence and distribution of body hair, fat, etc. Since male and female sex glands each produce both male and female hormones, though in different proportions, we have here not so much a sharp dichotomy as a gamut or mosaic of traits. The actual constellation of these traits, within a wide but normal range, can cause much mental anguish in the adolescent, whose body is undergoing these physical changes. In fact, even thoroughly male and female changes can cause shock or distress. Additionally, physical traits that offend cultural stereotypes, for example, shortness in a man or tallness in a woman, can cause suffering and psychological scars in individuals otherwise entirely normal sexually. I once knew a male psychiatrist, now deceased, who suffered from a height that was excessively "masculine" for a man of his generation, but would pass unnoticed in the taller present generation. Again, in our wealthy country, a middle- or upper-class woman has to struggle hard to keep thin, whereas the admired woman in traditional Turkey would be regarded as extremely fat by our standards.

What cannot be too emphatically noted here is the plain fact of wide but *normal* variation in these physical-hormonal traits of maleness and femaleness; nor are they necessarily in one-to-one matching with the more valuable traits of psychic masculinity and femininity. Furthermore, biological evolution depends upon the basis of *differences* within the species, so that we should abhor too standardized a conformity to pattern. What would seem a physical anomaly now (say, Shetland-like compactness of body) conceivably may be ecologically the wave of the future. Young people who yearn to achieve their own specific individuality, though they may not achieve it as much as they think or would like, are probably right in terms of biology. For cultural evolution, also, depends upon psychological uniqueness in culture-heroes, so that we should actively seek those socio-politico-economic conditions that promote, protect and cherish a high degree of individuality. From a personal point of view, we should learn to take these secondary variations as not much more important than being blond or brunet or redheaded. Again, racial variations are precious for the future of the total human species, since unforeseeable vicissitudes (say, massive atomic radiation) might select for differential survival precisely on the basis of skin color; indeed, racial hybrids might preserve a larger and more varied human gene pool. It is an irony of vast proportions that, here in America, through lucky historical accidents, we have large pools of Mongoloid genes in the American Indian, of Negro genes through importation of African slaves, and of Caucasoid genes through European migration—and yet some anthropologically ignorant people are unhappy about our enormous, undeserved, and unsurpassed opportunities for hybrid vigor in the future! Anyone can therefore be mildly gratified at representing racial traits in his body, though he can take no moral credit for it personally. At the same time, having a black or white or red or yellow skin has been vastly overrated in the past as indicating any special relationship to *individual* cultural potentiality. Such differences are largely social, hence, obviously, we should continue to bend our efforts toward equality of opportunity for individual achievement. Civilization requires for its purposes a wide range of variety in people, however much these differences have frightened people in tribal days of the past. Meanwhile, physical differences in secondary sexual characteristics are just not that important to one's potential as a human person. And gross physical traits can be misleading too. In parachute school the most "gutsy" and virile man I knew was a fragile-looking little college professor, whereas several of the giant athletic males were physical and moral cowards.

In addition to these primary and secondary sexual characteristics, therefore, there is a category I call "tertiary sexual characteristics." These are the psychological traits of "masculinity" and "femininity"—and henceforth my talk will deal mostly with these. "Masculinity" and "femininity" are not at all the simple dichotomy of traits that they seem to be. There are three or four aspects of tertiary sexuality that must be discriminated here. One is, the *sex of assignment* in rearing. Most boys are reared as males, and most girls are reared as females. But, commonly enough, pathological parents will rear a boy in feminine fashion, or a girl in a masculine fashion. It is not simply a question of dressing a boy in girl's clothing. It is a more subtle matter. Each parent is of one sex or the other and each has definite ideas, conscious and unconscious, about the fact of his or her sex. Further, each parent has attitudes toward the other sex, toward the spouse in particular, toward sons versus daughters, and toward one son or daughter versus another son or daughter. Sometimes a neurotic family seems even to select unconsciously the individual who will be officially "sick" for it, although psychiatrically the others may be just as sick or even sicker. Also, the relationship of parents to one another may change and develop, and hence children born at different times in changing circumstances are subjected to a different parental climate. The sex-age constellation in the family is also part of the complex "accidents" that have real and permanent psychological effects.

For example, having many sons masculinizes a father. A father who really does not like women (in spite of great "masculine protest" in his official hypervirility—but admiring only all things male) may in effect masculinize his daughter simply because, unconsciously to both, he has rewarded her selectively for masculine behaviors, but has taught her contempt for feminine behavior and femaleness. A more authentically virile father would have admired, and hence elicited through reward, feminine traits in her as a girl, in addition to fomenting them through his unabashed admiration of her mother. Plainly, tertiary sexual characteristics are to a large degree psychologically learned. Again, a hysteroid mother may subtly behave quite seductively or castratively toward an older son but not toward the younger ones; or she may treat all her sons as contemptuously as she does their father. Sometimes the unconscious conflict between parents over *sex of assignment* to a child will directly shape conflict in the child over his or her sexual identity. To summarize: sex of assignment is a category that applies not merely to the extreme case of a male child reared in dresses, and not merely to the familiar parent-shaped "sissy" or "tomboy," but in subtler ways that probably apply to every single human being. The matter can reach unsuspected complexity in cases we see clinically. For example, a mother may acknowledge her son's maleness but teach him to despise it. Or a father may court his daughter's femininity and teach her to overvalue it.

In addition to *sex of assignment*, there are other aspects of tertiary sexuality: *gender role* and *gender orientation*. Both are learned, and both are established in the social rearing process. In fact, just as there is apparently an "imprinting" period during which one does or does not learn to speak, so also there is an "imprinting period" between three and five years of age in which gender role and gender orientation are sometimes irrevocably set. Gender role is the teaching of what males are like and females are like, with respect to the society's contemporary stereotypes.

Let me describe the nature of gender role through an anecdote. The late Dr. Alfred Kinsey was really a fine fellow, with a connoisseur's knowledge of exotic ethnic foods. But when he interviewed me, now some decades ago, it was soon clear to me that he was enormously naive anthropologically and psychiatrically. I did not tell him so at the time. But after World War II, since I had both an anthropological and psychiatric training, he asked me to join his research group. I declined, because his research questionnaire had already taught me its severe limitations. I do not mean the usual errors of sampling, class, regional, and race bias, etc., for which he has already been amply criticized. I mean something far more basic and pervasive.

Ignoring all the methodological defects of his pioneering work, what did Kinsey actually discover? Basically that "the human male" is extremely oversexed, in spite of the varied "outlets" he manages to find for himself. This view is easy enough to adopt. In the first place it fits our stereotypes; it is also rather flattering; and in the third place, every human male that ever lived has surely had some problem in the management of his sexual impulses (as, conceivably, human females have had too). When Kinsey's first book on *The Human Male* was published, I remember telling my wife, "Aha! So that's it? Now I will predict for you what *The Human Female* is like!" And, sure enough, Kinsey complied: the human female is grievously undersexed; she is not interested in sexual fantasy, in male nudity, in pictures, in pornographic words, in short, in anything properly (or improperly) sexual. Indeed, she couldn't care less; and if it were left to her sexual desires alone, the human race would become extinct in one generation. Now, perhaps this characterization is a bit exaggerated. His "facts" certainly are. But that is the essential message of the second volume. A later generation, one of whose sources of mythology about sex has been *Playboy* magazine, knows that Kinsey's notions about women are simply not so. Cool sex takes no time, or effort, or involvement at all. Just as every male is, of course, an instant stud, with nothing so unmanly or stultifying as taste or preference, so also that fold-out girl is one-hundred-percent willing, and was just waiting for you to come along. Cool sex is as simple as turning the TV or hi-fi set off or on. Plainly, what Kinsey (or you) had discovered is only gender role, that is, the *folklore about sex* in that society in his generation. He had been the ethnographer of contemporary sex, not the comparative world anthropologist concerning males and females. And so *Playboy* in its time. That is to say, each generation has sets of largely unconscious stereotypes about male and female, and these are part of a covert and unofficial but changing culture. A generation maturing in the early seventies, for example, in contrast with a Victorian one at least, has decided that there is really not very much difference psychologically between men and women (having been reared coeducationally, in the same classes, and sometimes in the same sexually integrated dorms). Being of another generation, I am quite sure I do not subscribe to that view either. Females are *not* "more equal" ("human" = male) than males!

A moment's reflection would demonstrate that all these *must* be stereotypes, to change so much in each generation. If the male is really the more urgently sexed, why did Holy Writ (in which all things are true) represent that it was Adam who was seduced by Eve? It looks as though a quite different cultural stereotype were unconsciously at work here! And what about those late-medieval *chansons de geste*? In one of them, a knight is riding along in the woods, his mind on lofty and important things like crusades and tournaments and Holy Grails and such—"His strength was as the strength of ten because his heart was pure" (and, besides, his oversexed wife was safely locked as she should be in a chastity girdle back in the castle)—when he comes to the humble woodcutter's hut where he must spend the night. Now, I cannot repeat in this public place, and before a mixed audience, all the details about the woodcutter's daughter. But the large ethnographic generalization one could make is that, if he could not care less, she was surely urgently oversexed, even rapaciously predatory. As a matter of fact, given our differing stereotypes and expectancies, she was what a modern Swedish woman seems to an American man (some may remember the shock, now some years back, when a prominent Swedish actress behaved as though a woman had a legitimate right to be interested in sex—and, worse yet, acted as if she had a choice in the matter!). This is no isolated finding. There are many societies in which female sexual aggressiveness is represented as surpassing the male's, for example, the Cubeo of northwest Amazonia, among whom the men complain that the women are too ardent. And among the upper-class Tuareg of the Sahara, the female courtiers and troubadours are the sexual aggressors and the males the guardians of decorum. An upper-class Tuareg warrior would blush deeply in the love court of the lady troubadour, if his veil slipped (men wear veils here, not women).[2]

In addition to the matter of gender role—what people think males and females are like in nature and behavior—there is another dimension in tertiary sexuality, *gender orientation*. As opposed to gender role (which is a *cultural* model of expectancies), gender orientation is an individual perspective. This is a question of (a) self-judgment as to *how one fits* the fashions in sexual behavior; (b) one's conscious and unconscious *preferences* about how he feels and what he wants to be, sexually; and also (c) the "objective" *judgment of others* as to how well or ill the individual matches the stereotypes of gender role in his behavior. These are all really different. A man whom women loathe may think himself a Don Juan, and men may envy him. And a girl might think that (a) she had managed to present a seemly façade for modest feminine behavior, but (b) she secretly wished she had a man's choices and freedom—whereas (c) others judged her as having cat's claws in her velvet gloves (the female view of her), or as a predatory but frustrating "teaser" (the male view).

Perhaps a sharper focus can be given by using comparative ethnographic material.[3] Every Plains Indian, male or female, young or old, knew what the gender role of an adult male was: he was an "instinctual" and total warrior. Most of his life energy was bent toward killing enemy men, collecting scalps and other body-trophies, and capturing as many women and horses as he could. To this end, about puberty, he set out on a lone vision quest, to fast and pray four days and nights so that (he hoped) he might obtain "medicine power," a kind of packaged virility that would help him carry out his male roles. If he were lucky he actually got this package, that is his "medicine bundle" of supernatural magical malehood. Perhaps he would find a feather or some strange-looking lucky stone or bone, or a weasel would run by and he would shoot it for his medicine bundle container (the Blackfoot actually had so many medicine bundles that they constituted the major wealth that was traded back and forth). There was some variation in the result: some men got medicine power not to kill but to cure. These individuals became "medicine men" or shamans, and they could do everything from curing wounds, diagnosing causes and discovering the persons sending disease, and sucking out disease-producing objects, to seeing the enemy impossibly far off in space, or distant in future time, and from supernaturally protecting his war party to controlling the weather. There were only two kinds of male gender role in the Plains: warrior or medicine man.

There was, however, still a third kind of male, the "not-man" or *berdache*.[4] Lewis and Clark and other early explorers and scouts give us many accounts of the *berdaches* in the tribes they encountered. Many thought they were "hermaphrodites" or at least sexually perverse, when as a matter of fact they were not necessarily either. The *berdache* or not-man was first and foremost only a social transvestite. That is, he wore women's clothes and performed women's chores. His "not-man" status of being neither a warrior nor a medicine man was simply announced by his wearing women's clothes. Like everyone else, he knew perfectly well the male gender role, but had a stubborn preference for his own gender orientation. Psychologically, it is fairly easy to explain the *berdache* to a generation that can imagine other things that a male might do besides (a) going off to be killed in Viet Nam or (b) collecting a lot of symbolic green-colored paper instead of war bonnet feathers.

Perhaps, psychologically, the *berdache* may even have had a more vivid and imaginative view of the male gender role than the average man; that is to say, he can imagine all too well what it would be like to be killed or scalped or mutilated, so much so that he longs to "get out of that bag." But the male gender role is so straitly defined that he has literally only one way to do so: to become a male "drop-out" or transvestite. The discrepancy here between gender role and gender orientation is so great that Plains Indians have to rationalize it on supernatural grounds. As an example, when one *berdache* went out on his pubertal vision quest, instead of a snake or bear or Thunderbird or Sun, there appeared to him the Moon. In one hand she held a bow and arrow, in the other an elk rib such as women use to scrape skins in tanning. Naturally, he reached out for the bow and arrow. But the Moon smiled, crossed her arms, and what he grasped was the elk-rib scraper. Thus when he came back from the vision quest, he had to take up women's work and robes. He had no choice. We would say that the supernatural compulsion came from his subconscious mind: his "castration anxiety" about being scalped or mutilated was so intense that his social role was mutilated. But no matter how we explain the rationalization it came to the same end: under some powerful sanction he could never go to war and collect scalps and horses and feathers for a war bonnet like a proper man.

The price of abdicating the proud masculine game of prestige-warfare and its status-rewards was to wear feminine garb. Perhaps we can understand the emotional intensity of these visual signals of a preferred role. In our society an older generation still goes into frenzy if a young male lets both his face-hair and his head-hair grow at the same time. It is as confusing and anxiety-arousing as when boys and girls wear much the same clothes and have much the same attitudes toward the world. They do not fit the sharp dichotomies an older generation expects and is comfortable with, or at least struggles to conform to.

Further details concerning the *berdache* are interesting and edifying. Having made the public transvestite "statement" and having paid the price in potential status, the *berdache* now has some freedom of conscious and unconscious choice sexually. One *berdache* may marry, hunt, and have children, all the while wearing women's clothing. Married to a not-man, his wife would seem to be a lesbian, but she emphatically is not when she bears his children. Another *berdache* may elect to be a permanent bachelor or rather a permanent "spinster," a complete sexual drop-out. Another may become a kind of surreptitious male prostitute for other men. And still another, being officially a woman, may marry another man; among the Mohave, in fact, the *berdache* may even pretend to menstruate by making his inner thighs bleed, or even pretend to bear children.[5] But, curiously, it is not the *berdache* but the man who marries one who suffers social obliquy from such a marriage. The Indian rationale is clear. So male-centered a system is it that, being after all anatomically a male, the *berdache* is expected to do women's work even better than women can. A high form of praise for a woman might be that "she does beadwork as fine as a *berdache*'s!" This is not, however, the cause of the shame of the husband of a *berdache*; after all, a man is entitled to as fine a beadworker in his spouse as he can get. The shame, rather, is that the *berdache* might go hunting buffalo for "her" husband. And this is the last straw. It is not fair. The poor-stick-of-a-man husband of the *berdache* is giving up the ultimate male role, that of hunting game for his family.

In this, Indians feel something like we do when a man marries a rich woman. True, he gains buying power, which among us is the basis of male prestige. But this buying power gives him no status, and no validation of his masculinity, because the wealth depends on the prior activity of another male, his wife's father or her former husband(s). And, besides, he gains wealth not in the masculine way, by earning it in direct competition with other men, but in a feminine way, by marrying it. The man who marries a rich woman is really no better than a woman who has married only for money. Worse yet, he has sold his male birthright in the game of status-competition—and for mere money. The irony is that the husband of a *berdache* is only a high-class male whore.

Plains Indians have one more way of escaping the burdensome and anxiety-laden job of being a male. But this way is one of extremely high prestige, because it is hyper-"masculine." He becomes a "Crazy Dog." In many Plains tribes, a man rises in life through joining successively higher-ranked warriors' dancing-societies, as he has collected more scalps and horses and women and prestige by "counting coup"—that is, ritually touching in battle a fallen but still dangerous enemy with a little wooden coup stick. The warrior-and-dancing societies tend to be graded in prestige, like fraternities or college clubs, the difference being that a man moves from one to another as he rises in rank. Only a very high-ranking warrior would aspire to be a "Crazy Dog," for no one would take him seriously otherwise, and he chooses this role for himself. People would say, "He must be full of [supernatural] power," because he shows his new aspiration through stylized negativism, both in speech and in behavior. If he says one thing, he means the opposite. And he is so contrary that his wife must tell him to go away if she wants him to come to a meal.

But the real test of a "Crazy Dog" is his arrogant contrariness to common sense in war, when he exposes himself to extravagant dangers. Among the Kiowa Indians, for example, he wears a long sash that trails on the ground. In a hypothetical case, a party of Yanktonai Sioux are approaching, obviously on the warpath, so he shoots an arrow into the sash and tethers himself to the ground, as if he would not escape when the rest of his Kiowa mates sensibly retreat. What he is symbolically saying is, "I will take on alone all you Yanktonai buzzards, and all your Teton Dakota friends too, the Brulé, yes and the Hunkpapa also!" Understandably, most scholars regard this behavior as a form of ritual suicide, for this in fact is what it usually amounts to. But in what a blaze of glory the great warrior leaves life! If by remote chance he survives the onslaught and crawls back, minus scalp, an eye or a leg or so, he is accorded the greatest of respect and honor. He never has to prove anything further. Naturally, the mortality rate among Crazy Dogs is high, and there are never very many of them around. Perhaps in our society we have the equivalent in prestige terms: the man who makes a big killing on a stock market coup by the age of thirty-five—and then dies young of a coronary attack at thirty-six.

Thus we cannot suppose that there is any great number either of Crazy Dogs or of *berdaches* in any Plains tribe at one time, probably no more per capita than millionaires among us. The *berdache* is a monitory presence of what not to be, the Crazy Dog of model of extreme aspiration. Both are admittedly extreme cases. But they are recognized and socially visible roles, and are yet quite understandable in terms of their culture, its norms and its goals. Perhaps more usual would be my friend Bert Crowlance, now deceased so that his revealing visions can be told, and psychologists interpret them as they may. Bert had an accident that partly crippled him for work, so he hoped to get even a late vision that would reveal to him diamonds or, short of that, oil on his share in Oklahoma. The first time he went out, he tried and tried to get a vision, but without success. Finally, his mother appeared to him in a dream and said, "You might as well go back, Bert; you forgot your pipe." Next time, well armed with his tobacco pipe, he was flying through the air in fine fettle and spotted a place which would surely have diamonds or at least oil. But as he got closer, he was afraid to land. The place was full of frightening snake men. So Bert Crowlance never got oil, or diamonds either in Oklahoma.

It is apparent that there are additionally, then, *comparative cultural norms* for the tertiary sexual characteristics of "masculinity" and "femininity." Cross-culturally, some of these are merely behavioral expectancies: when two Berber men in North Africa walk hand in hand, it means nothing concerning their gender orientation, but only simple friendship. Fifty years ago, Appalachian males exchanged the mouth-to-mouth "holy kiss," before snake-handling meetings in church (the secular, heterosexual kiss in public would be unthinkable, and especially at church). Indeed, in earlier European times, men often kissed one another in public, as when knight greeted knight, or noble his cousin noble. In context, this was as meaningless sexually as men wearing silk, lace, high heels and powdered hair in eighteenth-century France. Louis XIV did, and he was probably the most powerful man of his time, and not notably inactive heterosexually either. In France, these customs were a matter of wealth and status difference, not of gender orientation or preference sexually.

Given the plethora of evidence available from comparative ethnography, it is perhaps understandable that theorists differ in their interpretation of the basic nature of "tertiary sexual characteristics." With his biology-based psychology, Freud believed that "anatomy is destiny," and I have already indicated that biology cannot be ignored in the ecological "hominization of man." But Paul Schilder differed sharply with Freud over the nature of psychological sex differences.[6] Schilder thought that, beyond differing actions relative to sexual anatomy, sex functions and behavior, all tertiary differences arose from social factors. In Freud's view, the psychological differences are intrinsic and in some sense innate; in Schilder's view, these differences are all socially learned. Freud's might be termed the *ethological*, Schilder's the *ethnological* view.

Today, the best known polemicist for the ethnological view is Margaret Mead in her study of three New Guinea tribes.[7] Among the Arapesh, both sexes manifest feminine-nurturant traits, because the main dichotomy for the Arapesh is not into male versus female, but rather into the grown versus ungrown person. Males and females are regarded as functionally so alike that they differ only in that the father feeds the fetus from his body before birth, whereas the mother feeds the baby at her breast after birth. A father may therefore be congratulated for his "hard work" in growing the baby! Again, a young man "grows" his adolescent fiancée by nurturing and feeding her. Premature sexuality between the young is frowned upon, not because of any Puritanical antisexuality as such in Oceania, but rather because one should achieve his or her own growth before contributing to new ones, i.e., babies. Given proper behavior in this respect, Arapesh can then believe in the self-fulfilling prophecy that "sexuality stunts growth" since both are full-grown before they practice intercourse. Among the fierce headhunting Mundugumor, both males and females are in our terms tough, self-sufficient, and "masculine," with competitive aggressive sexuality—perhaps because, as children, they were let out as hostages in enemy tribes, to keep the peace, and they had to learn to take care of themselves in a hostile and uncaring environment. And, finally, among the Tchambuli, women are "masculine" and men are "feminine" by our standards. In the old native days, men were preoccupied with headhunting and war rituals (surely a "masculine" enough business, initially), whereas women did most of the economically productive work. But when the British forbade headhunting and war, the Tchambuli men became technologically unemployed, and their old war rituals gradually developed into elaborately theatrical dramas. Men thereupon became extremely concerned with their dress and appearance. Being economically dependent on women, they were always worried about the impression they were making on the women. Women became the superior, confident, cool, cooperative, feet-on-the-ground, acerb, matter-of-fact and practical sex, while men were the narcissistic, aesthetic, sensitive, easily hurt, coquettish sex. It was not that women did not appreciate men and enjoy having them around. It was simply that men were merely decorative and entertaining, and not the important sex, and so they should not be taken too seriously. Thus, historically, and in the same tribe, men changed from being aggressively masculine to insecurely feminine, all on the basis of social change.[b]

As predominantly *learning* animals, human beings are evidently highly malleable. But not infinitely malleable! Anatomical differences remain on which a modestly "ethological" argument might be based, for physical dimorphism sexually is an incontestably cross-cultural phenomenon. Thus it could be pointed out that, even as a learning experience, growing up in a male body is a quite different psychological experience from growing up in a female body. For example (as discussed more fully in an earlier chapter of this book), as soon as a little boy learns that girls are anatomically different, then vulnerability to mutilation and loss of genitals for naughty acts or (*pan-human*) forbidden fanta-

---

b. In any "anthropology of knowledge," if social contexts are to be appealed to, then we might point out that Mead's ethnological argument is so regnant now possibly because of its availability for the polemics of "women's liberation." Some ethnographers have protested at the statistical improbability of one fieldworker on one island finding three tribes that neatly illustrated her thesis—rather than three different workers in three different parts of the world independently and accidentally (not from "problem-oriented" fieldwork) discovering the data that would support such an argument. It has also been pointed out that much of Mead's professional career has been devoted to "disproving" many of Freud's basic theses (that the sexes are innately different, that all humans go through the same ontogenetic stages of development, that adolescence in any society is an intrinsically stressful passage from a biologically dependent child role to the logically reciprocal adult role of providing for such dependency, among others).

sies gives a "castration complex" to a male different from that of a female. To her, who had already suffered a "loss," it is *not fair* that boys have what she does not—and what had she done to be so "punished"?—which gives an inevitably "paranoid" feeling about her femininity, added to which boys are quite unfairly stronger than girls, hence she is forced to learn quite different adaptive arts. Again, external genitals, the grossly distinctive features of males, are *present at birth*. But boys are insignificantly little compared to grown men. Therefore comparison, emulation, and competition are directly built into the male situation. A man always has to *prove* the distance he has moved from child to man—has dependence on the powerful and always significant mother *forced him to seek* dominance as an adult man?—and male creativity is always secondary and symbolic. A woman proves her womanhood, and superiority to men here for that matter, once and for all, by the only true creativity, the growing of a new human being. Who needs to write the Great American Novel if she can have a baby and produce a whole human lifetime in reality? But for this she has to wait. By contrast with boys and their anatomical distinctions, a little girl must also long wait for the distinctive overt trait of the adult female, breasts. She has not even a token promise for the future, as a boy does. Again, the experience of a nocturnal emission in a boy at puberty is quite different, psychologically, from the experience of menstruation in a girl. All her old guilts and inhibitions from earlier cleanliness training are reactivated, and if anything menstruation only confirms her earlier castration fantasies. In the boy, nocturnal emission is an awed, prideful, unalloyed body-zone pleasure. But menstruation, defloration, and childbirth all mean that female sexuality is associated with pain, and a girl may come to learn from older women a real resentment at the burden of being female (it takes a male much longer to learn that manhood has its burdens too). The female body is 23 percent muscle, the male 40 percent. And since each has differing vulnerabilities physically, the female and male stances toward life are bound to be different psychologically.

Every single male game (and athletics, despite women's entering some sports, is still quintessentially masculine) shows a projection of body image in competition. The runner and swimmer must do it faster than competitors, the shot-put must go further. The boxer knocks down his opponent to win, the wrestler pins the other down under him in submission. In baseball the lone man with the bat stands up against the whole other team. In golf the champion hits the ball harder and farther and more accurately toward the hole, and with fewer strokes. In all team games, one group of males tries to press another group backward, to force the symbolic ball into enemy territory or into his goal. And the winning football team can dismantle the goalposts as trophies; in basketball the winners can clip off the net from the basket. The very form of games is male in body image: to be the active overwhelming invader, and to avoid the passive fate of being invaded. Indeed, a male can understand women only in the projective terms of his own body. Hence, in his often unconscious terms, he may define some femininities as obscurely shameful or dirty (as their equivalents would be for him)—or even anxiously dangerous to him, as menstrual taboos all over the world will demonstrate.

Since males emulate, compare, and compete, males tend also to be the generalization makers, the rules and law makers, and the abstractionists of basic principles in comparisons. Partly this results from his different Oedipal fate. The male must give up the concrete, specific, dependent love he has learned for one woman, his mother, and generalize toward a protective-aggressive love of women. But having been forced to give up his one love does not necessarily make him a good monogamist among substitutes. From beginning to end the male simply loves women, though in physiologically different libidinal body zone ways, and with functionally different patterns of submission/dominance in child and man. Male sexuality is embattled, and burdened with proof, but it is psychologically less complex in its love-object. In a sense, there is something basically male even in the *berdache*: he *competes*, not in scalp-collecting but in beadwork.

By contrast, the female must change the sex of her love-object, from the little girl's mother, to her father, and then to some other man.[c] In the process, for good biological reasons, she is allowed to retain more of the child's biological dependency than the man, who must change the dependency relation completely. And to obtain her femininity in a baby, a woman must first obtain a man; her ultimate goal, in a baby, is more prominent, for a male seeks not so much fatherhood as sexuality with a woman. And seeking sexuality is not the same as seeking pregnancy. Again, a male can never be in doubt as to whether he is sexually aroused, but a woman actually may not know. Female sexuality is less embattled than male, but it is more obscure, more subtle, and more complex. A woman may become content to be, and she is sometimes puzzled at a man's seemingly endless and fierce striving to become. Why men love women is quite clear; they had good biological reasons for child-love of their mothers. But why women love men is difficult to see, even though a woman has physiologically more ways to love than a man does. Nevertheless, in her loving, the woman seems to be the concrete particularizer: she loves this baby and this man. If men cannot understand the prodigies of concern a woman can have for another who was once in her body, that may be because the male does not have a female body. There is also a "double standard" here that no one can do anything about: a male can impregnate an indefinite number of females in a short time, but when a female is pregnant it is by one man, and further, she experiences massive physiological changes quite lacking in the male. On all these biological grounds, it is quite difficult to disagree with Freud.

c. *Why* does a woman love men? She experienced no physical gratification from a father that both sexes had from the mother. Is her love an aspect of earlier dependency, transferred from mother, to father, to another man? Does her mother-identification reinforce her own mother-child symbiotic pleasure-narcissism, that extends to encompass her mate as well (for are not women better empathizers of men than men are of women?) Perhaps no male can know.

If tertiary sexuality is "learned," quite certainly in the *ethological* context of differently sexed bodies, it is equally certain that there are *ethnological* differences in the social context of conditioning. When I lived in China, in a remote region so conservative and backward that most older women still had bound feet, I was struck with the fact that the men seemed curiously devious, psychologically on the *qui vive*, and "feminine" whereas the women seemed hardbitten, matter-of-fact and "masculine." Only in time did I learn the cultural circumstances that might account for this "reversal." This remote and conservative southwestern part of China still had the old extended patrilocal and patrilineal family. This means that from the day he was born until the day he died (and even thereafter for that matter) a man was caught up in a complex fixed web of kinship relations that he had to adapt to, as son, nephew, cousin, etc. In the preservation of "face" (which is largely concern for the other person's status, dignity, personal feelings and the like), a male must learn to become a sensitive and astute psychologist in his complex relationships with other members of his permanent patrilineal family. Indeed, the old Confucian ethics was mostly a statement of ideal behaviors in different categories of interpersonal relationships.

By contrast, the female must always marry away from her father's family, and go to the patrilocal home of her husband. She entered an alien male-centered group as a daughter-in-law, under the tutelage of her mother-in-law, her husband's mother. There was no special sympathy or sexual solidarity among women, for the mother-in-law enforced the same stringencies she had once experienced as a daughter-in-law herself. A woman's status depended entirely on her ability to work for her husband's family and to produce children, preferably boys because only these would remain with the husband's patrilineage. It was not so much a sexual bias against the female as such (as I learned later was the case in pervasively stratified India), as it was a male kin-centered phenomenon. In her old age, a Chinese woman might enjoy high status as the oldest living ancestress in the group. But it was a status she had worked hard for. That is to say, in this classical Chinese situation the "life space" of a male puts a premium on developing adaptive psychological skills—as was the case for women among us, certainly fifty or a hundred years ago. For the Chinese woman, by contrast, the premium was on working hard and getting ahead on her own in an alien group. Thus some *characterological traits* we confidently categorize as "masculine" and "feminine" are not universal sexual absolutes at all. They are rather *characteristic human responses* psychologically to differing culturally defined roles for the sexes. It is probably impossible ever to discriminate completely the ethological from the ethnological, and to know what men and women "naturally" are. The reason is that, in despite of there being two sexes in every society, in every society we know these sexes always occur in a specific culture of one sort or another. Man invents himself. There is no "natural" man culturally.

Given the parallax available from two different time periods in the same society, we may reach another perspective on the matter. The Israeli *kibbutz* has been an important social experiment, notably in discovering sharp discrepancies between assumptions and conclusions. The utopian feminism of earnest early socialism sought the emancipation of women from child care, through basic changes in the traditional system of marriage, the family, and sex role differentiation in economic employment. Once baby crèches and child care dormitories for older children were established, women would be free to enter all occupations, even heavy agricultural labor. At the same time, men might be employed in the service occupations, such as the communal laundry, cooking and cleaning, and the like. All adults ate together, but sexual pairs lived together alone in small conjugal apartments. Nevertheless, as Zwi Shatz observed, "the need for family is very deep and organic." It was women, not men, who progressively brought children back from the common nursery-dormitory to a reconstituted nuclear family home. And, by their own choice, women gradually withdrew from heavy agricultural work, despite the greater prestige of "productive" jobs in which they were intrinsically "not interested"—whereas men, by similar free choice, gravitated from the "service" to the heavier agricultural jobs. Is it not possible that riding a jolting tractor does not favor pregnancy in a woman? Is it not true that women, with smaller muscles but larger fat reserves, have greater endurance in long but lower level expenditures of energy? Is it not true that male bodies have nearly twice as much muscle as female bodies?

Thus, whereas the older pioneer *kibbutzim* had a cultural explanation for sex-role differentiation, the *kibbutz*-reared *sabra* would argue a biological explanation. The "new human beings" turn out to be very human indeed. In the words of one founder of the Kiryat Yedidim *kibbutz*, "We came here to discover man." Perhaps they did—in all this species' complex ambiguity.

Evidently, then, there can be not only comparative cultural definitions of sexuality, but also *differences of pattern in time*. In every generation, in every tribe, we set up rigid norms—and then are unhappy either that statistically few individuals can actualize them or that, because they are sometimes illogical, the sexes blithely fail to fit them. For example, among Americans there is the cliché that only males can create great art (we have already pointed out that perhaps only males psychologically *need to*, because they cannot make babies)—but that only females may be preoccupied with and enjoy art, which is a patent absurdity. It never occurs to thoroughly virile European males that anyone should bully them out of enjoying Baroque music or Italian Renaissance painting. It is far more a matter of education and economic class (though working-class Italian males can be heard singing operatic arias in the streets) than of XX-XY chromosomes.[d] Further, why is it that the most virile among

---

d. Only a decade ago, male ballet stars suffered gender-orientation obliquy, perhaps because only females were then allowed such primary bodily exhibitionism. But ballet has flourished in a generation less bothered about gender-role. In fact, a male ballet dancer must develop enormous strength in his arms and shoulders in order to produce a smoothly legato drift down from an

American men (as defined by their being self-made millionaires), like Morgan and Mellon and Carnegie and Frick and Kress, should choose to enjoy and to collect art? And why is it that engineers, who typically have very high scores for masculinity on the Terman-Miles MF Test, should so commonly enjoy the music of Bach? Perhaps the music of Bach has nothing to do with XX-XY chromosomes: but if engineers enjoy Bach counterpoint, then it may only be that engineering minds relish complex dynamic structures of whatever kind. Meanwhile, it is absurd to argue that Rubinstein's performance of Mozart's 20th Piano Concerto is "better" than Clara Haskil's for all that Mozartian style is notably adapted for small nimble hands. They are different, yes—but both marvelous.

We cannot be human unless we have elaborate codes for behavior. But perhaps Herbert Marcuse[8] is right in asking: what are the codes that will deliver the greatest amount of potential enjoyment and self-fulfilment in return for the least cost in inhibition and repressive discipline? Or, in other terms, is man made for culture, or are cultures made for man?[9] Actually, in its tertiary sexual characteristics (for complex economic and other reasons), every changing generation is made up from a mosaic of traits taken from both father and mother, just as genetic physical traits are. Let me give a simple example of what I mean. In our society at present, the doctor enjoys high social status, in part indicated by the high income of doctors, in part by our legislative attempts to subsidize doctors through health insurance and other means, strangely enough against the doctors' own most extreme and vociferous objections. Why this irrational fight against self-interest? From teaching many generations of young doctors in medical schools I think I have an answer. In my judgment, a good doctor has some intensely "masculine" traits with respect to desire for competitively high status, intention to have a respect-worthy income, intensity of discipline to remote ends, willingness to accept responsibility and the like. The doctor wants to be symbolically the father, so far as his complete authority goes, and thus his objection to any governmental authority he sees as a dilution of his own total male authority. But at the same time, every good doctor also has gotten from his mother a "feminine" concern for other people, especially the weak and sick, that is more than the ordinary "natural" endowment of the male, and is really closer to the normal biological roles of the female in nurturing and protecting life. Thus, without in any way impugning the essential maleness of the doctor, it is plain that in this matter he is a mosaic of parental masculine and feminine traits.[e]

---

elevation of his partner in a *pas de deux*. And even in solo, a *premier danseur* must develop magnificent prodigies of athletic control of his body, far more difficult and demanding far longer discipline than in any mere sportsman. A tough little labor sociologist once told me, quite unselfconsciously, that at the ballet he watches the men because he can empathize with their feats; the women are merely ravishing spectacles, and he can see that any day on the campus.

e. At the same time, social institutions like medicine may have been rigidly though unconsciously defined in traditional sex terms, sometimes quite illogically. Witness the earlier extreme difficulties of women in becoming doctors, for all that in some specialties they might naturally be

Rattray Taylor,[10] in fact, thinks that one of the major hidden motors in social change is just this mosaic of identification, in which each generation subtly changes. A generation which primarily identifies with the father is "patrist" and one that identifies primarily with the mother is "matrist." The patrist ethos is authoritarian, directive, paternalist, and restrictive; the matrist, libertarian, nurturant, and openly egalitarian. Socially and politically, the patrist is absolutist and conservative, as befits a categorical father-identification; the matrist, relativist and progressive. The patrist father-identifier has a resentment of women because the mother is the base of conflict between father and son; to patrists, women are inferior, sinful, and trouble-makers unless restrained. But with the mother-identifier, women have a high status and freedom. Patrist orthodoxy is countered by matrist freedom of inquiry. Interference with a patrist regime is crime; intervention in a matrist regime takes the form of nurturant social insurance and welfare. The father-identifying patrist is a rigid and fiercely loyal traditionalist; the matrist is a spontaneous creative innovator. The patrist distrusts research and intellectual inquiry as weakening authoritarian orthodoxy; the matrist espouses research to change the regime for the better, and hence the matrist trends toward formal "heresy." Patrists, who love and exalt male things, have anxiety over homosexuality; mother-close matrists, over incest. Patrist prostitution is opposed to matrist promiscuity or free love or sexual emancipation. The patrist seeks to maximize sexual differences conceptually and in dress; the matrist minimizes sex differences. A quick mental review of presidents since the matrist FDR would probably produce a consensus regarding later ones. Surely the patrist-matrist orientation of voters and of geographic regions is an important factor in socio-political issues, all the way from Viet Nam to Israel, and from the Panama Treaty to the Equal Rights Amendment and other contemporary issues. It is important to remember that women too may be "patrists" and men "matrists," and a regime like Carter's be confusingly ambiguous.

Of course it is possible to reject identification with both parents, and to abandon the values of both for a drop-out pattern of age-mate living and values that are essentially antinomian. The hallmark of this kind of anomie is aimlessness, instability over time, and the tyranny of conformity to disconformity that is highly stereotyped and limiting. The differences among patrist, matrist, and age-mate kinds of ethos are pervasive and deep, and they tend to provoke strong feeling and argument. Some prefer the "right-thinking" security of (sometimes terrorist or bullying) orthodoxy, under which the main problem is enforcing obedience to conformity. Others prefer the freedom, the anxiety, the excitement, and the adventure of relativism. In an extreme alienation, in the age-mate ethos, the rejection of authority will be pervasive, whether

---

better than men, say in pediatrics, gynecology, etc. At the same time, since nursing is traditionally a feminine occupation, the "male nurse" encounters many aspersions on his masculinity, for all that male muscles are highly adapted for nursing chores that demand physical strength.

the authority be that of the parents, the President, the Papal authority, the police, the college administration, or the Establishment in general. Men overwhelm opposition, women undermine it, adolescents flatly confront it, hence all these styles differ from one another. In the ethos of a decent society, if there do exist essentially masculine and feminine traits, perhaps we need both, since the extremes are either distressing anomie and aimless relativism, or cramping imprisonment in Right-Thinking.

I have suggested two handfuls of ways in which we may discuss human sexuality. Probably there are more; but at least there exist these. The problem is that we can not always pretend to know to which any specific item should be assigned. Perhaps that is to be expected—or is as it should be. Humans are values-secreting animals, inventing themselves throughout history. Man is like an existentialist spider, spinning webs of symbolism and hypothesis out of his own yearning substance, flinging them over the unknown void—and then walking on them, to catch we know not what. To be human is to be burdened with self-definition. And perhaps so long as individuals continue to grow, the achieving of any absolute or static identity may continue to elude us. I have tried to steer a careful course between ethological givens and ethnological possibilities, between Scylla and Charybdis, the rock of absolutist dogma and the whirlpool of relativist chaos, espousing only the principle that we should not fear but should cherish all manner of human differences. Ulysses encountered many tumultuous, even frightening predicaments (and also had some interesting adventures on the way). More than one time, Ulysses seemed lost, but he did finally make it home to Ithaca. However you may redefine home, and whatever the turmoils, I hope you will make it too.

Reference Notes

1. For tertiary differences, see Eleanor E. Maccoby (ed.), *The Development of Sex Differences* (Stanford: Stanford University Press, 1966).
2. Irving Goldman, *The Cubeo Indians of the Northwest Amazon* (Urbana: Illinois Studies in Anthropology, No. 2, 1963), cited in M. K. Opler, "Anthropological and Cross-Cultural Aspects of Homosexuality," in Judd Marmor (ed.), *Sexual Inversion: The Multiple Roots of Homosexuality* (New York: Basic Books, 1965), p. 117. The best book for distinguishing the diverse dynamics of transvestism, homosexuality, and transsexualism is by Robert J. Stoller, *Sex and Gender* (New York: Science House, 1968).
3. A summarizing of the Plains Indian ethos may be found in W. La Barre, *The Ghost Dance: Origins of Religion* (New York: Delta Paperbacks, 1972).
4. Classic sources on the *berdache*: Ruth Benedict, "Sex in Primitive Society," *American Journal of Orthopsychiatry* 9 (1939), 570–74; Ralph Linton, *The Study of Man* (New York: Boni & Liveright, 1924); La Barre, *Ghost Dance*, pp. 138–40, 156–57, and 179–81. A summary is by Henry Angelino and C. G. Shedd, "A Note on Berdache," *American Anthropologist* 57 (1955), 121–26; extensive bibliography may be found in W. W. Hill, "Note on the Pima Berdache," *American Anthropologist* 40 (1938), 338–40. For a complementary phenomenon, see O. Lewis, "Manly-Hearted Women Among the Northern Piegan," *American Anthropologist* 43 (1941), 173–87.

5. George Devereux, "Institutionalized Homosexuality of the Mohave Indians," *Human Biology* 9 (1937), 498–527.
6. Isidore Ziterstein, "Paul Ferdinand Schilder," in F. Alexander, S. Eisenstein, and M. Grotjahn (eds.), *Psychoanalytic Pioneers* (New York: Basic Books, 1966), p. 467.
7. Margaret Mead, *Sex and Temperament in Three Savage Societies* (New York: William Morrow & Co. 1935); see also her *Male and Female* (New York: Morrow, 1949).
8. Herbert Marcuse, *Eros and Civilization* (Boston: Beacon Press, 1955); also (New York: Vintage Books, 1962).
9. A sharp critique of our tribal customs: Jules Henry, *Culture Against Man* (New York: Random House, 1963).
10. G. Rattray Taylor, *Sex in History* (New York: Vanguard Press, 1954).

7. The Influence of Freud on Anthropology

Any homage worthy of Freud demands two things: a patient seeking of the human data; and an astringent, disenchanted assessment of things as they are. Few men have had to such a degree as Freud the quality that Henry James's hero sought—that essentially "masculine character, the ability to dare and endure, to know and not to fear reality, to look the world in the face and take it for what it is." If this intransigent maleness of mind has caused many to hate and to fear Freud, it is nevertheless the same quality for which others respect and admire him.

In assessing Freud's influence on anthropology this chapter uses three techniques: *statistical* (a self-estimate of anthropologists replying to a questionnaire), *historical* (a recounting of individual influences in the development of the new anthropology), and *bibliographical* (a résumé of official periodicals and texts, and a classified listing of works and representative dynamic-psychological interests). The first source of information is the Fellows of the American Anthropological Association. Because of generous criteria in the Association as to what constitutes a Fellow, this latter group includes without question, and almost exhaustively, all the mature scholars and active teachers in the field of American anthropology. We are further fortunate in having within the field an identifiable body of students—an interest-group rather than a formal "school" perhaps—concerned with a new dynamic kind of anthropology. Some members of this "culture-and-personality" group either deny or do not know their historical origins in psychoanalytical thinking. In any case, those frankly influenced by analysis we might expect would fall within even a loosely conceived "culture-and-personality" group.

In order to investigate the opinions of Fellows in these matters, the following simple questionnaire was prepared:

I regard myself in general as one of the current culture and personality group
.... Yes .... No
I have had analytic training for .... months.
I have read .... one, ... five, ... ten, ... more than 10

This essay was intended to emulate and to continue Clyde Kluckhohn's classic comprehensive study of "The Influence of Psychiatry on Anthropology in American During the Past One Hundred Years," in J. K. Hall, G. Zilboorg, and H. A. Bunker (eds.), *One Hundred Years of American Psychiatry* (New York: Columbia University Press, 1944). The same job needs to be done for the last two decades. First published in *The American Imago* 15 (1958), 275–328. Reprinted by permission.

original sources (Abraham, Ferenczi, Jones, Freud, Jung, Adler, Rank) of book length in the field.

I have read .... secondary sources or derivative books.

I teach a course in the general culture and personality area of interest.

.... Yes   .... No

....
Name (optional)

The format was that of a stapled double postcard. The reverse of the questionnaire card contained the researcher's university address. Pasted on the attached card was the addressee's name and address, from labels furnished by the Executive Secretary of the Association corrected to October 1955; the reverse of this bore a request to fill in and mail the self-addressed half of the card.

Of 635 questionnaires mailed to Fellows in the United States and Canada, 331 replies were received within precisely one month. Despite the open postcard and the specified option of signing, all but forty of the replies were signed. The results of the inquiry are presented here in tabular form.

The quantitative treatment of units as various as human beings must always yield data of but modest depth and reliability. We discovered, with satisfaction, that anthropologists are perhaps as restive of classification as any other group of scholars. Indeed, though courteously yielding enough data to be useful quantitatively, they edified and instructed more in their purely individual statements. From the raw data the following inferences may be drawn. In the first place, considering that many of the Fellows of the American Anthropological Association are archaeologists, linguists, and physical anthropologists—many of whom nevertheless generously responded to an essentially cultural questionnaire—the more than 50 percent response is indicative of individual interest in the survey. The signing of responses must further be taken as evidence of candor and responsibility.

Considering the variety of scientific interests among Fellows, the fact that between a fourth and a fifth of the fellows now regard themselves as being in the general culture-and-personality group is highly significant. Others expressed interest and goodwill, though they did not regard themselves as members of the group, whether from not having researched, published and taught in the area, or from having other preeminent scientific interests. A few of the results are obviously to be expected: members of the C/P group are much better read both in basic and in secondary sources (this is true both of total Fellows and of analyzands, viewed as members versus nonmembers). But one rather astonishing result is that 20 persons who do not regard themselves as members of the C/P group nevertheless teach courses in the general C/P area and six more such persons have taught such courses in the past! One does not quite know how to interpret this result, whether indicating that academic interest in the subject outstrips the number of persons qualified to teach it, or

Fellows of the American Anthropological Association

	Analytic training	Basic reading					Secondary sources			Teaching of C/P courses				
		None	One	Five	Ten	Ten+	Mean	Median	Range	Teach	Do not	Have taught	No answer	Uncertain
Members of C/P group (n = 70)	25[1]	2[2]	3[3]	14[4]	7[5]	41[6]	37.7	16	0, 4–200	41	24	1	3	1
Non-members of C/P gr. (n = 244)	12[7]	25	34	72	17	36	9.1	6	0–100	20	224	6		
Teachers of C/P Courses														
Teachers of C/P courses (n = 70)	17	1	7	21	7	34	25.7	12.5	4–150	70	8	8	26	3
Analyzands in the American Anthropological Association														
Members of C/P group	25			1	2	21	94.2	75	9–150	16	7	2		
Not members of C/P gr.	12[8]			3	1	8	49.9	25	9–100	1	10	1		

1. Of member-analyzands, the reported time (in months of analysis) was: 2, 6 (three persons, 7 (currently), 10, 12 (two persons), over 12, 18 (two persons), 20, 24 (three persons), over 24, 30, 36 (two persons), 48, 60, 72, 84, "many months," and "have been analyzed." All but two signed their names. Most of those with over a year's analysis are prominent and productive workers in the culture-and-personality area.

2. This category was voluntarily added to the questionnaire by respondants. One of those who has done no basic reading teaches in the C/P area.

3. Two of these teach in the C/P area.

4. Seven of these teach in the C/P area.

5. Four of these teach in the C/P area.

6. Of these better-read C/P members, 26 teach C/P courses, 1 has taught, 1 is uncertain, and 14 do not teach such courses.

7. The reported time (in months of analysis) was: 2, 3, 6, 10 (two persons), 12 (two persons), 24, 42, 36 (two persons), and "several years." One analyzand of three months, not a member of the C/P group, writes, "I practiced [lay] analysis both in a hospital clinic and privately 1920–1923; perhaps that is why could not subsequently identify with Cult.-&-Pers." Additionally, one MD writes, "I have had psychiatric training for several years. I regard a good deal of the so-called Personality and Culture work as dilettantism or quackery." Readers will draw their own conclusions from both these statements.

that some persons teach in the area mainly to deny the validity of their subject matter. From comments on replies, it is probable that both are in some measure true.

Possibly self-estimates about reading may throw further light on the matter. It is our impression that the majority of respondants have inflated notions about the amount of reading they have done in primary and secondary psychoanalytic sources. But whether this is true or not, replies in the lower reading brackets are quite surprising. One C/P teacher-member states he has done no basic reading in analysis; two teacher-members had read only one basic source; seven had read only five; and four had read only ten books. This further raises grave question of the qualifications of teachers in the C/P field. The better-read persons tend to teach, according to the tables, but not all teachers are well-read.[1] Two or three persons wrote vehement comments on the obvious assumption in the questionnaire that persons operating in the culture-and-personality area might legitimately be expected to know something about basic or derivative psychoanalytic literature.[a]

On this point more must be said. In the first place, the data themselves indicate that more than a third of the members of the culture-and-personality group have had personal analyses of varying lengths—which belies any suggestion that culture-and-personality studies "have nothing to do" with psychoanalytic competence and interests. In the second place, it is possible to be quite explicit about the historic intellectual origins of culture-and-personality studies.

Culture-and-personality studies essentially began in the 1930s at Yale University, when Edward Sapir and John Dollard began the first seminar on "Culture and Personality."[2] Throughout his professional career, John Dollard has been notable for his repeated crossing of departmental lines, being at once sociologist, psychologist, anthropologist, and lay analyst for many years—an "interdisciplinary" team in one person, though he has constantly associated himself with members of each of these groups in his professional researches. Edward Sapir had a great linguist's almost preternatural *sense of dynamic pattern*. It was he, among the first, who early became restive with traditional Boasian anthropology, which was physical-science oriented, field-data collecting, essentially hostile to all generalizations save those established in reconstructed diffusionist-history, and on the whole a science of atomistic behaviorism

---

a. It is possible that this is a reflection of a professional characteristic. Kluckhohn writes that "to this day, anthropologists as a group are relatively unsophisticated in broad intellectual matters. In large part, this tendency may be traced to a major condition of their intellectual lives: the time which other social scientists may give to work in the library the anthropologist must give to field work, to preparation for field trips, to the study of difficult non–Indo-European tongues. Such attention as the earlier American anthropologists gave to strictly theoretical questions was almost entirely confined to diffusion versus independent invention and various other 'historical' issues" (see reference note 1.). There is some indication that this tendency is changing among anthropologists in recent years. But the great glory of Boasian field-oriented anthropology is at the same time its major disadvantage.

centered on establishing descriptive culture-patterns. There can be no question, in all fairness, of the basic sanity and usefulness of Boasian[b] anthropology. Boas's field-orientation was a healthy counterattack on armchair theorizing in the social sciences. Indeed, his anti-theory bias has set the tone of American anthropology, which seems to regard as its mission the "cutting down to size" of the great generalizing theories in anthropology that have proceeded in the past almost wholly from England, France, and Germany—all the while that Americans unwittingly borrow theory to incorporate into a complacently ragtag-and-bobtail "nontheoretical" position.[3]

Sapir's sense of form and pattern has had profound influence in two important directions: in linguistics in the now-celebrated "Sapir-Whorf hypothesis."[4] and in ethnology in the culture-and-personality movement. In linguistics, Sapir and his students developed as tools the phonemic concept, the Indo-Europeanist methods of establishing starred forms and primitive linguistic stocks, such quantifiable quests for time-perspective as glottochronology, and the like. In cultural studies, Sapir was convinced that an essential tool for the field worker was a personal "didactic" analysis, which would alert him to a whole new universe of relevance and meaning in his data. He not only listed for reading the works of Freud, Abraham, Ferenczi, Jones, Jung and others; he also actively encouraged many of his students to obtain a psychoanalysis. This latter accounts, to an appreciable degree, for the probably higher percentage of analyzands among anthropologists than among comparable social scientists like sociologists and psychologists. Sapir's own thinking and teaching was unquestionably influenced, and deeply, by Freudian psychoanalysis; and he was until his death a close friend of the late Harry Stack Sullivan, whose own theories of interpersonal relations have been influenced by Sapir. A survey of courses in culture and personality, taken from university catalogues eighteen years ago and made by the present writer, showed that by far the majority of teachers of such courses at the time were Sapir's own students or secondarily influenced by them.[c]

Another trend eventually culminating in culture-and-personality studies began within American anthropology at large, stimulated primarily by Boas himself. In reaction partly to the French collectivist psychology of Durkheim and Levy-Bruhl, field workers began to be interested in the *individual* in the tribe, not merely in monolithic patterns of behavior shared by all. Was individuality as we know it nonexistent among primitive peoples? What range of difference could be found among the allegedly standardized members of a primitive so-

---

b. Leslie White has criticized Boasian anthropology vigorously for a generation, chiefly in the interests of a neo-evolutionism based on Lloyd Morgan; White is thus one of the rare exceptions to the usual non-theoretical pose of American anthropologists until the last two decades. The most recent of many critiques of Boas, citing also earlier sources, is that of Murray Wax (see reference note 3).

c. Kluckhohn writes that "to him [Sapir], more than to any other single person must be traced the growth of psychiatric thinking in anthropology" (see reference note 2).

ciety? With his usual provocativeness, Sapir stated the extreme position that "There are as many cultures as there are individuals in the population."[5]

In this period there began, therefore, the collecting of life histories of primitive individuals. Perhaps the most famous was Radin's *Crashing Thunder, the Autobiography of a Winnebago Indian*, but there were in time many others,[6] even though some of them were viewed merely as a new technique for approaching traditional culture-patterns. The most useful guide in the making of such studies is John Dollard's *Criteria for the Life History*. The best critique is Kluckhohn's paper on *The Personal Document in Anthropological Science*.[7]

Not all the restiveness with Boasian descriptive ethnography was Sapir's alone, however. Leslie White has also long been an influential and vocal critic of Boas. Likewise, Malinowski's "functionalism" was an independent attempt to go beyond the mere descriptiveness of Boasian anthropology; the same is true of Radcliffe-Brown's social configurationism. But Malinowski never achieved a genuinely dynamic view psychologically. Nor did his active neglect of history satisfy the American anthropologists, who were themselves largely preoccupied with historical reconstructions. Nor, for all his initial impetus, did all culture-and-personality studies remain Sapir's in inspiration, or even exclusively Freudian. Nevertheless, culture-and-personality studies do remain essentially Freudian in concept and outlook—for which reason they are most often and most vehemently attacked, notably by academic psychologists. But when, like Kluckhohn, we attempt to find examples of inspiration from other schools of psychology—for, after all, in the psychological understanding of culture, *any* psychology would, in theory, be equally available for the purpose—we find almost none. Whiting's *Becoming a Kwoma*[8] while in form a study in Stimulus-Response psychology, was nevertheless influenced by psychoanalysis and by Sapir. Radin predicted in 1929 that Jung would have a greater influence on anthropology than any other of the analytic group, which prediction has far from materialized.[9] The only Rankian influence upon an American anthropologist that we have been able to discover is in a brief paper by Kilton Stewart.[10] Of Adler, only three incidental references are known in the general anthropological literature.[11]

An early secondary influence on a large public was the configurationist approach of Ruth Benedict in her *Patterns of Culture*. Reviewed gingerly by Kroeber on its first appearance, this work subsequently has come under repeated professional attack.[12] It employs a dated and purely literary Spenglerian-Nietzschean dichotomy of "Apollonian" and "Dionysian" cultures. It is essentially a static Gestaltist picture, untouched by any sense of dynamics either from genetic psychology or from psychoanalysis. Benedict never asked how Zuni children *became* Zuni, and edited, misused or misunderstood such material when she did touch upon it. *Patterns of Culture* has set no tradition and enjoyed no successors, unless the equally criticized[13] *Chrysanthemum and the Sword* may be counted as such; it might stand as the last, and brilliant, effort of a purely static descriptive ethnography—except that the literary constraints of the basically dubious Apollonian-Dionysian dichotomy have raised doubts in the minds of most anthropologists as to the accuracy of the book even as descriptive ethnography. A defense, if defense it is, is that in both these books Benedict was not always writing from first-hand field experience, but was using sources secondarily to promulgate a thesis. In any case, no literary-impressionistic picture of an *ethos*, however brilliant, will satisfy a modern intellectual public, though *Patterns of Culture* has had a phenomenal popular success because of its felicitous literary style.

It was mainly in reaction to such literary impressionism[d] that the Rorschach[14] and other projective techniques,[15] group approaches like the Columbia University Research in Contemporary Cultures,[16] and interdisciplinary attacks like those of the Yale Institute of Human Relations, the Department of Social Relations at Harvard, and others elsewhere, have been instituted; such research gives added usefulness also to regional specializations like those at Cornell, Michigan, Northwestern, Pennsylvania, Syracuse, and elsewhere.

Of greater influence than Benedict, however, both with a lay public and among experts, has been Margaret Mead. Mead has always shown in her work a sharp sense of the ontogenetic origins of character, which Benedict largely lacked, a keener sense of problem, and a better command of method. The influence of Sapir on Mead[e] is obscure, but there is no question of her own origins in psychoanalytic thinking. Abraham, Spitz, and Róheim[f] first focused her interest on psychosexual zones and their importance in personality development, and Mead also acknowledges an intellectual debt to Erik Homburger Erikson.[17] From the beginning, her field work has been problem-centered. Eclectic, analytically influenced, a fine and perceptive field worker, she has produced voluminously.[18] Of enormous and continuing influence are her justly famous *Coming of Age in Samoa* and *Growing up in New Guinea*, and her Balinese and New Guinea studies are too well known to be more than mentioned here. The combined influence of Sapir and Mead has inspired a whole new approach to field work, which emphasizes the dynamic problem of *how*

---

d. The first anthropological use of the Rorschach Test in the field, according to Hallowell (see reference note 14), was that of D. B. Shimkin on the Wind River Shoshone, but unfortunately it was never published. But it is to Hallowell himself that the major credit must be given for pioneering this method in modern culture-and-personality studies. The National Research Council's Committee on Primary Records (Division of Anthropology and Psychology) will shortly begin publishing a series under the editorship of B. Kaplan to be entitled "Publications of Primary Records in Culture and Personality." These will contain in microfilm a large number of unpublished protocols of Rorschachs, TATs, Mosaic Drawing, and other projective tests, as well as life histories and dreams.

e. "How much of the parallelism in the writings of Benedict, Mead, and Sapir is pure convergence and how much represents the influence of Sapir upon Benedict and Mead is a difficult question. I agree with Goldenweiser that a careful reading of *Patterns of Culture* 'can leave no doubt that on several occasions Benedict found inspiration in the writings of the late Edward Sapir' " (Kluckhohn, reference note 17).

f. A debt to Róheim is again acknowledged in Mead's "Researches in Bali" (see reference note 17). For Mead's own selection of her early papers that are psychoanalytically oriented (see reference note 18).

the individual acquires the peculiar culture of his society. The literature of this "culture-and-personality" approach is now formidable;[19] it has been partly anthologized by Kluckhohn and Murray, and by Haring,[20] and has inspired a number[21] of critiques[g] and surveys.[22] But if there is one contemporary figure identified in the public mind with culture-and-personality studies, this is without question Margaret Mead. Probably because of a modified but implicit Freudian inspiration, she is also a major figure of attack. But she stands as well as the pioneer of modern problem-oriented field work, with all its advantages and disadvantages, as over against an older holistic field work. There can be little question of her large and permanent influence on American anthropology.

The Sapir-Sullivan friendship produced no manifest published documents, though it was followed by a number of anthropologist-psychiatrist collaborations, among which might be mentioned that of Mekeel with Erikson, the Henrys, Mirsky and Bunzel with Levy, Aginsky with Wilbur, Chapple with Lindemann, Du Bois with Oberholzer, and Kluckhohn with Fries, Alexander and Dorothea Leighton, and H. A. Murray. But the first major collaboration between a psychoanalyst and an anthropologist which eventuated in large-scale theoretical advances was that of Abram Kardiner and Ralph Linton. Linton was one of the great field workers of his generation, but he never pretended to a specialist's psychiatric sophistication. That such psychiatric good sense could be made of his field work was as much of a surprise to Linton as to anyone else; that the gatherer and the interpreter of the data were two different persons also made a deep and lasting methodological impression on otherwise indifferent or skeptical anthropologists. Kardiner's works have been major landmarks in the field of culture and personality.[23]

A more controversial, but historically important, figure is Géza Róheim. So far as his reception among American anthropologists was concerned, Róheim had the double disadvantage of a European education and viewpoint in anthropology and a vigorously intransigent orientation to classical psychoanalysis. A field worker and a practicing psychoanalyst, a voluminous writer, it must almost be said that he wrote for an analytically sophisticated audience alone, save for a very few anthropologists. But Sapir, Mead, Devereux, and La Barre have acknowledged Róheim's influence upon them, and his reputation will continue to grow.[24] The major difficulty is that Róheim (like his great mentor Ferenczi) demands a profound and extensive understanding of the psychoanalytic literature for his best appreciation—and this is not commonly come by, among American anthropologists at least. Róheim's field work between 1928 and 1931 was in Somaliland, Central Australia, Normanby Island, and among the Yuma of Arizona. His greatest work, in the present writer's opinion, is *The Origin and Function of Culture*, but his writing was voluminous.[25] Róheim also founded and edited the first three volumes of *Psychoanalysis and the Social*

g. It is notable that the most tendentious critiques of a movement in anthropology have come from academic psychologists and sociologists, who often manifest little understanding either of psychoanalysis or of field methods of validation in anthropology.

Sciences. His sixtieth-anniversary *Festschrift* was a belated statement of the appreciation in which he had come to be held.[26] As Devereux has stated, "Róheim's true stature, as a creator of the first rank in the field of the psychoanalytic study of society and in the field of culture and personality problems, is just beginning to be recognized."[27] His awareness that much of culture is an autistic defense mechanism has already taken root in anthropological theory.[28]

In the analysis-cum-anthropology tradition of Róheim, undoubtedly the major figure today is George Devereux, a brilliant and subtle mind, thoroughly sophisticated analytically, fecund in ideas and articulate in writing of them. He has published widely on an incredible variety of subjects. Among anthropologists he is best known for his series of publications on the Mohave,[29] but his papers on theory far outnumber even these. When his Mohave papers are gathered together from their scattered and sometimes obscure sources, and placed in proper ontogenetic order as below, it will readily be seen that Devereux's Mohave are more completely covered on subjects in which the psychiatrist is interested than any other tribe. Like Róheim, Devereux is an intellectuals' intellectual; but there is no doubt in the profession of anthropology that he is the ranking analytically oriented student in the field.

In the period between 1928 and 1939, Kluckhohn noted the names of Ernest and Pearl Beaglehole, Cora Du Bois, John Dollard, A. I. Hallowell, Scudder Mekeel, and M. E. Opler as anthropologists who have received major influences from psychiatry.[30] In 1948, La Barre stated that—although they are by no means all oriented psychoanalytically—a list of those who had shown in their writings an interest in psychologically oriented anthropology would have to include Ashley-Montagu, Barton, Dyk, Ford, Gillin, Henry, Herskovits, Hill, Johnson, Joseph, Klineberg, Landes, M. K. Opler, Simmons, Thompson, and Underhill, in addition to those previously mentioned.[31] At that date should also be mentioned Belo, Bunzel, Erikson, Gayton, Goldfrank, Gorer, Hoebel, A. H. and D. Leighton, Lesser, G. Newman, E. C. Parsons, H. Powdermaker, Seigel, Speck, Tax, C. and E. W. Voegelin, and J. W. M. and B. B. Whiting—in addition to names already mentioned. There are now over thirty-seven Fellows of the American Anthropological Association who have had a personal psychoanalysis, and this must be viewed as having influenced their work whether they are in the culture-and-personality field or not. In 1958, however, so many persons, well-equipped or ill, regard themselves as followers of the new anthropology that it would be temerarious and unfair to make any statement of their contributions, short of an exhaustive and compendious bibliography. The amount of fine field work—its armamentarium of questions added-to by culture-and-personality insights—is today formidable indeed.

But we run the risk of a biased view. These developments, to a degree, are all *within* the culture-and-personality movement in general. What of a larger and more diffuse influence upon American anthropology as a whole? In answering this question we must again seek some sort of objective indices. For this purpose the best source is undoubtedly the official organs of the American

Anthropological Association. Here, however, our conclusions must be somewhat less sanguine, for there has been a very slow acceptance that can be demonstrated. In the *General Index of the American Anthropologist 1888–1928* Freud is not mentioned; only one work of Freud is ever reviewed; and there is no entry under "Psychoanalysis" or the like. In the *Index* for the period 1929–1938, no work is Freud is reviewed; but the "Subject Index" lists items for 1929 and for 1933 under the rubric "Psychoanalysis and Anthropology." In the next decade there is still no listing of Freud, but under "Psychoanalysis and Culture" there is one listing in 1946 for Meggers' attack on culture-and-personality studies, and in 1948 of Devereux' review of Róheim's first volume of *Psychoanalysis and the Social Sciences.*[32] Scarcely a large official recognition!

In the following eight years prior to this writing (at the time unindexed), however, the content of articles involved with a dynamic viewpoint increased. In the writer's judgment, perhaps some twenty-eight such articles would fall under this description.[33] Not all were by any means favorable—but at least they do deal with psychological questions critically, and this represents an advance. Encouragingly also, the Book Reviews in the *American Anthropologist* introduced in 1952 a section on "Psychoethnography," inaugurating it with La Barre's review of Barnouw on Chippewa personality,[34] and continuing it more or less regularly to date.

Another possible criterion of influence might be the mention of indexing of Freud and of psychoanalysis in the standard textbooks in anthropology. Here again the picture is disappointing. Beals and Hoijer, Chapple and Coon, Gillin, Lowie, Shapiro, Slotkin, and Turney-High all list no work of Freud in their bibliographies, and list neither "Freud" nor "Psychoanalysis" in their Indexes. Lowie even managed to write a book on *Social Organization* with all these same omissions![35] In the Boas-edited *General Anthropology* there are only two—and singularly ill-informed—mentions in an article by Gladys Reichard. Goldenweiser lists no books and makes no mention of "Psychoanalysis" in his index, but alone of textbook writers of his generation he makes three informed and generous mentions of Freud. Herskovits, in his first edition, mentions *Totem and Taboo*, and makes two index references to Freud, both of which are critical; his second edition makes several more generous mentions. Hoebel lists *Totem and Taboo* only in his bibliography (which he calls Freud's "unfortunate essay into anthropology"), and contains but three index references. In Kroeber's revised edition, he cites his own review of *Totem and Taboo*, and is largely negative in another brief discussion of Freud. Linton merely lists *Totem and Taboo*, but has no index reference to Freud. In his *History of Ethnological Theory*, Lowie ignores Freud both in bibliography and index, but cannot quite manage to pass psychoanalysis by without a disparaging reference to Rivers and a wholly misconceived reference to Malinowski's relationship to Freud, to be discussed later. Titiev, listing no Freud in his bibliography and ignoring psychoanalysis in his index, has one brief mention praising Freud and criticizing his followers.[36]

It is possible to regard the above as merely a demonstration that anthropologists are as much laymen as anyone else in assessing a difficult subject like psychoanalysis. But psychoanalysis fares hardly better in the hands of one better informed. George Peter Murdock states in the preface to his *Social Structure* that he has had fifteen months of analysis; but he remains somewhat ambivalent to psychoanalytic theory. He regards the Oedipus situation as probably universal in the nuclear family, and states that "Freud's theory . . . provides the only available explanation of the peculiar emotional intensity of incest taboos." But at the same time, "we must admit that his ventures into cultural theory are little short of fantastic"; and in another place, after citing Freudian explanations at length, he states that "Freudian theory fails us at this point"—on a question of the family and society! In an extraordinary preface to his book, Murdock writes that psychoanalysis "is probably destined to disappear as a separate theoretical discipline as its findings are gradually incorporated into some more rigorous scientific system such as that of behavioristic psychology" and apologizes to his readers that he has "been compelled to use unassimilated Freudian theory" in discussing avoidance and joking relationships and incest taboos![37]

Kluckhohn, another important and influential figure among contemporary American anthropologists, also manifests the same tentativeness toward psychoanalysis in his popular book, *Mirror for Man*. Psychoanalysis is "the first really comprehensive psychological system" and is mentioned respectfully in the "findings of psychoanalysis, anthropology, and the psychology of learning." Yet in another place he imputes an inexactly stated concept to psychoanalysis, and then "criticizes" it with Navaho data. The origin of conscience is in "dread of the community." Kluckhohn is critical of "Freud's assumption of an aggressive instinct," and after mentioning Freud and Einstein on war goes on to discuss "a more scientific approach" of his own.[38] But in his more professional writing, he is at great pains to achieve a just statement about "Freud and other psychoanalysts [who] have depicted with astonishing correctness many central themes in motivational life which are universal."[39] Such judicial-mindedness is the more appreciated in a man whose considerable prestige among anthropologists is founded on just such judicial-mindedness and knowledge.[h]

The attitudes of the ranking American anthropologist today, A. L. Kroeber, have been even more interesting and significant. In 1920 Kroeber wrote the first article in an American anthropological journal to discuss psychoanalysis, his famous and influential review of *Totem and Taboo*. His treatment was generous, but critical, concluding that "with all the essential failure of its finally avowed purpose, the book is an important and valuable contribution,"

h. Another respected and influential anthropologist, Hallowell, writes that "the Freudian model of personality structure and its derivative formulations have provided the most useful constructs so far but not necessarily the final ones," and Mead mentions the influence of Freudian concepts in theories of "National Character" (see reference note 39).

and "thus is one that no ethnologist can afford to neglect."[40] As Kluckhohn has remarked, "Herein Kroeber appeared much wiser than many American anthropologists, down to the present. . . . The conventional American anthropologist dismissed Freud's anthropology as bad and his conclusions as worthless. With regrettable but familiar illogic, psychoanalytic method and theory were therewith rejected."[41] There have been two chief reasons why American anthropologists have virtually unanimously rejected Freud's *Totem and Taboo*. First of all, Freud chose to rely on an older anthropology, that of the English "cultural evolutionists," whose method assumed a psychological unity of mankind in symbolic content, and an analogy with biological evolution which the Americans had already heavily impugned. This first, if we may so characterize it, was a "Jungian" defect in some of Freud's early ethnological thinking and was compounded further by the assumption that by some sort of "archetypical" memory the sons subsequently through all cultural history remembered the original sin of murder of the father in the "primal horde." Surely this was a "Just-So Story" (Freud's own words, in remarking on Kroeber's review of *Totem and Taboo*). What everyone, anthropologists and psychiatrists alike, should come to see it that *given the nuclear family as a universal human institution, the same conditions for the rise of the typical Oedipus complex exist in every individual and generation*. Anthropologists, like other mere human beings, have of course the same resistances to seeing the reality of the universal Oedipal *predicament*; but this cannot impugn the scientific fact of the universal incest taboo ethnographically.

This "Jungian" phrasing of a basic ethnographic fact has been most unfortunate, for American anthropologists, again following Kroeber[42] and their own common knowledge that culture is socially inherited and historically diffused, not biologically inherited as an archetypical mneme, has led them uniformly and universally to reject Jungian psychology on this basic point. Indeed, in a remarkable later review of *Totem and Taboo* nearly two decades later, Kroeber himself stated this matter with entire fairness.[i] If we take the Oedipal predicament, not as one single far-off historical event, but as a typically recurrent situation,

---

i. Kroeber quite properly scouted "the assumption, apparently typical of the [Jungian] school that the symbols into which the 'libido' converts itself are phylogenetically transmitted and appear socially. The machinery of this assumed process is not examined. Its reality is considered established by the adduction of examples which may be so interpreted. Now, if the [Jungians] are right, nearly all ethnology and culture history are waste of effort, except in so far as they contribute new raw materials. If, on the other hand, current anthropological methods and the psychological assumptions underlying them are correct, the phylogenetic theories of Jung and his collaborators are only a mistaken excrescence on their sounder work. Mutual understanding will not progress as long as the two tendencies go their conflicting ways in ignorance of one another" (see reference note 42). Whether they are aware of it or not, American anthropologists would universally take the Freudian position on symbolism, best expressed by Ernest Jones (reference note 42). But there has been a recent (and by anthropologists almost universally rejected) recrudescence of the phylogenetic Jungian view in the fantasies of the Harvard "sociobiologists"—whose fault is not that they are biologistic but that they do not argue species-specifically, and take their analogies falsely from insect and infrahuman societies, thus committing the familiar "animal series fallacy."

here we obviously are on better ground. . . . Stripped down in this way, Freud's thesis would reduce to the proposition that certain psychic processes tend always to be operative and to find expression in widespread human institutions. Among these processes would be the incest drive and incest repression, filial ambivalence, and the like; in short, if one like, the kernel of the Oedipus situation. After all, if ten modern anthropologists were asked to designate one universal human institution, nine would be likely to name the incest prohibition; some have named it as the only universal one. Anything as constant as this, at least as regards its nucleus, in the notoriously fluctuating universe of culture, can hardly be the result of "mere" historical accident devoid of psychological significance.[43]

Unfortunately, Freud's ambiguity in stating a timeless psychological process as if it were a single historical event, and his casting it in the form of the inheritance of an acquired characteristic as if this did not clash with standard opinion both in biology and in the social sciences, have together constituted an intellectual rationale—in the service of irrational individual resistances—for the rejection of the single most important insight into the nature of culture.[44] Kroeber concludes his review with these words:

I trust that this reformulation may be construed not only as an *amende honorable* but as a tribute to one of the great minds of our day. . . . We, on our part, if I may speak for ethnologists, though remaining unconverted, have met Freud, recognize the encounter as memorable, and herewith resalute him.

Unfortunately, this honorable statement remains true only of Kroeber himself: most American anthropologists, having accepted the first review out of Kroeber's great prestige, have *not* met Freud and have *not* encountered his ideas from firsthand reading, certainly not much beyond a cursory look at *Totem and Taboo*, that most grievously Jungian of all Freud's works.

It is interesting to note how Freud fared with other members of the first generation of anthropologists after Boas. Elsie Clews Parsons, with her insatiable and searching interest in all things anthropological, indicated some knowledge of Freudian theory in a brief note published in 1915 in an analytic journal. In a footnote to a paper first published in 1918, A. A. Goldenweiser also betrayed some knowledge of Freud; and later, in a book, Goldenweiser repeatedly mentioned Freud and devoted space to a systematic *résumé* of theories. But Goldenweiser was an individualist, of a noble and disappearing older breed; and there is little doubt that his status among his fellows suffered somewhat because of his candid and atypical appreciation of Freud.[45]

Second only to Kroeber, it was another respected contemporary, Lowie, who did most to set the typical American anthropologist's attitude toward psychoanalysis. It is a melancholy chapter in intellectual history, for Lowie—unlike Kroeber—manifestly never came to understand, or even thoroughly to know, the position he attacked. American anthropologists have been peculiarly innocent when it comes to assessing matters of theory, notoriously dependent on others for opinions in such abstruse concerns, and in this trait strangely standardized for otherwise so splendidly maverick a crew. Given the traditional Boasian windmilling at all except historical generalizing in ethnology, it has seemed only to require someone to speak loudly enough in an authoritative voice to set opinion on any matter of theory. Let him be well- or ill-informed, if only his critique be *negative*—for then a fellow can relax by damning and thenceforth ignoring the whole vexatious theory itself! This is no doubt a serious indictment. However, this has happened not once but many times in American anthropology: a parallel case has been the curiously monolithic and standardized opinion on the Kulturkreislehre School at the hands of Boas—for evidently few others ever read this literature at first hand. It took a fresh assessment by Kluckhohn, who did read the literature, to make us aware of our illiteracy. Another example has been that of totemism. After a lively and fruitful discussion of its problems for some years both in Europe and in America, it took but one ukase from Boas and the subject was dropped, almost never to be discussed in succeeding decades in America. It is worth detailing the still further instance of Freud, and his treatment by Lowie and Malinowski.

In 1920, Lowie gave some space to "refuting" Freud on the mother-in-law taboo. In 1924 he published a book on primitive religion which managed never once to mention Freud or psychoanalysis, or even psychiatry! In 1937, in his standard text on ethnological theory, Lowie further displayed the extent of his knowledge of analysis. He maintained that Rivers (an English medical man much influenced by Freud) "does not seem to have done more than to paraphrase ethnographic facts in psychiatric jargon"—which is less than justice to Rivers, who was one of the pillars of an earlier success of analysis in Britain than in America. Lowie further writes of "Malinowski's synthesis of psychoanalytic concepts with his ethnographic findings"—which is more than justice to Malinowski. There is doubtless good reason for Lowie's modesty in saying in his preface that "he is prepared to admit his inability to appraise definitely the latest fashions." The question is, why, then, did he pretend to do so? Lowie's statement about Malinowski is absurd.[j] For Malinowski never at any time had any either profound or reliable knowledge of psychoanalysis. Nor was he ever in any sense a synthesizer of analysis and ethnology. Witness Malinowski himself on the matter:

---

j. Since writing the above, I have come across some almost startling parallels to my judgment on Malinowski. Kluckhohn writes that "to some anthropologists in Europe and to perhaps the majority of the older professionals in the United States Malinowski appeared as little better than a pretentious Messiah of the credulous." Kluckhohn accuses Malinowski of "Flamboyant flogging of dead horses"; Lowie [in Kluckhohn] taxes him with an "adolescent eagerness to shock the ethnological bourgeois." Kluckhohn concludes that one of the "great weaknesses in Malinowski's theory [was] the lack of a workable psychology.... As for psychology, Malinowski remained rooted in an outmoded behaviorism. His publications show no mastery of contemporary leaning theory. Psychoanalytic theory he influenced importantly [?], but he was never analyzed, and psychoanalysis failed to become part of his systematic thinking" (see reference note 46). Strangely enough, Malinowski even uses the word "irresponsibility" of himself!

The observations to be recorded in this chapter were mostly done before my psycho-analytic interest was stimulated. . . . It did not take me long to see that dreams did not play the part among the Trobrianders ascribed to them by Tylor and others, and after that I did not trouble much more about them. Later only, stimulated by some literature sent to me by Dr. C. G. Seligman and by his advice, did I begin to test Freud's theory of dreams as the expression of "repressed" wishes and of the "unconscious."

This was the extent of his knowledge, an example of his "testing," and a sample of the quality of his knowledge and understanding. Later on in the same book is a typically oblique reference to psychoanalysis in connection with homosexuality; and the final paragraph of his book is a characteristic Malinowskian mixture of arrogance and ignorance about psychoanalysis. It is difficult to see the grounds for Lowie's statement. *Sex and Repression in Savage Society* and *Crime and Punishment in Savage Society* were both attacks (and are so generally understood) on a poorly understood Freudianism (and this is not so generally known, the more especially since Lowie sets up Malinowski as the arch-exponent of Freud). Both books are of course intellectually irresponsible, or worse, for Malinowski never troubled to become familiar with what he was "testing" or criticizing. As he himself writes, "I have come to realize since the above was written that no orthodox or semi-orthodox psychoanalyst would accept my statement of the 'complex,' or of any aspect of the doctrine" as misconceived by Malinowski. If Malinowski thus mangled psychoanalytic concepts he did not understand, and if so sober and reputable a scholar as Lowie could regard this as a "synthesis of psychoanalytic concepts with his ethnographic findings," what then is the poor student, at fourth hand (and unaccustomed to consult sources on theory in any case), to think of Freud and of psychoanalysis! In his next paragraph, Lowie immediately embarks upon a savage attack on Malinowski, the supposed exponent of psychoanalysis: whatever relevance it may have to Malinowski personally, it certainly has no relevance to psychoanalysis or to Freud. Lowie knew that Lowie didn't know; but Lowie did not know that Malinowski also didn't know psychoanalysis. To quote Lowie himself, these "apocalyptic utterances," this "battering down wide open doors" is so complex an intellectual shambles that it would be comic were it not that several generations of anthropologists have shaped their opinions on this venerable text.[46]

But there is still another method of assessing the influence of Freud on anthropological matters. This method is to examine the extent to which, unacknowledged or not, Freudian insights have influenced a preoccupation with new subject matters. Since Freud has borne the obliquy and the abuse, there is surely no injustice in imputing to him the impetus to study of dreams. In the general anthropological literature, this has been a considerable preoccupation,[47] both among British and American "standard" anthropologists, most of them by no means committed to a classic psychoanalytical viewpoint.

Two papers of Freud stimulated a psychoanalytic interest in the materials

abundantly available in folklore, and several of his early followers made notable contributions to the study of folklore. Freud himself gives major credit
to Riklin, Abraham, Rank, Jones, Storfer, and Jung for the early analytic study
of folklore and myth.[48] But without doubt the chief modern analyst of folklore
is Géza Róheim, whose voluminous writings contain many analyses of folklore
in psychoanalytic terms. Probably the major organ for publication of folkloristic analyses in English is *The American Imago*.[49] Elsewhere, in the classical
tradition, have appeared other studies of fairy tales.[50] Other modern studies are
varied. Codellas shows how modern Greek folklore preserves in distorted form
etiological myths about anthrax in goat herds; La Barre, using ethnobotanical
data, has sought to show how peyote folklore, viewed respectfully in symbolic
terms, actually records accurate observations; Zeid indicates how Egyptian
folk literature gives disguised satisfaction of repressed desires, and his fellow-
countryman El Saggad has studied Egyptian psychology from their folksongs;
M. E. Opler and R. F. Fortune have both written on the symbolism of the
snake; and Engle has made a series of fine psychoanalytic studies of classic
Greek folklore.[51] Psychiatrists also have used folkloristic materials for study.
Marie Bonaparte has repeatedly written on modern modern folk myths.[52] From
a psychoanalytic point of view, Moellenhoff has written on Mickey Mouse,
and Grotjahn on Ferdinand the Bull; Vowinckel-Weigert has made a brilliant
study of the cult and mythology of the Levantine mother-goddess, with which
should be mentioned Kohen on the Venus of Willendorf, and Ferenczi and
Coriat on the Medusa.[53] Karlson wrote an early paper, and Marett a book specifically on folklore and psychology.[54] Among analytically influenced American
anthropologists, Kluckhohn has written a theoretical paper on mythology;
Goldfrank on Hopi, and Jacobs on Chinook myths; Opler and Obayashi
showed how current psychological tensions in Japanese internment camps
found expression in *senryu* folk-poetry; the content of the "normal unconscious mind" was examined by La Barre through the use of limericks, and the
same author has done analytic studies of obscenity and of the popular cartoons
of William Steig. Honigmann has also written on obscenity. Charles has shown
how the ritual clown's function integrates with local tensions in given societies;
Dollard has written on an American Negro tension-reducing game; and Sterba
on a Dutch festival, Hallowe'en, and the World War II popular legend that
"Kilroy Was Here."[55] This sampling of studies does not pretend to be exhaustive
but is merely representative of the wide range of subjects that may be illuminatingly treated through the use of a dynamic viewpoint.

A vulgar allegation against Freud is that his psychoanalysis is "culture-
bound." The present writer has commented on how poorly made is this point—
particularly since the equally criticized "biological orientation" of Freud makes
psychoanalysis peculiarly well available for cross-cultural studies.[56] Indeed, Freud
was especially aware of the cultural pressures shaping neuroses and psychoses[57]
and has ranged no less in anthropological space than in historical time.[58] Out
of such interests has emerged what might fairly be called the beginnings

of a new "Comparative Psychiatry," in a number of studies.[59] The influence of Sapir and others, arising from an interest in the individual in culture,[60] has alerted anthropologists to collect detailed psychiatric material on specific cases of neurotics and psychotics in non-Western societies.[61] Directly in the psychoanalytic tradition is the only fully reported psychoanalysis of a non-Western individual, George Devereux's *Reality and Dream*, the psychotherapy of a "Wolf" Indian—in which, additionally, Devereux develops the interesting thesis of a "culture-area personality" arising from the common elements in the ddtritus of various Plains cultures.[62] More numerous are comparative psychiatric materials focused on a specific tribe.[63] Incidental remarks of psychopathological interest are not uncommon in the older ethnographic accounts, of which the following afford a representative sample.[64] But this is in marked contrast with a modern awareness that cultures *shape and define* psychoses. As early as 1934, Ruth Benedict was struck with the ease with which "abnormals" in our society would function in certain other cultures, concluding that "culture may value and make socially available even highly unstable human types," such as epileptic shamans or homosexual *berdaches*. Her view was that "each culture is a more or less elaborate working-out of the potentialities it has chosen." Certainly, she felt, "These illustrations force upon us the fact that normality is culturally defined."[65] But such relativistic thinking soon brings up the question: what is your baseline, your pan-human norm? Otherwise, how can your clinical labels "paranoid," "megalomaniac" and the like rise above mere cross-cultural name-calling?[66]

In this slowly emerging field of "Comparative Psychiatry," probably the most articulate statements have been those of George Devereux.[67] But there have been others aware of his problem arising from the collaboration of psychiatry and anthropology. In 1934, the anthropologist J. M. Cooper wrote on "Mental Disease Situations in Certain Cultures: A New Field for Research"; and in "A Note on Adjustment and Culture" discussed what psychiatrists would term the contrasting "autoplastic" solution of Oriental societies, and the "alloplastic" solution of Western societies.[68] The psychiatrist Coriat also contributed to this question in a paper on "Psychoneuroses among Primitive Tribes."[69] Earlier, De La Tourette had glimpsed the same problem.[70] John Dollard, in 1934, wrote on "The Psychotic Persons Seen Culturally," and L. K. Frank has developed these ideas in several publications, as have Eric Fromm and Karen Horney among psychiatrists.[71] Among anthropologists who have written on the question are Green, Hallowell, Henry, Honigmann, Hsu, Kroeber, La Barre, Linton, Warner, and Westermarck, in addition to those mentioned previously.[72] Others who have considered the question include the psychiatrists Kirby, Róheim, Schilder, Skliar and Starikowa, and Von Domarus,[73] and sociologists and psychologists including Klineberg, Smith, and Unwin.[74]

Of further interest to both psychiatrists and anthropologists are specific studies among primitive groups of alcoholism,[75] amok,[76] arctic hysteria,[77] and homosexuality among primitives,[78] latah,[79] mali-mali,[80] myriachit,[81] schizophrenia[82] and suicide among primitives,[83] tarantism and the "jumping" hysteria,[84] the use of drugs,[85] and the windigo psychosis.[86]

A further evidence of stimulation from the psychoanalytic movement is a trend among anthropologists to an interest in psychotherapeutic techniques found among primitive peoples.[87]

In sum, from an historical point of view, a great many people, varyingly equipped in training, have "climbed upon the bandwagon" of culture-and-personality studies. But from another, and perhaps fairer, point of view, the initial impetus of dynamic psychiatry's influence on anthropology has now become generalized—attenuated and diffuse perhaps, but all the more solidly entrenched and accepted by persons of different theoretical persuasions. Many of these do not know their debt to Freud through Sapir and Róheim, so much has psychoanalysis become part of the climate of thinking. Nevertheless, the awareness that culture is not a mere descriptive congeries of "traits" that mechanically "diffuse" geographically, but is rather a configuration of dynamically meshed and significantly interrelated parts *operating always in individual human beings*—that culture, in short, has psychological dimensions and psychiatric meanings—is here to stay, a revolution accomplished.

But what of the future? Here imagination takes flight—for the major premise of the analytically astute anthropologist must necessarily be that *nothing human can escape illumination* from the penetrating, pan-human, and holistic psychology of Freud. To establish this point, let us take first that anthropological science most improbably susceptible at first blush of yielding analytic insights: archaeology. Here we have only human artefacts and human remains. But if humans have made or ever touched an object, that object is potentially able to communicate to us across time. Already we have a first few brilliant essays in "analytic archaelogy." Kohen, for example, remarks on the curiously unspecified features of paleolithic fertility-goddesses, and Heilbronner contrasts the impressionistic profiles of male figures and animals in the Aurignacian period with the Magdalenian realistic frontal views of human females (often with the indistinct, schematized faces of the Oedipal nightmare)—undoubtedly a change in artistic preoccupation which should yield further insights into social structure when viewed with the Flügel-Taylor hypothesis of sex and social structure in history. Anthony Wallace has done a brilliant "palaeopsychological" reconstruction of the *ethos* of the ancient Maya—by examining their art and sculpture with the eye of modern projective techniques. Doris Webster has given us an uncanny, almost Schilderesque insight into the body-image meaning of the signs of the zodiac. Suzanne Bernfeld has left no doubt in our minds about the Oedipal meanings of archaeology, and Bryce Boyer has shown us how mere sculptures can tell us much about psychic states.[88]

Probably all Old Stone Age art should be looked at again with an analytically sophisticated eye. Certainly some properly equipped person should study, in body-image and symbolic terms, the art and the arts of primitive peoples.

Why, for example, is the elongated nose attached to the navel or to the penis in many Melanesian masks? What can be discovered analytically about the pig-motif in Melanesian art? What is the meaning of the bird-man symbolism in Oceania, from Melanesia to Easter Island? What are the analytic meanings of the fetishisms in Guinea Coast sculpture? What is the relevance of distortion of proportions in body-image terms in West African sculpture? What meanings can be discovered in the elegant animal-motifs in Scythian art? Might not a psychoanalytically astute person reassess the feline-motif in Chavin, Tiahuanaco and other South American sculpture and religion? And the weeping god of Tiahuanaco and elsewhere? The whole of the rich Middle American art should be looked at again psychoanalytically. Indeed, all primitive art—a peculiarly neglected area in contemporary anthropology—could well be carried beyond mere sterile description.

Primatology and human biology need more psychoanalytic insights. What, for example, are the psychosexual meanings of preferred marriage patterns, of avoidance and joking relationships, of kinship structures, both in nomenclature and in behavior patterns? The psychological process of raciation, native ideas of "beauty" and selective mating need to be explored. The meaning and therapy of race prejudice, a subject already soundly founded, needs more anthropological-psychiatric exploration. No one has ever exhaustively studied the Southern psychosis of post-Civil War times in this matter.[89]

Since its whole subject matter is symbolism and human structural artefacts, linguistics can also well use a psychoanalytic viewpoint. The Sapir-Whorf hypothesis should leave no doubt of the fertility of this field. The linguists Garvin, Trager, and Newman have all done subtle psychological studies on language; and Henry, Goldfrank, and Thorner have also contributed brief but valuable notes on these matters. In this same general area of symbolic communication, Birdwhistell, Klineberg, and La Barre should be joined by others interested in emotional expression and gesture. Obviously one such interesting study could be made by taking off from the ancient Hindu *Natya*, through Indonesian posture dancing and dance drama, and continuing out into the Oceanic attenuated forms of gesture language.[90]

Basic problems of *process* should be looked at psychoanalytically by anthropologists. What, for example, are the complex psychological factors involved in differential diffusion of traits? What are the hidden symbolic compatibilities and incompatibilities? What are the psychic rationales of culture conflict and culture change? All these matters require psychoanalytic insight for their fuller understanding.

Another area which, like archaeology, would seem unpromising for psychological treatment, is material culture. But Darlington has shown us the psychiatric dimensions of making clay pots! We would like to see further investigations of certain peculiar compulsive mechanisms in the manufacture of basketry in the Southwest. And, indeed, the whole area of primitive economic behavior should be studied psychoanalytically, as Weisskopf has already done for Western man. Tausk, Schilder, and Lorand (we believe) are really indispensible to the student comprehensively interested in material culture and inventions. What, for example, is the relation of the body image to invention and discovery? Hanns Sachs' essay on the Greek "delay of the machine age" and Yu-lan Fung's on China's have already shown how much more profound our potential understanding of technology could be through psychoanalysis.[91]

This, of course, by no means exhausts the relevance of psychoanalysis to the study of material culture. What more could we not learn from a restudy of bodily mutilations, decorations and adornment, concerning the body image, the erotization of body parts, and other finer points of ethos? No comparative study has been made, either, on primitive equivalents of Flügel's brilliant psychology of clothing, though the material is rich and available. Again, what bearing has the division of labor by sex upon oedipal constellations and social structure? What is the relationship between house-type and sleeping arrangements upon such diverse matters as primal scene mythology, projective religion, and political organization; and how, in specific tribes, are family and kin structure and child care related to the political structure of the state? The analytically sophisticated reader will immediately see from these few examples that it is not a matter of problems but rather the lack of analytic method that alone prevents further work in the area of material culture. If cultures are constructed by human beings, if culture traits are thus functionally interrelated in unexpected ways, and if the unconscious does exist, then the possibilities of insight are well-nigh limitless. That the demanding and difficult analytic method is shared as yet by but few anthropologists need not stem our heuristic enthusiasm for these possibilities.

Primitive literature and religion as projective systems will undoubtedly continue to be the most rewarding of all fields of anthropology for the scholar equipped with analytic tools. Regrettably, Jane Harrison came to an awareness of Freud only in the third of her great works on religion, but Cornford and Engle and others will carry forth this tradition in classical studies, the insights of which might well enough be applied also to the study of primitive folklore and literature. No anthropologist henceforth should suppose that he knows enough to write about primitive religion, unless he has read Freud, Jones, Kardiner, Reik, and Weigert.[92] For example, the entire problem of totemism needs to be reopened, and specific studies made of the Egyptian theriomorphic gods, of the Levantine rain-bull of the Neolithic (with its offshoots into East African cattle ritualism, Hindu cow worship, the Minoan-Cretan bull cult, the Orphic-Dionysian bull-murder, and the Roman and Spanish bull-fight), of the complex Semitic pig-totemism, of the worldwide genital mutilations, and of the great intercontinental snake-symbolism and its ancient meanings. Every primitive religious system deserves, of course, a treatment illuminated by analytic insight—thus far lacking except for the already cited books of Kardiner, the work of Freud and Reik on Judaism, and occasional papers like Daly on Hinduism, and Engle, Weigert, and Cornford on classical Greek subjects. Furthermore, even Christianity is incompletely understood as yet in psychoanalytic terms. And why has no one written a psychoanalytic study of the Southern snake-handling cult of contemporary times?

Freud, Alexander and Healy, Fries, Stanton and Stewart, Honigmann, Yap, Lasswell, West, and De Grazia should all be read by anthropologists interested in political organization, the state, and law—perhaps especially Indonesian *adat* and the sophisticated West African legal systems.[93] Applied anthropology should look, for various purposes, to Brill, Davidson, Dollard and Harten, Frank, Hadley, Kris and Leites, Maskin and Altman, Rinaldo, Stephenson and Cameron. And the value even to physical anthropology of psychoanalytic insights has only begun to have been shown by La Barre.[94]

One could elaborate almost indefinitely further. What is obviously needed, however, is that all students of all the humanities should ideally have some analytic understanding. If only we have the techniques of insight, then all humanistic data will yield up their secrets, we know not what beforehand. We return to our earlier premise: in the hands of the analytically astute anthropologist and humanist, nothing human can escape illumination from the penetrating, pan-human and holistic psychology of Freud. These are but samples.

Reference Notes

1. Clyde Kluckhohn, "The Influence of Psychiatry on Anthropology in America during the past One Hundred Years," in J. K. Hall, G. Zilboorg, and H. A. Bunker (eds.), *One Hundred Years of American Psychiatry* (New York: Columbia University Press, 1944), pp. 590–91.
2. Kluckhohn, *Influence of Psychiatry*, pp. 600–5; quotation from p. 601.
3. Murray Wax, "The Limitations of Boas' Anthropology," *American Anthropologist* 58 (1956), 63–74.
4. The Sapir-Whorf Hypothesis had its origin in Sapir's "Conceptual Categories in Primitive Languages," *Science* 74 (1931), 568, contained in D. G. Mandelbaum (ed.), *Selected Writings of Edward Sapir* (Berkeley & Los Angeles: University of California Press, 1949). The thesis was developed in Benjamin L. Whorf's *Four Articles on Metalinguistics* (Washington: Foreign Service Institute, 1949), and in *Language, Thought, and Reality* (Cambridge: Technology Press of the Massachusetts Institute of Technology, 1956). The most important critique of the hypothesis to date is H. Hoijer (ed.), *Language in Culture* (Menasha, Wisc.: Memoirs of the American Anthropological Association 79 [1953]), especially the papers by Joijer and Fearing.
5. Ruth Benedict in "Obituary of Edward Sapir," *American Anthropologist* 41 (1939), 465–68, p. 467. A representative sample of the literature inspired by these questions would include: W. Beck, *Das Individuum bei den Australien* (Leipzig: R. Voigt Länder, 1924); W. Koppers, "Individualforschung unter den Primitiven im besonderen unter den Yamana auf Feuerland," in W. Koppers (ed.), *Schmidt-Festschrift* (Vienna: Mechitharisten-Congregations-Buchen, 1928), pp. 349–65; R. H. Lowie, "Individual Differences and Primitive Culture," ibid., pp. 495–500; M. Mead, "The Role of the Individual in Samoan Culture," *Journal of the Royal Anthropological Institute* 58 (1928), 481–96; R. Thurnwald, "Werden, Wandel und Gestaltung von Staat und Kultur," in *Die Menschliche Gesellschaft* 4 (1935), sub "Persönlichkeit"; A. Vierkandt, "Führende Individualen bei den Naturvölker," *Zeitschrift für Sozialwissenschaft* 11 (1908), 1–28; W. D. Wallis, "Individual Initiative and Social Compulsion," *American Anthropologist* 17 (1915), 647–65; and H. Webster, "Primitive Individual Ascendance," *Publications of the American Sociological Society* 12 (1918), 44–60.
6. John Adair, "Life Histories of Six Zuni Young Men," in Bert Kaplan (ed.), *Microcard Publi-*

cations of Primary Records in Culture and Personality (Madison, Wisc.: University of Wisconsin Press, 1956 [hereinafter referred to as *MPPRCP*]); Hamed Ammer, *Growing Up in an Egyptian Village* (London: Routledge & Kegan Paul, 1954; E. G. Anderson, *Chief Seattle* (Caldwell, Idaho: Caxton Printers, 1943); Rufus Anderson, *Memoir of Catherine Brown, a Christian Indian of the Cherokee* (London: B. J. Holdsworth, 1825); Anonymous, *Memoir of the Distinguished Mohawk Indian Chief, Sachem and Warrior, Captain Joseph Brant* (Brantford, Ont.: C. E. Stewart & Co., 1872); William Apes, *A Son of the Forest*, 2nd ed. rev. (New York: The Author, 1831); S. M. Barrett (ed.), *Geronimo's Story of His Life* (New York: Duffield, 1907); R. F. Barton, *Philippine Pagans: The Autobiographies of three Ifugaos* (London: Routledge & Kegan Paul, 1938); R. A. Bauer, *Nine Soviet Portraits* (New York: Technology Press of Massachusetts Institute of Technology, 1955); E. and P. Beaglehole, *Some Modern Maoris* (Wellington: N. Z. Council for Educational Research, 1946); F. L. Beals, *Chief Black Hawk* (Chicago: Wheeler Publishing Co., 1943); J. Beckett, "Marginal Men: A Study of Two Half-Cast Aborigines," *Oceania* 29 (1958), 91–108; G. Bennett, "An Account of Elau, a Malayan Papuan Child," *Australian Medical Gazette* 2 (1883), 255–58; Black Hawk, *Life of Ma-Ka-Tai-Me-She-Kia-Kiak* (Boston: Russell, Odiorne & Metcalf, 1834); H. Blodgett, *Samson Occom* (Hanover, N.H.: Dartmouth College Publications, 1935); T. D. Bonner (ed.), *The Life and Adventures of James P. Beckwourth, Mountaineer, Scout, and Pioneer and Chief of the Crow Nation of Indians* (New York: Harper & Bros., 1856); B. Bonnerjea, "Reminiscences of a Cheyenne Indian," *Journal de la Societé des Americanistes de Paris* 27 (1935), 129–43; E. Bourguignon, "A Life History of an Ojibwa Young Woman," *MPPRCP* 1 no. 10, 1956; D. Bray, *The Life History of a Brannul* (London: Royal Asiatic Society, 1913); G. Brown, "Life History of a Savage," *Australian Association for the Advancement of Science* 7 (1898), 778–90; E. M. Bruner, "The Life History of a Fort Berthold Indian Psychotic," *MPPRCP* 2, 1957; F. Bryk, *Dark Rapture* (New York: Walden Publications, 1939).

J. W. Caughey, *McGillivray of the Creeks* (Norman: University of Oklahoma Press, 1938); Buwei Yang Chao, *Autobiography of a Chinese Woman* (New York: John Day, 1947); Nirad C. Chaudhuri, *The Autobiography of an Unknown Indian* (New York: Macmillan, 1951); A. D. Clerc, *Chitlangou: Son of a Chief* (London: Lutterworth Press, 1950); Cyrenus Cole, *I Am A Man: The Indian Black Hawk* (Iowa City: State Historical Society of Iowa, 1938); June M. Collins, "John Fornsby: The Personal Document of a Coast Salish Indian," in Marian W. Smith (ed.), *Indians of the Urban Northwest* (New York: Columbia University Press, 1949); Elisabeth Colson, "Autobiographies of Three Pomo Women," *MPPRCP*, 1956; George Copway, *The Life, History, and Travels of Kah-Ge-Ga-Gah-Bowh*, 6th ed. (Philadelphia: James Harmstead, 1847); Paul Cuffe, *Narrative of the Life and Adventures of Paul Cuffe, a Pequot Indian* (Vernon, N. H.: Bill, 1839); Benjamin Drake, *The Great Indian Chief of the West* [Black Hawk] (Cincinnati: Applegate & Co., 1851); idem, *Life of Tecumseh, and of his Brother the Prophet* (Cincinnati: E. Morgan & Co., 1841); Walter Dyk (ed.), *The Son of Old Man Hat: A Navaho Autobiography* (New York: Harcourt Brace, 1938); Rupert East, *Akiga's Story, the Tiv Tribe as Seen by One of its Members* (London: Oxford University Press, 1939); C. A. Eastman, *Indian Boyhood* (New York: McClure, Phillips & Co., 1902); E. Eggleston and L. S. Seelye, *Tecumseh and the Shawnee Prophet* (New York: Dodd, Mead & Co., 1878); Edward S. Ellis, *The Life of Pontiac, the Conspirator, Chief of the Ottawas* (New York: Beadle & Co., 1861); idem, *Tecumseh, Chief of the Shawanoes* (New York: E. P. Dutton & Co., 1898); Enimikeeso, *The Indian Chief* (London: William Nichols, 1867); Margaret J. Field, *Akim-Kotoku, an Oman of the Gold Coast* (London: Crown Agents for the Colonies, 1948); Clellan S. Ford, *Smoke from Their Fires* (New Haven: Yale University Press, 1941); Grant Foreman, *Sequoyah* (Norman: University of Oklahoma Press, 1938); H. A. Forsbrook, "The Life of Justin: An African Autobiography," *Tanganyika Notes Record* 41 (1955) 31–57; George E. Foster, *Se-quo-yah, The American Cadmus and Modern Moses* (Philadelphia: Office of the Indian Rights Association, 1885); Anna Foster, *The Mohawk Princess* [E. Pauline Johnson] (Vancouver: Lion's Gate Publishing Co., 1931); G. H. Franz, *Tau, the Chieftain's Son* (Natal: Dundee, 1929); Donald Frazer, *Autobiography of an African* (London, Seeley, Service & Co., 1925); W. D. Funkhouser, *Autobiography of an Old Man* (Lexington, Ky: [no publisher], 1941).

R. H. Gabriel, *Elias Boudinot, Cherokee, and His America* (Norman: University of Oklahoma Press, 1941); S. Garst, *Chief Joseph of the Nez Perce* (New York: Messmer, 1953); G. A. Gollock, *Lives of Eminent Africans* (New York: Longmans, Green & Co., 1928); W. Grant,

"Magato and His Tribe," *Journal of the Royal Anthropological Institute* 35 (1905), 266–70; A. I. Hallowell, "Shabwán, A Dissocial Indian Girl," *American Journal of Orthopsychiatry* 8 (1938), 329–40; M. R. Harrington, "The Life of a Lenape Boy," *Pennsylvania Archaeologist* 3 no. 4; G. R. Hebard, *Sacajawea, a Guide and Interpreter of the Lewis and Clark Expedition* (Glendale, Cal.: Arthur W. Clark, 1933); J. J. Honigmann, "The Life History of a Pathan (Pakistan) Young Man," *MPPRCP* 1 no. 5 (1956); Helen A. Howard, *War Chief Joseph* (Caldwell, Idaho: Caxton Printers, 1941); Howard Oliner, *Famous Indian Chiefs I Have Known* (New York: Century, 1907); idem, *Nez Perce Joseph* (Boston: Lee & Shepard, 1881); Pingying Hsieh, *Autobiography of a Chinese Girl* (London: Allen & Unwin, 1945); J. N. Hubbard, *An Account of Sa-Go-Ye-Wat-Ha, or Red Jacket* (Albany: Munsell, 1886); J. G. Huddle, "The Life of Yakobo Adoko of Lango District," *Uganda Journal* 21 (1957) 184–90; Thomas Hughes, *Indian Chiefs of Southern Minnesota* (Mankato, Minn.: Free Press Co., 1927); C. M. Jaramillo, *Romance of a Little Village Girl* (San Antonio: Naylor & Co., 1955); A. E. Jenks, *Childhood of Jishib, the Ojibwa* (Madison, Wisc: The American Thresherman, 1900); W. Fletcher Johnson, *Life of Sitting Bull and History of the Indian War of 1891* (Philadelphia: Edgewood Publishing Co., 1891); Charles H. L. Johnston, *Famous Indian Chiefs* (Boston: L. C. Page & Co., 1909); Peter Jones, *Life and Journals of Kah-ke-wa-quo-na* (Toronto: A. Green, 1860); Mohamed L. Kazem, "Autobiographies of Five Egyptian Young Women," *MPPRCP* 2 (1956); D. Kidd, *Savage Childhood* (London: A. & C. Black, 1906); A. R. King, "The Dream Biography of a J. Maiden," *Character and Personality* 11 (1943), 227–34; C. Kluckhohn, "A Navaho Personal Document," *Southwestern Journal of Anthropology* 1 (1945), 260–83; W. La Barre, "The Autobiography of a Kiowa Indian," *MPPRCP* 2 (1957); Chester A. Lee, *Chief Joseph* (New York: Wilson-Erickson, 1936); Francis La Flesche, *The Middle Five* (Madison: University of Wisconsin Press, 1963); A. and D. Leighton, "Gregorio, the Hand-Trembler: A Psychological Personality Study of a Navaho Indian," *Papers of the Peabody Museum of American Archaeology and Ethnology* 40 (1949); idem, "Navaho Lives," Chap. 8 in idem, *The Navaho Door* (Cambridge: Harvard University Press, 1944); F. B. Linderman, *American, The Life Story of a Great Indian* (New York: John Day, 1930), idem, *Plenty-Coups, Chief of the Crows* (Lincoln: University of Nebraska, 1930); idem, *Red Mother* (New York: John Day, 1932); R. T. Lobsang, *The Third Eye: The Autobiography of a Tibetan Lama* (London: Secke & Warburg, 1956); Chief Buffalo Child Long Lance, *Long Lance* (New York: Cosmopolitan Book Corporation, 1928); Martha P. Lowe, *The Story of Chief Joseph* (Boston: D. Lothrop & Co., 1881); Albert Luthuli, *Let My People Go* (Johannesburg: Collins, 1946).

Bertlil Malmberg, *Ake and His World* (New York: Farrar & Rinehart, 1940); Thomas B. Marquis (ed.), *Wooden Leg: A Warrior Who Fought Custer* (Minneapolis: Midwest Co., 1931); Alice Marriott, *Maria: The Potter of San Ildefonso* (Norman: University of Oklahoma Press, 1948); J. J. Mathews, *Wah'Kontah, The Osage and the White Man's Road* (Norman: University of Oklahoma Press, 1932); N. Matson, *Memories of Shaubena* (Chicago: Donnelley, Cassette and Lloyd, 1880); L. V. McWhorter, *Yellow Wolf, His Own Story* (Caldwell, Idaho: Caxton Press, 1940); A. B. Meachem, *Wi-ne-ma and Her People* (Hartford, Conn.: American Publishing Co., 1876); Truman Michelson, "The Autobiography of a Fox Indian Woman," *Annual Report of the Bureau of American Ethnology* 40 (1919), 295–349; idem, "Narrative of an Arapaho Woman," *American Anthropologist* 35 (1933), 595–611; idem, "Narrative of a Southern Cheyenne Woman," *Smithsonian Miscellaneous Collection* 87 (1932); T. Mofolo, *Chaka* (London: Humphrey Milford, 1931); G. Moore, "Amos Tutuloa, A Nigerian Visionary," *Black Orpheus* 1 (1957), 27–35; R. Morenus, *Crazy-White-Man* (New York: Rand McNally & Co., 1952); William H. Murray, *Pocohontas and Pushmataha* (Ardmore, Okla.: Paine, 1924); J. G. Neihardt, *Black Elk Speaks* (New York: William Morrow & Co., 1932); S. Y. Ntara, *Man of Africa* (London: Religious Tract Society, 1934); A. K. Nyabonga, *The Story of an African Chief* (New York: Scribner's, 1935); M. E. Opler, "Dirty Boy: A Jicarilla Tale of Raid and War," *Memoirs of the American Anthropological Association* 52 (1938); J. M. Oskison, *Tecumseh and His Times* (New York: Putnam, 1938); Elsie C. Parsons, "Waiyautitea of Zuni, New Mexico," *Scientific Monthly* 9 (1919) 443–57; J. B. Patterson (ed.), *Autobiography of Ma-Ka-Tai-Me-She-Kia-Kiak, or Black Hawk* (St. Louis: Continental Publishing Co., 1882); Margery Perham (ed.), *Ten Africans* (Evanston, Ill.: Northwestern University Press, 1936); Ebenezer W. Pierce, *History, Biography and Genealogy: Pertaining to the Good Sachem Massasoit* (North Abingdon: Zerviah Gould Mitchell, 1878); A. H. E. Poinant, *Piccaninny Walkabout: A Story of Two Aboriginal Children* (Sidney: Angus & Robertson, 1957); Saxton T. Pope, "The Medical History of Ishi," *University of California Publications in American Archaeology and Ethnology* 13 (1920), 175–213; Ricardo Pozas A., *Juan Pérez Jolote, biografía de un Tzotzol* (Mexico, D.F.: Fondo de Cultura Económica, 1952); Paul Radin, "The Autobiography of a Winnebago Indian," *University of California Publications in American Archaeology and Ethnology* 16 no. 7 (1920), 281–473; Santha Rama Rau, *Home to India* (New York: Harper, 1944); O. F. Raum, *Chaga Childhood* (London: Oxford University Press, 1940); Rebecca H. Reyher, *Zulu Woman* (New York: Columbia University Press, 1948); A. I. Richards, *Dezba: Woman of the Desert* (New York: J. J. Augustin, 1939); idem, *Spider Woman: A Story of Navaho Weavers and Chanters* (New York: Macmillan, 1934); Wolf Sachs, *Black Hamlet* (London: Geoffrey Bles, 1931); M. Sandos, *Crazy Horse: The Strange Man of the Oglalas* (New York: Knopf, 1942); Edward Sapir, "The Life of a Nootka Indian," in E. C. Parsons (ed.), *American Indian Life* (New York: B. W. Huebsch, 1922); William C. Sayres, *Sammy Louis: The Life History of a Young Mic-Mac* (New Haven: Compass Publication Co., 1956); J. W. Schultz, *My Life as an Indian* (New York: Houghton Mifflin Co., 1907); W. H. Scott, "Boyhood in Sagada (Philippines)—Igorot," *Anthropological Quarterly* 31 (1958), 61–72; L. E. Simmons (ed.), *Sun Chief: The Autobiography of a Hopi Indian* (New Haven: Yale University Press, 1942); M. F. Smith, *Baba of Karo, A Woman of the Muslim Hausa* (London: Faber, 1954); M. G. Smith, "Dark Puritan, The Life and Work of Norman Paul," *Caribbean Quarterly* 5 (1959), 34–47; E. Spicer, "Juan Pistola," in idem, *Pascua, a Yaqui Village in Arizona* (Chicago: University of Chicago Press, 1940); A. J. Splawn, *Ka-Mi-Akin, Last Hero of the Yakimas* (Caldwell, Idaho: Caxton Printers, 1917); Luther Standing Bear, *My People the Sioux* (Boston: Houghton Mifflin, 1928); J. H. Steward, "Panatübiji, An Owens Valley Paiute," *Bulletin of the Bureau of American Ethnology* 119 (1938), 185–95; idem, "Two Paiute Autobiographies," *University of California Publications in American Archaeology and Ethnology* 33 (1934), 423–38; William L. Stone, *The Life and Times of Red Jacket* (New York: Wiley, 1841); idem, *Uncas and Miantonomob* (New York: Dayton & Newman, 1842).

Lakshmibai Tilak, *I Follow After* (Madras: Oxford University Press, 1950); P. Tirabutana, "A Simple One: The Story of a Siamese Girlhood," *Southeastern Asia Program Data Papers* 30 (Ithaca: Cornell University Press, 1958); Glenn Tucker, *Tecumseh: Vision of Glory* (New York: Bobbs-Merrill, 1956); Ruth M. Underhill, "The Autobiography of a Papago Woman," *Memoirs of the American Anthropological Association* 46 (1936); J. W. Vanstone (ed.), "The Autobiography of an Alaskan Eskimo," *Arctic* 10 (1957), 195–210: Stanley Vestal, *Sitting Bull* (Boston: Houghton Mifflin, 1932); idem, *Warpath: The True Story of the Fighting Sioux Told in a Biography of Chief White Bull* (Boston: Houghton Mifflin, 1934); M. Waldraven-Johnson, *The White Comanche: The Story of Cynthia Ann Parker and Her Son Quanah* (New York: Comet Press Books, 1957); O. Walker, "Tiurai, le guérisseur," *Bulletin de la Société des Etudes Océaniennes* 10 (1925), 1–35; A. F. C. Wallace, *King of the Delawares, Teedyuscung* (Philadelphia: University of Pennsylvania Press, 1949); Heluiz C. Washburne, *Land of the Good Shadows: The Life Story of Anauta, an Eskimo Woman* (New York: John Day Co., 1940); H. Wassen, "Original Documents from the San Blas Indians, Panama," *Ethnologiska Studier* [Gothenburg] 6 (1938), 24–69; Virginia Watson, *The Princess Pocahontas* (Philadelphia: Penn Publishing Co., 1916); T. T. Waterman, [Ishi, the last surviving Yahi] in "The Yana Indians," *University of California Publications in American Archaeology and Ethnology* 13: 35–102; Andrew Welch, *A Narrative of the Early Days and Remembrances of Oceola Nik-kanochee, Prince of Econchatti, a Young Seminole Indian* (London: Hatchard & Son, 1841); Clarence Wharton, *Satanta, Great Chief of the Kiowas and His People* (Dallas: B. Upshaw, 1938); Leslie A. White, "Autobiography of an Acoma Indian," *Bulletin of the Bureau of American Ethnology* 136 (1943); W. Whitman, "Xube, A Ponca Autobiography," *Journal of the American Folklore Society* 52 (1939), 180–93; F. E. Williams, "The Reminiscences of Ahuia Ova," *Journal of the Royal Anthropological Institute* 49 (1939), 11–44; Gilbert L. Wilson, *Goodbird the Indian, His Story* (New York: Fleming H. Revell Co., 1920); Clark Wissler, "Smoking Star, a Blackfoot Shaman," in E. C. Parsons (ed.), *American Indian Life* (New York: B. W. Huebsch, 1922), pp. 45–62; Su-Ling Wong and Earl Cressy, *Daughter of Confucius* (New York: Farrar, Straus & Young, 1952); Norman B. Wood, *Lives of Famous Indian Chiefs* (Aurora, Ill.: American Historical Publishing Co., 1906); Parahansa Yoganana, *Autobiography of a Yogi* (Los Angeles: Self-Realization Fellowship, 1947); and C. L. Zimmerman, *White Eagle: Chief of the Poncas* (Harrisburg, Pa.: Telegraph Press, 1941).

7. John Dollard, *Criteria for the Life History* (New Haven: Yale University Press, 1935); Clyde Kluckhohn, "The Personal Document in Anthropological Science," in L. Gottschalk, C. Kluckhohn, and R. Angell (eds.), *Social Science Research Council Bulletin* 53 (1945), 79–173.

8. J. W. M. Whiting, *Becoming a Kwoma* (New Haven: Yale University Press, 1941).

9. P. Radin, "History of Ethnological Theories," *American Anthropologist* 31 (1929), 26–30. One Jungian psychiatrist has, however, used ethnological materials: William Morgan, "Navajo Diagnosticians," *American Anthropologist* 33 (1931), 390–402; idem, "Human Wolves among the Navajo," *Yale University Publications in Anthropology* 11 (1936), 3–43.

10. K. R. Stewart, "A Psychological Analysis of the Negritos of Luzon," *Man* 39 (1939), 10.

11. Radin, "Ethnological Theories," p. 26; E. Sapir, "Personality," *Encyclopedia of the Social Sciences* 12 (1934), p. 86; and A. A. Goldenweiser, "Some Contributions of Psychoanalysis to the Interpretation of Social Facts," in H. E. Barnes and F. B. Becker (eds.), *Contemporary Social Theory* (New York: Appleton-Century, 1940), pp. 401–2. These references are owed to Kluckhohn, "One Hundred Years," p. 590.

12. B. W. Aginsky, "Psychopathic Trends in Culture," *Character and Personality* 7 (1939), 331–43; H. Codere, "The Amiable Side of Kwakiutl Life," *American Anthropologist* 58 (1956), 334–51; E. S. Goldfrank, "Socialization, Personality and the Structure of Pueblo Society," *American Anthropologist* 47 (1945), 516–40; idem, "A Linguistic Note to Zuni Ethnology," *Word* 2 (1946), 191–96; E. A. Hoebel, *Man in the Primitive World* (New York: Knopf, 1945), pp. 449–52; An-che Li, "Zuni, Some Observations and Queries," *American Anthropologist* 39 (1937), 63; M. E. Opler, "On Method in the Writing of Anthropological Monographs," *American Anthropologist* 45 (1943), 329–32; and H. J. Wegrocki, "A Critique of Cultural and Statistical Concepts of Abnormality," *Journal of Abnormal and Social Psychology* 34 (1939), 166–78. See also article by Paul Schilder, "The Sociological Implications of Neurosis," *Journal of Social Psychology* 15 (1942), 3–21.

13. R. Beardsley, "National Character: The Japanese Talk Back," Paper read at the 1952 meeting of the American Anthropological Association; J. W. Bennett and M. Nagai, "Echoes: Critique of the Methodology of Benedict's *Chrysanthemum and the Sword*," *American Anthropologist* 55 (1953), 404–11.

14. A. I. Hallowell, *Culture and Experience* (Philadelphia: University of Pennsylvania Press, 1955), p. 384. A valuable summary and bibliography of Rorschach work in the field may be found in J. Henry and M. E. Spiro, "Psychological Techniques: Projective Tests in Field Work," in A. L. Kroeber (ed.), *Anthropology Today* (Chicago: University of Chicago Press, 1953), pp. 417–29. The following should be added: C. J. Adcock and J. E. Ritchie, "Intercultural Use of Rorschach," *American Anthropologist* 60 (1958), 881–92: O. Billig, J. Gillin, and W. Davidson, "Aspects of Culture and Personality in a Guatemalan Community: Ethnological and Rorschach Approaches," *Journal of Personality* 16 (1947–1948), 326–68; M. Bleuler, "Rorschach's Ink-blot Test and Racial Psychology: Mental Peculiarities of the Moroccans," *Character and Personality* 4 (1935), 97–114; W. Caudill, "Japanese-American Personality and Acculturation," *Genetic Psychology Monographs* 45 (1952), 3–102; F. Cheng and H. Rin, "A Personality Analysis of the Ami and its Three Subgroups by the Rorschach Test," *Acta Psychologica Taiwanica* 1 (1958), 131–43; G. De Vos, "A Quantitative Rorschach Assessment of Maladjustment and Rigidity in Acculturating Japanese Americans," *Genetic Psychology Monographs* 52 (1955), 51–87; C. Du Bois and E. Oberholser, "Rorschach Tests and Native Personality in Alor, Dutch East Indies," *Transactions of the New York Academy of Science* 4 (1942), 168–70; T. Gladwin and S. B. Sarason, "Truk: Man in Paradise," *Viking Fund Publications in Anthropology* 20 (1953); A. I. Hallowell, "Rorschach as an Aid in the Study of Personalities in Primitive Societies," *Rorschach Research Exchange* 4 (1940), 106; idem, "The Rorschach Method as an Aid in the Study of Personalities in Primitive Societies," *Character and Personality* 9 (1941), 235–45; idem, "The Rorschach Technique in the Study of Personality and Culture," *American Anthropologist* 47 (1945), 195–210; idem, "The Rorschach Test as a Tool for Investigating Cultural Variables and Individual Differences in the Study of Personality in Primitive Societies," *Rorschach Research Exchange* 5 (1941), 31–34; idem, "The Rorschach Test in Personality and Culture Studies," in idem, *Culture and Experience*, pp. 32–74; idem, "Use of Projective Techniques in the Study of Socio-psychological Aspects of Acculturation," *Journal of Projective Techniques* 15 (1951), 27–44; P. A. Hauck, "Ute Rorschach Performances and Some Notes on Field Problems and Methods," *Anthropological Papers, University of Utah* 23 (1955); J. Henry, "Rorschach Technique in Primitive Cultures," *American Journal of Orthopsychiatry* 11 (1941), 230–35; B. Kaplan, "A Study of Rorschach Re-

sponses in Four Cultures," *Papers of the Peabody Museum of American Archaeology and Ethnology, Harvard University* 42 no. 2 (1954); R. E. Newman, "La Téchnica de Rorschach aplicada a un grupo Otomi," *América Indigena* 15 (1955), 57–68; R. Ribeiro, ["Rorschach Responses of a Cult Priestess in Brazil"], *Revue Internationale d'Ethnopsychiatrie Normale et Pathologique* 1 (1956), 161–81; G. J. Sanchez, "Importancia del Test de Rorschach en el Estudio de la Personalidad y de la Cultura," *Revista de la Sanidad de Policia* 18 (1958), 133–40; A. H. Schachtel, Jules and Zunia Henry, "Rorschach Analysis of Pilagá Indian Children," *American Journal of Orthopsychiatry* 12 (1942), 697–712; and A. Murray and Jacqueline H. Straus, "Personality Insecurity and Sinhalese Social Structure: Rorschach Evidence for Primary School Children," *Eastern Anthropologist* 10 (1957), 97–111.

15. Among these may be cited: T. M. Abel, "Free Designs of Limited Scope as a Personality Index: A Comparison of Schizophrenics with Normal, Subnormal and Primitive Culture Groups," *Character and Personality* 7 (1938–39), 50–62; A. Anastasi and J. P. Foley, "An Analysis of Spontaneous Drawings by Children in Different Cultures," *Journal of Applied Psychology* 20 (1936), 689–726; idem, "A Study of Animal Drawings by Indian Children of the North Pacific Coast," *Journal of Social Psychology* 9 (1938), 363–74; F. L. Goodenough, "The Measurement of Mental Functions in Primitive Groups," *American Anthropologist* 38 (1936), 1–11; R. J. Havighurst, M. K. Gunther, and I. E. Pratt, "Environment and Draw-a-Man Test: The Performance of Indian Children," *Journal of Abnormal and Social Psychology* 41 (1946), 50–63; J. and Z. Henry, "Doll Play of Pilagá Indian Children," *American Orthopsychiatric Association Research Monograph* 4 (1944); W. E. Henry "The Thematic Apperception Technique in the Study of Culture-Personality Relations," *Genetic Psychology Monographs* 35 (1947), 3–135; idem, "Trukese TATs," *American Anthropologist* 56 (1954), 889; J. J. Honigmann and R. N. Carrera, "Cross-Cultural Use of Machover's Figure Drawing Test," *American Anthropologist* 59 (1957), 650–54; A. Joseph, R. B. Spicer, and J. Chesky, *The Desert People: A Study of the Papago Indians* (Chicago: University of Chicago Press, 1949); A. Joseph and V. F. Murray, *Chamorros and Carolinians of Saipan* (Cambridge: Harvard University Press, 1951); C. Kluckhohn and J. C. Rosenzweig, "Two Navaho Children over a Five-Year Period," *American Journal of Orthopsychiatry* 19 (1949), 266–78; D. Leighton and C. Kluckhohn, *The Children of the People* (Cambridge: Harvard University Press, 1948); G. Macgregor, *Warriors Without Weapons* (Chicago: University of Chicago Press, 1946); G. Paget, "Some Drawings of Men and Women made by Children of Certain Non-European Races," *Journal of the Royal Anthropological Institute* 62 (1932), 127–44; G. Róheim, "Play Analysis with Normanby Island Children," *American Journal of Orthopsychiatry* 11 (1941), 524–30; idem, "Children's Games and Rhymes in Duau (Normanby Island)," *American Anthropologist* 45 (1943), 99–119; A. Schubert, "Drawings of Orotchen Children and Young People," *Journal of Genetic Psychology* 37 (1930), 232–44; Edward Sherwood, "On the Designing of TAT Pictures, with Special Reference to a Set for African People Assimilating Western Culture," *Journal of Social Psychology* 45 (1957); M. Steggerda, "Racial Psychometry," *Eugenical News* 19 (1934), 132–33; idem, "The McAdory Art Test as Applied to Navaho Indian Children," *Journal of Comparative Psychology* 22 (1936) 283–85; idem, "Testing Races for the Threshold of Taste, with PTC," *Journal of Heredity* 28 (1937), 309–10; idem, "Form Discrimination Test as given to Navaho, Negro and White School Children," *Human Biology* 13 (1941), 239–46; M. Steggerda and E. Macomber, "Mental and Social Characteristics of Maya and Navaho Indians as evidenced by a Psychological Rating Scale," *Journal of Social Psychology* 10 (1939), 51–59; W. S. Taylor, "A Note on the Cultural Determination of Free Drawing," *Character and Personality* 13 (1944), 30–36; L. Thompson and A. Joseph, *The Hopi Way* (Chicago: University of Chicago Press, 1944); and E. Z. Vogt, "Navaho Veterans: A Study of Changing Values," *Papers of the Peabody Museum of American Archaeology and Ethnology* 51 (1952).

16. The earlier work of this group has been reported in W. La Barre, "Columbia University Research in Contemporary Cultures," *Scientific Monthly* 67 (1948) 239–40. Somewhat later is M. Mead, "Research in Contemporary Cultures," in H. Guetzkow (ed.), *Groups, Leadership and Men* (Pittsburgh: University of Pittsburgh Press, 1951), pp. 106–18. One important publication of the group since Mead's report is R. B. Métraux and M. Mead, "Themes in French Culture," *Hoover Institute Studies*, Series D, no. 1, Stanford, Cal., 1954.

17. M. Mead, "The Mountain Arapesh, II. Supernaturalism," *Anthropological Papers of the American Museum of Natural History* 37 (1940), 330–31; idem, "Educative Effects of Social Environment as Disclosed by Studies of Primitive Societies," *Environment and Education, Supplementary Monographs* 54, Chicago, 1942; idem, "Researches in Bali," *Transactions of*

the New York Academy of Science ser. 2, II, 1–8. Kluckhohn, "One Hundred Years," p. 601, citing A. A. Goldenweiser, "Leading Contributions of Anthropology to Social Theory," in H. E. Barnes (ed.), *Contemporary Social Theory* (New York: Appleton-Century, 1940), p. 489.

18. M. Mead, "The Use of Primitive Material in the Study of Personality," *Character and Personality* 3 (1934), 10; for more recent items, see M. Mead and G. Bateson, "Balinese Character," *New York Academy of Science*, Special Publication 2 (1942). See also Kluckhohn. "One Hundred Years," pp. 599–600, for an appreciation of Mead's early work until around 1940.

19. Bibliographies of this literature may be found in: J. Gillin, "Personality in Preliterate Societies," *American Journal of Sociology* 4 (1939), 681–702; B. J. Meggers, "Recent Trends in American Ethnology," *American Anthropologist* 48 (1946), 176–214; C. Kluckhohn, "The Personal Document in Anthropological Science"; W. La Barre, *A Classified Bibliography of the Literature on Culture and Personality* (Mimeographed, February 1952); and G. Devereux and K. A. Menninger, *A Guide to Psychiatric Books* (New York: Grune and Stratton, 1960).

20. C. Kluckhohn and H. A. Murray (eds.), *Personality in Nature, Society, and Culture* (New York: A. A. Knopf, 1948); and D. G. Haring (ed.), *Personal Character and Cultural Milieu* (Syracuse, N.Y.: Syracuse University Press, 1948).

21. J. W. Eaton, "In Defense of Culture-Personality Studies," *American Sociological Review* 16 (1951), 98–100; R. Endleman, "The New Anthropology and Its Ambitions: The Science of Man in Messianic Dress," *Commentary* (Sept. 1949), 284–91; B. J. Meggers, "Recent Trends"; F. L. K. Hsu (ed.), *Aspects of Culture and Personality: A Symposium* (New York: Abelard-Schuman, 1954); A. R. Lindesmith and A. L. Strauss, "A Critique of Culture-Personality Writings," *American Sociological Review* 15 (1950), 587–99; H. Orlansky, "Infant Care and Personality," *Psychological Bulletin* 10 (1949), 1–48.

22. The best surveys of the literature are: Alex Inkeles and D. J. Levinson, "National Character: The Study of Modal Personality and Sociocultural Systems," in G. Lindzey (ed.), *Handbook of Social Psychology*, 2 vols. (Cambridge: Harvard University Press, 1954), ch. 26, II:977–1020; Otto Klineberg, "Recent Studies in National Character," in S. S. Sargent and M. W. Smith (eds.), *Culture and Responsibility* (New York: Viking Fund, 1949); C. Kluckhohn, "Culture and Behavior," in Lindsey, *Handbook*; and J. M. W. Whiting and I. E. Child, *Child Training and Personality* (New Haven: Yale University Press, 1953). G. H. Seward, *Sex and the Social Order* (New York: McGraw-Hill, 1946) makes an able précis of much of the literature until 1946. At the suggestion of the late Ralph Linton, and under the sponsorship of the Viking Fund, an interdisciplinary conference was held in New York in 1947; the proceedings of this conference were issued as *Culture and Personality* (New York: Viking Fund, 1949). In a recent encyclopedic compendium of the anthropological sciences are articles by Margaret Mead on "National Character" and A. I. Hallowell on "Culture, Personality, and Society," in A. L. Kroeber (ed.), *Anthropology Today* (Chicago: University of Chicago Press, 1953), pp. 642–67 and 597–620 respectively. See also G. Bateson, "Cultural Determinants of Personality," in J. McV. Hunt (ed.), *Personality and the Behavior Disorders* (New York: Ronald Press, 1944).

23. A. Kardiner, *The Individual and His Society* (New York: Columbia University Press, 1939); and idem, *The Psychological Frontiers of Society* (New York: Columbia University Press, 1945). See also idem, "The Concept of Basic Personality Structure as an Operational Tool in the Social Sciences," in Ralph Linton (ed.), *The Science of Man in the World Crisis* (New York: Columbia University Press, 1945), also reprinted in D. G. Haring (ed.), *Personal Character* (rev. ed., 1949), pp. 431–37. Linton's major works in the culture-and-personality area include: "Culture, Society and the Individual," *Journal of Abnormal and Social Psychology* 33 (1938), 425–36; "The Effects of Culture on Mental and Emotional Processes," *Research Publications of the Association for Research in Nervous and Mental Diseases* 19 (1939), 293–304; "Psychology and Anthropology," *Journal of Social Philosophy* 5 (1940), 115–27; and his short book, *The Cultural Background of Personality* (New York: D. Appleton-Century Co., 1945).

24. For an appreciation of Róheim, see Kluckhohn, "One Hundred Years," pp. 605–6; and W. La Barre, "Geza Róheim: Psychoanalysis and Anthropology," in F. Alexander, S. Eisenstein, and M. Grotjahn (eds.), *Psychoanalytic Pioneers* (New York: Basic Books, 1966), pp. 272–81.

25. Roheim's chief works are: *Australian Totemism* (London: G. Allen & Unwin, 1925); *Animism, Magic, and the Divine King* (London: K. Paul, Trench, Trubner & Co., 1930); "The Psychoanalysis of Primitive Cultural Types," *International Journal of Psycho-Analysis* 13 (1932), 1–224; "The Evolution of Culture," ibid. 14 (1933), 387–418; *The Riddle of the*

Sphinx (London: Hogarth Press, 1934); *Primitive High Gods* (Supplemental Volume to *Psychoanalytic Quarterly*, 1934); "The Study of Character Development and the Ontogenetic Theory of Culture," in E. E. Evans-Pritchard, Raymond Firth, Bronislaw Malinowski, and Isaac Schapera (eds.), *Essays Presented to C. G. Seligman* (London: Kegan Paul, Trench, Trübner and Co., 1934), pp. 281–92; "The Psychoanalytic Interpretation of Culture," *International Journal of Psycho-Analysis* 22 (1941), 147–69; "Transition Rites," *Psychoanalytic Quarterly* 11 (1942), 336; *The Origin and Function of Culture* (New York: Nervous and Mental Disease Monographs, 1943); *The Eternal Ones of the Dream* (New York: International Universities Press, 1945); and *Psychoanalysis and Anthropology* (New York: International Universities Press, 1950).

26. G. B. Wilbur and Warner Muensterberger (eds.), *Psychoanalysis and Culture: Essays in Honor of Géza Róheim* (New York: International Universities Press, 1951). This volume contains a bibliography of Róheim's works, pp. 455–62.

27. G. Devereux, "Obituary of Géza Róheim," *American Anthropologist* 55 (1953), 420.

28. W. La Barre, *The Human Animal* (Chicago: University of Chicago Press, 1954). See also the recent writings of Howard F. Stein.

29. George Devereux: "Mohave Indian Infanticide," *Psychoanalytic Review* 35 (1948), 126–39; "Mohave Indian Obstetrics," *American Imago* 5 (1948), 1–47; "The Mohave Neonate and its Cradle," *Primitive Man* 21 (1948), 1–18; "Mohave Beliefs Concerning Twins," *American Anthropologist* 43 (1941), 573–92; "Post-partum Parental Observances of the Mohave Indians," *Transactions of the Kansas Academy of Science* 52 (1949), 458–65; "Mohave Orality," *Psychoanalytic Quarterly* 16 (1947), 519–46; "Cultural and Characterological Traits of the Mohave Related to the Anal Stage of Psychosexual Development," *Psychoanalytic Quarterly* 20 (1951), 398–422; "Notes on the Developmental Pattern and Organic Needs of Mohave Indian Children," *Transactions of the Kansas Academy of Science* 53 (1950), 178–85; "Mohave Indian Autoerotic Behavior," *Psychoanalytic Review* 37 (1950), 201–20; "The Social and Cultural Implications of Incest among the Mohave Indians," *Psychoanalytic Quarterly* 8 (1939), 510–33; "Institutionalized Homosexuality of the Mohave Indians," *Human Biology* 9 (1937), 498–527; "The Primal Scene and Juvenile Heterosexuality in Mohave Society," in Wilbur and Muensterberger, *Psychoanalysis and Culture*, pp. 90–107; "Status, Socialization, and Interpersonal Relations of Mohave Children," *Psychiatry* 13 (1950), 489–502; "The Mohave Male Puberty Rite," *Samiksa* 3:11–25; "Heterosexual Behavior of the Mohave Indians," in G. Róheim (ed.), *Psychoanalysis and the Social Sciences* 2 (1953), 85–128; "Mohave Paternity," *Samiksa* 3:162–93; "Mohave Soul Concepts," *American Anthropologist* 39 (1937), 417–22; "The Function of Alcohol in Mohave Society," *Quarterly Journal of Studies on Alcohol* 9 (1948), 207–51; "Magic Substances and Narcotics of the Mohave Indians," *British Journal of Medical Psychology* 22 (1949), 110–16; "Psychodynamics of Mohave Gambling," *American Imago* 7 (1950), 1–13; "Mohave Chieftainship in Action," *Plateau* 23 (1951), 33–43; "Mohave Voice and Speech Mannerisms," *Word* 5 (1949), 268–72; "Some Mohave Gestures," *American Anthropologist* 51 (1949), 325–26; and "Mohave Etiquette," *Southwest Museum Leaflets* 22 (1948), 1–9.

30. Kluckhohn, "One Hundred Years," pp. 606–7.

31. W. La Barre, "Folklore and Psychology," *Journal of American Folklore* 61 (1948), 382–90, p. 387. The list is based on the useful chronologically ordered bibliography of B. J. Meggers, "Recent Trends," pp. 197–202.

32. The *General Index* of the American Anthropological Association publications is published approximately every decade. Those referred to above are: Vol. 32, no. 3, pt. 2, 1930 (for 1888–1928); Vol. 42, no. 4, pt. 3, 1940 (for 1929–1938); and Vol. 53, no. 4, pt. 2, 1951 (for 1939–1948).

33. A. W. Green, "Culture, Normality, and Personality Conflict," *American Anthropologist* 50 (1948), 225–37; L. Thompson, "Attitudes and Acculturation," 50 (1948), 200–15; A. K. Cohen, "On the Place of 'Themes' and Kindred Concepts in Social Theory," 50 (1948), 436–43; W. Caudill, "Psychological Characteristics of Acculturated Wisconsin Ojibwa Children," 51 (1949), 409–27; D. Eggan, "The Significance of Dreams for Anthropological Research," 51 (1949), 177–98; F. Voget, "A Shoshone Innovator," 52 (1950), 53–63; A. F. C. Wallace, "Psychology and Anthropology in America in 1841," 52 (1950), 287; K. L. Little, "Methodology in the Study of Adult Personality and 'National Character,'" 52 (1950), 279–82; B. D. Paul, "Symbolic Sibling Rivalry in a Guatemalan Indian Village," 52 (1950), 205–18; A. I. Hallowell, "Personality Structure and the Evolution of Man," 52 (1950), 159–73; J. F. Em-

bree, "A Note on Ethnocentrism in Anthropology," 52 (1950), 430–32; J. Henry, "National Character and War," 53 (1951), 134–35; M. E. Spiro, "Ghosts, Ifaluk, and Teleological Functionalism," 54 (1952), 479–503; D. Eggan, "The Manifest Content of Dreams: A Challenge to Social Science," 54 (1952), 469–85; D. G. Mandelbaum, "On the Study of National Character," 55 (1953), 174–87; J. W. Bennett and M. Nagai, "Echoes: Reactions to American Anthropology," 55 (1953), 404–11; D. B. Shimkin and P. Sanjuan, "Culture and World View," 55 (1953), 329–48; I. N. Mensch and J. Henry, "Direct Observations and Psychological Tests in Anthropology," 55 (1953), 461–80; N. Lurie, "Winnebago Berdache," 55 (1953), 708–12; M. E. Spiro, "Human Nature in its Psychological Dimensions," 56 (1954), 19–30; E. Bourguignon, "Dreams and Dream Interpretation in Haiti," 56 (1954), 262–68; B. J. James, "Some Critical Observations concerning Analysis of Chippewa 'Atomism' and Chippewa Personality," 56 (1954), 283–86; A. I. Hallowell, "Southwestern Studies of Culture and Personality," 56 (1954), 685–708; W. E. Henry, "Trukese TATs," 56 (1954), 889; H. Angelino and C. L. Shedd, "A Note on Berdache," 57 (1955), 121–26; J. Henry et al., "Projective Testing in Anthropology," 57 (1955), 245–70; J. Gillin, "Ethos Components in Modern Latin American Culture," 57 (1955), 488–500; and S. Arieti, "Some Basic Problems Common to Anthropology and Modern Psychiatry," 58 (1956), 26–39.

34. V. Barnouw, "Acculturation and Personality among the Wisconsin Chippewa," *Memoirs of the American Anthropological Association* 72 (1951), in *American Anthropologist* 54 (1952), 249–250.

35. R. L. Beals and H. Hoijer, *An Introduction to Anthropology* (New York: Macmillan, 1953); E. D. Chapple and C. S. Coon, *Principles of Anthropology* (New York: H. Holt & Co., 1942); J. Gillin, *The Ways of Men* (New York: Appleton-Century-Crofts, 1948); R. H. Lowie, *An Introduction to Cultural Anthropology*, rev. ed. (New York: Farrar & Rinehart, 1940); H. Shapiro (ed.), *Man, Culture, and Society* (New York: Oxford University Press, 1956); J. S. Slotkin, *Social Anthropology* (New York: Macmillan, 1950); H. H. Turney-High, *General Anthropology* (New York: T. H. Crowell, 1949); and R. H. Lowie, *Social Organization* (New York: Rinehart, 1948).

36. F. Boas (ed.), *General Anthropology* (New York: D. C. Heath, 1938); A. A. Goldenweiser, *Anthropology* (New York: Johnson Reprint Corporation, 1970); M. J. Herskovits, *Man and His Work* (New York: Knopf, 1948); idem, *Cultural Anthropology* (New York: Knopf, 1955); E. A. Hoebel, *Man in the Primitive World* (New York: McGraw-Hill, 1949): A. L. Kroeber, *Anthropology* (New York: Harcourt, Brace & World, 1948); R. Linton, *The Study of Man* (New York: D. Appleton-Century, 1936); R. H. Lowie, *The History of Ethnological Theory* (New York: Farrar, Rinehart, 1937); and M. Titiev, *The Science of Man* (New York: Holt, Rinehart & Winston, 1954).

37. G. P. Murdock, *Social Structure* (New York: Macmillan Co., 1949), pp. 12, 280, 291, 293 quoted (on universality of Oedipus and incest taboos in the nuclear family); quoted pp. 292, 294, xii, respectively.

38. C. Kluckhohn, *Mirror for Man* (New York: Whittlesey House, 1949), quoted pp. 217 and 226; 201; quoted pp. 214, 55, and 54.

39. C. Kluckhohn, "Universal Categories of Culture," in A. L. Kroeber, *Anthropology Today*, pp. 507–23, quoting p. 515 from another publication of Kluckhohn and Morgan; Hallowell, p. 604; Mead, in ibid., pp. 643–44 and 651.

40. A. L. Kroeber, "*Totem and Taboo*: An Ethnologic Psychoanalysis," *American Anthropologist* 22 (1920), 48–55, quoted pp. 53 and 55.

41. Kluckhohn, "One Hundred Years," p. 594.

42. A. L. Kroeber, review of C. G. Jung, [Collected Papers in] *Analytic Psychology and the Psychology of the Unconscious*, in *American Anthropologist* 20 (1918), 323–24. On this question, see W. La Barre, "Elementargedanken Noch Einmal?" *American Anthropologist* 57 (1955), 862–63; and Ernest Jones, "The Theory of Symbolism," *Papers on Psychoanalysis* 5th ed. (Baltimore: Williams and Wilkins, 1948), pp. 87–144.

43. A. L. Kroeber, "*Totem and Taboo* in Retrospect," *American Journal of Sociology* 45 (1939), 446–51.

44. I have argued this question at greater length elsewhere; see W. La Barre, *Human Animal*, Chap. 12, "Why Man Is Human." See also, idem, "Family and Symbol," in Wilbur and Muensterberger, *Psychoanalysis and Culture*, pp. 156–67—appropriately here in Róheim's *Festschrift* because this thinking was to a strong degree influenced by Róheim.

45. E. C. Parsons, "Ceremonial Consummation," *Psychoanalytic Review* 2 (1915), 358–59; A. A.

Goldenweiser, *History, Psychology, and Culture* (New York: A. A. Knopf, 1933); and idem, *Early Civilization* (New York: A. A. Knopf, 1922).

46. R. H. Lowie, *Primitive Society* (New York: Boni and Liveright, 1920), pp. 91–94; idem, *Primitive Religion* (New York: Boni and Liveright, 1924); idem, *The History of Ethnological Theory* (New York: Farrar & Rinehart, 1937), pp. 172 (on Rivers), 234 (on Malinowski), and vii (on Lowie). These are the only allusions (psychoanalysis and Freud are not discussed at all) in the standard American book on theory. W. H. R. Rivers's books include *Dreams and Primitive Culture* (Manchester: University Press, 1917–18), *Mind and Medicine* (Manchester: University Press, 1919), and *Psychology and Ethnology* (New York: Harcourt, Brace & Co., 1926). B. Malinowski, *The Sexual Life of Savages*, 2 vols. (New York: H. Liveright, 1929), 2:385 (quoted), 472, and 572; and *Sex and Repression in Savage Society* (New York: Harcourt, Brace, 1927), p. 75. C. Kluckhohn, "Bronislaw Malinowski, 1884–1942," *Journal of American Folklore* 56 (1943), 209, 216; B. Malinowski, Foreword to *The Sexual Life of Savages* (London: G. Routledge and Sons, 1932), p. xxix.

47. V. Elwin, "A Note on the Theory and Symbolism of Dreams among the Baiga," *British Journal of Medical Psychology* 16 (1937), 237–59; R. Firth, "The Meaning of Dreams in Tikopia," in Evans-Pritchard et al., *Essays Presented to C. G. Seligman*; A. I. Hallowell, "Freudian Symbolism in the Dream of a Saulteaux Indian Man," *Journal of Social Psychology* 9 (1938), 47–48; E. S. C. Handy, "Dreaming in Relation to Spirit Sickness in Hawaii," in R. H. Lowie (ed.), *Essays in Anthropology Presented to A. L. Kroeber* (Berkeley: University of California Press, 1936), pp. 119–27; A. R. King, "The Dream Biography of a J. Maiden," *Character and Personality* 11 (1943), 227–34; K. Luomala, "Dreams and Dream Interpretations of the Diegueno Indians of Southern California," *Psychoanalytic Quarterly* 5 (1936), 195–225; W. Morgan, "Navaho Dreams," *American Anthropologist* 34 (1932), 390–405; P. Radin, "Ojibway and Ottawa Puberty Dreams," in Lowie (ed.), *Essays*, pp. 233–64; D. M. Schneider, "An Analysis of Yir Yoront Dreams," ms.; D. M. Spencer, "Fijian Dreams and Visions," in D. S. Davidson (ed.), *Twenty-fifth Anniversary Studies* (Philadelphia: University of Pennsylvania Press, 1937), pp. 199–209; and W. J. Wallace, "The Dream in Mohave Life," *Journal of American Folklore* 60 (1947), 252–58. To this list should be added D. Eggan, "Significance of Dreams," and "Manifest Content of Dreams," and the frequent use of dream materials in the works of Devereux and Róheim. The chief book on the subject is by J. S. Lincoln, *The Dream in Primitive Cultures* (London: Cresset Press, 1935; reprinted New York: Johnson Reprint Corp., 1970).

48. S. Freud, "The Occurrence in Dreams of Material from Fairy Tales," *Collected Papers* 4:236–43, and "The Theme of the Three Caskets," ibid., pp. 244–56.

Karl Abraham, *Dreams and Myths* (New York: Nervous and Mental Disease Monograph Series 15, 1913); Otto Rank, *The Myth of the Birth of the Hero* (N&MDMS 18, 1913); idem, *Das Inzestmotiv in Dichtung und Sage* (Vienna: Franz Deuticke, 1912); Ernest Jones, "The Symbolic Significance of Salt in Folklore and Superstition," chap. 4 in *Essays in Applied Psycho-Analysis* (London: Hogarth Press, 1923); and Franz Riklin, *Wishfulfillment and Symbolism in Fairy Tales, N&MDMS no 21, 1915*.

S. Freud, in *Collected Papers*, 1:230. A summary of works up to 1948 may be found in W. La Barre, "Folklore and Psychology," *Journal of American Folklore* (1948), 382–90. The following reference note lists items published 1948–1952.

49. In the *American Imago* have appeared the following studies: Sidney Tarachow, "Totem Feast in Modern Dress," 5 (1948), 65–69; H. L. Cox, "The Place of Mythology in the Study of Culture," 5 (1948) 83–94; R. Sterba, "Kilroy Was Here," 5 (1948), 173–91; idem, "On Hallowe'en," 5 (1948), 213–24; L. and S. Fraiberg, "Hallowe'en: Ritual and Myth," 8 (1950), 289–328; W. H. Desmonde, "Jack and the Beanstalk," 8 (1951), 287–88; idem, "The Bull-Fight as a Religious Ritual," 9 (1952), 173–95; G. Róheim, "The Evil Eye," 10 (1952), 351–63; idem, "The Language of Birds," 10 (1952), 3–14; and D. F. Zelig, "Two Episodes in the Life of Jacob," 10 (1952) 181–203.

50. S. Ferenczi, "Gulliver Fantasies," *International Journal of Psycho-Analysis* 9 (1928), 283–300; S. Lorand, "Fairy Tales and Neurosis," *Psychoanalytic Quarterly* 4 (1935), 234–43; idem, "Fairy Tales, Lilliputian Dreams, and Neurosis," *American Journal of Orthopsychiatry* 7 (1937), 456–64; and J. Mather, "The Unconscious Significance of Fairyland," *Australian Journal of Psychology and Philosophy* 1 (1934), 16–32.

51. P. Cordellas, "Modern Greek Folklore: The Smerdaki," *Journal of American Folklore* 58 (1945), 236–44; W. La Barre, "Kiowa Folk Sciences," ibid., 60 (1947), 105–14; A. Abou Zeid, "La psychanalyse des mythes," *Egyptian Journal of Psychology* 2 (1946); M. M. El-

Sayyad, "The Psychology of the Egyptian People from Folksongs," ibid., 1 (1945), 151–71; M. E. Opler, "Japanese Folk Belief Concerning the Snake," *Southwestern Journal of Anthropology* 1 (1945), 249–59; R. F. Fortune, "The Symbolism of the Serpent," *International Journal of Psycho-Analysis* 7 (1926), 237–43; B. S. Engle, "Attis: A Study in Castration," *Psychoanalytic Review* 23 (1936), 363–72; idem, "Lemnos, Island of Women," ibid., 32 (1945), 353–58; idem, "Melampus and Freud," *Psychoanalytic Quarterly* 11 (1942), 83–86; and idem, "The Amazons in Ancient Greece," ibid., 512–54.

52. Marie Bonaparte, "The Myth of the Corpse in the Car," *American Imago* 2 (1941), 105–26; idem, "The Legend of the Unfathomable Waters," ibid., 4 (1946), 20–31; and idem, "Saint Christopher, Patron Saint of the Motor-Car Drivers," ibid., 5 (1947), 49–77.

53. F. Moellenhoff, "Remarks on the Popularity of Mickey Mouse," *American Imago* 1 (1940), 19–32; M. Grotjahn, "Ferdinand the Bull," ibid., 33–41; E. Vowinckel-Weigert, "The Cult and Mythology of the Magna Mater," *Psychiatry* 1 (1938), 347–78; M. Kohen, "The Venus of Willendorf," *American Imago* 3 (1946), 49–60; S. Ferenczi, "On the Symbolism of the Head of the Medusa," in *Further Contributions to the Theory and Practice of Psychoanalysis* (London: Hogarth Press, 1926), 360; and I Coriat, "A Note on the Medusa Symbolism," *American Imago* 2 (1941), 281–85.

54. K. J. Karlson, "Psychoanalysis and Mythology," *Journal of Religious Psychology* 7 (1914), 137–213; R. R. Marett, *Psychology and Folklore* (London: Methuen & Co., 1920).

55. C. Kluckhohn, "Myths and Rituals: A General Theory," *Harvard Theological Review* 35 (1942), 45–79; E. S. Goldfrank, "The Impact of Situation and Personality on Four Hopi Emergence Myths," *Southwestern Journal of Anthropology* 4 (1948), 241–62; M. Jacobs, "Psychological Inferences from a Chinook Myth," Paper read at the 1951 Meeting of the American Antrhopological Association; M. K. Opler and F. Obayashi, "Senryu Poetry as Folk and Community Expression," *Journal of American Folklore* 58 (1945), 1–11; W. La Barre, "The Psychopathology of Drinking Songs," *Psychiatry* 2 (1939), 203–12; for a comparative study, idem, "Obscenity: An Anthropological Appraisal," *Law and Contemporary Problems* 20 (1955), 533–43; idem, "The Apperception of Attitudes," *American Imago* 6 (1949), 3–43; J. J. Honigmann, "A Cultural Theory of Obscenity," *Journal of Criminal Psychopathology* 5 (1944), 715–33; L. H. Charles, "The Clown's Function," *Journal of American Folklore* 28 (1945), 23–34; J. Dollard, "The Dozens: Dialectic of Insult," *American Imago* 1 (1939), 3–25; R. Sterba, "A Dutch Celebration of a Festival," *American Imago* 2 (1941), 205–8. See also Sterba, "Kilroy Was Here," and "On Hallowe'en."

56. La Barre, *Human Animal*, pp. xii-xiii.

57. S. Freud, *Civilization and Its Discontents* (London: Hogarth Press, 1930). This trend in Freud's thinking has been illuminatingly continued in H. Marcuse, *Eros and Civilization* (Boston: Beacon Press, 1955), which Kluckhohn has well praised in *New York Times Book Review Section*.

58. S. Freud, "A Neurosis of Demoniacal Possession in the Seventeenth Century," *Collected Papers* 4:436–72.

59. P. Alphandery, "De quelques documents médiévaux relatifs à des états psychastheniques," *Journal de Psychologie Normale et Pathologique* 26 (1929), 763–87; S. E. Jeliffe, "Some Random Notes on the History of Psychiatry in the Middle Ages," *American Journal of Psychiatry* 10 (1930), 275–86; G. W. Kisker, "A Study of Mental Disorder in Ancient Greek Culture," *Psychiatry* 4 (1941), 535–45; J. J. Moreau, *La Psychologie Morbide dans ses Rapports avec la Philosophie de l'Histoire* (Paris: Victor Masson, 1859): T. K. Oesterreich, *Possession, Primitive, Middle Ages, and Modern* (New York: R. R. Smith, 1930); and J. R. Whitwell, *Historical Notes on Psychiatry* (Philadelphia: Blakiston's, 1937). J. C. Flugel, in *Man, Morals and Society* (London: Duckworth, 1945); Eric Fromm in various books; and G. Rattray Taylor, *Sex in History* (New York: Book Find Club, 1956) have continued this trend.

60. E. Sapir, "Cultural Anthropology and Psychiatry," *Journal of Abnormal and Social Psychology* 27 (1932), 229–42; idem, "The Contribution of Psychiatry to an Understanding of Behavior in Society," *American Journal of Sociology* 42 (1937), 862–70; idem, "The Emergence of the Concept of Personality in a Study of Culture," *Journal of Social Psychology* 5 (1933), 408–15; idem, "The Unconscious Patterning of Behavior in Society," in E. Dummer (ed.), *The Unconscious: A Symposium* (New York: A. A. Knopf, 1929), pp. 114–42; and E. Sapir, "Why Cultural Anthropology Needs the Psychiatrist," *Psychiatry* 1 (1938), 7–12. These papers represent the core of Sapir's contribution to culture-and-personality studies; they are most accessibly reprinted in E. Sapir, *Selected Writings in Language, Culture and Personality*, D. G.

Mandelbaum (ed.), (Berkeley: University of California Press, 1949). Sapir's *Festschrift*, L. Spier, A. I. Hallowell, and S. S. Newman (eds.), *Language, Culture, and Personality: Essays in Memory of Edward Sapir* (Menasha, Wisc.: George Banta, 1941), contains a number of valuable contributions to culture-and-personality studies elsewhere cited.

61. V. Barnouw, "The Phantasy World of a Chippewa Woman," *Psychiatry* 12 (1949), 67–76; I. H. Coriat, "Psychoneuroses among Primitive Tribes," *Journal of Abnormal and Social Psychology* 10 (1915), 201; C. Du Bois, *The People of Alor* (Minneapolis: University of Minnesota Press, 1944); A. I. Hallowell, "Shabwan: A Dissocial Indian Girl," *American Journal of Orthopsychiatry* 8 (1938), 329–40; W. La Barre, "A Cultist Drug Addiction in an Indian Alcoholic," *Bulletin of the Menninger Clinic* 50 (1941), 40–46; A. H. and D. G. Leighton, *Gregorio*; M. Mead, *Sex and Temperament* (New York: W. Morrow, 1935); M. F. Molina, "Study of a Psychopathic Personality in Guatemala," *Psychiatry* 10 (1947), 31–36; C. G. Seligman, "Temperament, Conflict, and Psychosis in a Stone Age Population," *British Journal of Medical Psychology* 9 (1929), 187–202; and M. E. Spiro, "A Psychotic Personality in the South Seas," *Psychiatry* 13 (1951), 189–202. Róheim, of course, has made many such observations in his field work. Undoubtedly the psychiatrist most experienced with exotic and preliterate populations is Burton G. Burton-Bradley, M.D., formerly of Singapore, now of Papua, New Guinea. Among prominent Western-trained psychiatrists are P. M. Yap of Hong Kong and Kwang-iel Kim of Seoul, Korea, both of whom publish in the area of comparative psychiatry. In Africa, the most active group is in Nigeria. Russian psychiatry, by Western standards, is almost hopelessly antiquated.

62. George Devereux, *Reality and Dream: Psychotherapy of a Plains Indian* (New York: International Universities Press, 1951). There also exists in manuscript an analysis of an Indian woman by Devereux.

63. E. Beaglehole, "Culture and Psychosis in New Zealand," *Journal of the Polynesian Society* 48 (1939), 144–55; idem, "Culture and Psychosis in Hawaii," in E. and P. Beaglehole (eds.) *Some Modern Hawaiians* (University of Hawaii Research Publications No. 19, Honolulu, 1939): J. W. Eaton, R. J. Weil, and B. Kaplan, "The Hutterite Mental Health Survey," *Mennonite Quarterly Review*, Jan. 1951, 3–21; J. Gillin, "Magical Fright," *Psychiatry* 11 (1948), 387–400; Arnold W. Green, "Culture, Normality, and Personality Conflict," *American Anthropologist* 50 (1948), 225–37; A. I. Hallowell, "Fear and Anxiety as Cultural and Individual Variables in a Primitive Society," *Journal of Social Psychology* 9 (1938), 25–47; L. Halpern, "Some Data on the Morbidity of Jews and Arabs in Palestine," *American Journal of Psychiatry* 94 (1938), 1215–22; R. Landes, "The Abnormal among the Ojibwa Indians," *Journal of Abnormal and Social Psychology* 33 (1938), 14–33; A. H. and D. Leighton, "Some Types of Uneasiness and Fear in a Navaho Indian Community," *American Anthropologist* 44 (1942), 194–209; J. E. Lind, "Phylogenetic Elements in the Psychoses of the Negro," *Psychoanalytic Review* 4 (1917), 303–32; B. Malzberg, "Mental Disease among Negroes in New York State," *Human Biology* 7 (1935), 471–513; idem, "Migration and Mental Disease among Negroes in New York State," *American Journal of Physical Anthropology* 21 (1936), 107–13; W. Morgan, "Human Wolves among the Navaho," *Yale University Publications in Anthropology* 11 (1936); L. A. Nichols, "Neuroses in Native African Troops," *Journal of Mental Science* 90 (1944), 862–68; M. C. Randle, "Psychological Types from Iroquois Folktales," *Journal of American Folklore* 65 (1952), 13–21; H. Rusillon, *Un Culte Dynastique avec Evocation des Morts chez Sakalaves de Madagascar, Le "Tromba"* (Paris: Alphonse Picard et Fils, 1912); E. Saindon, "Mental Disorder among the James Bay Cree," *Primitive Man* 6 (1933), 1–12; G. Sandeschejew, "Weltanschauungen und Schamanismus der Alaren-Burjaten," *Anthropos* 23 (1929), 976ff; C. G. Seligman, "Temperament, Conflict, and Psychosis in a Stone Age Population," *British Journal of Medical Psychology* 9 (1929), 187–202; D. M. Shelley and W. H. Watson, "An Investigation concerning Mental Disorder in the Nyassaland Natives," *Journal of Mental Science* 82 (1936), 701–30; S. M. Shirokogoroff, *Psychomental Complex of the Tungus* (London: K. Paul, Trench, Trubner & Co., 1935); idem, "Social Organization of the Manchus," *Royal Asiatic Society (North China Branch)*, Extra Volume III (Shanghai, 1924); and R. B. Stevens, "Racial Aspects of Emotional Problems of Negro Students," *American Journal of Psychiatry* 103 (1947), 493–98.

64. H. Basedow, *The Australian Aborigine* (Adelaide: F. W. Preece and Sons, 1925), p. 229; W. Bogoras, *The Chukchee* (New York: G. E. Stechert, 1909), pp. 45ff.; J. Crawfurd, *History of the Indian Archipelago*, 3 vols. (Edinburgh: Archibald Constable & Co., 1820), I:66–70; M.

Dobrizhoffer, *An Account of the Abipones*, 3 vols. (London: J. Murray, 1822), ch. 22, II:233–37; J. H. Driberg, *The Lango* (London: T. F. Unwin, 1923); W. B. Grubb, *An Unknown People in an Unknown Land* (London: Seeley & Co., 1913), p. 205; A. Hrdlicka, "Physiological and Medical Observations among the Indians of the Southwest," *Bulletin, Bureau of American Ethnology* 34 (1908), 171–214; idem, "Indians of Sonora, Mexico," *American Anthropologist* 6 (1904), 83; P. Hyades and J. Deniker, *Mission Scientifique de Cap Horn* (Paris: Gauthier-Villars et fils, 1891), 7:227–30; E. Pechuel-Loesche, *Völkerkunde von Loango* (Stuttgart: Strecker & Schröder, 1907), pp. 21–25; S. Reinach, "Le Laos Français," *Revue Indo-Chinoise* (1900), 82ff, pp. 150–52; W. H. R. Rivers, *The History of Melanesian Society*, 2 vols. (Cambridge: At The University Press 1914), I:345; J. Roscoe, *The Baganda* (London: Macmillan & Co., 1911), 22ff.; idem, *The Bakitara or Banyoro* (Cambridge: At the University Press, 1923), 290ff; idem, *The Banyankole* (Cambridge: At the University Press, 1923), p. 117; H. Ling Roth, *Natives of Sarawak and British North Borneo*, 2 vols. (London: Truslove, 1896), I:95–96, 296; H. Safford, *In Court and Kampong* (London: 1897), pp. 78–80; G. Schweinfurth, *The Heart of Africa*, 2 vols. (New York: Harper & Bros., 1874), 2:310: W. W. Skeat and C. O. Blagden, *Pagan Races of the Malay Archipelago*, 2 vols. (London: Macmillan, 1906), 2:246–47; V. Solomon, "Extracts from Diaries Kept in Car Nicobar," *Journal of the Royal Anthropological Institute* 32 (1902), 202–38; E. W. Smith and A. M. Dale, *The Ila Speaking Peoples of Northern Rhodesia*, 2 vols. (London: Macmillan & Co., Ltd., 1920), 1:239; M. Steggerda, "Maya Indians of Yucatan," *Carnegie Institute Publications* 531 (1941); P. A. Talbot, *The Peoples of Southern Nigeria*, 4 vols. (London: Oxford University Press, 1926), passim; and E. M. Weyer, *The Eskimo* (New Haven: Yale University Press, 1932), pp. 118–19.

65. R. Benedict, "Anthropology and the Abnormal," *Journal of General Psychology* 10 (1934), 64, 73, 72; idem, "Anthropology and the Abnormal," *Journal of Genetic Psychology* 128 (1940), 2.

66. Such, for example, has been the common criticism leveled against R. M. Bricker, *Is Germany Incurable?* (Philadelphia, 1943); and R. M. Bricker and L. V. Lyons, "A Neuropsychiatric View of German Culture," *Journal of Nervous and Mental Diseases* 98 (1943), 281–93. I have tried to make clear the predicament of Benedict's relativism in *The Human Animal*, pp. 233–66.

67. George Devereux, "A Sociological Theory of Schizophrenia," *Psychoanalytic Review* 26 (1939), 315–42; "Maladjustment and Social Neurosis," *American Sociological Review* 4 (1939), 844–51; and in a forthcoming book.

68. J. M. Cooper, "Mental Disease Situations in Certain Cultures: A New Field for Research," *Journal of Abnormal and Social Psychology* 29 (1934), 10–17; also abstracted in *Publications of the American Sociological Society* 28 (1934), 129; "A Note on Adjustment and Culture," *Primitive Man* 12 (1939), 57–69. The terms above are of course those of Ferenczi.

69. I. M. Coriat, "Psychoneuroses among Primitive Tribes," *Studies in Abnormal Psychology*, series 6 (1915), 201–8.

70. G. De La Tourette, *Traité clinique et therapeutique de l'hysterie*, 3 vols. (Paris: E. Plon, Nourrit, 1891–1895), 1:1–19 and passim. Others were K. Hilficker, "Critique of Freud's Views on Ideation of Schizophrenic Patients and Primitive Peoples," *Allgemeine Zeitschrift für Psychiatrie* 89 (1928), 97–108; A. Hirsch, *Handbook of Geographical and Historical Pathology*, 3 vols. (London: The New Sydenham Society, 1883–1886), 3:516–29; and O. Hovorka and A. Kronfeld, *Vergleichende Volksmedizin*, 2 vols. (Stuttgart: Strecker & Schröder, 1909), 2:179ff and 241ff. Indeed, the great taxonomist in psychiatry, Emil Kraepelin, was already aware of the problem of differential incidence of mental disorders in various groups (E. Kraepelin, "Vergleichende Psychiatrie," *Centralblatt für Nervenheilkunde und Psychiatrie* 27 [1904], 433–38; and in *General Paresis* [New York: Nervous and Mental Disease Monograph Series 14, 1913], p. 140; see also his *Manic-Depressive Insanity* [Edinburgh: E. and S. Livingstone, 1921], pp. 170–71).

71. L. K. Frank, "Physiological Tensions and Social Structure," *Papers and Proceedings, 22nd Annual Meeting, American Sociological Society* (1928), 74–82; idem, *Society as the Patient* (New Brunswick: Rutgers University Press, 1948); and idem, "Cultural Control and Physiological Autonomy," in Kluckhohn and Murray, *Personality*, pp. 113–16; E. Fromm, "Individual and Social Origins of Neurosis," in Kluckhohn and Murray, *Personality*, pp. 407–13; idem, "On the Problem of German Characterology," *Transactions of the New York Academy*

of Science II, 5 (1942–1943), 79–83: K. Horney, *The Neurotic Personality of Our Time* (New York: W. W. Norton, 1937); idem, *New Ways in Psychoanalysis* (New York: W. W. Norton & Co., 1939).

72. A. W. Green, "Social Values and Psychotherapy," *Journal of Personality* 14 (1946), 199–228; A. I. Hallowell, "Culture and Mental Disorder," *Journal of Abnormal and Social Psychology* 29 (1934), 1–9; J. Henry, "The Inner Experience of Culture," *Psychiatry* 14 (1951), 87–104; J. J. Honigmann, "Culture Patterns and Human Stress," *Psychiatry* 13 (1950), 25–34; F. L. K. Hsu, "Sex Crime and Personality, A Study in Comparative Cultural Patterns," *American Scholar* (Dec. 1951), 57–66; A. L. Kroeber, "Cultural Anthropology," in I. M. Bentley (ed.), *The Problem of Mental Disorder* (New York: McGraw-Hill, 1934), and "Psychosis or Social Sanction," *Character and Personality* 8 (1940), 210–15; W. La Barre, "The Age Period of Cultural Fixation," *Mental Hygiene* 33 (1949), 209–21, reprinted as "Wanted: A Pattern for Modern Man" in the pamphlet series of the National Committee for Mental Hygiene; idem, "Social Cynosure and Social Structure," *Journal of Personality* 14 (1946), 169–83; idem, "Toward World Citizenship," *Survey Graphic* 85 (1949), 153–56 (reprinted, *Foreign Service Institute*, Department of State, Washington, D.C., as a training document); and idem, "Child Care and World Peace," *The Child* 13 (1949), 156–57 (also reprinted as a FSI training document); R. Linton, "The Effects of Culture on Mental and Emotional Processes," *Research Publications, Association for Nervous and Mental Diseases* 19 (1939), 293–304; W. L. Warner, "The Society, the Individual and His Mental Disorders," *American Journal of Psychiatry* 94 (1937), 275–84; and E. Westermarck, *The Origin and Development of the Moral Ideas*, 2 vols. (London: Macmillan, 1906), 2:269–72.

73. G. H. Kirby, "A Study of Race Psychopathology," *New York State Hospital Bulletin*, March 1909; G. Róheim, "Racial Differences in the Neurosis and Psychosis," *Psychiatry* 2 (1939), 375–90; P. Schilder, "Cultural Patterns and Constructive Psychology," *Psychoanalytic Review* 27 (1940), 159–77; idem, "The Sociological Implications of Neuroses," *Journal of Social Psychology* 15 (1942), 3–21; N. Skliar and K. Starikawa, "Zur vergleichende Psychiatrie," *Archiv für Psychiatrie und Nervenheilkunde* 88 (1929), 554–85; E. Von Domarus, "Anthropology and Psychotherapy," *American Journal of Psychotherapy* 2 (1948), 603–14.

74. O. Klineberg, *Race Differences* (New York: Harper & Bros., 1935), chap. 18, esp. pp. 294–99); M. H. Smith, "A Comparison of the Neurotic Tendencies of Students of Different Racial Ancestry in Hawaii," *Journal of Social Psychology* 9 (1938), 395–417; J. D. Unwin, *Sexual Regulations and Cultural Behaviour* (London: Oxford University Press, H. Milford, 1935).

75. R. Bunzel, "The Role of Alcoholism in Two Central American Cultures," *Psychiatry* 3 (1940), 361–87; and D. Horton, "The Functions of Alcohol in Primitive Societies," in Kluckhohn and Murray, *Personality*, pp. 540–50.

76. F. Adelman, "Toward a Psycho-Cultural Interpretation of Latah," *Davidson Journal of Anthropology*, Spring 1955; H. C. Clifford, *Studies in Brown Humanity* (London: G. Richards, 1898), pp. 189–95; idem, *In Court and Kampong* (London: G. Richards, 1897), pp. 78–80; H. Codet, "Psychonevroses exotiques, l'amok et le lattah de Malaisie," *Le Progrès Médical* 42 (1927), 241–42; J. Crawford, *History*, 1:66–70; W. G. Ellis, "The *amok* of the Malays," *Journal of Mental Science* 39 (1893), 325–38; W. Fletcher, "Latah and Amok," *British Encyclopedia of Medical Practice* (London: Butterworth, 1938), pp. 641–50; D. J. Galloway and H. O. O'Brien, "Amok," *Journal of the Royal Asiatic Society* 85 (1922); C. Hose and W. McDougall, *The Pagan Tribes of Borneo*, 2 vols. (London: Macmillan, 1912), 2:130; E. Kraepelin, *Psychiatrie*, 4 vols., 8th ed. (Leipzig: J. A. Barth, 1909–1915), 1:155–58, 3(2):1105, 1137; 4(3):1655; E. Metzger, "Einiges über Amok und Mataglap," *Globus* 52 (1897), 107–10; C. Rasch, "Ueber Amok," *Neurologisches Centralblatt* 13 (1894), 550–54 and "Ueber die Amok-Krankheit der Malayen," *ibid.* 14 (1895), 856–59; G. Tarde, "Les maladies de l'imitation," *Revue Scientifique* 45 (1890), 737–48 and *ibid.*, 46 (1891), 6–11; P. C. Z. Van Brero, "Latah," *Journal of Mental Science* (1895), 537; F. H. G. Van Loon, "Amok and Latah," *Journal of Abnormal and Social Psychology* 21 (1926), 434–44, and "Protopathic-instinctive Phenomena in Normal and Pathological Malay Life," *British Journal of Medical Psychology* 8 (1928), 264–76.

77. D. Aberle, "Arctic Hysteria and Latah in Mongolia," *Transactions of the New York Academy of Science*, Series II, 14 no. 7 (1952), 291–97; J. Armangue y Tuest, "Mimicismo o neurosis imitante, " *Revista de Ciencias Medicales de Barcelona* 10 (1884), 574, 583, 613, 680, 715, 746–77; W. Bogoras, *The Chukchee*, 450ff; A. Brill, "Piblokto or Hysteria among Peary's

Eskimo," *Journal of Nervous and Mental Diseases* 40 (1913), 514–20; M. A. Czaplicka, *Aboriginal Siberia* (Oxford: Clarendon Press, 1914), pp. 305–25; S. Novakovsky, "Arctic or Siberian Hysteria as a Reflex of the Geographical Environment," *Ecology* 5 (1924), 113–27; and H. P. Steensby, "Contributions to the Ethnology of the Polar Eskimo," *Meddelelser om Grønland* 34 (1910), 377–78.

78. H. Angelino and C. L. Shedd, "A Note on Berdache," *American Anthropologist* 57 (1955), 121–26; G. Devereux, "Institutionalized Homosexuality of the Mohave Indians," *Human Biology* 9 (1937), 498–527; E. W. Gifford, "The Cocopa," *University of California Publications in American Archaeology and Ethnology* 31 (1933), 294; W. W. Hill, "Notes on the Pima Berdache," *American Anthropologist* 40 (1938), 338–40, and "Status of the Hermaphrodite and Transvestite in Navaho Culture," *American Anthropologist* 37 (1935), 273–79; F. Karsch-Haack, *Die gleichgeschlechtliche Leben der Naturvölker*, 1911; A. L. Kroeber (ed.), "Handbook of the Indians of California," *Bulletin of the Bureau of American Ethnology* 78 (1925), pp. 46, 190, 497, 500, 647, 748, 803; W. La Barre, *The Ghost Dance: Origins of Religion* (New York: Delta Books, 1972), pp. 138–40, 156–57, 179–81; N. Lurie, "Winnebago Berdache," *American Anthropologist* 55 (1953), 708–12; E. C. Parsons, "The Study of Variants," *Journal of American Folklore* 33 (1920), 87–90, and "The Zuni la'mana," *American Anthropologist* 18 (1916), 521–28; C. G. Seligman, "Sexual Inversion among Primitive Races," *Alienist and Neurologist* 23 (1902); L. Spier, "Klamath Ethnography," *University of California Publications in American Archaeology and Ethnology* 30 (1930), 51–53, and *Yuman Tribes of the Gila River* (Chicago: University of Chicago Press, 1933), pp. 242–43; C. Voegelin, "Tübatulabal Ethnography," *Anthropological Records, University of Carlifornia* 2 (1938), 78–80; and E. Westermarck, *Origin and Development*, 2:456–78.

79. I have a duplicate set of a well-nigh exhaustive bibliography on *latah* and *amok* collected by Dr. Alfred G. Smith, of the Department of Sociology and Anthropology at Emory University, Georgia, but he has not yet published on it.

80. W. E. Musgrave and A. G. Sison, "Mali-mali, a Mimic Psychosis in the Philippine Islands," *Philippine Journal of Science* 6 (1910).

81. W. A. Hammond, "Myriachit," *New York Medical Journal* 39 (1884), 191; idem, "Myriachit," *Aesclapian* 1 (1884), 57–60; and idem, "Myriachit," *British Medical Journal* 1 (1884), 758.

82. M. Amir, "Criminal Schizophrenics among Bataks," *Geneesk Tijdschrift van Nederlandsch Indie* 75 (1935), 24–33; N. J. Demerath, "Schizophrenia among Primitives," *American Journal of Psychiatry* 98 (1942), 703–7; R. E. L. Faris, "Some Observations on the Incidence of Schizophrenia in Primitive Society," *Journal of Abnormal and Social Psychology* 29 (1934), 30–31; C. Lopes, "Ethnographische Betrachtungen über Schizophrenie," *Zeitschrift für die gesammelte Neurologie und Psychiatrie* 142 (1932), 706–11; W. Plattner, "Race Mixtures and Relation between Racial and Constitutional Types in Schizophrenia," *Allgemeine Zeitschrift für Psychiatrie* 9 (1933), 410–31; and P. H. M. Travaglino, "Schizophrenia and the Javanese Psyche," *Psychiatrische und Neurologische Blätter* 31 (1927), 416–25.

83. R. Lasch, "Der Selbstmord aus erotischen Motiven bei den primitiven Völkern," *Zeitschrift für Sozialwissenschaft* 2 (1899), 578–85; S. R. Steinmetz, "Suicide among Primitive Peoples," *American Anthropologist* (old series) 7 (1894), 55–60; R. Weichbrodt, *Der Selbstmord* (Basel: S. Karger A. G., 1937); E. Westermarck, *Origin and Development* 2:229–40; and J. Wisse, *Selbstmord und Todesfurcht bei den Naturvölkern* (Zutphen: W. J. Thieme & cie., 1933).

84. H. F. Gloyne, "Tarantism, Mass Hysterical Reaction to Spider Bite in the Middle Ages," *American Imago* 7 (1950), 29–42. G. M. Beard, "Experiments with the 'Jumpers' of Maine," *Popular Science Monthly* 18 (1880), 170–78; idem, "Some Remarks Upon the 'Jumpers' or Jumping Frenchmen," *Journal of Nervous and Mental Diseases* 5 (1878), 526; H. F. Day, *Pine Tree Ballads* (Boston: Small, Maynard & Co., 1916); Gilles de la Tourette, "Etude sur une affection nerveuse," *Archives de Neurologie* [Paris] 9 (1885), 19ff and 158ff; P. Le Gendre, "La maladie de Gilles de la Tourette," *Union Médicale* [Paris] 3me sér. 40 (1885), 109–14; and F. Vizioli, "Sul Miryachit e sul Jumping," *Giornale di Neuropatologia* [Naples] 2 (1884), 164–80.

85. J. E. Dhunjibhoy, "A Brief Résumé of the Types of Insanity commonly met with in India, with a full Description of 'Indian Hemp Insanity' peculiar to the Country," *Journal of Mental Science* 76 (1930), 254–64; W. La Barre, *The Peyote Cult*, 4th ed. (Hamden, Conn.: Shoe String Press, 1975, and New York: Schocken Books, 1975).

86. D. Boyle, "The Killing of Wa-sak-apee-quay by Pe-se-quan and Others," *Annual Archaeologi-*

cal Report 1907, Appendix to the Report of the Minister of Education, Ontario (Toronto: L. K. Cameron, 1908), pp. 91–121; idem, "The Killing of Moostoos the Wehtigo," ibid., (1904), pp. 126–38; A. Burgesse, "Windigo," *Outfit* 277 (1947), 4–5; J. M. Cooper, "The Cree *wihtigo* Psychosis," *Primitive Man* 6 (1933), 20–24; J. E. Guinard, "Witiko among the Tete de Boule," *Primitive Man* 3 (1930), 69–71; F. W. Hodge (ed.), *Handbook of the Indians North of Mexico*, 2 vols. (Bulletin of the Bureau of American Ethnology 30 [1907], 2:930 sub "Weendigo"; R. Landes, "The Abnormal Among the Ojibwa Indians," *Journal of Abnormal and Social Psychology* 33 (1939), 14–33; S. Parker, "The Windigo Psychosis in the Context of Ojibwa Culture and Personality," *American Anthropologist* 62 (1960), 603–24; K. Pinkerton, *Windigo* (New York: Harcourt Brace & Co., 1945); J. E. Saindon, "Mental Disorders among the James Bay Cree," *Primitive Man* 6 (1933), 1–12; A. Skinner, "The Plains Ojibway," *Anthropological Papers, American Museum of Natural History* 11 (1914), part vi, pp. 500–5; F. G. Speck, *Neskapi* (Norman: University of Oklahoma Press, 1935), pp. 71–74. The paper by J. M. Cooper, "The Cree Witiko Psychosis," in Alan Dundes (ed.), *Every Man His Way* (Englewood Cliffs, N.J.: Prentice-Hall, 1968), pp. 288–92, has a basic bibliography on *windigo*; the best modern interpretation is that of V. Barnouw, "A Psychological Interpretation of a Chippewa Origin Legend," *Journal of American Folklore* 68, nos. 267–69 (1955), 73–85, 211–23, and 341–55. A curious parallel is reported by W. M. Bolman, "Hamburger Hoarding: A Case of Symbolic Cannibalism Resembling Whitico Psychosis," *Journal of Nervous and Mental Disease* 142 (1966), 424–28.

87. E. H. Ackerknecht, "Psychopathology, Primitive Medicine and Primitive Culture," *Bulletin of the History of Medicine* 14 (1943), 30–67; E. Beaglehole, "A Note on Cultural Compensation," *Journal of Abnormal and Social Psychology* 33 (1938), 121–23; idem, "Emotional Release in a Polynesian Community," ibid., 32 (1937), 319–28; H. S. Darlington, "An Instance of Primitive Psychotherapy," *Psychological Review* 25 (1938), 205–8; idem, "Confession of Sins," *Psychoanalytic Review* 24 (1937), 150–64; G. Devereux, "Primitive Psychiatry," *Bulletin of the History of Medicine* 8 (1940), 1194–1213, and 11 (1942), 522–42; idem, *Reality and Dream*; idem, "The Mental Hygiene of the American Indian," *Mental Hygiene* 26 (1942), 74–81; J. Gillin, "Magical Fright," *Psychiatry* 11 (1948), 387–400; A. I. Hallowell, "Sin, Sex and Sickness in Saulteaux Beliefs," *British Journal of Medical Psychology* 18 (1939), 191–97; W. W. Hill, "Navaho Rites for Dispelling Insanity and Delirium," *El Palacio* 41 (1936), 71–75; D. Jenness, "An Indian Method of Treating Hysteria," *Primitive Man* 6 (1933), 13–20; W. La Barre, "Primitive Psychotherapy in Native American Cultures: Peyotism and Confession," *Journal of Abnormal and Social Psychology* 42 (1947), 294–309; A. and D. Leighton "Elements of Psychotherapy in Navaho Religion," *Psychiatry* 4 (1941), 515–23; W. Morgan, "Navaho Treatment of Sickness," *American Anthropologist* 33 (1931), 390ff; M. E. Opler, "Some Points of Comparison and Contrast between the Treatment of Functional Disorders by the Apache Shamans and Modern Psychiatric Practice," *American Journal of Psychiatry* 92 (1936), 1371–87; O. Pfister, "Instinctive Psychoanalysis among the Navahos," *Journal of Nervous and Mental Disorders* 76 (1932), 234–55; R. Rirz, *Exorcismus und Heilkunde auf Ceylon* (Berne, 1941); S. L. Rogers, "Early Psychotherapy," *Ciba Symposia* 9 (1947), 602–32; K. Stewart, "Dream Therapy in Malaya," *Complex* 6 (1951), 21–33; M. W. Stirling, "Jivaro Shamanism," *Psychoanalytic Review* 20 (1933), 412–20; and H. C. Wyman, "Navaho Diagnosticians," *American Anthropologist* 38 (1936), 236–46.

88. S. C. Bernfeld, "Freud and Archaeology," *American Imago* 8 (1951), 107–28; L. B. Boyer, "Sculpture and Depression," *American Journal of Psychiatry* 106 (1950), 606–15; J. C. Flugel, *Man, Morals*; P. Heilbronner, "Some Remarks on the Treatment of the Sexes in Palaeolithic Art," *International Journal of Psycho-Analysis* 19 (1938), 441; Kohen, "Venus of Willendorf"; G. Rattray Taylor, *Sex in History*; A. F. C. Wallace, "A Possible Technique for Recognizing Psychological Characteristics of the Ancient Maya from an Analysis of their Art," *American Imago* 7 (1951), 3–22; D. Webster, "The Origin of the Signs of the Zodiac," *American Imago* 1 (1940), 31–47.

89. Anyone who thinks of writing seriously on the dynamics of racism should know at least: B. Bettelheim, "The Psychoanalysis of Anti-Semitism," *Complex* (Fall 1930), pp. 35–41; O. Fenichel, "Psychoanalysis of Antisemitism," *American Imago* 1 (1940), 24–39; H. Leiblowitz-Leonard, "A Psychoanalytic Contribution to the Problem of Antisemitism," *Psychoanalytic Review* 32 (1945), 359–61; R. M. Lowenstein, "The Historical and Cultural Roots of Anti-Semitism," in G. Róheim (ed.), *Psychoanalysis and the Social Sciences* (New York: Interna-

tional Universities Press, 1947); A. Lurie, "The Jew as a Psychological Type," *American Imago* 6 (1949), 119–55; R. Sterba, "Some Psychological Factors in Negro Race Hatred and Anti-Negro Riots," in Róheim, *Psychoanalysis*, pp. 411–27. The best dynamic-anthropological understanding of the Jew and anti-Semitism is by Howard Stein, in an article forthcoming in the *Journal of Psychohistory*; the analysis of ethnicity as a defense mechanism is to found in Howard F. Stein and R. F. Hill, *The Ethnic Imperative* (University Park: Pennsylvania State University Press, 1977).

90. E. Sapir, "Symbolism," *Encyclopedia of the Social Sciences* (New York: Macmillan Co., 1937), 14:492–95, reprinted in D. Mandelbaum (ed.), *Selected Writings of Edward Sapir*; P. L. Garvin, "Standard Average European and Czech," *Studia Linguistica* 3 (1949), 65–85; G. L. Tregar, mss. and projected work; S. Newman, "Analysis of Spoken Language of Patients with Affective Disorders," *American Journal of Psychiatry* 94 (1938), 913–94; idem, "Personal Symbolism in Language Patterns," *Psychiatry* 2 (1939), 177–84; idem, "Behavior Patterns in Linguistic Structure; A Case Study," in L. Spier et al. (eds.), *Language* pp. 94–106. On communication see: J. Henry, "The Linguistic Expression of Emotion," *American Anthropologist* 38 (1936), 250–56; E. S. Goldfrank, *Linguistic Note*; L. Thorner, "German Words, German Personality, and Protestantism," *Psychiatry* 8 (1945), 403–17; R. Birdwhistell, ms. and projected work; O. Klineberg, "Emotional Expression in Chinese Literature," *Journal of Abnormal and Social Psychology* 33 (1938), 517–20; and W. La Barre, "The Cultural Basis of Emotions and Gestures," *Journal of Personality* 16 (1947), 49–68, reprinted in D. G. Haring (ed.), *Personal Character*.

91. H. S. Darlington, "The Primitive Manufacture of Clay Pots: An Exposition of the Psychology of Pot-Making," *Psychoanalytic Review* 24 (1937), 392–402; W. A. Weisskopf, *The Psychology of Economics* (Chicago: University of Chicago Press, 1935); V. Tausk, "On the Origin of the Influencing Machine in Schizophrenia," *Psychiatric Quarterly* 2 (1933), 519–56; P. Schilder, *The Image and Appearance of the Human Body* (London: K. Paul, Trench, Trubner & Co., 1935); S. Lorand, "A Note on the Psychology of the Inventor," *Psychoanalytic Quarterly* 3 (1934), 30–41; Hanns Sachs, "The Delay of the Machine Age," *Psychoanalytic Quarterly* 2 (1933), 404–24; and Yu-lan Fung, "Why China Has No Science," *International Journal of Ethics* 32 (1922), 258–59.

92. J. E. Harrison, *Epilegomena to the Study of Greek Religion* (Cambridge: At the University Press, 1921); F. M. Cornford, "The Unconscious Element in Literature and Philosophy," *Proceedings of the Classical Association*, 1922; B. S. Engle, "Attis," "Lemnos," "Melampus," and "Amazons," ref. note 59; S. Freud, *Moses and Monotheism* (London: Hogarth Press, 1940); idem, *The Future of an Illusion* (London: Hogarth Press, 1928); idem, "Obsessive Acts and Religious Practices," *Collected Papers*, 2:25–35; E. Jones, *Symbolic Significance of Salt*; idem, "Psychoanalysis and the Psychology of Religion," in S. Lorand (ed.), *Psycho-analysis Today* (New York: Covici, Friede, 1933); A. Kardiner, *Individual and His Society*; idem, *Psychological Frontiers*; idem, *Basic Personality Structure*; T. Reik, *Ritual: Psychoanalytic Studies* (New York: Farrar, Straus & Co., 1940); idem, *Dogma and Compulsion* (New York: International Universities Press, 1951); and E. Weigert, *Magna Mater*.

93. S. Freud, "Psychoanalysis and the Ascertaining of Truth in Courts of Law," *Collected Papers*, 2:13–24; F. Alexander and W. Healy, *Roots of Crime* (New York: A. A. Knopf, 1935); M. Fries, "National and International Difficulties," *American Journal of Orthopsychiatry* 11 (1941), 562–73; A. H. Stanton and S. E. Perry (eds.), *Personality and Political Crisis* (Glencoe: Free Press, 1954); J. J. Honigmann, "Morale in a Primitive Society," *Character and Personality* 12 (1944), 228–36; P. M. Yap, "The Mental Illness of Hung Hsiu-Ch'uan, Leader of the Taiping Rebellion," *Far Eastern Quarterly* (May 1954), 237–304; H. D. Laswell, *Psychopathology and Politics* (Chicago: University of Chicago Press, 1930); R. West, *Conscience and Society: A Study of the Psychological Prerequisites of Law and Order* (London: Methuen & Co. 1942); S. de Grazia, "A Note on the Psychological Position of the Chief Executive," *Psychiatry* 8 (1945), 267–72.

94. A. A. Brill, "The Psychopathology of Selections of Vocations," *Medical Record* [New York] 23 February 1918; S. M. Davidson, "Anxiety States Arising in Naval Personnel Afloat and Ashore," *New York State Journal of Medicine* 42 (1942), 1654–56; J. Dollard and D. Horton, *Fear in Battle* (New Haven: Yale University Press, 1943); L. K. Frank, "Psychosomatic Disturbances in Relation to Personnel Selection," *Annals of the New York Academy of Science* 44 (1943), 439–622; E. E. Hadley, "Unrecognized Antagonisms Complicating Business Enter-

prise," *Psychiatry* 1 (1938), 13–31; E. Kris and N. Leites, "Trends in Twentieth Century Propaganda," in Róheim, *Psychoanalysis and the Social Sciences*, pp. 393–410; M. H. Maskin and L. L. Altman, "Military Psychodynamics: Psychological Factors in the Transition from Civilian to Soldier," *Psychiatry* 6 (1943), 263–69; J. Rinaldo, *The Psychoanalysis of the Reformer* (New York: Lee Publishing Co., 1921); G. U. Stephenson and K. Cameron, "Anxiety States in the Navy," *British Medical Journal* 2 (1943), 603–7; and W. La Barre, *The Human Animal*, pp. 98–109.

III. Applied

8. Social Cynosure and Social Structure

Advertisements, movies, popular fiction, and other vehicles of publicity, amusement, and fantasy unite in demonstrating to us that in our society it is the nubile young female who achieves the most attention, who is the cynosure of all eyes. Indeed, this is so true that the statement itself appears a naïve laboring of the obvious. But although this situation may seem to us inevitable, and indeed quasi-biological, a closer study reveals that it is a culturally arbitrary and historically conditioned phenomenon.[a]

The status of women in American society is derived partly from the prior culture of the west-European settlers in our country, and partly from later historical accidents. Under the conditions of frontier society, woman achieved high status through an economically useful contribution that was enhanced by her scarcity value.

This achieved status has never been abdicated in later American culture-history, though it has been greatly modified. Most of the economic functions of woman, in the manufacture and preparation of food and clothing and the like, have been removed from the home, to be performed by specialized extra-familial commercial institutions. With woman no longer valuable in terms of her sex-patterned economic activity, and no longer valuable as a statistical rarity, she seeks to retain her status through an artificial scarcity, a competitive, cultivated invidiousness of sexual appeal.

This is so evident that prestige now accrues to woman as *consumer*, rather than as producer: it is as a suitable vehicle for the display of male buying power that a woman is now valued. Her socially useful contributions as a producer or worker carry no prestige at all, save in competitive-masculine terms. It is woman as a cosmetic creation, as clotheshorse, and as conspicuous consumer who is valued.

This essay appeared considerably earlier than the Women's Liberation movement, and perspectives have changed along with social change. Nevertheless, it is presented as it first appeared, as indicating an anthrolopological perspective and sympathy with women in their arbitrarily truncated role culturally—in a struggle for recognition as persons that is currently by no means entirely won.

First published in the *Journal of Personality* 14 (1946), 169–83. Copyright © Duke University Press. Reprinted by permission.

a. The illuminating studies by Dr. Helene Deutsch on the origins and development of feminine narcissism (in *The Psychology of Women*, 2 vols., New York, 1944 and 1945), impressive and convincing as they are, may need to be qualified as applying perhaps only to women *in our culture, now.*

In this competition for overt sexual desirability, youth on the part of the woman is the greatest ally. Thus, our advertisements are, with heavy preponderance, concerned with pictures of young women.

A striking exception to this occurs in wartime and was as true of the advertisements of the First World War as of the Second. With the same unanimity, advertisements become preoccupied with the young male as soldier. Usually he is discreetly nude and bathing in groups overseas, or alone at home in a bathtub; or he is presented as sleeping, eating, and drinking, or in other appealing circumstances. The sentimentality (overly patterned affects) toward the soldier is as stereotyped in wartime as the corresponding attitudes toward the nubile female are in peacetime.

But the social usefulness of the male appears nowhere so clearly and so poignantly as in his potential sacrifice in the ultimate defense of the society. His temporary position as cynosure is regarded by most people as earned, together with the increase in narcissism signalized by the uniform, etc. (we feel that there is distinctly nothing unvirile in a paratrooper's insignia, corps identification, or in the bright colors of ribbons won for courage and unselfish valor).

The most excruciating of advertisements are those which attempt in wartime to indicate that face-powder and lipstick are somehow subtly more important than gunpowder and airplanes. The picture of leisure-class women at home gallantly buying the right perfume in order magically to succor their men in the raddled agony of battle and death is extravagantly absurd. Yet even here, such a woman is by implication a mere appanage of the male, and hardly a person in her own right.

That clothes-narcissism *is* permitted women in our contemporary society and is regarded as appropriate to their role, while it is *not* permitted or appropriate to the male in peacetime, is indicated, I believe, by the rather usual adult male attitude toward the pastel sweaters, the green pork-pie hats, the ravishing ties, and the fancy shoes of the fashion plates in certain self-announced "magazines for men." Here the appeal is to the collegiate adolescent, the tout, and the sharpy; the bachelor man-about-town overprotesting his virility; and to other persons unsure of or dubious in their masculinity and maturity.

Most adult men find such advertisements obscurely effeminate. The socially approved male exhibitionism in our society is largely the symbolic one of competitive accomplishment in athletics, business, or science, rather than the direct exhibition of the person. This is so much the case that, however undeserved, there clings about the radio crooner, the male actor, dancer, and movie star (and even the professional strong man with his spectacularly masculine body) a distinct aura of the effeminate or the sexually inappropriate act. Even the politician dare not be too unusually handsome lest, like several British and Americans who could be named, his real abilities be overshadowed and obscured. And, however indulgent and approving we may feel toward the public nudity of the female in contexts of entertainment, by contrast the ultimate horror and crime is the exhibition of male genitals.[b]

Thus it is, as I have stated, that the great majority of our advertisements are centered on pictures of young women. These pictures are doubly significant: they constitute reader appeal for both sexes (evidencing that the young woman *is* the cynosure of our society), and they further make appeal to the woman as consumer (in their concern for the correct bodily shape, texture, cleanliness, scent, haberdashery, sartorial *brouhaha*, and general impedimenta of the female).

The unhappiness of modern woman is traceable in part to her recognition that her status is somehow factitious in its grounds. As clotheshorse her status is dependent upon the logically prior activity of the male, and woman is the mere vehicle of the masculine prestige gained through competitive achievement of buying power. Her value is her sexual marketability, not her value as a human being or as a person. Her real social value as mother and wife is by no means as conspicuously attended to and rewarded; still less her value in the economic production of goods and services. She may well feel that this is a most unfair evaluation of the relative worth of womanly roles.

But in movies and popular fiction, the focus of attention is upon the competitive nubility of the young woman. The type-fantasy is the Cinderella saga, of irresistible feminine beauty winning the bearer of masculine status and wealth. She need not know how to cook, she need not be able to read a newspaper intelligently, she need not even belong to the right book club: cutaneous texture and subcutaneous contour are all she needs to bring buying power ravening at her feet. The appalling emptiness of values in this transaction is highlighted by the fact that the male, too, is depersonalized. It is true that he is required to have cosmetic charm, though of a recognizably lower candle power than the female's, but he need possess none of the variety of signs of masculine worth, provided he embodies buying power.

The startling fact is that the movie usually ends in the "final clinch," after the cut-and-dried vicissitudes of the boy meeting, losing, and refinding the girl. For all that the bulk of movie fare gives witness, life ends at this point. The excitements, the problems, and the rewards of maturity are, comparatively speaking, little noticed in this art. Popular music is even more exclusively obsessed with the anxieties of mate-finding and mate-losing, so drearily and so

---

b. Since this article was written, nowhere has social change been more evident than in attitudes toward male nudity. Perhaps its very shock-value made it of greater use for a counter-establishment generation. Fifty years ago men's room grafitti were solely preoccupied with a lozenge-and-dot female symbol that can be traced back to the middle-European neolithic. But male nudity, ever since *Hair, O Calcutta, Equus* and other plays is a commonplace on Broadway, and *Playgirl* magazine even has a centerfold to match that in *Playboy*. However, Freud pointed out that, aesthetically considered, genitalia are essentially unattractive, and Kinsey maintained that women do not have the same interest in male nudity as men do in women's. If so, then even pornography has a sexist bias.

masochistically so that one is moved, with profane exasperation, to wish for, at least once, a forthright cock-crow of possession and triumph.

But the status of glamour girl can be lost through the years, or indeed, in a season. So compelling is the pattern, though, that even when it is no longer useful or appropriate to the legal spouse and matron, the woman still endlessly strives toward it. Thus our society is witness to the obscenity of grandmothers still archly affecting the bobby socks, the jumpers, and the youthfully styled haircuts of their remoter descendants, still smearing onto their sagging jowls the greases and the colored dirts of synthetic youth. The fripperies of dress and the general hallucinations of attitude continue with a sad shamelessness, all the more tragic in that the patterned imprisonment in immaturity disenfranchises the woman of the far richer experiences open to her as a functioning adult.

Thus, the status of cynosure is by no means a blessing to its bearer. And when thus realistically dissected, the arbitrariness and extravagance of popular myth and behavior make it clear that the status of cynosure is a cultural construct, and the contingent product of social, economic, and historical forces.

Success in our society is *invidious*. And yet, in its essence, it need not necessarily be so, nor is it the case in a number of societies which we could cite. The fundamental problem of the stability and even of the viability of a given culture may be involved with the question of the extent to which individual members of the society may really achieve "success," in the terms with which the society defines success. By *definition* success in our capitalistic society means the obtaining of what others may not have; it is the exclusiveness of achieving the statistically rare. Yet, strangely, perhaps a majority of humble supporters of this dispensation empathize the figure on the dizzy pinnacle, ignore their own statistical chances of this indivious success, and delude themselves with the fantasy that it could be they.[c] The "hard-headed" small businessman planning his empire is as equally capable of this empathy and this cavalier and irresponsible attitude toward the cold statistics of the matter as the shopgirl dreaming of the movie queen. Were this not true, the society would not enjoy such stability as it does. But with this definition of success, the majority of people are permanently infantilized as mere spectators of the feast of life. However, it is an open question whether mass satisfactions need be real or merely empathized, and the anthropologist is by no means prepared to insist that stability requires genuine rather than fantasied satisfactions, when he observes our own society in the thirteenth century.

We may now summarize two points: (a) The cynosure of a society may be an individual, an age and/or sex group, a class, caste, or occupational group,

c. The irony concerning the American "upward-mobility" myth is that built-in class attitudes (toward education, science, higher culture, etc.) effectively imprison persons of lower-class origins in a lower-class ethos, so that even with middle- and upper-class economic status, in bored frustration and inchoate puzzlement, they retain lower-class souls.

such that some individuals and not others receive the bulk of attention, gratification of narcissism, and public prestige. One may be born to the status of cynosure, one may achieve it, and one may in some cases lose it. (b) Not all individuals in a given society are permitted to achieve success, within the culture's definition of success; therefore, some individuals must be emotionally disenfranchised for the benefit of those others. Although success is not necessarily invidious in all societies, the percentage of those in a given society who achieve it may differ widely from the percentage of those who achieve success in the terms of another society.

The ideal society would possess a *variety* of cynosures such that every age, sex, occupational and other group could fit into a number of respectable alternatives, or at least such that the total list would exhaust the whole variety of conditions of man in that society. This is merely to say that such an ideal society would achieve a democratization of prestige and would abolish its single or exclusive cynosure statuses. Or, put in other words, a stable and satisfying society would embrace within its patterns of success the greatest possible number of individuals.

Is it possible that we may find relationships between the conservatism and the tempo of social change, the percentality of success, and the nature of cynosures? The following information from a variety of cultures other than our own will illustrate, if it does not answer, some of these questions.

We have noted that the status of cynosure or focus of attention and prestige may be reached in a wide variety of ways. In one of the most stable, conservative, and perhaps individually most satisfying of all cultures, the classical Chinese, *any individual may achieve it in time if he is biologically normal.* For here parenthood is the criterion of cynosureship. While it may appear that age makes one the cynosure, this is not strictly the case; for without the creation of a family during the years one is attaining to that age, in the familial organization of Chinese society, one would be a cynosure without an audience, an absurdity. The aged eunuch and the celibate Buddhist monk lack this respect. And while it may appear that the father is the cynosure (for he can demand the obedience and respect of even a middle-aged married son), nevertheless, the mother too, for all the alleged superiority in status of the male to the female, may similarly enjoy the status. That the true criterion is parenthood, and not age or sex, is evidenced by the fact that the matriarch, too, shares in the ultimate prestige, and also perhaps by the fact that these same values are extrapolated further into the supernatural world, in ancestor worship. For all its faults (and it has them) classical Chinese culture did in time embrace within its forms of prestige and success the vast majority of the members of its society. The reverence and respect for the parent is also involved with the teacher and preceptor as cynosure, and it is certainly true that the scholar in China was similarly a social cynosure. But with intelligence and hard work any man can achieve the status whatever his social origins, and the system remains democratically open. By contrast, the occupations traditionally admired in many other societies, those of warrior and merchant, in China were despised and held far below the occupation of husbandman, that other promoter of increase.

Again, all individuals may achieve the status of cynosure *in time if of the requisite sex.* In the Central Australian gerontocracy, every male need only survive to old age to be its beneficiary. Here the exclusion of the women from ceremonial and other prestigeful areas of life is striking, so that half the society, unlike the Chinese, is disenfranchised by the accident of birth. It is important to note that the cynosure also has considerable significance in the economic and social functioning of Central Australian culture. It is no trick at all to manipulate food taboos in such a manner that the most desirable food is taboo to youngsters and to women, although as in the case of exploiters of most societies the process is hardly conscious. The tempo of change in a gerontocracy is also notable. By contrast with the breathless faddism and precipitate change in our own youth-oriented society, Central Australian native culture is among the most unchanging in the world, and the most conservative. It is not without significance, perhaps, that its mythology is oriented toward the remote past, the "alchuringa-time," a mythic past mysteriously present now in ritual, and the sanction for behavior is that it has always been done this way, not that this way is "new."

This suggests a dynamism perhaps significant in Western society. In America the authority figure has been dethroned by a successful revolution against a British tyrant, and in the resultant sibling society, youth and dizzy change reign. The symbolic oedipal revolution is won. In British society, however, the king still reigns, though he does not rule. Undethroned, he is reduced to political impotence, but remains still the cynosure of an empire. Thus, English affects cluster around the familiar, the old and the loved, in a word, the traditional; and social change comes with some reluctance, lagging far behind the indubitably intelligent and realistic judgment of the electorate. Modern England has had economic and political revolution, but without a complete social and symbolic revolution. Modern America has had a political and symbolic revolution, but without a complete social and economic revolution. Modern Russia has presumably undergone a social and economic revolution, but in its retention of absolutism, it has completed neither the political nor the symbolic revolution. And, quite clearly, Catholic and dictatorial South American countries, for all their many spurious revolutions, have achieved neither political, social, economic, nor symbolic revolution, for although the personnel changes, the system and the practices remain.

An extreme of catholicity in cynosure selection is reached in parts of Indonesia. Here the status is achieved *automatically in time by every individual.* It is, however, a somewhat empty status from our own unbelieving point of view, since it is reached only in death. Not so to the Indonesians:

Powerful though the beliefs in magic and spirits are, probably the most important cult in Indonesia has to do with the ghosts of the dead and the ancestors. In few other places in the world do funeral ceremonies involve so much time, energy, and sacrifice. In many tribes the dead receive not only one, but two and even three successive funerals, at each of which the bones of the deceased are exhumed or removed from their tombs for cleaning. The ways of disposing of mortal remains are extremely varied. In the island of Sumatra alone, for instance, the different tribes bury, cremate, entomb, abandon, conceal in caves, and seal in trees the bodies of their dead. Even within the same tribe diverse methods of disposal may be employed, depending upon the age, rank, sex, and manner of death of the deceased.

This obsession with death and the dead reaches its culmination in the all-important ancestor cult. The ancestors have passed beyond, to the realm of the spirits, and, if kept satisfied, are in an excellent position to aid the living. Therefore they receive endless sacrifices, and the people dread offending them in any way. This, indeed, is a great reason for the conservativism of the Indonesians, as the ancestors are likely to be angered by any alteration in the ways they were used to on earth.[d]

Thus, whatever the frustrations and failures of this life, one could at least look forward to becoming dead in Indonesia, and to enjoying lively revenge as an ancestral ghost. However, this raises the question (if it has not already been suggested by our own culture) of the social cost of the cynosure, and whether its support is ultimately worth while in terms of return to the society.

Alternatively, cynosure status can be closely exclusive, *achieved by birth by one individual in each generation, or by one family only.* Here should be mentioned the Emperor of Japan, in whom the cynosureship of his society was dazzlingly focused as the descendant of the Sun Goddess, Amaterasu o Mikami. This is wholly consonant with the male orientation and the tightly feudal structure of prewar Japan. The Royal Family of England is an excellent example of the second. The breathless concern with Royal household trivia by the citizens of a far-flung Empire equals, indeed, the tireless voyeurism of the sexuality of the cinema great by the avid readers of movie magazines in America.[e]

The individual may become a cynosure *by election* of one sort or another. The "divine kings" described in such detail by Sir James Frazer in *The Golden Bough* probably belong in this category. The divine king, somewhat in the manner of the President among us, is the scapegoat of the society, however, and is regarded as being magically responsible, both positively and negatively, for the success or failure of the crops, the well-being of the cattle, and the like.

d. Raymond Kennedy, *Islands and Peoples of the Indies*, Smithsonian Institution, War Background Studies, No. 14, p. 48.

e. Again, with the change of movie cynosure from female to male since the time of first writing of this article, such figures are now, rather, the popular songsters of both sexes. But the principle remains the same in changing mass publications. The adulation is of similar magnitude and reward, as though lasting social eminence were merely a matter of publicity; yet the essential triviality of their accomplishment is signalized in their evanescence and early oblivion.

The position of cynosure here is subject to sudden vacation by death, if weakness and old age, or anything untoward like a drought or crop failure reveals the senescence of the cynosure. In Mexico the bravest captive enemy youth chosen to impersonate the war god enjoyed all the available delights and prestige which the society could give them; but this was for a term only, and ended in the use of such individuals in human sacrifice. In the case of the divine king and the god-impersonator, therefore, the status of cynosure, though elective, carried many prerogatives and great prestige, but it was paid for by the individual's death. The dynamics of hostile affect in the ruthless Aztec society and in absolutist societies with divine kings would be an interesting subject for study. The question of the price of being cynosure to the individual is also obvious.

Similarly punishing to the individual may be the cynosureship won *by either sex if the right activities are performed,* as in the case of ascetics in India. The enormous prestige which accrues to the "holy" person practicing austerities in India must be witnessed to be believed; even the Hindu gods can compel one another to their will, and at times the very structure of the universe has been threatened in Hindu myth by ascetic individuals piling up the capital of supernatural virtue in extraordinary amounts through their penances. The institutionalized masochism of these individuals is functionally of a piece with the fantastically sadomasochistic structure of Indian culture.

In some societies the individual may become the cynosure *by sex, age, and activity.* The case of the soldier in Germany from the time at least of Frederick the Great is an illustration of this. The saber-scarred cheek of the duelist was the badge of this society, and the soldier was the darling of German society in the last war to the extent that economic, social, and sexual values were bent to his service. The extent to which military values and the philosophy of force have permeated German history is evident to any student of prewar German history and German philosophy. The history of Hitler is the shrewd implementation of his magical political formulae with police and military power.[f]

The warrior as cynosure is not an uncommon phenomenon, as a matter of fact, among primitive societies; thus one may attain the status *by successful sex-patterned activity.* Possibly the culture of the Plains Indians carried this to the greatest logical extreme. The idea of *power,* a sort of male *mana,* underlies Plains culture. One may acquire supernatural power through the vision quest, or through purchase (as with the Blackfoot medicine bundles), but only two formal roles were open to men in the exploitation and display of this power. A man might become a warrior or a medicine man—and little else. Secular success in warfare probably carried greater prestige than magic success in doctoring, but between the two of them, these roles absorbed practically all the

---

f. If the magic force of Hitler was in the political realm, the Marxist and Russian faith is in the magic of economics; but this faith nevertheless implements itself with a tight social, cultural, political, and military control of its communicants. The British-American faith is in law and orderly social process.

prestige of cynosureship available in the society. The fiercely competitive and individualistic struggle for success in war, through scalp-taking, horse-stealing, counting coup, and other quixotic displays of daring, has given to the typical Plains Indian the qualities of character, the aggressiveness and the extroversion, which we regard as fundamentally "masculine" since they conform to our own cultural male-ideal.

But the psychological pressures of the male pattern in Plains society—the systematic and repeated exposure of oneself to mutilation and death—must have been enormous indeed, because success in its terms was commonly so threatening and impossible that a semiofficial status was set up for the frequent enough "failures" in this society. This was the famous institution of the *berdache*, the nonman who did not go to war like other males, signalized by the feminine dress and feminine activities (and sometimes quasi-female sexuality) of these individuals. The *berdache* is the product of the fierce exclusiveness of concentration upon the warrior as cynosure, and not all men in the gamut of individual temperament and character variation could take on the severely defined traits of the warrior's role. Our own concentration upon the acquisition of economic buying power as the prime and essential masculine value, and the central and only worthwhile male activity, might well be examined in the light of the psychodynamics of Plains culture.

Successful sex-patterned activity finds a less traumatogenic expression elsewhere. In France, it is the mature and sexually functioning woman who is the cynosure of the society. Nowhere, certainly not in Europe, is there so well developed an appreciation of woman as woman, as sexual object and mother alike. That there is the split-image of woman as official wife and as mistress in French society does not negate this fact; it is rather an evidence of the double role of woman as mother and as sexual object, which in no society may be the same individual. It was in France that femininity reached its highest *chic*, and Paris was long the true home of feminine *haute couture*, millinery, and perfume.[g] It was the France of that feminine Don Juan, George Sand, of the ageless Ninon de l'Enclos, the imperishable Sarah Bernhardt, the fabled Kiki, and the indestructible Mistinguette.

The achievement of cynosure status by successful sex-patterned activity is by no means undesirable in itself: it all depends upon what the sexually patterned activities and roles are, and what their social usefulness may be. In late medieval and early modern times, the condition and outward appearance of pregnancy and approaching motherhood brought such prestige and was considered aesthetically so satisfying that stomachers were introduced into fashionable dress to imitate the condition. Similarly, in the prolific Victorian period, fashion emphasized the elegance and the importance of the female pelvis in the bustle. Inasmuch as maternity is a genuine social value, and since there is much

g. If, as it may indeed be contended, the English cynosure was the young statesman and public servant (the young Pitt, Anthony Eden, e.g.), then it is appropriate to find London the analogous center of male style.

to be gained for all individuals concerned through its satisfactions, the value of the mother as cynosure is easily recognized. Indeed, whatever of stability medieval Europe knew, after the disintegration of the classical cultures, centered on the forms and institutions of mariolatry and recrudescent Mediterranean mother-goddess religions. That this same culture can in other times produce institutionalized social, economic, political, and emotional infantilisms is another problem, and an instance of the dangers of overemphasizing any one human role.[h]

On the other hand, since one male can produce many pregnancies and his own role in child-bearing is a relatively minor one, the appurtenances of individual virility are biologically and socially less valuable and indispensable. Thus, the similar expression of male exhibitionism in dress, in the late fifteenth- and early sixteenth-century codpiece, quickly reached competitive extremes which were ridiculously and patently spurious. The well-established psychiatric significance of suckling children at the breast, as an undeniable social value, gives, on the other hand, a dignity and a perennial satisfaction to the display in dress of the female bosom throughout the history of style. But these are *functional* values of woman as mother and as mate, and of incomparably greater worth than woman as conspicuous consumer in the competitive seeking to capture male buying power. It is surely at least arguable that a focused cultural appreciation of wise maternity and a connoisseurship of the finesses and intricacies of intelligent and well-considered motherhood constitute as worthwhile and as satisfying a social cynosure as the French connoisseurship of woman as sexual object. And certainly both are more real creatures than the cold, compulsive-masked, cosmetic beauty of the professional glamour girl and cinema queen, who is less the maturely functioning female than prenuptial mantrap.

Other cultures, too, have been aware of the charm of youth. Our traditionally antisexual and youth-oriented American society chooses to concentrate attention upon the young female before the time of sexual fulfilment. This is a cynosureship achieved *by the appropriate sex at a given age and subsequently lost*. Among the Greeks of the fifth century before Christ, the cynosure of society was just as distinctly the adolescent and maturing young male. There are rich philosophical, metaphysical, theological, psychiatric, and didactic overtones to this fact, both in classic times and later, but these as much merit extended study elsewhere as does our own social cynosure.[i]

The case of Bali, in which the very young, preadolescent girl is the social cynosure, is even more striking, but the choice of the breastless female child is

---

h. In the postwar France of Sartre and Lévi-Straus, the cynosure (based on earlier literary figures) has emerged as *the single currently reigning intellectual*. But the French still behave as though they had invented sexuality.

i. For a fuller delineation of the cultural, artistic, and philosophical significance of the Greek *ephebe*, see W. La Barre, *The Ghost Dance: Origins of Religion* (New York: Delta Books, 1972), pp. 433–553.

quite probably another index of the pathology of this ignorantly admired and profoundly schizothymic culture. Her fate is to grow up and become the wicked witch of a mother, whose frustrations (subjective and objective, active and passive) regenerate the whole trauma and tragedy.

One final type of cynosureship comes to mind in this not necessarily exhaustive list. That is the case of the Northwest Coast Indians, in whose society the cynosure is the prestige-creating, property-destroying potlatching chief. In one sense he is the cynosure as recipient of prestige created by his ancestors, and in another sense he is the cynosure as creator of prestige for his descendants. However, a *nouveau riche* or *arriviste* potlach-giver cannot gain prestige *for himself*, but only *for his descendants*. The cynosureship is here, more correctly, a *property-purchased prestige which is inherited*. Something of the sort is familiar to us in our own society, in which full gentility lags a generation, and in which the length of time the family has had money is significant.

Indeed, it is in terms of the social cynosure that we might most usefully view the Northwest Coast culture. Ruth Benedict's *Patterns of Culture* has had the well-deserved influence of a pioneering attempt to apply the insights of psychiatry to ethnology. And like all truly significant books, it instructs us even in its errors. Not the least of its values has been the teaching of caution about the extrapolation of clinical categories from the field of *psychiatric* description of *individuals* to the *ethnological* description of *cultures*. Sapir, like many another later investigator, has pointed out that if Northwest Coast culture is descriptively "megalomaniac," then the megalomaniac individual in it is in close, non-conflictful conformity with the culture. That is, the individual who (in our clinical sense) is megalomaniac there, is then *well adjusted* to his culture; while the nonmegalomaniac individual (the "sane" man in our judgment) is a bad misfit. It is clear that the dynamic situations of the descriptively megalomaniac individual in Northwest Coast culture on the one hand, and such an individual in our culture on the other hand, are not only different, but diametrically opposite.

The danger of this line of thought is evident when would-be scientific description and analysis degenerate into name-calling. Spengler labels cultures "carnivorous" and "herbivorous," and leaves us in no doubt as to which he regards as superior. But it is equally crude on our part to call Nazi culture "paranoid." Casting aside nationalistic emotion and ethnocentric value judgment, such description is to be criticized on the same grounds as the Northwest Coast instance. If we are satisfied with an impressionistic first approximation of *description*, well and good: Nazi culture *was* arrogantly "megalomaniac" in its racism, "persecutory" in its political ideology, "amoral" in its behavior, and pathological in its sexuality. Its leader, Hitler, *was* hypochondriac, and from abundant evidence very possibly a classical clinical case of paranoia. Descriptively there is much evidence of the paranoid here; but we must consider more deeply the problem of the *dynamics* of the "abnormal" milieu, in which the abnormal individual is at home.

The concept of cynosure may be a useful refinement of description in dealing with the Northwest Coast culture. Actually it is only the potlatching chief who is the functioning megalomaniac, in one sense. It is he who is the focus of his group's economic activity; it is he who recklessly and arrogantly destroys great amounts of property in the social manufacture of prestige. Of course the group empathizes its potlatch chief and of course its members share the cultural values of their chief, but it is the chief who is the cynosure. And although other individuals share the culture of the chief, to what extent are the commoner and the chief actually identical in their psychological functioning as individuals?

In so far as the Northwest Coast culture and our own are wry caricatures of each other, its study is illuminating in the critical examination of our capitalist culture. Has not Veblen already adequately demonstrated that property among us is utilized not so much for its sound biological contributions to our well-being as for its prestige value? Do we not "consume" (destroy, or withhold from the use of needful others), motivated by invidious conspicuousness, and are we not thus grossly wasteful of social effort? Does not the invidiousness of success as we define it exact a fearful emotional toll in the psychological disen-franchisement of the majority of men and women, and their systematic infan-tilization as voyeurs rather than partakers of success? And, since all our values must be cast in pecuniary terms, do we really have the best cynosures that money can buy?

9. Authority, Culture Change, and the Courts

The enormous charisma of the courts is a moral capital that must be constantly replenished. As in all institutions ultimately founded on moral prestige, this charisma must be functionally earned, in this case through continued dispensation of wisdom and of justice. True, like the presidency, courts bring with them much sheerly historical sanction; but in our democratic system all sanctioned power must be continually legitimated—otherwise, the moral capital behind the institution is eroded, and the charismatic "money in the bank" is spent and no longer earns interest.

But to discuss social institutions in the abstract, without understanding the human animal these institutions express and serve, is to be feckless and *simpliste*. Behind all patterns of authority—of courts, police, presidents, prelates or popes—there lie forces deeply rooted in the human condition, most specifically in the nuclear family of our earliest shaping and experience. The family is unique to man. Most animal species bear young well-equipped with ready-made instincts: and after a very brief period of dependency they are adapted to be on their own as adult animals. By contrast, the human individual has an almost extravagantly prolonged *childhood*.[a]

Fully one-seventh of a baby's birth-weight is brain, the rest of his body almost an afterthought, and brain still grows rapidly after birth, because man is a learning animal with *drives* to be disciplined, not rigid instincts to take over for him. Big brain and long childhood both point unmistakably to the fact that man is a *learning animal*, not so much instinctual as moral in his nature—a fact shown again in the great variety of his tribal moral systems. Nearly a third of life is spent growing the infantile body into an adult one, in the meantime learning in detail how to become a human being, as "human" is defined in any particular tribe and time. Other animals are built to be what they are: humans are built only to learn what they are to become.

Culture is not in the chromosomes, customary law must be learned, indeed socially enforced. In learning how to become human we manifest another trait, the universally human incest taboo, absent in all other animals. This means that, first, for some decades in a "family of origin" we grow physically and learn emotionally and intellectually—our effective "environment" being not

This chapter was originally an address delivered at the 27th Annual Judicial Conference of the United States Courts of the Fifth Judicial District, on 27 May 1970, in Hollywood, Florida, and published in the *Loyola Law Review* 18 (1972), 481–92. Reprinted by permission.

a. The biological consequences (in race, culture, language, religion) of this peculiar species-specific *neoteny* in man are traced in W. La Barre, *The Human Animal* (Chicago: Phoenix Books, 8th printing, 1968) and in *The Ghost Dance* (New York: Doubleday & Co., 1972).

so much instinct-met unedited nature, but rather the highly self-editing injunctions of the bigger and stronger human animals around us, the precipitate of which is character and conscience. Then a universal categorical imperative requires each maturing individual to leave his family of origin (where his biological business was to be a child), and to form a new "family of procreation" where his biological job now is to provide a stable framework for the dependency and growth of new individual personages. We take our basic human nature far too much for granted, for in these specifically human social structures we differ widely even from our closest ape relatives.

Adolescence, the transitional or "hiatus status" between these two family-types, is therefore a universal human phenomenon.[b] Adolescence is *the time that history is made*. At first blush, this seems like a nonsensical statement; everybody knows that adults make history, not children. Men make history—but they are themselves finally *made* at adolescence. The whole tone of a generation's attitude toward the immediate past derives from the emotional complexion of that generation's relationship to its parents—whether and in what ways to emulate or to rebel against what the parents are, culturally and personally. For parents do not change the future; youth does. Parental maturity *is* the past—that is, what happened to parents as *they* grew up. The moving present is the meeting of the generations and, in the sense that history is change, adolescence (and what happens at adolescence) is the pivot-point of history. Biologically speaking, the inevitable death of individual animals is what makes biological progress possible; culturally speaking, change is possible only if the older persons' values die, to be replaced by new ones. Perhaps, demographically, the present dizzying rate of change will be slowed by the survival of more persons to old age. But change will come. If adolescence is the crucible of change, the family is the laboratory of personality.

The chief psychic task of adolescence is, nevertheless, somehow largely to identify with adults, to learn past tribal lore and adult roles, often aided in this transition by dramatic and sometimes painful puberty rites. There are possible pathologies in this learning process. For example, fathers may abdicate their fatherhood (viz., actual greater age, strength and real experience) and pretend to be "buddy-buddy" siblings, of the same status and ignorance as sons, and therefore fail to serve as foils for the son's growth and identity. Or, mothers and female teachers may pretend to be fathers; but adult males, everywhere larger than children and females, are the ultimate sanctioners of morality, biologically speaking. Hence many adolescents clearly evidence a kind of moral muckerism and throw out all female-mediated values in their search for masculine identity, the pattern for which they did not find in their fathers.

Meanwhile, external social history always happens to individuals at their different stages in personal growth, so that in a sense it is not the same history.

b. The best statement of this is *Normal Adolescence: Its Dynamics and Impact*, by the Committee on Adolescence, Group for the Advancement of Psychiatry (New York: Scribner's, 1968); also GAP Report V I, no. 68, 751–858.

Take for example the present parental generation. Affluence means different things to us, and to our children. In our adolescence we experienced the Great Depression; and many of us witnessed our fathers struggling manfully, sometimes heroically, just to hold the family together economically. As one result, our generation highly values—perhaps even overmuch—basic economic security, and takes pride in giving each son and daughter expensive clothes and car and college education and travel and all the rest. In our blind well-meaning way, this is what to us (when lacking it) meant success as a parent.

However, having known these comforts and securities all their lives, the present middle-class generation of youth couldn't care less about them. Money to them is no problem—just ask Dad!—and they have wholly unrealistic notions about established economic practices. Some youngsters in fact are willing to be antimaterialistic down to their parents' last dollar. But have we not somehow, through our very goodwill and success in providing, bereft the young of having to learn important techniques of coping with a stressful economic world, so that the frustrating imperfection of that world comes to them as if it were a unique and shocking discovery of their own, and for which we are personally to blame. Meanwhile, in their eyes, parents have miserably failed to do the real job: to protect the young against *their* anxieties, the Bomb, the perfidiousness of politicians, the population explosion, the pollution of the environment.

"Stop the world, I want to get off!" says one of their poets.[c] But history is what you cannot resign from. Because contemporary history is we people, here and now, at our various ages and states of grace. To suppose that one can "drop out" from the past is wholly fatuous, because it is right here, now. Furthermore, the dropout ethic is a prime technique for never growing up at all, and for remaining in a feckless, deprived, incompetent and irresponsible adolescence forever. If the biological hallmark of human maturity is *responsibility*, one hesitates to imagine what spiritual "Skid Row" many of the present generation may one day inhabit. For they have much unfinished characterological business, which is somehow (if only partially) to identify with and *constitute* some kind of establishment (which is only a jargon-word for ongoing human society). And what, then, will *their* children say of them as parents, and of the kind of world, if any, left them?

Every maturing man and woman must sometime learn to distinguish between what he has learned and what he has been taught—and the more rapidly culture-history changes, the wider the gap between the two. It is the *business* of adolescents to criticize the past, because finally they have to grapple with contemporary products of the past. It has become customary to view our social problems as evidence of a "generation gap." I do not think this is a realistic

---

c. Peter Orlovsky. Mr. Orlovsky has written other plangent lines, which an older generation living on the surface of its skin (or even, as advertised "image," quite outside it) might well ponder for their ethical overtones: "When I go out, I always wear my belt/Cause everything inside my belt/Belongs to me."

concept: generations succeed one another without break, and the only significant "gap" is each succeeding age-gap between the cohort of parents and the
youth cohort of their own children. The time gap is always there, biologically
constant and chronic, and the culture gap is only especially acute in times of
rapid social change. Parenthood is at best a self-taught and hugger-mugger
amateur job; and parents (say the young) are people who are twenty years out
of date—which is why, as grandparents, our wisdom is of no use to those bent
infallibly on making their own kind of parental mistakes.

This counterpoint of the generations is the hidden essence of history. What
happens at home fundamentally shapes institutions cumulatively in the outside
world. The family is the laboratory of personality. But we must also realize
that *typical* contemporary experience in any youth cohort makes the bridge
between individual personalities and the cultural *ethos* of that new generation,
and psychology is transformed into history. Culture is history; but adolescence
is the crucible of change. Each successively maturing youth cohort is the moving finger of history. For youth is not the eternally timeless time it seems to be
at the time; it is later than they think. For at the end of adolescence comes a
"hardening of the categories"—and another adult generation, for better or
worse, just as arrogant and just as fallible, to provide a foil for the childhood
and adolescence of another new one. Somehow, what was once infinitely
promising formative Personality has now hardened into imprisoning codified
Culture.

One greatly ignored dynamic of history is the changing *styles* of parent-child
relationships and differing concepts of their nature and status. However inevitable and self-evident the parent-child relationships seem to be at any one time,
the brute fact is that they do change in historic time. Some argue, in fact, that
childhood itself is an invention of the 20th century; they point for example to
early American painting, in which figures of children are naively presented
simply as undersized adults—wearing the same clothes and having the same
body-proportions, but only smaller in size. This ignoring of what we nowadays
see as almost the crucial distinction among people is quite like the ignoring of
culture and history in Italian painting, wherein Biblical figures are naively
shown in contemporary High Renaissance clothing and backgrounds, quite as
if Biblical people and times were not greatly different.

An early American pioneer childhood could not be the same as a modern
childhood, if only because the fact of childhood was not recognized in the
terms we see it. More than that, the whole dynamic psychosocial context was
different. In America's early agrarian days, a boy was constantly around his
father, helping with the chores. He learned without thinking how to become a
man and what it was like to be a man. At the same time a girl was constantly
with her mother, learning properly feminine work. Parents then did not have
to think about being parents, but only to get their work done. In consequence,
sexual differences were highly polarized in those days: a woman was afraid to

appear unwomanly or unladylike, and a man was afraid of being thought unmanly.

By contrast, in a modern suburban setting, ubiquitous Mom is the arbiter of morals to children of both sexes, with father largely absent earning a living in some remote, complex, and unknown specialized way. Conditioned similarly, now boys and girls seem to be much more alike than formerly. Admittedly, women know how to deal with children, that is before sexual differentiation. However, women do *not* know how to teach boys to become men. Given a human mother's hypermammalian body, she correctly knows that all children are equally dear—that is, equally in need of nurturance, and equally able to give her pleasure in this. But men, hardened in an acerb world outside the family, know well that all men are not equal. In *adult* performances, some men are better than others, whether in strength, in wisdom, or in some assiduously learned competitive skill. Here it is not who you are (mother's categorical darling) but what you are (competitively, in a man's world) that makes the difference now.

An exclusively woman-raised boy therefore knows only that he is lovable, or in need of love. A man has to know how to earn respect in adult ways. Thus when such a woman-raised boy suddenly meets the world outside the pseudo-matriarchal family, he wonders why he is not automatically as good as the next one (chronic inferiority feelings), or why he is not accorded instant status (envious, because he does not know status-earning *process*). It is not enough passive-magically to let hormones produce the impressive advertisement of a male beard (for the least significant aspect of manhood of all is the cosmetic), to dress up in some fantasy-part (an adult male role is not a costume-party charade) or even to act-out sexuality without responsibility (which is the critical adult role economically and socially). In growing up, it is not enough to witness endless one-way boob-tube nonhappenings about cow-boys, play-boys, and other nonpersons. There must be direct and reciprocal father-and-son encounter, psychologically real give and take, and mutual learning (how else can a father grow up, or a son?). Otherwise, not having learned political process from early encounters with adult male authority and social power, the adolescent can only resort to the temper tantrums of the Chicago Seven, or in the other stereotyped ways of the present youth-generation, such as passive picketing to arouse maternal guilt, to coerce and bully Mom. (Happily, in very recent time, these infantile knee-jerk reactions to frustration are being replaced by more effective political know-how—significantly modeled, by the way, on the constitutionally mature behavior of men the whole political spectrum from Senators Ervin to Fulbright).

In army and in civilian life, men have a sense of hierarchy that women do not understand at all. Men know that some men are their betters, and even in detail why. After all, the major difference between boy and man is potency and power, hence in achieving manhood a boy inevitably makes comparisons in body and spirit, and he competes for real and symbolic potencies and powers. Only in a man's world does a boy learn to become a man, because only males live in male bodies. As I shall indicate in a moment, many current crises in the use of power come from pathologies and disturbances in the father-son moral experience of one another. Maturing sons can and do teach those fathers who are able to learn the mature wisdom of reasonableness, and who understand that the real authority of fatherhood is not absolute but functional, based on protection and character-shaping. And wise fathers similarly can teach sons the complex contingencies of mature manhood, which is by no means the supposed omniscient, omnipotent, or even omnibenevolent status as it is when seen from the child's-eye view of the father and the man.

One current difficulty is that in the modern middle-class father-absent family the boy often cannot see why college skills, seriously acquired, should be necessary for a job like his father's. At the same time, in acquiring a masculine identity, a boy has to alienate himself from everything mother-mediated, including even abstract adult rules. With mostly women teachers throughout childhood, no wonder most Americans are muckers about anything intellectual!—in the face of the notorious fact that status everywhere in our complex society depends upon specialized learned skills. To reclaim his masculinity in a feminine setting, a boy almost has to hate school and to rebel against it. Again, girls, raised with boys in school even through college, do not have to take technical learning seriously either—because, after all, they are girls.[d] As a result, somehow schools teach contempt for education (and contempt for women), hardly their proper goal. As another result, the sexes are far less polarized in femininity and masculinity than biological fate may demand or a parental generation feel comfortable with. There is still no surer way to "bug" the older generation than modern youth's symbolic transvestitism in hair-do and clothing.

When he finds himself living in a strange tribe, the anthropologist tries to discover *pattern* in the behavioral chaos surrounding him. And surely anyone over thirty is a stranger in the world surrounding him today! When I look at today's world, the most all-encompassing pattern I can discern seems to be a crisis in all sectors in the operation of *power* and *authority*. Ultimately, I believe, there is a basic social pathology in the current adult male role. One could give a long disquisition on how Americans destroyed de-legitimated authority in deposing a British king and set up a sibling-society by social contract; how the frontier experience destroyed feudal social hierarchy and shaped a new

---

d. Additionally, in America we allow a certain face-saving class muckerism about education, despite the fact that economic class is markedly education-stratified. Europeans are thoroughly aware of this fact and therefore take education with desperate seriousness. In England and France, the whole politico-social and intellectual élite is funneled through a surprisingly few institutions of higher learning, and competition is intense for the limited number of academic positions. In Scandinavia, for example, a university professor ranks formally just below a cabinet minister. In America, however, the academic intellectual is viewed ambivalently, either as "egghead" or Einstein.

American character with the promethean Ahab obsessively hunting down Moby Dick, the white whale, and so on.

But I have time only to suggest the current endpoint: a kind of deep schizophrenia we show between the Cowboy and Playboy as male roles, and the Dagwood and Blondie syndrome. In our favorite fantasy the Cowboy still preserves his frontier autonomy, himself his own law; cigarette ads present the vacant virile Montana face, all hormones but no mind behind it; and at each cookout grill each suburbanite fantasies himself a pioneer still mystically close to nature. In the classic cowboy movie there could not be too much kissing; and after rescuing the beleaguered maiden and restoring the rustled cattle or stolen goldmine to her aged father or widowed mother, the cowboy wandered off into the sunset with his trusty steed, with or without his subordinate playmate Tonto. These are not sexually involved or socially integrated men! In a modern more urbanized setting, Playboy too, never settles down to an adult, male, fatherly role, but remains only an adolescent would-be stud. Sexuality for Playboy is just one more gadget: every well-appointed bachelor apartment should have an instant turn-on, turn-off Playgirl-of-the-Month female, just as it should have a push-pull AC-DC, AM-FM, UHF TV-tape recorder-radio-phonograph. For Playboy, the female is never so complex a thing as a person, with her own perhaps different psychological needs; she is just another instantly available gadget to satisfy male sexual whim. No Personality, no problem. But this is a purely youth's-eye view of sexuality!

Now, for complex culture-historical reasons, Americans have come to worship quite slavishly the shallow and fleeting attractions of youth. We greatly minimize the dignities and the satisfactions of responsible maturity—that are, indeed, a much longer time with us during a lifetime. In this youth-cult, Americans lead world-style, curiously even in Russia and even in Red China—which is one reason that, as anthropologist, I would view with alarm the total Americanization of our culture-various world. But note our psychotic dichotomy. As consumer, as clothes-horse, as play-boy and athlete, the young male in our society is lavishly admired and attended to. The young female is the cynosure of all eyes; but neither youth nor female, I assure you, is the usual social cynosure in the majority of the world cultures that we know.[e] Again, significantly, in America the moment the individual passes the line from childlike irresponsibility and activity as consumer to that of parental responsibility and producer, he markedly changes status. Glamor Girl becomes Mom, a nag and a shrew, controlling mate and child alike.

With marriage and fatherhood, the glamorous and envied Playboy turns into Dagwood, a buffoon and figure of fun. Social pathology, to be sure, also lies in seeing womanly role only as female foil to the phallic male. The compulsive

e. Parents, for example, were the social cynosure in classic China; old men, among Australian Bushmen; the pre-adolescent girl in Bali; in Indonesia, the dead, etc. (W. LaBarre, "Social Cynosure and Social Structure," chap. 8 this volume).

worship of youth thus disfranchises adult roles in both sexes. There is a degradation of the male, both as man and as father; perhaps an adult male nowadays, when he reflects on it, can feel a little what it must have been to be a female in the 19th century, or a Negro, now. In popular folklore like the "funnies" and TV shows, male adulthood is presented as mere foolishness, a big joke. In our proper concern for the rights of women and the rights of children, we seem to have lost sight entirely of the rights of man as male, as adult, and as father. This demeaning of fatherhood is at the core of the pathology of secondary symbolic father-and-son authority relationships; and it infects all our social institutions from courts to the presidency, and from the papacy and police to international relations.

It is not a mere "generation gap" in the family, it is more exactly an "authority gap" in most of our social institutions. There is, for example, a widening gap between the historic authority of the Pope and the views of his communicants on very personal matters such as birth control and the celibacy of the clergy. Some churchmen argue that birth control dogma does not take into account a changed demographic-ecological situation, makes poverty inevitable, promotes war and degradation of the environment, produces unwanted children and all the psychiatric consequences of this, does not cope with the population explosion but only exacerbates it, creating further problems for the frighteningly foreseeable future. Celibacy of the clergy is felt as institutional infantilization and robbery of manhood, militating against adult male sexual and psychological rights. Some theologians regard these two issues as potentially the most disruptive since the Protestant Reformation. I will not enter into any merits of either case, but only point out here the modest proposition that this is an instance of crisis in authority and the exercise of power.

Universities, in part perhaps because they institutionally house middle-class adolescence itself, are a conspicuous locale of authority-conflict. Many young people cannot cope with authority structures because they have not learned to cope with the authority of a father earlier. Confrontation politics, with non-negotiable ultimatums, is a fascist use of terrorism and raw force to bully Alma Mater with temper tantrums. Significantly, at least 30 presidents of major universities have left their post in the last three years. In 1960, tenure of office averaged 7.4 years; but today a college president in the job for 2 years has seniority over half the presidents of the Association of American Universities.[f] It would seem that intellectual authority is the most gentle and bearable of all,

f. William K. Stevens, "University Presidents Say They've Given up Power," *New York Times*, 15 March 1970, Section K. A partial list of college and university heads who have left or announced their intention to do so within the last 3 years: Harvard, Brandeis, California, Columbia, Minnesota, UCLA, Colorado, Kansas, Ohio, Michigan State, Indiana, San Francisco State, Hawaii, Alabama, Iowa, Georgia Institute of Technology, Colgate, Nebraska, Northwestern, California Institute of Technology, Delaware, Stanford, Fordham, Holy Cross, Duke, City College New York, Brown, Cornell, Hunter, Oberlin, Wesleyan.

since with learning the student comes to embody that modest, contingent and self-critical authority himself. I would only suggest that there is such a thing as intellectual authority—that comes from hard won, often decades-long patient familiarizing oneself with information, with problems, and with miscellaneous thinking about data and theories. Intellectual authority merely presents for judgment the reasons for scientific opinion on specified matters.[g] But, emotionally rich enough for certain, many present-day college students seem to have lacked experience of masculine astringency in thinking. For various reasons I judge myself as being particularly close to my students; yet I was really taken aback in an advanced seminar when a student bitterly accused me of being a "rational empiricist" because of habitual attempts to think in orderly and articulate ways about experience. One can understand why TV-ad-nurtured youth would relish the ironic and wry "put-on" of Zen mockery of rationalism, but the more recent preoccupation with noodle-headed Vedantism and psychedelic drugs seems to indicate an emotional *preference* for ineffable subjective indulgence over the harsh "authority" of object-encountering empiricism.[h]

The authority of the law and legal institutions meets with the same angry defiance. In particular since the Chicago Convention, there is a wide gap between the authority of police-sanctioned law and a youthful generation that would gladly battle all the "Pigs" between them and the Establishment. Mayor Daley's police, some feel, in part destroyed a liberal presidential candidacy. Others feel that police treatment of the Black Panthers destroys any majority-legitimated power of white people to direct racial reform. Many, and not only lawyers, have wondered whether judicial behavior at the trial of the "Chicago Seven" has not seriously eroded the charisma of American courts at large. As to the intellectual authority of knowledge, many teachers like myself see the antiintellectual trends of our time only heightened by activist attacks on the freedom and even continued operation of our colleges and universities—for which the murder of dissenting students is no cure. A conservative Administration's attacks on constitutionally legitimate dissidence of the press, public of-

g. If blacks are correct (and I think they are) that the most effective way to change one's economic class status is through education, then it is not immediately apparent why they are the best judges of what is "relevant" to that education. (At a movie on campus, a white student sitting behind me once disgustedly marveled that his roommate was spending a whole semester reading Thucydides' *Peloponnesian War*; I longed to tell him there is hardly any classic in all world literature *more relevant* to concern with the Viet Nam War that his dress and ornaments proclaimed—hence student-run classes might tend to a sharing of ignorance, as in the usual "bull-session.") Self-chosen segregation into classes, dormitories and exclusive clubs does not appear especially to favor desegregation either, nor is special grading in special curricula a real encounter with white competitors. Political insistence on "upgrading" (i.e., funding) separate black colleges, law, and medical schools is actually a *reinforcing of segregation,* under the political pressure of incompetent vested academic interests and misguided black separatism. It is the old "separate but equal" fallacy in new guise.

h. Likewise, I am astonished that "elitism" has recently become a pejorative term. After all, is not evolution itself, as well as any social structure anywhere, in a sense elitist?

ficials, and individuals can only infuriate informed Jeffersonians; and reactionary attacks on the Bill of Rights seem to me not so much "strict constructionism" as dangerously subversive activity.

It is hardly necessary to point to the ultimate irresponsibility of both the Departments of State and of Defense in the present international shambles. But did not LBJ erode our confidence in the presidency even before Mr. Nixon and his "gambles," regarded by some as presidential crimes against the Constitution? Will Viet Nam continue to ruin both American prestige abroad, and both democracy and the economy at home? Can we trust those who give us industrial consumer-abundance not to wreck the planet as a place for human beings to live in? With only the moon as yet in our precarious grasp, are we sure we have "invented a throw-away planet"[i] here on earth? How much real moral energy does an Administration put into solving basic problems, and how much into improving its publicity "image" and conniving merely to entrench itself in political power?

In many if not most areas, young people simply do not trust the traditional depositories of authority. Perhaps, indeed, authority has at times been arbitrarily abused. Their increasing political involvement is at any rate a more hopeful and realistic power-technique than their earlier "confrontation" tantrums and ceremonial sign-carrying, which is mainly symbolic magic. If change is needed then let us by all means preserve the most effective process of change we know about. I believe that the division of powers in our Constitution is the most brilliant political invention in history since the Greeks invented democracy itself. What all men of goodwill must remember is that within this American system no power is absolute in sanction but, like the courts, lives only through continuing *functional legitimation*. But in the quest for custom-made values, beware of what you want, because you will get it. And when you seek some adequate authority for your acts, remember that it serves a father right for having been a son.

i. Allen Ginsberg in, I believe, an as yet unpublished poem.

10. The Patient and His Families

The title of this paper expresses the point of view that every patient and every client of the medical social worker has *several families*—at least three. Indeed, the existence of these families is an expression of the covert structure of every hospital. The patient has these families naturally and normally, and in the course of his business of being a human being. The first of these several families is the "family of origin" of every human being, that is to say, the family into which he was born. This family of origin is the place of origin and growth of the individual both biologically and psychologically. In the process of becoming human in his local society's terms, every human being serves an apprenticeship in the form of a long, dependent childhood. During this childhood, and within the uniqueness of his own individual family, he learns both his society's culture and also his own private personality through his unique experiences in his family of origin. This family, the source of his personality, is also, of course, the source of all his later transference attitudes with which medical social workers, doctors, and nurses may have to deal.

The second of these families is the person's "family of procreation." By definition, and by the universal human taboo concerning incest, every member of the family of procreation must be different from every member of the family of origin, with the single exception of the individual himself. Having had the role of consuming security, exploiting dependency, and learning his culture and his personality, the individual now assumes an entirely opposite role as a parent by providing security, supporting dependency, and teaching his culture and, in a sense, his personality to his children. That is to say, in his second family, as parent, each individual fills those roles that he *did not* fill as a child in his original family, and thus rounds out the cycle of familial roles—often enough unconsciously duplicating or imitating his parents' roles and attitudes which he himself learned from observation as a child.

In addition to these two families—the one in which a person is shaped and the one in which he does the shaping of personalities—there is a third kind of family, also intimately involved in medical casework, and for this I shall coin the name "family of extrapolation." The family of extrapolation exists in many diverse forms and is, in the last analysis, the basis of all our social institutions. The family of extrapolation exists when we speak of the "Fatherhood of God" or the "brotherhood of man"; when we address a priest as "Father" and a nun as "Mother" or "Sister"; when we impute a fatherly role to the President or to

From an article in *Casework Papers*, published by the Family Service Association of America, 1958, later reprinted in *Child Family Digest* 18 no. 1 (1959), 9–18. Reprinted by permission of Family Service Association of America.

the Supreme Court; when a social caseworker finds herself in a motherly role; and in every single men's organization— from college fraternity to secret brotherhood—which builds itself upon the symbolism of the enlarged or synthetic family.

Modern social casework everywhere is a highly professionalized endeavor to preserve the integrity of individual families; and, if this cannot be done, casework itself attempts to serve as a substitute for these lacking or inadequate family functions or to find somewhere else a social institution or form which can take the place of necessary family functions. The theme of this meeting of the Family Service Association is "Family Cohesion in a World of Stress," and it well demonstrates, to my mind, the medical worker's awareness of this basic casework precept concerning the family. I find this orientation most congenial, because it matches my own anthropological-dynamic-psychiatric conviction about the universality and the centrality of the family to the human animal. If casework works to preserve the integrity of the family, then, to my mind, it is reaching directly into the heart of the matter.

All social institutions are ultimately based upon the family. By this I mean that so thoroughly are we imbued with familial attitudes during childhood and throughout our lives that it is quite impossible to be human anywhere without using again these same old familial, "familiar" symbolisms. On the primitive level, the biological family—its symbols and forms extended to include other people—inevitably becomes the "blood brotherhood." That is to say, when real blood kinship does not exist or is no longer known, we have to create ritually the synthetic "blood-brotherhood" family through initiation. All men's fraternity rituals of whatever kind are pathetic ritual attempts of males to do what women can do biologically—to create in their genuinely related children the blood relationships of siblings. These ritual creations of male pseudo-families are the very basis of the larger society. Typically, in primitive initiation ceremonies, the person being initiated is kidnapped away from his mother-family and taken into the mysterious wilds, where he is "killed" and "eaten" symbolically by the great supernatural, whose voice is the "bull-roarer" about which women and children may know nothing, on pain of death. After this, the initiate undergoes a mystic rebirth as a new member of the male tribal group.

We can all recognize the bogus nature of such "blood brotherhoods"— brotherhood that has to be ritually manufactured specifically where it does not exist—but we are bound to respect the fact that the original forms of these new social creations are rooted in the biological family. Perhaps primitive men are right: women do not understand these ritual male mysteries. But then again, why should they, when women can create real blood relationships through their bodies? A point worth emphasis, however, is that we have given to us, in our anatomy and in our physiology, the answer to the problems of the proper relationship of child to mother and of man to woman—but we do not have any anatomical answers to the problem of the relationship of father to son and of man to man. The expression of the old animal relationship of males was simply to fight and to kill one another; but if we are going to have human societies larger than families, it is inevitable that we call upon the symbolisms of the family in order to shape them. It is for this reason that all human associations, like that of the state (in which we seek paternal authority combined with brotherly justice), and all human institutions, like that of religion, invariably use the structural and the emotional language of the family. All human groups, of whatever kind, necessarily embody basic transference attitudes derived originally from the nuclear family.

If this reasoning is sound, social casework as an institution is, without question, going to be built upon familial implications like every other human institution. As one kind of casework, then, medical social work is not unique in this and will inevitably be committed to familial modalities both in theory and practice. How, in specific ways, is medical casework involved with the basic "familial nature of man"? How can an understanding of these emotions and these social structures illuminate and guide medical casework practice?

To discuss these matters properly, I suggest that readers accompany me into the hospital as anthropological field workers visiting a strange foreign tribe, and together we shall look at the "culture of the hospital"—its strange rituals, its mysterious tribal customs, its bloody ceremonials, its magic cures. What we shall see are people cast into different roles: patients, doctors, nurses, and still another mysterious priestess, the medical social worker. What is it that makes the whole hospital necessary as an institution? Very simply, it is the health inadequacy of selected individuals from the outside, larger society which requires of them a sojourn, long or short, within the walls of this institution, the hospital.

Immediately we see how the complex web of normal familial relationships is disrupted. If the patient is a child, he is alone, torn from his family, threatened with mysterious and body-damaging acts of strange adults. Ideal medical care would deal not only with the organs of the frightened and sick child, but also with his psyche. I hope that some day, in every hospital, as a routine matter, the function of medical social workers will include the handling of the anxieties of every child patient before he undergoes an operation; it probably would save psychiatrists a great deal of work later. And, after children are taken care of, why not extend this medical casework practice to include adult patients as well? I am aware that traditionally medical casework deals mainly with the problems of the patient's family which have been occasioned by his illness. One might ask why this additional proposed function—of allaying the patient's fears— should not be performed by the nurse. But this seems to me a matter definitely requiring casework skills and, if my later analysis of their situation is correct, the nurse and the social worker are in radically different emotional and psychological roles.

In our analysis let us look first at that august figure in the hospital, the doctor. Very quickly we perceive that, in transference terms, the doctor is very definitely the father. His is the ultimate authority during the entire affair of the patient's stay in the hospital as a socioeconomically inadequate person or child. The doctor has the knowledge, the power, the responsibility. Even grown men—however potent or important their role in the outside world—are required to submit in an unquestioning childlike way to the categorical authority of the benevolent and wise father, the doctor. The doctor is properly outraged at the disobedient patient who, placing himself in the doctor's hands, does not obey implicitly the doctor's orders. The doctor, when he is an opponent of socialized medicine, is struggling vehemently against the imposition of another alternative authority—that of the state—which shall come between his parental authority and his patient. The doctor, in his role as such, is not even the whole man, but only the father: he is professionally required to be only the sexless and remote father-figure in his relations with his pseudo children, and the worst thing a doctor can do is to become involved as a man and male with a woman patient. If he does so, he has stepped out of his role as father-figure and is appropriately punished by society. In fact, in role terms, the doctor should marry the nurse, if the unconscious pattern is to be fulfilled.

And what of the patient? Very clearly, we soon discern his role is that of the child in this new pseudo family of the hospital. Indeed, his illness has made him a child in socioeconomic terms. Nowhere is this role change seen more clearly than when an adult male becomes the patient. Men are notoriously bad patients because they have to struggle with the problems of the most contrastive role differences. From being an adequate, self-directing and self-supporting citizen, providing for the security of others, the man changes into a dependent and a consumer of security—in a word, symbolically the child. But not only symbolically; everyone connected with hospitals knows of the severe regressions all patients undergo. The patient becomes self-involved and narcissistic, forgets and ignores most of the world outside his suffering body. He literally "cares" only for himself. His emotional horizons contract to those characteristic of the child. He is unreasonable, demanding, "me first," irritable—in a word, *childish*.

What about the nurse? If the doctor is the institutional ghost of the father, and the patient of the child, then the nurse is clearly *one aspect of the mother image*. I wish particularly to insist upon this, because I believe that there is a split image in the mother role in hospitals as between the nurse and the medical social worker. Let me provisionally discriminate the role in this way: the nurse is primarily the "id" mother of the patient; the medical caseworker is primarily the "ego" mother of the patient's family. Since the nurse's role is contrastive with the caseworker's—as is also true of her temperament and professional training—it may be useful to sketch in the picture we observe of the "culture of the nurse." The nurse, as mother-image ministering to the id, occupies a peculiar place. She must at the same time be warm and feminine, and yet impersonal as a woman. She must tread the narrow line between a concern for the sick patient and emotional involvement with a real person. The patient finds the breakup of his normal routines a change in itself and in his social role; but in addition he encounters pain, anxiety, uncertainty, threats to his bodily integrity or real dangers to it, threats to his own family integrity created by his temporary separation from them—and all this in a strange place and among strange people.

In the situation of regression, the patient typically creates transference relationships. The nurse is the object of transference attitudes of dependency upon the mother, just as the doctor is the object of transference attitudes toward the original father. It is possible to trace all these matters in the folklore and stereotyped attitudes of the hospital. When the patient begins to show signs of reacting as a person to the nurse as a person, he is getting well, and the situation must be particularly managed by the nurse and her professional mannerisms. In the culture of the hospital it is schematically wrong for the nurse to return in personal terms the love she may have elicited in her recovering patient. Nurses will sometimes severely criticize another nurse who has mixed up her roles and exploited as a woman her role as a nurse.

Again, in the unconscious pattern sense, the nurse should marry the doctor, as the mother has married the father. In this changing situation let us note the nurse's defenses. She defends herself by infantilizing the patient, depersonalizing him, and thrusting him back into the child role. She is bossy, like a mother who knows what is best for you, and no nonsense either. She uses a brisk, impersonal baby talk: "And how did we sleep last night? I see we ate a good breakfast." She is mistress of the "brush off" if the patient tries to treat her as a person. To protect herself, she depersonalizes her patient: "My gallbladder case was a perfect lamb last night." In other words, the nurse must be warmly feminine, without being sexually a woman to the patient. In a word, she is in the role of a mother. The job of the nurse is in fact to help the patient become a person again, economically, socially, physically, and psychologically, but in the helping process the nurse must nevertheless preserve her status role. These intangible things are probably never taught or learned in any formal classroom in nursing schools, but in nursing practice this culture is inevitably taken on, largely unconsciously, just as, in the teaching of medical students, the role of the doctor is not always formally taught, but is nevertheless unconsciously learned.

The major problem of the nurse is to maintain a kind of "social distance" from her patient. When the patient is very sick, no amount of tender, warm, reassuring care is inappropriate, but when the patient begins to "sit up and take notice," she has to free herself from a growing personal involvement. This repeated personal disengagement from a case, as sensitive nurses have sometimes described it to me, seems very much like the feeling I have as a college professor when the senior class graduates and leaves the campus. It is an endless and repeated grief of a lost paternity of many children.

When the nurse's defense—of bossiness and crisp maternity—is carried to extreme, she may become too lacking in femininity or tenderness and too much the "battle ax." Such an individual then often becomes an administrator, no longer in such close contact with the patient as is the nurse.

The pattern of the family is surely laid in all human beings. So naturally do we assume that a nurse must be a woman that the male nurse is an uncomfortable and pattern-contradicting anomaly. Although genuinely male strength is rationally an appropriate trait in handling certain kinds of patients, the male nurse nonetheless suffers from adverse imputations cast upon his masculinity, much as the woman doctor somehow seems masculinized because she does not fit role expectancies. We note that a doctor commonly refuses to treat as a patient any member of his own family. This relationship would be too much a mix-up of his role as a real father and his role as an institutionalized or professional father. We note, too, that nurses are threatened, like the doctor, when for one reason or another the patient refuses to play his child role vis-à-vis their parental roles, and some instances when the nurse becomes the rival of the patient's real mother. These, and many other examples, make it clear that we are not merely imagining the parental roles of doctors and nurses, but that reactions in terms of family patterns are, so to speak, built into all human personalities.

Now what of the role of the medical social worker who, in most instances, is a woman? I believe our best understanding of her derives from contrasting her with the nurse. I have taught nurses, both in college classes and in nursing schools, just as I have for several years taught students in a medical school. I also have considerable personal and professional acquaintance with social workers. What I have to say at this point cannot perhaps be statistically validated, but it does represent the most accurate statements, qualitatively, that I am able to make on the basis of my experiences. In my observation, the typical nursing student is a very uncomplicatedly feminine woman, warm, psychologically not notably astute as women go, and ordinarily not self-examining or self-reflective. Temperamentally, this kind of woman is self-selected for the kind of role a nurse is called upon to perform as the intuitive "id" mother of the patient, as I have suggested.

On the other hand, the caseworker seems to be more highly sophisticated psychologically, much more self-aware, much more inclined to self-scrutiny and professional self-evaluation. Perhaps part of this difference lies in the differences of roles involved. The medical caseworker is not ordinarily so closely involved with the physical and psychological concrete person of the patient as is the nurse. On the contrary, she is more involved with individual family members as social persons, as role fillers, as functioning people, even when overburdened by the illness of a family member. This does not mean that the medical caseworker does not at times indeed function as a mother-surrogate, or even as a substitute mother. For example, if the sick person is a mother with a family, the caseworker must contrive through housekeepers, child care, and other means directly to take up the slack occasioned by the social absence of the family's real mother. I think of the medical caseworker as the "ego" mother of the now socially sick or threatened or temporarily disintegrated family. It is she who is primarily saddled with the responsibility of aiding the reality orientation of the family. For the temporarily bereft husband, she is the wife as wise planner and counselor, and as such she fills many of the roles women perform for men. For the overworried relative, she is the wise and reassuring woman, one who shares the wisdom of the doctor.

Whereas the nurse's face is turned toward the patient, and the nurse's role and temperament are adapted to this situation, the caseworker's face is turned toward the outside world. Nurse and doctor can become so preoccupied with hospital routines and hospital culture as to forget the outside world at times; the caseworker, never. If the doctor and nurse are busy knitting up a raddled or sick body, the medical caseworker is busy knitting up raddled family and socioeconomic situations. The doctor and nurse focus almost exclusively on the patient, while the caseworker must always remain aware of the family and social context. It is my opinion that potential misunderstandings lie here. As handmaiden to the doctor and in her professional subservience to him, the nurse is able to function smoothly in this harness, since both have the same goals and differ only in the masculine and feminine roles involved. There is the danger, however, the the doctor may seek to make of the social worker another handmaiden, to the degree that he has not understood the nature of the caseworker's role and the differences in her preoccupations and goals. Doctors, indeed, may be peculiarly blind—whether by personality or by training—to the sociocultural *person* who exists beyond the physical body they learned about in anatomy and physiology classes. Since medicine has moved into the hospital and out of the home, and since medical specialities still proliferate, the doctor is much too likely to look at the patient merely as a skinful of organs, in one or two of which he is professionally interested. This situation may be unavoidable since specialization is inevitable as knowledge increases. Perhaps the specialist would be more sympathetic and understanding if he realized that the caseworker is a "medical" specialist too; in some ways she is only restoring the functions of the fine old figure, the old-fashioned country doctor and general practitioner. That wise old individual would not need to be indoctrinated with the value of the medical caseworker. He saw the patient whole, both as physical body and as social organism; he knew the whole family; he saw them in their functioning context when he visited the homes of his patients; he concerned himself with the total problem of physical illness in the family.

The old-fashioned doctor tried in all kinds of unstated and inexplicit ways to help with the social and economic problems of his patient as well as the psychological and the medical ones. Indeed, it is my central point that as medicine specializes and the doctor concentrates on the mere anatomy and physiology of his patient, these other social problems still remain crying out for solution. These become specifically the concern of the medical caseworker. Of all the types of casework, medical social work makes the most demand on the worker for a quick and accurate assessment of a situation to determine where the major problem lies. Other kinds of casework may allow more time for study or may deal with simpler problems, but every medical case is in some sense an emergency.

Does the patient regress emotionally under illness? Is illness itself a threat to the adequacy of egos in the family? If so, in either case, the medical caseworker must be quick to perceive the answer to these questions: "Where must I fill in the lacking ego functions in this specific situation, and how must I find and support the strengths and the reality orientation of this specific family?" In one instance she may chiefly function to facilitate the medical care itself—emotionally, economically, and socially. If she must handle unreal anxieties in one case, in another she may need only to interpret the simple medical facts, to be supportive in real adjustments of the family to illness, and sometimes simply to inform the responsible remaining members of the family about community resources and other agencies. In all of this, it seems to me, the medical caseworker functions as a kind of "ego mother" in a stress situation—taking over temporarily the ego functions of the sick person and the disorganized family.

Doctors need to be shown that medical casework skills are long since traditional in their profession; they were part of the medical practice of the old horse-and-buggy doctor. If they sometimes misunderstand the meaning of medical casework, it is well that they be reminded of these facts: that modern hospital medicine is clinically very specialized and that the whole treatment of the whole patient even in the old-fashioned sense necessarily involves a skilled and developing medical casework service, based on an understanding of projective transference from roles learned in everyone's nuclear family.

11. "The Worm in the Honeysuckle": A Case Study of a Child's Hysterical Blindness

Part One, by Maurine Boie La Barre

The philosophical background of social casework, nurtured by the descriptive sociology of the early twentieth century, has been enriched in recent decades by the study of anthropology. Cultural concepts, particularly as they have been integrated with psychoanalytic concepts, have deepened the case-worker's awareness of the molding influence of tradition and the tribe upon patterns of child care, the development of roles in the family and the group, and social resolutions of conflicts between impulses and cultural demands. Caseworkers may also make a contribution to the study of the complex and profound relation between psychic and cultural factors by analyzing case data in both cultural and psychological terms. We also struggle constantly to learn to use our deepened understanding creatively in the service of the client.

Cultural factors are more easily identified in the lives of people reared in a tradition-bound racial, regional, or national subculture and transplanted to a fluid, transitional environment. The heterogeneity of the adaptive patterns they encounter in their new environment clearly plays a dynamic role in the inner psychic stress of the individual and may also affect his resistance to, or readiness to accept, professional help. For example, classical hysteria, as Freud described it, has rarely been encountered in psychiatric practice in urban areas in recent decades,[1] but in some sections, notably in the southern United States, *its incidence is significantly higher.*[a] With children at the Child Psychiatry Unit, Department of Psychiatry, University of North Carolina Medical School, clinical experience has shown that, in mild cases, symptom relief sometimes occurs quickly, spontaneously, or with a minimum of psychiatric intervention.

Maurine La Barre was professor of social casework, Division of Child Psychiatry, Duke University Medical Center in Durham, North Carolina, and was earlier in the Child Psychiatry Unit of the University of North Carolina Medical School in Chapel Hill, North Carolina. An organizer of the Durham Child Guidance Clinic and founder of the School for Pregnant Schoolgirls, Mrs. La Barre was onetime Editor of *The Family*, now *Social Casework*, and author of *The New York City Baby Book*.

Reprinted from *Social Casework* 47 no. 6 (July 1965), 399–413. Copyright by the Family Service Association of America. Reprinted by permission.

a. In the six years of operation (1952–1958) of the North Carolina Memorial Hospital 600 inpatients have been given a diagnosis of conversion reaction; 22, or about 4 percent, of these were children under sixteen years of age. Moreover, the percentage of conversion reactions among children evaluated in the Child Psychiatry Outpatient Clinic of the Hospital has been relatively higher than that reported from clinics in other areas.

The staff has found it difficult, however—indeed, impossible, with very few exceptions—to engage the patient's family in plans for extended psycho-therapy for the child. This resistance seems to be related to cultural attitudes, which have been recognized in the etiology of hysteria.[2] How the realities of the family culture are related to dynamic processes in the individual's neurosis requires further elucidation.

The case study presented in this article illustrates the interplay of external and internal stresses in the etiology of a child's hysteria and in the choice of the conversion symptom; the meaning of the symptom to the child, her family, and the social group; and the roles played by the child's family, religious belief, and the psychiatric service in the treatment of her illness.[b]

Nancy, a ten-year-old black girl, was referred to the inpatient pediatric ser-vice of the hospital by the local ophthalmologist; four days before the referral she had suddenly become blind, having complained of intermittent headaches for four days previously, and having had an upper respiratory infection two weeks before. The results of physical examination on admission were within normal limits except for photophobia in bright light and absence of pupillary reflex, thought to be due to myotonic pupils. Neurological examinations showed no organic basis for the blindness. The ophthalmologist demonstrated (by dis-simulation) that her vision was 20/20 in both eyes. Psychiatric consultation was requested, and a diagnosis of conversion reaction was made.

On the basis of psychological studies, Nancy's intelligence was assessed in the dull-normal range. She was somewhat preoccupied with religious activities and with Bible stories. The thought of highways and of railroad tracks was extremely disturbing to her, apparently because she had received so many warnings of their dangerousness. It seemed likely that much of her training had been based on fear, punishment, and warnings of dire results from bad behavior. Rorschach responses suggested anxiety and preoccupation with pri-mal scene memories or fantasies. It seemed possible that her blindness was selective.

Daily psychiatric interviews were held with Nancy during her eight days of hospitalization. She appeared to be in no distress, but was timid and shy, and bit her fingers and stuttered. She reported the onset and progress of her illness without much emotion: on the morning she became blind, she said, she went into her parents' bedroom and then "saw darkness." She denied seeing any-thing in the room that morning and did not remember ever sleeping there. At times she could remember seeing shadows on her mother's face and hands waving. She was aware that her blindness prevented her going to school; and

b. This case study was prepared in the Child Psychiatry Unit, Department of Psychiatry, Uni-versity of North Carolina Medical School, when Maurine La Barre was a member of the staff. The study was supervised by Harold Harris, M.D.; the psychiatric resident working with the child was Mike Zarzar, M.D.; the child psychologist was Mrs. Sophia Martin. The study was presented at the Department of Psychiatry Grand Rounds; the discussion, led by Weston La Barre, Ph.D., and Wilfred Abse, M.D., Professor of Psychiatry, University of North Carolina School of Medicine, has been incorporated into this report.

she remembered having wished in the past that she did not have to go. She denied having any boy friends and avoided talking about the subject. She said her father was a preacher in the Holiness Church and remembered that his most recent sermon had been about kings.

In the hospital Nancy could sometimes see the light and follow directions by gesture, but at other times she could not. The psychiatrist observed that whenever she had to take responsibility for doing something, she said she could not see; but if seeing something was suggested to her— that is, if the therapist took responsibility for seeing—she could see. Her play was limited because of her vision. She was able to draw a few things, however, and chiefly drew sweets, such as candy and ice cream; she was unable to draw a boy, and her female figures lacked hands and showed an absence of continuity in the body configuration. She daydreamed of having a house all to herself, with a television set, a table and chairs, and a bathroom. While in the hospital she had a dream of a black snake going in and out of a hole. Her associations to *bed, mattress, sheet,* and *pillow* were in terms of wind, storm, and fire. One day she said, "I don't want to see," and then she expressed a strong fear of snakes, remembering various occasions when a snake came near her house or relatives saw snakes and grabbed the children and ran. She also said she was afraid of scorpions, lizards, and the like. She said she felt she "ate the small snake in the honeysuckle" and this made her blind. Several indications of oral dependency needs were observed by the psychiatrist, to whom Nancy soon developed a positive transference of an oral-dependent type. Psychotherapy consisted chiefly of exploring her fears and wishes, reassuring her, and suggesting that her sight was returning. Her ability to see improved somewhat while she was in the hospital.

Though the prognosis for symptom relief was good, a problem was presented by the fact that the family lived 150 miles from the hospital and had a very limited income. The psychiatric social service was requested to interview the parents and explore the possibility of placing Nancy in short-term foster home care in the community so that she could receive outpatient treatment for a few weeks.

The social worker's exploration of the realities of Nancy's psychocultural situation had four different facets, so to speak, and primacy was given sometimes to one and sometimes to another. The first objective, in terms of my social work function, was to develop rapport and a good working relationship with the family in order to help them deal with medical recommendations and in order to secure background information that could serve as a basis for child guidance counseling. I needed to find out what kind of people and parents they were and to understand their way of engaging themselves in Nancy's treatment program. I also had to assess the relationship I developed with them.

My second purpose, as a member of the orthopsychiatric team, was to secure data of dynamic significance that would contribute to the understanding and treatment of Nancy's illness. In her own words, she became blind because she "ate the worm in the honeysuckle." Who had taught her this bit of folklore? What meaning did it have in terms of her illness? Was it likely that if she was relieved of her current hysterical symptom, others would appear at another season?

My third purpose was to utilize community resources on behalf of the child. Placement had been recommended as a means of keeping her accessible for therapy. This possibility raised a number of questions: How would the parents feel about their child's living in another home? What could be learned about the quality of Nancy's home life that would be useful in selecting a foster home? Would the experience of placement itself be therapeutic for Nancy? What kind of readjustment would she face on returning to her own home?

My fourth objective was to explore the potential of the case as a basis for studying the etiology of conversion reactions in children and the resistance of parents to plans for therapy. I had to assume the participant-observer role and be concerned both with therapy and with research.

The only discussion between the clinic staff and the parents had been a review of Nancy's medical history by the admitting physician. When I first met them a week later, my impression was that they were pleasant, self-respecting people. They were neatly, though shabbily, dressed. The mother, aged twenty-six, was comely, deep-bosomed, and maternal and grave in manner; the father, aged thirty-two, was boyish looking and rather dapper, and had an engaging manner.

I explained to Nancy's parents that thorough medical examinations had been made and no physical disorder found; that the doctors thought her blindness might be caused by worry or upset feelings. The parents wondered whether her "eye trouble" could be a "family condition."

Nancy's mother thought she "studied" too much about school: "That's all she cares about; she works at her books all the time, ever since she learned to read. Sometimes I hears her talking in her sleep about a 'rithmetic problem. She has to get all her work just perfect. She reads the Bible a lot and knows all the stories." The mother said Nancy was a good little girl and never caused them any trouble. With twinkling eyes, she added, "Course I switches them sometimes, so they'll know I is the mama." She reported that Nancy had always been "real healthy" and that this was the first time she had ever had to be "carried to a doctor."

I explored the onset of the blindness carefully with the parents and elicited no new information. When I said that Nancy thought it was the honeysuckle that made her blind, the mother replied, "You know what that is? Them doctors didn't know what I was talking about." Nancy had told her mother that during recess the children ate the honeysuckle growing near the school, and her mother had warned: "You shouldn't do that, 'cause if you eat the worm in the honeysuckle, it will run you blind." "My mama told me that when I was a little girl; so I told her that." The father laughingly said he'd eaten honeysuckle when he was a boy, that all the children did and that it had never made them blind. "Course, I didn't eat the worm."

The father said Nancy was "real good in school" and he thought she was bright. The week before he had taught her Sunday-school class and she had understood the lesson about Saul and David and David's sin in forcing his son's wife. Asked what was the difference between the sins of the two kings, Nancy had said, "David repented." The father had explained to the class that fornication was an immorality, not a sin.

The father said that Nancy had wanted to be in the school band but he had not allowed her to because he was planning to arrange private music lessons for her; maybe she had been disappointed about that.

The father wondered whether Nancy's blindness might be a family disease—because the previous year his wife's brother had not been able to open his eyes unless he propped them open with his fingers. He was taken to the local doctor, the eye doctor, and the hospital, but they never could find out what was the matter. (A medical report secured later revealed that when the local doctor advised ligation for the uncle's wife, he "could not keep his eyes open" and never was able to sign permission for the sterilization.)

A talk with the mother alone about sex education revealed that Nancy's menarche had not yet occurred, but since the mother's own periods had begun when she was ten years of age, she had told Nancy about menstruation a few months before. The mother said, "My own mama never told me nothing; it was a white lady that told me." The mother said she had not told Nancy anything about babies but thought she knew from other children. The mother had had two babies in the hospital and the others at home. When her time comes, she sends the children to their grandmother's home. The mother also wondered whether Nancy's blindness could be "some family condition" because her husband's mother "don't seem right." "She cans on Sunday." The mother has tried to talk with her about it, but the grandmother just says, "We got to live."

The mother then spontaneously related that three years before, about a month after one of her children was born, she went to church, and "after a while," she said, "I don't know what come over me; I could still hear and see people but it didn't mean anything." She was like that for several days. Her husband took her to two doctors, but they couldn't find anything wrong, though they "knows some women is like this after childbirth." They were going to send her to a state mental hospital, but there wasn't room. (Application for admission was confirmed by the local clerk of court.) Then the people from the Holiness Church came in, and someone stayed with her night and day, praying and singing, and she just gradually got all right. That was when she got saved. Of course she had been saved before, but this time she repented. When asked what she had repented of, the mother said she used to smoke and gossip and say slanderous things. The mother evidently associated her breakdown with Nancy because she next told about the child's stuttering, which had begun about three years before. Some of the father's relatives stuttered too.

With both parents I discussed plans for further care of Nancy and the possibility of foster home placement so that she could have outpatient treatment. The mother said that if it would help Nancy, she would do anything. The father said that if I could assure him that it was a good home, he would be willing; he said that he brings his children up to know that "not everybody is alike" and that he would want to know whether the home was a good one.

The father works in a cotton mill, earning $40 a week, and is a preacher in a small, rural, Holiness church. He lost a day's pay by coming to the clinic and had to pay $14 to rent a car because his old one was broken down. There are nine children in the family, of whom Nancy is the oldest.

After this interview I summed up my impressions. Nancy's parents seemed intelligent, warm, naïve but verbal, and more communicative than most black patients. I felt that the mother had quickly established a positive relationship with me, but her criticisms of her mother and mother-in-law were clues to the hostility underlying her dependency. I should have explored whether the father's idea of a "good home" was the same as mine, but my attention had turned to the fourth facet of my undertaking, the fascinating research possibilities in the religious and folklore beliefs of this family. I also wanted to please the doctors and effect placement. I asked the resident how long Nancy might stay in the hospital, and we discussed the parents' tentative agreement to placement. The next day I conferred with the local department of public welfare and with the department of welfare of Nancy's home county, explaining our special research interest in childhood hysteria and asking their cooperation. Both agencies responded splendidly and made special exceptions to their usual procedures to facilitate immediate placement. Reports were given them as background for the selection of the foster home and for application for Aid to the Blind.

Before the department of welfare could take any action, however, the parents came to the clinic and asked to take Nancy home for a faith healing service on Sunday. They promised to bring her back to see the psychiatrist the following week. He tried to dissuade them, but they were determined.

The psychiatrist thought that the parents wanted to follow the same pattern of treatment for Nancy that they had followed in the case of the mother's psychiatric illness because they were doubtful about how much we could help her. I told the parents that Nancy's sight was returning and that at times she could see quite well. And I explained that the doctors would like to help her further.

The father spoke enthusiastically about various healers, mentioning certain people who had been healed, including his wife "when she was insane." The mother showed me her testimony in a mimeographed church pamphlet she had brought with her. The father wanted me to read, particularly, the testimony about a child who had been cured after having been examined by twenty doctors, and the testimony about the daughter of one of the elders of his church who was healed of a squint just a week before the onset of Nancy's blindness.

The father explained that the church had split into three groups because some members could not accept the things others did. Nevertheless, the various churches meet together for a faith crusade once a month. He discussed tithing in the Holiness Church, saying that many of his congregation make only $2 a day and he doesn't know how they give as much as they do. The Holiness churches believe that they should help their own so that they need not go to the welfare department for help, but the father doesn't feel it's a disgrace to ask for public assistance. He pointed out that he had lost two days' work that week, but said he had arranged to buy another car so that he would not have to rent one to come to the clinic in the future.

The mother looked depressed and withdrawn. She said she would rather have the father bring Nancy to the hospital each Saturday than to have her away from home. When I said she must miss her little girl, she responded warmly that this was so. She felt she should "do for her." The mother then seemed much more responsive.

The mother spontaneously told me that she had all her children after marriage; she had been married at the age of fourteen, and it was more than a year before Nancy was born. Everyone says she is a wonderful mother—she does so much for her children. Many a night she has gone to bed hungry because she has given her piece of bread to one of the children. She weaned and toilet trained each baby before the next one came; her mother-in-law helped her with this. Nancy was toilet trained at eight months and weaned at ten months. The mother gets up every day between five and six o'clock, washes and irons at night, and sometimes scrubs the floor twice a day. Her mother taught her about housework. Her mother works on a farm now; fifteen years ago a splinter flew in her eye, and she has had a glass eye since. The mother never saw her father. He was "mean, lazy, alcoholics, and no good." Any food her mother gave him, he sold for liquor. He left home for good before she was four years old. Her mother had had three children by him and nine by a second husband, who was a good stepfather. The mother told me about how good and patient her husband is with her and the children.

The father said he felt faith helps some people, though not everyone. This doesn't mean he hasn't confidence in doctors, but he does believe that faith helps. He had prayed over Nancy the day she became blind, and she was better for a few hours but then couldn't see again. Maybe he didn't have enough faith. The father asked what I thought of taking Nancy to Oral Roberts, the famous white faith healer, on the way home. I easily dissuaded him from this, saying I thought it would be better to go to the faith healers he knew. I told the parents I could understand that they would rather "do for Nancy" at home and that it would mean a lot to them to take her to the faith healing meeting. As the father spoke further of the faith healing meetings, I asked where they were held and whether visitors came. The father assured me I would be very welcome—that his people believe in treating everyone alike and that I would not be "looked over." I told them that if I could arrange it, I would come to the service and visit them at home, and I asked them how they would feel about my doing so. Both expressed pleasure. Before they left, they assured me several times that they would bring Nancy back to see the doctor.

On Sunday I drove 150 miles to the family's church. When the mother saw me she broke into a beatific smile, exclaiming joyously, "She did come!" She said that she and the father had talked all night about my coming, wondering if I would drive so far. The father said that Nancy was "seeing some better" since she had been in the hospital.

The father's church was a small, decrepit building, without electric lights, bare except for wooden benches and a box draped with cloth, which serves as an altar. Seven women, four men, and fifteen children were present. The informal and formless service included gospel songs and spirituals, sung from memory, accompanied by a bass drum and two tambourines. Impassioned prayers were made by the elders, in which others joined in with "Amen," "Hallelujah," "Praise God," and the like. Testimonies offered by most of the adults expressed gratitude to God for "waking up in their right mind in the morning," for being able to clothe and feed themselves, and for having been "baptized, sanctified, and saved." The amount of audience participation and emotion expressed were striking, though characteristic of white Holiness services as well.

The father walked up and down the platform, looking boyish, making smiling remarks, saying he knew the members of the congregation came to church to sing and pray and *enjoy* themselves. He complained he did not feel like preaching—and I felt he was inhibited by my presence. The members encouraged him: "Go on and preach. We're waiting. The congregation will answer you back."

The father then called out the chapter and verse of passages in the Bible about faith, salvation, and healing, which various women read. He carefully pointed out a difference between two promises in the Scriptures: If you believe and call on the name of the Lord, "you *shall* be saved," whereas, in the healing passages, the Bible says, "you *may* be healed." Nancy was called forward; the members stood in a semicircle around her, and the minister and elders anointed her head and eyes with olive oil. The minister began praying, and the others joined in with individual prayers, above which the minister's voice soared in a musical chant. Impassioned pleas were made to the Father and Jesus to heal the child. (At no time was sin mentioned, or repentance or forgiveness.) The members became more and more stirred up, stamping their feet and crying out, their bodies shaking and trembling; the emotional tension was contagious—what the group meant by "feeling the spirit." Nancy's mother sobbed hard and began "speaking in tongues," as did one of the men. One elder did a shuffling dance step. The father jumped and leaped, doing various acrobatic and dance steps. The mother ran back and forth, throwing her arms over her head, sobbing, crying out in syllables, quite hysterically. The congregation again encouraged the father to preach, and he then began dramatically acting out the story of Elijah the Prophet challenging the false prophets of Baal. The congregation became very elated, and the minister, seemingly orgiastic.

Before the dramatization of the Bible story was completed, the father suddenly stopped, gave great rasping sobs, and then, in a matter-of-fact voice, made a number of announcements. He asked me to stand—but he had forgotten my name. The mother whispered that I did not have to speak but that they would all be pleased if I said a few words. The father laughingly told about a doctor at the hospital: he couldn't understand half of what the doctor said. (Knowing of the snake-handling cult in the Holiness Church, the doctor had mentioned this to the father, and the father had thought him ridiculous. There were only two kinds of snakes he was scared of—big ones and little ones.) He told the group I had asked if I would be embarrassed at coming to the service. They all know, he said, that they are not welcome in white churches, but white visitors are welcome in theirs. He referred to the sin of Noah's son (looking on his father's nakedness), which had caused them to be black. "But on judgment day we will all be . . . "—and the congregation cried as one—"white as snow." He thanked me for coming so far to see Nancy and for coming to the church, and he asked if I would say a few words. Having been to such churches before, I had anticipated his invitation and had thought a long time about what I might say. I told the congregation I knew it was true that they were not welcome in most white churches and so appreciated the privilege of worshiping with them. I told them that everyone at the hospital was interested in helping Nancy. We had many patients, grown-ups and children, who were afflicted, like her, with sudden blindness or deafness, and some couldn't walk or talk. The cause wasn't a physical disease that medicine or an operation would cure, but something that troubled their minds and hearts. I myself believed that God's spirit of compassionate love lived in human beings and, through the skills of doctors, nurses, teachers, and preachers, helped to heal the troubled minds of the sick, just as our doctors had helped Nancy to begin to see again. I said I was glad I could pray and give thanks with them for her recovery.

During the service the children sat quietly; several fell asleep, as Nancy did. When the service reached its highest emotional pitch, the children looked at the adults with rather puzzled expressions. I could not detect any change of expression in Nancy. Her mother led her about, and she appeared to be unable to see.

The services ended with a prayer for my safe journey home. All the members of the congregation came up to shake hands with me and expressed warm appreciation of my having come and also having spoken. The mother said that Nancy had told her that the white people at the hospital treated her "so nice." The women said dryly, "Must be different from people 'round here."

I talked with Nancy and encouraged her to go back to school.

The next day I had conferences with the local welfare department, Nancy's teacher, and the family doctor. They verified a number of points and all confirmed my evaluation of the family as being self-supporting and self-respecting.

To each of the community people with whom I spoke I expressed the hospital's appreciation of their cooperation, and I discussed the hospital's psychiatric services and our mutual concerns for Nancy. Using this child as an example, I also discussed various manifestations of emotional disturbances in children, the high proportion of patients with conversion reactions at the hospital, and our interest in research. I felt that, in addition to serving my immediate purposes, my consultations with community resources helped to develop good public relations for the medical center and contributed to mental health education.

I also made a visit to Nancy's home, which was on the outskirts of the town. The four-room house was very dilapidated and the rooms crowded with beds, but it looked clean and neat.

The father told me more about his own life: his father is an "alcoholics," and his parents had separated four years before. The father had first belonged to a Methodist church and had been offered a chance to go to a seminary. But he hadn't agreed with the minister and had felt he was doing most of the work in bringing the people in while the minister got the credit; so he got a church of his own.

They used to have a very nice house, he said, with all their own furniture, good furniture. He had seven suits and enough white shirts to change twice a day, and his "old woman" had lots of shoes. But they lost everything in a fire. He had been working in the fields and saw smoke. All he thought of was that he had left three little children in bed at home (Nancy was then around four). The house was in flames when he reached it, and just as he got the children out, the roof fell in. They lost everything they had. Asked what kind of work he had been doing then, he said, "I was mean, I did everything—drinking, gambling, selling white corn." After the fire they moved to an old house where three men had been killed. The father said he "never did see or hear anything," but he thought about it a lot, "that it might be him that got killed or killed someone." One night he had a dream—"Some folks call it a vision, but I thinks it was a dream." In the dream the Lord came, dressed all in black, and one of the apostles with him, dressed all in black, and six white angels—their robes and faces all as white as white. The Lord called him, but he wouldn't go. The apostle called him, and somehow he killed him. Then the Lord looked sorrowful, and turned, and went through a big gate, and the angels after him, one by one. Just as the last angel got to the gate, the father called, "Wait!" and then woke up in the bed calling, "Wait!" It seemed a sign. He began "to hunt him revival meetings" to see if that would help him, and finally he was saved.

While we were talking, a Negro man drove up and asked how Nancy was. He was astonished to learn that she could see, and asked to take her home with him; the father, with some reluctance, agreed. Shortly afterward the mother returned from the fields and worried about Nancy—she didn't know the man who took her off in his car; those people didn't call on them and had no small children, and you can never tell what men will do with a little girl.

The mother said that Nancy had wanted to go to school that morning, but the mother had been fearful of letting her go, lest she strain her eyes. I encouraged her to let Nancy go back because her eyes seemed to be getting better and she would enjoy ending the school year with her class, even though she didn't do much work. I talked with the mother about our feeling that Nancy was a fearful little girl and suggested that she could help her by being reassuring if she worried about her school work or was slightly naughty. I also suggested that, since Nancy seemed to be afraid to stay alone at night, they might get some relative or older girl to stay with the children if the mother went out to an evening meeting with the father.

During our conversation, the little children came up for hugs from the mother, and she told me a little about each child. When I left, the mother said, "I don't know why it is, but I pure loved you when I first saw you."

It was after the home visit that I went to the doctor's office; and the father followed me there. (Perhaps he was worried about what I might tell the doctor.) He had a question to ask, he said: "Could it be someone put a hex on Nancy and that was why she went blind?" He could not remember who suggested this; maybe it was someone who knew about hexing. The doctor and I both reassured him, explaining that hexing could not really injure you, though some people might worry themselves sick if they believed in it. We pointed out that the doctor and the prayers together seemed to be making Nancy better.

As is usual in clinic practice, the orthopsychiatric team conferred frequently to evaluate data and to plan, taking into account reality factors that affected the patient's problem and our treatment goals. Our clinical experience with other cases of childhood hysteria had demonstrated the advisability of setting limited goals, such as symptom relief, environmental changes, and counseling with parents about medical care and methods of handling selected areas of stress for the child. It is usually not feasible to engage the family in long-term plans for therapy, largely because psychiatric clinics cannot compel them to utilize therapy for their children. Our responsibility is to inform them of the nature and seriousness of the child's condition and to try to help them resolve misunderstandings, resistances, and apprehensions about psychiatric treatment. Thus, our goals are determined not only by the nature of the psychiatric problem and the various methods of treatment available but also by situational reality factors and by the family's motivation, understood in the larger terms of the family's own values and social adjustment.

In Nancy's case many factors were weighed by the team. Our first goal, diagnostic evaluation, was accomplished. The second goal, symptom relief, was also achieved, although perhaps not as effectively as it might have been through our plan for continued psychotherapy during foster home placement. Distance from the clinic and the family's economic situation limited continued outpatient treatment. In addition, reality factors in the clinic situation had to be considered, such as the facts that the resident treating Nancy was leaving the service and that the pressure of waiting lists limited the possibility of reassignment. The third goal was giving consultation service to the local physician, teacher, and welfare agency so that these community resources would be better prepared if further service needs should arise. In this context, counseling was given the parents about methods of easing the child's overconscientiousness and fears, and about the availability of medical care.

In addressing ourselves to these goals, we evaluated the family's motivation for, and capacity to use, various kinds of psychiatric service and tried to determine the kind of service that would be most effective, given the family's personal-social gestalt or adjustment. For Nancy and her family, the realities of limited employment opportunities, low income, family size, and cultural milieu presented many environmental problems, both for the present and for the future, which psychiatric service could not resolve or change. In the data available about the life histories and personalities of the parents, as well as of the child, there were indications of many inner and outer conflicts and pressures that threatened the precarious balance of ego control and social adjustment.

With increasing knowledge of the cultural and psychological factors in the family's situation, we saw that the chief social institutions upon which this family relied were its own unity as a family and its church. Thus, another objective was included in our brief service, that of resolving the dilemma of choosing between religion and medicine, the church and the hospital. I endeavored to effect this resolution through my community visit and participation in the church service, supporting, rather than weakening, the value of religion to the family, while enabling them to return for further medical care when needed.

The Saturday after my visit the father did indeed bring Nancy to the clinic. He felt her sight was improving, although still not as good as it was before her blindness. He said she was getting around all right and could take care of herself. She could tell time by the clock, but she had not been trying to read and did not go back to school, because the mother thought she should stay at home. As far as he could tell there had not been any marked change, although she said she could see better after the faith healing service. He spoke again of his wife's healing—"She was real insane." She got worse and worse and finally was completely out of her mind: didn't know anybody, fought so that he had to tie her hands and feet to the bedstead; she screamed and talked nonsense and bit him and the children if they came near her. She had never been like that before or since. He mentioned again that he used to be mean, and that he was mean to his wife. He didn't mean to say that he beat her, but he would drink a lot and was ugly. She was upset and always "wanted they should live better; so she was real glad when he was saved." He said they always got along well together— not like some people he knew. He spoke again of the mother's tendency to worry about everything and said she had always been nervous like that since he met her, when she was a girl. He wished he could be that way just one time so that he would know what it was like, because he doesn't worry about anything. When I remarked that we thought Nancy was a worrying little girl too, he agreed and related several episodes he remembered. Nancy seemed to be so scared of snakes, he said, and one day she thought she saw one in the yard. Another time, she said there had been a man in the house; another time she said she saw a woman in the house, who lay down on the bed with her. Using these examples of Nancy's fearfulness, I suggested to the father, as I had to the mother, that someone should stay with her in the house at night. The father referred to the dilapidated condition of the house. They had moved out there from town because it was quiet in the country. He wondered if it might help Nancy if they moved back into town where there were more lights and people. I agreed she might feel safer with neighbors close at hand and mentioned the fact that there would be other children for her to play with. The father thought he was lucky to have his job at the mill, because there are few places where a Negro man can earn so much as $40 a week. He made a little at his preaching, and sometimes people brought him food and clothing. They also bought a battery and tires for his car. The people in the church were still talking about my visit and about how much they appreciated what I'd said.

In view of the fact that Nancy's eyesight was improving and her psychiatrist was leaving the service, I told the father that we felt she was on the way to recovery and would not need to come to see the doctor regularly. But, I said, we would like to know how she was getting along.

A month later Nancy wrote to her doctor saying she could see much better and would go back to school in September; she was having fun playing and hoped the doctor would write to her soon.

Three months later I made a follow-up home visit. The family had moved to a better house, with indoor plumbing. It was in a slum district, and the mother kept the front door locked when working out back because of the "drunks." The mother said that she was very glad to see me, as she often thought of me, and that she wanted me to know she believed people need both doctors and the Lord. Nancy had started school and liked her teacher very much. Her eyes were all right, but she was still having headaches. The mother took her to a new local doctor, and he said she "must have been poisoned all over her body." The mother herself is not well. She has missed periods for four months, but she has not "felt life." She went to the doctor and he said she had tumors and should come back in a month to see about an operation. For the past month she has been bleeding steadily and is afraid of cancer. I encouraged her to go back to the doctor as soon as she could. The mother also pointed out various medical needs of her children—one child had a clubfoot for which the doctor was going to prescribe orthopedic shoes; another had a "knot" above his eye. The mother had had a few days' work on tobacco, and one of the women in the church kept the two smallest children for her. She has also helped with school clothes. I sent greetings to the church members and asked the mother to let me know whether she had an operation and how they got along.

Part Two: Discussion, by Weston La Barre

In a psychiatric-cultural view of the realities of this child's life situation, a number of factors are significant. Sociologically, the family was upwardly mobile. Both parents came from poor, uneducated, tenant-farmer families. The grandfathers were alcoholic; the grandmothers were the stronger, more stable parental figures. Nancy's father broke away from the semi-peonage of tenant farming. With only a third-grade education, he considered himself lucky to have a regular job earning a dollar an hour, this being a relatively high income for a black laborer in that section of the country. His salary of $40 a week was supplemented somewhat by church collections and gifts from his congregation. For a family with nine children, such an income can scarcely provide minimum necessities. The father's intelligence, capacity for leadership, and ego strivings, and the mother's housekeeping standards, maternal devotion, and desire "to live good" had raised the family above the morass of poverty, ignorance, and low social standards surrounding them. With white authority figures, the parents maintained a reputation for self-support and self-respect, and they struggled to avoid a dependency relationship with the welfare department and the hospital social worker. They were trying hard to make something of themselves against formidable environmental handicaps and were determined to transmit to their children their hard-won values.

Their social striving had exacted instinctual renunciation on the part of this couple. Their ego and superego ideals denied them the easy money and fine clothes the father had been able to get from gambling and bootlegging, and gratifications such as smoking, drinking, and premarital and extramarital sexual indulgence. In their precarious struggle with external realities and internal stresses, the family drew upon such ego supports as were available to them, as will be seen in the discussion of faith healing.

The dynamics underlying their social striving may be glimpsed in the father's history: in his unresolved oedipal and sibling rivalry; his rebellion against authority and group mores in his semi-delinquencies; his search for ego and superego support in the church; his rivalry and break with the Methodist minister who got the credit for his efforts; his identification with the Holiness group that cured the mother; the rivalry in this group also, in which various members could not agree and split off into separate churches; and the father's success in establishing a church "of his own," where he was sole and undisputed leader. Although the parents had differed during the early years of their marriage about the way of life they wanted, they came to share the same goals, which were the basis of the strong bond between them. The father's role was that of social leader, preacher, and head of the family, and his wife's that of homemaker and mother. They shared their parental responsibilities and their religious beliefs and activities, and supported each other in them.

The father's unsatisfied educational ambitions placed pressure on Nancy, his oldest child. The mother's needs also played a role in the child's anxiety. She herself had been shaped early to a pattern of hysterical overreaction and anxiousness, compulsiveness, and maternal responsibility by her own mother. Her compulsiveness had manifested itself in her early toilet training of Nancy, which had placed a heavy burden on the child, and her emphasis on cleanliness, neatness, and good performance was clearly reflected in Nancy's overconscientiousness about her school lessons. In other cases of childhood hysteria we have noted a similar overemphasis on, and anxiety about, schoolwork, to meet the needs of the parents and win approval, and as a defense against threatening impulses, such as curiosity about sexuality.

Both the parents' and Nancy's conflicts about oral, visual, and sexual impulse gratification, and the mechanisms they used to deal with these conflicts, were repeatedly and variously highlighted in the data. Inadequately satisfied hunger, particularly, was a constant reality for them, and anxiety about food was a recurrent theme. The mother's father deprived his wife and children of food by selling whatever was given them in order to buy drinks. The father's mother sinned against her son's new religious mores by preparing food on the Sabbath—"because we got to live." The mother often went to bed hungry because, with maternal self-sacrifice, she had given her piece of bread to one of the children. Nancy's fantasies were predominantly concerned with sweets, and her oral-dependent relationship to her mother was reflected in her transference to the psychiatrist.

The causes of the mother's psychotic breakdown are unknown, but her symptoms were described in oral terms: "She talked out of her head," and she bit her husband and children. Moreover, the mother's cure was attributed to the singing and praying and the mothering of the Holiness congregation. She was then "saved" by repenting and renouncing her sins of smoking and slandering. In the church she found a socially accepted and rewarded channel for hysterical expression, in gesturing, crying, and "talking in tongues." And it is not insignificant that Nancy's stuttering, which the father considered a family trait, developed after the mother's breakdown.

The father's history also revealed his conflict about impulse gratification, renunciation, and sublimation. He had identified with his father's alcoholism and indulged himself in drinking, gambling, and aggressive behavior. Through the traumatic experience of the fire that destroyed his fine furniture and clothes and endangered the lives of his children, his anxiety and guilt were awakened. He then saw his former gratifications as "bad" and feared they might lead to uncontrollable aggression, to murder or his own death. The dream—which he recognized as a dream, not a mystic vision—manifested his rebellion against parental authority in his refusal to follow the Lord; his rivalry, in his murder of the apostle, "perhaps by choking him with his hands"; and his decision to submit to the demands of the superego when he finally answered the call of the good father. He interpreted the dream as a "call" and then sought salvation through revival meetings, where the contagious emotion of the group, expressed in singing, praying, confessing, and repenting, supported his ego resolve to renounce the alcoholic gratification of his overwhelming need. Preaching, taking a leadership role, provided substitute socially permitted and rewarded sublimations.

Another factor in the overdetermination of symptom choice is indicated in the coincidence of ocular symptoms throughout the social group: the mother's mother wore a glass eye because of an injury she had incurred while chopping wood, a man's job; an uncle developed a hysterical inability to keep his eyes open when requested to sign permission for his wife's sterilization; the mother had been healed of the need to wear glasses several years before; and, perhaps most significantly, another little girl had been healed of a squint by the father just a week before the onset of Nancy's blindness. Since Biblical stories and symbolic imagery about blindness, and cures through repentance and healing, are numerous, Nancy's knowledge of the Bible and her religious preoccupation as well as the emotional impact of the healing services may also be recognized as predisposing factors in the development of her hysterical symptom. In this verbal family, the child doubtless heard retold many times the stories of the fire, her father's conversion, her mother's cure, and the like, so that her own memories have become fused with family and religious lore.

A major dynamic in the hysteria was the child's exposure to sexual stimulation while the family mores concealed and denied the reality of sexuality. Nancy slept in her parents' bedroom until she was four years old; and in such a small, poorly built house real privacy is impossible even in adjoining rooms. Moreover, there are hints—in the father's account of his drinking orgies and quarrels, in his orgiastic exhibitionism in church, and in the mother's frequent pregnancies, which she did not explain to the child—that Nancy saw and heard more than she was permitted to know. Nancy herself said that when she became blind she saw only darkness and the moving shadows on her mother's face and arms; she feared that strange people would break into the house while her parents were away; and she admitted her fear of seeing snakes and dreamt of a snake going in and out of a hole. Her responses to projective tests clearly pointed to the traumatic effect of exposure to the primal scene. That Ham became blind and black as punishment for looking upon his drunken father's nakedness is yet another source of Nancy's choice of symptom, deriving both from tradition and from her family's gestalt.

As Nancy neared the menarche, her mother's hysterical anxiety and overprotective concern for her first-born child, with whom she identified, focused on the sexual dangers that might befall the child, and these were expressed in excessive warnings. The mother herself took pride in the fact that she bore her first child only after she had been married more than a year, because children in this racial-cultural group mature early socially, and often are involved in sexual relationships that result in illegitimate pregnancy. The family's cultural sexual anxiety was conveyed in the folk proverb, which the mother had learned from her mother: "If you eat the worm in the honeysuckle, it will run you blind." Thus, in the precipitating events we see the confluence of anxiety and guilt-provoking impulses of oral incorporation (sucking the honey and eating the phallic symbol) and of visual gratification (sexual knowledge). Nancy was tempted to eat the forbidden sweet, both wishing and fearing to see and eat the snake, and became blind, as a punishment for her impulse and a defense against her wish. In her history we may glimpse also the layer of unresolved oedipal conflict—the mother forbidding and threatening punishment, being overly anxious about Nancy's libidinal interest in the male figure. The child's conflict was activated by approaching adolescence, the information given her about the mysterious changes about to take place in her body, and her father's teaching about King David's sin in forcing his son's wife; perhaps, too, the conversation of other children at school about "where babies come from." The conversion symptom was an attempt to resolve the unbearable tension, anxiety, and guilt about her conflicting impulses, punishing her and preventing her from seeing and eating what she had seen and longed to see and eat. The symptom also provided a secondary gain for the child in her mother's solicitude and the dramatic attention she received from her father and the church members, being looked at because she could not see, and appealing to her father's power to heal her as he healed the child with the squint.

The child's symptom had, furthermore, symbolic content and significance for her family and the group. The parents' first response to Nancy's blindness was to use home remedies and prayer. When, in their search for medical aid, they were confronted with the idea that Nancy's blindness had an emotional cause, they tried to deny their own involvement and attribute the illness to inheritance, each parent pointing to relatives in the other's family. In other ways, as well, they externalized and projected dangerous, intrapsychic impulses onto malevolent forces in the outer world—the worm in the honeysuckle and hexing. They sensed, naïvely, the identificatory process in symptom formation. Faced with the possibility of foster home placement so that Nancy's psychiatric treatment could continue, they chose to utilize the institutional means with which they had had previous successful experience, faith healing. Our psychiatric intervention threatened to take away from them the secondary gains with which their own methods of treating the illness provided them.

The mother's need to prove her goodness as a mother was threatened by the plan for foster home placement, and she became depressed and withdrawn, as if she felt deprived and rejected. When her wish and right "to do for" her daughter was recognized and accepted, she could re-establish her positive transference to the social worker. She still sought and needed the approval of a mother figure, but her ambivalence in the hostile dependency played its role in her determination to assert and maintain her control. Her love for "the white lady who explains things" was genuine, but it lasted only so long as there was no threat to take her control from her, as long as she could show she was "the mama," who had the authority to decide whether Nancy should return to school.

For the father, too, the child's symptom and its treatment had profound meaning. At faith healing meetings, he had seen other leaders heal people, and he had ventured to try to heal too, once that we hear of, successfully, the girl with a squint. Now, assured that his daughter's blindness was not a physical disease, he correctly judged that an emotionally caused blindness might be cured by emotional methods. While not entirely refusing the doctor's treatment, he needed to demonstrate—to the child, his wife, his congregation, and, perhaps chiefly, himself—his power to heal by words, by power from the Lord, while he struggled with his self-doubt, wondering whether he had faith enough. Faith healing was a *means of communicating* to Nancy, by and through the family culture, that her guilt impulses need not be overwhelming and could be forgiven.

To the group, also, the child's symptom and its cure had much meaning. Everyone had heard about the preacher's daughter who had become blind. The teacher, doctor, and welfare workers were collaborating to secure medical treatment; but the father's congregation had a special stake and role in Nancy's cure. Clearly, the church group identified with the psychodynamics of the family, as did the family with those of the group. The church bulletin published accounts of successful faith healing where medicine had failed and reported the mother's cure through the local congregation and the recent healing of the girl with a squint in the father's church; at each Sunday service members were encouraged to testify to their sanctification and healing, and they attended the monthly healing meetings held jointly with other Holiness churches, supporting and enlarging their identification with their beliefs and practices. The members of such churches are the "different" ones, individualists who have separated from the more conventional church affiliations of the majority, such as the Baptists and Methodists, and they prefer to worship outside denominational structure and theology; they choose preachers with healing power rather than an educated ministry. Their services lack formality and ritual; they permit much audience participation and foster emotional expression. While Bible stories, sermons, hymns, and prayers stress the repression of impulses, to conform with religious ethics, the church provides an opportunity for emotional catharsis and a kind of therapy, in abreaction, orgiastic acting out and exhibitionism. The members of the congregation come to church to enjoy themselves and they literally "dance their joy before the Lord," like David; they jump, shout, weep, cry, and "speak in tongues." Hysterical symptoms and faith healing serve as concrete evidence of the importance of their faith, its living reality and power. The other realities in the lives of these people are poverty, deprivation, restriction, and limitation; to these realities their beliefs add further restrictions and renunciations of gratification. But they also provide compensatory group gratifications. These believers have reason for their simple prayers of gratitude for their daily bread and for "waking up in their right mind"— and for this one institutional means available to them for the enjoyment of feeling and for group support of ego striving. Such religious beliefs can be considered a kind of group delusional defensive system (depending on denial, undoing, projection, and catharsis) that enables the congregation to live more comfortably and hopefully; the mutual participation in processes of gratification, renunciation, and sublimation, strengthens group cohesion as it assists group survival. And perhaps the ego formation of people who seek this kind of religious experience requires continuous group support of this nature. Also, to do by faith what white doctors cannot do with knowledge is not a negligible ego gratification for a minority group that has suffered the disdain of the powerful majority.

It is interesting that one of the few hints we get of the way in which Nancy's parents handled their aggression, as they walked the tightrope of race relations, was given in the church service. The white visitor's name was forgotten, but, she was "invited" to say a few words, and she was "put on the spot" by the introduction. Some minimal expression of aggression, through humor and innuendo, was permitted in the criticisms of discrimination in white churches. But the hostility was handled primarily through denial, rationalization, and projection; it was removed from the present to the past and the future. The congregation's pleasure in the triumph of Elijah over the prophets of Baal lay in their identification with the victory of the righteous minority over the powerful but wicked majority. The Biblical folk rationalization for their color, as punishment for Noah's son's sin was cited, and the religious hopes of a future life was stressed, in which "they shall all be white as snow."

Religion had many values for this family, permitting gratifications, sublimations, catharsis. In their valiant, precarious struggle to lift themselves and their children out of a morass of ignorance, poverty, and lack of standards, the church provided a bulwark of support to ego strengths and family cohesion. In their efforts to be self-supporting and self-directing, to preserve and transmit to their children their hard-won values, and to cope with racism, they avoided dependency relationships with the welfare department and other authority figures. They "managed" their relationship with the caseworker with charming skill, never saying a direct and discourteous "no" to her offers of foster home and welfare aid. By subtle means they tested her understanding of, and respect for, their values and their autonomy as human beings. As they felt assured of her willingness to give supportive help to their ego efforts, within their definition of the situation, they shared more of their history, their problems, and their strivings with her. In response to her respect for their family integrity and the value of their religious beliefs to them, they granted her the privilege of participating in their actual social situation. In the church she could express, in the group's own language, their common ground—concern for Nancy and mutual trust in the therapeutic effect of the compassionate love that underlies both religious faith and psychotherapy. In this way a resolution was offered of the dilemma of faith healing as against psychiatric treatment, church against hospital. The value of the church to the family was supported, and the door was left open for further medical and social service.

It is a delicate task to investigate the living situation of a family, for by so doing, we enter into it and thereby play a role in it, willy-nilly. It is difficult to do this with some therapeutic benefit, at least without disturbing the intricate balance of the family's personal-social development—particularly in a biracial situation, complicated by regional stereotyped traditions and peculiar religious beliefs. To succeed, the participant-observer must be aware of, and responsive to, subtle indications of the group's feelings and the relationship of the patient to the group; and he must be genuine in his own feeling, for the group is sensitive and reacts to it. Moreover, effective service and investigation in psychiatric-cultural treatment and research depend on teamwork. In this case the social worker fulfilled her function as a member of the orthopsychiatric team as she developed a working relationship with the family, which was therapeutic in nature, to help them with problems of medical care and to counsel them in connection with their parental responsibilities; as she obtained data of dynamic significance for the understanding and treatment of the psychiatric illness; as she utilized community resources on the child's behalf; and as she served as a medium for mental health education.

By being aware of the many facets of such a case, the psychiatric social worker may also contribute to the deepening of insight and the increase of clinical skill—the goal of research based on case studies.

Reference Notes

1. See Earle Somers, "Some Regional Aspects of Conversion Reactions," a paper presented at the meeting of Southern Branches of the American Psychiatric Association, Miami, Florida, December 1, 1958. See also James Proctor, "Hysteria in Childhood," *American Journal of Orthopsychiatry* 28 (April 1958), 394–407.
2. Albert Linch, "Certain Cultural Influences on a Group of Clinic Patients," *Psychiatry* 21 (1959), 301–5.

12. Aymara Folklore and Folk Temperament

Folklore may be looked at as the projective-test protocols of a society, the data for a kind of cultural Rorschach. By using the techniques of content-analysis, one can derive some notion of the people's preoccupations, anxieties, and even to a degree their group temperament or ethos. This I propose to attempt through a content-analysis of a one hundred percent sample of Aymara folktales collected in connection with ethnographic field work.

On the bleak, windy, and cold semidesert plateau of Lake Titicaca, at 12,500 feet above sea-level and upward, the life of the Aymara is difficult and precarious. Without *both* their marginal agriculture and their herds of domesticated llamas the Aymara probably could not survive in this environment. The agricultural staples are *chuñu*, potatoes frost-dried into corky chunks, and, to a much lesser degree, *quinoa*, the small seeds from a plant of the spinach family. The meat of the llama is dried into *ch'arki* (borrowed by the Spanish as "charqui" and anglicized in Texas as "jerky" whence, by a false back-formation, "jerked meat"); sometimes, two species of fishes, netted, speared or hooked from giant-reed *balsa* boat-shaped rafts, are also dried for later use. Little hunting is done, except for small wild rodents. Llamas are used for land transport, and their wool, like that of alpacas, is spun and woven on horizontal looms for clothing: mid-calf-length bottom-split trousers and shirt for men, worn with a knitted helmet or ear-flapped *gorro*; multiple knee-length wool skirts, with a shirt and sleeveless jacket, and a crude native-made bowler-like felt hat for women. Llama-dung or *taquia* and a semisubterranean resinous plant resembling a woody cauliflower, *yareta*, are used for fuel in the largely treeless altiplano. The Aymara make rude pottery and have some native bronze metallurgy. Houses are of turf, with thatched wood-framed gabled roofs. Social organization is arranged around the *ayllu* or patrilineal sib.

Aymara religion is primarily apotropaic magic designed to protect people, crops, and animals against the malevolence of witches and a host of evil spirits including ubiquitous place-demons. Indeed, the salient feature of Aymara culture is the great variety of categories of black-magicians, omen-takers, diagnosticians, diviners, dream-interpreters, chiropractors, surgeons, herbalists and other medicine men, with varied curing techniques which they may practice simultaneously with black magic. The *materia medica* of the Aymara form one

First published in *Journal of the Folklore Institute* 2 no. 1 (June 1965), 25–30. See also, W. La Barre, "The Aymara: History and Worldview," *Journal of American Folklore* 79 no. 311 (1966), 130–44, republished in John Greenway (ed.), *The Anthropologist Looks at Myth* (Austin: University of Texas Press, 1966), pp. 130–44. Copyright 1966 by the American Folklore Society. All rights reserved.

of the most enormous yet found among a primitive people. Their folk-thought concerning disease and pathology is highly developed; indeed, the Collawayus, an Aymara subgroup southeast of the Lake, are famous all over South America, even as far as Buenos Aires and Rio de Janeiro, as folk-doctors.

Psychologically, the Aymara live in an unhappy, hostile, and insecure world. Children's souls are liable to be kidnapped by place-demons in the earth; in traveling, even adults must be solicitous to placate these spirits. Women must be careful to cover the nape of the neck with a woolen wimple in traveling or at night lest they be attacked by the terrible bodiless vampires or flying heads of Aymara legend. Witchcraft and counter-witchcraft spells are constantly flying back and forth in the air, as men seek to harm one another's llamas, crops, children, and persons. When one makes an enemy's nose bleed in a fight, one must drink some of his blood so the defeated enemy's witchcraft will not harm the aggressor. One of the best ways to get rid of a disease is to cast it into magic materials that are left at a crossing of paths, so that the next unwitting traveler may carry the disease away. The unfaithfulness of lovers and spouses is only to be expected from the widespread use of love-magic and spells. And, as Tschopik writes,[1] the Aymara "seek omens in nearly all manifestations of nature and possess an elaborate series of techniques for divining the future; indeed, the total culture of the Aymara might best be characterized as apprehensive."

What are some other psychological characteristics described by informed students of the Aymara? I found them truculent, hostile, silent, and unsmiling; Forbes called them "intensely suspicious and distrustful . . . [with] the most deep-rooted and inveterate hatred for their white oppressors"; Grandidier considered the Aymara "cruel," Walle "hard, vindictive, bellicose, rebellious, egotistical, and jealous of his liberty . . . lacking in will, except the will to hate." Squier says they are "a people notoriously morose, jealous, and vindictive" and "more sullen and more cruel" than the Quechua. Hewitt wrote that "they are the most difficult of all Andean peoples to cultivate; in fact, it is well-nigh impossible to establish friendly relationships with them." Yet even the Aymara is no match for the *cholo* or half-blood "who units in himself the treachery, stupid cupidity, morbid distrust, hostility, and fantastic brutality of both his ancestries."[2] These forceful and uncompromising statements, it must be remembered, are not the projected "racial stereotypes," say, of a Bolivian white class that notoriously exploits the Aymara; they are the considered judgments of professionally trained ethnographers, of quite varied national origins and, presumably, of the most diverse personality themselves. The consensus is the more notable since such conclusions conflict with the usual experience of ethnographers who, in love with their subject-matter, more usually end up with affection for their subjects.

Let us now more fully illustrate these "subjective" assessments of the Aymara by summarizing[3] the "projective" materials furnished in the folktales of the Aymara themselves. Then, if we can establish thus the "hardness of the data," it will be time enough later to offer hypotheses and theories to explain the data. While they omit much of the emotional coloring of the tales, the following synopses of folktales collected in original Aymara text give some notion of the typical content:

Fox, starving, goes to the mountain to seek food. He meets Condor and, bethinking himself of his own bushy tail and Condor's naked feet, he gets Condor to agree that the one who can sit longest in the cold snow will eat the other; but in the end it is Fox who is eaten.

Vixen asks why Gull's children are so white and is told that this is the result of baking in an oven. Vixen burns all her children to death in trying this, and then bursts herself angrily trying to drink up Lake Titicaca to get at, kill,[a] and eat up Gull and her children.[4]

Skunk has a friend, a little llama herder, but she dies. He takes funeral foods to her family; when he is gone, these are found to be scarabs, lizards and leaves.

Sparrow warns Linnet that Hawk is after Linnet's fledglings. Hawk, seeking to eat Sparrow in revenge, angrily chases Sparrow into a hole in a wall whence Sparrow escapes by outwitting Hawk.

In a famine, Mouse and Sparrow agree to store their joint food in Mouse's burrow. Mouse treacherously eats it all up, and when they fight gives Sparrow the stripes on his head which may be seen to this day.

Condor, in the guise of a tall man, steals the chief's daughter. Hummingbird bargains his aid to bring her back; henceforth Condor never comes down from Illimani to where Hummingbird flies among the crops gathering his reward.

The Inca destroy Llogheta, reducing it to a pile of stones, and massacre all its inhabitants because they do not submit.

Every night the foxes untie the burro, and he wanders about eating the crops. For this he is beaten daily until in revenge he pretends to be dead. The foxes tie themselves to the burro to drag him home, intending to make *charqui* of him; but the burro jumps up and drags all the foxes before the chief, who kills them.

Several songs were also collected:

A young woman deceives a young man by saying she has a hundred sheep, a yoke of bulls, a llama-load of coins, and that she is a good spinstress and weaver—but none of this is true.

Two lovers leave each other, the one to seek a woman made of mud, the other, a man carved of dry wood.

An ensorcelled youth seeks the witch Sparrow to release him from a hopeless love, but Sparrow only laughs at him.

---

a. Tschopik has another tale consistent in tone with this: Mouse as a handsome young man marries a woman. She brings his lunch to the field but, not finding him there, breaks the head of the mouse. Mouse returns home with his head bound, saying, "It was I." The woman then angrily kills their baby, at which Mouse runs away with all their food. (H. Tschopik, "Aymara Texts, Lopaca Dialect," *International Journal of American Linguistics* 14 [1948], 108-14).

Another song is a lament of an Aymara soldier in the Chaco war at what his faithless wife has done while he was gone.

Such is the unhappy and hostile world in which the Aymara live. If these, then, are the data, how do we explain them? The present suggestion pretends to be no exhaustive explanation but only one overtone of the well-developed timbre of the phenomenon, and merely attempts to put ethnographic and historic facts into meaningful juxtaposition with each other. For the historical experience of the Aymara people is consistent with Aymara temperament and Aymara culture patterns; Aymara culture and personality are jointly an historical accumulation.

From our earliest knowledge of them the Aymara have had an authoritarian, class-stratified society such as is not uncommonly found among peoples of some agricultural development. Chiefs, it appears, even in ancient "Colla" times had much autocratic power and were carried about in wickerwork litters by their servants, and something like nobles are mentioned; the incumbent of the one chieftainship which has survived into modern times is deeply reverenced. The megalithic ruins of Tiahuanaco in the heart of the Aymara country also argue a highly centralized, theocratic society not unlike that of the Inca who built Cuzco to the north.

The Colla, or colonial-period Aymara, had had states that long resisted the hegemony of the Inca theocratic society, and Inca history recounts that they had repeatedly to reconquer the constantly revolting Aymara. Insofar as they were conquered, the Aymara came under the intense centralization and autocracy of the Inca political and economic structure, the details of which are well known. When Pizarro and his Spaniards conquered Peru, they had scarcely but to effect a palace revolution and place themselves at the apex of a hierarchy already provided them in the prior society and its culture. Indeed, the military miracle was possible, as in Mexico, only because both Inca and Aztec were tightly integrated societies, much centralized, with harshly sanctioned habits of conformity.

With the revolt from Spain, the Aymara in Bolivia came under one of the most unmitigatedly savage and exploitative of peonages to be found anywhere in the New World—a fact that may partly explain why there have been more "revolutions" per year of national life in Bolivia than in any other country in history. Most of these "revolutions" have seen only a circulation of personnel, a demogogic leader coming into power and then exploiting personally the unchanged system as ruthlessly as before—and some of them have been tyrants of the notorious stripe of Francia, Rosas, and Melgarejo. The gambit of the moderately successful is to escape with the loot to Lima; a really successful exploiter escapes to Paris, where some have been known to marry Bourbon royalty on their fortunes. Recently, some of these revolutions have been in part Communist-inspired, as when American personnel were kidnapped as hostages, though their release was finally procured by the central government, mindful of huge subsidy aids from the United States. But if a Communist revolution becomes successful in Bolivia, this will be a replacement by a no more benign totalitarianism than the Aymara have known many times before.

We know something of the results in behavior and morale from experiments of psychologists with varyingly "autocratic" and "democratic" organization of groups of nursery children to advance our hypothesis: if the Aymara, as evidenced in their folktales (and indeed throughout the rest of their culture), are apprehensive, crafty, treacherous, violent, and hostile, one reason for this may be that such a character structure is an understandable response to their having lived under rigidly hierarchic, absolutist, tyrannical economic, military, and religious controls—for perhaps as long as a millennium.

Reference Notes

1. H. Tschopik, "The Aymara," *Handbook of South American Indians, Bulletin* 143, *Bureau of American Ethnology* 2 (1946), 501–73.
2. W. La Barre, *The Indians of the Lake Titicaca Plateau, Bolivia* (= Memoir 68, *American Anthropological Association*, AA 50, no. 1, pt. 2 [January 1948], pp. 39–40, where full references may be found).
3. Complete translations of the folktales on which these preliminary summaries are based, together with a more intensive psychological and psychiatric item-analysis, have since been published in an anthology edited by John Greenway, *The Anthropologist Looks at Myth* (Austin: University of Texas Press, 1966), pp. 130–44.

13. Obscenity: An Anthropological Appraisal

The anthropologist discovers no absolutes with respect to the descriptive content of the obscene representation or word or act. The customary law, so to speak, is always logically prior to the behavior: nothing is obscene that has not been previously defined culturally as such. It is as if, where the culturally styled corset would have its society appear thin, there, and there alone, does the renegade flesh choose to bulge with the imperfectly disguised tension that is the obscene—for that society.

It is true that, since immediately sexual behavior is prohibited in all societies in some contexts (viz., the universal incest taboo)[1] or otherwise in some manner culturally restrained,[2] the sexual is a characteristic root of the obscene. Nevertheless, if public coitus in Yap and Taiwan[3] —even ceremonially open coitus in the Society Islands and elsewhere[4] —is the pattern, then any "obscenity" of the matter disappears here, along with the social disappearance of the neurotic or legally reprehensible voyeur. The same is true with respect to other physiological acts that in our society are a common root of the obscene. Thus, where public micturition and defecation are both condoned and practiced, there the "obscene" exhibitionism of the acts also disappears;[5] and unless cleanliness training has been sufficiently rigorous in a society to obtain the necessary repressions, then its culture will lack scatological humor or obscenity.[6][a]

In these discussions of obscenity, therefore, we must guard against any facile assumption that our parochial patterns, however deeply engrained both emotionally and legally, necessarily constitute human absolutes. For example, there exists in the museum of the University of San Marcos, in Lima, Peru, a reserved section containing collections that are shown only to qualified persons. The ancient Peruvians—not only the Inca proper, but the Chimu and Nazca and others as well—were accustomed to depict in their portrait jars the entire round, without exception, of their daily life, material and non-material.[7][b] Thus, among the scenes portrayed are various styles of coitus and other sexual acts, grotesquely ithyphallic drinking jars, and the like. The point to be made is this: the existence of this segregated "reserved section" is an ethnographic

Reprinted with permission from a symposium entitled Obscenity and the Arts, appearing in *Law and Contemporary Problems* 20 no. 4 (Autumn 1955), 533–43, published by Duke University School of Law, Durham, North Carolina. Copyright 1955 by Duke University.

a. E.g., the *koyemshi*, or obscene "mud clowns," of the Pueblo peoples are the converse of their strict cleanliness training (see reference note 6).

b. The practice has been of inestimable value to botanists, archaeologists, anthropologists, and even psychologists and sexologists. In this last connection, it may be of interest to note that Dr. Alfred Kinsey has a fine representative collection of "obscene" Peruvian pottery (see reference note 7).

commentary on our own society, not on that of the ancient Peruvians. The same principle holds for the Christian tourist viewing the "obscene" carvings on the famous Hindu temple at Kajaraho; he may have met all these things before in Krafft-Ebing, but he finds them unexpected or out of context in a religious edifice.

The relativity of verbal obscenity is even more readily apparent and may be demonstrated by almost mechanical procedures. For example, a major soap-maker recently was considering a name for a new soap powder and had the business acumen to ask a group of linguists to investigate any possible untoward meanings of the name in some fifty foreign languages. In English and in most of the other European languages, it meant "dainty"; in Flemish, it meant "aloof"; in Gaelic, it meant "song"; in Afrikaans, it meant "horse"; in Persian, it meant "hazy" or "dim-witted"; and in Korean, it sounded very much like a word for "lunatic." These were bad enough. But in all the Slavic languages, it was obscene. The proposed new name was hastily abandoned.[8]

The obscene is psychologically close to the humorous in our society—to the sexually and scatologically humorous at least. But whereas such humor, accepted, releases tensions, the obscene arouses anxiety.[9] When relatively "harmless" or lightly repressed materials return to consciousness, then the unregenerate animal wish has skillfully outwitted the psychic censor implanted by social conditioning, and we have a successful "return of the repressed"[10]—though it may still need to retain some protective disguises or maintain a disingenuous ambiguity into which pretended innocence may retreat. For this reason, puns, plays on words, or fortuitously overlapping symbolisms are highly desirable as release-mechanisms for our repressed sexual, sadistic, or scatological components. Scratch any culture-bearer and find a Rousseauist: the brother Adam in us all admires the skill with which the wit both obtains the wish and retains apparent cultural probity. Wit consists precisely in the skillful searching out of these masking ambiguities and overlaps and in their clever contextual compositionings, so that in this sense, our appreciation borders on the esthetic.

Actually, from the point of view of the unconscious, the cliché should be reversed: "I don't care if it's funny, just so it's dirty." But as the strength of repression varies in different individuals—and there may have been varying severity of conditioning even among individuals in the same society—we may, therefore, expect to find that what is "funny" for one person is "dirty" for another. Protective anxiety (disgust) will then lead the latter to withdraw his franchise from the transaction and resume the standard moral pose of the society. Perhaps his superego requires further liquidation in alcohol.

The obscene, relatively to the accepted "humor," is, on the other hand, the word or act which in its direct and blatant form is likely to meet the standard resistance and repressions of the entire group. Once again, the cultural dimension of this is evident, for we can observe subgroup differences. The same upper-class sophisticate who enjoys the virtuoso bedroom or bathroom joke at a cocktail party will be entirely bored with the endless shallow innuendo of popular songs—stating much the same things, but with varying repression-tensions, and hence requiring less intellectual work to circumvent the repression. The victory is too easy, the opponents too undisguised; and since class membership is, in part, attained and kept by varying disciplines of immediate wish, then the immediately scatological is rejected as "vulgar," which is a class-designator rather more than it is a moral judgment.

In a sense, also, obscenity occupies a position midway between the (possibly) reprehensible-humorous and outright-criminal. For example, father-daughter incest in our society is so utterly unthinkable that it is immediate classified as the categorically criminal. Yet, in American Indian stories of the supernatural tricksters "Coyote" and "Raven" (and among the Eskimo, even in sacred myths, as of the seagoddess Sedna), father-daughter incest frequently recurs as a motif in humorous context.[11] Possibly some of the graffiti in our men's rooms occupy this position intermediate between the obscene and the criminal. A good test case of this intermediacy is found in a field experience I had among the Aymara Indians of the region south of Lake Titicaca in Bolivia.[12] These Indians have been subject to European influences since Spanish colonial times, though in remoter regions, they remain relatively unacculturated. I had been questioning an old man at Tiahuanaco on the thoroughly banal kinship system of the group and had asked the native term for "sister-in-law." The old man said something in response and then, for some reason, fell into an evil chuckling. My interpreter, a somewhat mission-acculturated *mestizo*, did not interpret this and tried to brush it off as unimportant or irrelevant. But I persisted, fearful of missing some new point that is the meat of ethnographic research. Finally, but only after considerable resistance, the interpreter translated the old man's response for "sister-in-law" as *spare wife*—thus establishing the conjectural possibility of a former type of polygamy in which a man may marry his wife's sister also.[c] The old man was sufficiently close to the old life to find this funny (as a prohibited, but conceivable, behavioral possibility); but the younger man, indoctrinated with the Christian prohibition of polygamy, was shocked and attempted to protect the ethnographer from the morally reprobated information (as an unthinkable act).

In our society, it must be insisted, obscenity inheres in a definable list of things that may not necessarily be prohibited elsewhere: in the use of tabooed *artistic representations* or *words*, in *nudity* of certain parts of the body, and in the performance of publicly prohibited *acts*. We have already touched upon the first in discussing ancient Peruvian pottery (a variation in "obscenity" in ethnographic space); but variations in "obscenity" are possible in culture-historical time also within the same tradition (e.g., the nudity of classic Greek

---

c. It is true that later my professor at Yale, Dr. G. P. Murdock, an expert in these matters, took me sharply to task on this, but for scientific rather than moral reasons. He properly criticized me for not distinguishing then between "sister-in-law" as brother's wife versus wife's sister, for which English has only one common term. I should make it clear that my Aymara informant was guilty perhaps only of the latter, sororal polygyny, not of fraternal polyandry.

statues and Renaissance sculpture was covered with a fig leaf in Reformation and Victorian times). It is perhaps enough to remark further here that we have no reason to suppose that the large and unmistakably phallic—indeed, essentially and contextually phallic—wooden statues of the ancestors used in Melanesian religious ceremonies evoke any other emotions than awe, reverence, and perhaps fear. Any "obscenity" involved is the artefact of our own cultural projections.

Indeed, in other contexts, the shoe may be on the other foot, and *we* may be accused of obscenity when none, certainly, is intended. A cultivated Chinese gentleman, for example, once remarked that the pronounced and regular rhythms of the Sousa march, "The Stars and Stripes Forever," played by a Marine band, seemed to him almost unbearably lascivious and suggestive of coitus; Chinese classical music, even in dealing with love episodes, is quite discernibly different. For us, however, this vigorous and bombastic music evokes only the masculinity of marching men, the martial theme, and the Fourth of July oratory. With far more ease, we might be persuaded that Liszt's "Liebestraum" was flagrant pornophony, complete with nocturnal emission, since that was its announced programmatic content.

The cultural relativity of the obscene might further be illustrated by an innocent picture which appeared during the war in the North African edition of *Stars and Stripes*. The picture purported to be that of an American GI teaching an Arab the homely art of dunking doughnuts. But what actually is happening here? Is the GI really teaching, or even essentially teaching, the Arab all there is to know about doughnut-dunking? Doughnut-dunking implies a flouting of the injunctions of Emily Post, a male vacation from females who are striving for vertical social mobility, Jiggs and Maggie, the revolt of the American he-man from "Mom"—and much else. The archly bent finger is an American lampoon of the effete tea-drinking Englishman and reminds us of 1776—and who, after all, won that war? It implies the masculine frontier, class muckerism, and Boston versus the rest of the country. There may even be echoed a robust Anglo-Saxon parody of Norman-French manners in Montmorencys and Percivals, and thus recall 1066 and all that. It may be all this and more. But is the Arab, in fact, being "taught" all these culture-historical implications of an alien tradition—about which our GI, in all probability, is neither conscious nor articulate? On the contrary, the Arab brings to it his own cultural apperceptions and interpretations. To be sure, the Arabs knew all about coffee (and sugar too, for that matter) long before Europeans; in fact, the common European names for these two things are derived from the Arabic. The Arab is far more likely to be worried about another matter: is this oddly shaped breadstuff perhaps cooked (O abomination!) in pork-fat; and is this act of eating it not so much naughtily humorous as filthily blasphemous? But perhaps he may be reassured that the cooking fat does not derive from an unclean animal, and he can be happy that it is cottonseed-oil or peanut-oil, possibly laced with beef suet, none of which were prohibited by the Prophet. Where, then, can he search for an explanation of the GI's manifest amusement at himself in doughnut-dunking? Ah, at last it is clear: the doughnut is an obscene symbol for the female (such as is common in Arab life), with coffee "black as night, hot as hell, and sweet as a woman," as the Arab prefers it. Now, perhaps, in universal male confraternity, he can join with his GI friend in tasting the sweetness of women. But these outlandish paynim kaffirs are certainly peculiar buzzards in their symbolisms! However, we are reassured, for these are the Arab's ratiocinations, not ours; we are only dunking doughnuts, and vast disparate cycles of culture history are tangential at only one point—in the dipping of this comestible in this potable.

Blasphemy is, no doubt, also cognate with the obscene in another way. Blasphemy is the utterance of words prohibited of the sacred, but obscenity may be utterance of the tabooed with respect to the secular. A primitive may be forbidden by his religion to utter the name of a dead kinsman or even a word in which a syllable suggests the name or part of the name of his dead relative. But these tremendous sanctions may be no more potent emotionally than those which make taboo to us the utterance of certain thoroughly secular and commonplace words. In a medical work, we may write learnedly of feces; and the missionary back from China may speak of night-soil before the Ladies' Aid Society. Rose fanciers may discuss a preferred manure, animal or vegetable, quite openly at the Elite Garden Club; and even the Bible speaks earthily of dung. Wholly unexceptionable literary works may discourse on excrement, poets may write of ordure and effluvia, and Sir James George Frazer deal insightfully with exuvial magic. An entirely nice girl may tell her college roommate that her boyfriend's line is just so much bull; and little boys playing double-dares yell "chicken" and Mamma does not scold. In heated political discussion at the Faculty Club, the previous Republican government-by-adagency might be pronounced thorough crap (or crud), nobody's feelings be hurt, and the discussion continue on the same high intellectual plane. But under no circumstances, scholarly or otherwise, may one give public utterance to that homely four-lettered Anglo-Saxon vocable, about which, in all conscience, I must leave my readers to guess. The emotional strength of that taboo is quite on a par with the primitive prohibition of the name of the deceased, for all that we, when mourning is over, may mention the name even of a dead spouse with equanimity.

English is fantastically rich and sensitive in its vocabulary categories, but that is because of the peculiar historical experiences of the speakers of English. Genteel and obscene vocabulary categories are a direct descendant, culturally, of the Norman Conquest. The duchess perspires; the middle-class matron is in a rosy dew; but greasy Joan sweats as she keels the pot. Stomach began with the Greek word for "mouth," and then became the esophagus, but now seems to have settled temporarily at the midriff; but no matter—we have many variously colored alternatives: entrails, guts, insides, abdomen, belly, "Little Mary," "bread-basket," tummy, enteron, and coelem besides. The point to be made here is that because of their peculiar historical and philological origins, these words in English are actually gradations of a very fine sort on a gamut from the unexceptionable to the obscene. "Compassion," "sympathy," and "fellow-feeling" all mean literally the same thing, *feeling with* another. But compassion is lofty and abstract; sympathy is kinder, though still a bit formal; and fellow-feeling is downright friendly. What needs to be noted, however, is that the extraordinarily sensitive semantics and contexts of English in its vocabulary categories is a thing by no means to be taken for granted. The Hopi language, for example, has no "proper" versus "obscene" words.[13] All words are on the same mundane, matter-of-fact level, with the exception, perhaps, of a vocabulary-category for "baby-talk," in which ordinary words are mutilated grammatically in stereotyped ways. In the absence of class differences, there are no "educated" versus "vulgar" vocabularies; and if certain matters are tabooed in discussion with certain relatives, they are categorically tabooed with *any* vocabulary. American Indians, in general, are much more sensitive than we are to the *who* in kinship situations; and whereas anything goes with respect to rough verbal or physical horseplay between a man and a woman who are in a kin-determined "joking relationship," those who are in "avoidance relationship" kin-wise will be inordinately shy and bashful in their relationships socially. For example, in one field situation among the Kiowa Indians, I had an old man as informant and his daughter-in-law as the only available interpreter. Since these are governed by a strict "avoidance-relationship," and since I knew almost no Kiowa, the old man talked off into space and not to his daughter-in-law directly, while she talked directly to me in English; in return, she appeared to be talking pointlessly to me in Kiowa (which the old man unofficially heard), after which he talked off into space again and the whole process began all over. Mary Buffalo told me, in high moral dudgeon, that "those Comanche got no shame," because the Comanche happen not to be possessed of some such taboo which the Kiowa had. Possibly we are doing no better than Mary Buffalo when we adduce as universals what are merely our own tribal taboos and obscenities. It is edifying to note, too, that it is precisely in such societies as have the taboo that we find "Coyote," in the funny stories told about him, shamelessly speaking directly to his daughter-in-law and indulging in "joking relationship" behavior or worse. It is funny because it is shockingly incongruous, or funny because it is prohibited—and plainly in the category of the obscene.

On the other hand, whatever our own reactions, the Aztec are not being obscene when they refer to gold as the "offal of the Gods."[14] They are merely relating an etiological myth. Similarly,

In the Brihadáranyaka Upanishad—one of the finest of the Upanishads—there is a passage in which instruction is given to the man who desires a noble son as to the prayers which he shall offer to the gods on the occasion of congress with his wife. In simple and serene language it directs him how—"when he has placed his virile member in the body of his wife, and joined his mouth to her mouth," he should pray to the various forms of deity who preside over the operations of nature: to Vishnu to prepare the womb of the future mother, to Prajapati to watch over the influx of the semen, and to the other gods to nourish the foetus, etc. . . . Yet the gross details of physical union were obviously not unclean to the writers of this and similar passages in the Upanishads.[15]

On the contrary, the Hindus regard the Upanishads as the very highest flights of their religious and philosophical literature; and when it is realized that the worst fate that can befall a man is to die without a son to perform his rites and the cult of his soul after death, then we may guess how deeply serious and religious this language is in Hindu terms.

In the matter of nudity of the body or of body-parts in females, our male-dominated society is, perhaps understandably, ambivalent. Characteristically, in the case of a "living statue" display at the Chicago World's Fair, the law, with sensitive fidelity to the mores, decided that the exposure of both breasts was "obscene," but that the exposure of only one was "art," thus satisfying both church-goers and art-connoisseurs. Two decades ago, it was still being argued whether, with safety to public morals, the male torso might be exposed above the waist on bathing beaches; but for some centuries in our society, the ultimate obscenity has been the display of male genitals, or even their representation in painting and sculpture. Many Malayan and southeast Asiatic peoples are even[d] more rigorous in this respect and do not permit the exposure of male nudity even before other males. The intensity of this repression is shown by the powerful projective sanction of the "evil eye" in which seeing the person does damage to him.[16] But it is impossible to maintain that the total nudity in males of all ages among such people as the Nilotic Nuer[e] can ever have any implication of obscenity to the Nuer themselves.[17] Among the Kwoma of New Guinea, it is not lifelong nudity which is obscene, but the indiscreet public erection.[18] A considerable number of people hide the penis, but not the scrotum, in a phallocrypt; the Sakai of Malaya, for example, slit the perineal T-band to cover the penis but expose a testis on each side.[19] At the other extreme, in Africa, we have "the prudish Baganda, who made it a punishable offence at one time for a man to expose any part of his leg above the knee [though] the wives of the king would attend at his court perfectly naked."[20] The total nudity of one sex but not the other is, of course, a commonplace in ethnological accounts, as is also nudity at one age but not another, or nudity of some status-group but not another, or in one social or religious context but not another.

Indeed, there is a scholastic discrimination of minutiae in obscene versus

d. A variant of this is found among the Atjehnese of northern Sumatra, among whom accidentally catching sight of a male nudity is considered "unlucky" to the viewer (see reference note 16).

e. Nilotics, like the Nuer, among whom the men go naked, dislike clothing; the Nuba-Fung peoples, among whom men also go naked, apparently do not actively dislike clothing (see reference note 17).

nonobscene nudity that approaches the precision even of English vocabulary-categories. The Etruscans and the classic Greeks (in particular the Spartans) regarded total public nudity of males in some contexts with complete unconcern. It was not the exposure of the penis which was obscene, but of the glans. Decorum demanded, therefore, that all men who had to show themselves naked in public, such as boxers, gymnasts, or actors, should wear a *ligatura praeputii*, or *kynodesme*, as is abundantly evidenced in Greek and Etrurian pottery. A similar discrimination is found among the Marquesans of Polynesia, though in other peoples, male infibulation has additional motives.[21]

The total or partial nudity of the female body is quite as much a commonplace among peoples of the world. It may be didactically useful, perhaps, to emphasize the atypicality of what our own tribe senses as obscene: in far and away the majority of peoples of the world and on all continents, the exposure of the breast in nursing a child is quite without any connotation of obscenity whatever, nor is permanent exposure above the waist in women. Indeed, in ancient India, uncovering the breasts was a sign of deference to men on the part of lower-caste women and a sign of respect to superiors. That such a sense of modesty regarding the breasts is almost wholly European is indicated by the Marotse practice of covering the bosom with a mantle when a strange European approaches, though ordinarily this mantle is worn across the back; such behavior is a direct and clear artefact of European missionary attitudes.

Also, it is quite plain that modesty sense by no means always pertains to the genitalia. The famous story is told by Sir Richard Burton of a Moslem woman in Africa who accidentally fell off a camel. Her skirts were around her head, but her husband regarded the contretemps with equanimity. It was no matter that other men knew that his wife was female—for had she not kept her face covered? Curiously, among the Touareg, it is the men who are veiled and do not expose the face, even before other men in eating. A Haida Indian woman is embarrassed to be caught by a strange man without her labret or lower lip plug. Among many Negro groups in Africa, propriety requires the buttocks to be covered, not the genitals. Philippine Islanders and Samoans think it indecent for the navel to be exposed, though every other part may go uncovered. In China, it is an obscenity for a woman to expose her artificially deformed feet to a strange man. Foot modesty is probably a very ancient Asiatic pattern, for it is found also among the Siberian Koryak, and an Eskimo woman in her igloo may be stripped down to a tiny bikini skin garment before strange men if only she keeps her boots on, since removal of the boots has a sexual connotation. Among the Canary Islanders, a people isolated perhaps from Neolithic to early modern times, it was immodest for a woman to expose her breasts or feet. The Koryak regard it as deeply sinful to look upon the face of a dead person. Ainu women cover the mouth when speaking to a man. Some of the body parts involved with modesty seem strange indeed. Rameses III (1198–1167 B.C.) boasted in one of his inscriptions that his rule was so successful that he had made it possible for an Egyptian woman to go anywhere she liked *with her ears exposed*, and no stranger would molest her. The Japanese have erotized the nape of a woman's neck.[22]

With respect to obscene or publicly prohibited *acts*, there is the same lack of universality in what we happen to regard as obscenity. We have already seen that public coitus,[f] repeatedly attested to in firsthand accounts,[23] is by no means unknown in Oceania, though normative ethicists would make this perhaps the very first of obscenities "universally" abhorred by all peoples of the world. Nor among physiological acts is it only coitus that is obscene in public contexts. In some cases, *eating* is an obscene act when performed in the presence of other people or in public; and the same Tahitians who copulated in public would eat separately and privately. The Maldive Islanders ate always in solitude, retiring for this purpose to the innermost part of the house and covering the windows lest passersby observe them; the practice is reported for other Oceanic peoples as well. Many of the "divine kings" in Africa and elsewhere, collected by Sir James G. Frazer in a volume of *The Golden Bough*,[24] never ate in public; perhaps some of the same reasons are involved in the fact that the Pope never dines in public, nor does an American admiral on his flagship.

The Manchus regard kissing in public by men and women as the utmost obscenity, almost as a perversion, although husband and wife as well as lovers may kiss each other stealthily since it has a shameful significance.[25] And yet

> on account of the Manchu system of class in the house, the frankest love intercourse can take place in the room, where several persons are sleeping. The people then show that they see nothing, hear nothing. The husbands of these women, if all regulations and customs are observed, are not shocked at all by their wives' unfidelity with their [the husbands'] young relatives.[26]

Even more striking, from our point of view, is that among the same Manchu who regard public kissing with such horror, it is quite customary for a mother to take the penis of her small son into her mouth and to tickle the genitals of her little daughter in petting them in public.[27]

Ceremonial dances not infrequently imitate the coitus of animals or of humans, often in the most sacredly religious of contexts. The coitus of animals is imitated especially in Siberia; of humans, perhaps most commonly in Africa and Oceania.[28] But what seems another curious inconsistency to us occurs among the classical Japanese. From the Héian period onward, and perhaps earlier, the Japanese have had the sacred *kagura* dance performed on the stage of a Shinto shrine at village festivals. In the early days, the sacred *kagura* was a naïvely erotic dance which "adopted so primitive a form of vulgar indecency that it could not be performed today."[29] Something resembling the ancient *kagura* may still be viewed in remoter Japanese villages, but western-acculturated

---

f. The practice appears to be established especially for Tahiti (where it was reported by Captain Cook and numerous others), but it was also found in the Margonne and Caroline Islands and perhaps elsewhere.

Japanese authorities, with a sensitive attention to "face," attempt to keep these from the view of European visitors. Nevertheless, it is the same Japanese with their perfectly candid *kagura* dance who so vehemently object to the "obscenity" of public kissing[30] that modern American movies must be drastically edited before showing to Japanese audiences.

This discussion has attempted to show, through comparative examples, the anthropological relativity of obscenity, whether in words, artistic representations, nudity of various parts of the body, or publicly prohibited acts. But it should be noted that we have largely included only those matters relevant to what we in our society would consider obscene. We perform with indifference a great number of acts (such as drinking milk, blowing the nose, eating a beefsteak, or holding food in the left hand) which various oriental peoples view with inexpressible horror. Nowhere can we find those absolutes which normative ethicists desire to discover in order to support their own tribal rationale through a naïve *consensus gentium*. There are no such human universals. Infrahuman animals lack "obscenity" as they lack "modesty," and the various tribes of men have widely varying concepts of both. All such notions are the artefact of culture and tuition. All that we can postulate of the social animal, man, is that he has the *capacity* for repression through socialization or enculturation, and hence can have very intense *reactions* to the prohibited or the obscene as defined by his society—but so far as any "universality" of descriptive *content* of these categories is concerned, this is wholly the prescription, cultural or legal, of his own social group or subgroup.

Reference Notes

1. Weston La Barre, *The Human Animal* (Chicago: University of Chicago Press, 1954), pp. 121–30.
2. See chaps. 6, "Father Comes Home to Stay," and 7, "And Makes it Legal," in La Barre, *Human Animal*, pp. 98–111.
3. C. S. Ford and F. A. Beach, *Patterns of Sexual Behavior* (New York: Harper & Bros, 1951), p. 68.
4. Paolo Mantegazza, *Sexual Relations of Mankind* (New York: Anthropological Press, 1932), pp. 34, 37, 135.
5. John G. Bourke, *Scatologic Rites of All Nations* (New York: Johnson Reprint Corporation, 1968).
6. Matilda C. Stevenson, "The Zuñi Indians, Their Mythology, Esoteric Fraternities, and Ceremonies," *Annual Report of the Bureau of American Ethnology* 23 (1904), 3-608. See also John G. Bourke, *The Urine Dance of the Zuni Indians of New Mexico*, Privately Printed (1920).
7. *Ancient Peruvian Erotic Art*, slide lecture narrated by Alfred Kinsey, at the Central States Anthropological Society, 6 May 1955, Bloomington, Indiana.
8. See Ryan, "Business Enlists the Gift of Tongues," New York Times, 15 May 1955, sect. 3., p. 1, col. 2.
9. Sigmund Freud, "Wit and its Relation to the Unconscious," in *The Basic Writings of Sigmund Freud* (New York: Modern Library, 1938), p. 633. See also John J. Honigmann, "A Cultural Theory of Obscenity," *Journal of Criminal Psychopathology* 5 (1944), 715-33.

10. Weston La Barre, "The Psychopathology of Drinking Songs," *Psychiatry* 2 (1939) 203–12.
11. "Coyote" tales: G. A. Dorsey, *Pawnee Mythology* (Washington: Carnegie Institution, 1906), pp. 430, 433, 438, 439, 447, 451, 453, 460, 463–65. "Raven" tales: Franz Boas, "Kwakiutl Tales," *Columbia University Contributions to Anthropology* 2 (1910) and 26 (1935). Sedna legends: Franz Boas, "The Central Eskimo," *Annual Report, Bureau of American Ethnology* 6 (1888), 399–699, pp. 583 ff.
12. Weston La Barre, *The Aymara Indians of the Lake Titicaca Plateau, Bolivia*, Memoirs of the American Anthropological Association 68 (1948).
13. Benjamin Lee Whorf, *Four Articles on Metalinguistics* (Washington: Foreign Service Institute, 1949).
14. Paul Radin, *The Story of the American Indian* (New York: Boni & Liveright, 1927), p. 104.
15. Edward Carpenter, *Intermediate Types Among Primitive Folk* (London: G. Allen & Co., 1914), pp. 132–33.
16. C. Snouck Hurgronje (trans. A. W. O'Sullivan), *The Achehnese*, 2 vols. (Leyden: E. J. Brill, 1906), 2:42.
17. C. G. and B. Z. Seligman, *Pagan Tribes of the Nilotic Sudan* (New York: Humanities Press, 1950), p. 17. For those interested in nudity, the best summary of primitive materials is to be found in Edward Westermarck, *The History of Human Marriage*, 3 vols., 5th ed. (London: Macmillan & Co., 1925), 1:418–54 and 497–571.
18. John W. M. Whiting, *Becoming a Kwoma* (New Haven: Yale University Press, 1941), pp. 49, 51, 75–77, 86–87.
19. N. Annandale and H. C. Robinson, *Fasciuli Malayensis* (New York: Longmans, 1903–4), pp. 32–33.
20. Westermarck, *Human Marriage*, 1:545, citing H. H. Jonston, *The Uganda Protectorate*, 2 vols. (London: Hutchinson & Co., 1904), p. 771.
21. E. J. Dingwall, *Male Infibulation* (London: J. Bale Sons & I Danielsson, 1925); C. J. Eberth, "Ethnological Remarks," in "Die männlichen Geschlechtsorgane," *Handbuch der Anatomie des Menschen*, Bd. 7, Teil 2, Abteilung 2 (Jena: G. Fischer, 1904); N. E. Himes, *A Medical History of Contraception* (Baltimore: Williams & Wilkins, 1936), pp. 320–31.
22. Weston La Barre, "The Cultural Basis of Emotions and Gestures," *Journal of Personality* 16 (1947), 49–68. See also L. Hopf, *The Human Species* (New York: Longmans, Green & Co., 1909), pp. 307–8; Cook, "The Aborigines of the Canary Islands," *American Anthropologist* 2 (1900), 451–70; Waldemar Jochelson, *The Koryak* (Jessup North Pacific Expedition, Publ. 6, 1908); J. Batchelor, *The Ainu of Japan* (New York: F. H. Revell Co., 1895), p. 35; J. H. Breasted, *A History of Egypt*, 2nd ed. (New York: C. Scribner's Sons, 1919), pp. 484–85.
23. C. P. C. Fleurieu, *Voyage autour du Monde par Etienne Marchand, An VI* [1797], 6 vols. (Paris: Imprimerie de la République, An VI–VIII [1798–1800]), 1, pp. 52–53, 60, 171–74. For other early voyages, see La Barre, *Human Animal*, p. 344 (pp. 353–54 in 4th and later editions).
24. J. G. Frazer, *The Golden Bough*, 3rd ed., 12 vols. (London: Macmillan & Co., 1919), 3:116–19.
25. S. M. Shirokogoroff, "Social Organization of the Manchus," *Journal of the North China Branch of the Royal Asiatic Society*, 3rd Extra Volume (1924), p. 101.
26. Shirokogoroff, *Manchus*, p. 151.
27. Ibid., p. 122.
28. M. C. Kahn, "Notes on the Saramaccaner Bush Negroes of Dutch Guiana," *American Anthropologist* 31 (1929), 468–90, esp. 468–85.
29. *Japan Year Book, 1939–40* (Foreign Affairs Association of Japan, 1939), p. 813.
30. A. E. Crawley, *Studies of Savages and Sex* (New York: Johnson Reprint Corporation, 1959), pp. 113–36.

14. Psychoanalysis and the Biology of Religion

An answer has never been forthcoming, indeed few seem ever to have asked the question: *why*, given the empirical inadequacies of magic and the flagrant lack of consensus regarding religious "truths," are both magical and religious behaviors so fervent, ubiquitous, and persistent among all the peoples of the earth? A flaccid cliché has it that both magic and religion represent "wishful thinking." But *what experiences lend plausibility* to the wish? And how can mere wish become a "collective representation"? Theorists have provided numerous etic explanations, such, for example, as that religion serves societal functions—the religious believers' subjective stance being regarded as objectively irrelevant. But function is not essence. Nor has it occurred to behavioristic observers to enter the emic minds of practitioners, in order to examine the notorious epistemological anomalies of these beliefs. In fact, however, all human infants *learn ontogenetically* the affective stances that are behind both magic and religion, a thesis that can be demonstrated in species-specific human biology. Indeed, the very differences between magic and religion can also be thus explained, and even the differences between types of magic.

To explain the omnipresent differences between magic and religion, anthropologists have commonly sought objectivist external clues, for example that magic is private and religion social. This view can scarcely be maintained when it is obvious that magic rituals are very often social (whether in context, content, function, or intention) and that much of religion is ineffably private. Further, in objective ethnographic fact, magic and religion are not infrequently co-present, and sometimes mixed. In default of empirical proofs and in view of the lack of consensus concerning the efficacy of magic acts and religious behaviors, it would seem that the distinctions between them must be sought elsewhere, viz., in *differing subjective stances*. Much criticized for being "too biologistic," Freudian body-based psychology is here peculiarly available for explaining these elusive differences, which, moreover, obtain cross-culturally in human biology.

Fifty years ago, cultural anthropologists were concerned to emphasize the exotic specificities of each society, in order to attack culture-bound notions of what "human nature" consisted in, and to criticize unproven Fraserian as-

This chapter is excerpted from the Plenary Session Address at the annual meeting of the American Psychoanalytic Association, Quebec, 30 April 1977. It later appeared in the *Journal of Psychological Anthropology* 1 (1978), 57–64. Reprinted by permission. The complete address, "Freudian Biology, Magic, and Religion," was published in the *Journal of the American Psychoanalytic Association* 26 no. 4 (1978), 813-30

sumptions concerning "the psychological unity of mankind"—as though to "test the limits" of variability in human cultural behavior (for example, Malinowski's critique of the Oedipus complex). Twenty years ago, anthropologists sought to show, now on much better empirical grounds, just what were the pan-human characteristics generic to all mankind (for example, the nuclear family and the universal mother-son incest taboo). At the present time we are criticizing some of the overly sharp distinctions then made between human behavior and that of infrahuman primates, some of whom now seem to be incipient hunters and at least occasional meat-eaters, to use tools, and even at times to exhibit something like learned group-culture. My present purpose is to criticize certain extremes of this last position and to show that there do exist species-specific traits in some human institutions, namely magic and religion.

Recently, psychologists have stated that "elephants wave branches at the moon with what our observer might infer is superstitious reverence," and that golden hamsters are superstitious because they can be induced experimentally to show behaviors which the human observer can then judge are "irrational." These interpretations seem to me naive anthropomorphic projections, which show a poor sense of what magic and religion are really like. To refine our understanding of these transitional animal/human traits, we would do better to contrast human with higher-ape behaviors, rather than with those of elephants and golden hamsters.[1]

One striking difference is that higher anthropoids do not lachrymate, whereas human babies, and indeed their later adult counterparts, do cry with lachrymation when they are physically or psychologically discomfited. Ashley Montagu[2] has suggested that whereas infrahuman primate babies are characteristically carried about clinging to the mother's fur, by contrast human babies are not, but are sometimes left physically separate, while the mother is busy with other affairs. This means that when hungry, or otherwise in pain, the baby must cry loudly, and often at length, to summon the mother with triumphant success, whereas the clinging ape-baby need only seek the proximate pectoral source for sustenance.

Now, the cells responsible for the sense of smell die when they are dried out; and, in crying at length, the passage of large amounts of air over the nasal mucous membranes would tend to dry them out. Lachrymation, then, is at first not so much a form of communication (such as it may later become in compelling interindividual response) as it is a new adaptation of normally present eye lubrication to the additional task of repairing nasal membrane desiccation. This thesis is confirmed in the fact that we sometimes also "laugh until we cry" when the emotions involved are subjectively quite the opposite, but while the same physiological need for lachrymation remains identical, viz., from the passage of large amounts of air over the nasal membranes. Such species-specific differences have relevance to the uniqueness of magical behavior and religious beliefs in man. Certainly the magic cry is *successful* for infants in summoning help for their needs, in spite of such physiological danger as would attend it without lachrymation. Hence, we must assume that such complex behavior is *adaptive* in the neotenous human.

No theory other than the present psychoanalytical one, we repeat, has ever attempted to show *why*, or even to note the presence of the problem, when magical and religious behaviors are so often disconfirmed by other later experience, they are nevertheless firmly, even fervently believed in and resorted to. A rigorously oriented human biology will explain this, and indeed much more. For all neotenous and largely noninstinctual human beings pass through phases of ontogenetic ego growth, during which each one of these behaviors is *temporarily adaptive and relevant*. But in each case, the limits of such phase-usefulness are reached each time a new *kind* of object-adaptation is required of the maturing individual.

The big-brained human baby, in a sense prematurely born with respect to any instinct-guided adult-like adaptations, is well equipped for *experiencing*, but very poorly equipped for *direct accomplishment* of, its biological wishes and needs. That is, the highly and long dependent human being is a learning animal, such that personal psychological learning and cultural adaptations from the past experience of the group tend to replace rigidly but narrowly once-and-for-all adaptive animal instincts, and indeed much of culture tends to discipline and edit the expression of remaining raw animal impulses.

Functionally, the human fetus is omnipotent in his first womb environment, for in that phylogenetically perfected Eden all biological needs are equivalent to their instant accomplishment. Small wonder, then, that societies repeatedly fantasize some far-off original Eden in the infancy of man (it lay, rather, in the infancy of the individual), and that in the "cosmic consciousness" of mystics and pantheists, the individual fantasizes a oneness with the universe, as though organism and environment were still symbiotically one through some omnibenevolent placenta (that original universe was the womb). But at birth, cast rudely out of that Eden, the erstwhile fetus must learn a new oxygenation technique in breathing, new body-heat homeostasis, and a new mode of food intake. Fixation at nonbreathing obeys Thanatos, as does marasmatic fixation at noneating; only breathing and suckling obey Eros, each a new synthesis with an object, with oxygen in the extra-uterine world, and milk in the mother's breast.

It is significant that in Upanishadic attempts to re-reach that Nirvanalike state of mystic desirelessness—"O thou jewel in the flower of the lotus!" the fetus in the womb (or, perhaps more literally in Hinduist thought the male principle, spirit, ensconced in the female, materia)—the control of breathing should be the technique ritually used; or that hells awaiting the sinful are fiery or frozen, too hot or too cold for human comfort; or that in bargains with the supernatural, fastings and food-taboos and food-sacrifices should be so prominent. Of course it is true that all other mammals save the monotremes are womb-born and hence have the same need for new postnatal adaptations. However, these higher mammals are biologically more mature and better prepared for birth, whereas only humans have the extravagant discrepancy between large, experiencing brains and protracted, near-total dependence *on others* in their physically immature postnatal state. In this lie the roots of magic and religion.

In the contemporary trend to minimize animal/human differences, much is made of the possibility that, with considerable effort and manipulation, chimpanzees can be taught limited kinds of human speech and even symbolizing. Much of this may be simple conditioning in an intelligent ape; certainly ape cries in the wild appear to be semantically "closed," with precious little of what we could interpret as generative grammar. In any case, the quantitative difference between human symbolic behavior and that of apes is so enormous as to mean that, in quantum leap, both culture and language have species-specific qualitative difference in humans.

Consider that, after years-long experience of infantile dependency, and of an impotence during which the magic cry successfully commands the presence of mother, the human individual—that is, by and large, all individuals in all human societies—then learns to talk. Human speech is in quality a biologically unprecedented technique for precise interindividual communication. Consider also that after years-long experience of physical dependence and helplessness, the individual, at about the same time, learns to walk. Both walking and talking, *especially after such long delays*, are enormously significant to the individual emotionally. Much of desire remains inchoately nonverbal throughout life. But one has only to observe the differences in ego terms between the babe-in-arms and the toddler to realize that talking and walking dramatically enhance the relationship to the human and physical environments respectively.

And now consider the two nearly universal types of sympathetic magic, homeopathic or effigy magic, and contagious or exuvial magic. Effigy magic is based on the belief that as the wax image *symbolizes* the enemy, so malevolent damage done to the image will also damage the enemy, "like for like." When Adam names the animals paraded before him, the name magically *is* the animal—and Plato still believed that the word *creates* the thing. What godlike power the use of symbols now gives us! Similarly, learning to walk gives another powerful new adaptation, a real potency of the physical body in a larger real universe. Indeed, the emotive "reality" of the physical universe begins in an ability to *handle* it. Further, the ability to manipulate the physical environment is the basis of our whole "alloplastic" human evolution, the control and creation of things outside the genetic body and organism-skin.

Contagious magic believes that if we can obtain a part of the enemy's organism—his hair, blood, sputum, feces, or other exuviae—we can then control his body, part-for-whole. Thus, symbolic effigy-magic overextrapolates the real powers we learned from symbolizing in speech: the symbol is considered to be the thing. Likewise, contagious part-for-whole magic illegitimately overextrapolates our personal experience of the nature of organism: the feces and sputum are *no longer functionally part* of our enemy's organism, and they are never part of one's own.

Hence, while walking and talking *do* give us new powers, they do *not* preserve the omnipotence that we once knew in the womb or in infantile management of mother and that we think we still have in any discrepancy between wish and world. Old adaptations are seductive precisely because of their experienced power. We must sometimes *unlearn* old adaptations to make new ones. The magic of words has its limitations. At one time the magic cry did in fact summon mother and procure help for needs, and magic words still seem miraculously to manipulate the human universe. But, alas, even the most powerfully abusive word-magic will not control a stubbornly nonfunctioning internal combustion engine. The wise child learns that "Sticks and stones will break my bones / But words will never hurt me"—at the same time that he can still magically use them against others in symbolic effigy-magic.

Hovering behind magic is Lady Luck, an inchoate but cherishing mother-figure, always ready to edit physical reality for her favored one. And rubbing Aladdin's lamp brings at least a vaguely anthropomorphic, male, magically omnipotent genie outside one, but still categorically owned. The magician pulls quasi-neural strings to which nothing is attached, certainly not the organism of his enemy, whether stimulated or particulated. The mystic supposes some placental attachment to an omnibenevolent environment still to exist, the religionist more specifically to the omnipotent-others, his parental gods.

Thus, religion, the belief in spiritual beings, requires a more highly developed experience of individual identity and, through our projection of *experienced subjectivity*, of the emotional reality[a] of other subjectivities around us. (Of course we can also overextrapolate this *anima* illegitimately to sun, moon and stars, streams, winds, and whatever, because these move or are warm like ourselves.) Intense experience of *subjective personality* and intense libidinal ties to loved *persons* are required in order to suffer the death of others or to imagine the possibility of one's own. I think cows do not know or fear death, insofar as they lack both intense personal subjectivity and intense libidinal ties.

---

a. "The last and logically irrefutable word of the pure intellectuality of the ego on the relationship to other objects is a solipsism, which cannot equate the reality of other living beings and the whole outside world of personal experience, and speaks of them as more or less living phantoms or projections. When Freud ascribed to the unconscious the same physical nature which one traces as a quality of one's own conscious ego, he made a step that was only probable in logic but never demonstrable in the direction of positivism. I do not hesitate to compare this identification with those which we recognize as the prerequisite of libidinal transference. They lead ultimately to a kind of personification or animistic conception of the entire world around us. All this is 'transcendent' viewed from the logical-intellectual standpoint. We ought to replace this mystic sounding word by the expression 'transference' or 'love,' and courageously assert that the knowledge of a part, perhaps the most important part, of reality is not intellectual but only to be obtained *experientially* as conviction." (Sandor Ferenczi, "Contraindications to the 'Active' Psycho-Analytic Technique," in *Further Contributions to the Theory and Technique of Psycho-Analysis* [London: Hogarth Press, 1926], p. 229.)

But death is surely one of the major preoccupations in world religions.

Religion and magic constitute not so much objective differences in the nature of any cosmic or social reality as they do differing *subjective attitudes* toward these extrasomatic not-self realities. Magic arrogantly *commands* impersonal external reality to obey the mana power of omnipotent wish. But religion *beseeches* person-like spirits or the ghosts of persons, parents, and ancestors, omnipotently to accomplish our needs *for us*. Each of us knew this adaptive technique in early childhood—and experienced success of it. Thus, while not necessarily earlier in cultural history, in life-history the impersonal magical commanding, or projection and incorporating, of ambiguously placed mana represents an *earlier individual phase* of adaptive ego growth than does religion, a later phase-development which knows in emotional reality the existence of persons. (Hence there can be no historic "cultural evolution" of magic and religion, with spurious questions of which-came-first, and both may occur mixed at any point of time or complexity in cultures.)

Magic and religion are near-ubiquitous responses in human societies because they represent universally human experiences in individual ego-growth, but illegitimately extrapolated or regressed-to adaptations to new objects: persons and things. We must learn the limitations of our hands and our mouths, organisms, and symbols, if we would become chastened to a scientific stance, there with enormous new alloplastic potencies since, in surrendering still more narcissistic omnipotence, we have accorded the object a new emotional reality and independence of the self. We buy adaptive potency each time the baby in us surrenders another fragment of its initial illusory omnipotence, and by abdicating godhood discovers the world, the objective dignity of other persons and things. In each case, a long powerlessness is followed by real power. The gold of self is traded for love; the paper money of narcissism is exchanged for the nourishment of object-love.

Yet organisms dare not completely surrender the arrogant ownership and temerarious control of one part of the world, that within the organic skin. The perigenetic defenses of germ plasm (Ferenzci) extend beyond the metazoan body even to the bounds of society and culture themselves (Roheim). Some narcissism is necessary for life: any organism must preserve its finicky homeostases, psychic or physiological, in order to remain an organism, with contingent power over skin-contained reality, however finite in space and time.

Thus, when individuals and societies reach the limit of ego-adaptive techniques, at each new threat to this remaining narcissism, in the face of new historic vicissitudes, they tend to regress to using earlier successful adaptive techniques. Each authentically new ego adaptation to environment enhances Eros, in ever-more-improbable and complex life; fixation or regression, Thanatos, the more-probable, death.

Shamans and their societies represent Oedipal-regressive relationships, in which the paranoid shaman has the parental omnipotence or the magic power, and his clients a childlike dependence on him. Given Freudian ontogenesis of the self in the neotenous human animal, we need not suppose that, because of learned convictions, magical and religious stances are now adaptive in the new crisis cult. Nor do noncommonsensical beliefs, passing back and forth between shaman and society, pose any epistemological or group-fallacy problem, since all in the group have experienced these once-useful power techniques, and both shaman and society wish to believe. The eerily supernatural omniscience and compelling power of charisma, streaming from the shaman like irresistible magnetic mana, is the exact measure of his appeal to his clients' conscious and unconscious wish-fantasies. He is so unerringly right because he so pinpoints these wishes. In personal or societal crises, promulgation of the shaman's new wish-messages is effective because, in crisis, the supernatural cult diffuses quite like secular culture in any other of its manifestations, and shaman and society regress together to ontogenetically earlier techniques of adaptation.

An animal without *prolonged infancy* in a *nuclear family* has no *experiential basis* for regressive belief in magic or religion. Elephantine waving of branches at the moon, whatever it is ethologically, is not ethnologically religious behavior, and the conditioned irrationality of golden hamsters is not superstitious magic. Only long-dependent infants can invent magic. Only Oedipal apes can have religion.

Reference Notes

1. Ronald K. Siegel, "Religious Behavior in Animals and Man," MS 1976, citing R. Carrington, *Elephants* (New York: Basic Books, 1959), and I. Douglas-Hamilton and O. Douglas-Hamilton, *Among the Elephants* (New York: Viking Press, 1975). Timothy Keith-Lucas, unpublished experimental work on golden hamsters at Duke University.
2. Ashley Montagu, "Natural Selection and the Origin and Evolution of Weeping in Man," *Science* 130 (4 December 1959), 1572–73; "Natural Selection and the Origin and Evolution of Weeping in Man," *Journal of the American Medical Association* 174 (24 September 1960), 392–97; *The Human Revolution* (New York: Bantam Books, 1967), pp. 98–102.

15. Countertransference and the Beatniks

Adolescents, who have not yet joined our tribal cult, have an uncanny ability to be provocative of their parents. The reason for this, perhaps, is that adolescents, from personal experience, have a close knowledge of the vulnerabilities of their parents and know how to combat parents' imposed and unwelcome cultural burdens; children also well know how to punish parents for discrepancies between pretense and behavior. Adolescence is *par excellence* a time of conflict between the individual and his society. Each generation is a ready critic of the failure of parents to provide some needed security, psychological or otherwise. The parents seemed to promise to the child omnipotence, omniscience, and omnibenevolence—and now at adolescence what happens to these pretenses to godhood? Youngsters are by no means necessarily adequate critics of the long-range past, because they do not really know it. But as critics of the immediate cultural past in the person of their parents, they are uncanny and unbeatable.

All beatniks are not adolescent in chronological age. And yet they are somehow doing what is functionally the job of adolescents in our culture. The critique of the old by the young is the moving finger of history and cultural change. And on the other side, when we observe the magisterial tones of such adult "squares" as John Ciardi, in his witty article, "Epitaph for the Dead Beats,"[1] or Robert Brustein on "The Cult of Unthink,"[2] it is hard not to discern the defensive and angry tone of the parent.

To the parental generation, the ingrate beatnik seems to be the true *Rebel Without a Cause*—for have not we who lived through the Great Depression made prosperity permanent and hence earned the right to feel superior to our parents and to be admired by our children? What, after all, could anyone imaginably ask beyond what we lacked, material security? Haven't we more than supplied our parents' lacks that we, of all things, should be accused of new lacks as parents and as people? Isn't the cult of success self-evidently right, now and forever? We have set our national house in order, and now they complain about the international scene? We are successes as private persons, and so they have to criticize us for being failures as public persons? What are they fussing about? Why, if beatniks would only consent to become true Americans, like us they could be maggots drowning in butter! We have poop

The Group for the Advancement of Psychiatry at its twice-yearly meetings, in addition to three-day committee meetings, has a general Sunday Symposium organized by the various working committees. The committee on Adolescence, to which I served as a consultant at twenty-three meetings, presented one such symposium on beatniks, with Allen Ginsberg, Peter Orlovsky, Francis Rigney, and myself as speakers. This chapter on now historical ethnography has not been published before.

fins on our cars, eight lights in front and sixteen in the back, and yet they still complain?

The beatnik centers originally in San Francisco, one of the most distinctive and culturally diverse cities in the Western world. Beyond a colorful and extensive Chinatown, upper Grant Street climbs Telegraph Hill and becomes the haunt of the beats, "Endsville" as opposed to "Squaresville" where the rest of us live. Formerly an Italian quarter, Endsville is now a Bohemia of several blocks on Grant Street between Columbus and Filbert and on near-adjacent cross streets. North Beach habitués congregate in such places as The Co-Existence Bagel Shop (né Herb's Delicatessen, co-proprietor Peter Bury), The Coffee Gallery (the bohemia's art gallery), The Place (its Town Hall), The Anxious Asp (its pub), and The Cellar (its dim smoky subterranean night club).

These places typically have sawdust-strewn floors, the walls are hung with angry nonrepresentational avant-garde paintings, and there are tables around which habitués sit for hours, often wordlessly but with bitter stares into their espresso cups or into the void. These are the scenes of poetry reading and jam sessions, drinking and declamation. For example, The Place, a small beer-and-vino bistro holding twenty-five people—according to Fire Department regulations only—has a "Blabbermouth Night" every Monday: from a soapbox on a tiny balcony over the bar one may declaim on any subject, whether obscene or facetious, for three minutes, often followed by rebuttal speeches, and sometimes sardonically or seriously a Message is launched to the highly vocal audience. The crowd changes constantly, for, to "make the scene," one goes ceaselessly from bar to bar. Interspersed among these meeting places are many tiny hole-in-the-wall "art galleries" such as The Scene, and gift shops; a characteristic object for sale in one of these last is a small flat cobblestone inked with the imprint of a grasping hand in red ink and labeled "Weapon, World War IV."

A beard is the badge of a practicing beatnik, and sandaled feet. Clothing is elaborately casual, preferably offbeat in an individualistic fashion—though inevitable conformity does creep in—dirty, ideally, beyond description. But such a picture is oversimplified. There are also the highly stylized motorcycle hoods who march turgid-aggressive up to the beatnik bars, all black leather and toughness and group insignia, phallic feckless brutality in black belts and boots. Others present have the Ivy Look in clothing, but many of these phonies are weekend beats or amateurs from Bay area colleges. The beatnik girl affects the carefully nondescript in dress as well—a beat-up blouse, preferably of alien ethnic origin, and any kind of skirt or toreador pants or whatever, perhaps black cotton stockings, fetid and frayed once-white cotton sneakers, no makeup on a fishbelly-white and bitter-vacant face, and with either a peeled-onion ponytail or stringy long Charles Addams hair. One typically untypical young female wears custom-built shoes, jet high-heeled and pointed like tight Edwardian highbuttons but ending at the top metamorphosed into cowboy boots. Padrice Seamus O'Sullivan, an unkempt thirty-some man with a deep-lined face, self-styled "the last of the great romantic poets," affects high boots and a longplumed hat. Blacks, almost invariably male and variably plausible, are a constant feature of the scene; their complete acceptance is a fetish of the beats. All the above are the "professional beats" and exhibitionist phonies, usually despised by the working artists and poets, intellectuals, and novelists.

There is a special in-group lingo of the beatnik. A "swinging cat" must "make the scene" and "get with it Daddy-O" lest he be a "square." He seeks "kicks" of any kind, he may "whiff the pod," "take a fix" or be "flying high on tea." He may "dig Existentialism the most" or be "way out" on Zen Buddhism—"crazy, man" and all that "all-right jazz." He may "have it made" with a "way-out chick," i.e. "share the rent" of a "pad" (also used as a verb, e.g. "Pad me, Joe baby, let's blast off"). Even on a "chicken-run" the keynote is "cool," for "life is a lousy drag" of infinite ennui and bottomless despair. If youthful cheerfulness keeps breaking in, it must be raucous and ironical, covering a base of centuries of disenchanted experience.

In beatnik bars the men's rooms bear grafitti on the walls, from the mock-profound "Some day the steel will ring" or "Red is a Ned-swinger" (meaningless, as Red, present in The Cellar, when questioned, laughingly informed the square ethnographer), to the cynical and blasphemous pseudo-ad "Jesus saves, Why don't you? (Bank of America)" or the tantalizing "Americans, go home!" and the bitter Easter message, "Man, they nailed me!" The men's room of The Anxious Asp is papered with the Kinsey Report on the sexual behavior of the human female. My social-worker companion said the "chicks' john" was evidently less written-on, although one acid comment advised, "Never love a beatnik!"

The beatniks represent a "wide spectrum of behavior—happy, sick, tragic, creative and just plain no-good," to quote Dr. Francis Rigney of the San Francisco Veterans Administration Hospital, from whom I take the following figures. He thinks there are altogether only five or six hundred authentic beatniks. One-third of the "hard core" class themselves as "writers," one-fourth as "painters" and one-sixth as "musicians." The average age of the men is thirty; of the girls, twenty-three; and males outnumber females three to one. Their average education is two years of completed college work. In origin, 20 percent are from the Bay Area and 50 percent from the East Coast, including 10 percent from New York City alone. Dr. Rigney finds three types among them, the character-neurotic, the chronically anxious, and the passive-aesthetic—all of whom "have made society the verbal scapegoat of their own neuroticism." The beatniks, he says, "have walked out on society and like any group of sick people they want to be left alone."

But some beats, surely, are ambivalent about their shunning of society; one sometimes thinks that whatever substance of identity these have found for themselves would fade, were there not "squares" to be their foils and audience. Indeed, their curiously conformist "nonconformism" derives its own tyrannical style from the fact that it is merely the psychopathic negative of the square—who, in being so conformist himself, sets a rigid countertype to be avoided. Furthermore, the beatniks are quite self-conscious and aware of themselves as, in part, a creation of journalistic publicity. They may protest their wish to be alone, and they doubtless genuinely despise the squares who boorishly invade their domains, and yet at times they seem desperately to need an audience, if only to discover who they themselves are. Without their Boswells of the press, they would also miss some special opportunities for shock and denunciation. The Grayline Bus now includes Grant Street in its tours of San Francisco By Night with much the same sight-seeing attitude as the trip to Chinatown on the lower reaches of the street. Squares are given the "turn-on." The Old Lady from Dubuque may shock her Friday Morning Garden Club with tales of the chick seen naked from the waist up talking to two men at the window above the Bagel Shop—but it is the chick who is closest to the window, and she is performing partly for the tourists' benefit, quite as night-life attitudinizing is done to edify visiting squares. This last is strictly a "benefit performance," partly arcane hipster jargon, partly fool-gulling innuendo, served up with a frosty glance that returns the insult. (And, indeed, if you treat people like natives they will act like natives, and the tourists, one must admit, have largely "asked for it.")

Whatever beatniks are or are not in themselves, they are often thoroughly upsetting to many people. They are likewise uncannily attractive, though they also often arouse attitudes defensive of our own vested cultural interests, and they are often firmly rejected as being one kind of person it may be personally desirable or socially useful to be. In turn, from the beginning, beatniks have made no bones about their hatred and contempt for contemporary American society and its values. The poet O'Sullivan especially feels the persecution of the "cossacks," and one policeman said "I am here to break their backs," and another, "If Jesus Christ came down here barefooted, I'd rap him with a 'vag' charge." In its representatives, Society replies in kind to the beatniks' contempt. Few literary critics or writers show any sympathy for them. Wallace Stegner[3] calls their culture "a dreary borrowing, an inward-turning if there ever was one, a death wish in a crying towel." "The simple fact is that they go around with their heads in their armpits, complaining about how the world smells," writes James Shock. "They are a group of individuals, psychologically ageless, living individual existences, confirming one another's presence from time to time, waiting not for Godot but for time to run out," as Thomas Albright[4] writes.

It is their intellectual pretensions that seem most to infuriate society with the beatniks. Kerouac, their high priest, has been called "a man belligerently exalting his own inarticulateness" by the critic Robert Brustein. "He is hostile to the mind, petulant toward tradition, and indifferent to order and coherence." The beats are "expatriates of the past . . . having abdicated the traditional responsibilities of the avant-garde—that of facing existing culture squarely and honestly if only to criticize, condemn, or demolish it—they seem to slough off all responsibility whatever." Pretending vaguely to be intellectual, the beats are anti-intellectual[a]—quite as much as are the American squares of whom they are so contemptuous. Theirs is not so much a reverence for life, as in a similarly disillusioned Schweitzer, as a reverence for death. Kerouac, in *The Subterraneans* voices the catchword of this group: "I don't know, I don't care, and it doesn't make any difference."

In their quest for the bizarre, many of them profess Zen Buddhism. Some of these the true beats frankly recognize as "phonies"—for how well do they understand Zen intellectually and emotionally anyway? They in fact accept no discipline of the mind in the Zen search for quietism. Instead, they "swim downstream" and "look for kicks" of new sensation, madly hipstering over America, not so much geographically since all roads lead to nowhere, but searching for something to believe, categorically knowing beforehand they will not find it. Some say that they are Existentialists. But how poorly do they understand Camus, for one, who is the very epitome of the man morally "involved" in his times. The beatniks are the irresponsibly *un*committed, by self-definition. Theirs is a feckless and purposeless rebellion with no social relevance. They are not even like Britain's "Angry Young Men," condemning the Establishment with cogent criticism. They are as stupefyingly inarticulate about their unknown goals as an Eisenhower press conference.

In his famous once-banned poem *Howl*, Allen Ginsberg calls the beatniks "the best minds of my generation." But who would take him seriously? As a literary movement (its roots ultimately in Hemingway's "lost generation"?), their best novelists surely do not derive, say, from that great innovator, James Joyce, for they are mucker ignoramuses, whereas Joyce was an almost monstrously learned man, and creator of the most cunningly wrought style of any writer of our time. Who are the models of Jack Kerouac and Allen Ginsberg? Not James Joyce but more nearly James Jones, whose book *From Here to Eternity* was a blind revolt against any authority whatever, whether of persons or of self-imposed stylistic discipline or form; and the later James Jones, with a blustering pride in incompetence that takes itself far too seriously. (And only his sharp intelligence saves Norman Mailer from being another inarticulate narcissist.) Out of the bored beat blab no Message ever comes. Theirs is no Whitmanesque love, however inchoate and ambiguous, for America. It is a blind and un–self-discerning hatred. It is a barbaric yawp that is fundamentally mindless.

Kerouac is himself authority for the statement that the Beat Generation are

a. And yet this is not always true of of authentic dedicated beatniks. I was struck this morning by one tiny fact of scholarship, and it is this. The generic name for *ayahuasca*, the narcotic "vine of the Spirits" of some South American Indians, used to be called *Banisteria caapi*. But the genus has recently been remonographed, and I note that my friend here, Allen Ginsberg, used the correct new generic name, *Banisteriopsis caapi*—and found this out from the head of the Harvard Botanical Museum, who is the world authority on Amerindian native narcotics! Furthermore, Brustein is surely incorrect in supposing that authors like Allen Ginsberg and Lawrence Ferlinghetti are not critics, articulate and vehement, of our society.

"the Beatifics." But whoever saw such a group so conscientiously full of *Weltschmerz* since *The Sorrows of Young Werther*? Who *are* their avatars? "The Bird" (Harry Hilmuth Pastor), the giant proprietor of The Party Pad, an old produce warehouse which gives the harrassed police of San Francisco a constant headache, and the press a constant source for tongue-clicking. Larry Ferlinghetti is a poet, a Ph.D., and a respectable businessman, a bookseller and patron of literary talent, the original publisher of Ginsberg's *Howl*. There is a fringe of older poets, Kenneth Patchen and Kenneth Rexroth; perhaps Henry Miller and Robinson Jeffers are their literary ancestors also. But their end is cultural and intellectual nihilism, and their means to this a complacent muckerism. As Jim Shock puts it, "The intellectual level of the average North Beach beatnik is on a par with that of an uninformed ape." And again, "They are for nothing and against nothing for to be interested enough in anything to take sides would not be cool." Besides, they are not literate enough in the many alternatives of our rich cultural past to make informed and discriminating choices of any kind whatever.

Beatniks, say all these critics, embody a kind of intellectual delinquency, not moral direction of any kind. Society at large, then, can reject pretensions to the intellectual of the beatnik. The beatniks are the flunk-outs from life's colleges. They are the exhibitionistic masochists who burn their bridges before they get to them.

Very well. The squares have had their say. But now—having paraded all our angry adjectives, having in general expressed a middle-aged parental spleen— what about our own attitudes of *countertransference* (that sophisticated psychiatric term) to the beatniks as functional adolescents? Is our anger really "uninvolved"? Do not the beats—with the infallible sureness of adolescents in searching out the chinks in the armor of parental personalities and cultures— almost mercilessly caricature our own helplessness and uncertainty, our own insecurity and indirection, our left-undone cultural business. And how adolescent are parents in America anyway? With what models have we provided them? Does hot indignation merely cover guilt?

Who, indeed, was *Waiting for Godot* in presidential elections as far back as we can remember, and for all I know in next week's also? Who, terrified in *The Age of Anxiety*, brought the mindless and uncommitted charisma of Dynamic Conservatism, which when it moves at all, goes round and round in blind do-nothing circles, happy to escape responsibility with yet another game of golf, leaving the dirty work to a sufficiently dirty vice-president? The charming, lovable American boy-man and his play-morality exalted to political cynosure and putative dictator of our society? Will the next election provide us with anything better than younger versions of the same? Who has given moral direction to our present most essentially American internal problem, our struggle for desegregation? The beatniks have even bettered us in this! Who is solving the basic problem of education in a democratic, technological world? The picture weeklies?

Who has reacted responsibly to the sheer survival-necessities for the species *Homo sapiens* and firmly banned all atomic weapons testing? Will TV's soothing syrup save us from strontium fallout embedded in our babies' bones? What mere hood could hope to mimic Hitler in the magnitide of his social psychopathy? What "rumble" can match Buchenwald and Dachau? Or, for that matter, what switchblade can equal the bombs on Hiroshima or Nagasaki? Are the Men of Berlin—or wherever this week's crisis will focus—the moral betters of the Men of Munich? Is our highest ethical message only higher poopfins on our preposterous motorcars, more functionless lights for the gathering darkness? In our government-by-Madison-Avenue ("credibility" not integrity is the word, "image" not character), who would not hoot with *Mad Magazine* and our TV-commercial-surfeited youngsters at any cozening or tranquilizing Message?[b]

Perhaps our anger is with ourselves. Our anger at the beatniks is come by quite dishonestly. Let us look for a moment at current "serious" literary and intellectual leaders, our "official" spokesmen for the times, to discern if we can the common predicament of ethical relativity, which says that man is responsible for his own values. First, that great modern saint, Dr. Albert Schweitzer, burdened intellectually with rationalizing a fossil folklore, who nevertheless still strove for loyalty to his fathers in his *Quest for the Historical Jesus*. With an immense scholarship and a bedrock intellectual integrity, Schweitzer found Him not—and had the emotional honesty to know and to state this desperate conclusion. This adornment of European civilization no less firmly and finally resolutely abandons that civilization than the beatniks abandon theirs, gives up the questing for moral forefathers, goes guilt-laden to Lambarene, and waits quietly for death and the eschatological promise of his race's childhood he can no longer rationally believe in. Is this intellectual defeatism in the face of intellectually indefensible stands much different from the moral defeatism of the beatniks?

---

b. For those who did not live through the violent history contemporaneous with the beatniks and later, and who might tend to see the young as arbitrarily "rebels without a cause," it may be salutary to point to some historic events: the bullying and contemptible Bay of Pigs episode, engineered by our Federal government; the arrogantly unconstitutional acts of our secret police; the Chicago convention; the charnel house of My Lai; the six-million-dollar "Camelot" contract given grandiose sociologists to subvert an evidently needed counter-colonialist revolution; the "experimental" Army use of LSD on unsuspecting subjects; Van Doren's betrayal, on a quiz show, of the dignity and honor of a professor; the governmental use of "social security" taxes to finance the unspeakable Vietnam War, the progress of which was consistently lied-about by the commanding generals and the political powers; and finally the betrayal of a whole people by repeated public Presidential lying over the Watergate crimes. In the context of these events, reactions to them become more understandable (while still not justifying the consequences): the corruption of academic life from Berkeley to Columbia by obsessive political "activism" in extrapolitical institutions (since official organs had become so fanatically unheeding) and, indeed, the destruction of some scholarly interest-groups (from anthropological-area specialists to linguists) by incessant "politicization" of nonpolitical functions. The simple fact is that in some of its aspects our society had become morally insufferable; and when adult public opinion finally did catch up, it uncannily mirrored many of the earlier-espoused positions of the young.

Or take Paul Tillich, another of our greatest theologians. After a masterful analysis of history and our times in *The Courage to Be*, Tillich comes to fundamental unbelief, his choice clearly seen to be between an existentialist and humanist neo-stoicism, and the historic narcissistic fantasy of God-and-immortality. Does he opt for humanistic man, an animal that must take care of itself like any other animal? No, for him, as for Nietzsche, "God is dead"—and yet, at the end of his profound and courageous book, what does Tillich do but postulate in despairing cowardice a "God Beyond God," a new *credo quia absurdum* in which he really cannot believe? How is this different from *Growing Up Absurd*? Is the dead God any more promising than the gods of alien cultures like India and Japan?

Again, consider our most publicized contemporary historian, Arnold Toynbee. What has he to offer a beat Britain and the larger Western world except a nativistic Ghost Dance and a return to the sacred sixteenth century of Henry the Eighth, his Message only that the lessons of History should lead us by the hand back into the dim cathedrals of Anglo-Catholicism! Is Karl Jaspers any less anti-intellectual than Kerouac—and if it should come to that, are the prose style of Heidegger and Kierkegaard any whit less murky than those of Kerouac or James Jones? And I, for one, must confess I can understand what Lawrence Ferlinghetti is talking about far better than I can Jean-Paul Sartre, despite equally earnest application to both.

Shall we follow a preciously pained T. S. Eliot out of *The Wasteland* back to neo-romanism, royalty, and reaction—O a far cry from his American St. Louis! Does not Kafka, too, represent the Upper Beatniks in his picture of the unbearable helplessness of modern man in *The Castle* and in *The Trial*, not even knowing and facing his historic guilts, and in the nausea of self-contempt in the fable of the cockroach-man? Who invented being beat anyway! *All the Sad Young Men* have long been around, certainly since F. Scott Fitzgerald's time. The beatnik with his beard and Hemingway-grouch in a Grant Street bistro is blood brother to the mindless alcoholics of *A Farewell to Arms* and *The Sun Also Rises*. Is the message of *Death in the Afternoon* any different from that of the Grant Street *macho*, the motorcycle hood? What difference is there between real hair on the face and false hair on the chest? The *Old Man of the Sea* has only himself on his shoulders, like Proteus and the rest of us.

And Samuel Beckett—how many more times must we endure the maundering death of another senile-psychotic *Murphy* or *Molloy* or *Thing*, prototypes of our senescent society? How long, indeed, must we hang around, *Waiting for Godot*? Is there really *No Exit* for *The Flies*? And who can stand before the immense and slick *Last Supper* of Dali in the National Gallery in Washington and not be nauseated by his Madison Avenue "sincerity"—at least the terrifying nausea of Picasso's *Guernica* means desperately what it says! Is Aldous Huxley any less noodle-headed for using mescaline to find the Word than beatniks flying high on tea? Is not Huxley's seeking to open those *Doors of Perception* just another search for epistemological "kicks"? Can switchblade rumbles of *Rebels Without a Cause* be any more meaningless than the senseless murder in *The Stranger?*

Tennessee Williams, our major American dramatic talent, has told us (how many times!) that mature love is unattainable and beset with crippling dangers. In one fashion or another the impossibility of adult heterosexual love is the burden of *The Glass Menagerie, A Streetcar Named Desire, Camino Real, 27 Wagons Full of Cotton, One Arm, Hard Candy, Orpheus Descending (Fugitive Kind,* on the screen), *The Rose Tattoo, You Touched Me!, The Roman Spring of Mrs. Stone, Cat on a Hot Tin Roof, Suddenly Last Summer*—and now, in *Sweet Bird of Youth,* it is all spelled out exactly in the hysterectomy of the girl and the castration of the boy. The whole canon of Williams repeats the same dismal theme. Is that all this superb dramatic writer has to say? And is it true anyway? Could not an *Esquire-* or *Playboy*-fan or a beatnik brooding over his espresso cup have told us the same profundities? And is not Zen, in any case, a likelier source for the higher morality than Nabokov's savage parable in *Lolita* of an America rotten before it was ripe, or Capote's picaresque *Breakfast at Tiffany's.* Are the heroines of Nabokov and Capote any less beatnik for being female and ending up in the Bronx and Africa, instead of Grant Street? These writers to our official culture have superb literary gifts. But do they in the end have anything more profound to tell us than Kerouac *On the Road,* on the beatnik perpetual vacation of the id?

Psychiatrists are familiar with the characteristic "schizophrenogenic family" and know how the officially "well" members manage to choose one of the family members to be the "sick" one for them. In society, as in the family, perhaps all of us are in it together. Are beatniks those that the official society has "chosen" to be the sick ones for us? Are all these defensive tricks to distance ourselves from them not strangely familiar psychiatrically? No one has to choose finally to be a beatnik, but can we not see them as somehow symptomatic of a sick society? Meanwhile, psychiatrists, who are professionally adept at self-discernment, might be willing to look with an anthropologist at the social-countertransference aspects of this cultural phenomenon. It may be that every society has the critics it deserves. If so, let us not waste the beatniks! For it may be that noisy indignation at the beatniks only covers defensively our own society's guilt.

Reference Notes

1. John Ciardi, "Epitaph for the Dead Beats," *Saturday Review* XLII no. 6 (6 February 1960), 11–13, 42.
2. Robert Brustein, "The Cult of Unthink," *Horizons* 1 (September 1958), 38ff.
3. Wallace Stegner, "The West Coast: Region with a View," *Saturday Review* 2 (May 1959), 15–17, 41.
4. Thomas Albright, in James Shock, *Life is a Lousy Drag* (San Francisco: Unicorn Publishing Co., 1958). John Clellon Holmes' paperback *Go* is a *roman à clef* in which Stofsky is Allen

Ginsberg; Carlo Marx is Ginsberg in Kerouac's *On the Road*. Lawrence Lipton writes knowl-edgeably in *The Holy Barbarians*, and Paul Goodman in *Growing Up Absurd*. Seymour Krim has edited *The Beat Scene*: Norman Podhoretz' article on "The Know Nothing Bohemians" is worth reading, as also is Diana Trilling's on "The Other Night at Columbia" in the *Partisan Review*, and Donald Cook's article in *Playboy*. The paperback, *The Beat Generation* by Albert Zugsmith (New York: Bantam Books, 1959) is a cheap, sensational book made into a sleasy movie by MGM, neither of which has insight into or even any special relevance to the beatniks.

IV. Kinesics

16. Paralinguistics, Kinesics, and Cultural Anthropology

Gregory Bateson has taught us that *all culture is communication*. Unfortunately, the uses of such communication are often to a high degree those of *recognition* of ingroup/outgroup-boundaries among groups and subgroups, and hence serve both identity and separateness alike. This identification function is present in "ethnic gesture"—those *paralinguistic* elements that accompany, often unconsciously, all spoken language—as well as those *kinesic* motor acts, facial expressions and general "body language" that carry semantic significance in the absence of speech. A layman's cliché is that "we could not speak each other's language, so we made ourselves understood by gestures," which is fatuous in its assumption that paralanguage is humanly universal or that it is not culturally learned quite as much as language is. Indeed, however impeccably one speaks, say, French in its phonemic (timbre), intonational (FM), dynamic (AM), prosodic (temporal) and other exactitudes, he is still not likely to be mistaken for a true Frenchman in the absence of the appropriate kinesic garnishments to accompany it. And, for the rest, *ethological* species-wide gesture is at best limited and dubious, and the bulk of it is properly *ethnological*.

Despite the potential riches in the cultural approach, the usable sources are limited in number.[a] For example, Gordon Hewes' two papers are fine distri-

---

Nonverbal communication has become a major interest within all the behavioral sciences. The essay-components of the present study have been anthologized and translated more than two dozen times, but the scope has been enlarged here to include art, music, and other humanistic concerns.

This chapter is a consolidation of "Paralinguistics, Kinesics, and Cultural Anthropology," in T. A. Sebeok, A. S. Hayes, and M. C. Bateson (eds.), *Approaches to Semiotics* (The Hague: Mouton, 1964), pp. 191–220, reprinted by permission; "Ethology and Ethnology," *Semiotica* 6 no. 1 (1972), 83–96, reprinted by permission; and portions of my review of R. L. Birdwhistell, *Kinesics and Context: Essays on Body Motion Communication*, in *American Journal of Sociology* 77 no. 5 (1972), 999–1000.

a. Allport, G. W., and P. Vernon, *Studies in Expressive Movement* (New York, 1933), a psychological approach to gesture, gait, and many other semantic motor acts; Birdwhistell, R. L., *Introduction to Kinesics* (Louisville, 1952), by the pioneering taxonomist and lexicographer of kinesics, who has devised that initial tool of study: a method of recording kinesic data; Crichtley, MacDonald, *The Language of Gesture* (London-New York, 1939), an older work but still usable, including gestures and speech, deaf-mute language, and gesture as a precursor to language; Darwin, C. R., *Expression of the Emotions in Man and Animals* (New York, 1955), a statement of what might be called the traditional instinctivist theories of kinesic expression; Feldman, S., *Mannerisms of Speech and Gesture* (New York, 1959); Hall, E. T., *The Silent Language* (New York, 1959), a very readable and justly popular book on cultural semantics, the fundamental and indispensable primer for all modern studies; Hayes, F., "Gestures: A Working Bibliography," *Southern*

bution studies, but largely limited to nonsemantic kinesics such as postural and motor habits; it is pioneering and monumental effort to glean sporadic data from ethnographic monographs which largely neglect to cover the subject except incidentally. Two tribal "kinesic lexicographies" stand alone: Flora Bailey's Navaho motor habits, and Devereux's brief but model lexicon of Mohave paralinguistic gestures accompanying speech.[1] Basic lexicographies are adequate for such kinesic or allelolanguages as the Plains Indian sign language, the sign language of Australian aborigines, the silent gestural language of European monks, designed to avoid interrupting the meditations of others, an allegedly international language of medieval traveling monks, reliably dated from, at the latest, the fourth century A.D. onward; the hand-language of deaf-mutes and those who would communicate with them; the gestural argots or kinesic trade-jargons of truck drivers, Hindu merchants, Persians, gypsies, carnival folk, burglars, street urchins, tobacco auctioneers, and others; the elaborate gestural language of the Hindu *natya* dance-dramas; the ritual hand-poses or mudrás of Buddhist and Hindu priests in Bali; the drum languages of West and Central Africa, the Mayans, Jivaros, Melanesians, Polynesians, and Javanese; the "whistling language" of the Canary Islanders and some West Africans; the special camphor-gathering language of the Jakun, and the allusive communications of Patani fishermen and many other hunting peoples—but these are beyond the scope of the present preliminary work-paper. The Mediterranean peoples are rich in kinesic communication, and on the ancient Hebrews, the Ashkenazi Jews, and Neapolitans we have something like adequate lexicographic materials to work on. Gestures pictured in the Mayan codices might well be studied by linguists as an aid in breaking this refractory code; and Andrea del Jorio makes the reasonable proposition that if we understood the gestures of modern Neapolitans, we might with some success interpret the

---

Folklore Quarterly 21 (1957), 218–317, an excellent source which does not pretend to be exhaustive; Hewes, G. T., "The Anthropology of Posture," *Scientific American* 196 (Feb. 1957), 123–32, the only systematic, traditional distribution-study, a pioneering work that sacrifices depth for range, along with "World Distribution of Certain Postural Habits," *American Anthropologist* 57, no. 2, pt. 1 (April 1955), 231–44); La Barre, W., "The Cultural Basis of Emotions and Gestures," *Journal of Personality* 16 (1947), 49–68, an argument against "instinctive gesture" and summarizing statement of an anthropological view that, like any form of social behavior, kinesic codes must be learned; Mira y Lopez, E., *Myokinetic Psychodiagnosis* (New York, 1958), one of the first "applied" works on kinesics; Paget, Sir Richard A. S., *Human Speech* (New York-London, 1930), a fundamental work in gesture study, perhaps the best statement of the view that speech arises from nativistic gesture, a currently unfashionable position but one not to be ignored; Ruesch, J., and Bateson, G., *Communication, the Social Matrix of Society* (New York, 1951), a richly suggestive fusion of analytic psychiatry, cultural anthropology, and the "information theory" of communications engineers; Reusch, J., Bateson, G., and Kees, W., *Nonverbal Communication* (Berkeley, 1956), an objectivist and naturalistic approach, of many details of which the cultural anthropologist may be critical, but not to be overlooked; Schilder, P., *The Image and Appearance of the Human Body* (New York, 1950), an odd, pioneering, brilliant, sometimes incomprehensible book, but a psychiatric classic nonetheless; Young, P. T., *Emotion in Man and Animals* (New York, 1943).

A few other items may need to be added, but this brief list embodies most of our basic working library, though other fundamental works exist on slightly more specialized subjects.

gestures of the ancient Greeks, especially those on classical vases.[2] The covert signs of bidders at auction and those persons working in noisy situations (hand-gestures of those directing crane-operators and earth-mover operators, etc.) might also be worthy of scholarly attention.

The pioneer and acknowledged master of kinesics, however, is Ray Birdwhistell, as he is also the chief *agent provocateur* of further kinesic studies. His demonstration of kinesics in our society is not so much an academic lecture as it is pure theater. Longtime avid Birdwhistell-watchers agree that the spectacle of the old maestro himself—making with the forehead, the mouth, the eyebrows and the pelvis—is a show that, if it ever comes to your town, should not be missed. Birdwhistell estimates that a human being puts out between 2,500 and 10,000 bits of information per second in various modalities, which gives one a sense of the magnitude of the observer's task. What multivectored polygraph could monitor this universe of information? What computer contain it? Semantically, how to reduce this staggering complexity even of descriptive motor and related behaviors to meaningful and communicable, since communicated, kinemes and kinemorphs? What are the lexic allo-variants and the diacritical modifications of these? The human (?), the ethnic, the regionally dialectic, the idiolectic locale of such variants?

It is apparent that Birdwhistell is beholden in his thinking to sophisticated modern linguists, notably McQuown, Pike, Hockett, Smith, Trager, Hall, Sebeok, and Wells—and in turn has contributed to the whole large new field of sociolinguistics or psycholinguistics, ably anthologized by Dell Hymes, and others.[3] But it is no slavish dependency. Much nonverbal communication is in fact paralinguistic (accompanying speech), but Birdwhistell is quick to reject any easy and false analogy with linguistics that does not in fact fit his peculiar kind of data, and he is as astute methodologically[4] as he is preternaturally perceptive of the complex data. His modesty and empirical alertness alike are evident in his recognition that the very complexity of the data requires us to go back to a natural history phase, which some anthropologists have skipped in their eagerness for generalizations and for prestigeful but false exactitude in heavy method prematurely used. The fear of data is the beginning of wisdom. And these data are formidable indeed, with a virtually clinical complexity. The reader ready to protest at the horrendously difficult kineme-notation system in his *Introduction to Kinesics*[5] should keep Birdwhistell's sense of this complexity in mind and remember that serious involvement with kinesics is no easy amateurism but often sheer hard work.

Fortunately, Birdwhistell has gathered together a volume of his articles, often from obscure and inaccessible publications, with some new essays added.[6] The reader will refind old favorites and discover new ones in this varied collection. The little study entitled "There Are Smiles" is typically sensitive and articulate with regard to regional and contextual differences, and, unimprisoned as he is by instinctivist theory, Birdwhistell might extend this, indeed, to a worldwide study of smiling. The Kentucky mountaineer and the bluegrass-country contrasts in the kinesics of expressing illness is a witty little gem of observation by a master. The little essay on "Masculinity and Femininity" (compare Robert Stoller on the psychodynamics of gender) in sheer brilliance of clinical observation rivals the skill of even such uncanny virtuosi as the psychiatrists Grete Bibring and the late Harry Stack Sullivan. "The Family and Its Open Secrets" again displays a sharp clinical eye. "Theatre and Family Meals" is elegant functionalist ethnography (and better social anthropology than most) in perceiving the related styles of these two media of communication. The split-second minimal-gestural drama of driver and hitch-hikers and the famous Cigarette Scene of course are already modern classics.

A rather surprising discovery is that there is not necessarily any one-to-one counterpoint in time line between the kinesic and the linguistic streams of communication by a subject, though these may be semantically related, much as two discrete melodic voices are, musically. Birdwhistell is evidently right concerning the linguistic "openness" and "productivity" inherent in kinesic communication—I am tempted to suggest polysynthetic syntax of Eskimo affixes, in which it is the whole package that counts. He repeatedly warns us not to expect a final neat lexicon of body gestures like a Babylonian or Jungian dream book, though he suggests that a final kineme catalog for one society (50–60 for Americans) may be little more compendious than the 15–50 phonemes Trager finds in any one language.

The reality of ethnicity in kinesic communication is proven in the fact that from movies alone and with sound track off, it is possible to tell which language Fiorello La Guardia, who spoke Yiddish, Italian, and English, was using. I am easily persuaded of this: I can demonstrate offhand a dozen distinct ethnic walks which are easily recognizable. (For a description of some of these, see later in the present essay).

One fundamental question that needs to be investigated in kinesics is the precise boundary line between instinctual movements, expressions, and acts *versus* the numerous culture-based kinesic codes that must be learned like any arbitrary, invented, symbolic system. A great deal of speculative nonsense has been indulged in by the older instinctivist theorists and much of what they uncritically attributed to innate inherited responses can now be clearly seen to be culturally learned responses—but the question is by no means finally settled at our present stage of knowledge. It is obvious that many body motions—for example, breathing and heartbeat—are basically structural-functional, for all that nonphysiological modalities (psychological and cultural) can plainly be seen to cause a change of rate in both. The sucking-reflex, the grasping-reflex, and the startle-reflex are about as close to anything we know that we would wish to call "instinctual" in humans. They are present in the neonate as muscular movements, long before the myelination of other tracts is completed at about the age of 36 months; and they serve (or served in ancestral primates) adaptive purposes. And although eye movements and eye focusing are sometimes present in very young babies, it would appear that these muscular movements are already an intimate mixture of structurally given and environmentally induced learning. Eye-blinking at the approach of a noxious stimulus and "automatic" retroflexion of limbs from painful stimuli would appear to involve even more of the learned response.

The fruitful work of modern animal ethologists might well be animadverted to at this point. Overly facile extrapolation can easily commit the "animal series fallacy" here, and the marked neoteny of man indicates that, with the very long-delayed maturation of the human infant, a change of phase has occurred between humans and infrahumans, so that man is predominantly a learning animal. Man has certainly very little of the species-specific motor acts such as we observe in the courting and fight-or-flight reactions of sticklebacks, birds, and some quadrupeds. Birds, goats, and monkeys appear to have definable periods, within which internally given and environmentally stimulated elements join to give adaptive responses, and outside of which periods (both before and after) environmental stimulation produces no adaptive learning. Perhaps human speech itself is one of these: for all that speech is admittedly everywhere cultural in its content (phonemics, lexemics, and syntactics), our meager data on feral children would seem to indicate that there is an optimal period for learning to talk, after which, in the absence of prior environmental stimulation, the individual can never learn to talk. Perhaps the psychiatrists might join me here in speculating that something like this may happen in the complex phatic-semantics of mother-child relationships in some schizophrenics traumatized in the early oral, preverbal epochs of their lives. Furthermore, the abundant psychoanalytic materials on "fixation" convince me that there are maturational states-of-preparedness in the individual during which, in the absence of appropriate environmental stimuli, there can be the grievous and "fixated" mislearnings that we call neuroses and psychoses. A clinical exposure to the data would, I believe, convince anyone that Karl Abraham[7] was essentially correct in correlating the symptomatology of the major psychoses and neuroses with traumata in specific maturational stages of the individual life-history. But here I approach the borderline of the territory of other specialists at this conference and must be content to indicate at least one cultural anthropologist's willingness to learn from these specialists.

The complexity of the matter, on this other borderline of human ethology and cultural kinesics, is indicated in the fact of walking. For all that I have been among those modern students insistent upon the profound significance of man's bipedality, both on physical anthropological and evolutionary grounds, I am still not prepared precipitately to conclude that walking in humans is a simple instinctual matter. It really belongs in the area of human ethology. Structurally, the physical anthropologist Thieme[8] has argued that the lumbar curve is ontogenetic rather than phylogenetic in man; and functionally, again the meager evidence we have on feral children would seem to indicate that anatomically the young child, bereft of the broad cue of bipedal adults in the environment, can get about quadrupedally about as well as other children can make it bipedally, and perhaps even better. Furthermore, experienced field workers will be unregenerate kinesiologists in this matter: people simply do walk differently in different societies. There are culturally induced *styles of walking*. Old hands in Burma, during the last war, could detect the difference between the lowland Shan walk (arms are swung in planes parallel to the sagittal plane of the body) and the highland Kachin and Palaung walks (arms swung in arcs obliquely forward of the body). In my observation, the Bengali walk differently (all elbows and knees, with considerable foot-lifting) from the Punjabi (with a more puppet-like rigidity and verticality), south Chinese very differently from the Singhalese even when both are barefooted—for all that the difference in walk between the Amerindians and other American males might be imputed, in part, to differences in terrain and footgear. Amazonian men and women have very different styles of walking that may *not* be imputed to differences in trochanters, but rather to sex-dichotomized styles.[9] And even in the lower East side of New York one can still see what I have called the "Ashkenazi shuffle" in Jews of Eastern European origin. I would even go so far as to argue "idiolects" in walking: by purely auditory cues I am able to identify the walk of any member of my family, and even to surmise something about their emotional states. If McQuown, Newman, Trager, and other linguists can diagnose psychiatric syndromes purely on the basis of intonation, so also can psychiatrists like Kempf,[b] Ostwald, Sullivan, and Schilder on purely kinesic grounds. Birdwhistell is so uncannily perceptive in this area that he could probably tell you what the patient wants for dinner! Walking styles undoubtedly have semantic-kinesic functions. For example, the jointless glide (as if on wheels) to indicate the Oriental woman in a movie; in my judgment, Myrna Loy could do this best, in a manner most similar to the Singhalese walk of those that I have observed. Also, in American movies, the suggestion of a sinister inhuman monster—see any Frankenstein-monster movie—is gained by a peculiarly stereotyped, stiffly wooden and deliberate gait.[c] Any addict of Western movies, I believe, can quickly decide which is the hero and which the villain by the position of the pelvis in walking and motor tempo and use of the eyes and head (plus-or-minus a dangling cigarette). Styles of standing change historically too: it is amusing to note that the modern "hood slouch" is not unlike the stylish posture of debutantes in the 'twenties in its loose pelvic forward thrust, and both are similar to the aristocratic manner of standing observable for eighteenth-century Kandyan Singhalese nobles (male, and still earlier in the Sigiriyan frescoes of females) in Hinayana Buddhist paintings. The approved pose of "attention" has also differed markedly from World War I to World War

b. For a copiously illustrated work on kinaesthetic tonuses in art works and in psychiatric patients, see Kempf's book cited in reference note 7.

c. T. A. Sebeok has made to me, in correspondence, the interesting suggestion that this stereotyped kineme may be traced to the old German silent film, *The Golem*, which deals with a medieval Jewish legend. Sebeok also maintains that there is a quite distinctive urban-Swedish style of walking. I consider the most beautiful walk that I have ever seen to be the Florentine, illustrated by Claudia Cardinale in the Fellini movie *8½*. But Danish women walk stunningly too.

II: in the former, the lumbar curve was maximized; in the latter, minimized. Stylized differences in the "dress parade walk" of the British, Americans, Russians, and Germans (describable in terms of degree of knee flexion: marked for Americans, minimal for British, absent for the Russian and German "goose-step") need only to be alluded to to be remembered.

Acts perhaps closer to the strictly ethological in humans may be seen in laughing and crying (or, more specifically, lachrimation). Gorillas cannot weep, but human babies can and do. Ashley Montagu has advanced the brilliant and provocative theory that lachrimation is a species-specific adaptive act in humans.[10] Because of its extravagantly infantile helplessness, the human baby must needs summon succor from adults, often from a distance, loudly, and for a long time. To be sure, the vocables adults use may be learned vocal segregates; vociferous, phonemically indiscriminate vocalization is sufficient for the infant's purpose: technical "noise" or something appallingly close to it would do. But prolonged crying means that large masses of air must pass over the nasal membranes, tending to dry them out, whereas sensitive olfactory membrane cells must be kept moist or they quickly die. Lachrimation, therefore, has the adaptive function of keeping cells moist that are threatened by the adaptive necessity of the helpless infant's summoning attention and aid. I would add that, because large masses of desiccating air are also involved in prolonged adult laughter, Montagu's theory has the advantage of explaining that otherwise inexplicable phenomenon of "laughing until you cry."

Laughter, as a kinesic phenomenon, is also probably pan-human, but more complex. I consider that laughter is the kinesic concomitant of "letting the cat out of the bag" of cultural repression, a tension-release of now "innocently permitted" expression of otherwise forbidden aggressive, erotic (and possibly also fearful and embarrassed) states of mind—though just why this kinesic modality is used remains a mystery, except that it utilizes an inveterate and habituated oral modality in humans (perhaps higher primates "laugh" also). But laughter is deeply embedded in the specific cultural context of the person who is laughing—Japanese and African and American Negro laughter are sufficient cases in themselves alone to demonstrate this point. Furthermore, the things that people laugh at, in this "return of the repressed" or the "discomfiture at incongruity" will vary depending upon what cats have, by enculturation, been put into what cultural bags.[11] Humor is notoriously as difficult to export as ethos, and for much the same reasons.

Smiling, as opposed to laughter, I consider an as yet unexplained phenomenon. Older theorists, whom we would now classify with the ethologists, were sure that the smile was a disguised snarl, symbolically exposing the canine teeth; but hominid canines haven't been much use for fighting since phylogenetically remote times, nor is it clear why a hostile gesture should be used as friendly one. The behaviorist psychologist E. B. Holt "physiologized" the smile as being ontogenetically understandable as the relaxation of facial muscles in the infant replete from nursing.[12] But this leaves me unconvinced, when the same infant will make the same "smile" in its sleep, from the *pain* of colic, as well as the *pleasure* of amusement.

As for other physiological modalities in man—defecation, micturition, coitus, and even childbirth—these kinetic acts surely have their anatomical substrates, but they just as surely have their kinemic contexts when they become loaded with cultural semantics and stylization, as every good and complete ethnographic monograph should indicate they do.[13] In the approved kinetic and parakinetic styles of these acts, Havelock Ellis, Malinowski, and others have adequately edified us; and Kinsey has sufficiently adumbrated class-differences in these phenomena in America. Obviously, like ballroom dancing, all the above have their sex-dichotomized aspects as well; and Kinsey, in one of his rare truly cross-cultural excursions, has stated that there are even preferred modalities in perverse acts among British (sodomy), American (fellation), and French (mutual onanism) homosexuals. In this section of the present paper, then, the gamut from weeping to sexuality shows a complete range from the rather purely ethological to the clearly ethnological. One's guess is that this may be, in part, a function of the chronological *time of appearance* of the phenomenon: the child's cry at birth, at its first breathing, is most clearly cut-and-dried physiology; whereas sexual behavior already at adolescence has long since been sicklied o'er by the pale cast of culture and ontogenetic conditionings.

We enter more firmly onto sure cultural ground with such motor sememes or kinesic isolates as pointing and head-movements (for "yes" and "no"). Though man is everywhere a notably "handed" animal, pointing with the forefinger and other fingers curled palmward is a limitedly cultural phenomenon, probably of Old World origin and dispersion (American Indians, on both New World Continents, point with the lips, as also do Shans and other Mongoloid peoples; in other groups, pointing is done with eye-movements, or nose- or chin-and-head movements, or head-movements alone). As for negation and affirmation kinemes, behaviorists and other psychologists have sought to explain our "yes" nod as the movement of the infant seeking the breast, the "no" as avoiding it. But here the psychologists have reckoned without their cultural hosts: they have an elegantly universalistic explanation for a phenomenon which is not humanly universal, a common pitfall for any social scientist who ignores culture. Cultural anthropologists can supply us with many alternative kinemes for "yes" and "no" in various cultures.[14] For example, shaking the hand in front of the face with the forefinger extended, is the Ovimbundu sign of negation, while Malayan Negritos express negation by casting down the eyes. The Semang thrust the head forward in affirmation. In fact, there are even regional "dialects" of affirmation in the Indic area: crown of the head following an arc from shoulder to shoulder, four times, in Bengal; throwing the head back in an oblique arc to the left shoulder, one time, somewhat "curtly" and "disrespectfully" to our taste, in the Punjab and Sind; curving the chin in a downward leftward arc in Ceylon, often accompanied by an indescribably beautiful parakineme of back-of-right-hand cupped in upward-facing-palm of the left hand, plus-or-minus the additional kineme of a crossed-ankle curtsey.

Greeting kinemes vary greatly from culture to culture. In fact, many of these motor habits in one culture are open to grave misunderstanding in another. For example, the Copper Eskimo welcome strangers with a buffet on the head or shoulders with the fist, while the northwest Amazonians slap one another on the back in greeting. Polynesian men greet one another by embracing and rubbing each other's back; Spanish-American males greet one another by a stereotyped embrace, head over the right shoulder of the partner, three pats on the back, head over reciprocal left shoulder, three more pats. In the Torres Straits, the old form of greeting was to bend the right hand into a hook, then mutually scratching palms by drawing away the rigid hand, repeating this several times. An Ainu, meeting his sister, grasped her hands in his for a few seconds, suddenly released his hold, grasped her by both ears and gave the peculiar Ainu greeting cry; then they stroked one another down the face and shoulders. Kayan males in Borneo grasp each other by the forearm, while a host throws his arm over the shoulder of a guest and strokes him endearingly with the palm of his hand. When two Kurd males meet, they grasp one another's right hand, raise them both, and alternately kiss the other's hand. Andamanese greet one another by one sitting down in the lap of the other, arms around each other's necks and weeping for a while; two brothers, father and son, mother and daughter, and husband and wife, or even two friends may do this; the husband sits in the lap of the wife. Friends' "goodbye" consists in raising the hand of the other to the mouth and gently blowing on it, reciprocally. At Matavai a full-dress greeting after long absence requires scratching the head and temples with a shark's tooth, violently and with much bleeding. This brief list could be easily enlarged by other anthropologists.

Kissing is Germanic, Graeco-Roman, and Semitic (but apparently not Celtic, originally). Greek and Roman parents kissed their children; lovers and married persons kissed one another, and friends of the same or different sexes; medieval knights kissed, as modern pugilists shake hands, before the fray. Kissing relics and the hand of a superior is at least as early as the Middle Ages in Europe; kissing the feet is an old habit among various Semites; and the Alpine peasant kisses his own hand before receiving a present, and pages in the French court kissed any article given them to carry.[15] Two men or two women exchange the "holy kiss" in greeting before meetings, in the earlier Appalachian-highland version of the snake-handling cult of the Southeast; the heterosexual kiss is a secular one, not used in public. Another admired gambit is to move the rattlesnake or copperhead back and forward across the face, and closer and closer, until the communicant's lips brush the flickering-tongued mouth of the snake; one Durham minister once offered to kiss the police officers who had raided a snake-handling meeting, to show "no hard feelings", but this offer was not accepted. Kissing, as is well known, is in the Orient an act of private lovemaking, and arouses only disgust when performed publicly: thus, in Japan, it was earlier necessary to censor out the major portion of love scenes in American-made movies. Tapuya men in South America kiss as a sign of peace, but men do not kiss women (nor women, women) because the latter wear labrets or lip plugs. Noserubbing is both Eskimo and Polynesian. Djuka Negroes of Surinam show pleasure at a particularly interesting or amusing dance step by embracing the dancer and touching cheek to cheek, now on one side, now on the other—the identical attenuation of the "social kiss" (on one cheek only, however) between American women who do not wish to spoil each other's make-up. And one of the hazards of accepting a decoration in France is a bilateral buss in the name of the Republic. Ona kissing in Tierra del Fuego is performed only between certain close relatives and young married couples or lovers; and not lip-to-lip, but by pressing the lips to the head, cheek, or arm of the other, accompanied by a slight inward sucking.[16]

Sticking out the tongue is a kineme with indisputably diverse significance in varied cultures. In Sung Dynasty China, tongue protrusion was a gesture of mock terror, performed in ridicule; the tongue stretched far out was a gesture of surprise (at the time of the novel, *Dream of the Red Chamber*); in modern south China at least (Kunming), a quick, minimal tongue protrusion and re-traction signifies embarrassment and self-castigation, as at some social *faux pas* or misunderstanding; it can vary in context from the humorous to the apologetic. Among the Ovimbundu of Africa, bending the head forward and sticking out the tongue means "you're a fool." In India, the long-protruding tongue in the statues of the goddess Kali signifies a monumental, welkinshat-tering rage, a demon-destroying anger as effective as a glance from the Saivite third eye in the forehead. In New Caledonia, in wooden statues of ancestors carved on houses, the protruded tongue means wisdom, vigor, and plenitude, since the tongue "carries to the outside the traditional virtues, the manly deci-sion, and all the manifestations of life which the word bears in itself." Perhaps this is the meaning, in part, of similar New Zealand carvings, although here there may be other overtones of ancestral fertility or the like. (The meaning of the connecting of the elongated nose and mouth to umbilicus and genitals in Melanesian carvings is unknown to me). In the Carolines, however, the gods are disgusted at the lolling tongues of suicides by hanging, and for this reason refuse entry to the souls of such among the deities. In at least one of the eigh-teen "Devil Dance" masks in Ceylon, specialized for the exorcistic cure in spe-cific illnesses, the black mask has a protruding red tongue, probably synergistic (to judge from other cognates in the India area) with the extremely exophthal-mic eyes which are characteristic of all eighteen of these masks: to frighten out the demons regarded as causing the specific diseases. In Mayan statues of the gods, the protruded tongue signifies wisdom. In Tibet, the protruded tongue[d]

---

d. The desirability of multiple sources on such a matter is indicated here: according to Mallery, Tibetans put out their tongues in polite deference to a police official in Lhasa investigating their provenience and purposes, but scratched their ears and put out their tongues at Europeans when they break out their pictures, microscopes, etc., some with their mouths open in awe. But Hayes

is a sign of polite deference, with or without the thrust-up thumb of the right hand, scratching the ears, or removing the hat. Marquesans stick out the tongue as a sign of simple negation. In America, of course, sticking out the tongue (sometimes accompanied by "making a face") is a juvenile quasi-obscene gesture of provocative mockery, defiance, or contempt; perhaps the psychiatrists can explain why this is chiefly a little girl's gesture, though sometimes used playfully by adult women, or by effeminate men. One might also conjecture a European "etymology" behind this gesture in American child-culture, based on this chronological sequence: apotropaic (a stone head with thrust-out tongue and "making a face" on a Roman fort in Hungary, although this etymon may also include a note of defiance as well), protective-defiant (gargoyles with thrust-out tongue on Gothic cathedrals), mock-affirmative (the subordinates of the demon Malcoda in Dante acknowledge a command by sticking out their tongues and making a rump-trumpet)—all with an obscure overtone of the obscenely phallic—whence the modern child-gesture of derision (and there comes to mind a similar "shame on you gesture," using the left-hand pointing gesture and using the similarly held right hand in an outward whittling movement, repeated). But such precarious kinemic "etymologies" must await more adequate ethnographic documentations, and these we largely lack. The Eskimo curl up the tongue into a trough or cylinder and protrude the tongue slightly, but this is not a kineme; it is rather a motor habit, used to direct a current of air when blowing a tinder into a flame.

Gestures of contempt are a rich area for study also. A favorite Menomini Indian gesture of contempt is to raise the clenched fist palm downward up to the level of the mouth, then bringing it downward quickly and throwing forward the thumb and the first two fingers. Malayan Negritos express contempt or disgust by a sudden expiration of breath, like our "snort of contempt." Neapolitans click the right thumbnail off the right canine in a downward arc. The *mano cornuda* or "making horns" (first and little fingers of the right hand extended forward, thumb and other fingers folded) is primarily used to defy the "evil eye." The *mano fica* (clenched right fist with thumb protruding between the first and second fingers) is an obscene kineme symbolizing the male genitals; in some contexts its meaning is the same as the more massive slapping of the left biceps with the right hand, the left forearm upraised and ending in a fist; a less massive, though no less impolite, equivalent is making a fist with all save the second ("social finger") and thrusting it upward.[e] Mediterranean

writes that "in Tibet, customary greeting to a fellow traveler [is the] thrust up thumb of the right hand and thrust out [of] the tongue." Bailey writes, "In Tibet a respectful salutation is made by removing hat and lolling out the tongue." In Japan, "Formerly every *Sambaso* [a kind of prologue to a classical play, Kabuki as well as Bunraku] doll or mask had its tongue thrust out in accordance with the greatest obeisance performed in Tibet, from which, according to the late Rev. Ekai Kawaguchi, *Sambaso* was introduced" (see reference note 16).

e. The Boro and Witoto of Amazonia have a sign to express desire for coitus, but this is a mere jest or ribald suggestion: the right elbow is grasped with the left hand, the elbow being flexed so as to have the right hand extend upwards; it is, in fact, the letter Z of the deaf-and-dumb alpha-

peoples are traditionally rich in such gestures; I believe, though with admittedly unsatisfactory evidence, that the "cocked snout" came from Renaissance Italy as a gesture of contempt about the same time as the fork arrived in England in the reign of Elizabeth.

Beckoning gestures have been little collected. In a restaurant, an American raises a well-bred right forefinger to summon a waiter. To express "come here!" a Latin American makes a downward arc with the right hand, almost identical with an American jocular gesture of "go away with you!" The Shans of Burma beckon by holding the palm down, moving the fingers as if playing an arpeggio chord. The Boro and Witoto beckon by moving the hand downward, not upward, as with us, in our face-level, wrist-flexing, cupped-hand "come here!" signal.

Gestures of politesse are equally sparse in ethnographic sources. The Hindu palms-together, thumbs about the level of the chin, is a greeting, a "thank you," and a gesture of obeisance, depending on the context. A Shan, on being done a kindness, may bend over and sniff the sleeve of the benefactor's coat; the meaning is "how sweet you smell," not entirely unlike the Indian "shu-kriya" (sweetness) meaning "How sweet you are!" Curtseys and bows (almost infinitely graded in depth of bend in the Orient, to express a wide gamut of deference or mock-deference, depending on the social context) are both European and Asiatic. Indic and Oceanic peoples sit down to honor a social superior; Europeans stand up. In both Africa and Melanesia, hand-clapping is a gesture of respect to chiefs and kings. Covering and uncovering the head in deference to gods, kings and social superiors, is complex, and sometimes contradictory in nature, in Europe and Asia. Taking off or putting on articles of clothing is also full of subtleties of politesse: in classic south India a woman uncovers the upper part of her body in deference, but in America a man puts on his coat to show respect to a lady. The psychology of clothes[f] and the motor habits in handling one's clothing can benefit from much more study: a Plains Indian warrior, for example, could express a wide variety of emotional states, simply through the manner in which he wore his outer robe or cloak. Quite as many gentlemen object to ladies hiking down their skirts or girdles, as ladies object to gentlemen hiking up their pants; and I once witnessed the interview with a young psychiatrist of a female hysteric in which a lively and wholly unconscious colloquy was carried on: she with various tugs at her bodice, skirt-hem, and other parts of her dress and underclothing, he with corresponding "business" with his tie, trousers, etc.[g] Hands were veiled in the

---

bet—somewhat the opposite of the American obscenity, so far as right and left arm are concerned (see reference note 14).

f. The British psychoanalyst J. C. Flugel has shown an exquisite sensitivity to meanings in his monograph on clothes (see reference note 17).

g. In this same psychiatric clinic, at another time, I also observed a self-justifying male patient giving a long song-and-dance about himself, while slightly to his rear beside him, his psychiatrist (of German descent) gave a complete editorial comment on his patient's story, entirely through

clothing before a superior in ancient Rome; traces of this are found in Christian art; and when cardinals approach the Pope to do homage or to receive the hat, they veil their hands in their capes; Moslems also cover the hands before a person of higher rank or when making a visit. The vast folklore on clothing and nudity, the various and changing erotizations of body parts can only be alluded to here; but much of it has relevance to kinesics and paralinguistics.

Conventionalized motor acts in both Occidental and Oriental acting are of relevance to kinesics also. Chinese opera is full of them; Hindu epic drama is a whole gesture language in itself; American silent movies are an excellent source, as are the pantomimes from Chaplin to Marcel Marceau. Stage and movie motor-"business" in modern Russian acting (e.g., in the films "Alexander Nyevski" and Dostoievsky's "The Idiot") seem extravagant and ludicrous to American audiences. Notable in American films are the rapid changes of style in motor acts, so that they are quickly out of date and soon absurd (as also with the gestural tics of some television performers such as Ed Sullivan, used to express affability or endearingly folksy pseudo-embarrassment); notable in oriental drama is the stability of conventionalizations, such that they remain the same for centuries and over many countries.

Conversational gestures are multitudinous: the shaken right forefinger of accusation, sharp criticism, and threat; the recriminatory gesture of right hand thrust out and shaken palm upward (also used for subjective dis-incrimination with a slight variation, lifting in an upward, outward arc, sometimes with head movements); the eighteenth-century tapping of the right nostril with the right forefinger to express extravagant and amused incredulity; the forefinger spiral above the right cranial hemisphere, to express much the same thing, plus grave doubts about the speaker's mental status; the arched eyebrow for interest, surprise, disbelief. French and Americans use the forehead quite differently, as also do American males and females. In Indo-Persian art, biting of the fingers expresses surprise. The Argentine "ademanes" are a particularly complete repertoire available for editorial comment on another speaker or the passing scene: kissing upward-held bunched fingers ("Magnifico!"), shaking the bunched fingers ("What a crowd!"), touching beneath the eye with a forefinger ("Do you take me for a sucker?"), stroking beneath the chin with the back of the palm ("I haven't the faintest idea about it" plus-or-minus "And I couldn't care less!"), moving the hand forward, palm down, fingers out lackadaisically ("Don't be spastic! Take it easy! Relax! No sweat! *Mañana!*")—and so on.

Much nonsense, in racist terms, has been uttered on "ethnic gesture"; and yet, at different times and places, social groups display quite varying volubility kinemically. "Anglo-Saxons" in a long-current stereotype are supposed to be

---

facial gestures and motions of the head—fully as skillful a performance as John O'Hara's in the original short story version of "Pal Joey" in which a self-justifying heel condemns himself out of his own mouth.

both rigid and impoverished in kinesic communication (at least intentionally); and yet Englishmen of the first half of the eighteenth century gesticulated freely, and their American counterparts were, if anything, even less inarticulate kinetically in frontier times. The "grand manner" of oratory lasted until the mid-nineteenth century in England at least, so far as elocutionary gesture is concerned, and has survived even later in some rural areas in America. The gestures of American politicians on TV seem, by comparison, merely inapposite clumsy and distracting. The Sephardic Jew Disraeli spoke with great economy of gesture and is credited with introducing the more restrained "Victorian" style, although another stereotype has it that Jews as such are highly gesticulatory. (What is meant is that, at least in modern times, many Ashkenazi Jews are.) The French are also thought to be great gesturers; but they were not in the sixteenth century! French courtiers, before the arrival of the Italian Catherine de Medici, made few gestures and thought them vulgar, but "âmes sensibles" of the Restoration gesticulated freely. Historically, Italy (and those areas, I believe, under ancient Greek influence especially, and not the mid-northern nucleus of early Rome) has been a major source of European gestures. Silicians are reputed to have first elaborated a gesture language under the tyrant Denys l'Ancien in which they could communicate entirely without words; "legend has it that all the details of the bloody 'Vespro Siciliano' (Sicilian Eve), 1282, in which the people of Palermo massacred several thousand officers and soldiers of the French Army of occupation, were discussed and arranged on the streets by means of gestural signs and symbols only." [17] De Jorio collected an exhaustive "vocabulary" of traditional Neapolitan gesture (some of which I consider goes back to Greek sources).

Psychologists have done some excellent work on kinesics. The foremost among these, undoubtedly, is M. H. Krout. [18] More recently D. Efrón has made a careful comparative study of the gestures of Jews and Italians. His general conclusions are as follows:

> The radius of the gestures of the ghetto Jew seems to be much more confined than that of the Southern Italian. A great deal of his gestural activity appears to be taking place within the immediate area of his chest and face. Whereas in the Italian the gestural sweep often coincides with his arm's length, in the Jew it very seldom reaches a limit above the head or below his hips. In the ghetto Jew the upperarm participates seldom in the movement, and often is more or less rigid and attached to the side of his body. The axis of gestural motion is often centered at the elbow. [19]

(An old joke is to grab the wrists of a person to "shut him up"; "I talked my arm off" is scarcely a mere figure of speech). The contrasts (extracted passim from Efrón) could be summarized as follows:

Jew
Frontal plane depth, centripetal
One hand

Choppy
"Address"
Staccato
"Familiarity" with person of interlocutor (grabs lapels)
Disjunctive
Crowds interlocutor
Gestures punctuate
Nervous energy
Restricted
Elbow pivot
Simultaneous, both persons, dual monologue
Emphatic "attention!" intensificatives

Italian
Lateral, centrifugal surface plane away from body
   Symmetrical, both
   Sweeping
   "Display"
   Legato
   Manipulates, touches parts of own physique
   Synergic
   No contact with interlocutor
   Gestures "illustrate"
   Animal force
   Spacious, ample
   Shoulder pivot, even with finger gestures
   Alternating, dialogue
   At least 125 manual "words"

Samples of Italian gestures are: "What do you want?" (bunched fingers of both hands before, move twice upward toward body); good, sweet, pretty (gesture of drinking thumb; or moustache twisting—the latter identical with a classic *natya* gesture in India); "I don't care" or "La Barbe" (more exactly, "Je m'en fiche" or "Je m'en fou", = fingernails under chin, flip open and out with pivoted hand [sometimes with a "bouche mouée"]); and "The Pepper" = "he's nuts" (left fingertips bunched at right elbow, right arm vertical, rotate right hand with fingers slightly bunched).[h]

With gesture a paralinguistic, meaning-bearing phenomenon, it is not surprising that one of the theories of the origin of language should be that speech originated in gesture. The theory is of venerable antiquity. Most recently of anthropologists, La Barre has suggested that speech may have originated from

---

[h]. Anthropologists should not neglect other contributions of psychologists to kinesics: "Numerous experiments based on the meaning of gesticulation have been made and reported on, especially since about 1920. A number of these have been included in the [Hayes] bibliography. Students of folk gestures will find a mine of valuable information in the "Psychological Abstracts," published monthly by the American Psychological Association (see under entries: Gesture, Face, Hand, Emotion, etc.). See Hayes bibliography (p. 292) at beginning of present chapter.

the *vocal* gestures of higher primate "phatic" communication, i.e. those vocalizations involved with danger-warning, territorialism, fighting, courtship, and the like—vocalizations "international" from ape group to ape group, communicating no more than the affective or hormonal state of the utterer (a statement about the subjective, not the objective, world, as in semantic speech), a "social hormone" that readies the ape group for synergistic action. The notion is one owed to Edward Sapir; but before him the chain of theorists in this vein include Rousseau, Vico, Lucretius, Epicurus, and Democritus. It is important to note, however, that in the later theorists at least the notion always implies primate and hominid *vocalization* or "vocal gesture," that is, the change from "phatic" cries to semantic speech. The relevant quotation from Sapir is that

> It is likely that most referential symbols go back to unconsciously evolved symbolisms saturated with emotional quality, which gradually took on a purely referential character as the linked emotion dropped out of the behavior in question. Thus shaking of the fist at an imaginary enemy becomes a dissociated and finally a referential symbol of anger when no enemy, real or imaginary, is actually intended. When this emotional denudation takes place, the symbol becomes a comment, as it were, on anger itself and a preparation for something like language. What is ordinarily called language may have had its ultimate root in just such dissociated and emotionally denuded cries, which originally released emotional tension.[20]

But this is not what is meant by the psychological theorists, i.e. that *speech* originated from *gesture*. The foremost theorists of this tradition are Paget and Johannesson.[21] The notion would be that "ideas," like the "subsistential entities" of the New Realist philosophers, are all neurological or perhaps *motor sets*—operational (or subacute) thought-tonuses in an organism whose life-interests are served thereby and therethrough. No external reality totally corresponds to them; they are nevertheless existential in the sense that muscular tonuses and subacute or residual electrical potentials are existential. These ideas are "motor sets" so long as they are unspoken, i.e. verbalized, expressed overtly; they are a species of "emotive language." (I am aware that, as "devil's advocate," I may have added physiological rationales that, for me, would be required to give plausibility to this kind of theory.) However, for all that speech is after all a motor act, the theory has a wide chasm to jump between purely muscular gesture to specifically *vocal* muscular behavior, and I am unable to surmise how this might occur; at the very least, one would have to postulate some kind of meaningful vocalization as an intermediary step, hence the theory has more technical problems to solve than the speculations of Sapir which, in any case, remain in the area of vocalization. I do not find Paget-Johannesson theory convincing, because as a cultural anthropologist I find difficulty in discovering anything like "instinctual gesture" in any kineme (which an absolutist "Babel" theory would seem to require), and because semantic gesture often appears to be a back-formation exploiting logically prior linguistic locutions; but perhaps it is better to leave this specialized problem to our colleagues, the linguistic experts.[i]

One very provocative variant of this kind of thinking is the theory of S. F. Nadel that music came into existence from the wish of primitive peoples to have a special means other than ordinary speech for the purpose of communicating with the supernatural.[22] That is, music is a kind of allelo-language. To my mind, however, music does not appear to have sufficiently fixed and conventionalized meanings certainly to have *accomplished* this end. To be sure, some musical meaning *is* conventionalized, e.g. the *leitmotifs* in Wagnerian music, but these are mainly musically repetitive melodies that serve as "cognomens" of characters, or musical allusions to other scenes in the musical drama of the Ring.[j] On the other hand, it is my private impression that, in the music of Tschaikovsky, there is a probably unconscious use of horns in orchestration to indicate the blatant and harshly disruptive entrance of the forbidding or commanding father into the languishing violins indicating the mother-relationship—but this is a question of one composer and not Western music at large, the responses of perhaps only one listener and not of a sophisticated musical audience at large (both of which would seem to be required if music is to be a sufficiently "tight" system of meaning-communication). Similarly, I know the musically sophisticated wife of an analyst who says of Ravel's *Valse*, "This expresses exactly what I feel about life." (I would paraphrase her opinion something like this: "It is an Existentialist piece of music. It starts off singing its melody with childlike innocence and confidence, then *bang!* some trauma enters the psychological Eden; afterward the melody picks itself up and sings again, somewhat waveringly, but more or less intact; then *wham!* the cold winds of the cosmos crash in and knock the melody sprawling, this time rather maiming the melody, which nevertheless gathers itself together bravely, somewhat fragmentarily singing its song again and gradually gaining confidence, but now with the knowledge that further vicissitudes are in store before the final catastrophe.") But, again, this is a private apperception of the music. Music, I believe, is rather more a tonal Rorschach, inviting us to private fantasy, than it is a firmly semantic system of "communication."

i. The Chomskian position seems to me insupportably Lamarckian and mystical. My own view more nearly approximates that of David Kronefeld: " I question the elaborateness of the 'innate' knowledge of the basic form, shape, and function of the grammatical rules which Chomsky claims a child must possess in order to learn to speak when it does. I propose a minimal set of cognitive skills the possession of which would allow such language learning, and show that most of these skills are equally involved in non-linguistic activity. My minimal set of innate skills allows us to consider how speaking animals evolved from non-speaking ones, which Chomsky's does not" (see reference note 21).

j. Of course, Nadel's theory does not suffer from the necessity of explaining *written* music, which is a phenomenon after the fact of actual vocally or instrumentally produced music. Musical notation, it is true, is an internationally understood symbolic system with *instructions to action* (apart from the largely Italian expressive instructions which are purely linguistic), and as such are chronologically and logically *posterior* symbolic systems, strictly of the order of Laban's dance notation and Birdwhistell's system of descriptive kinesic notation.

Nevertheless, I once had a musically and otherwise very sophisticated student (now a New York psychiatrist) who, on entering an acquaintance's room would look, not at the books, but at the music he found there. For him, the presence of much Bach was indicative of an intricate, orderly, compulsive personality (engineers, he believed, have the neat and mathematical minds that commonly prefer Bach). Mozart indicated the "oral personality," Beethoven "masculine protest," Wagner the exhibitionistic and narcissistic "phallic personality," and Tschaikovsky the hysterical and perverse with much problem concerning father-figures. I can agree with much of what he says, but once again this is primarily of diagnostic significance, at best; and, like the reading of a Rorschach protocol, is mere methodological window-dressing for psychiatric insight which may in fact derive from other cues such as knowledge of the biography and personality of the composer, which is methodologically illegitimate. Furthermore, composers often give their own verbal explications of their intentions and meanings, which is again methodologically illegitimate if we are supposed to obtain sure "communication" directly from the music itself. Most experienced listeners tend to prefer "absolute" music rather than "programmatic" music such as, e.g., Tschaikovsky's *Nutcracker Suite* (here one also has to take the nauseatingly saccharine timbre of the celesta in the "Dance of the Sugar-plum Fairy"); though there exist other more interesting programmatic compositions like Moussorgsky's witty *Pictures at an Exhibition*, Respighi's *Fountains* and *Pines of Rome*, or Copland's *Billy the Kid* and *Appalachian Spring*. Similarly, I am content to listen, as instructed, to an ancient Russian fertility dance in Stravinsky's *Sacre du printemps*, but find my teeth set on edge by Walt Disney's reprogrammatizing of this in *Fantasia* as the evolution of cartooned dinosaurs (Beethoven's *Pastorale* is spoiled for me because I cannot avoid seeing cartooned centaurs lolloping over the landscape: my own apperceptive fantasies are better than Disney's!). In the 'twenties and earlier, program notes to concerts contained an immense amount of apodictic aestheticist nonsense about what one was supposed to hear in a given piece of music; this condescending snobbism was often a mere vehicle for the would-be literary exhibitionism, and not very good at that, of the musical poseur. And for all that, perhaps anyone's apperceptive comments on music may grate on the ears of another listener busy with his own preferred phantasies, just as many listeners "can't stand" the personalities of Wagner, Strauss, Bruckner, or Liszt, as revealed in their music.

Nevertheless, in societies other than our own, music *does* have more fixed semantic conventions. For the Greeks, modes (or tonal key-progressions or "scales") had well-recognized and distinct emotional significance or "ethos." Thus the Dorian mode was virile, vigorous, masculine, and martial, whereas the Lydian mode was soft, cloying, enervating, and effeminizing in its very femininity. The intricate Hindu *raga* system is also elaborately conventionalized in its connection with context, god addressed, mood, time of day to be used, etc. Arabic *maqáms* or "melody types" have ethos of a sort also. It is a puzzle to Westerners just how Greeks were able to discern modal differences (e.g., Hypomixolydian from Lydian), for these are not like pianoforte "keys" in successively higher or lower pitches, are far more complex than our major-minor key dichotomy, and depended upon perception of pure configuration for perhaps a score of authentic and their derived plagal modes.

On the other hand, Hindu *raga* music contains the helpful cues of the *alapa* (preliminary statement of the unmodified *raga* "scale," which is then freely improvised upon just as, in American jazz, the "melody type" or composition [e.g. "St. Louis Woman" or "Tiger Rag"] is stated before being improvised upon by instrumentalists, alternating in melody versus accompaniment roles, in otherwise unrecognizable ways), as well as conventionally associated instrumental ornamentations (e.g. *portamento* for one *raga*, slow and increasingly rapid *tremolo* for another, etc.), appropriate instruments (e.g. the *vina* for the goddess Sarasvati, flute for Krishna, etc.), and other helpful contextual cues such as place, time of day, season, etc. Balinese music, because of different levels of acculturational style (Old Polynesian, Hinduist, Chinese, Moslem, European) has many recognizable styles such as *pelog* (narrow-interval scale) and *selendero* (wide-interval pentatonic scale), varied further in tempo, etc.[k]

Like the Hindu *raga* music, Chinese classical music, from the Confucian period onward, also had "ethos" and of a distinctly moral tone, but connected in China with numerology, magic, and government. There was, for instance, the fabled "yellow bell" or *huang chung*, whose sacred absolute pitch a ruler had to ascertain before he could be sure his regime was firmly established in the cosmic scheme. "It was said that the morals and even the future of the state could be known by examining its music, so that the king might use this means of learning whether his vassals ruled their territories well or ill.[23] Confucius (*Analects* XV,10) urged as a model the music of the ancient Succession Dance, "for the tunes of Chêng are licentious"—however, the Prince of Wei liked the music of Chêng and Wei because they at least kept him from falling asleep in his full ceremonial gear, which the traditional music did not.[24] Native-discerned musical categories are of course notable for the Japanese also; but the cate-

---

k. It is interesting that, on much the same historical and class-bound grounds, Western music also has musical "vocabulary categories" similar to those of words (Norman genteel, Anglo-Saxon vulgar, neo-Latin and neo-Greek intellectual and scholarly words, advertising neologisms sometimes woefully aping these, profanity, obscenity, and obscenity-avoiding circumlocutions, book-writing vocabularies, cant, trade and other jargons, colloquialisms, dialect-regional words and phrases instantly identifiable, oratorical words, baby talk—all categories commonly absent in preliterate languages), of which every careful stylist must be constantly aware. Likewise, our categories in music are classical (almost infinitely divisible by periods and composers, from meterless ictus of Gregorian plainsong to successively discernible types so real that they can be satirized, whether by Prokofief or Alex Templeton), jazz (again subdivided by the knowledgeable into blues, ragtime, swing, bebop, rock, etc. by technical scale differences, tempo, timbre, ornamentation, etc.), as well as "hillbilly" (used in both sacred and secular contexts easily discernible), oldtime-popular music of several periods (Stephen Foster versus *Dardanella* versus *Smoke Gets in Your Eyes* versus *The Peppermint Twist* versus *Sergeant Pepper*, etc.), children's sing-song verses, often of great antiquity—most of which musical categories are immediately recognized by most persons in our culture).

gories of such American Indians as the northern Athapaskans were *functional* categories (for hunting, ceremonies, love, canoe-songs, etc.)—long before Bartok's "Gebrauchsmusik"—and not in the present sense stylistically different; indeed, only two musical "styles" are found in the whole of North America (standard and Yuman, characterized by rests and change of register), although I believe to have discerned distinct styles in Amazonian music quite different, for example, from familiar Andean style.

What needs to be emphasized, however, is that the ethos of all these mode-systems had to be learned, and were in no sense "racially" innate.[l] Similarly, the musical signals of specific groups have to be learned. For example,

> ... in the days when raids by Burman dacoits were common, the scattered Karen who were hiding in the jungle, fearing lest some of their foes were still in ambush, would signal to one another by playing certain notes on ... jew's-harps. Familiar with the sounds thus produced, which were unintelligible to their enemies, they were able to find one another and come together again.[25]

The Mura, also, when separated by a wide river could, allegedly, "carry on a conversation" by the use of the Quechuan five-stopped flute.[26] But these conventionalizations in musical communication are strictly on a par, so far as their arbitrariness is concerned, with the gestural kinemes of the many Bantu and Sudanic Negroes[m] who have a rich quasi–"sign language."[27] Probably the repertoire of such sporadic "musical languages" is no greater than that of our own military bugle calls (i.e. a limited number of sound-configurations or "tunes" to which conventionalized word meanings have later become attached, though all but the tone-deaf should be able to apprehend the meaning by pitch and rhythm patterns alone). Likewise, I have not encountered evidence to convince me that any African group had a sign language in the sense that the Plains Indians did: African gestures appear to have about the same level of complexity as American Indian trail signs, and no more.

On the other hand, West Africans in particular are rich in symbolic allusiveness. Each Ashanti gold weight refers to a moralistic proverb (e.g., one figure

---

l. For instance, a Chinese gentleman once remarked that he found Sousa's march, *The Stars and Stripes Forever*, embarrassing because of its marked "erotic" rhythms, which is not our apperception (as virile, aggressive, soldierly, patriotic). On the other hand, I have heard Chinese operas in which the libretto indicates a father's grief at the death of a son but the music a wholly inappropriate "jaunty" tempo as of joy, to my ear. Naive travelers' apperception of the "sad" or "minor key" music of primitives is largely nonsense, therefore; the natives merely have different scale systems which we mis-hear, culturally.

m. Since these are not so well known as some other gestural systems, it may be well to describe a few of these for the Ovimbundu. Among them, gestures of anger and contempt are common, and certain actions are used to communicate with deaf persons. Counting can be done from one to ten with a moderately complex system of finger gestures. An insulting gesture is made by holding up the left arm with the fist closed, the left wrist grasped and shaken by the right hand (meaning that one is so angry that he can't find words). Drawing the right index finger across the mouth means completion, as does rubbing the palms quickly together. "Go away" is a scratching motion of the fingers on the extended hand (see reference note 27).

in which two crocodiles at right angles to each other have separate heads and tails but the same body means family food-sharing since there is only one stomach; and another of a man smoking and carrying a powder-keg on his head refers to a proverb roughly translatable as "Discretion is the better part of valor"). In Dahomey a gift of parrot eggs was a delicate hint to an aging divine king that he should commit suicide for the good of his people. However, the cowrie language, for example, had a considerable elaboration. For the Yoruba, sending one cowrie shell with a hole in the back meant defiance; two cowrie shells fastened face to face meant "I want to see you," though when tied back to back, "Go away and stay away." Up to forty cowries were used in messages of the powerful Ogboni league, the meaning depending on the number of shells used, the method of stringing, and the nature of objects placed between the cowries, e.g., a piece of charcoal meant that the prospects of the sender were gloomy. A piece of wood such as was used to clean the teeth meant "As I remember my teeth in the early morning, and during the day, so I remember you as soon as I get up, and often afterwards." A kola nut means peace, welcome, and good health. A bit of sugar signifies "There is no enmity between us."[28] The Uraons of India also have a symbolism of objects:[n] water and mango, "life"; rice, nuts, dates, "fertility"; grinding stone, "home" (cf. our "hearth"); the color blue, "opulence"; bamboo, paddy, "marriageable girl", etc.[29] In such object-communication via conventionalized symbols, animals are often used to indicate human characteristics. For example, among the Boro of Amazonia, the snake symbolizes evil; the tapir, blindness and stupidity; dog, cunning deceit; agouti or capybara, wit and practical joking (since it is a trickster like the North American Indian coyote and raven, or like the African hare, all of whom outmaneuver others); boa constrictor, silence and strength; parrot, irresponsibility (as in chattering women who betray secrets); peccary, constancy; tiger, bravery; monkey, tenacity of life (because, when shot, it may hang onto a limb with its hands for some time after death; sloth, laziness; hawk, cunning, and so forth.[30] Similarly, among the Sinhalese, the *hamsa* or sacred goose of Hinduism, stands for discrimination (since it is supposed to be able to drink milk only from a bowl of mixed milk and water), and (unaccountably!) for its beautiful gait; and, in erotic poetry, for the breasts of women. The lion, the mythical ancestor of the Sinhalese, stands for majesty and power.[31] In the Indic

n. This is to be compared with the European "language of flowers," in which such flowers as the forget-me-not, lily, rose, pansy, rue, Parma violet, etc. have a symbolic significance. The Palaung of Burma have a similar "language of leaves," used in love-making and courtship. To be compared also are color-symbolisms such as the red-green-yellow of navigation lights and traffic signals, "yellow" (of a male who shows the white feather), blue (in mood, for both sexes), "black-hearted," "green with envy," red (for passion), black (for mourning), white (for purity), yellow (signifying in late-medieval England, I believe, "carrying the torch" of unrequited love), as well as the rich color systems of, especially, Southwestern American Indians, often connected with ritual objects, gods, directions; and also the color symbolisms of many other peoples. Compare also the elaborate ways in which feathers of specific birds are notched, dyed, and tipped, to indicate further information on the Plains Indian war bonnet.

culture sphere, the elephant stands for the male, royalty, or the god Indra (for whom elephants, monsoon clouds, are the *vahana* or vehicle, much as the bull is Shiva's *vahana*, the peacock Saraswati's, the mouse Ganesha's, etc.). In legends of Krishna, the elephant's head and trunk symbolize male genitals; and since Buddhist times, the lotus symbolizes the female—a list which the cultural anthropologist could extend almost indefinitely. But all these symbolisms are connected with specific objects, used or worn or sent or mythologized, and are not kinemically significant with respect to motor acts as such, hence they are beyond the scope of the present study.

More relevant to our subject, perhaps, are the kinetic-semantic systems which embody more elaborate symbolisms and more sustainedly articulate communications. Some of these are not adequately known: the drum-language of the Maya; the whistle language and slit-gong xylophone "talk" of the northern Chin of Burma; Kwoma communication by drumming on tree-roots; humming "language" of the Chinese of Chekiang; whistling communication of the Mazatec, Ibo, Veda, and perhaps also Zapotec and Tlapanec. Perhaps we should mention here syllabic substitution (*Fernruf*) for the Lokele, Duala, and Yaunde, Jabbo falsetto, and Alpine yodelling. The Mexican Kickapoo are said to have some sort of whistling system, but we have no examples of it.[32] It is probable that the whistling systems vary all the way from simple conventionalized signal-isolates, to fairly complete replications of speech. For example, a man in Ashanti wanted his tobacco pipe and told the messenger in whistled tones exactly where the pipe would be found; Lobi and Builsa men also employed a whistling language.[33] Although not enough is reported to be certain of the point, it is probable that the African whistling languages exploit the tonemic patterns in language similarly to drum language. The Canary Islanders' whistled language, however, whatever its aboriginal form, now operates by whistling substitutes for the actual phonemes of spoken Spanish (i.e. not tonemes)—a complete speech surrogate.

The musical and other instruments on which semantically configurated sounds are transmitted, comprise a wide variety: whistles and horns (Chin of Burma; horns only, Kru of Africa), flutes (Lhota Naga), hollow-seed membranophone (Chinese boys of Fukien), lute (Olombo of the Congo), musical bow and zanza (Africa), membrane drums, iron gongs, slit gongs, and xylophones (Africa, Maya, and perhaps tropical South America), wood troughs (Haka Chin), wooden canoes (Fiji, Choco of Colombia), canoe paddle shaft used as a two-toned instrument (Congo), buttress roots of trees (Melanesia and Indonesia).[34] It is of course well known both to linguists and to communications engineers that any medium whatever can communicate any information whatever through the use of only two differentiated signals or, indeed, only one (present/absent, as in electronic computers with a two digit system of on/off).

The best known systems, of course, are the drum languages of West Africa. Communication in these, basically, replicates the tonemic patterns of oral language in two musical tones or drum-timbres; but it also contains a number of "short-hand" arbitrary conventionalizations. For example, "So close is the articulation between speech and abridged communication among the Tumba (Congo) that the drummer often hums the message he is sending."[35] On the other hand, the Ewe (Togo) have adopted drum-signaling from their Ashanti neighbors, and have taken over signal-messages based on spoken Tshi, i.e., set sentences that become conventionalized; similarly, in another case, when a man signals his wife, "I feel hungry," the three-syllable spoken utterance takes seventeen syllables when drummed; and in the four-toned system of horn signal-melodies, not speech-melody but its abstractions are transmitted.[36] But drum languages should properly be left to the linguists, and need only to be alluded to here.

Nonverbal, muscle-communication, again, has become so familiar in the work of Birdwhistell that it requires no more than mention here. These are of the sort also discussed by Ashley Montagu: the (unconscious) flexing of the foot upon the lower leg in a context of embarrassment; also, marked voluntary contraction of the external sphincter ani muscle; inflation of the vestibule of the lips; lowering of the head when standing, crouching low when sitting; lowering the head, half covering the eyes with the hand; contraction of the muscles of the throat; and elevation of the left shoulder and slight lowering of the head, etc.[37]

The fields of kinesics and paralinguistics, though relatively new, are so rich in suggestions for the cultural anthropologist that one almost apologizes for the amount of material one needs at least to allude to, even in passing. The present section is a potpourri of examples which may stimulate the ideas of experts at this conference.

Many primitives believe that motor acts of the wife at home will affect the luck of the hunter: Old Stone Age drawings in Africa and Europe often show a line running from the hunter to the woman very likely expressing this notion (sometimes from the bow, weapon, or male genitals to the female genitals, suggesting a symbolic equation of weapon and phallus, or hunting and coitus, which, indeed, is attested to in some American Indian legends, as of a hunter drawing a bow whereupon the deer he is to shoot turns into a beautiful woman whom he marries). Similarly, "Ikpakhuak had bad luck in hunting one day, and Higilak discovered through her familiar spirit that she had been sewing too much deerskin clothing, while Ikpakhuak had also been at fault by hammering too much on the stones while loosening them for caches, neither of which things should be done to excess on the path of the migration [of caribou]."[38] Peruvian ceramic art, New Zealand wood carving, ancient Hindu art, and a famous temple in Konarak portray motor acts, often of an erotic nature.

The Balinese have a marked kinesthetic need to remain oriented to the directions "mountainward" versus "seaward," so much so that they become anxious when this habitual orientation is inadvertently lost. Calvin Coolidge is said to have had the presidential bed in the White House oriented north-south and placed on glass saucers, in order to obtain the health benefits of terrestrial magnetism.

> The Hebrew imagines himself to be facing east and describes east, west, north, south by the expressions "before," "behind," "left," "right." . . . The Indo-European peoples picture themselves as facing north and call the hand towards the rising sun the better hand, the dexterous one, and the other (although the Greek veiled it by euphemisms) the sinister. The Etruscans, on the contrary, thought of themselves as looking south; the Roman augurs continued the tradition and considered the left the lucky hand.[39]

For this reason, "thunder on the left" had a different significance as an omen for the Greeks and the Romans. In Eskimo engravings on ivory, time-sequence in drawings goes from right to left (rather than as in, for example, American cartoons, from left to right, in accordance with the linear sequence of our writing), *viz.* a running reindeer, then one shot with an arrow, then one fallen, the hunter, the winter hut, and finally hides drying on poles.[40] The various directions of writing, including the Greek "boustrophic" (back and forth as the ox plows), will of course be familiar to linguists—left to right writing perhaps being dictated by the necessity, in pen and ink writing, of not smudging the part already written (given the normal right-handed person). The predominance of right-handedness even in ancient humans, incidentally, is indicated by positive and negative hand paintings on Old Stone Age cave walls; the matter is not without importance because of the left-brain position of the speech center.

A chased silver flask, made in Kashmir, which I obtained in the present Pakistan, has a stopper which opens by unscrewing clockwise, and closes by screwing counterclockwise—a matter which has alerted me to the fact that many motor habits in India are "backwards" when judged in terms of our own. Sir George Watts has written on this matter that

> there is a peculiarity of all Indian needlework that may in passing be mentioned in this place since it doubtless has something to say to the styles of work produced, namely, the fact that the needle is pulled away from, not drawn toward, the operator. In other words, the action of sewing adopted in India is just the opposite to that pursued in Europe. The persistence with which the inhabitants of Eastern countries work is this so-called "opposite direction" seems due to the lesser development of the extensor muscles of the body and not a perversity of character. To the same circumstance is due the crouching gait of the people, of the plains of India more especially—the leg being swung, not pulled forward, and in consequence is never fully extended. Of the same nature is the overhead habit of swimming and the jerking of the playing marble by the forefinger of the right hand from between the forefinger and thumb of the left, instead of being propelled by the forcible extension of the thumb. Hence, to

the same cause also, whatever it may be, must be attributed all the agri-cultural and industrial operations where strength and skill are put forth in pulling and drawing, not in pushing or propelling.[41]

The matter is perhaps, an occasion, of considerable practical importance, in such concerns as industrial design, the manufacture of tools and imple-ments, etc.

The various kinds of "arrow release" will be familiar to all Americanists. Motor habits in canoeing, etc., might be worthy of study, but have not yet, to my knowledge, been examined. Clockwise and counterclockwise movements in the Sun Dance and other rituals are well documented; in the peyote cult, the proper over-and-under passing of staff and water drum is rigorously specified by purists, because of the symbolisms involved. Motor habits of specific tribes in making artifacts might possibly have some diagnostic value for archeolo-gists, if these can be detected in the artifact in question (weaving, pottery, core flints, knives, awls, skin scrapers, etc.). Sex dichotomized motor acts might be studied more fully also; e.g., all Yahgan women can swim, but this is a skill unknown to males.[42]

Art conventions, with respect to positioning, perspective, duplication of view, and the like, of objects in visual art, are known to all students of primi-tive art. Distortion of body parts (e.g. of the lower leg, thigh, etc., to indicate strength or speed) is notable in Bushman-Hottentot art, and is almost in itself diagnostic of this style. Body-proportion distortions, indeed, are a significant feature of all West African art, in properly diagnosing the tribal style involved. A Yoruba *ibeiji* figure, for example, can be instantly recognized because of the convention of not joining the lips at the edges on the carving. The leaving unfinished of a weaving sequence, when a ritual design is put on a secular trade article, will come to mind to all students of Southwestern Indians.

A paper by Doris Webster has long aroused my admiration because of her uncanny ability to make sense of the signs of the zodiac in terms of the body image and the position of body parts (the Fishes, crossed feet; Libra, arms extended, as in balancing; Sagitarius, arch of one foot placed on the knee in a sideways plane of the other leg, etc.).[43] The paranoid science of astrology with its delusions of reference could relevantly be studied in the light of her paper. The classic paper by Tausk[44] on the "schizophrenic influencing machine" as a symbol of parental coitus should also be mentioned here. Treatment of body parts in ancient and primitive art has been used with great brilliance diagnos-tically in the study of both Stone Age figurines and Maya statues.[45] Diagnostic signs of depression have likewise been discerned through the study of sculp-ture; and the art expert André Schoeller maintains that the motor "language" in the brush strokes of a painter is as crammed with personal quirks as hand-writing. The psychoanalyst, Ernst Kris, diagnosed the Viennese Baroque sculp-tor Messerschmidt as paranoid, largely on the basis of examples of his curiously distorted busts, a diagnosis easily confirmed by an examination of the sculp-tor's letters and reports from his acquaintances.[46]

The Chinese have a complex gestural language of assignation, and most of the courtesans are very expert in their interpretation. A forefinger rubbed below the nose means that a man finds a woman attractive and would like to make a more intimate acquaintance; a forefinger tapping the tip of the ear means "No!" while the right hand slapping the back of the left hand means the same. Closed fists, but with the forefingers and second fingers of both extended and rubbed together as if sharpening knives, or putting the two hands together and shaking them like castanettes, have meanings easily imagined. The most infamous of these signs would only be used by the most vulgar of coolies; shoving the right forefinger in and out of the closed palm of the left hand. By means of signs the price and the hour of meeting are also communicated; or else the fan is used to indicate the appropriate information. I have no doubt that similar signs are used on the Spanish Steps in Rome, but I do not know these; the "language of the fan" was known to all coquettes in eighteenth-century court circles in France. In Calcutta I was taught a gesture which effectively got rid of the beggars that besiege Americans as insistently as flies, but unfortunately I never learned what it means.

In advertising the hand symbol for a well-known beer (to indicate "Purity, Body, Flavor" by touching forefinger and thumb, the last three fingers extended) is a gesture equally well known to kinesiologists as an ancient and obscene European gesture for coitus. Made with the raised right hand and quickly moved forward it now means "fine" or "OK." Kinsey has made a minor contribution to kinesiology in the following passage:

> The toes of most individuals become curled or, contrariwise, spread when there is erotic arousal. Many persons divide their toes, turning their large toes up or down while the remaining toes curl in the opposite direction. Such activity is rarely recognized by the individual who is sexually aroused and actually doing these things, but the near universality of such action is attested by the graphic record of coitus in the erotic art of the world. For instance, in Japanese erotic art curled toes have, for at least eight centuries, been one of the stylized symbols of erotic responses.[47]

The erotization of body parts (foot, nape of neck, ear, etc.), on the other hand, appears to vary ethnographically quite widely.[48]

To my mind, the artist William Steig has an uncanny ability to portray psychiatric syndromes (especially in his classic book of cartoons, The Lonely Ones) largely through the postural tonuses of his figures.[49] From a study of daily column-wide wordless cartoons entitled "Tall Tales" that have appeared during the last two years, I am prepared to give, with exhaustive proofs, and in the appropriate context, a fairly complete psychiatric profile of the artist, Jaffe; I would venture the same, on the same grounds, for Gladys Parker of the series "Mopsy" and for Charles M. Schultz of "Peanuts." One of my students, expert in the Goodenough "Draw-a-Man" projective technique, applied this to the study of "Little Orphan Annie" with extraordinary results; and another has done a brilliant study on the psychological complexes of Pablo Picasso, through a study of his paintings.

The gesture language of the Japanese "tea ceremony" has been adequately described by ethnographers, but never sufficiently analyzed by kinesiologists.

A study of the approved stances and motor modalities in various sports might well be made from the point of view of kinesiology. Particularly absorbing to me has been the observation of the motor "business" and mannerisms of baseball, as observed in the Little League playing of my second son. Various athletes, I maintain, can be matched with their sport, by merely noting the way they sit in classrooms or walk across the campus; and like many other local fans I particularly admire the walking style of the Duke runner, David Sime, especially after he gave up football.

The Abbé Dubois made an exhaustive study of the motor acts of an orthodox Brahman, in connection with attendance to excretory acts.[50] Sex-dichotomized motor habits of this sort for men and women are well known to everyone in our society; but these are by no means the same for the appropriate sex in all societies.

Spitting in many parts of the world is a sign of utmost contempt; and yet among the Masai of East Africa it is a sign of affection and benediction, while the spitting of an American Indian medicine man is one of the kindly offices of the healer. The enormous variety and flexibility of male punctuational and editorial-comment spitting is especially rich, I believe, in Southern rural regions. Urination upon another person (as in a famous case at the Sands Point, Long Island, country club, involving the late Huey P. Long) is a grave insult among Occidentals,[51] but it is a part of the transfer of power from one medicine man to another in Africa, or to the patient in curing rituals and initiations.

Hissing in Japan (by sudden breath-intake) is a *politesse* to social superiors, implying the withdrawal of the subject's inferior breath in the presence of the superior person thus complimented. The Basuto applaud by hissing; but in England hissing is rude and public disapprobation of an actor or a political speaker.

The extraordinary complexity of motor and paralinguistic acts involved with drinking liquids in Africa is the subject of an article by A. E. Crawley.[52] The elaborate modesties of eating are also known to ethnologists with respect to India, Polynesia, and Africa.

It is easy to ridicule[53] kinesiology as an abstruse, pedantic, and unimportant study by pure scientists. But I believe kinesiology is, on the contrary, one of the most important avenues for better understanding internationally. Consider, as one small example, how Chinese hate to be touched, slapped on the back, or even to shake hands; how easily an American could avoid offense by merely omitting these intended gestures of friendliness! Misunderstanding of nonverbal communication of an unconscious kind is one of the most vexing, and unnecessary, sources of international friction. (Consider, for example, the hands-over-the-head self-handshake of Khrushchev, which Americans interpreted as an arrogant gesture of triumph, as of a victorious prize-fighter, whereas Khrushchev seems to have intended it as a friendly Communist gesture of international brotherhood.)

Gregory Bateson taught me in Ceylon the great value of attending Indian-made movies as an inexpensive kind of easily available fieldwork; and I have since, gratefully, assiduously attended foreign movies of all kinds. I should like to conclude this subject, as a final example, with some conjectures based on the Russian movie, *The Cranes Are Flying*, which I believe explain some-what the famous United Nations episode of Khrushchev's banging his shoe on the desk in the presence of that august body. I do not understand Russian, so that my comments are based entirely upon observation of the motor acts of the characters in two scenes of this movie. First scene: a soldier in a military hospital receives news that his sweetheart has married another man. Much uncontained total emotion, kinetically; raging, tearing at bandages with the teeth, so that there is potential danger to his war wounds; hospital manager is summoned in person to quell the one-man riot, and bring the social situation back to normal. No stiff-upper-lip Anglo-Saxonism here! The assumption seems to be that the mere feeling of an emotion by a Russian is sufficient legitimation for the expression of it. Anyone, even the highest authority in the context, it is assumed, can legitimately be called upon to help contain it, since the experiencer of the emotion cannot, need not, or is not expected to. (In this connection one recalls the finding of Gorer that the Russian infant is swaddled because, despite his small and unthreatening size, he is regarded as a center of dangerous and uncontained emotion; whereas Polish swaddling is done be-cause the human being is an infinitely precious and fragile thing, in need of this protection.)

Second scene: a little ragamuffin boy, quite self-contained and stolid as a street-urchin alone in the snow, comes into a warm canteen full of Russian women; some minor contretemps in which the little boy's wish is crossed, then: not merely a simple temper tantrum in the child (pan-human phenomenon) *but* all the women begin running around, dropping everything else, as if it were the most natural and necessary thing in the world to help the exploding indi-vidual contain his emotion through attention and pacification. Hypothesis: if this is the expectancy of the Russian child in the enculturation experience and evidenced both in his behavior and in that of the soldier, it is possible that Khrushchev was unconsciously using a coercive modality, plausible and under-stood and unconsciously taken for granted in Russian culture, that wholly missed its mark, certainly for the Anglo-Saxon expectancies of Americans and British present? Or was it a merely paralinguistic intensificative to indicate "sincerity"? My reasoning is tenuous; it needs to be supported by masses of ethnographic fact before even being respectfully listened to. But the point I wish to make is that such kinesic and paralinguistic communication is of para-mount importance in international relations. Would Pearl Harbor have occurred if we had been able to read the "Japanese smile" of the diplomats as they left their last fateful meeting with Secretary of State Cordell Hull?

Slightly later than Birdwhistell's "kinesics" there has developed another related field, called "proxemics" by Hall. This deals with significant animal uses of space, including man's, and promises the same subleties as kinesics.[54] Some of the first "experimental" evidence that is likely to satisfy those who need quantitative proof of the existence of the qualitative, is presented by Michael Watson,[55] and in an earlier collaboration with T. D. Graves.[56] Watson summarizes the now familiar animal materials: territoriality and escape-flight distance in various species; Christian's deer on James Island; Calhoun's "behavioral sink" in crowded Norway rats;[57] visual, auditory, olfactory, and thermal space; architectural and urban space; sociofugal and sociopetal acts and structures, etc. But the list is by no means exhaustive. It omits, for example, Hall's summarizing article and the extensive discussion, by a *Current Anthropology* international panel of experts, that follows it.[58] Watson appears to repeat some of the misdirections of Hall, to be discussed later; nor is he sufficiently critical of sources, as when Ardrey and Schaller are cited as though their work were equally authoritative.

Some anthropologists have thought proxemics a lode soon mined. But Watson is not prey to this illusion. In his *Current Anthropology* paper he writes that "the field of proxemic research is potentially vast." But, curiously, he evinces in this study no very large appetite for detailed group-specific cultural emics, so that the approach seems more like that of the experimental etic psychologist than of the field ethnologist. In its beginnings, proxemics has been an exciting natural science, a kind of sensitive "bird watching" depending on exquisitive sharpness of observation. But it has also been grossly inexact in identifying human universes of application, no doubt because it was erroneously considered ethological and inadequate in other ways. As it becomes more experimental it also becomes more dull, not only because of confusion in theory but also because we have not sufficiently bounded the universe of significance in our impatience to be exact about what little we already know. We need to lay bare these theoretical confusions in early proxemics. And meanwhile, in the vein of Boas on cephalic indices of immigrants' children, we would suggest there is no use measuring skulls until we know better what skull measurements measure, and what they mean.

Historically, proxemics seems to have emerged from studies in animal ethology. However, if we are to respect the notoriously species-specific nature of *Homo sapiens*, we may be led to suspect that feisty sticklebacks, anomie-suffering deer, and ghettoized rats are at best irrelevant, if indeed they are not anthropomorphisms; and that certain sleazy and inept speculations on human "territorialism" and "instinctive aggression" are in turn zoomorphisms. Specifically, even slime molds might seem grist for the proxematic mill since, after an indefinitely "protozoan" amoeba-like vegetative independence, the individual cells swarm into a slug-like metazoan, the head of which becomes a stalk up which tail cells migrate, there sexually to produce spores for further asexual reproduction. But this is surely hormonal, not human communication.

In short, human proxemics deals primarily with ethnological not ethological phenomena, as noted earlier was the case with kinesics. Proxemic behavior in humans is learned cultural behavior, of society-wide not species-wide scope, and such communication affiliates rather with kinesics and paralinguistics than with instincts or hormones. We should abandon analogies with sticklebacks and slime molds and look instead to the primates for edification. Now, data for an authentic human ethology may indeed exist. But we look for them on the wrong level of complexity. It is true that some primates have species-specific phatic cries (but even there the physiological possibilities could still be learned by imitation of others). However, we should not expect to encounter the pan-human in any precise semantic content of an utterance, inasmuch as species-wide phatic cries of apes have "opened" to become the arbitrary but only society-wide languages of men, even supposing there was once a single human *Ursprache*. We by no means understand the phylogenesis of speech, yet we know something of its ontogenesis in the individual. In early childhood there is an ontogenetic imprinting period available for learning *any* human language; and if the requisite social stimulation is lacking, then the forever speechless feral child may result (though this is certainly no simple linguistic phenomenon). But the ethology of abstract *propensities* is a far cry from fixed *semantic content* in any species-specific animal communication, especially the human.

In an earlier essay in the present volume, on sexuality and the hominization of man, a contrast was drawn between the ecologically "closed" band of baboons in food foraging and the "opening" of early hominid bands through male hunting of animals, surely of adaptive significance since it was followed by the massive species-specific "trimorphism" of human beings in their potential for culture. In the human separation-and-return of human males, *the new use of animal space is a new ecology*. And as far as space is concerned, one might speculate on the contrastive proxemics of eyesight in baboon foraging and human hunting, and the selective pressures placed on cortical development in a new ecologically different space.

Since primates are visual rather than olfactory mammals (probably owing to their arboreal phase in which olfactory cues were much diluted), it is likely in the proxemics of sight that we might best seek the elusively pan-human. Schaller's studies of the gorilla[59] have shown us the importance of visual communication by silver-backed males of cues for group movement, and the importance of the averted gaze in preventing threat behavior from turning into an attack charge (much admiring the courage of Schaller's conviction in proving his hypothesis). And, indeed, it is not so much that visual cues have have decreased in importance in humans (for, if anything, paralinguistic communication has proliferated in society-wide "linguistic" fashion), as that auditory cues should have so tremendously outstripped the visual in the species-specific proliferation of speech. After the ear, the eye is still certainly the most important sense in human communication—nonverbal, kinesic, proxemic, or whatever.

Are there still enough occasions for aggression[60] in human males that each must watch the watcher? We still hurt or feel insulted from being stared at, as if there were an "organism-invasion" (Diebold)[61] in such looking. At the same time, the centripetal pull of mutual eye engagement across crowded rooms can both initiate and cement marital, friendly, and hostile relationships between individuals—but are not these open semantic-contextual rather than closed ethological phenomena? Or does quick eye-aversion in public among mutually unknown males mean more than bored uninterest and serve the same placative function as in Schaller's apes, or at least set disjunctive nonengagement? Dark glasses do not really hide the narcissistic, but merely make them more conspicuously exhibitionistic, even slightly insulting in their accepting but not providing visual feedback. Does the dark-glassed voyeur not wish to be seen seeing? And what is so insulting as an official public not-seeing by acquaintances, an aggressive staring past the other—a kind of not *countenancing* the other rather than mere gaze aversion? Gaze aversion additionally seems often to state submission in a dominance-hierarchy context. The "same thing" is so different that we need a kind of *morphosememics* in both kinesics and proxemics!

Perhaps we need also a science of "chronemics" in the social uses of tardiness, quantitative waiting and the like in hierarchic statements of relative status. As for dominance hierarchies mediated mostly by sight in primates in general, how much does "hierarchizing" depend not merely on neoteny but also on human monotocicity (much as birth in litters may serve pack-learning in dogs) such that siblings are born serially, size- and age-different? One is reminded here of horripilation in many mammals and feather-fluffing in birds, both of which enhance the size or decrease the apparent distance of the opponent in frightening ways. Posture seems in part to be the equivalent in primate threat displays, including man's.

Since vagueness in group designation has flawed most early proxematic descriptions, Lynch[62] quite properly urged Hall toward subcultural refinement. If we are correct in the apposition of proxemics to linguistic communication, then we should anticipate that this paralanguage would show something successively like linguistic-stock, language, dialect, and even idiolectic differences, perhaps not unlike those we encounter in kinesics. For example, I have noted marked regional differences even in the eastern United States, again in the matter of visual proxemics:

> Like many Americans from the northern part of the United States, I am still surprised that total strangers on the streets of my Southern Piedmont town often greet me as though I were a personal friend. At first I interpreted this as extreme friendliness that goes beyond normal American ex-

troversion. I have since learned, however, that it is the result of my unconsciously looking at people in Northern urban fashion. In the South, looking directly at people implies you know them, so that, with varying degrees of incertitude or diffidence, people respond to a mere look with a "friendly" greeting, a phenomenon that can be easily demonstrated experimentally. Also, if for some reason one wants formal anonymity in public, even when passing close by, by not looking at the other person one is officially not there (though he may remind you later, a bit aggressively or chidingly, that he saw you on the street, which both knew).

. . . In private colloquy, two Southern business men will stand together on a street-corner, somewhat closer together than elsewhere in the United States, but studiously avoid one another's eyes, gazing about explicitly almost anywhere else. By contrast, two professional men of Northern origin will stand somewhat farther apart in private conversation, but will exchange repeated "frank" looks into the other's eyes with constant "checking" on facial expressions, often raising both eyebrows in direct or skeptical gaze. The contrast is so marked that one can predict regional origin on the basis of this clue alone.[63]

To leave animal ethology still further behind, there is a humanistic realm regarding the symbolic and aesthetic use of space that I would be tempted to dub the "kinaesthetic," were the term not already preempted by neurology for proprioceptive awareness (to which indeed, it may be synaesthetically related, psychologically). Like many other form-conscious persons, I take acute pleasure in responding to the idiolectic proxemics of some painters. *Le Moisson* by Van Gogh, for example, in exquisite use of near/distant colors has a blue cart in mid-distance profile beyond successively blued-sandy, orangish-yellow, umbered bluish-gray, dark green, and orangish strips of garden plants, this whole foreground against oranged-chartreuse, apple green, and orange-yellow fields, with two successively farther tan blue-shadowed barns, and another distant orange-lit red-roofed barn against the blue hills and finally eggshell sky (like some passages in Mozart, the barns are in compositional relation that *could be no other*), the vivid horizontals forming a whole with a startling space-depth of almost measurable feet.

Again, in an actually smallish painting of men with dogs returning in the snow from the hunt, with skaters far below and a vast landscape beyond, Breughel has uncannily swept hundreds and hundreds of cubic miles of space. The *Sleeping Gypsy* of Rousseau is silhouetted against a poignantly lonely desert and an infinity of moon-haunted sky. Dutch painting of the eighteenth century has a space-appetite for immense lucent skies above the finite earth, quite unlike the homely man-scaled intimacies of British landscape painting of the same period. Are contrastive population densities and social structures accountable for the differences? Or time-bound ethnic proxemics?

Italian Renaissance painters are astonishingly intelligent in portraying motion on a static plane; and as has been suggested, I believe by Sir Kenneth Clark, in Florentine painting it is always a spring morning, but in Venetian a golden summer afternoon. Florentine painting usually is also spatially intimate, Venetian grandiose in its distances. Italian Renaissance portraits throughout are replete with proxematic subtleties. How is it that Botticelli's perfectly healthy *Venus* has an earthly weight of approximately one gram, while Michelangelo's *Pietà* carries the weight of the world? Paolo Veronese's gigantic paintings are, despite their size, knit into units by insistent diagonals, while a Mannerist painting full of violent spaghetti nudes is kept from exploding only by a compositionally obsessive triangle.

Compare also the almost extravagant violence of "motion" in Verrocchio's *Tobias and the Angel* with the still strangely kinetic but lesser vigor of Botticelli's *Birth of Venus*, the mere lively squirming of the baby in Murillo's *Virgin and Child*, and the successively "slower" movement in Pieter de Hooch's mother and child in *The Pantry*, and the downright stately tempo of Vermeer's *Lady and Gentleman Drinking Wine*. Compare the commercial bustle of Canaletto's merely spacious outdoor view of *The Doge's Palace* with the echoing vastness of Pannini's *Interior of St. Peter's, Rome*; because of spatial differences, these two paintings almost *sound* different. Compare also the *similar noise level*, conveyed by "motion," in Breughel's jaunty dancing peasants, but with lesser motion in his peasant wedding meal; the placid and quiet movements of the eight variably distant figures in Hobbema's rural *Avenue, Middelharnis*, and progressively onward to the quite soundless static peasants of Le Nain. And how does Piranesi get such stupendous architectural immensities into his merely large prints?

Or contrast, in a single painting, Dali's *Metamorphosis of Narcissus*, beyond the double visual pun on Latin "orchis," the *static punning echo* (with its manifest psychiatric overtones) of mirrored hand and figure in the foreground, with the *noisy restlessness* of the background figures. Or note the kinaesthetically tender space-tempo in Michelangelo's not-quite-touching hands of Adam and God in the Sistine *Creation of Man*. And *what time* is it: is life slowly beginning to stir in the languid Adam, or is his perfected static body still awaiting the touch of life?

Figures in Picasso's "blue period" are anguishedly lonely, but together; whereas in the placidly neat family groups of Le Nain, each individual is space-limned apart in psychic solitude. In Wyeth's painting of a table-corner bearing a cup, knife, and plate, with a small-paned window behind looking onto two logs lit by a slanting sun, there is a wholly unsentimental but still almost erotic passion for seen space. And, for that matter, *what time is it*, early morning or late afternoon? In Wyeth's *Christina's World*, many miles of lonely mid-day grassland seem to stretch out in every direction. Great painters, of course, make their own proxematic rules, and yet all contrive to be so kinaesthetically correct and inevitable that they compel us to see as they do. One main difference between great art and *kitsch* is just this mastery, and the unmistakable authority of a great painting can be almost palpably experienced. Right position is also essential especially in English composition—as shown for example in Chomsky's famous grotesque, *I see the white big house*—whereas kinaes-thetic measure is critical in inflected Latin poetry that subordinates word-po-sition to its prosodic ends: *Ante mare et terras et quod tegit omnia caelum / Unus erat toto naturae vultus in orbe / Quem dixere chaos*, from Ovid's *Meta-morphoses* will serve. And how different kinaesthetically must be the reading of Chinese ideographs, full as they are with visual metaphors.

And how infallibly buildings (as ultimately kinemic constructs) reflect the personality of the architect—Coit Tower versus the Telegraph building in San Francisco—or of the donors: Kennedy Center for the glory of a family versus the Taj as the expression of a rajah's love for Mumtaz-i-Mahal; the rhetoric of the SUNY-Albany campus versus the friendliness of nondescript Princeton or Chapel Hill, or of single buildings such as classic Whig-Clio and that frumpy Victorian matron, Alexander Hall; the time-right grace of Charlottesville Georgian versus Duke perpendicular-Gothic, a jejune copy of Yale Harkness, itself a copy of Trinity College in Cambridge (though at Yale with some farci-cal pratfalls, like an archway Gothic on York Street and Georgian in the quad).

The visual-kinaesthetic is an important nexus in proxemics. Individuals dif-fer markedly in their preference for proximity to or distance from the movie screen, and quite apart from any visual correction with glasses or dizziness caused from too rapid a pan shot in poor movie-making. One individual may like comfortably to distance himself as passive unseen watcher; another seems to seek being lost in the dramatic action as participant observer. Preference for seats at the ballet may depend on greater enjoyment of *tout ensemble* move-ment patterns, versus delight in the detail of an elegant *pas de deux*. Precise timing and spacing of dancers is imperative in an ensemble movement, for pattern is otherwise hopelessly mutilated. A *danseur noble* like Igor Yousou-poff in a *Swan Lake pas de deux* may be embarrassingly miscast in a frivo-lous "Aurora's Wedding" with different space tempo, and a miscast *prima ballerina assoluta* is catastrophe indeed. Photographed ballet can be infuriat-ing, if the film editor stupidly cuts to irrelevant chopped close-up when both the eye and aesthetic logic demand ensemble, or when the camera whisks away from enchanting detail to tiresome *tutti*; it is as frustrating as a tone-deaf sound engineer monitoring the recording of a symphony. Such annoying edi-torial interference leaves no choice to the connoisseur who knows how he wants to watch ballet, and often enough the ballet-film editor follows cliched movie-technique alternation of close-up and distance-shot merely because it is available in the camera—though in the hands of an aware artist this spatial counterpoint can be exhilarating and witty in movies themselves. Swift zooms of course should be confined to proxemic jokes and kinesic farce; slow zooms in love scenes are merely sticky.

One of the reasons that watching amateur 'home movies' is often so uncom-fortable or embarrassing is that the subjects, as in a still photograph *look at* the movie taker, whom they may know better than the viewer (to his discomfort) knows them—whereas, in professional movie the rigid convention that the actor *never* looks directly at the camera. (Even as a child one felt angry and exploited when Peter Pan looked to his audience to succor the dying Tinker Bell; at least one moppet might gladly have killed them both off for this brutal invasion of emotional privacy and the right to see as suits fantasy; this gambit of Barrie should be made as "unconstitutional" as plastic Musak in airports and other public places.) Both in movies, and on the stage, for the actor to "look" even at a distance involves the audience and sharply disrupts the dramatic illusion that one is watching, unseen, a "real life" situation. It has the shock of farce, which, indeed, frequently exploits this broadly as "double-take." By contrast, the magnificently natural understanding of audience involvement through the use of high side-proscenium and indiscrimination between stage-preparation and play proper, turned the whole theatre in the New York production of *Hair* into pure tribal rock. Perhaps the therapy of modern alienated man could look into such proxemizing techniques. By contrast, the excessive back-staging in the movie of Woodstock and incessant panning back and forth from stage to audience produced cynical turn-off in many, since exploitative commercialism so saliently emerged.

The contrast between home and professional movies was brilliantly exploited in one of the Burton-Taylor movies, when home movies were indicated very simply and unmistakably by the actors' looking directly into the camera and putting on the self-consciousness of the amateur who knows he is being "taken." By habitually looking into the camera, certain masters of ceremony and public figures *always* look amateurish, in spite of contrived tics of folksy disembarrassment like popping the cuffs, touching the nose, etc. That TV commercials so often involve actors looking at the viewer is, perhaps, another reason why some people particularly dislike them and feel their privacy has been rudely or oafishly invaded by the "gall" of total strangers acting, without consent, as if they knew you, and in your own living room at that. It becomes a positive pleasure and privilege to turn them off and annihilate them with a turn of the wrist. Only a trusted newscaster like Walter Cronkite, with his magnificently candid editorializing face that lets you know exactly how he feels about each item of news and intervening advertisement, can be allowed to look directly into one's private family room. Also, until the end of 1970, his distance from the TV camera was exactly right for both dignity and friendliness; unfortunately, since early 1971, the camera has been moved up too close, which is too presuming, and in distracting zooms that destroy rapport. He has here become "too personal" and too manipulated to serve as trusted oracle. Politicans should understand, or perhaps not understand too well, how to look at people when speaking. The two Presidents, LBJ and Nixon, should never have attempted the "frank look" because both were so indescribably bad at it that they conveyed the impression of chicanery and disingenuousness through their very honesty of self-presentation.

Historically, plays and movies and their natural extension, television, have taught us new ways of looking. But most nonshow TV is merely visual radio, so poorly have the unused visual potentialities of TV been understood. Advanced science should produce color TV—only to produce a soap-ad or a football game?—or a NET documentary on living biology! By contrast with these electronic modalities, one of the secrets of successful *viva voce* public speaking, especially at some distance on a podium, is to look constantly into the eyes of one specific individual after another, not merely to sample feedback, but also to "engage" the audience. Only a few get looked at, but everyone feels the speaker is interested in one's personal reactions; one is not an ignored fraction of a captive audience exploited by mere self-indulgent loquaciousness but becomes a partner in dialogue. Feedback and counterfeedback, mutually reinforced, can mount into a very frenzy of agreement and approbation. The speaker must really lose himself to find his audience.

Experienced teachers are well aware of a *topographic* element in teaching: apple-polishers, especially the pretty but not-so-bright girls, sit in the front row of the classroom, whereas the more detached and independent minds sit a few rows farther back, interested but not captured. In academic public lecturing other than classes, the degree of interest in the subject may be indicated by the distance of the listener from the speaker he does not know.[o] Here the speaker will do well to watch the first rows, and not those further back, at least until he is in full swing. And even experienced lecturers feel chagrined when the audience chooses to congregate mostly in the back of the room, and constantly adjure people, not always successfully, to "move up closer" to get all the promised goodies.

Another facet is the topographic *context* in proxemics: many teachers have the reputation of having "eyes in the back of their head." The reason is fairly simple. As they sit, students do not ordinarily see one another's faces, hence to see more of the others and to be seen by fewer of them from the back seems to confer increasing anonymity and psychological privacy as they sit farther toward the rear of the room. This is an illusion, as any lecturer knows. Again, because of the sensitivity of the eye to peripheral movement, all the teacher need do during an examination is to turn his erstwhile vacant gaze immediately upon a head rising up, for that student to be convinced the teacher has

o. Larger geographical space is sometimes important. "The Pentagon March of October 1967 had a significant spatial component. Four barriers separated five levels of commitment and action. Overcoming the barrier of geographical distance was largely a function of psychological distance; those most alienated were willing to travel farthest. The participants showed clear evidence of spatial differentiation as a function of commitment at each successive level of confrontation." Somewhat contrastively, the Gidsingali of Northern Arnhem Land and the Dalabon of the Beswick Reserve in Australia have an elaborate system of restrictions on the dangerous proximity of objects, places, and activities (see reference note 63). In this context, I particularly relish the attitude of a lady who lives in one of my favorite cities, when I said, "The only trouble with San Francisco is that it is so far away"—"From *what*?" she replied.

been watching him specifically the whole time. A smile by the teacher makes it even worse, in mobilizing the guilt of a possible cheater. Also, an occasional stroll and pause at the back of the room, where the student is seen but does not see the seer, induces a very panic of honesty.

The early scandal of the arms-length coupled pair in the Viennese waltz changed the proxemics of an eighteenth-century Sir Roger de Coverley group-style of dancing, and proximations that had been coy and courtly became downright flirtatious or worse. After World War I came the still more shocking proxemics of the bunny hug and the foxtrot, next changed to the Charleston, only to yield after World War II to the sad separateness of the frug style of dancing, which is more a provision of spectator sport for others than paired participant engagement. The ballroom now again becomes a whole group, not romantic self-focused couples. The whole choreographic world of primitive and folk dancing should be reexamined from the viewpoint of proxemics and kinesics. Is the dance mutually experienced, individually exhibited, or group-performed?

There is a *sex component* of proxemics to be attended to. At faculty parties in the United States, men and women notoriously tend to place themselves on either side of an imaginary line, diagonal or otherwise across the room when they sit down; the wise hostess has known when to give freedom of choice in another room, after her fixed sex-alternation at the dinner table (the great innovation of the Ghost Dance in the Plains consisted in sex-alternation in one circle, replacing the older unisexed concentric circles in opposite motion, but some conservatives could only bring themselves to hold handkerchief corners in the new style). This is not a matter of sex-relevant topical interests either, for many women complain bitterly at missing the masculine conversation, since they can talk to women any day at the supermarket. Furthermore, men tend to sit farther apart and to move about more restlessly, e.g., in argument; women sit more closely and tend to keep one place. However, in an intellectually or socially nonpretentious "fun" party, every one of the above descriptions must be modified, even though the identical people are involved. Again, the topography and passage patterns of rooms in different houses makes for quite different parties, as well as do relative space-numbers and space-proximities.

There is an *age-component* in proxemics, perhaps related to historic generation-change but not simply so. A large outdoor deck-cum-living-room-cum-patio-cum-family-room can hold sixty uncrowded high school students, two or three dozen adults easily at another time in a standup cocktail and buffet, but only a party of eight in a relaxed dinner-party more extravagantly consuming space. Again, to adults at the high school party, students tended to accord larger space bubbles than they themselves maintained.

Hence there is probably a *status* component in proxemics also. The poet Auden, who was not unselfconscious about the dignity and charisma of the bard, who was acutely sensitive proxemically (especially to architecture and ethnic space),[p] and who sharply delineated his private and public selves, was only half-playful when he wrote, "Some thirty inches from my nose/The frontier of my person goes."[64] Arthur Schlesinger[65] noted that on the news of Senator John Kennedy's election to the presidency, the people who had been closely associated with his campaign and even intimate friends immediately behaved as though his space-envelope had suddenly expanded enormously, like some impenetrable plateglass *mana* inviolably there; John Kennedy was also acutely sensitive to the proxemics of politics and privacy, and he astutely modulated all his personal modalities thereto. In a 1964 survey of how the American public ranks nonunique occupations, a Supreme Court Justice ranks highest (congressman, cabinet member, and college professor surprisingly share the same four-point-lower rank); and yet at a cocktail party of Federal Court judges, the usual large "public" space-bubble of one revered Supreme Court Justice shrank democratically to one indiscernible from these of his subordinate judges. Hence *context* modifies proxemic status.

Proxemics thus far has been largely an American preoccupation. Among Europeans, the ideas of Bernhard Bock[66] of Brunswick, Germany, seem to me the most provocative and stimulating. Bock has drawn attention to the circadian "rhythms of density" (rush hours, night hours) in city life; the person's fluctuant wish for solitude, company, and crowds; the contrast in effect of crowded or partly full public performances; and the changes in geographic and social environment in moving to a new place. How, he asks, are proxemic patterns affected by childhood neglect, overprotection, adolescent difficulties, and life traumata? What are the individually differing proxemic needs for company in danger or stress? How do only children and children from large families differ proxematically? children from different social classes, ethnic groups, rural/urban residence? What are the contrasts of formal proxemic patterns and real feelings, perhaps even deviant, in individuals and groups; and what are the effects of these contrasts? What is the proxemic significance of first-naming among acquaintances and friends, the *tu-vous* and *du-Sie* in friendship, love, and kinship, and of group-argots and vocal amplitudes? The influence of radio and TV on mass proxemics? The proxematic differences among the respectively increasing-distance senses of touch, taste, smell, hearing and sight? (And their phylogenetics?) The proxemics of games, dancing, sports (e.g., swimming/tennis/baseball/basketball/football)? The changing communications networks, e.g., of specialists and scholars? (And with age and status?) The symbolisms of contact and fellowship, of miming (the "stage whisper," the visual whisper), prelinguistic sounds, the handshake and the kiss (Crawley has

---

p. Hall has written with his usual perceptiveness on sociopetal and sociofugal patterns of furniture arrangement in houses and in hospitals; of Latin versus North American interview patterns in offices; of American, Japanese, and Arabic floor plans; and of German, Arabic, and American feelings about basements (see reference note 64).

assembled older data on these), physical embraces (and ethnic differences, stereotypes)?

Edmonson[67] points out the relevance to proxematic interests of *Lebensraum*, the "ten-foot pole," close and distant relatives (to which one might add the Southernism of "kissing-cousins"), psychic contagion (the "evil eye") and pollution (caste in India, the sacred head of the *mana*-laden Polynesian first-born chief), and of "keeping in touch"—this last with so many gradations of meaning as to reach the extreme "not if I see you first." There are indeed almost endless subjects that come to mind: space-consciousness and kinaesthesia, space-derangement and psychotropic drugs; the imagined spaces of mathematicians. There exist the proxemics of furniture, clothing, institutional planning of hospitals, asylums, public buildings; proxemics and transportation, roads, real estate, ecology, car design size, and engineering. Does "space-travel" really "bring a whole nation together?" Or do flatulent Madison Avenue-isms like "astronaut" ("voyager among the stars," for circumterrestrial or sublunar rocketeers; it is lately, still more fatuously, "cosmonaut") in a context of more pressing world issues, tend rather to divide and stratify?

The anthropologist and the sociologist have many proxematic problems to ponder: proxemics and motor habits, settlement patterns, village orientation, migration; seasonal changes in proxemic state, as of a winter teacher and public lecturer to the summer scholar and writer; the proxemics of work versus vacation, of trade-travel and transhumance; social class or occupation and the proxemic scope, range, and variety of friends, colleagues, professional memberships, and travel; the "world village" of modern mass communications; travel-appetite and -fear; silent barter and other trade-proxemizers like the *kula*, the *potlach*, space and folk-ethnology (northern Athapaskans) and -myth; the distinct space-differences between Florence and Rome, London and Paris, Chicago and New Orleans, New York and San Francisco; sexual space adaptations in deep-sea fish and other spatially dispersed species; Gauguin's flight to Tahiti and Joyce's self-exile from Ireland; the doublebed, twin-bed, and other sleeping patterns; the telephone-booth game and car-crowding of adolescents; "sensitivity training" and touch; proxemics and race problems, urban/suburban living, social conscience and the tax structure, busing and schools, parks, swimming pools; the knee-child, lap-child, sibling-sex order, and character.

Psychosomatics and proxemics seem to me to promise especially fruitful insights. Psychosomatics and proxemics are already partly understood with reference to asthma, perhaps also to skin diseases like eczema, but what of acne, warts? Agoraphobia, acrophobia, claustrophobia, eremophobia? Charisma and ego-syntonic space? Space consciousness, body ego, schizophrenic depersonalization, vertigo and *kayak-angst*, proprioception, tics—the ethologist Peter Klopfer suggests that play may be proprioceptive experiments in adaptive "fit" and that even abstract aesthetic preferences may serve preadaptive ends.[68]

Workers with delinquents persuasively insist that there is a kind of kinaesthetic intelligence quite different from verbal and conceptual intelligence. What also of proxemics and Robert Stoller's acute studies of sex and gender in the *spatial* parent-child psychogenesis of transvestism, homosexuality and trans-sexuality?[69] The hodophobia of William Ellery Leonard and the Locomotive God?[70]

There are further psychic and even metaphysical proxemics still to explore. Michael Balint[71] once suggested that some individuals characteristically operate in terms of *matter and place*, whereas others operate in terms of *process and space*. It would seem that Parmenidean (nominal) metaphysics of the Plenum represented the former, and Heraclitean (verbal) metaphysics of Change and paths to the Empyrean the latter. In the one, pure packed Being admitted of no motion or change; in the other, pure Becoming had nothing for change to happen to. It took the pre-Socratic Atomists Leucippus and Democritus to transcend the two with atoms and the Void (space), in a magnificent tradition that extends down to Einstein's $E = mc^2$. There is also the curious mystic system of para-anthropology, with representatives in Mesopotamian astrology and Protagorean Sophism, the paranoid Hellenistic confusion and assimilation of microcosm and Macrocosm, Gnostic and Kabbalistic fantasy on the model of the *Anthropos*, and zodiac correspondence to body-parts—a whole metaphysical system of the schizoid body-image as world-view.

We are in a stage of exciting perceptions, one tumbling over the other, their relations only dimly discerned, a stage of weak verification and, ironically enough, poor delineation of the demographic and conceptual *locus* of our phenomena. The biological use of time is one of the great cosmic themes, and the use of space perhaps not less so. Instinctual territoriality in man may indeed be dubious. But in a learning animal there are still more promising and far more interesting vistas to explore.

Reference Notes

1. Flora L. Bailey, "Navaho Motor Habits," *American Anthropologist* 44 (1942), 210–34; George Devereux, "Some Mohave Gestures," *American Anthropologist* 51 (1949), 325–26.
2. Some older sources: W. P. Clark, *Indian Sign Language* (Philadelphia: L. R. Hamersly & Co., 1885); L. F. Hadley, *Indian Sign Talk* (Chicago: Baker & Co., 1893); S. H. Long, "The Indian Language of Signs," in *Account of an Expedition From Pittsburgh to the Rocky Mountains*, 2 vols. (Philadelphia: H. C. Carey and I. Lea, 1823), I:378–94; G. Mallery, "Sign Language among North American Indians," *Bureau of American Ethnology, Annual Report* 1 (1879–80), 263–552, and "A Collection of Gesture-Signs and Signals of the North American Indians with Some Comparisons," *Bureau of American Ethnology, Miscellaneous Publications* 1 (1880), 1–329; H. L. Scott, "The Sign Language of the Plains Indians of North America," *Archives of the International Folk-Lore Association* 1 (1893), 1–206; and W. Tomkins, *Universal Indian Sign Language of the Plains Indians of North America* (San Diego: W. Tomkins, 1926). In this context should be mentioned J. E. Ransom's paper on "Aleut Semaphor Signals," *American Anthropologist* 43 (1941), 422–77; R. M. Berndt, "Notes on the Sign Language of the Jaralde Tribe of the Lower River Murray, South Australia," *Royal Society of South Australia, Trans-*

actions and Proceedings and Report 64 (1940), 267–72; A. C. Haddon, "The Gesture Language of the Eastern Islanders [of Torres Straits]," Report of the Cambridge Anthropological Expedition to the Torres Straits 3 (1907), 261–62; A. W. Howitt, Native Tribes of Southeast Australia (London and New York: Macmillan, 1904), 723–35; M. Meggitt, "Sign Language among the Walbiri of Central Australia," Oceania 25 (1954), 2–16; C. P. Mountford, "Gesture Language of the Ngada Tribe of Warburton Ranges, Western Australia," Oceania 9 (1938), 152–55; C. G. Seligmann and A. Wilkin, "The Gesture Language of the Western Islanders," Report of the Cambridge Anthropological Expedition to the Torres Straits 3 (1907), 255–60; and Edward Charles Stirling, in Baldwin Spencer (ed.) Report on the Work of the Horn Scientific Expedition to Central Australia, 4 vols. (London and Melbourne: Dulau & Co., 1896), 4:111–25. For other sign languages, see G. Rijnberk, Le language par signes chez les moines (Amsterdam: North-Holland Publ. Co., 1953); "Lexicon of Trade Jargon," Federal Writers' Project (MS in the Library of Congress, Washington); C. G. Loomis, "Sign Language of Truck Drivers," Western Folklore 5 (1956), 205–6; D. C. Phillot, "A Note on the Mercantile Sign Language of India," Royal Asiatic Society of Bengal, Journal and Proceedings N.S. 3 (1906), 333–34, and idem, "A Note on the Sign-, Code-, and Secret-Languages, etc. Amongst the Persians," Royal Asiatic Society of Bengal, Journal and Proceedings N.S. 3 (1907), 619–22; O. Ribsskog, Hemmilige Sprak og Tegn, Tatersprak, Tivilifolkenes Sprak, Forbrytersprak, Gattegutsprak, Bankersprak, Tegn, Vinkelog Punktskrift (Oslo: J. G. Tanum, 1945); Anon., "Tobacco Auctioneer Gestures," Greensboro [N.C.] Daily News, 29 September 1944 (see also painting of similar gestures in U.S.A. national magazines in advertisements for Lucky Strike cigarettes in 1942). For India, see A. and G. Coomaraswamy (translators) of Nandikesvara, The Mirror of Gesture, 2nd ed. (New York: E. Weyhe, 1936), and Russell Meriwether Hughes [La Meri, pseud.], The Gesture Language of the Hindu Dance (New York: Columbia University Press, 1941); cf. Tyra af Kleen, Mudras, The Ritual Hand-poses of the Buddha Priests and the Shiva Priests of Bali (New York: E. P. Dutton & Co., 1924). For Greek, Jewish and Italian gestures, see Robert Young, Analytical Concordance to the Bible (New York: Funk & Wagnalls, 1936, sub "Hand," "Embrace," "Greet," "Kiss," "Salute," "Bless," "Head," etc.); D. Efron, Gesture and Environment: A Tentative Study of Some of the Spatiotemporal and "Linguistic" Aspects of the Behavior of Eastern Jews and Southern Italians in New York City (New York: Kings Crown Press, 1941); A. de Jorio, La mimica degli antichi investigata nel gestire napoletano (Naples: Fibreno, 1932). The profusely illustrated work of F. T. Elworthy, Horns of Honour (London: J. Murray, 1900) is world-wide in scope, occasionally over-speculative, but it is an indispensable source for kinesiologists.

Recent studies include: Paul A. Bouissac, La Mesure des gestes: Prolégomènes à la sémiotique gestuelle, Approaches to Semiotics 3 (The Hague; Mouton, 1973; Mary R. Key, Paralanguage and Kinesics: (Metuchen, N.J.: Scarecrow Press, 1975), and idem, Nonverbal Communication: A Research Guide and Bibliography (Metuchen, N.J.: Scarecrow Press, 1975); I. M. Schlesinger, "The Grammar of Sign Language and the Problem of Language Universals," in John Morton (ed.), Biological and Social Factors in Psycholinguistics (Champaign-Urbana: The University of Illinois Logos Press, 1970); William C. Stokoe, Semiotics and Human Sign Languages, Approaches to Semiotics 21 (The Hague: Mouton, 1972).

3. Dell Hymes (ed.), Language in Culture and Society: A Reader in Linguistics and Anthropology (New York: Harper & Row, 1964). See also: W. Bright (ed.), Sociolinguistics (The Hague: Mouton, 1970); Roger Brown, A First Language: The Early Stages (Cambridge: Harvard University Press, 1973); A. Capell, Studies in Socio-Linguistics (The Hague: Mouton, 1966); J. A. Fishman, Advances in the Sociology of Language, 2 vols. (The Hague: Mouton, 1965, 1972), idem (ed.), Readings in the Sociology of Language (The Hague: Mouton, 1968); P. P. Giglioli (ed.), Language and Social Context (Baltimore: Penguin Books, 1972); Judith Green, Psycholinguistics (Baltimore: Penguin Books, 1973); J. J. Gumperz and Dell Hymes (eds.), Directions in Sociolinguistics (New York: Holt, Rinehart & Winston, 1972); W. Labov, Sociolinguistic Patterns (Philadelphia: University of Pennsylvania Press, 1973); Stanley Lieberman (ed.), Explorations in Sociolinguistics (Bloomington: Indiana University Press, 1967); Norman Markel, Psycholinguistics (Homewood, Ill.: Dorsey Press, 1969); and D. I. Slobin, Psycholinguistics (Glenview, Ill.: Scott, Foresman, 1971). For a therapeutic use of psycholinguistics, see Louis Gottschalk (ed.), Comparative Psycholinguistic Analysis (New York: International Universities Press, 1961).

4. Ray Birdwhistell, Kinesics and Context: Essays on Body Motion Communication (Philadelphia: University of Pennsylvania Press, 1970).

5. Ray Birdwhistell, *Introduction to Kinesics*, rev. ed. (Louisville, Ky.: University of Louisville, 1956).

6. Birdwhistell, *Kinesics and Context*. See also idem, "Kinesics and Communication," in E. S. Carpenter and M. McLuhan, *Explorations in Communication* (Boston: Beacon Press, 1960).

7. Karl Abraham, "A Short Study of the Development of the Libido, Viewed in the Light of Mental Disorders," in *Selected Papers of Karl Abraham* (London: Hogarth Press, 1927), pp. 418–501. Edward J. Kempf, *Psychopathology* (St. Louis: C. V. Mosby, 1921).

8. F. P. Thieme, "Lumbar Breakdown Caused by the Erect Posture in Man," *Anthropological Papers, Museum of Anthropology, University of Michigan* 4 (1950).

9. W. La Barre, "The Cultural Basis of Emotions and Gestures," *Journal of Psychology* 16 (1947), 62–63.

10. M. F. Ashley Montagu, "Natural Selection and the Origin and Evolution of Weeping in Man," *Science* 130 (1959), 1572–73.

11. M. F. Ashley Montagu, "Why Man Laughs," *Think* 26 no. 4 (April 1960), 30–32. See also the chapter on obscenity in the present volume.

12. E. B. Holt, *The Freudian Wish* (New York: Henry Holt, 1915).

13. Havelock Ellis, *Studies in the Psychology of Sex*, 4 vols. (New York: Random House, 1936), III:393ff., gives numerous examples indicating that coitus, micturion, defecation, and walking are culture-conditioned, as also is the kinesics of childbirth.

14. W. La Barre, "Cultural Basis," pp. 50–51.

15. E. Crawley, "The Nature and History of the Kiss," in his *Studies of Savages and Sex* (New York: Johnson Reprint Corporation, 1969), pp. 113–36.

16. John M. Cooper, "The Ona," *Bulletin, Bureau of American Ethnology* 143 (1946), I:107–25, esp. p. 118. R. D. Mallery (ed.), *Masterworks of Travel and Exploration* (Garden City, N.Y.: Doubleday, 1948), pp. 271, 275; Hayes, *Gestures*, pp. 223, 226; H. Bayley, *The Lost Language of Symbolism*, 2 vols. (London: Williams & Norgate, 1912), II:128; A. Sakai, *Japan in a Nutshell*, 2 vols. (Yokohama: Yamagata, 1949) I:131.

17. D. Efron, *Gesture and Environment*, pp. 25, 30–31, 38, 43, 59. J. C. Flugel, *The Psychology of Clothes* (London: Hogarth Press, 1930). I have not seen E. B. Hurlock, *The Psychology of Dress* (New York: Ronald Press, 1929) or F. A. Parsons, *Psychology of Dress* (Garden City, N.Y.: Doubleday, Page, 1921).

18. The major relevant works of M. H. Krout are: "Autistic Gestures," *Psychological Monographs* 46 (1935), 1–126; *Introduction to Social Psychology* (New York: Harper & Bros., 1942), esp. pp. 313 et seq.; "Symbolic Gestures in Clinical Study of Personality," *Transactions of the Illinois State Academy of Science* 24 (1931), 519–23; "The Social and Psychological Significance of Gestures," *Journal of Genetic Psychology* 47 (1935), 385–412; "A Preliminary Note on Some Obscure Symbolic Muscular Responses of Diagnostic Value in the Study of Normal Subjects," *American Journal of Psychology* 11 (1931), 29–71; "Further Studies in the Relation of Personality and Gesture: A Nosological Analysis of Autistic Gestures," *Journal of Experimental Psychology* 20 (1937), 279–87; and "Understanding Human Gestures," *Scientific American* 49 (1939), 167–72.

19. D. Efron, *Gesture and Environment*, p. 43.

20. W. La Barre, *The Human Animal* (Chicago: University of Chicago Press, 1954), p. 169, citing Edward Sapir from *Selected Writings* (Berkeley: University of California Press, 1945), p. 465; see also La Barre p. 349 (361 in the 4th and subsequent editions).

21. Sir Richard A. S. Paget, "Gesture Language," *Nature* 139 (1937), 198; "Gesture as a Constant Factor in Linguistics," *Nature* 158 (1946), 29; *Human Speech* (New York and Harcourt, Brace & Co., 1930); "Sign Language as a Form of Speech," paper read at the Royal Institute of Great Britain (1935); *Babel, or the Past, Present, and Future of Human Speech* (London: K. Paul, Trench, Trubnen & Co. 1930), esp. chap. 1; *This English* (London: K. Paul, Trench, Trubner & Co. 1935); and "Origin of Language, Gesture Theory," *Science* 99 (1944), 14–15; A. Johannesson, *Origin of Language* (Reykjavik: H. F. Leiftur, 1949); *Gestural Origin of Language* (Reykjavik: Leiftur, 1952); "Origin of Language," *Nature* 157 (1946), 847–48; and "Origin of Language (in Imitation of Gestures)," *Nature* 162 (1948), 902; David B. Kronefeld, "Innate Language?" Paper delivered at the 75th Annual Meeting of the American Anthropological Association, Washington, 1976, *Abstracts*, p. 44.

22. S. F. Nadel, "The Origins of Music," *Musical Quarterly* 16 (1930), 538–42.

23. H. G. Creel, *The Birth of China* (New York: Reynal & Hitchcock, 1937), p. 331.

24. L. C. Goodrich, *A Short History of the Chinese People*, 2nd ed. (New York and London: Harper & Bros., 1943), p. 52, fn. 20.
25. H. T. Marshall, "The Karen People of Burma," *Ohio State University Bulletin* 26 no. 13 (1922), p. 163.
26. G. E. Church, *Aborigines of South America* (London: Chapman and Hall, 1912), p. 138.
27. W. D. Hambley, *Source Book for African Anthropology* (Chicago: Field Museum of Natural History, Anthropological Series 26 [1957], pp. 318–19).
28. Hambly, *Source Book*, p. 320.
29. MacEdward Leach, review of W. G. Archer's book on Oraon poetry, in *American Anthropologist* 57 (1955), 183–84.
30. T. Whiffen, *The North-West Amazons* (London: Constable and Company, 1915), p. 243.
31. A. K. Coomaraswamy, *Medieval Singhalese Art* (Broad Campden: Essex House Press, 1908), pp. 81ff.
32. Theodore Stern, "Drum and Whistle Languages: An Analysis of Speech Surrogates," *American Anthropologist* 59 (1957), 487–506.
33. Hambly, *Source Book*, p. 318.
34. Stern, *Drum and Whistle Languages*, pp. 492–93.
35. Ibid., p. 488.
36. Ibid., pp. 490, 491, 496.
37. M. F. Ashley Montagu, review of an article by L. A. Dexter, in *Psychiatry* 6 (1943), 255–56.
38. Diamond Jenness, "The Life of the Copper Eskimo," *Report of the Canadian Arctic Expedition* 12 (1923), p. 185.
39. *Hastings Encyclopedia of Religion and Ethics*, X:73–74.
40. Charles Singer, E. J. Holmyard, and A. R. Hall, *A History of Technology*, 5 vols. (New York and London: Oxford University Press, 1954), I:41, Figure 24.
41. Sir George Watt, *Indian Art* (London: J. Murray, 1904), pp. 370–71.
42. Review by R. H. Lowie in *American Anthropologist* 40 (1938), 495–503, esp. p. 496.
43. Doris Webster, "The Origin of the Signs of the Zodiac," *American Imago* 8 (1951), 31–47.
44. Viktor Tausk, "On the Origin of the Influencing Machine in Schizophrenia," *Psychoanalytic Quarterly* 2 (1933), 519–36.
45. P. Heilbronner, "Some Remarks on the Treatment of the Sexes in Palaeolithic Art," *International Journal of Psycho-Analysis* 19 (1938), 441; A. F. C. Wallace, "A Possible Technique for Recognizing Psychological Characteristics of the Ancient Maya from an Analysis of their Art," *American Imago* 7 (1951), 3–22.
46. L. B. Boyer, "Sculpture and Depression," *American Journal of Psychiatry* 106 (1950), 606–15. *Time* magazine XLIX, 23 (9 June 1947), p. 45. E. Kris, "Ein geisteskranker Bildhauer," *Imago* 19 (1933), 384–411.
47. Alfred C. Kinsey et al., *Sexual Behavior in the Human Female* (Philadelphia: Saunders, 1953), p. 620.
48. Weston La Barre, "The Erotization of Body Parts in Various Cultures," address to the Yale University Anthropology Club (1936).
49. Weston La Barre, "The Apperception of Attitudes, Responses to 'The Lonely Ones' of William Steig," *American Imago* 6 (1949), 3–43.
50. Abbé J. A. Dubois, *Hindu Manners, Customs and Ceremonies*, 3rd ed. (Oxford: Clarendon Press, 1906).
51. Abraham, *Selected Papers*, pp. 280–98; see also references to the urethral personality in Weston La Barre, *They Shall Take Up Serpents: Psychology of the Southern Snake Handling Cult* (Minneapolis: University of Minnesota Press, 1962), p. 197, n. 120.
52. A. E. Crawley, "Drinks and Drinking," *Hastings Encyclopedia of Religion and Ethics* 5:72–82.
53. *Horizon* 21 no. 4 (1960) 122–25.
54. E. T. Hall, *The Silent Language* (New York: Doubleday, 1959). See also his *Beyond Culture* (Garden City, N.Y.: Anchor Press, 1976).
55. O. Michael Watson, *Proxemic Behavior: A Cross-Cultural Study* (= *Approaches to Semiotics* 8 [The Hague: Mouton, 1970]).
56. O. Michael Watson and T. D. Graves, "Quantitative Research in Proxemic Behavior," *American Anthropologist* 68 no. 4 (1966), 971–85; O. M. Watson, "On Proxemic Research," *Current Anthropology* 10 nos. 2–3 (1969) 222–23.

57. N. Tinbergen, "The Curious Behavior of the Stickleback," *Scientific American* 187 no. 6 (1952), 22–26; John J. Christian, "Factors in Mass Mortality of a Herd of Sika Deer (*Cervus nippon), Chesapeake Science* 1 (1960), 79–95; John J. Christian, Vagh Flyger and David E. Davis, "Phenomena Associated with Population Density," *Proceedings of the National Academy of Science* 47 (1961), 428–49; John J. Christian and D. E. Davis, "Social and Endocrine Factors are Integrated in the Regulation of Growth of Mammalian Populations," *Science* 146 (1964), 1550–60; John B. Calhoun, "A Behavioral Sink," in Eugene L. Bliss (ed.), *Roots of Behavior* (New York: Harper, 1962), pp. 295–316; and idem, "Population Density and Social Pathology," *Scientific American* 206 (1962), 139–46; see also Peter H. Klopfer, *Habitats and Territories: A Study of the Use of Space by Animals* (New York & London: Basic Books, 1969).

58. Edward T. Hall, "Proxemics," *Current Anthropology* 9 nos. 2–3 (1968), 83–95, with discussion pp. 95–108; idem, "The Study of Man's Spatial Relations and Boundaries," in I. Galdston (ed.), *Man's Image in Medicine and Anthropology* (New York: International Universities Press, 1963), pp. 422–45; and idem, *The Hidden Dimension* (New York: Doubleday, 1966); idem, *Handbook for Proxemic Research* (American Anthropological Association: Society for the Anthropology of Visual Communication, 1974); idem, "A system for the Notation of Proxemic Behavior," *American Anthropologist* 65 (October 1963), 1003–26; Ruth Tringham (ed.), *Territoriality and Proxemics: Distribution Patterns Within Settlements* (New York: Warner Module Publications, 1973); O. M. Watson, *Symbolic and Expressive Uses of Space: An Introduction to Proxemic Behavior* (Reading, Mass.: Addison-Wesley Modules in Anthropology, 1972).

59. George Schaller, *The Mountain Gorilla: Ecology and Behavior* (Chicago: University of Chicago Press, 1963).

60. Weston La Barre, review of M. F. Ashley Montagu (ed.), *Man and Aggression* (New York: Oxford University Press, 1958), in *American Anthropologist* 71 (1969), 912–15.

61. A. Richard Diebold, "Comments," *Current Anthropology* 9 nos. 2–3 (1968), 97–98.

62. Frank Lynch, "Comments," *Current Anthropology* 4 nos. 2–3 (1968), 102–3.

63. Weston La Barre, "Comments," *Current Anthropology* 9 nos. 2–3 (1968), 101–3. See also M. Argyle and J. Dean, "Eye-contact, Distance, and Affiliation," *Sociometry* 28 (1965), 289–304; J. J. Gibson and A. D. Pick, "Perception of Another Person's Looking Behavior," *American Journal of Psychology* 76 (1963), 386–94. Clarke Akatiff, "The March on the Pentagon," *Annals of the Association of American Geographers* 64 no. 1 (1974), 26–33. Kenneth Maddock, "Dangerous Proximities and Their Analogs," *Mankind* 9 no. 3 (1974), 206–17.

64. W. H. Auden, *About the House* (New York: Random House, 1965), p. 4. Edward T. Hall, "Quality in Architecture: An Anthropological View," *Journal of the American Institute of Architecture*, July 1963, unpaged.

65. Arthur M. Schlesinger, Jr., *A Thousand Days* (Boston: Houghton Mifflin, 1965), pp. 98–104, and chap. 4, passim.

66. Bernhard Bock, "Comments," *Current Anthropology* 9 nos. 2–3 (1968), 96–97.

67. Munro S. Edmonson, "Comments," *Current Anthroplology* 9 nos. 2–3 (1968), 99–100.

68. Peter Klopfer, "Sensory Physiology and Esthetics," *American Scientist* 58 no. 4 (1970), 399–403.

69. Robert J. Stoller, *Sex and Gender* (New York: Science House, 1968).

70. William Ellery Leonard, *The Locomotive God* (New York and London: Crofts, 1927).

71. On Michael Balint, see Weston La Barre, *The Ghost Dance: Origins of Religion* rev. ed. (New York: Delta Paperbacks, 1972), pp. 507–8.

Index